COMPETITIVE FRONTIERS

DEDICATION

From Nancy J. Adler: To the women of my history and roots – Laura, Nina, Lilly, Mizzi, Martha, Cecil, and especially my mother, Liselotte; to the women of my generation – Phyllis, Kristi, Jane and Alyson; and to Sarah, who in all her giggling two year old splendor is welcoming in the new generation.

From Dafna N. Izraeli: To the memory of my mother, Rachel Gewurz, who taught me the difference between myth and reality, and provided me with a room of my own.

COMPETITIVE FRONTIERS

Women Managers in a Global Economy

Edited by

Nancy J. Adler and Dafna N. Izraeli

This collection copyright © Basil Blackwell Ltd 1994

First published 1994

Blackwell Publishers
238 Main Street
Cambridge, Massachusetts 02142
USA

108 Cowley Road
Oxford OX4 1JF
UK

Library of Congress Cataloging-in-Publication Data
Competitive frontiers: women managers in a global economy / edited by
    Nancy J. Adler and Dafna N. Izraeli.
        p. cm.
    Includes bibliographical references and index.
    ISBN 1-55786-510-8
    1. Women executives.   2. International business enterprises—
Management.   I. Adler, Nancy J.   II. Izraeli, Dafna N.
    HD6054.3.C67   1993
    331.4'816584—dc20   93-19121
                                                              CIP

British Library Cataloguing in Publication Data
A CIP catalogue record for this book is available from the British Library.

Typeset in Plantin 10 on 12 pt by Best-set Typesetter Ltd. Hong Kong
Printed in the United States of America

This book is printed on acid-free paper.

CONTENTS

LIST OF CONTRIBUTORS

NANCY J. ADLER is Professor of Organizational Behavior and Cross-Cultural Management at the Faculty of Management, McGill University, Montreal. She received her BA in economics and her MBA and PhD in management all from the University of California at Los Angeles.

Dr. Adler conducts research and consults on strategic international human resource management, expatriation, women in international management, international negotiating, developing culturally synergistic approaches to problem solving, and international organization development. She has authored numerous articles, produced the film *A Portable Life*, and published the books *International Dimensions of Organizational Behavior* (Second Edition, 1991) and *Women in Management Worldwide* (1988).

Dr. Adler has consulted to private corporations and government organizations on projects in Europe, North and South America, the Middle East, and Asia. She has taught Chinese executives in the People's Republic of China, held the Citicorp Visiting Doctoral Professorship at the University of Hong Kong, and taught executive seminars at INSEAD in France and Bocconi University in Italy. She received McGill University's first Distinguished Teaching Award in Management (1986) and was its recipient again in 1990.

Dr. Adler has served on the Board of Governors of the American Society for Training and Development (ASTD), the Canadian Social Science Advisory Committee to UNESCO, the Strategic Grants Committee of the Social Sciences and Humanities Research Council, the Executive Committee of the Pacific Asian Consortium for International Business, Education and Research and has held leadership positions in the Academy of International Business (AIB), the Society for Intercultural Education, Training, and Research (SIETAR), and the Academy of Management. She received ASTD's International Leadership Award (1990) and SIETAR's Outstanding Senior Interculturalist Award (1991). She was selected as a 3M Teaching Fellow (1991), honoring her as a top university professor, and was elected to the Fellows of the Academy of International Business (1992).

CAROLINE ANDREW is Professor of Political Science at the University of Ottawa and a former Coordinator of its Women's Studies Programme. She has published in the areas of urban development, municipal politics, and women and politics. She researches women in politics and administration, and municipal activities of interest to women.

ARIANE BERTHOIN ANTAL is Director of the International Institute for Organizational Change, IOC-Ashridge, Archamps, France. She holds an MA in international relations from Boston University and a doctorate from the Technical University of Berlin. Before joining IOC, she was Senior Fellow at the Wissenschaftszentrum Berlin für Sozialforschung. Her research and consulting are international and focus on innovation in organizations and promoting individual and organizational learning. Her publications include *Comparative Policy Research: Learning from Experience* (edited with M. Dierkes and H. Weiler and published by Gower); *Making Ends Meet: Corporate Responses to Youth Unemployment in Britain and Germany* (Pinter and the Anglo-German Foundation); *Corporate Social Performance: Rediscovering Actors in Their Organizational Contexts* (Campus Verlag and Westview). In addition, she has published many English and German articles on women in management, organizational culture, and social innovation processes. She is Consultative Member of the Board of the European Women's Management Development Network, of which she was previously President.

AUDREY CHAN is Senior Lecturer at the Faculty of Business Administration, National University of Singapore. She has a PhD in human resource development from Texas A&M University. Dr. Chan does research in strategic human resource management, career development of professionals, managerial reform in the People's Republic of China, and Asian business enterprises. She has published over twenty journal articles, book chapters, and conference papers. She was a visiting research scholar at the University of Southern California, University of Michigan at Ann Arbor, INSEAD in France, and China Enterprise Management Association in the People's Republic of China. Dr. Chan is active in consulting and executive training of Asian managers. Since 1984, she has directed the Human Resource Management Executive Program and General Management Program at the National University of Singapore. She has also conducted numerous in-company senior executive programs for established institutions such as the National Computer Board, Port of Singapore Authority, Neptune Orient Lines, Singapore Airlines, and the Indofood Group in Indonesia.

WEI-YUAN CHENG is Professor of Sociology at the National Taiwan University where he teaches economic sociology, industrial relations, and rural sociology. He has written on problems of development, economic attitudes, and labor relations in the Third World. Professor Cheng has coauthored two books with Professor Lung-li Liao, *Changing Women in Taiwan* and *The Poor in Taiwan*. He received his BA from the National Taiwan University, his MA from Michigan State University, and his PhD from University of Missouri-Columbia.

CÉCILE CODERRE is Associate Professor of Social Work at the University of Ottawa. She has published in the areas of women and management, feminist theory, and pornography. Her present research examines the development of the women's movement in western Quebec, women and management, and employment equity.

VIRGINIA CROCKETT-TELLEI is Marketing Administrator for Micronesian Telecommunications Corporation (MTC), a subsidiary of GTE Hawaiian Tel located in Saipan, Commonwealth of the Northern Mariana Islands. Prior to joining MTC, she served as Associate Director of the Pacific Asian Management Institute at the University of Hawaii at Manoa, where she was responsible for the administration of international business training programs and for coordination of research projects on business and international education. She received her BA in Asian studies from the University of California, Berkeley and her MA in geography from the University of Hawaii under the auspices of the East-West Center's Population Institute. Ms. Tellei holds a certificate in advanced Indonesian from Malang Teachers College in Indonesia. Her most recent research focuses on Indonesian women and management development issues.

CORINNA T. DE LEON is Senior Lecturer and the Subject Leader of Marketing at the Faculty of Business, City Polytechnic of Hong Kong. Previously, she taught at the Faculty of Business Administration, National University of Singapore. Dr. de Leon has conducted research on ethnic identity of overseas Chinese, gender differentiation, social representations of cross-cultural categories, structural and situational power in negotiations, organizational acculturation in expatriate management, product involvement effects on advertising miscomprehension, and cultural aspects of service quality. She has held senior management positions in marketing organizations and been a management consultant on executive development and applied research in the private and public sectors in Hong Kong, Singapore, the Philippines, England, and Sweden. She received her MA in social-industrial psychology from the Ateneo de Manila University in the Philippines and her PhD in social psychology from the University of Sussex in England. Dr. de Leon was awarded long-term research scholarships by the Japanese Ministry of Education and the British Council. She was the recipient of research grants from the National University of Singapore and the City Polytechnic of Hong Kong.

ANN DENIS is Professor of Sociology at the University of Ottawa and was the first Coordinator of the university's interdisciplinary Women's Studies Programme. She has published on gender, ethnicity, and post-secondary education. Her current research focuses on women and employment, especially women in management, and the interrelations among higher education, women's employment, and their unpaid activities – both domestic and in the community.

RONEL ERWEE is Professor in Organizational Behavior and Deputy Director of Research at the Graduate School of Management, University of Pretoria. She received her BA, MA, and DPhil from the University of Pretoria and completed part of her doctoral work at Michigan State University. Her research focuses on career development, entrepreneurship, and women in management, and she consults and publishes in these areas. Professor Erwee serves on the Board of Directors of the Small Business Development Corporation, the Women's Bureau, the Institute of Personnel Management (Publication Board), and the Free Market Foundation. She is only the ninth woman since 1965 to receive the Four Outstanding Young South Africans Award, and she conducts the only Women as Executive Program currently offered by business schools in South African universities.

ELLEN A. FAGENSON is Assistant Professor of Management at George Mason University. She received her PhD from Princeton University and was a postdoctoral fellow at Columbia University. She is the author of *Women in Management: Trends, Issues and Challenges in Managerial Diversity* (1993) and has published articles in such journals as the *Journal of Applied Psychology, Journal of Applied Behavioral Science, Journal of Organizational Behavior, Journal of Vocational Behavior, Journal of Business Venturing, Journal of Business Ethics, Group and Organization Studies,* and *Entrepreneurship: The Theory and Practice.* Dr. Fagenson's research has been reported by the *New York Times, USA Today,* the *Associated Press,* and *United Press International.* Her research and consulting activities focus on organization development, mentoring, power, women managers, and entrepreneurs. She serves as a management and psychology reviewer for several journals and is on the editorial review board of *The Executive.* She is the former Chair of the Women in Management Division of the Academy of Management.

VALERIE HAMMOND is Chief Executive, Roffey Park Management Institute, West Sussex, United Kingdom. Her current research examines management for the future, cultural and organizational change, and women in management. Ms. Hammond is Director of Business Leadership for Women, a program that resulted from her extensive research on women in management. Most recently, she led the research team whose work led to the creation of Opportunity 2000, the United Kingdom's business-led initiative for women's economic development. Before joining Roffey Park, Ms. Hammond was Director of the Ashridge Management Research Group, having previously worked with the Rank Organization, Friden Ltd., Mobil Data Services Ltd., and Petroleum ITB. She was a founding member and then President of the European Women's Management Development Network and remains actively involved in the international development of women in management and professional roles.

EVA HÄNNINEN-SALMELIN is Research Manager and Trainer of the International Women's Management Institute in Tampere, Finland. She received her MA in political science from the University of Helsinki. She has been a researcher and acting lecturer at the University of Tampere. Her research focuses on women in management, women in politics, and power in the changing society. She has published articles in *Unfinished Democracy, Women in Nordic Politics* (1985) and *Women and Public Administration, International Perspectives* (1992).

SUK-CHING HO is Senior Lecturer of Marketing at the Chinese University of Hong Kong. She is also the Chair of the Marketing Department and Director of

Studies in Consumer Research. She received her BBA from the Chinese University of Hong Kong and her MBA from Indiana University. Ms. Ho has conducted research and authored many articles on gender issues in management and marketing, particularly in Hong Kong.

WENDY HOLLWAY is Senior Lecturer at the University of Bradford, United Kingdom. She received her BA in psychology from the University of Sheffield and her PhD, also in psychology, from the University of London. Her interests range from gender discrimination in organizations and the history of work psychology to poststructuralist theories of subjectivity and gender and psychoanalytic psychotherapy. She is the author of *Work Psychology and Organizational Behavior: Managing the Individual at Work* (1991) and *Subjectivity and Method of Psychology: Gender, Meaning and Science* (1989) and coauthor of *Changing the Subject: Psychology, Social Regulation and Subjectivity* (1984). Her research on obstacles to women managers' advancement in the Tanzanian civil service led to her development of *Women into Senior Management,* a course for women managers in the East African Civil Services.

VIKI HOLTON joined Ashridge Management College in England in 1978, where she is currently a Senior Researcher with the Management Research Group and a specialist in issues concerning women's employment. Her most recent work was a survey on the future profile of senior information technology managers and the implication of this on women's development and the career development processes of men and women in the IT industry in the UK. The research was commissioned by the Women into Information Technology Foundation. She also was part of the research team for Opportunity 2000, the national business-led campaign in the United Kingdom to help women's involvement in organizations. Ms. Holton is editor of the quarterly newsletter of the European Women's Management Development Network and a member of its board. As a result, she has considerable knowledge of women's management development both in Europe and internationally.

DAFNA N. IZRAELI is Professor of Sociology at Bar-Ilan University, Israel and formerly Chair of the Department of Sociology. She has written numerous articles in professional journals and encyclopedias on organizational politics, gender work, and social policy. Her published volumes include *The Double Bind: On the Position of Women in Israel* (with A. Friedman and R. Schrift, 1982); *Women's Worlds* (with M. Safir, M. Mednick and J. Bernard, 1985); *Women in Management Worldwide* (with N. J. Adler, 1988); *Dual-Earner Families: International Perspectives* (with S. Lewis and H. Hootsmans, 1992); and *Women in Israel: Studies of Israeli Society* (with Y. Atzmon, 1993). Dr. Izraeli is academic advisor for the programs on women in management at the Israel Management Center and the Open University.

JANICE J. JACKSON is Chair of the Management and Marketing Department at Virginia State University. She received her doctorate of business administration from Memphis State University with a major concentration in management and minors in marketing and psychology. Dr. Jackson began her teaching career working with emotionally disturbed preschoolers and then taught English and mathematics in elementary and secondary schools. Before her arrival at Virginia State University, she was member of the management faculties at Memphis State University and George Mason University. She has taught a wide range of graduate and undergraduate courses including business strategy, organizational behavior, principles of management, business communications, organizational theory and business statistics. Dr. Jackson's research and publications focus on managerial communication, women in management, minorities in business, and equity issues. She is currently Chair of the Business Disciplines, a reviewer in the Women in Management Division of the Academy of Management, and a member of the Organizational Behavior Teaching Society and the Southern Management Association.

BOGDAN KAVČIČ is Senior Consultant and the Co-owner of ITED–Management Consulting Institute. He also is the Coordinator of the Slovenia directed research project in Organizational Sciences at the Ministry of Science and Technology. From 1976 to 1991, Professor Kavčič taught at the Faculty of Sociology, Political Science and Journalism, University of Ljubljana Yugoslavia. He was first Vice-Dean and later Dean of the Faculty of Sociology, Political Sciences and Journalism, at the university. He received his bachelor's degree in psychology and philosophy and his masters and PhD in sociology all from the University of Ljubjana. In 1987, he received a scholarship from the Japanese Science Association and spent two months at the Chuo University in Tokyo. Professor Kavčič's extensive research on management of work organizations and his participation in several international research projects has led to the publication of seventeen books and over 200 articles in professional journals. The results of his research have been presented at a number of international workshops and congresses of the International Sociological Association.

KAREN KORABIK is Associate Professor in the Department of Psychology at the University of Guelph, Canada. She received her BA, MS, and PhD from St. Louis University. She has published many articles on women in management, including studies of leadership and conflict resolution style; stress, coping, and social support; turnover; and acculturation. She was the Guest Editor of a special issue of *Equal Opportunities International* on Women in Management: Recent Developments in North America. She carried out interviews with women managers in the People's Republic of China in 1985 and 1990.

CAMILLA KREBSBACH-GNATH is Partner of KG&D Management und Unternehmensberatung, Kronberg, Germany – a company that concentrates on corporate development and organizational learning. She was formerly Division Head with Battelle Institute in Frankfurt and Head of Corporate Development at one of the major German banks, where she was in charge of organizational change and restructuring the corporation. She has recently published "Managing Change," FAZ-Blick durch die Wirtschaft, Frankfurt (December 1992).

JEAN LEE is Lecturer at the Faculty of Business Administration, National University of Singapore. She received her BA from the National University of Singapore and her MEd and PhD from the University of Massachusetts. Dr. Lee's research focuses on cross-cultural management, women in management, and Chinese management. She has published articles in international and regional journals and proceedings of international conferences. She is currently the Associate Editor of the *Asia Pacific Journal of Management,* published by the Faculty of Business Administration, National University of Singapore. Dr. Lee is actively involved in many executive development programs. She is the Director of the Human Resource Management Executive Programs for the China Electronics International Trading Cooperation and the Commission of Economics and Trade of Qingdao Municipal Government, People's Republic of China. She has conducted management training for Singapore Airlines and many regional and local companies. She has been an OD consultant to the Bina Surya Group in Indonesia since 1988.

OROSE LEELAKULTHANIT is Assistant Professor at the Graduate School of Business Administration, National Institute of Development Administration (NIDA), Bangkok. She was Associate Dean for Aacdemic Affairs and has served on the Executive Committee of the Executive MBA program at the Graduate School of Business Administration, NIDA. She received her BS in pharmacology from Mahidol University, her MBA from Thammasat University in Thailand, and her PhD in business administration from Indiana University. Dr. Leelakulthanit has conducted research on quality of life in Thailand, quality of work life, and business ethics and competitive strategies for Thai Garment Manufacturing Association. She has taught executive seminars in various universities, institutions, and private and public enterprises.

LUNG-LI LIAO is Professor of Social Work at the National Taiwan University where he teaches human resource management. Mr. Liao received his BA from National Chung-shing University in Taiwan and his MSW from Yeshiva University Wurzweiler School of Social Work in New York City. He also was trained in the School of Social Service at the University of Chicago. Mr. Liao is a consultant on management issues for both public and private agencies in Taipei. He has advised the Executive Yuan (the Cabinet) Civil Service Training Committee and lectured at the Chinese Management Development and Consultation Center in Taipei. Mr. Liao published a textbook on social work management and supervisory techniques. Most recently, he and Mr. Ng coauthored *Supervisory Management and Quality Control for Social Service* (Hong Kong Christian Service). Mr. Liao and Dr. Wei-yuan Cheng coauthored a book and several articles on women managers in Taiwan.

NORMA MANSOR is Associate Professor at the Faculty of Economics and Administration, University of Malaya, Kuala Lumpur, Malaysia. She received her BEcons from the University of Malaya and her MPA and PhD from the

University of Liverpool, England. Dr. Mansor conducts research and does training and consulting on strategic human resource management, corporate culture, and international management. She has authored numerous articles and coauthored *Women Managers of Malaysia* (1991). Dr. Mansor has conducted executive training programs for public and private sector companies in Malaysia. She received a Fulbright Fellowship (in 1990) and the Mitsubishi Award for Young Scholars (in 1991). Dr. Mansor has been a visiting scholar at Stanford University (1990–91), the Massachusetts Institute of Technology (1991), and Waseda University, Toyko (1992).

LAETICIA K. MUKURASI has recently become Programme Officer for Gender Development with the United Nations Development Programme. She is responsible for ensuring gender issues are appropriately addressed in UN projects. Previously she was Human Resource Development and Administrative Manager at Fibreboards (Africa) Limited, a public company in Tanzania. She holds a BA in public administration and international relations, a postgraduate degree in personnel management and an MA in gender and development from the University Sussex. Ms. Mukurasi has done consulting and research in human resource management and gender issues for a number of international and national organizations. Her projects included Workers Participation in Management, Gender Issues in Management, designing Transformative Gender-Oriented Policies and Evaluation of Gender-Oriented Training. She has authored a number of articles; a book, *Post Abolished: One Woman's Struggle for Employment Rights in Tanzania* (1991); and a chapter in *Women and the Industrial Decade in Africa* (United Nations Economic Commission for Africa, 1986). Ms. Mukurasi was a member of Executive Committee of the Association of Tanzania Employers, an Assessor of the Industrial Court of Tanzania, and a member of the General Council of the Tanzanian Trade Unions.

HELEN J. MULLER is Associate Professor and Coordinator of the Organizational Behavior Program at the Anderson School of Management, University of New Mexico. She holds a BA in cultural anthropology from the University of Wisconsin, a masters in public health from the University of Hawaii, and a PhD in public administration from the University of Southern California. She is the coauthor of *Public Health in a Retrenchment Era*, and other publications on issues such as: reframing management education; health services administration; and women, work, and management in developing countries. She initiated new college courses on women in management and diversity in organizations. Her research focuses on comparative management and gender issues, both domestically and internationally.

TUULIKKI PETÄJÄNIEMI has been the Equality Ombudsman in Finland since 1991. She received her LLB from the University of Helsinki and LLM (trained on the Bench) at the Turku Court of Appeals. She has been a member of Parliament and a member of the Nordic Council from 1979 to 1987. Before her appointment to the Equality Ombudsman, she was Assistant General Manager in the Union Bank of Finland Ltd. Her honorary positions include President of the National

Council of Women of Finland, Chair of the working group for the development of job evaluation in Finland, and Finland's Representative to the United Nations Commission on the Status of Women.

SHEILA M. PUFFER is Associate Professor at the College of Business Administration, Northeastern University and a fellow at the Russian Research Center, Harvard University. She is a graduate of the Plekhanov Institute of the National Economy in Moscow and was awarded her PhD from the University of California, Berkeley. Professor Puffer has published 25 articles on motivation, rewards, and disciplinary action; chief executive succession; and Russian management. She has also coauthored *Behind the Factory Walls: Decision Making in Soviet and US Enterprises* (Harvard Business School Press, 1990), and edited *Managerial Insights from Literature* (PWS-KENT, 1991) and *The Russian Management Revolution: Preparing Managers for the Market Economy* (M.E. Sharpe, 1992).

EVELYNE SERDJÉNIAN is an independent sociologist and management consultant. She received her "Licence" in ethnology, her MBA in economics and sociology from the University of Paris X, and her PhD in sociology from the Ecole des Hautes Etudes en Sciences Sociales, Paris. She has authored articles and reports on women and management and published two books, *L'égalité des chances ou les enjeux de la mixité* [*Equal Opportunity and the Mixity Challenge*] (1988) and *Les femmes et l'égalité professionnelle – Des moyens d'action* [*Women's Equal Opportunity – Action Tools*] (1987). Dr. Serdjénian conducts research on equal opportunity programs, management development, and access of women to economical and political power. She received an IBM grant and a German Marshall Fund fellowship to conduct research in the United States in 1985 and 1988. Dr. Serdjénian spent twenty years with IBM France and Europe in various management positions and now consults on personnel issues to banks, industrial companies, public authorities and international organizations.

RENATA SIEMIENSKA is Professor at the Institute of Sociology, University of Warsaw. She received her MA in geography and her MA and PhD in sociology from the Jagiellonian University in Cracow, Poland, and her habilitation (the highest academic degree in Poland) from the University of Warsaw. Dr. Siemienska's research and publications center on cross-cultural analyses of value systems of different populations and local leaders in particular. She also studies women's participation in public life. She is the author of numerous articles published in Polish, English, French, and German. Her books include *New Life in a New Town* (1969), *Power of Tradition and Power of Interests: About Sources of the White Ethnic Movement in the United States* (1978), *Gender, Occupation and Politics: Women's Participation in Public Life in Poland* (1990), and *Gender Inequality: A Comparative Study of Discrimination and Participation* (with M. Vianello et al., 1990). She is the Editor of *Polish Systems of Values and Models of Consumption: Diagnoses-Prognoses* (1984), *System of Values and Ideology as Determinants of Functioning of Polish Political System* (1988), and two special volumes of the international journals,

Women in Politics (1985) and *Political Values and Their Correlates in Socialist and Nonsocialist Comparative Perspective* (1988). Dr. Siemienska has served as the expert of UNESCO and member of the Executive Council of the International Political Science Association. Dr. Siemienska is a member of the Board of the United Nations International Research and Training Institute for the Advancement of Women and the Steering Committee of the European Network for Women's Studies.

SUNUNTA SIENGTHAI is Associate Professor and Associate Dean at the Faculty of Commerce and Accountancy, Thammasat University Bangkok. She received her BA in English from Chulalongkorn University, and her MA and PhD in labor and industrial relations from the Institute of Labor and Industrial Relations, University of Illinois at Urbana-Champaign. Dr. Siengthai conducts and publishes her research on labor management relations and productivity, human resource management, cross-cultural management, human resource development in the ASEAN countries, labor migration, male–female earnings differentials, and public enterprise management. She has taught in the executive development programs in various universities and institutions, both public and private, for-profit and not-for-profit. She was a JSPS scholar at Kyoto University in 1976 and a Citibank Fellow at the Kenan-Flager Business School, University of North Carolina at Chapel Hill in 1992. She has served on several subcommittees on wages for the Department of Labor.

PATRICIA G. STEINHOFF is Professor of Sociology and Director of the Center for Japanese Studies at the University of Hawaii. She holds a BA in Japanese language and literature from the University of Michigan and a PhD in sociology from Harvard University. Her books include *Abortion Politics: The Hawaii Experience and Conflict in Japan* (coedited with Ellis Krauss and Thomas Rohlen). She has also published nearly 50 articles on women's reproductive issues in the United States and on protest, social control, and social movements in Japan.

KAZUKO TANAKA holds degrees in sociology from Tokyo Metropolitan University and the University of Hawaii. She is Assistant Professor of sociology in the Faculty of Law, Kokugakuin University, Tokyo, Japan, and is an active participant in the Ochanomizu Women's University Women's Studies Group. She is the co-editor of three books (in Japanese): *Toward a Sociology of Women* (1981), *Creating Women's Studies* (1981), and *Concise Dictionary of International Women's History* (1986).

LORNA WRIGHT is Director of the Centre for Canada-Asia Business Relations at Queen's University, Kingston, Canada, and Associate Professor in the School of Business. She received her BA in psychology from Wilfred Laurier University, her MA in applied linguistics from the University of Essex, her MIM (masters in international management) from the American Graduate School of International Management, and her PhD in business administration from the University of

Western Ontario. Dr. Wright conducts research and consults on cross-cultural negotiations, international organizational development, preparing managers for international assignments, and women in management in Asia. She speaks Thai, Indonesian, and Japanese. Dr. Wright has taught at Nagoya University in Japan and Mahidol University in Thailand. She is a member of the Advisory Council of the Canada ASEAN Centre in Singapore, the editorial board of the *Journal of Southeast Asia Business* and was National Chair of the Canada Indonesia Business Council from 1988 to 1990. She received the Queen's University Commerce Society Award for Teaching Excellence in 1992.

ACKNOWLEDGMENTS

It is impossible to thank all of the people who have helped to create the possibility and the reality of this book. We would especially like to thank Rolf Janke, our editor, who skilfully guided Adler's first book, *International Dimensions of Organizational Behavior* to press, and has impressively guided *Competitive Frontiers* from a set of chapters into a published book. We would also like to thank the entire team at Blackwell Publishers in the United States and England for enthusiastically supporting the idea of *Competitive Frontiers*. We would like to thank the authors for searching for and finding the best available information on women in management in each of their countries around the world. Equally important, we would like to thank the many colleagues who helped us to better understand the subtle global dynamics of women managers working in a worldwide economy, including Gunilla Masreliez-Steen (Sweden), Victoria Hoffarth (The Philippines and England), Federica Olivares (Italy), Susan Bartholomew (Canada), Kathleen Brewer Doran (United States and Canada), and Homa Mahmoudi (United States). We would like to extend a special thanks to Rosalind Finlay, without whose calm, patient professionalism, there would be no book.

PART I

INTRODUCTION

Competitive Frontiers: Women Managers in a Global Economy

Dafna N. Izraeli and Nancy J. Adler

> The best reason for believing that more women will be in charge before long is that in a ferociously competitive global economy, no company can afford to waste valuable brainpower simply because it's wearing a skirt.
>
> *Fortune* (21)

World business has become intensely competitive. Top quality people allow corporations to compete. Yet, while outstanding human resource systems provide competitive advantages, companies worldwide draw from a restricted pool of potential managers. Although women represent over 50 percent of the world population, in no country do women represent half, or even close to half, of the corporate managers. Even in the United States, where many believe the proportion of women executives to be outstanding, reality belies the belief: whereas 46 percent of the American workforce is female, women constitute only three percent of the senior executives (6;51), and less than half of one percent of the highest paid officers and directors (20).

What has prevented the movement of women into management and, especially, into the executive suite? What have countries, companies, and women themselves done to increase women's representation in management? *Competitive Frontiers: Women Managers in a Global Economy* traces the changing nature of world business and its impact on the role of women managers. It reviews the role of women managers working within their own countries as well as those working across national boundaries. Unlike many books and articles written about women in management, *Competitive Frontiers* takes a global perspective and goes beyond the parochial determinism of each individual country's unique cultural, social, legal, economic, and political history of domestic business. Throughout *Competitive Frontiers* we ask if globally competitive firms dare to limit their potential talent pool to half of the human race.

Cross-national Comparisons: A Multidomestic Perspective

Until the late 1970s, women remained virtually invisible as managers, and their absence was generally considered a nonissue (8). Since then, women managers have become increasingly visible in many countries. *Competitive Frontiers* describes

---

Authors' names listed in reverse alphabetical order.

women managers in 21 countries and four continents. Each chapter views women in management through the lens of the broader societal context, linking the behaviors of individual women and men with the societal forces shaping their opportunities, motivations, and choices. Each country reveals a growing number of qualified women seeking managerial positions and an emerging cadre of women successfully pursuing management careers.

From one perspective, the picture is positive. In each country, changing societal patterns have resulted in significant increases in the number of women managers. These patterns include favorable economic and demographic conditions, supportive government policies, changing family roles, and emerging support systems, in addition to women's positive responses to their new opportunities.

From another perspective, the picture is not so positive. In each country a similar story is told of societies in which men control the centers of political and economic power and of management as a profession controlled primarily by men – a profession in which women remain relative newcomers, especially at the top. In all countries, major barriers retard women's progress in management, including such obstacles as stereotypical perceptions of women's abilities and qualifications, traditional attitudes towards women's family roles, women's minimal access to the social networks from which companies recruit managers and executives, and broadly based discrimination against women (30). Beyond the international commonalities underlying women's exclusion from the centers of managerial power and authority lies the uniqueness of local conditions in each country that produces the variety of women's experiences worldwide.

Systematic investigation of women's progress in management is relatively new. It began in North America – primarily in the United States – in the early 1970s, in Western Europe in the early 1980s, in Asia toward the mid-1980s, and in the former Communist countries of Eastern Europe, as well as in the People's Republic of China, only toward the end of the 1980s. Some chapters in this volume represent the first major study of women in management in that particular country.

In all countries, broad societal forces during recent decades resulted in more women entering lower-level managerial positions. In the economically developing and recently industrialized countries, a shift took place between the 1950s and early 1970s from agrarian toward manufacturing economies. This shift, along with the development of labor-intensive industries, primarily by multinational corporations, created a demand for cheap labor that brought many women into the urban labor force. Governments saw increasing labor force participation by women as essential for national economic growth and development, and they therefore encouraged women's economic activity. These governments, however, had no special interest in the promotion of women into management. Moreover, the traditional male ethos associated with manufacturing industries made industrial firms less friendly towards women managers than the developing wave of service sector firms.

In both the industrialized and industrializing worlds, the expansion of banking and other financial services opened opportunities for women in lower- and middle-level management positions. In most countries in the 1970s and 1980s, the growing public sector also absorbed many of the increasingly educated women into lower-level managerial positions. As new jobs were created, women moved into management and men moved up the hierarchy. The expansion of the public and service sectors became major factors promoting women's initial breakthrough into management. Reference to positive stereotypes – such as recognizing Asian women's traditional experience in the management of family finances and regarding women as more honest and trustworthy than men – helped employers rationalize women's presence in what had previously been a male domain (13;14;55;59). In both the industrialized and industrializing worlds, economic growth and increasing global competition heightened the demand for top quality managers. Economic enterprises began to take advantage of the growing availability of qualified women to fill the new positions.

In each country, the specific processes used to bring about changes differ. In the United States, powerful women's groups used the political process and the courts to help establish regulations that held employers responsible for implementing equal opportunity within their organizations (18). Such political and legal changes made it in organizations' self-interest to open their doors to women for lower-level managerial positions. However, neither the political nor the legal changes were sufficiently powerful to counter resistance to women entering the most senior managerial levels.

In France, legislation passed in the 1980s gave unions responsibility for negotiating equal opportunity on behalf of women. Progress, however, was very limited. The French unions appear to have lacked sufficient motivation to effect the previously legislated societal changes. Many French observers believe that the union leaders, most of whom are men, share management's prejudicial attitudes against women (52). In Hong Kong, where government intervention in commerce has been intentionally minimal and sex discrimination in employment continues to be legal, the proportion of women among corporate managers remains negligible (16).

In the social welfare states of Western Europe and Israel, social democratic parties created large public service bureaucracies that became the principal employers of women and thereby provide an important channel for women moving into management. Not surprisingly in these countries, gender segregation emerged along sectoral lines, with women managers concentrated in the public sector and men in the private sector (23;29).

Under Communist rule, Eastern European countries and the former Soviet Union set quotas for women in local-level management. However, women remained highly under-represented in more senior and national positions. In the former Yugoslavia, for example, opportunities for women managers depended on the political interests of the Communist party (32). Women's chances for promotion were best during periods of economic growth and political calm. However, during the times when political unrest was greatest, the proportion of women promoted into and within management dropped. At those times, the Communist party allocated positions either to men known to be loyal to the party or to men whose loyalty it needed to secure. In Poland, since women rarely filled managerial positions in state enterprises, few now have sufficient experience to draw upon for managing in the new market-oriented economy (54). The large women's organizations in certain former Communist countries, such as Poland and the Soviet Union, operated essentially as extensions of the Communist party. As such, they served primarily a social control function for the party, rather than filling an advocacy role for women (46;54).

Countries recently freed from Communist rule appear to be experiencing a backlash against many of the policies that were supportive of women's employment, professional advancement, and general freedoms (40). For example, high unemployment has increased competition, including competition for managerial positions, most often to women's detriment. In addition, due to a lack of funds, most former Communist countries have chosen to severely reduce the extensive network of childcare services, thus further increasing unemployment among women managers, who have been forced to quit working because too few acceptable childcare options remain available. Moreover, the belief that a woman's place is in the home is replacing the quota system that guaranteed women's representation in lower- and middle-level management in most former Communist countries. For example, under pressure from the Catholic church, the Polish parliament is currently enacting one of the most limiting antiabortion laws in the world. In Russia, Poland, former Eastern Germany, and parts of former Yugoslavia, women face a difficult struggle ahead to maintain or regain their previous representation in the economy (9;32;46;54). Only now are women in these transitional economies beginning to organize to advance their professional and political status and interests (40).

Other countries, such as Singapore, Malaysia, Indonesia, and Zimbabwe, have only recently emerged from extended periods of colonial rule. Colonialism's impact on women differed in important ways from its impact on men. For example, in colonial Indonesia, the Dutch recruited upper-class men for roles in the civil service and reinforced women's exclusion from public life (61). Moreover, the Dutch in Indonesia did not develop an educational system for the local people. In contrast, the Americans introduced universal education in the Philippines, thus giving Philippine women a decided advantage in urban labor markets compared with women from many other postcolonial countries (25). In Zimbabwe, where white men control the private business sector and black men control family life, black women continue to face a double challenge both as women and as black women (41). Similar patterns also exist in South Africa (17).

In most postcolonial countries, women participated in the struggle for liberation. A number of them later became members of their countries' new governments, thus providing role models for other women. However, because they were brought into government positions only by these unusual circumstances, the token women leaders did not necessarily become harbingers for the continued involvement of succeeding women in the centers of economic or political power. More commonly, they emerged as exceptions to a pattern that generally continues to exclude women from power (41). This exclusion has most frequently reasserted itself with the passing of the original leadership.

Women as Senior Executives: Managing above the Glass Ceiling

In recent years, the proportion of women managers has increased significantly in all countries for which data are available, although at a faster rate in some countries than in others. Yet, the anticipated "breakthrough" into the centers of organizational power seems even less likely today than it did twenty years ago, when the groundbreaking book *Breakthrough: Women into Management* noted: "It's when and how, not if, women move up. The groundwork has been laid" (35:15).

This optimism was reflected in many of the countries described in our earlier book, *Women in Management Worldwide* (1988), the first to provide a multinational perspective on women in management. In each country, people believed that the developments that had led to women's entry into the labor force and subsequently to their entry into management had unleashed a dynamic that would result in a more equal distribution of women throughout the profession. We were cautioned, however, to separate myth from reality by analyzing the gains carefully (33).

Whereas the optimism about women's movement into management appears to have been well grounded, the optimism about women moving up into executive positions now appears to have been premature. Conditions that we, like other observers, expected would remove the barriers to women's progress in management left most women well below the glass ceiling, where they could glimpse but not enter the executive suite. Women's increased investment in higher education and greater commitment to management as a career, as well as new equal opportunity legislation and the shortage (or anticipated shortage) of highly qualified managers, did not result in a significant breakthrough into the executive ranks. Regardless of the proportion of women managers at lower levels, women in every country remain only a tiny fraction of those in senior positions (51). According to *Business Week*, "at the current rates it will be 475 years before women reach equality in the executive suite" (56:76).

Our earlier work, as well as that of others, had failed to appreciate the important distinction between entry into management and upward mobility within management. We implicitly assumed that the movement of women managers into the executive level involved similar dynamics to those of women's initial entry into management. We were perhaps overly impressed with the thin trickle of extraordinary women, operating under exceptional circumstances in each country, who had succeeded in breaking through the glass ceiling to assume senior executive positions. The mass media heightened public exposure to their presence. In all countries, articles and feature stories in women's magazines and some mainstream business journals made these exceptional women highly visible. Visibility had the benefit of increasing the women executives' impact as role models, but also the unfortunate consequence of reinforcing the illusion that substantial numbers of women had and could make it to the top (27;28). The reality, however, is that the executive suite has remained highly resistant to women's entry.

To date, there has been no systematic research documenting the characteristics of the few executive women of almost every nationality who have succeeded in assuming very senior positions: however, they appear to come from the same societal groups as do male executives. For example, in cultures which draw executives primarily from the upper classes, such as the Javanese *priyayi* in Indonesia, both the few women executives and their male counterparts most frequently come from elite families in which personal connections smooth the way for business success (61). Similarly, in places such as Hong Kong, where family businesses define the dominant enterprise structure, both senior women and men most commonly run their families' businesses (16). In such cultures, executives generally view themselves as working in the service of their families. However, for a woman, working as an executive in a family business is not necessarily recognized as qualifying her to assume a similar executive position in a nonfamily enterprise. For example, in the Malaysian province of Kelantan, where women have traditionally dominated both business activity and family finances while men worked primarily in agriculture, the proportion of women who have been promoted into upper-level managerial positions in nonfamily enterprises and government organizations remains negligible (36).

Given these patterns, women's promotion into senior positions appears to be related to their access to the channels from which firms recruit executives; channels that tend to differ from those from which firms recruit entry-level managers. Becoming a manager generally requires appropriate credentials, whereas becoming an executive requires, among other things, belonging to the appropriate networks. For example, in Israel, women's near total exclusion from the senior ranks of the military deprives them of experiences that firms consider crucial for managing complex organizations. Their very limited access to senior positions both in the military and in political parties excludes them from links to social networks that are extremely important for access to positions of power in the civilian economy. Based on such exclusion, Israeli women remain unlikely to obtain significantly more powerful positions in the near future (29). Such definitions of appropriate experience eliminate women from consideration for senior corporate positions in other ways. For example, the requirement of many British firms that candidates for board member positions must have had prior board experience in a public company – which few women have had – eliminates most British women from consideration and explains, in part, the paucity of women board members (22).

Clearly, the situation facing women executives has not been the same as that of women managers. A fuller understanding of both the differences between "moving into" and "moving up within" management and the barriers that have limited women's advancement will better equip organizations to select more effective policies. Such policies will allow firms to remedy the current situation, rather than forcing them to remain trapped within prior, self-limiting perspectives.

Understanding the Barriers That Have Limited the Advancement of Women Managers

Until recently, a single set of questions dominated discussion about women managers worldwide: why are women under-represented, under-utilized, and skewed in their distribution among the levels of management? Only in the 1990s has the need for global competitiveness and transnational efficacy begun to transform and complement these initial equity-based concerns. Although the specific explanations offered for this worldwide phenomenon have varied, they reflect three essentially different perspectives. The first perspective emphasized individual-level differences, the second focused on organizational context, and the third analyzed institutional-ized discrimination. Whereas all three perspectives have made important contri-butions to our understanding of the historical barriers faced by women in management, each alone has been insufficient to fully explain the situation or to indicate appropriate ways to redress the balance. This is in part because many organizations did not perceive it to be in their interest to change. To understand the organizational reality faced by today's women managers worldwide, we need all three perspectives as well as a fourth that takes into account senior managers' greater power and authority. This fourth perspective includes senior managers' greater ability to influence – and to limit – women's access to executive positions and the history of societal and organizational dynamics pressuring them to do so. Such a multiperspective approach builds on accumulated knowledge and takes our understanding a step forward toward understanding the business environment of the 1990s and the twenty-first century. It thereby provides more adequate explana-tions and a more realistic understanding of what needs to be done if more women are to become senior managers – thus enabling firms facing global business dynam-ics to compete more effectively.

Perspective 1: A reliance on individual-level differences between women and men

Using an individual-level perspective, managers and scholars initially explained the paucity of women in management in terms of perceived personality and behavioral differences between women and men. Taking men's characteristics and behaviors as the norm for effective managerial performance, proponents of this perspective presumed that women's actual or perceived divergence from male norms explained women's limited representation in the managerial ranks (see articles and annotated bibliography (57;58)). Perceived differences between women's and men's manage-rial behavior were usually attributed either to gender differences in childhood socialization or to innate biological predispositions.

This individual-level perspective had the advantage of not assuming that women were identical to men. However, it also had three serious shortcomings in explain-ing why women were under-represented, under-utilized, and skewed in their dis-tribution among management levels. First, as will be highlighted in the second perspective, most studies that compared women and men managers in similar jobs found negligible differences (15;42;45;47). Second, the contemporary em-phasis on the manager as a "team player and coach," especially in today's increas-ingly knowledge-intensive industries (see (44)), suggested that a more people-oriented leadership style might render women more qualified than men for contemporary management positions. Similarly, the increasing emphasis on inter-national and transnational management, and with it the heightened importance of relationship-building skills, again puts a premium on the very characteristics that have been presumed to be women's strengths. Third, focusing on the individual ignored and concealed the importance of organizational factors affecting women's managerial careers.

Perspective 2: An emphasis on organizational context

The limitations of the individual-level perspective led observers to examine the organizational factors affecting women's managerial careers (31). Explanations shifted from gender-related individual differences to organizational factors facilitating and impeding women's careers in management. According to this perspective, characteristics of organizations – such as women's under-representation in management, the uneven distribution of women and men in various roles, as well as the greater opportunities organizations provide for men than for women to gain access to power, prestige, and monetary rewards – shaped attitudes and behavior much more than did individual personality traits. For example, research suggested that opportunities for promotion, more than gender-related individual differences, influenced women's and men's ambitions. Specifically, women's concentration in low-ceiling positions and in career tracks that limited their opportunities for promotion helped to explain women's supposedly lower level of ambition in relation to their jobs, careers, and organizations. Similarly tokenism helped to explain the dynamics associated with being the only woman in a senior management position – such as higher visibility and more stereotypical responses from colleagues. These dynamics both increased the performance pressures on women and reduced their prospects for success. Proponents of the organizational context perspective argued that these and other difficulties associated with tokenism would disappear when women represented a substantially greater proportion of the managers in an organization, since colleagues would then respond to them primarily as individuals and not as stereotypical representatives of a group (31).

In focusing on organizational context, this second perspective enriched our understanding of the factors affecting women's nonpromotion into and lack of upward movement within management as well as explaining some of the difficulties faced by the few token women who had succeeded in being promoted into more senior positions. However, similar to the first perspective's explanations based on individual differences, explanations based on organizational context also had serious shortcomings. First, they ignored the effects of broader societal forces on the organization as well as on a woman's place within the organization (37). Organizational context explanations failed to situate women managers and potential managers in the wider context of the society in which women live – the society that defines their existence, values, and options, as well as the costs for countering established societal expectations. Since a woman's organizational status and role are inseparable from her status and role in the greater society, one must include societal influences beyond the organization to understand women's experiences inside the organization (5;62). *Competitive Frontiers* is an explicit attempt to begin to add a cultural and societal context to our understanding of women's roles in management.

A second limitation of the organizational context perspective was its implicit assumption that organizations are essentially gender-neutral (1;11); that is, that our culturally based ideas about women and men do not inherently influence our organizational concepts and practices. Essentially, organizational context explanations implicitly assumed that organizations treat women and men the same. Unfortunately, viewing organizations as gender-neutral allowed managers and scholars to ignore the gender specificity of organizational choices and responses. For example, according to organizational context explanations, being a token in a group creates strong performance pressure on the token person (31). Moreover, the presence of a token in a team, whether a woman or a man, heightens team members' awareness of their own gender identity as well as of the differences between themselves and the token. Given this heightened awareness of differences, the second perspective explained that the organization would be more likely to treat the token in a stereotypical manner; that is, as a representative of a group rather than as an individual. While true, what this argument concealed was that societal stereotypes of women and men differ and that, therefore, tokenism has very different consequences for token women managers than for token men managers (26). Specifically, organizations frequently derail token women managers to less powerful, more peripheral jobs, whereas they often promote token men managers up the hierarchy. An easily visible example of the latter in many countries is the rapid rate at which banks promote token male tellers into supervisory and managerial positions compared with the negligible promotion rates of their equally qualified women colleagues. Consequently, although problematic for a woman, being a token often works to a man's advantage. By inaccurately equating the experiences of women and men tokens, organizational context explanations obscured masculinity's connections with power and privilege – connections that are embedded in the broader society and reflected in organizations.

A third limitation of the organizational context perspective was its assumption that power negates the influence of gender (31). According to this assumption, once a woman manager achieves a certain level of power, her status as a woman becomes irrelevant. However, what actually happens is that women who attain positions of power become more likely, rather than less likely, to experience a backlash against them (19). Thus, in reality, rather than eliminating the significance of gender, power often heightens it.

Fourth, organizational context alone inadequately explained the persistence and replication of the gender-based division of authority and power. Even in organizations in which women managers held a sizeable proportion of lower- and middle-level managerial positions, men continued to dominate the top positions. Theories that suggested that organizations and bureaucracy were gender-neutral did not adequately account for this continued structuring based on gender (1).

Perspective 3: The unveiling of institutionalized discrimination

The third perspective rejected the view that organizations were gender-neutral. Rather, it argued that established, taken-for-granted understandings about organizations have built-in assumptions about gender and that these assumptions explained women's persistent under-representation, under-utilization, and especially their skewed distribution in management (1;11;12). This third perspective demonstrated that organizations were neither objective nor gender-neutral. Fundamentally, it argued that gender discrimination was embedded in managers' basic assumptions about society and organizational life.

> To say that an organization . . . is gendered means that advantage and disadvantage, exploitation and control, action and emotion, meaning and identity are patterned through and in terms of a distinction between male and female, [between] masculine and feminine (1:146).

By contrast, the first perspective, which focused on individual differences and often assumed that the core problem lay in the shortcomings of individual women, never questioned the influence of gender on the organization. Also by contrast, the second perspective, which focused on organizational context, denied that assumptions about gender were embedded in managers' perceptions of all aspects of the organization, including the allocation of positions and the distribution of power and authority. From this third perspective, the significance of gender was seen to permeate all aspects of the organization. For example, the third perspective did not view management as simply a gender-neutral set of technical, human, and conceptual skills associated with various management positions. Rather, it viewed management as an occupation in which the assumptions about who was suitable to be a manager, including which social and personal characteristics were required, were based on societal assumptions about women and men. For example, common managerial beliefs were shown to privilege the life-style that societies most frequently reserve for men. Beliefs such as that successful managers must prove their worth by their early thirties, that career breaks to care for family members indicate a lack of organizational commitment, and that being the last person to leave at night demonstrates exemplary organizational commitment, all advantage a life-style more easily pursued by men than by women.

In most countries, including many described in this book, societies expect women to act subserviently towards men and therefore assume that men – but not women – will exercise authority over other people, especially over other men. These societal expectations form part of the everyday taken-for-granted reality of organizations. Organizations only marginally violate such expectations when they promote highly qualified women into lower-level managerial positions, since these women frequently supervise other women. However, organizations generally perceive women as neither natural nor acceptable in positions of real power and authority and consequently overlook them for higher-level positions. When this happens, it rarely occurs to anyone that it should be otherwise.

In Western countries, research found that both women and men managers perceived the characteristics of the ideal manager to be those they associated with the typical man but not with the typical woman (49;50). A more recent study found that by the late 1980s these perceptions were still held by men but no longer by women (10). Similar studies from other cultures, such as Hong Kong, also found that male managers held more prejudicial attitudes against women than did female managers (16). The widely supported belief by men managers that typical male characteristics are requisites for effective management revealed the close coupling of management with masculinity. "A 'masculine ethic' of rationality . . . [has given] the managerial role in the West its defining image for most of the twentieth century" (31:22).

> This 'masculine ethic' elevates the traits assumed to belong to some men to necessities for effective management: a tough-minded approach to problems; analytic ability to abstract and plan; a capacity to set aside personal emotional considerations in the interests of task accomplishment and a cognitive superiority in problem-solving and decision-making" (24:20–21).

 The specific image of an ideal manager varies across cultures, yet everywhere it privileges those characteristics that the culture associates primarily with men.

According to this third perspective, three implicit and explicit processes produced and reproduced discrimination against women managers. These processes explained the persistence of institutionalized patterns of gender discrimination in organizations.

First, organizations emphasized gender differences by using deceptively circular logic. The circular logic begins by organizations presuming that women and men have different personality predispositions and occupational interests, even when such managerially relevant differences have yet to be proven to exist. Based on such presumed differences, organizations then assign women to different jobs from those assigned to men, with those assigned to women incorporating less prestigious tasks, lower rewards, and fewer opportunities for advancement. The organization then uses the contrasting patterns of jobs held by women versus men to reinforce its belief that differences between women and men are inherent, rather than in fact constructed by the organization itself (60). For example, when organizations assume that men have a tougher-minded approach to problem solving than do women, they tend to hire mostly men for managerial positions that they believe require such tough-mindedness. They then interpret women's absence from such positions as evidence of an inherent shortcoming among women; namely, that women lack a sufficiently tough-minded approach to problem solving. Neither women's actual tough-mindedness nor the assumption that such a characteristic is the best way to achieve desired results is questioned or tested. Once such a pattern is established, organizations then use women's absence from the initial managerial categories to justify women's continued exclusion from both the initial and similar managerial positions. Thus, the first process reproducing institutionalized discrimination was organizations' assignment of women and men to different categories of jobs.

The second process reproducing institutionalized discrimination was the tendency of managers to promote people who most resembled themselves, those "who shared their own backgrounds, life-styles, prejudices, politics and goals" (38:25). Some observers used the nature of managerial work to explain this pattern. They stated that since managerial work is highly indeterminate, full of uncertainty, and fraught with difficulty in discerning the direct consequences of actions and decisions, managers want to work with people they feel they can trust (31;39). Moreover, since ambiguity precludes any form of direct assessment and control, only similarity can form a basis for trusting new managers, rather than any form of more precise performance measurement. Since senior male executives perceived women as being different and therefore as not being completely like them, they tended not to select women for senior management positions. Selecting new managers on the basis of similarity secured the status quo regarding the distribution of rights, privileges, and rewards for the current, primarily male, cohort of managers and executives (43).

According to this perspective, the third process reproducing institutionalized discrimination stemmed from the hierarchical interactions taking place daily between women and men in society and in organizations. Hierarchies structure interaction into patterns of dominance and subordination, most commonly between senior men and junior women, including between male bosses and women secretaries. Such male-dominated hierarchical interactions create and reinforce power and positional distinctions between women and men and make them appear natural. When such gender distinctions form part of the organization's taken-for-granted reality, managers rarely question them. Moreover, individuals who are aware of such organizational discrimination often have difficulty obtaining sufficient support for their views to change the patterns. Thus, by hierarchical gender relationships becoming a part of the taken-for-granted reality of organizational life, organizations sustain women's absence from the centers of power.

An important contribution of this approach was that it exposed the underlying gender-based assumptions embedded in the way people think about organizations. It challenged taken-for-granted definitions of reality and revealed many of them to be reflections of the pro-male bias embedded in society and organizations, rather than of objective, rational definitions of the best, or most effective, approaches to management. While the institutionalized discrimination perspective was highly instructive for understanding the persistence of discrimination, its primary shortcoming was that it failed to explain why, despite existing discrimination, women have nonetheless moved into lower and even middle management positions. In addition, this perspective has not been particularly helpful in explaining what would be required for women to assume executive positions, short of transforming the entire societal and organizational culture. Beyond the institutionalized discrimination perspective, a greater appreciation of power was needed to understand the role of senior management in monitoring women's promotion into the executive suite.

Perspective 4: Revealing power's influence in the organization

From the fourth perspective, societal and organizational institutions that privilege men have persisted because individuals and groups with a vested interest in their persistence have had the power to pre-empt change. From this perspective, one reason current managers limit the number of women managers has been simply that they do not want more competition. Managers at each level in the hierarchy have not differed in their desire to limit competition but rather in their ability to do so. Only those at the top, most of whom are men, have had the power and authority to determine an organization's rules, including determining the criteria for promotion close to and into their own ranks. Senior executives are more able than lower-level managers to protect their sphere of influence from outsiders – including from the entrance of both women and all but selected other men.

In all countries surveyed, the proportion of women among lower-level managers increased significantly when a rising demand for managers created a shortage of equally qualified men (48). During times of rising demand, it has been in organizations' interest to hire and promote the most highly qualified women and men managers available. The women hired did not replace male managers as much as they filled newly created positions. Senior executives remained largely unaffected by this dynamic because, given the limited number of executive positions, there has yet to be a scarcity in any country of interested and qualified male candidates. Moreover, because societies generously reward senior executives, firms are unlikely to suffer from a serious shortage.

In the United States, pressures to comply with affirmative action regulations and to establish the firm's image as an equal opportunity employer encouraged senior executives to create incentives for lower- and middle-level managers to promote women (18). Legislated affirmative action, a policy unique to the United States, was ostensibly intended for senior as well as lower-level management. In reality, however, it successfully opened the entry-level, but not executive positions, to women.

Not only have senior executives been protected from such affirmative action pressures, but they have also been exposed to pressures to exclude women from the most senior ranks. Managers who promoted women to senior positions could rarely do so without social support. For example, Ralph Ablon, chairman of American Ogden Corp., number 74 on *Fortune's* list of the 100 largest diversified service companies, recently appointed a woman as Ogden's chief financial officer. Ablon explained, "When I became CEO 29 years ago, I don't believe I could have been as liberal, and I couldn't have gotten away with appointing a woman as CFO. Today I could" (20:42). Why was Ablon able to do today what he was unable to do in the past? Perhaps it was because societal norms in the United States have changed. Ablon implicitly explained his (and his colleagues') past choices not to select a woman to be the CFO as emanating in part from his assessment of the potential cost to himself and to his company had he done so. Due to societal pressure, discrimination against women has often actually been rational from the perspective of individual senior executives, since behaving otherwise has usually elicited criticism from their peers (34).

Adding the dynamic of power to the institutional discrimination perspective helped explain why some patterns have changed and others have not. It helped explain why, despite management's masculine image, women have succeeded in entering the lower levels of management, but, once in, have failed to move up into senior management. Similarly, it helped to explain why individual and organized pressure has been needed from government and other public organizations as well as from the women prepared to move up. However, even this perspective, like its three predecessors, failed to account for the impact on women in management of the increasingly competitive business dynamics faced by today's international and transnational firms (3).

Policy Implications

Each alternative explanation for women's under-representation, under-utilization, and skewed distribution in management suggested different change strategies for improving the situation. In fact, the recommendations are interrelated since change at each level has implications for conditions at all levels. For purposes of actually improving the situation, firms should consider strategies encompassing multiple levels of change. For clarity, however, we will discuss the recommendations separately in relation to each of the four perspectives presented in this chapter.

First, when the situation is understood as caused by individual-level differences between women and men, as in the first perspective, the most common recommendation has been that women themselves have to change – that women must increase their self-confidence, become more strongly motivated to move up the career ladder, and exhibit more stereotypically male approaches to management. However, women have been cautioned to remain "feminine enough" to avoid challenging or offending prevailing sex-role conventions (53). According to this perspective, if women are to make it in management, they have to learn to "fit in."

As captured in the first perspective, the societal and organizational messages conveyed to women managers in most countries have been that women themselves are an important part of the problem and that, therefore, women have to take primary responsibility both for the current situation and for changing it. To comply with the dictates of this common appreciation of the problem, women, on their own initiative, have increasingly turned to business schools, economics programs, and special management training courses to obtain the requisite qualifications to "fit in." Women managers, entrepreneurs, and professionals have also organized networks to provide mutual support and greater access to needed opportunities and resources.

By contrast, when the situation is understood as an organizational context problem, as in the second perspective, then individual women gaining qualifications previously held predominantly by men is not sufficient. From this perspective, the responsibility for solving the problem shifts from individual women to employers. It is organizations themselves that need to eliminate barriers and provide incentives for increasing the number of women managers. For instance, organizations must create career paths for women and men managers with an equal probability of leading to the top, rather than continuing to constrain women's upward mobility by concentrating them in low-ceiling positions. Mechanisms such as affirmative action programs have enabled organizations to recruit and hire women managers and to place them into higher-ceiling managerial job hierarchies, thus creating greater opportunities for upward mobility.

When the situation is understood as one of institutionalized discrimination, as in the third perspective, then both women and men managers need first to acknowledge the discrimination itself "because sexual discrimination is insidious, and when inequality is not overtly acknowledged, it's harder to address" (51:74). Once acknowledged, eliminating discrimination requires senior management's commitment to change along with the cooperation of the total organization. The policy recommendations stemming from the institutionalized discrimination perspective have thus been more far-reaching than those based on the first two perspectives, since they require changing managers' basic assumptions about organizations and society. For example, companies have mandated sessions to educate all managers – senior and junior – about the patterns of implicit and explicit discrimination and have trained them in new nondiscriminatory behaviors.

When the situation is understood as a consequence of power dynamics, as in the fourth perspective, then the interests of the organizations' most powerful members must change. The benefits of including more women executives and the costs of excluding them must become more apparent to senior executives. Some observers already argue that the "number of qualified women will soon be so great that ignoring them will be bad business" (51:76). Although this may well be true, those in power need to recognize the broader economic and competitive advantages of sharing the executive ranks with more women.

The power perspective emphasizes the need for current executives to understand that it is in their own and their companies' best interest to welcome more women into the executive suite. The intensification of global competition has become a major influence compelling executives to view women managers as a competitive advantage rather than as a legislated necessity. Global competition challenges corporations to maximize the effectiveness of their human resources. The successful performance of growing numbers of women managers offers firms an opportunity to outperform their more prejudiced competitors by better using women's talents. A number of leading transnational firms have already accepted this reality and begun to act accordingly (2;3).

In additon, in some countries, organizations promoting equal opportunity for senior-level women – such as Catalyst in the United States and the Federation of Business and Professional Women in South Africa – provide firms with prestige incentives (such as awards) for advancing women into senior management. Similar national initiatives offer broader incentives and support to senior executives for providing equal opportunities for women managers and executives. For example, a team of chief executives and directors of leading British companies established the national Opportunity 2000 campaign to improve women's economic opportunities and progress and, concomitantly, their own companies' economic competitiveness (22). Under the sponsorship of the Prince of Wales, Opportunity 2000's membership grew from seventeen organizations in 1990 to 220 by the end of 1993. Whether Opportunity 2000 will also bring significant numbers of women to the highest levels of organizations by the year 2000 remains to be seen. Pressure from powerful societal groups – including significant competitors and stakeholders – continues to be an important force in this direction.

Global competition and the need for top quality managers are making women's promotion into senior management a business issue, rather than strictly an issue of equity. For success, continued change is needed at the individual, organizational, and societal levels. Future business leaders will build their success on equity, not on archaic patterns of under-representation, under-utilization, and skewed distributions of women in management.

References

(1) Acker, Joan (1990) "Hierarchies, Jobs, Bodies: A Theory of Gendered Organizations," *Gender & Society* 4(2):139–158.

(2) Adler, Nancy J. (1987) "Pacific Basin Managers: A Gaijin, Not a Woman," *Human Resource Management* 26(2):169–191.

(3) Adler, Nancy J. (1994) "Competitive Frontiers: Women Managing Across Borders," in Nancy J. Adler and Dafna N. Izraeli (eds.), *Competitive Frontiers: Women Managers in a Global Economy*, pp. 22–40. Cambridge (USA)/Oxford (England): Blackwell Publishers.

(4) Adler, Nancy J., and Izraeli, Dafna N. (eds.) (1988) *Women in Management Worldwide.* Armonk, N.Y.: M. E. Sharpe.

(5) Adler, Nancy J., and Jelinek, Mariann (1986) "Is 'Organizational Culture' Culture Bound?" *Human Resource Management* 25(1): 73–90.

(6) Ball, Karen (1991) "Study Finds Few Women Hold Top Executive Jobs," *Washington Post*, August 26, p. A-11.

(7) Bartlett, Christopher A., and Ghoshal, Sumantra (1989) *Managing across Borders: The Transnational Solution.* Boston: Harvard Business School Press.

(8) Berthoin Antal, Ariane, and Izraeli, Dafna N. (1993) "A Global Comparison of Women in Management: Women Managers in Their Homelands and as Expatriates," in Ellen A. Fagenson (ed.), *Women in Management: Trends, Issues and Challenges in Managerial Diversity*, Vol. 4. Newbury Park, Calif.: Sage.

(9) Berthoin Antal, Ariane, and Krebsbach-Gnath, Camilla (1994) "Women in Management in Germany: East, West, and Reunited," in Nancy J. Adler and Dafna N. Izraeli (eds.), *Competitive Frontiers: Women Managers in a Global Economy*, pp. 206–223. Cambridge (USA)/Oxford (England): Blackwell Publishers.

(10) Brenner, O. C., Tomkiewicz, Joseph, and Schein, Virginia Ellen (1989) "The Relationship between Sex Role Stereotypes and Requisite Management Characteristics Revisited," *Academy of Management Journal* 32(3):662–669.

(11) Calas, Marta B. (1988) "Gendering Leadership: The Differe(e/a)nce That Matters." Paper presented at the annual meetings of the Academy of Management, Anaheim, Calif.

(12) Calas, Marta B., and Smircich, Linda (1992) "Re-writing Gender into Organization Theorizing: Directions from Feminist Perspectives," in M. I. Reed and M. D. Hughes (eds.), *Re-thinking Organization: New Directions in Organizational Research and Analysis.* London: Sage.

(13) Chan, Audrey, and Lee, Jean (1994) "Women Executives in a Newly Industrialized Economy: The Singapore Scenario," in Nancy J. Adler and Dafna N. Izraeli (eds.), *Competitive Frontiers: Women Managers in a Global Economy*, pp. 127–142. Cambridge (USA)/Oxford (England): Blackwell Publishers.

(14) Cheng, Wei-yuan, and Liao, Lung-li (1994) "Women Managers in Taiwan," in Nancy J. Adler and Dafna N. Izraeli (eds.), *Competitive Frontiers: Women Managers in a Global Economy*, pp. 143–159. Cambridge (USA)/Oxford (England): Blackwell Publishers.

(15) Chusmir, Leonard H., and Mills, Joan (1988) "Resolution of Conflict: Managerial Gender Differences." Paper presented at the annual meetings of the Academy of Management, Anaheim, Calif.

(16) de Leon, Corinna T., and Ho, Suk-ching (1994) "The Third Identity of Modern Chinese Women: Women Managers in Hong Kong," in Nancy J. Adler and Dafna N. Izraeli (eds.), *Competitive Frontiers: Women Managers in a Global Economy*, pp. 43–56. Cambridge (USA)/Oxford (England): Blackwell Publishers.

(17) Erwee, Ronel (1994) "South African Women: Changing Career Patterns," in Nancy J. Adler and Dafna N. Izraeli (eds.), *Competitive Frontiers: Women Managers in a Global Economy*, pp. 325–342. Cambridge (USA)/Oxford (England): Blackwell Publishers.

(18) Fagenson, Ellen A., and Jackson, Janice J. (1994) "The Status of Women Managers in the United States," in Nancy J. Adler and Dafna N. Izraeli (eds.), *Competitive Frontiers: Women Managers in a Global Economy*, pp. 388–404. Cambridge (USA)/Oxford (England): Blackwell Publishers.

(19) Faludi, Susan (1991) *Backlash: The Undeclared War against American Women*. New York: Crown Publishers.

(20) Fierman, Jaclyn (1990) "Why Women Still Don't Hit the Top," *Fortune*, July 30, pp. 40–62.

(21) Fisher, Anne B. (1992) "When Will Women Get to the Top?" *Fortune*, September 21, pp. 44–56.

(22) Hammond, Valerie, and Holton, Viki (1994) "The Scenario for Women Managers in Britain in the 1990s," in Nancy J. Adler and Dafna N. Izraeli (eds.), *Competitive Frontiers: Women Managers in a Global Economy*, pp. 224–242. Cambridge (USA)/Oxford (England): Blackwell Publishers.

(23) Hänninen-Salmelin, Eva, and Petäjäniemi, Tuulikki (1994) "Women Managers, the Challenge to Management: The Case of Finland," in Nancy J. Adler and Dafna N. Izraeli (eds.), *Competitive Frontiers: Women Managers in a Global Economy*, pp. 175–189. Cambridge (USA)/Oxford (England): Blackwell Publishers.

(24) Hearn, Jeffrey, and Parkin, Wendy P. (1988) "Women, Men, and Leadership: A Critical Review of Assumptions, Practices and Change in the Industrialized Nations," in Nancy J. Adler and Dafna N. Izraeli (eds.), *Women in Management Worldwide*, pp. 17–40. Armonk, N.Y.: M. E. Sharpe.

(25) Hoffarth, Victoria (1993) "Women's Participation in Philippine Management and Organizational Performance," Working Paper. Manila: Women for Women Foundation (Asia), Inc.

(26) Izraeli, Dafna N. (1983) "Sex Effects or Structural Effects?: An Empirical Test of Kanter's Theory of Proportions," *Social Forces* 62(3):153–165.

(27) Izraeli, Dafna N. (1987) "Women's Movement into Management in Israel," *International Studies of Management and Organization* (Fall-Winter):76–107.

(28) Izraeli, Dafna N. (1988) "Women's Movement into Management in Israel," in Nancy J. Adler and Dafna N. Izraeli (eds.), *Women in Management Worldwide*, pp. 186–212. Armonk, N.Y.: M. E. Sharpe.

(29) Izraeli, Dafna N. (1994) "Outsiders in the Promised Land: Women Managers in Israel," in Nancy J. Adler and Dafna N. Izraeli (eds.), *Competitive Frontiers: Women Managers in a Global Economy*, pp. 301–324. Cambridge (USA)/Oxford (England): Blackwell Publishers.

(30) Izraeli, Dafna N., and Zeira, Yoram (1993) "Women as Managers in International Business: A Research Review and Appraisal," *Business & The Contemporary World* V(3): 35–46.

(31) Kanter, Rosabeth Moss (1977) *Men and Women of the Corporation*. New York: Basic Books.

(32) Kavčič, Bogdan (1994) "Women in Management: The Case of the Former Yugoslavia," in Nancy J. Adler and Dafna N. Izraeli (eds.), *Competitive Frontiers: Women Managers in a Global Economy*, pp. 286–298. Cambridge (USA)/Oxford (England): Blackwell Publishers.

(33) Keller Brown, Linda (1988) "Female Managers in the United States and in Europe: Corporate Boards, M.B.A. Credentials, and the Image/Illusion of Progress," in Nancy J. Adler and Dafna N. Izraeli (eds.), *Women in Management Worldwide*, pp. 265–274. Armonk, N.Y.: M. E. Sharpe.

(34) Larwood, Laurie, Gutek, Barbara, and Gattiker, Urs. E. (1984) "Perspectives on Institutional Discrimination and Resistance to Change," *Group & Organization Studies* 9(3):333–352.

(35) Loring, Rosalind, and Wells, Theodora (1972) *Breakthrough: Women into Management*. New York: Van Nostrand Reinhold.

(36) Mansor, Norma (1994) "Women Managers in Malaysia: Their Mobility and Challenges," in Nancy J. Adler and Dafna N. Izraeli (eds.), *Competitive Frontiers: Women Managers in a Global Economy*, pp. 101–113. Cambridge (USA)/Oxford (England): Blackwell Publishers.

(37) Martin, Patricia Yancey (1981) "Women Labour Markets and Employing Organizations: A Critical Analysis," in D. Dunkerley and G. Salaman, *The International Yearbook of Organization Studies*. London: Routledge & Kegan Paul.

(38) Martin, Patricia Yancey, Harrison, Dianne, and Dinitto, Diana (1983) "Advancement for Women in Hierarchical Organizations: A Multilevel Analysis of Problems and Prospects," *Journal of Applied Behavioral Science* 19:19–33.

(39) Mintzberg, Henry (1975) "The Manager's Job: Folklore and Fact," *Harvard Business Review* 53 (July/August):49–61.

(40) Moghadam, Valentine M. (1992) *Privatization and Democratization in Central and Eastern Europe and the Soviet Union: The Gender Dimension*. Helsinki: WIDER Institute of the United Nations University.

(41) Muller, Helen J. (1994) "The Legacy and Opportunities for Women Managers in Zimbabwe," in Nancy J. Adler and Dafna N. Izraeli (eds.), *Competitive Frontiers: Women Managers in a Global Economy*, pp. 358–374. Cambridge (USA)/Oxford (England): Blackwell Publishers.

(42) Nieva, Veronica F., and Gutek, Barbara A. (1981) *Women and Work: A Psychological Perspective*. New York: Praeger.

(43) Offe, Carl (1976) *Industry and Inequality* (J. Wickham trans.). London: Edward Arnold.

(44) Peters, Thomas J., and Waterman, Robert H., Jr. (1982) *In Search of Excellence: Lessons from America's Best-Run Companies*. New York: Harper & Row.

(45) Powell, Gary N. (1988) *Women and Men in Management*. Newbury Park, Calif.: Sage.

(46) Puffer, Sheila (1994) "Women Managers in the Former USSR: A Case of Too Much Equality," in Nancy J. Adler and Dafna N. Izraeli (eds.), *Competitive Frontiers: Women Managers in a Global Economy*, pp. 263–285. Cambridge (USA)/Oxford (England): Blackwell Publishers.

(47) Ragins, Belle Rose (1991) "Gender Effects in Subordinate Evaluations of Leaders: Real or Artifact?" *Journal of Organizational Behavior* 12:259–268.

(48) Reskin, Barbara F., and Roos, Patricia A. (1990) *Job Queues, Gender Queues*. Philadelphia: Temple University Press.

(49) Schein, Virginia E. (1973) "The Relationship between Sex Role Stereotypes and Requisite Management Characteristics," *Journal of Applied Psychology* 57(2):95–100.

(50) Schein, Virginia E. (1975) "Relationships between Sex Role Stereotypes and Requisite Management Characteristics among Female Managers," *Journal of Applied Psychology* 60(3):340–344.

(51) Segal, Amanda Troy, and Zellner, Wendy (1992) "Corporate Women: Progress? Sure. But the Playing Field Is Still Far from Level," *Business Week*, June 8, pp. 74–76.

(52) Serdjénian, Evelyne (1994) "Women Managers in France," in Nancy J. Adler and Dafna N. Izraeli (eds.), *Competitive Frontiers: Women Managers in a Global Economy*, pp. 190–205. Cambridge (USA)/Oxford (England): Blackwell Publishers.

(53) Sheppard, Deborah L. (1989) "Organizations, Power and Sexuality: The Image and Self-Image of Women Managers," in Jeff Hearn, Deborah L. Sheppard, Peta Tancred-Sheriff and Gibson Burrell (eds.), *The Sexuality of Organization*. London: Sage.

(54) Siemienska, Renata (1994) "Women Managers in Poland: In Transition from Communism to Democracy," in Nancy J. Adler and Dafna N. Izraeli (eds.), *Competitive Frontiers: Women Managers in a Global Economy*, pp. 243–262. Cambridge (USA)/Oxford (England): Blackwell Publishers.

(55) Siengthai, Sununta, and Leelakulthanit, Orose (1994) "Women Managers in Thailand," in Nancy J. Adler and Dafna N. Izraeli (eds.), *Competitive Frontiers: Women Managers in a Global Economy*, pp. 160–171. Cambridge (USA)/Oxford (England): Blackwell Publishers.

(56) Spillar, K. (1992) quoted in Segal, Amanda Troy and Zellner, Wendy (1992) "Corporate Women: Progress? Sure. But the Playing Field Is Still Far from Level," *Business Week*, June 8, p. 76.

(57) Stead, Bette Ann (ed.) (1978) *Women in Management*. Englewood Cliffs, N. J.: Prentice-Hall.

(58) Stead, Bette Ann (ed.) (1985) *Women in Management*, 2nd edn. Englewood Cliffs, N. J.: Prentice-Hall.

(59) Steinhoff, Patricia G., and Tanaka, Kazuko (1994) "Women Managers in Japan," in Nancy J. Adler and Dafna N. Izraeli (eds.), *Competitive Frontiers: Women Managers in a Global Economy*, pp. 79–100. Cambridge (USA)/Oxford (England): Blackwell Publishers.

(60) West, Candace, and Zimmerman, Don H. (1983) "Small Insults: A Study of Interruptions in Conversations between Unacquainted Persons," in B. Thorne, C. Kramerae, and N. Henley-Rowley (eds.), *Language, Gender and Society*. Rowley, Mass.: Newbury House.

(61) Wright, Lorna, and Crockett-Tellei, Virginia (1994) "Women in Management in Indonesia," in Nancy J. Adler and Dafna N. Izraeli (eds.), *Competitive Frontiers: Women Managers in a Global Economy*, pp. 57–78. Cambridge (USA)/Oxford (England): Blackwell Publishers.

(62) Wolff, Janet (1977) "Women in Organizations," in S. Clegg and D. Dunkerley (eds.), *Critical Issues in Organizations*. London: Routledge & Kegan Paul.

2

Competitive Frontiers: Women Managing Across Borders

Nancy J. Adler

> It doesn't make any difference if you are blue, green, purple, or a frog,
> if you have the best product at the best price, they'll buy.
>> American woman manager based in Hong Kong

About the single most uncontroversial, incontrovertible statement to make about women in international management is that there are very few of them. The evidence is both subjective and objective (17). As an executive in a global firm, would you hire a woman for an international management position? Would you send her abroad as an expatriate manager? Would she succeed? Would hiring her increase or decrease your firm's competitiveness?

Global Competition

Business today increasingly competes on a worldwide basis. Few firms have the luxury of competing primarily within their own domestic market. Whereas some firms use country-specific multidomestic strategies, and thus compete in independent domestic markets, a much greater number have embraced globally integrated strategies structured around worldwide lines of business (11). As global competition continues to intensify, firms are evolving transnational strategies. Such strategies simultaneously require the local responsiveness demanded by multidomestic strategies, the worldwide integration demanded by global strategies, along with an increased emphasis on organizational learning and innovation (14). These business dynamics lead to:

> transnational networks of firms and divisions within firms, including an increasingly complex web of strategic alliances. Transnational firms . . . are less hierarchically structured than firms operating in the previous phases. Power is no longer centered in a single headquarters that is . . . dominated by any one national culture. As a consequence, both structural and cultural dominance are minimized, with cross-cultural interaction no longer following any predefined "passport hierarchy" (10).

These organizational changes are affecting the numbers and roles of women managers.

Women and Transnational Corporations

Given the increasing importance of transnational corporations, it is encouraging that their impact on women in management, to date, has been primarily positive. Transnational corporations include women in ways that domestic, multidomestic, and multinational firms do not. First, the extremely competitive business environment forces transnational firms to select the very best people available. The opportunity cost of prejudice – of rejecting women and limiting selection to men – is much higher than in previous economic environments. As *Fortune* succinctly stated, "The best reason for believing that more women will be in charge before long is that in a ferociously competitive global economy, no company can afford to waste valuable brainpower simply because it's wearing a skirt" (18:56). This competitive advantage is heightened by a growing worldwide education differential favoring women.

Second, whereas domestic and multidomestic companies hire primarily local nationals and, therefore, must closely adhere to local norms on hiring – or not hiring – women managers, transnational corporations are not similarly limited. Because the corporate culture of transnational firms is not coincident with the local culture of any particular country, transnationals have greater flexibility in defining selection and promotion criteria that best fit the firm's needs rather than those that most closely mimic the historical patterns of a particular country. Said simply, transnationals can and do hire local women managers even in countries in which the local companies rarely do so.

U.S.-based transnational corporations, for example, have often hired local women managers when local firms would not. This dynamic has been particularly pronounced in Japan, where foreign corporations have had difficulty attracting top-ranked male applicants (25;35). American firms have led the way in hiring well-qualified Japanese women, while Japanese firms are still extremely reluctant to hire them (36). Interestingly, while still hiring fewer women than most American firms, Japanese multinationals operating in the United States hire more women managers in their American affiliates than they do in their home country operations (33).

By hiring women, transnationals act as role models for firms in many countries that have not seriously considered promoting significant numbers of women into managerial positions. The greater the number of expatriates involved in foreign affiliates, the less likely they are to follow local human resource practices – including being less likely to restrict the number of women managers (33). The firm's transnational character allows it organizational freedoms and imposes competitive demands not present in domestic or multidomestic environments.

Third, transnational corporations have begun to send women abroad as expatriate managers (4). Because transnationals use expatriates and local managers, they can benefit from the greater flexibility that many cultures afford foreign women. As will be described, most countries do not hold foreign women to the same professionally limiting roles that restrict local women (6;23). The outstanding success of these women expatriate managers in all geographical areas – Africa, the Americas, Asia, Europe, and the Middle East – is encouraging firms both to continue sending women abroad (6;30) and to begin to promote more local women into management (23).

Fourth, whereas domestic, multidomestic, and multinational firms have been characterized by structural hierarchies, transnationals are increasingly characterized by networks of equals. Recent research suggests that women work particularly well in such networks:

> women . . . are countering the values of the hierarchy with those of the web. . . . when describing their roles in their organizations, women usually refer . . . to themselves as being in the middle of things. . . . Inseparable from their sense of themselves as being in the middle . . . [is] women's notion of being connected to those around them (22:52,45–46).

Not surprisingly, transnational firms see women managers as bringing needed collaborative and participative skills to the workplace (31).

Fifth, leading management scholars have identified innovation as a key factor in global competitiveness (14;21;32). An inherent source of innovation is well-managed diversity, including gender diversity (8). Women bring diversity to transnational corporations that have heretofore been primarily male dominated.

Transnational corporations thus include more women than their predecessors could (or would) and benefit organizationally from their professional contributions in new ways. They benefit both from women's increased representation at all levels of the organization as well as from their unique ways of contributing to the organization that complement those of men.

Fundamental Assumptions: Different Approaches

Given the current scarcity of women in the managerial ranks, transnational firms can use two approaches to unleash the potential of women managers: they can increase the number of women managers and executives, and they can encourage their unique contribution. Unfortunately, many of their predecessors – domestic, multidomestic, and multinational firms – adopted neither approach or limited themselves by focusing on only one of the two approaches.

As shown in Table 2.1, firms have traditionally made one of two fundamentally different assumptions about the ideal role of women in management. Although generally implicit, the first reflects an equity approach based on assumed similarity, while the second defines a complementary contribution approach based on assumed difference. The first focuses on increasing the representation of women managers; the second, on increasing their utilization at all levels of the organization.

The first, the equity approach, based on assumed similarity, has been used most pervasively in the United States. In this approach, firms assume that women are identical, as professionals, to men, and therefore equally capable of contributing in ways similar to those of men. From this equity perspective, the primary question is one of entry into and representation within management. Is the firm hiring and

Table 2.1 Two approaches to women in management

Assumptions	Equity approach	Complementary contribution approach
Fundamental assumptions	Similarity	Difference
Women's and men's contributions	Identical	Complementary
Fairness based on	Equity	Valuing difference
Strategic goal	Equal access	Recognizing and valuing difference
Assessment	Quantitative	Qualitative
Measured by	Statistical proportion of women at each hierarchial level	Assessing women's contribution to organization's goals
Process	Counting women	Assessing women's contribution
Measurement of effectiveness		
Women's contribution	Identical to men's	Complementary to men's
Norms	Identical for men and women	Unique to men and women
Based on	Historical "male" norms	Women's own contribution
Referent	Men	Women
Acculturation process	Assimilation	Synergy
Expected behavior	Standardized	Differentiated
Based on	Male norms	Female norms
Essence	"Dress for success" business suit	Elegant, feminine attire
Example	United States: "The melting pot"	France: "Vive la différence!"

Source: Nancy J. Adler (1986–7)"Women in Management Worldwide," *International Studies of Management and Organization* 16(3–4):3–32.

promoting sufficient numbers of women managers? Primary change strategies include affirmative action programs, equal rights legislation, and structural changes designed to avoid tokenism and to train women in managerial skills traditionally neglected during their formal education and informal socialization.

Given the equity approach's emphasis on equal entry into and equal representation within the male-dominated world of management, the equity approach's implicit goal for women managers is assimilation. Firms expected women to think, dress, and act like the men who had traditionally held the aspired-to management positions. Understandably, firms measured effectiveness against male norms: could she do what he had been doing as well as he had been doing it? Or, according to *Fortune* (31:58), "If you can't join 'em, beat 'em . . . the way to overcome [discrimination] is to . . . start outdoing men at their own game." The potential for women to make unique, but equally valuable, contributions to organizations remained outside the logic of the equity approach and therefore largely unrealized.

In contrast, the second approach, the complementary contribution approach, is based on the assumption of difference, not similarity. Originally used to describe Swedish managers (34), it has been pervasive throughout Europe and Japan and is evident in most other areas of the world. In the complementary contribution approach, firms assume women and men differ and therefore are capable of making different, but equally valuable, contributions to the organization (13;16;19;20;24; 26;27;28). Unlike in the equity approach, the goal is not assumed to be equal statistical representation but, rather, equivalent recognition of and benefit from women's and men's differing patterns and styles of contribution at all levels of the organization.

From this second perspective, change strategies focus first on identifying the unique contributions of women and men managers; second, on creating enabling conditions to encourage and reward both types of contribution; and third, on creating synergy – on combining women's and men's contributions to form more innovative and powerful organizational solutions to business challenges. Under this second set of assumptions, firms expect women managers to think, dress, and act like women. Women managers' thinking and behavior, though similar in many ways to that of their male colleagues, is seen to differ in important respects.

Progress, as measured by the equity approach, is quantitative – a statistical accounting of the proportion of women managers in the organization by rank, salary, and status. As measured by the complementary contribution approach, progress is qualitative – an assessment of the organization's track record in encouraging and rewarding women and men for making unique contributions and for building organizationally effective combinations of those contributions; that is, for increasing innovation and organizational learning.

Interestingly, each approach has tended to be labeled as heresy when viewed through the eyes of the other. From the perspective of the equity approach, viewing women (or any other distinct group) as different was seen as tantamount to judging them as inferior (16). Recognizing differences among women and men managers was implicitly equated with prejudice (8). From this point of view, only one best way to manage exists, and equity demands that women be given equal access to that one way. By contrast, the complementary contribution approach posits that there are many equally valid, yet different, ways to manage. The best approach, based on recognizing, valuing, and combining differences, is synergistic. From this second perspective, not to see a woman manager's uniqueness is to negate her identity and, consequently, to negate the potential for her unique contribution to the organization.

To predict what women's roles in management will be in the late 1990s and the twenty-first century, we must understand the underlying assumptions that firms make in each country about the role of women in management (15). To what extent is difference viewed as heresy as opposed to a potential resource? To what extent is uniqueness seen as a constraint rather than as a valuable asset? Unlike their predecessors, transnational firms view woman managers' increased representation and potentially unique contribution as complementary sources of competitive advantage rather than as either–or solutions, or, even more limiting, as societal constraints.

Unexpected Success: Women Managing Across Borders

Cross-border business is fundamental to transnational firms. Unlike their predecessors, such firms define managerial roles transnationally, with expatriate assignments forming a central component. Given the historical scarcity of local women managers in most countries, firms have questioned if women can function successfully in cross-border managerial assignments. They have believed that the relative absence of local women managers formed a basis for accurately predicting the potential for success, or lack thereof, of expatriate women.

Given the importance of these questions to future business success, a multipart study was conducted on the role of women as expatriate managers. The research revealed the story of a noun, *woman*, that appears to have gotten mixed up with an adjective, *foreign*, when predicting expatriate managers' success. It revealed a set of assumptions that managers and executives make about how foreigners would treat expatriate women, based on their beliefs about how foreign firms treat their own local women. The problem with the story is that the assumptions proved to be false. Moreover, because the assumptions fail to accurately reflect reality, they are inadvertently causing executives to make decisions that are neither effective nor equitable.

The first part of the study sought to determine the proportion of women that companies select for expatriate positions. It surveyed 686 major North American multinational firms. The firms reported sending over thirteen thousand (13,338) expatriate managers abroad, of whom 402, or 3 percent, were women. Thus, North American firms send 32 times as many male as female expatriate managers abroad (1;4). In comparison with this 3 percent in international management, women held 37 percent of domestic U.S. management positions, twelve times as many as they held abroad (38).

Although the 3 percent represents significantly fewer women working as expatriate managers than the proportion holding domestic management positions, this should not be viewed strictly as a poor showing but rather as the beginning of a new trend. The vast majority of women who have ever held expatriate management positions were sent so recently that they are currently still working abroad.

Given transnationals' needs for the best-qualified managers – whether women or men – the second, third, and fourth parts of the study sought to explain why so few women hold international management positions. Each part addressed one of the three most commonly held *myths* about women in international management:

Myth 1: Women do not want to be international managers.
Myth 2: Companies refuse to send women abroad.
Myth 3: Foreigners' prejudice against women renders them ineffective, even when they are interested in international assignments and are successful in being sent.

These beliefs were labeled "*myths*" because, although widely held by both women and men, their accuracy had never been tested.

Myth 1: Women do not want to be international managers

Is the problem that women are less interested than men in pursuing international careers? The study tested this myth by surveying more than a thousand graduating MBAs from seven top management schools in the United States, Canada, and Europe (3;5). The results revealed an overwhelming case of no significant difference: female and male MBAs display equal interest, or lack of interest, in pursuing international careers. More than four out of five MBAs – both women and men – want an international assignment at some time during their careers. Both female and male MBAs, however, agree that firms offer fewer opportunities to women than to men, and significantly fewer opportunities to women pursuing international careers than to those pursuing domestic careers.

Although there may have been a difference in the past, women and men today are equally interested in international management, including expatriate assignments. The first myth – that women do not want to be international managers – is, in fact, truly a myth.

Myth 2: Companies refuse to send women abroad

If the problem is not women's lack of interest, is it that companies refuse to select women for international assignments? To test if the myth of corporate resistance was true, human resource vice presidents and managers from 60 of the largest North American multinationals were surveyed (2). Over half of the companies reported that they hesitate to send women abroad. Almost four times as many reported being reluctant to select women for international assignments than for domestic management positions. When asked why they hesitate, almost three-quarters reported believing that foreigners were so prejudiced against women that the women managers could not succeed even if sent. Similarly, 70 percent believed that dual-career issues were insurmountable. In addition, some human resource executives expressed concern about the women's physical safety, the hazards involved in traveling in underdeveloped countries, and, especially in the case of single women, the isolation and loneliness.

Many of the women who succeeded in being sent abroad as expatriate managers report having confronted some form of corporate resistance before being sent abroad. For example:

Malaysia: "Management assumed that women didn't have the physical stamina to survive in the tropics. They claimed I couldn't hack it [in Malaysia]."

Thailand: "My company didn't want to send a woman to that 'horrible part of the world.' They think Bangkok is an excellent place to send single men, but not a woman. They said they would have trouble getting a work permit for me, which wasn't true."

Japan and Korea: "Everyone was more or less curious if it would work. My American boss tried to advise me, 'Don't be upset if it's difficult in Japan and Korea.' The American male manager in Tokyo was also hesitant. Finally the Chinese boss in Hong Kong said, 'We have to try!' Then they sent me."

A few women experienced severe resistance from their companies to sending any women managers abroad. Their firms seemed to offer them an expatriate position only after all potential male candidates had turned it down. For example:

Thailand: "Every advance in responsibility is because the Americans had no choice. I've never been chosen over someone else."

Japan: "They never would have considered me. But then the financial manager in Tokyo had a heart attack, and they had to send someone. So they sent me, on a month's notice, as a temporary until they could find a man to fill the permanent position. It worked out, and I stayed."

Although most of the women are sent in the same capacity as their male expatriate colleagues, some companies demonstrate their hesitation by offering temporary or travel assignments rather than regular expatriate positions. For instance:

Hong Kong: "After offering me the job, they hesitated: 'Could a woman work with the Chinese?' So my job was defined as temporary, a one-year position to train a Chinese man to replace me. I succeeded and became permanent."

These sentiments concur with those of 100 top-line managers in *Fortune 500* firms, the majority of whom believe that women face overwhelming resistance when seeking managerial positions in international divisions of U.S. firms (37). Similarly, 80 percent of U.S. firms report believing that women would face disadvantages if sent abroad (30). Thus, the second myth is in fact true: firms are hesitant, if not outright resistant, to sending women managers abroad.

Myth 3: Foreigners' "prejudice" against women expatriate managers

Is it true that foreigners are so prejudiced against women that women could not succeed as international managers? Would sending a woman manager abroad be neither fair to the woman nor effective for the company? Is the treatment of local women the best predictor of expatriate women's potential to succeed? The fundamental question was, and remains, the following: is the historical discrimination against local women worldwide a valid basis for predicting expatriate women's success as international managers?

To investigate the myth that foreigners' prejudice against women renders them ineffective as international managers, a survey was taken of over a hundred women managers from major North American firms who were on expatriate assignments around the world. Fifty-two were interviewed while in Asia or after having returned from Asia to North America (6;23). Since most of the women held regional responsibility, their experience represents multiple countries rather than just their country of foreign residence.

Who are the women expatriate managers? The women were very well educated and internationally experienced. Almost all held graduate degrees, the MBA being the most common. Over three-quarters had had extensive international interests and experience prior to their present company sending them abroad. On average, the women spoke two or three languages, with some speaking as many as six fluently. In addition, they had excellent social skills. Nearly two-thirds were single and only three (6 percent) had children.

Firms using transnational strategies sent more women than did those using other strategies, with financial institutions leading all other industries. On average, their international assignments lasted 2.5 years, with a range from six months to six years. The women supervised from zero to 25 subordinates, with the average falling just below five. Their titles and levels within their firms varied. Some held very junior positions – for example, assistant account manager – others held senior positions, including one regional vice president. In no firm did a woman expatriate hold her company's number one position in the region or in any country.

The women were considerably younger than the typical male expatriate. Their ages ranged from 23 to 41 years, with the average age being just under 30. This reflects the relatively high proportion of women sent by financial institutions – an industry that sends fairly junior managers on international assignments – and the relatively low proportion sent by manufacturing firms, which select fairly senior managers for expatriate positions (such as a country or regional director).

The decision to go   For most firms, the women expatriates were "firsts." Only 10 percent followed another woman into her international position. Of the 90 percent who were "firsts," almost one-quarter represented the first woman manager the firm had ever sent abroad. Others were the first women sent to the region, the first sent to the particular country, or the first to fill the specific expatriate position. Clearly, neither the women nor the companies had the luxury of role models or of following previously established patterns. Except for several major financial institutions, both the women and the companies found themselves experimenting, in the hope of success.

Most women described themselves as needing to encourage their companies to consider the possibility of assigning international positions to women in general and to themselves in particular. In more than four out of five cases, the woman initially suggested the idea of an international assignment to her boss and company. For only six women did the company first suggest the assignment.

Since most firms had never considered sending a woman manager abroad, the women used a number of strategies to introduce the idea and to position their careers internationally. Many explored the possibility of an international assignment during their original job interview and eliminated companies from consideration that were totally against the idea. In other cases, the woman informally introduced the idea to her boss and continued to mention it at appropriate moments until the company ultimately decided to offer her an expatriate position. A few women formally applied for a number of international assignments prior to actually being selected and sent.

Many women attempted to be in the right place at the right time. For example, one woman who predicted that Hong Kong would be her firm's next major business center arranged to assume responsibility for the Hong Kong desk in New York, leaving the rest of Asia to a male colleague. The strategy paid off; within a year, the company elevated their Hong Kong operations to a regional center and sent her to Asia as their first woman expatriate manager.

Most women claimed that their companies had failed to recognize the possibility of selecting women for international assignments, rather than having thoroughly considered the idea and then having rejected it. For the majority of the women, the obstacle appeared to be the companies' naiveté, not malice. For many women, the most difficult hurdle in their international careers involved getting sent abroad in the first place, not – as most had anticipated – gaining the respect of foreigners and succeeding once sent.

Did it work? The impact of being a woman   Almost all of the women expatriate managers (97 percent) reported that their international assignments were successful. This success rate is considerably higher than that reported for North American male expatriates. Although the women's assessments are subjective, objective indicators support the contention that most of the assignments, in fact, had succeeded. For example, the majority of the firms (after experimenting with their first woman expatriate manager) decided to send more women abroad. In addition, most companies promoted the women on the basis of their foreign performance or offered them other international assignments following completion of the first one.

Advantages   Given the third myth, women would be expected to experience a series of difficulties caused by their being female and, perhaps, to create a corresponding set of solutions designed to overcome each difficulty. This was not the case. Almost half of the women expatriates (42 percent) reported that being female served as more of an advantage than a disadvantage; 16 percent found it to be both positive and negative; 22 percent saw it as being either irrelevant or neutral; and only 20 percent found it to be primarily negative.

The women reported numerous professional advantages to being female. Most frequently, they described the advantage of being highly visible. Foreign clients were curious about them, wanted to meet them, and remembered them after the first encounter. The women therefore found it easier than their male colleagues to gain access to foreign clients' time and attention. The women gave examples of this high visibility, accessibility, and memorability:

Japan: "It's the visibility as an expat, and even more as a woman. I stick in their minds. I know I've gotten more business than my two male colleagues. . . . [My clients] are extra interested in me."

Thailand: "Being a woman is never a detriment. They remembered me better. Fantastic for a marketing position. It's better working with Asians than with the Dutch, British, or Americans."

India and Pakistan: "In India and Pakistan, being a woman helps in marketing and client contact. I got in to see customers because they had never seen a female banker before. . . . Having a female banker adds value to the client."

Again contrary to the third myth, the women managers discovered a number of advantages based on their interpersonal skills, including that the local men could talk more easily about a wider range of topics with them than with their male counterparts. For example:

Japan: "Women are better at putting people at ease. It's easier for a woman to convince a man. . . . The traditional woman's role . . . inspires confidence and trust, less suspicion, not threatening."

Indonesia: "I often take advantage of being a woman. I'm more supportive than my male colleagues. . . . [Clients] relax and talk more. And 50 percent of my effectiveness is based on volunteered information."

Korea: "Women are better at treating men sensitively, and they just like you. One of my Korean clients told me, 'I really enjoyed . . . working with you.'"

Many women also described the high social status accorded local women and found that such status was not denied them as foreign women. The women often received special treatment that their male counterparts did not receive. Clearly, it was always salient that they were women, but being a woman was not antithetical to succeeding as a manager.

Hong Kong: "Single female expats travel easier and are treated better. Never hassled. No safety issues. Local offices take better care of you. They meet you, take you through customs. . . . It's the combination of treating you like a lady and a professional."

Japan: "It's an advantage that attracts attention. They are interested in meeting a *gaijin*, a foreign woman. Women attract more clients. On calls to clients, they elevate me, give me more rank. If anything, the problem, for men and women, is youth, not gender."

In addition, most of the women described benefiting from a "halo effect." The majority of the women's foreign colleagues and clients had never met or previously worked with a woman expatriate manager. Similarly, the local community was highly aware of how unusual it was for North American multinationals to send women managers abroad. Hence, the local managers assumed that the women would not have been sent unless they were "the best," and therefore expected them to be "very, very good."

Indonesia: "It's easier being a woman here than in any place in the world, including New York City. . . . I never get the comments I got in New York, like 'What is a nice woman like you doing in this job?'"

Japan: "They assumed I must be good if I was sent. They became friends."

Some women found being female to have no impact whatsoever on their professional lives. Many of these women worked primarily with the overseas Chinese:

Hong Kong: "There are many expat and foreign women in top positions here. If you are good at what you do, they accept you. One Chinese woman told me, 'Americans are always watching you. One mistake and you are done. Chinese take a while to accept you and then stop testing you.'"

Asia: "There's no difference. They respect professionalism . . . including in Japan. There is no problem in Asia."

Disadvantages The women also experienced a number of disadvantages in being female expatriate managers. Interestingly enough, the majority of the disadvantages involved the women's relationship with their home companies, not with their foreign colleagues and clients. As noted earlier, a major problem involved the women's difficulty in obtaining an international position in the first place.

Another problem involved home companies initially limiting the duration of the women's assignments to six months or a year, rather than offering the more standard two to three years. While temporary assignments may appear to offer companies a logically cautious strategy, in reality they create an unfortunate self-fulfilling prophecy. When the home company is not convinced that a woman can succeed (and therefore offers her a temporary rather than a permanent position), it communicates the company's lack of confidence to foreign colleagues and clients as a lack of commitment. The foreigners then mirror the home company's behavior by also failing to take the woman manager seriously. Assignments become very difficult or can fail altogether when companies demonstrate a lack of initial confidence and commitment. As one expatriate woman working in Indonesia stated, "It is very important to clients that I am permanent. It increases trust, and that's critical."

A subsequent problem involved the home company limiting the woman's professional opportunities and job scope once she was abroad. More than half of the women expatriates experienced difficulties in persuading their home companies to give them latitude equivalent to that given to their male counterparts, especially initially. For example, some companies, out of supposed concern for the woman's safety, limited her travel (and thus the regional scope of her responsibility), thereby excluding very remote, rural, and underdeveloped areas. Other companies, as mentioned previously, initially limited the duration of the woman's assignment to six months or a year, rather than the more standard two to three years. For example:

Japan: "My problem is overwhelmingly with Americans. They identify it as a male market . . . geisha girls. . . ."

Thailand (petroleum company): "The Americans wouldn't let me on the drilling rigs, because they said there were no accommodations for a woman. Everyone blames it on something else. They gave me different work. They had me on the sidelines, not planning and communicating with drilling people. It's the expat Americans, not the Thais, who'll go to someone else before they come to me."

A few companies limited the women to working only internally with company employees, rather than externally with clients. These companies often implicitly assumed that their own employees were somehow less prejudiced than were outsiders. In reality, the women often found the opposite to be true. They faced more problems from home country nationals within their own organizations than externally from local clients and colleagues. As one woman described it:

Hong Kong: "It was somewhat difficult internally. They feel threatened, hesitant to do what I say, resentful. They assume I don't have the credibility a man would have. Perhaps it's harder internally than externally, because client relationships are one-on-one and internally it's more of a group; or perhaps it's harder because they have to live with it longer internally; or perhaps it's because they fear that I'm setting a precedent or because they fear criticism from their peers."

Managing foreign clients' and colleagues' initial expectations was one area that proved difficult for many women. Some found initial meetings to be "tricky," especially when a male colleague from their own company was present. Since most local managers had never previously met a North American expatriate woman who held a managerial position, there was considerable ambiguity as to who she was, her status, her level of expertise, authority, and responsibility, and therefore the appropriate form of address and demeanor toward her.

People's Republic of China: "I speak Chinese, which is a plus. But they'd talk to the men, not to me. They'd assume that I, as a woman, had no authority. The Chinese want to deal with top, top, top level people, and there is always a man at a higher level."

Asia: "It took extra time to establish credibility with the Japanese and Chinese. One Japanese manager said to me, 'When I first met you, I thought you would not be any good because you were a woman.'"

Since most of the North American women whom local managers had ever met previously were expatriates' wives or secretaries, they naturally assumed that the new woman was not a manager. Hence, they often directed initial conversations to male colleagues, not to the newly arrived woman manager. Senior male colleagues, particularly those from the head office, became very important in redirecting the focus of early discussions back toward the woman. When this was done, old patterns were quickly broken and smooth ongoing work relationships were established. When the pattern was ignored or poorly managed, the challenges to credibility, authority, and responsibility became chronic and undermined the women's effectiveness.

As mentioned earlier, many women described the most difficult aspect of the international assignment as getting sent abroad in the first place. Overcoming resistance from the North American home company frequently proved more challenging than gaining local clients' and colleagues' respect and acceptance. In most cases, assumptions about foreigners' prejudice against women expatriate managers appear to have been exaggerated. The anticipated prejudice and the reality did not match. It appears that foreigners are not as prejudiced as many North American managers had assumed.

The *Gaijin* Syndrome

One pattern is particularly clear: first and foremost, foreigners are seen as foreigners. Like their male colleagues, female expatriates are seen as foreigners, not as local people. A woman who is a foreigner (a *gaijin*) is not expected to act like the local women. Therefore, the societal and cultural rules governing the behavior of local women that limit their access to managerial positions and responsibility do not apply to foreign women. Although women are considered the "culture bearers" in all societies, foreign women are not expected to assume the cultural roles that societies have traditionally reserved for their own women. As one woman expatriate in Japan stated, "The Japanese are very smart: they can tell that I am not Japanese, and they do not expect me to act as a Japanese woman. They will allow and condone behavior in foreign women that would be absolutely unacceptable in their own women." Similarly a Tokyo-based personnel vice president for a major international bank explained that "Being a foreigner is so weird to the Japanese that the marginal impact of being a woman is nothing. If I were a Japanese woman, I couldn't be doing what I'm doing here. But they know perfectly well that I'm not" (29:1,27).

Many of the women expatriates related similar examples of their unique status as "foreign women" rather than as "women" per se:

Japan and Korea: "Japan and Korea are the hardest, but they know that I'm an American woman, and they don't expect me to be like a Japanese or Korean woman. It's possible to be effective even in Japan and Korea if you send a senior woman with at least three or four years of experience, especially if she's fluent in Japanese."

Asia: "It's the novelty, especially in Japan, Korea, and Pakistan. All of the general managers met with me. . . . It was much easier for me, especially in Osaka. They were charming. They didn't want me to feel bad. They thought I would come back if they gave me business. You see, they could separate me from the local women."

Pakistan: "Will I have problems? No! There is a double standard between expats and local women. The Pakistanis test you, but you enter as a respected person."

Japan: "I don't think the Japanese could work for a Japanese woman . . . but they just block it out for foreigners."

Hong Kong: "Hong Kong is very cosmopolitan. I'm seen as an expat, not as an Asian, even though I am an Asian American."

Conclusion

It seems that we have confused the adjective *foreign* with the noun *woman* in predicting foreigners' reactions to expatriate women. We expected the most salient characteristic of a woman expatriate manager to be that she is a *woman* and predicted her success based on the success of the local women in each country. In fact, the most salient characteristic is that expatriates are *foreign*, and the best predictor of their success is the success of other foreigners (in this case, other North Americans) in the particular country. *Local managers see women expatriates as foreigners who happen to be women, not as women who happen to be foreigners.* The difference is crucial. Given the uncertainty involved in sending women managers to all areas of the world, our assumptions about the greater salience of gender (female/male) over nationality (foreign/local) have caused us to make false predictions concerning women's potential to succeed as international executives and managers.

The third myth – that foreigners' prejudice precludes women's effectiveness as international managers – is, in fact, definitely a myth. Of the three myths, only the second myth proved to be true. The first myth proved false: women *are* interested in working internationally. The third myth proved false: women *do* succeed internationally, once sent. However, the second myth proved to be true: companies are hesitant, if not completely unwilling, to send women managers abroad. Given that the problem is caused primarily by the home companies' assumptions and decisions, the solutions are also largely within their control.

Recommendations

In considering women managers for international assignments, both the companies and the women need to approach the decision and the assignment in a number of new ways.

Recommendations to companies

Do not assume that it will not work.   Do not assume that foreigners will treat expatriate women managers the same way they treat their own local women. Our assumptions about the salience of gender over nationality have led to totally inaccurate predictions. Therefore, do not confuse adjectives with nouns; do not use the success or failure of local women to predict that of foreign women managers.

Do not confuse the role of a spouse with that of a manager.   Although the single most common reason for male expatriates' failure and early return from international assignments is the dissatisfaction of their wives, this does not mean that women cannot cope in a foreign environment. The role of the spouse (whether male or female) is much more ambiguous and, consequently, the cross-cultural adjustment is much more demanding for the spouse than for the employee (8). Wives have had trouble adjusting, but their situation is not analogous to that of women managers and therefore is not predictive.

Do not assume that a woman will not want to go abroad.   Ask her. Although both single and married women need to balance private and professional life considerations, many are very interested in taking international assignments. Moreover, the proportion of women interested in working abroad is identical to that of men and can be predicted to increase over the coming decade.

Offer flexible benefits packages.   Given that most expatriate benefits packages have been designed to meet the needs of traditional families (employed husband, nonemployed wife, and children), companies should be prepared to modify their benefits packages to meet the needs of managers who are single (women and men) and dual-career couples. Such modifications might include increased lead time in announcing assignments, executive search services for the partner in dual-career couples, and payment for "staying connected" (including telephone and airfare expenses) for couples who choose some form of commuting rather than both simultaneously relocating abroad.

Give women every opportunity to succeed.   Accord her full status at the outset – not that of a temporary or experimental expatriate – with the appropriate title to communicate the home office's commitment to her. Do not be surprised if local colleagues and clients initially direct their comments to male managers rather than to the new woman expatriate during their first meeting with her. However, do not accept such behavior; redirect discussion, where appropriate, to the woman. Such behavior from foreign colleagues should not be interpreted as prejudice but rather as a reaction to a new, ambiguous, and unexpected situation.

Recommendations to women expatriate managers

The women expatriates had a number of suggestions for the women managers who will follow in their footsteps.

Assume naiveté, not malice.   Realize that sending women abroad is new, perceived as risky, and still fairly poorly understood. In most cases, companies and foreign managers are operating on the basis of untested assumptions, many of which are faulty, not on the basis of prejudice. The most successful approach is to be gently persistent in "educating" the company to be open to the possibility of sending a woman abroad and granting her the status and support usually accorded to male peers in similar situations.

Be outstanding.   Given that expatriating women is perceived as risky, no woman will be sent abroad if she is not seen as technically and professionally well qualified. In addition, beyond being extremely well qualified, arrange to be in the right place at the right time.

Address private life issues directly.   For single women the issue of loneliness and for married women the issue of managing a dual-career relationship must be addressed. Contact with other expatriate women has proven helpful in both situations. For dual-career couples, most women consider it critical to have discussed the possibility of an international assignment with their husbands long before it became a reality and to have developed options that would work for them as a couple. For most couples, this means creating alternatives that have never, or rarely, been tried in the particular company.

Realize that expatriate status inadvertently helps to solve some of the role overload problems experienced by women who are managers, wives, and mothers.

Since most expatriate managers can afford household help while on an expatriate assignment, but not in their home countries, they are able to reduce substantially the demands on their time. As one American expatriate manager in Hong Kong stated, "It would be impossible for me to do what I'm doing here if I was still in the United States. There just wouldn't be enough time!"

Global competition is, and will continue to be, intense in the 1990s. Transnational corporations, faced with the most intense global competition, may well continue to lead in hiring and promoting women into significant international management positions. Can they risk not choosing the best person just because her gender does not fit the traditional managerial profile? Needs for competitive advantage, not an all-consuming social conscience, may answer the question, if not in fact define it. Successful companies will select both women and men to manage their international operations. The option of limiting international management to one gender has become an archaic "luxury" that no company can afford. The only remaining question is how quickly and effectively each company will increase the number and use of women in their worldwide managerial workforce.

Notes

I would like to thank the Social Sciences and Humanities Research Council of Canada for its generous support of the research reported here. I owe special thanks to Dr. Homa Mahmoudi for her creativity and professional insight in helping to conduct the Asian interviews. This article is based on Dr. Adler's recent work on transnationals (Adler, 1993; Adler and Bartholomew, 1992) and her research on women expatriate managers (Adler, 1979; 1984a; 1984b; 1984c; 1986; 1987; Jelinek and Adler, 1988). The equity and complementary contribution approaches were originally presented in Adler (1986–87) and Adler and Izraeli's first book, *Women in Management Worldwide* (1988).

References

All quotes by the women expatriates are taken from Dr. Adler's research interviews. While the names of the women cannot be released, each of them was working in the country listed at the time of the interview.

(1) Adler, Nancy J. (1979) "Women as Androgynous Managers: A Conceptualization of the Potential for American Women in International Management," *International Journal of Intercultural Relations* 3(4):407–435.

(2) Adler, Nancy J. (1984a) "Expecting International Success: Female Managers Overseas," *Columbia Journal of World Business* 19(3):79–85

(3) Adler, Nancy J. (1984b) "Women Do Not Want International Careers: And Other Myths About International Management," *Organizational Dynamics* 13(2):66–79.

(4) Adler, Nancy J. (1984c) "Women in International Management: Where Are They?" *California Management Review* 26(4):78–89.

(5) Adler, Nancy J. (1986) "Do MBAs Want International Careers?" *International Journal of Intercultural Relations* 10(3):277–300.

(6) Adler, Nancy J. (1987) "Pacific Basin Managers: A Gaijin, Not a Woman," *Human Resource Management* 26(2):169–191.

(7) Adler, Nancy J. (1986–87) "Women in Management Worldwide," *International Studies of Management and Organization* 16(3–4):3–32.

(8) Adler, Nancy J. (1991) *International Dimensions of Organizational Behavior*, 2nd edn. Boston: PWS-KENT Publishing.

(9) Adler, Nancy J. (1993) "Competitive Frontiers: Women Managers in the Triad," *International Studies of Management and Organization*, in press.

(10) Adler, Nancy J., and Bartholomew, Susan (1992) "Managing Globally Competent People," *Academy of Management Executive* 6(3):52–65.

(11) Adler, Nancy J., and Ghadar, Fariborz (1990) "Strategic Human Resource Management: A Global Perspective," in Rudiger Pieper (ed.), *Human Resource Management in International Comparison*, pp. 235–260. Berlin: de Gruyter.

(12) Adler, Nancy J., and Izraeli, Dafna N. (eds.) (1988) *Women in Management Worldwide*. Armonk, N.Y.: M. E. Sharpe.

(13) Aptheker, B. (1989) *Tapestries of Life: Women's Work, Women's Consciousness, and the Meaning of Daily Experience*. Amherst: University of Massachusetts Press.

(14) Bartlett, Christopher A., and Ghoshal, Sumantra (1989) *Managing across Borders: The Transnational Solution*. Boston: Harvard Business School Press.

(15) Berthoin Antal, Ariane, and Izraeli, Dafna N. (1993) "A Global Comparison of Women in Management: Women Managers in Their Homelands and as Expatriates," in Ellen Fagenson (ed.), *Women in Management: Trends, Issues and Challenges in Managerial Diversity, Women and Work*, Vol. 4. Newbury Park, Calif.: Sage.

(16) Calvert, Linda McGee, and Ramsey, V. Jean (1992) "Bringing Women's Voice to Research on Women in Management: A Feminist Perspective," *Journal of Management Inquiry* 1(1):79–88.

(17) Caulkin, S. (1977) "Women in Management," *Management Today* (September):58–63.

(18) Fisher, Anne B. (1992) "When Will Women Get to the Top?" *Fortune*, September 21, pp. 44–56.

(19) Fossan, J. (1989) "Women in Organization," *Implementing Strategies and Achieving Change*. Seminar Research Report. Berlin: Aspen Institute.

(20) Gilligan, Carol (1982) *In a Different Voice*. Cambridge, Mass.: Harvard University Press.

(21) Hammond, Valerie, and Holton, Viki (1994) "The Scenario for Women Managers in Britain in the 1990s," in Nancy J. Adler and Dafna N. Izraeli (eds.), *Competitive Frontiers: Women Managers in a Global Economy*, pp. 224–242. Cambridge (USA)/ Oxford (England): Blackwell Publishers.

(22) Helgesen, S. (1990) *The Female Advantage: Women's Ways of Leadership*. New York: Doubleday.

(23) Jelinek, Mariann, and Adler, Nancy J. (1988) "Women: World-Class Managers for Global Competition," *Academy of Management Executive* 2(1):11–19.

(24) Korabik, Karen (1988) "Is the Ideal Manager Masculine? The Contribution of Femininity to Managerial Effectiveness." Paper presented at the annual meetings of the Academy of Management, Anaheim, Calif.

(25) Lansing, P., and Ready, K. (1988) "Hiring Women Managers in Japan: An Alternative for Foreign Employers," *California Management Review* 30(3):112–127.

(26) Loden, M. (1987) *Feminine Leadership or How to Succeed in Business without Being One of the Boys*. New York: Times Books.

(27) Miller, Jean Baker (1976) *Toward a New Psychology of Women*. Boston: Beacon.

(28) Miller, Jean Baker (1982) "Women and Power," Working Paper. Wellesley, Mass.: Wellesley College, Stone Center for Development Services and Studies.

(29) Morganthaler, E. (1978) "Women of the World: More U.S. Firms Put Females in Key Posts in Foreign Countries," *Wall Street Journal*, March 16:1,27.

(30) Moran, Stahl, and Boyer, Inc. (1988) *Status of American Female Expatriate Employees: Survey Results*. Boulder, Colo.: International Division.

(31) Perry, Nancy J. (1992) "If You Can't Join 'em, Beat 'em," *Fortune*, September 21, pp. 58–59.

(32) Porter, Michael (1990) *The Competitive Advantage of Nations*. New York: The Free Press.

(33) Rosenzweig, Philip M., and Nohria, Nitin (1992) "Human Resource Management in MNC Affiliates: Internal Consistency or Local Isomorphism," Working Paper. Boston: Harvard Business School.

(34) Steen, Gunilla Masreliez (1987) "Male and Female Culture: A View From Sweden." Working paper originally presented at the International Federation of Training and Development Organizations conference.

(35) Steinhoff, Patricia G., and Tanaka, Kazuko (1988) "Women Managers in Japan," in Nancy J. Adler and Dafna N. Izraeli (eds.), *Women in Management Worldwide*, pp. 103–121. Armonk, N.Y.: M. E. Sharpe.

(36) Steinhoff, Patricia G., and Tanaka, Kazuko (1994) "Women Managers in Japan," in Nancy J. Adler and Dafna N. Izraeli (eds.), *Competitive Frontiers: Women Managers in a Global Economy*, pp. 79–100. Cambridge (USA)/Oxford (England): Blackwell Publishers.

(37) Thal, N., and Cateora, P. (1979) "Opportunities for Women in International Business," *Business Horizons* 22(6):21–27.

(38) *Yearbook of Labor Statistics* (1986) (1987) (1991) Geneva: International Labor Office.

PART II

ASIA

3

HONG KONG

The Third Identity of Modern Chinese Women: Women Managers in Hong Kong

Corinna T. de Leon and Suk-ching Ho

> Male dominance in Hong Kong exists at a much higher degree; there-fore, the female entrepreneurs in Hong Kong must make extra effort in discharging their triple responsibilities of running a home, caring for children, and establishing a business venture (14:228).

Covering an area of 1,075 square kilometers south of the People's Republic of China, Hong Kong is a modern, urban society where Eastern and Western cultures mingle. A British colony since 1842, Hong Kong has 5.8 million inhabitants, the overwhelming majority of whom are ethnic Chinese. Of all residents in the districts of Kowloon, Hong Kong Island, and the New Territories, 60 percent were born in the Colony and 34 percent were born in mainland China (46).

As in other industrialized countries, the rapid economic development of Hong Kong during the past few decades has created opportunities that facilitated women's entry into the labor market (16;41). For the third quarter of 1991, unemployment was 2 percent and under-employment was 1.5 percent (46). The 1991 census showed that 49 percent of the 5.8 million inhabitants of Hong Kong were women. Of the employed population of 2.8 million, 37 percent were women.

Although contemporary Hong Kong society has assumed a modern, deceptively Western outlook, the ethnic Chinese maintain a strong cultural identity (8). The central focus on the family in traditional Chinese society persists in contemporary Hong Kong (27). Familism is and will likely continue to be the predominant characteristic of Chinese societies (56). Despite the significant improvements in educational and employment opportunities for women, familism remains the critical factor determining the success or failure of women's pursuit of managerial careers in Hong Kong.

Familism in Contemporary Hong Kong

The ethical principle of filial piety in Confucianism emphasized kinship networks as the focus of Chinese culture. Traditionally, there was a sharp gender demarcation of labor. Men were expected to manage society, while women were expected to take care of the home and produce male heirs (52). The central importance of the family was predicated on married women being confined to domestic work and devoted to caring for their husbands and children. Under the influence of Westernization and modernization, such patriarchal traditions of Chinese culture have gradually been modified in Hong Kong to adapt to urban life-styles.

Conventional familism in China viewed the family as an integral part of society. In urban Hong Kong, "society is considered to be largely insignificant, and the family is to 'exploit' society for its own utilitarian purposes" (34:202). The dynamism of Hong Kong society has been attributed to *utilitarian familism*, in which families function as "the major reference groups with which an individual identifies and for whose material well-being he/she strives" (34:202). A similar observation is evident in the notion of *entrepreneurial familism*, referring to the family as being "the basic unit of decision-making and risk-bearing . . . [in which] resources are pooled and strategies devised to seek security and advancement" (55:15). There has been widespread agreement that "in order for people to live more happily, Honkongese should strengthen their ties with family members and relatives so that they can provide mutual help" (35:60).

The kinship network functions as an informal welfare system; the Hong Kong Chinese heartily assume the responsibility for providing financial assistance to relatives. There is widespread agreement that failing to take care of elderly parents should be punishable by law and that elderly parents should live together with their married children (33;34;35;55). Throughout their childhood, Hong Kong Chinese are taught that other family members must have priority over oneself (51). "The sense of mutuality, of being connected through affection, obligation, and responsibility to specific other people – the background theme which is absolutely critical to an understanding of Chinese social life . . . Chinese interdependence . . . is what makes life within one's family so supportive and sustaining; outside it, so rough and uncaring" (7:19).

Contemporary Chinese families are small but not confined to the nuclear unit, and the relatively extended membership is closely knit (35). The Chinese usually spend their spare time with their families and interact with other social groups only when utilitarian interests are involved. Family relationships among the Chinese become "a lifelong affair, with family activities continuing to absorb the lion's share of one's time and responsibility" (7:6). It is culturally assumed that a woman's major goal is "maintaining the well-being and continuation of the family" (56:7). Marriage and motherhood occupy central positions in a Chinese woman's sense of identity:

> To the Chinese, being a wife and mother is an honourable estate. While the view may not coincide with the more modern Western ideas, a married woman did not necessarily think of herself as a worthless drudge because she was confined to duties within the house, garden, and fields. Within the private, inside sphere she could exert great influence and enjoy affection and respect from the members of her immediate family. Thus to decry these traditional roles is to view them from a very different perspective from that of the women who made and make them their life's work (43:128).

Maternal identity of Hong Kong women

In Hong Kong, women professionals tend to marry later and have fewer children than other women (28). The proportion of managers who were never married is higher for women (28 percent) than for men (13 percent). This difference can be explained by the fact that more of the women managers are younger: 48 percent of female managers and only 27 percent of male managers are between twenty and 34 years old (19). Between 1985 and 1991, the proportion of never-married women administrators declined by 6 percent, from 34 percent to 28 percent, suggesting that marriage is now less widely regarded as restricting the pursuit of a managerial career than it once was (18).

Unlike the ethnic Chinese men in Singapore who prefer to marry "downwards," highly educated Hong Kong men tend to marry women of similar educational backgrounds (43). A wife is considered to be foremost a member of her husband's family which eventually becomes the major beneficiary of her education and career. Families of origin therefore encourage daughters to delay marriage and pursue careers, since, until they marry, daughters significantly increase the income of those families (43;47;48). Although never-married women are given more freedom and autonomy in their personal lives, they can never hope to achieve financial independence, since their incomes are treated as family resources (43).

Most women managers (67 percent) work fewer hours than the official work week of 44 hours, compared to 57 percent of men who work more than the official work week, to a maximum of 98 hours per week (19). This finding reflects women's concentration at the lower levels of management, where working hours are somewhat less demanding. Domestic responsibilities often compel women to avoid longer hours even when the job demands it.

Familial responsibilities are the major reason Hong Kong women leave the labor force. "Increase in volume of housework" (42 percent) or "childbirth" (11 percent) are the major reasons given by half of all women who left the working population in 1987. As 67 percent of women who left work were between twenty and 39 years old, and 86 percent of them were married, we may conclude that the women interrupted their careers for a number of years for childbearing and childrearing. In 1987, 21 percent of entrants to the labor force were women in their thirties, as compared to 2 percent for men in the same age range; and the major reason for entry given by most women was "more spare time available for work" (24).

Most Hong Kong Chinese are convinced that their children will have good opportunities to improve their social and economic status, and will eventually belong to the middle and upper classes (35;55). A 1987 survey found that the majority of Hong Kong parents wanted only two children, while 15 percent wanted one or none, mainly because they hoped to give every child "as much education as possible" (55). Chinese women executives put a priority on being "mothers of highly-accomplished children" (11). Consequently, mothers assume the duty of tutoring their children to ensure entrance and good performance in the highly competitive educational system (43). The dedicated contributions of Hong Kong parents to their children's educational development is accurately described as follows.

Childhood achievement is almost exclusively defined in academic terms. . . . The obsession with academic achievement remains today, since academic achievement is still a major escalator to higher position. . . . Parents exert massive pressure on their children to do well in school. Homework is supervised and extends for long periods, extracurricular activities are kept to a minimum, effort is rewarded, tutors are hired, and socializing is largely confined to family outings (7:18).

The majority of working women belong to dual-income families. Women's conflict between domestic and professional roles is eased by childcare substitutes and mother surrogates (2). Childcare centers are available in Hong Kong, with places for children under the age of six (36;46). However, resorting to public or private childcare centers is not popular among women managers, since they regard these as social welfare centers geared to the needs of lower-income families (4).

Women professionals in higher-income families prefer live-in help at home, either relying on relatives or employing domestic helpers (2;42). In 1990, over 60,000 households in Hong Kong, accounting for 4 percent of the total, employed domestic helpers who earned the minimum monthly wage of US$412 plus benefits with housing and food allowances (3;46). Demand for foreign domestic helpers increased in 1991 to 84,000, an increase of 20 percent since 1990. Nine out of ten of these helpers are non-Chinese women from the Philippines (46).

The major role of a woman in modern Hong Kong is still as a mother at the center of her family, which is the nucleus of society. For example, in the book *Hong Kong 1992* (46:60–61), three out of seven pictures of "leading business figures" are of senior women managers. The first picture is of Patsy Chang, described as a "representative of Hong Kong's 'high flyers,' at the crest of the new wave of business leaders, administrators, and entrepreneurs." Despite this description, her picture shows her as a motherly figure, playing with children at a charitable organization where she is the director.

Whereas the father is considered to be the disciplinarian, the mother is the source of care and concern for the Chinese child, who is brought up to regard home as a refuge (7). Although a wife can have a career, her primary commitment is to her home and family, for which she assumes major responsibility (11;44). However, many interviewed women senior executives reported conflicts between their career and family roles, saying that their family duties were of more concern to them than their careers (9). Maternal identity remains foremost even among modern Chinese women who have developed a strong professional identity.

Women managers want a husband who "becomes very prominent"; they are fully committed to caring for their husbands (11). The shared view is that the woman's career comes second in decisions affecting her and her husband and that she would willingly drop her own career to support his. In Hong Kong, husbands hold the view that a woman may work, as long she does not threaten the man's dominant position (43). Chinese women managers consider role reversal unacceptable and believe that "what wives with careers need most aren't house-husbands but supportive spouses" (5).

Gender identity of Hong Kong women

Gender identity of women managers in Hong Kong is based on the powerful male–female stereotypes in Chinese culture. Such gender differences appear more deeply embedded in Chinese than in Western societies (7). Print advertisements portray a woman's place as being in the home and women as lacking authority and as concerned with their physical appearance (21). Both female and male managers explain the paucity of women managers in Hong Kong as caused by women's lack of personal motivation (16). The majority believe that the managerial success of women is constrained by their lack of dedication to pursuing a career, minimal commitment to the employing organization, insufficient experience and education, and little interest in managerial roles.

The stereotypical perspectives of women's traits as inferior for leadership restrict women's entry into management (20). Men's attitudes toward working women were less favorable than women's, as shown in a large survey of business graduates of both genders (17;37). When questioned in the commercial districts of Hong Kong, men expressed less positive attitudes than women toward the managerial abilities of women and were less appreciative of managerial traits associated with women (49;50).

Another hindrance to women's career progress is men's anticipated difficulty in working with women as managers. Hong Kong Chinese male executives report avoiding arguing with women, hesitating to criticize women, and believing that women were not open-minded (1). Their evaluations regarding women's personality were more positive than were those regarding women's leadership ability and working style. However, women and men managers with direct experience of working with women held more favorable attitudes toward them (17;37). Attitudes toward women in management were more favorable among male executives who were older, held senior management positions, had worked or studied abroad, or had worked directly with women (1).

Women Managers: Emerging Third Identity

Fifteen years ago, 2 percent of employed women and 6 percent of employed men were managers and administrators (20); in 1991, the figures were 5 percent and 12 percent, respectively (24). Of all managers and administrators, 10 percent were women in 1976 and 20 percent were women in 1986 (46). Men were more likely to be self-employed employers (58 percent), compared with women (40 percent). Women managers were more likely to be employees (52 percent) than were men (42 percent). In 1991, 7 percent of women managers were unpaid family workers, compared with only 0.4 percent of men (24).

Discrimination and legislation

Discriminatory practices against women trying to attain higher managerial positions characterize Hong Kong business firms (20). A content analysis of recruitment advertisements found that business firms preferred men over women for the managerial/supervisory vacancies by a ratio of four to one (22). Firms recruited women mainly for lower-level positions or people-oriented staff functions, such as personnel manager and public relations executive. A study of recent advertisements for staff vacancies showed that hotels prefer male candidates for all management ranks, although women were highly visible in staff positions (12). In the thriving hotel industry in Hong Kong, men occupied over 65 percent of the senior and junior managerial positions and were employed in 88 percent of the line authority positions and 49 percent of the staff authority positions (12).

In 1985, the ratio of women's average earnings remained at two-thirds of men's wages, as was the case in 1976. The increase in the number of educated women has not diminished the wage differential, because women are more willing to accept lower salaries in the face of greater competition from equally qualified women. The preference of Hong Kong employers for male recruits over female applicants, irrespective of educational level, encourages higher salaries among men but not among the larger pool of educated women (53). A woman executive said, "I think there should be special laws to let women have equal pay for equal work" (39). However, another woman took the opposite view that "equal pay for equal work" would adversely affect the economy of Hong Kong" (29).

Married women in Hong Kong are generally believed to be discriminated against in hiring, promotion, and salary practices (6;16;38). Such discrimination curbs women's mobility between firms and consequently their opportunities for enhancing their careers. In one study, several women executives thought that they would not be able to find the same level of pay or benefits elsewhere and that they would, therefore, not seek alternative employment in the next few years (11).

Of those employed in the Hong Kong civil service in 1980, 25 percent were women; and at the directorate level, 5 percent were women (31). Equal pay in the civil service was introduced in 1973. Consequently, dismissal with gratuity of women upon marriage, followed by their re-employment on a temporary basis, was discontinued (43). Until 1981, women were not entitled to the housing allowances and medical benefits given to male civil servants. Furthermore, women civil servants took five years longer than men to achieve their current position, and were five times less likely to achieve senior status (43).

The Women and Young Persons's (Industry) Regulations were amended most recently in 1988. Women are forbidden from being employed in certain trades and industrial work, as well as from working more than ten hours a day and/or beyond 11 P.M., more than 96 hours per fortnight, more than six days a week, and more than 200 hours of overtime per year (54). Unfortunately, such "protective labour legislation serves to restrict women's competitiveness in the labour market" (43:119). There are no statutory restrictions on the hours adult male workers may work (54). Furthermore, until 1990, when separate taxation procedures were introduced, the wife's income was assessed jointly with her husband's.

Following the customary rights of property which have remained unchanged for more than a hundred years, the New Territories Ordinance legalized the restriction of land inheritance in Hong Kong's New Territories to male descendants. In 1992, a woman pursued a case in court to challenge the ancestral customs that had barred her from inheriting the land of her father, after the death of her mother, who had no sons (10). She petitioned to become the manager of her father's properties, which were being administered by a *village tso*, traditionally a committee of men set up by a landowner to manage his properties after his death for the benefit of his male descendants.

There is no legislation that makes gender discrimination illegal in Hong Kong (43). The social and economic development of women has been pursued by several women's associations; namely, the Hong Kong Association of Business and Professional Women, Hong Kong Council of Women, Zonta, Association of Women for Action and Research (AWARE), and the Association for the Advancement of Feminism. A lobby is pressuring the Hong Kong and British governments to revise discriminatory laws, although as yet without much success. In Hong Kong, the issues of discrimination against women include the male-only inheritance of land in the New Territories, job advertisements that cite gender preferences (for male managers and female secretaries), and personnel selection and promotion that is influenced by women's family obligations (15).

During International Women's Day in 1990, demands were made for Hong Kong to become a signatory of the International Convention on the Elimination of All Forms of Discrimination Against Women (ICEDAW), and the International Covenant on Economic, Social and Cultural Rights (ICESCR) (39). The United Nations adopted the ICEDAW twelve years ago. Although both Great Britain and the People's Republic of China became signatories, the Hong Kong government has not yet ratified the ICEDAW (15). A government working party on ICEDAW, made up mostly of male government officers, was organized in February 1992 (60). At that time, a male member of the International Women's Rights Action Watch commented that "it would need more than legislation to eliminate all kinds of discrimination and something needed to be done to change the culture of society . . . it would be difficult for the government to legislate against discrimination in the private sector" (60:3).

Professional identity of Hong Kong women

Several new women's magazines have begun to cater to an expanding professional class of women in Hong Kong, including the appropriately named *Woman at Work* (13). The local edition of the French journal *Marie Claire* promotes the image of the "modern, independent, middle-class woman who is interested in society and woman's rights." Another magazine called *Mary* caters to eighteen- to 35-year-old women who are "financially independent." In 1987, the Association for the Advancement of Feminism began circulating the *Women's Current*. Assuming the publishers' assessment of market potential was realistic, these magazines are a testament to the emergence of a class of women with a professional identity and special needs.

Hong Kong women with managerial positions, better education, and relatively high salaries attach great importance to their careers as the means to their "self-fulfillment" (11). However, they express dissatisfaction about the four job factors they highly valued – namely, freedom, accomplishment, self-development, and fringe benefits. They are more satisfied with factors they considered relatively unimportant – namely, others' respect, friendliness, and treatment.

College education is a critical factor for career progression in Hong Kong (28;35), and the expanding educational system is creating new opportunities for women. In 1981, of the Hong Kong residents between seventeen and twenty years of age, 5 percent were admitted to tertiary education. In 1992, 18 percent enrolled in the eight degree-granting institutions; namely, University of Hong Kong, The Chinese University of Hong Kong, Hong Kong University of Science and Technology, City Polytechnic of Hong Kong, Hong Kong Polytechnic, Hong Kong Baptist College, Lingnan College, and the Open Learning Institute of Hong Kong. The rapid expansion of the education system at the tertiary level is indicative of government plans to increase the available places by 25 percent by 1994–1995, partly as a countermeasure to the severe brain drain that has resulted from the high levels of emigration (46).

While competition in the Hong Kong school system remains extremely keen, the entrance requirements for tertiary institutions have changed. Since 1985, when the Chinese University of Hong Kong (CUHK) began basing students' entrance on their secondary school certificate examination, pending the results of an admissions test, the enrollment rate showed an 11 to 16 percent increase in women students (23). The government introduced a similar admissions procedure for all tertiary institutions in 1991. Its administration made it possible for applicants to submit a single application and receive provisional offers from several schools. The overall rise in student admissions and the greater chances for admission in alternative institutions should improve women's access to higher education and consequently to greater employment opportunities.

Currently, there are slightly more male than female students in degree programs. Women, however, are increasingly entering fields of study relevant to management. For example, at the Chinese University of Hong Kong, the proportion of women students in the business administration program increased from just over 5 percent in 1979 to almost 11 percent in 1989. By 1990, women made up 38 percent of graduates with bachelor's degrees in business administration at the Hong Kong Baptist College. By 1991, at the City Polytechnic of Hong Kong, 50 percent of graduates in the full-time undergraduate business program and about 35 percent of those in the part-time program were women; and 75 percent of the graduates in international business were women. At present, the educational profile of women managers in Hong Kong closely resembles that of men; that is, 45 percent have completed secondary education, and about 20 percent hold a university degree (24).

The future of women managers in Hong Kong

The certain dissolution of the legal existence of Hong Kong as a British colony make any predictions about the future of Hong Kong tentative. The Sino-British Joint Declaration of 1984 stated that the United Kingdom's administration and jurisdiction over Hong Kong will continue until June 30, 1997, at which time Hong Kong will become a Special Administrative Region (SAR) of the People's Republic of China. Based on the principle of "one country, two systems," a local government and legislature composed of Hong Kong inhabitants, with autonomy from China's socialist system, is guaranteed in the SAR for a period of 50 years (46).

It could be argued that since the legitimacy of British authority over the Chinese society has been tenuous, the turnover of Hong Kong to China is inevitable and will be beneficial; however, pessimism about the future permeates Hong Kong society. For the older generation, the majority of whom came as refugees from China after the Communist takeover, the imminent resumption of Chinese sovereignty over Hong Kong recalls bitter experiences. For the younger generation, the reversion from a capitalist to a Communist society raises many questions about Hong Kong's future.

Nine out of ten Hong Kong residents do not believe in their personal efficacy in influencing society or government policy (33;34;35). A large majority of Hong Kong Chinese expect that civil rights will be curtailed, individual liberty reduced, the legal system abridged, and that living standards will decline after 1997 (55). Most Hong Kong residents believe that the Chinese government will seriously endanger their interests, and many presume that they will not be free to either discuss or criticize government policies after 1997 (32). Hong Kong Chinese have asserted that "in the face of future uncertainties, we can only adjust as best as we can" (35:53).

The 1997 issue is the major impetus for the current exodus from Hong Kong. Many Chinese are choosing to leave rather than use their voice to express dissatisfaction. According to government estimates, the yearly number of emigrants had almost tripled to 60,000 between 1987 and 1991 (25;46). A recent survey showed that 30 percent of Hong Kong Chinese "hoped" to emigrate; and of the 10 percent who can satisfy the immigration requirements of their preferred destinations (Canada, USA, or Australia), many intend to do so (55). In a government survey conducted in 1990, 16 percent of Hong Kong residents stated that they had plans to emigrate (46). Facing the dim prospects of 1997, the Hong Kong Chinese are finding innovative means of expressing their family-centeredness: "Responding to the uncertain future, various families decide to diversify their physical and human capital and extend their networks globally. Through emigration the entrepreneurial form of familism is enhanced rather than decimated" (55:15).

A survey of business organizations in Hong Kong showed that the single largest category of emigrants (20 to 25 percent) are managers (30;40). One-third of the emigrants are in the professional, technical, administrative, or managerial occupations (46). Half of all emigrants in 1989 were between 25 and 44 years of age, whereas only about one-third of the general population is in that age group.

The brain drain is a primary concern to many companies, especially since the trend is expected to rise rapidly as 1997 approaches. On the assumption of a shrinking economy, Hong Kong residents are not confident that career opportunities will remain the same for women as for men after 1997, and most believe that employment opportunities will decrease more for women than for men (16). However, some argue that since many emigrants from Hong Kong are the highly educated and high-income elite, the brain drain is due more to perceived political threats than to an anticipated lack of future economic opportunities (55).

The increasingly urgent demand to fill the vacancies created by the emigrating managers may eventually lead to a greater appreciation of women as an untapped human resource in Hong Kong. An optimistic scenario predicts that chronic shortages of managers should make women a more attractive alternative and hence mitigate gender bias in recruitment practices. An officer of Zonta, a professional women's service organization with members throughout Southeast Asia, stated that "Hong Kong employers do have more of an open mind when it comes to hiring women" (26). For example, Baroness Lydia Dunn, originally from Shanghai, is considered to be "one of Asia's most powerful women." She is a director of several large multinational corporations and a senior member of the Executive Council of the Hong Kong government (5:55).

In 1980, women managers believed that they had been quite successful and had not been discriminated against (11). In 1986, they evaluated themselves as being "above average" in most managerial traits, although they were not satisfied with their creative abilities (28). More recently an accountant stated that "although there is no protection for the equality of women, I have never felt at a disadvantage because I am a woman" (39). A woman vice president of an executive search firm noted that modern Hong Kong encourages upward mobility more so than is the case in other Asian countries and that "it doesn't matter if you are a woman . . . if you're good, you're rewarded . . . the chances to shine – to perform outstandingly – are greater here" (26).

In Hong Kong, women executives have done better in the service fields, such as communication, marketing, advertising, personnel, and public relations, than in production-centered sectors (11). Recruitment advertisements present more opportunities for women in the service industries (retail enterprises, hotels, and airlines) than manufacturing, construction, communications, and storage (22). Service is the largest sector in Hong Kong: 27 percent of the workforce is engaged in the wholesale and retail trades, restaurants, and hotels, and 11 percent in finance, insurance, real estate, and business services (46). With an increasing shift away from manufacturing, the employment opportunities of women should grow alongside the development of Hong Kong into a service-oriented economy.

The development of women's managerial careers

Hong Kong has not been immune to the profound changes in the economic life of women in modern societies over the past 30 years. Rapid economic development creates employment opportunities at most managerial levels. Discriminatory employment practices, however, continue to limit women's vertical mobility. Furthermore, the conventional notions of maternal and gender identities of Chinese women seriously restrict their access to positions of power.

For the typical Hong Kong Chinese, the notion of success is aligned with the desire for monetary wealth. The most important personal goal is to make as much money as possible (35). Wealth is a "surrogate for security," the reward for one's efforts, and the evidence of work achievement (45). Success is attributed to personal characteristics, and "it is this rejection of fate as the determinant of one's future that propels Hong Kong Chinese to strive hard for success" (35:53).

Nonetheless, due to the strength of Chinese women's familistic orientation, the contradictions between their professional and personal lives remain unresolved. The ideology of familism seems to be the fundamental obstacle to women's pursuit of managerial success, and, since the centrality of familism has not declined and will not diminish in modern Hong Kong, women's entry into the executive echelons cannot be expected to improve via the slow transformation of this core cultural value.

In contemporary Hong Kong, women's professional achievement as well as that of men is still measured in terms of the benefits it provides to one's group or family rather than to oneself. It is therefore, defined by other people's standards of evaluation, and fulfilled within a network of personal ties (33;34;55;57;58). In the "Hong Kong context work is not seen as an individual woman's right [or] as a means of self-actualization. . . . Rather it is seen as an extension of typical female roles into the workplace for reasons that are to do with the greater good of the community or the benefit of the family" (43:127). The Hong Kong Chinese's strong work ethic is attributed to the "long tradition of obligation to the family, which sponsors seriousness of purpose" and to the "highly sensitive social networks and forms of group pressure" that predisposes individuals to secure their membership through industriousness (45:293).

Because family-centeredness persists in modern Hong Kong, a woman's interdependent relationships with her husband, children, and relatives underlie her sense of identity (7). Many women managers recognize the influence of family members on their occupational decisions (11). Many women entrepreneurs report that their careers have been influenced by an entrepreneurial father (14). Not surprisingly, many women business executives have fathers who were highly successful proprietors, managers, or professionals (28).

Currently a woman's managerial career remains subordinate to her responsibilities as a wife and mother. Nonetheless, strong maternal and gender identities may enhance rather than contradict the emerging professional identity of modern Hong Kong women. Women managers in Hong Kong expressed the view that "achievement in business would not hinder, but reinforce, the affirmation of their femininity" (11:12). Women entrepreneurs believed that "kinship is not a hindrance but an asset to entrepreneurship" (14:229).

The extension of family-centeredness to women's professional life is essential, because "for the Chinese, maturity means a movement towards a harmonious integration into the social fabric of the family" (59:44). Women entrepreneurs believe that achievement rather than independence is their primary motive, thus again indicating the strong family ties of the collective culture (14). Hence, the professional identity of modern Hong Kong women is and will remain predicated on kinship relationships. The conflict, however, between her professional and personal life is eased by the astute woman manager's flexibility in behavior and relativism in attitude.

> *Hence, whether the modern theme or the traditional theme occupies the central position will be contingent upon the situation at hand. The ready availability of the traditional outlook, however, means that private interests in Hong Kong can be curbed without too much difficulty, if collective interests in a particular situation can be demonstrated to be of supreme importance. Moreover, shifting back and forth between the traditional and modern outlooks is eased by the 'situational morality' of the Hong Kong Chinese, which does not impose hard and fast rule on moral choice (35:55).*

References

(1) Arnold, Margaret, and Lee, Eva (1990) "Perceptions and Attitudes of Hong Kong Chinese Male Executives about Women in Management," *Proceedings: The 3rd International Conference on Comparative Management*, June, Kaohsiung, Taiwan, pp. 190–196.

(2) *Asiaweek* (1992a) "Who's My Mommy," March 27, pp. 26–29.

(3) *Asiaweek* (1992b) "Hands Across the Seas," March 27, p. 27.

(4) *Asiaweek* (1992c) "Home Alone in Hong Kong," March 27, p. 29.

(5) *Asiaweek* (1992d) "Executives: Breaking the Barriers," August 21, pp. 54–57.

(6) Benitez, Mary Ann (1989) "Women on One-Third Lower Pay Than Men," *South China Morning Post*, November 10, p. 3.

(7) Bond, Michael Harris (1991) *Beyond the Chinese Face: Insights from Psychology*. Hong Kong: Oxford University Press.

(8) Bond, M. H. and King, A. Y. C. (1985) "Coping with the Threat of Westernisation in Hong Kong," *International Journal of Intercultural Relations* 9:351–364.

(9) Cashmore, E. E. (1989) *The Experiences of Successful Career Women in Hong Kong: A Study of Strategies for Overcoming Subordination*. Hong Kong: Department of Sociology, University of Hong Kong.

(10) Chan, Quinton (1992) "A Woman's Place Is in Her Home," *Sunday Morning Post*, August 9, p. 4.

(11) Chau, Theodora Ting (1980) "Woman Executives in Hong Kong," *The Hong Kong Manager* 16(1):8–12.

(12) Cheung, M. K. L. (1990) "Gender Discrimination: A Study of the Hong Kong Hotels' Junior and Managerial Staff Employment Situations and Practices, 1985–89," *Human Resources Journal* 6(2):23–37.

(13) Chiu, Vivian (1991) "The Magazine Market Fires a New Salvo," *South China Morning Post*, July 2, p. 13.

(14) Chu, Priscilla, and Siu, Wai-sum (1991) "Women Entrepreneurs in Hong Kong: An Exploratory Study," *Proceedings of the 1991 Conference of the British Academy of Management: Business Advancing the Horizons*, pp. 227–231.

(15) Daswani, Kavita (1992) "New Ray of Hope for Women in Equality Fight," *South China Morning Post*, March 1, p. 11.

(16) Dolecheck, M. M., and Dolecheck, C. C. (1987) "Discrimination of Woman in the Work Place," *Human Resources Journal* 3(1):37–44.

(17) Francesco, A. M., and Leung, A. Y. S. (1983) "The Effect of Males' and Females' Working Experience with Women on Other Attitudes Towards Women in Management," *Hong Kong Journal of Business Management* 1:49–55.

(18) *General Household Survey* (1985) Hong Kong: Census and Statistics Department.

(19) *General Household Survey* (1989) Hong Kong: Census and Statistics Department.

(20) Ho, Suk-ching (1976) "Women into Management – in Hong Kong?" *New Asia College Academic Annual XVIII*, pp. 273–282. Hong Kong: The Chinese University of Hong Kong.

(21) Ho, Suk-ching (1983) "Sex Role Portrayals in Print Advertisements: The Case of Hong Kong," *Equal Opportunities International* 2(4):1–4.

(22) Ho, Suk-ching (1985) "Women Managers in Hong Kong: A Content Analysis of the Recruitment Advertisements," *Equal Opportunities International* 4(2):30–33.

(23) *Hong Kong Annual Digest of Statistics* (1989) Hong Kong: Census and Statistics Department.

(24) *Hong Kong Annual Digest of Statistics* (1991) Hong Kong: Census and Statistics

Department.

(25) *Hong Kong Economic Times* (1990) "A Review of the Issues of Immigration in 1990," December 28, p. 3.

(26) *Hong Kong Standard* (1990) "Hong Kong a Haven for Working Women," November 28, p. 3.

(27) Hsu, F. L. K. (1971) "A Hypothesis on Kinship and Culture," in F. L. K. Hsu (ed.), *Kinship and Culture*, pp. 3–30. Chicago: Aldine.

(28) Keown, Charles F., and Lam, Mei Chu Yvonne (1986) "Success Factor for Hong Kong Women Executives," *The Hong Kong Manager* (May):19–29.

(29) Khor, Diana (1985) "Fetters of Feminism," *Hong Kong Psychological Society Bulletin* 14:1.

(30) Kirkbride, P. S., and Chan, E. (1988) "Emigration from Hong Kong," *Human Resources Journal* 4(2):5–17.

(31) Lai, Wong May Ling (1982) "Civil Service Attitudes towards Women in Hong Kong." Unpublished dissertation, University of Hong Kong.

(32) Lam, Jermaine T. M., and Lee, Jane C. Y. (1992) "The Political Culture of the Voters in Hong Kong Part II: A Study of the Geographical Constituencies of the Legislative Council in Hong Kong." Research Report, Department of Public and Social Administration, City Polytechnic of Hong Kong.

(33) Lau, Siu-kai (1982) *Society and Politics in Hong Kong*. Hong Kong: The Chinese University Press.

(34) Lau, Siu-kai (1984) "Utilitarianistic Familism: The Basis of Political Stability," in Ambrose, Y. C. King and Rance P. L. Lee (eds.), *Social Life and Development in Hong Kong*, pp. 195–216. Hong Kong: The Chinese University of Hong Kong.

(35) Lau, Siu-kai, and Kuan, Hsin-chi (1988) *The Ethos of the Hong Kong Chinese*. Hong Kong: The Chinese University of Hong Kong.

(36) Leung, Franz (1989) "Build More Crèches: Academic," *Hong Kong Standard*, November 10, p. 6.

(37) Leung, Yee-sheung Anita (1981) "The Effect of Direct Working Experience with Women Workers on Attitudes towards Women in Management." MBA Research Thesis, The Chinese University of Hong Kong.

(38) Marray, Denise (1989) "Female Workers Face a Battle for Rights to Equal Pay," *Hong Kong Standard*, March 4, p. 11.

(39) Marray, Denise, and Li, Angela (1990) "Women Call for Equality in Workplace," *Hong Kong Standard*, March 9, p. 4.

(40) *Ming Pao Daily* (1990) "Emigration of Managerial Personnel Will Peak Again after a Temporary Levelling Off," September 26, p. 4.

(41) Ngo, H. Y. (1989) "The Situation of Women's Employment: A Comparison of Hong Kong, S. Korea, Singapore and Taiwan," *Hong Kong Journal of Business Management* 7:71–83.

(42) Parton, Anne (1992) "Top Mums Find Time to Lead a Working Life," *South China Morning Post*, Special Report: Mother's Day, May 3, p. 1.

(43) Pearson, Veronica (1990) "Women in Hong Kong," in Benjamin K. P. Leung (ed.), *Social Issues in Hong Kong*. Hong Kong: Oxford University Press.

(44) Podmore, D., and Chaney, D. (1974) "Family Norms in a Rapidly Industrialising Society: Hong Kong," *Journal of Marriage and the Family* 36(2):400–407.

(45) Redding, Gordon, and Gilbert, Y. Y. Wong (1986) "The Psychology of the Chinese Organizational Behaviour," in Michael Harris Bond, *The Psychology of the Chinese People*, pp. 267–352. Hong Kong: Oxford University Press.

(46) Roberts, David (ed.) (1992) *Hong Kong 1992: A Review of 1991*. Hong Kong: Government Information Services.

(47) Salaff, Janet (1979) "Working Daughters in the Hong Kong Chinese Family: Female Filial Piety or a Transformation in the Family Power Structure," *Journal of Social History* 9:439–465.

(48) Salaff, Janet (1981) *Working Daughters of Hong Kong: Filial Piety or Power in the Family*. New York: Cambridge University Press.

(49) So, Stella L. M., and Young, Kitty (1989) "A Portrait of Women Executives in Hong Kong," *Proceedings of the Inaugural Meeting of the Southeast Asia Region, Academy of International Business*. (June):92–106.

(50) So, Stella L. M., and Young, Kitty (1991) "A Study of Women's Abilities in Managerial Positions: Male and Female Perceptions," in Fanny M. Cheung, et al. (eds.), *Selected Papers of Conference on Gender Studies in Chinese Societies*, Research Monograph 3, pp. 155–166. Hong Kong: Hong Kong Institute of Asia-Pacific Studies, The Chinese University of Hong Kong.

(51) Sun, Long-ji (1983) *The Deep Structure of Chinese Culture*. Hong Kong: Yishan.

(52) Tian, J. (1981) "Women in the Early Stages of Chinese Feudal Society," *Women of China*, July, pp. 35–36; August, pp. 42–43; September, pp. 20–21; October, pp. 34–35; November, p. 29.

(53) Turner, H. A., Fosh, Patricia, and Ng, Sek-hong (1991) *Between Two Societies: Hong Kong Labour in Transition*. Hong Kong: Centre of Asian Studies, University of Hong Kong.

(54) Williams, Kevin (1990) *An Introduction to Hong Kong Employment Law*. Hong Kong: Oxford University Press.

(55) Wong, Siu-lun (1992) "Emigration and Stability in Hong Kong," Social Sciences Research Centre Occasional Paper #7, Department of Sociology, The University of Hong Kong.

(56) Yang, C. F., and Kao, H. S. R. (1988) "Familism and Development: An Examination of the Role of Family in Contemporary Hong Kong, Taiwan, and Mainland China," Working Paper. Hong Kong: University of Hong Kong.

(57) Yang, Kuɔ-shu (ed.) (1988a) *Chinese People's Psychology*. Taipei: Gwei Gwan To Shu.

(58) Yang, Kuo-shu, and Tseng, S. C. (eds.) (1988b) *Chinese People's View of Management*. Taipei: Gwei Gwan Tu Shu.

(59) Yau, Oliver H. M. (1988) "Chinese Cultural Values: Their Dimensions and Marketing Implications," *European Journal of Marketing* 22(5):44–57.

(60) Yue, S. Y. (1992) "Group to Look at Sex Prejudice," *South China Morning Post*, February 27, p. 3.

4 INDONESIA

Women in Management in Indonesia

Lorna Wright and Virginia Crockett-Tellei

In Indonesia, much lip service is paid to the popular assumption that educated women have access to a wide variety of career choices. Although this appears to be the case, they also face serious obstacles to upward mobility. As expected, the data reviewed here confirm that Indonesian women are under-represented in managerial positions, especially in the private sector. However, as Indonesia's economy grows and shows an equally growing demand for skilled managers, it seems likely that educated women will find more doors opening to them, albeit more often in government than business. The estimated annual need for new managers in Indonesia ranges from 26,000 (57) to 100,000 (63).

Comparing the situation of Indonesian women managers with that of women managers in other countries in the region is informative. In 1980, Indonesia had a lower female workforce participation rate than her sister countries – 33 percent, compared to 47 percent in Thailand, 39 percent in the Philippines, 36 percent in Singapore, and 34 percent in Malaysia (19). The percentage increased to 45 percent by 1987 (4;41;64), which compares more favorably with Malaysia (35 percent), the Philippines (36 percent), and Singapore (39 percent) at roughly the same time period (4). Reasons suggested for women's increased participation are their higher education level and the need for more workers per household in economically hard times (64).

With regard to managers in particular, one report estimates the percentage of women in management (including administration) in Indonesia to be 0.035 percent in 1989 (4). Another report shows it to have been 0.03 percent in 1985 with no change since 1980 (64). Not only is this a low number in itself, but it is lower than any other county in the region. Of all managers and administrators in Indonesia in 1985, women constituted only 6.6 percent, which again was the lowest among all ASEAN countries. It compares with 25 percent in the Philippines, 22 percent in Singapore, 15 percent in Thailand, and 8 percent in Malaysia (70).

The Context: Economic Development, Management, and Women in Indonesia

Economic and demographic background[1]

Indonesia is an influential member of the Association of Southeast Asian Nations (ASEAN) and the Organization of Petroleum Exporting Countries (OPEC). It is the fifth largest nation in the world, with a population of 165.5 million in 1985 (39;26). Indonesia's five main islands – Sumatra, Java, Kalimantan (Borneo), Sulawesi (the Celebes), and West Irian – extend 3,200 miles across the equator in an archipelago populated by over 300 different ethnic groups (40). Fittingly, the national motto is "Unity in Diversity."[2] The Javanese constitute by far the largest ethnic group – about 60 percent of the population – and predominate in government and the military. The majority of Javanese follow the Islamic religion, but the form of Islam has been heavily influenced by earlier Hinduism and even earlier animistic practices. More traditional Islam is embraced in other parts of Indonesia, as are Christianity, Hinduism, and Buddhism.

From 1970 to 1978, Indonesia's real per capita gross domestic product (GDP) grew at the rapid rate of 5.9 percent (39), fueled to a large extent by oil production. In the period 1982 to 1984, the rate slowed to 2.7 percent (39), largely because of the world slump in oil prices. Between 1986 and 1988, GDP rose again to 5.5 percent, due to the government's switch in emphasis to non-oil and gas sectors. In 1990, GDP rose by an estimated 7.1 percent (72). Despite the government's commitment to deregulation and emphasis on non-oil and gas exports, and the enviable growth record of the past few years, Indonesia's economy still faces several major obstacles to growth.

Indonesia has a bottom-heavy age structure, with over two-thirds of the population under fifteen years of age (26), and a high population growth rate (2.3 percent per annum), which has resulted in a rapidly increasing labor force.[3] Notwithstanding, the World Bank approved the government's policies and assessed that Indonesia's reform agenda will enable her to meet the emerging challenge of a growing labor force, while also increasing productivity and reducing poverty (72).

Despite the incentives of the Suharto government for private sector development, the Indonesian economy remains highly centralized and closely controlled by the dominant state enterprises and influential military units. Three hundred and fifty years of Dutch economic guidance, and particularly their emphasis on agricultural rather than manufacturing production, have taken their toll.[4] In 1985, manufacturing represented only 9 percent of the total labor force. Agriculture, forestry, and fisheries, in contrast, employed over half of the total workforce – 55 percent. As Indonesia slowly urbanizes, the labor force in the cities is being absorbed into the tertiary sector. In 1985, 15 percent of the total workforce were in trade, 13 percent in public services, 3 percent in transportation and communication, and 0.4 percent in finance, insurance, real estate, and business services (27). Much of the tertiary sector is characterized by small-scale, impermanent, and low-capital businesses, dubbed the "informal" sector (37;55). In fact, the majority of Indonesian firms are small and family-owned (43). Large and medium-sized industries in Java employ fewer than one-third of those employed in manufacturing (72).

Management in Indonesia: Colonialism, Ethnicity, and Pancasila

The development of the Indonesian managerial ranks has been strongly influenced by three factors: Dutch colonial policies on education and administration; the legal and cultural constraints on various ethnic groups in relation to business activity; and the postwar government's involvement in the private sector.

During the period of Dutch colonialism (1619–1942), the Dutch held the higher-level management positions in government and the largest business concerns. The Javanese, the largest ethnic group in Indonesia, were employed mostly as lower-level civil servants. The Dutch neither encouraged the Javanese nor other Indonesians to engage in business; in fact, they enacted various legal restrictions on such involvement.[5] Traditionally, the Javanese nobility preferred government service, as they considered trade fit more for commoners and foreigners, such as the Chinese, Arabs, and other ethnic groups from the outer islands (56).[6] The disdain that the upper class (priyayi) held for business affairs meant that women often handled family finances – a factor that worked in favor of women when they entered the modern labor force.

Instead, immigrant Chinese and the descendants of the Arab merchants who had helped to bring Islam to Indonesia became active businesspeople and traders in Indonesian cities (5;15). At times, the Dutch granted them the privilege of conducting business while they prohibited indigenous Indonesians from doing so (9). Discussions of entrepreneurship in Indonesia, therefore, often focus on the Chinese, a minority of approximately 10 percent that exerts great influence on the nation's economy despite only being partially assimilated[7] and subjected periodically to purges during times of political unrest (65;67;68).

The development of entrepreneurial and managerial expertise among the indigenous Indonesian population (pribumi) has been hampered not only by the traditional values of the Javanese nobility, or the priyayi class, but also by the educational policies of the Dutch. Very few high schools were open to Indonesians, and those wishing a university education had to travel to The Netherlands.[8]

Not surprisingly, when most of the Dutch involuntarily relinquished their management positions in Indonesia at the end of the revolution in 1949, they left a vacuum that the untrained Indonesians found difficult to fill. Initially, most management training was conducted on the job (18). Although colleges began to provide courses in business management in the 1950s (mostly within departments of economics), only very recently has business become a formal course of study.[9] Five years ago, all graduate business schools were private institutions, and the degrees they granted were not recognized by the Department of Education and Culture. Since then, two of the most prestigious universities in Indonesia, University of Indonesia and Gadjah Mada University have set up MBA programs. Most recently, ITB (Bandung Institute of Technology) opened a postgraduate degree program in business administration and technology. At one institution in 1991, only nine out of 66 students were women (14 percent). However, the fact that there are any women at all is an encouraging sign.

Administrators and managers in the public and private sectors are drawn from a tiny pool of high school and university graduates, the upper ranks of the military, Chinese business families, and the aristocratic class of the Javanese (*priyayi*) along with certain other influential ethnic groups that constitute the Indonesian elite. Indonesian society is highly stratified and hierarchical. Social status and class have traditionally been based on hereditary nobility and land ownership. However, more recently, educational attainment and wealth have begun to play a part as well. Members of these privileged groups have the easiest access to higher education and value it greatly. The ubiquitous Indonesian name cards typically list all degrees and titles earned.

Traditionally, the elite, especially the wealthy Javanese and Chinese business families, sent their sons and daughters overseas to earn degrees in business or technical disciplines. Since there is little indigenous management science *per se*, Indonesians have been influenced by Japanese, European, and U.S. management advice (48;63). Yet, in practice, Indonesian social and cultural values are also consciously incorporated into management. In particular, Indonesians frequently debate the relationship between management and *Pancasila*, the five-part state philosophy that stresses belief in one Supreme Being, democracy, state unity, humanism, and social justice.[10] The government and the military exert a strong influence on business. State enterprises dominate many key industries and retired military officers hold many government and business positions (63).

Indonesian Women's Economic Roles

Indonesian women, especially those in the dominant Javanese ethnic group, have traditionally been active labor force participants and influential financial decision-makers within the family, especially among peasants (14;29).[11] They participated visibly and vocally in the tumultuous events of national, political, and economic development, particularly since the First Indonesian Women's Congress in 1928 (33). There are, however, significant class differences in women's work and autonomy, which may be traced to the influence of customary law (*adat*) and the two dominant religions of Hinduism and Islam.

Traditional law (adat)

In most of Indonesia's ethnic groups, customary law provided women with a rather strong economic position based on both property rights and inheritance (12). For example, in Java a married woman retained the right to her own property (69). However, other *adat* concerning marriage, in combination with Islamic law and Hindu custom, placed restrictions on women. For instance, arranged marriages at young ages were common, especially among the upper class.

Rural women's labor force participation rates have always been high. For example, in 1980, over 40 percent of rural women aged fifteen to 49 were employed (26). Women dominated market trading activities in Javanese villages and towns

(10), although by the 1970s this dominance appeared to be eroding (33). Women's earnings constitute a substantial proportion of total family income: up to one-half among the lower classes (23;34).

Historically, Chinese women have also been actively involved in family businesses, albeit in supportive roles. Unfortunately, very little has been written about Chinese women in Indonesian businesses, and available demographic data do not identify Chinese separately.[12]

Javanese noblewomen and the Indonesian women's movement[13]

The adoption of Hinduism (ca. 1400) and, subsequently, of Islam (ca. 1600) greatly affected the position of women in the aristocratic class. In accordance with the tenets of these religions, Javanese *priyayi* and noblewomen of other ethnic groups began to be secluded from public life, although they did not wear the veil.

The *priyayi* view of women stresses the roles of wife and mother. A women achieves high social status through the rank of her husband, whose position is reinforced by his wife serving as a gracious ornament at his side. Although the tradition of seclusion prevented most women from playing public roles, some upper-class women in colonial and precolonial times also achieved status and income through such means as becoming monarchs, special elite female bodyguards to the Javanese sultans, traders of batik and jewelry, and office workers during the Japanese occupation (34;50;59;69).

Dutch colonial rule, however, sustained the cloistered status of Indonesian noblewomen by providing civil service appointments for their husbands with high enough wages or access to indirect income (i.e., through perquisites and commissions) so that any economic contribution of the wives was generally not crucial to maintaining the family's social position (50).

The Javanese noblewoman Raden Adjeng Kartini personifies the upper-class Indonesian woman's aspirations for independence. She devoted her brief life at the turn of the century to developing educational opportunities for women. She saw education as the alternative to remaining bound, ignorant, and in a "golden cage" because of early arranged marriages (32). Acclaimed for starting vocational training for women (especially teachers' training), she is considered the pioneer of the Indonesian women's movement. An annual Kartini Day celebrates the progress women have made over the past century. True to her aristocratic upbringing, Kartini envisioned women of her class working only in certain types of occupations: "If I choose to work, it would have to be at something fitting! It is only work for pleasure which would not be a disgrace to my noble and highly placed family" (14).

The girls' schools that were set up following Kartini's example opened the door for Indonesian women to become vocal agents for change in society. Women's organizations proliferated during the 1920s. Their initial issues of concern were rights for women in areas such as education and marriage. However, the women's movement was soon diverted into the national struggle for independence from colonial rule, in which women played an active role.

Since the Indonesian revolution against Dutch rule (1945–1948), upper-class women, in particular, have become quite visible in political and public affairs. A proportion of seats in the national parliament is reserved for special functional groups, including women (who are allocated under 10 percent) (12). There have been several women cabinet ministers (33). Ikatan Wanita Pengusaha Indonesia (IWAPI, the Organization of Indonesian Businesswomen) is an active branch of the Indonesian Chamber of Commerce. Other professional associations for women have been formed, but about one-third of the women's organizations are actually wives' auxiliaries of men's professional groups, such as the Military Wives (PERSIT). The platforms of the women's organizations have focused on so-called female concerns such as maternal and child health, family planning, marriage law reform, education and vocational training (especially for teachers), and political representation for women.

Islam, as practiced by many Indonesians, is tempered by vestiges of Hinduism and animism, which have had a moderating effect on attitudes towards women's presence in the public sphere. Fundamentalism has not had the impact it has had in other parts of the world; and the government, interested in maintaining this status quo, attempts to balance Islam with the other religions that are also part of Indonesian culture. For example, a study of women's roles as portrayed in two Islamic magazines found that the ideal Indonesian Muslim woman is a wife and mother who has successfully pursued an academic or professional career after marriage and who has been active in community welfare, religious education, or politics, but has also put her children's and husband's needs before her own (71). An unmarried career woman is somewhat suspect. The fact that a career is part of the Indonesian Islamic view of the ideal Muslim woman is indicative of the fact that Islam is less of a barrier to women's advancement in Indonesia than it is in other Islamic countries.

Educated Women Workers and Managers in Urban Centers

Women's labor force participation rates[14]

There are important differences in labor force participation between the middle and upper classes. Middle-class women typically have a high school education and remain in the formal labor force (in teaching or sales) up to the time of marriage, after which they engage in full-time domestic responsibilities. However, many of these women conduct some informal, service-based business or trade out of their homes to supplement the family income. They also concentrate on "status-production work," such as membership in women's auxiliary organizations (e.g., Air Force Wives) (45). Upper-class women – those from noble, wealthy, or high-ranking military families – are more likely to have paid employment in the professions, civil service, or family businesses. They remain in the formal labor force after marriage, although they take out time when their children are born. The higher level of education attained by upper-class women partially explains this difference, as does the competitive advantage afforded elite women by virtue of their position in the power structure in acquiring white-collar jobs.

The interplay between religion and culture is complex. On the whole, fewer women from areas dominated by Christianity and orthodox Islam – West Java, Jakarta, and the outer islands – work outside the home than do those from Central and East Java, where *abangan*, or nominal, Islam reigns.[15] Among the educated, those from Central Java are still the most likely to work, although the differences are not dramatic (30).

Some other reasons why college-educated women represent the greatest proportion of those employed outside the agricultural sector are the influence of Western feminist values among the very cosmopolitan upper-class, the competitive advantage afforded them by their higher level of education, and their access to an income that allows them to maintain a high-status life-style. The high level of economic activity among unattached, independent women (household heads, unmarried women, and those with no children) indicates that marriage, motherhood, and a career are still not easily combined.

Women managers in business and government[16]

Do the available data support or refute the two following popular impressions?

> Finding executive women who occupy high-level management positions in business in Jakarta does not appear to be an easy task. It seems that most women in management hold dual functions: as owner/founder and manager of the enterprise. Even if there are some professional managers, they usually hold less visible positions such as office administrator (56).

> Business and management are regarded as a male domain (17).

How do women managers compare with their male counterparts? Are there any important variations between the characteristics of managerial women in business and those in government? Table 4.1 presents some of the major differences between women and men aged 25 to 44 years in managerial and administrative positions in both the government and private sectors.[17] As can readily be seen, there are more women managers in the public sector than in the private sector. In both sectors, more women managers are single than are men in management or than are women in any other category of white-collar women's employment. In 1976, nearly 39 percent of women administrators were single, compared with 12 percent of men (and 25 percent of businesswomen compared to under 6 percent of businessmen), even in the 25- to 44-year-old group, by which age most Indonesians have chosen to marry. Women in administrative positions obviously do not combine work and marriage as easily as do men. Women managers in the private sector are more likely to be married than are other white-collar women (as are men in the private sector). This partially reflects women's involvement in family businesses.

Unlike most other white-collar jobs, the age structure for business managers is similar for both women and men. The few women employed in private sector management have probably gained their positions through many years of work experience, high educational attainment, and/or family ties.

About half of the men (51 percent), in contrast to almost 60 percent of the women, in government administration have received higher education (see Table 4.1).[18] It appears that women must be more qualified than men in order to obtain

Table 4.1   Demographic profile of managers aged 25 to 44 (1976)

	Private sector		Government	
	Women (%)	Men (%)	Women (%)	Men (%)
Marital status: single	25.6	5.8	38.8	12.4
Educated	79.5	89.2	59.3	50.9
In management, administration, related work of all white-collar jobs	1.4	3.7	21.1	35.8

Population subset is composed of 26,112 men and 9,541 women.

Source: Derived from 1976 SUPAS II sample tape, Indonesia Central Bureau of Statistics (25).

government administrative positions, in spite of the civil service rules officially basing selection on educational degrees and entrance exams (36). Among private sector managers, more men are educated than women (89 percent compared to 80 percent). Apparently, women in business rely on family connections or other factors more heavily than on educational qualifications to compete with men for their positions. Yet, more women managers attain a higher level of education than do women civil servants (approximately 80 percent compared with 60 percent).

The data show that women managers are more likely to work in the public than in the private sector. They differ from their male colleagues in several important aspects. Women managers are generally younger, more likely to be single, and more highly educated. Women managers in business and government are somewhat different from each other, with government administrators being more often single and somewhat less educated, whereas the typical woman executive is more likely to be older, more highly educated, and less often single. She is also a rare breed, as yet barely represented in the managerial ranks.

From this broad overview, let us look in more detail at women managers in both sectors.

Corporate women managers

Little research has been carried out on the status of women managers, and the Ministry for the Role of Women, when contacted, had no information on the subject. Census statistics do not readily yield this information either. One encouraging sign that the situation is changing is the growing number of articles on women managers, directories of prominent women, and women listed among the executives for institutions and companies.

However, all sources provide only fragmented pictures of the presence of women in management in Indonesia. We still know very little about where women managers work. There is some evidence that the banking sector provides more opportunity for women managers than do other sectors. This may be so for several reasons. The banking sector expanded rapidly following a series of deregulations, and 57 new private banks opened between 1988 and 1990. Bank Indonesia also licensed eighteen foreign joint ventures and 653 smaller rural banks in that same time period (54), thereby creating an extreme shortage of trained staff and managers. The traditional belief that women deal with finances better than do men – and that women are more meticulous and more trustworthy – also works in their favor.

The Women Managers in Business Organizations (WMBO) project is the richest data source available on women managers in the ASEAN region and consequently on Indonesian women managers.[19] The overall project surveyed 275 ASEAN women managers and conducted interviews with selected women, some of which resulted in individual case studies. (see, for example, (1;2)).

The 53 women in the Indonesian section of the WMBO study were a very select group, and not representative of Indonesian women managers as a whole. However, it is the only research done to date on Indonesian women managers as a group, as opposed to the individual profiles in such magazines as *Eksekutif*. As such, it is a valuable addition to our knowledge.

The 53 women were drawn from a potential pool of 172 managers, each originally identified by soliciting nominations from various business sources and from culling directories and reports (21). Of these, 35 (66 percent) were corporate managers, twelve were entrepreneurs and the remaining six were managers of businesses owned or controlled by their families. These latter eighteen women (34 percent) were considered noncorporate senior managers.

Of the 35 corporate managers, ten were at the senior level and the remainder were middle managers. The survey found that 58 percent of the women belonged to the Malay people but did not indicate any particular ethnic group. Twenty-three percent were Indonesians of Chinese descent.

Another survey, currently being carried out by one of the authors, of both female and male managers in Indonesia found that the largest proportion of women responding were Javanese (69 percent; note that Javanese are part of the Malay people.)[20] In contrast to this, only one-quarter of the male managers responding were Javanese, with another quarter being ethnic Chinese.

More than half of the women managers in the WMBO study were Muslim (58 percent), 41 percent were Christian, and one family business manager was Hindu. More than 60 percent of the responding women were married. Only one-fifth were never married. Seventy percent of the women were also working mothers. The average number of children was 2.4 – lower than the national average of 3.8. Of the 43 women listed in the *Directory of Women Managers in Southeast Asia*, 32 (74 percent) were married, six were single, and three were widowed (70).

More than one-third of the women in the WMBO study worked in medium-sized companies while another third worked in large companies, 20 percent of whom were involved in firms with more than 1,000 employees. Among the latter was a noncorporate woman who established and managed one of the largest transport service companies in Indonesia.

All of the entrepreneurs and two-thirds of each of the family business managers and senior corporate executives were involved in general management. Even though most respondents believed that women excel at personnel and administration functions, these areas had the fewest women in the survey. A breakdown of responding women managers by functional area follows:

General management	42%
Marketing	25%
Production	15%
Finance	11%
Personnel	8%
Administration	8%

The overall distribution of women responding to the survey indicates that slightly fewer than half (47 percent) held the title of manager or head; 26 percent were managing directors or VP/directors, and the remainder were at the level of president (many of these were entrepreneurs), or left the level unspecified.

It is a characteristic of Indonesian businesspeople, women or men, that they may be involved with more than one business at the same time or head of several departments within the same company. In the *Directory of Women Managers in Southeast Asia*, ten of the 43 women indicated that they managed more than one department (70). Three women each managed two companies simultaneously; and one general manager oversaw four companies (all related).

The typical Indonesian manager in the WMBO survey considers natural talent to be her key success factor. This belief contrasts with that of Filipinas, for whom the key success factor is competence, and contrasts with Malaysian, Singaporean, and Thai women, for whom it is hard work (21). Another interesting contrast to their ASEAN sisters, among whom a majority saw great obstacles, is that more than half of the Indonesian women managers saw no major obstacles to their careers (19).

This view may be partially explained by the fact that women in senior management positions and top government roles tend to be from the country's leading families. In Indonesia, family status and family ties are very important, and can help a woman advance over a man with less influential connections (12;52). Most of the surveyed women came from privileged groups – 75 percent grew up in large cities; most had domestic help at home; and only one reported coming from a family in the low-income bracket. Almost three-quarters had fathers who were either government officials, entrepreneurs, or in one of the professions. Only 17 percent had mothers who worked outside the home.

For the women managers in the WMBO survey, the three most important reasons for working were pleasure in accomplishment, desire to earn their own money, and need for recognition. Economic need was more significant among middle managers. The second survey had similar findings, with the three most important reasons for working being self-satisfaction, respect from colleagues, and high salaries. The majority of women (85 percent) worked because of interest; only one indicated that she worked because of financial need.

Based on how they approached their jobs, most of the women (96 percent) reported trying to get to know their subordinates on a one-to-one basis while also attempting to keep the relationships from getting too informal. Two-thirds (66 percent) reported that indirectly influencing their subordinates proved more effective than giving them direct orders. Most (96 percent) believed in "networking." Although the term itself is foreign to Indonesia, the concept is not. Connections (*koneksi*) are very important in getting things accomplished in Indonesia.

Similar attitudes were found in a study of managers in the textile industry in a Central Javanese village (49). With a population of close to 9,000, there were 100 textile home industry units. Most were jointly owned by husbands and wives, with the women acting as managers. Some units operated on a medium scale (50 to 100 employees) while others operated on a large scale (over 100 employees).

The women generally expressed maternalistic attitudes towards their employees and considered them of lower status but part of the family. This maternalistic attitude is similar to that expressed by women managers in the WMBO project and not too different from traditional male *bapakism*. Many older women considered that they, rather than their husbands, did most of the work. This view is consistent with the concept of *priyayi*, which holds that it is beneath the dignity of a refined man to worry about wealth creation. Women's contribution to the textile industry is under-represented in the census data, since women frequently underplay their participation in management and ownership of home industries to male enumerators, thus leaving the unit to be listed as owned by the husband only.

The precedence of men in the public sector is illustrated by the Indonesian organization Dharma Wanita. The government is the largest employer in Indonesia, and all wives (but not husbands) of civil servants belong to Dharma Wanita, an organization of government wives. Wives of senior civil servants, who may have a career of their own, have no choice but to drop the career or put it on hold so as not to interfere with their duties as mandated by Dharma Wanita. Positions in Dharma Wanita parallel those of the husband, with the wife of a minister heading the branch of Dharma Wanita for that department. Although the organization promotes many excellent social welfare activities, it does not promote the professional advancement of its women members. The women are strictly treated as appendages of their husbands.

Many career women have ambivalent feelings about pursuing a career to the exclusion of family (20); however, they generally do not feel that they have to make a choice between career and family. Indonesian women do not perceive it to be the either/or decision it often becomes in the West.

An encouraging sign of changing attitudes in the second survey was that almost all the responding men felt women should continue working after they married, and 90 percent felt they should continue even after having children. However, of the married men, only 52 percent had a wife who worked, and only 43 percent had a wife who worked full-time. Almost two-thirds felt that a woman's primary responsibility was to her household.

Indonesian men generally viewed women in management as nonproblematic. Over half the men responding to the survey did not believe that women either had to be more competent or to work harder than men to achieve equal success, and a similar proportion disagreed that men could cope better than women with stressful situations. Similarly, the men did not see women as better managers because of a sensitive, supportive, "feminine" nature. More than four-fifths (81 percent) reported finding no sexual discrimination in their organizations. More than half felt that neither male nor female subordinates minded reporting to a woman superior.

Very few men responding to the survey admitted feeling any threat from the increased presence of women in business. Ninety percent of the men said they would hire women for managerial positions, while 10 percent said they would not. Eighty-three percent said they would not mind working for a woman boss, but not one man indicated that he would be happy about it, while 7 percent indicated they would be unhappy about it.

Women managers in government

Notwithstanding the fact that women have entered the civil service in increasing numbers, the number in senior management positions remains small. Table 4.2 presents the proportion of women in top-level positions (Echelon III to I) in the 22 government departments at the national level. These positions account for only about 7 percent of all civil service positions (31). In 1984, 11 percent of all managerial positions were held by women.

When it comes to state-owned enterprises, the picture is even bleaker. In 28 state enterprises, with a total of 377 senior positions, only fourteen (3.7 percent) were filled by women (7). Of these fourteen women, ten worked in three of the seven state banks, accounting for 5.7 percent of the 174 positions there. Four banks had

Table 4.2   Women in senior positions in government departments in 1984 and 1991

	1984		1991	
Department	Total personnel	Number of women	Total personnel	Number of women
Home Affairs	63	0	69	1 (1.4%)
Foreign Affairs	55	1 (1.8%)	58	2 (3.4%)
Defense and Security	44	0	56	0
Justice	48	3 (6.3%)	61	9 (14.8%)
Information	44	0	50	0
Finance	77	1 (1.3%)	83	4 (4.8%)
Trade	49	2 (4.1%)	55	3 (5.5%)
Cooperatives	30	0	38	1 (2.6%)
Agriculture	98	0	95	3 (3.2%)
Forestry	40	0	49	0
Industry	59	1 (1.7%)	67	1 (1.5%)
Mines and Energy	43	0	48	1 (2.1%)
Public Works	53	1 (1.9%)	59	1 (1.7%)
Communication	54	0	59	0
Tourism, Post, Telecommunication	25	1 (4%)	28	1 (3.6%)
Manpower	40	2 (5%)	41	2 (4.9%)
Transmigration	30	0	37	0
Education and Culture	64	2 (3.1%)	70	4 (5.7%)
Health	45	2 (4.4%)	62	8 (12.9%)
Religious Affairs	43	1 (2.3%)	50	1 (2.0%)
Social Affairs	47	4 (8.5%)	48	4 (8.3%)
Total	1,051	21 (2%)	1,183	46 (3.9%)

Sources: Standard Trade and Industry Directory of Indonesia (1991) 11th edn., Vol. 2 *List of Important Functionaries and Addresses; Buku Alamat Pejabat Negara* (1984) 13th edn. [*Book of Addresses of State Functionaries of the Republic of Indonesia*]. Jakarta: B. P. Alda.

no women in these positions. In 1984, there were only three senior women in state enterprises.

A more general study of women in the civil service provides evidence of significant improvement in their position over the ten years from 1974 to 1984 (36).[21] The number of women working in government more than doubled during that period, and the proportion of civil servants who were women increased from 18 percent to nearly 30 percent. Also encouraging was their advancement into higher wage levels within government. In 1974, most women were employed in the lowest of the four broad official classifications (*golongan* I), in which proof of only elementary school graduation is required. By 1984, the majority were found in *golongan* II, which requires a college degree or equivalent. Women at *golongan* III (postgraduate degree) had more than tripled from the 1974 level, thus indicating that progress has been made, although we cannot tell from *golongan* figures if the progress is into managerial ranks.

Conclusions

One can take both a pessimistic and an optimistic view of the situation for women in management in Indonesia. On the one hand, the rather pessimistic observations made by Indonesians writing in *Eksekutif* (17;47;57) are confirmed by the data. White-collar Indonesian women are under-represented in managerial positions, even though they are more highly educated than men. Entry into managerial positions in the private sector is more difficult for women in the absence of the formal selection criteria used by the civil service (36). Faced with this barrier, those in business apparently become entrepreneurs and managers in family enterprises or small companies rather than executives in corporations.

As Indonesia faces further challenges to growth and a continued demand for skilled managers, educated women may find more doors opening to them. However, women face a number of constraints in filling these positions. The principal obstacles are the cultural value placed upon wifely duty (*kodrat wanita*), the Indonesian style of organizational behavior, and the stereotypes held about women in management.

Chief among the sociocultural constraints is the conflict between the roles of wife/mother and career woman. The Applied Family Welfare Program (PKK), which was initiated in 1980 to ensure the participation of women in national development, outlined five roles for women: wife, housekeeper, childbearer, childrearer, citizen (62). In public discussions of this program, the ordering of the first four roles change, but the role of citizen invariably comes in fifth place (24). The roles of wife and mother clearly outweigh in importance the role of citizen for women. All of the managerial women profiled in *Eksekutif* cite the conflict between their family and work roles as significant in their own work histories. Given the strength of the cultural value attached to marriage and motherhood, it is not surprising that women managers are more likely to be single than are their male counterparts.

The "femininity values" in organizational behavior that characterize Indonesia affect women and men differently and inhibit women's upward mobility (see (22)). Indonesian society discourages ego motives, self-advancement, and individual competitiveness; mutual aid (*gotong royong*) and collective achievement are the standard. Women who pursue a career may appear to neglect home life and thus be criticized for being selfish and self-advancing at the expense of others.[22]

Furthermore, the high value placed on patron–client relationships ("strongly collectivist" (22)), ascribed status ("high-power distance" (22)), and maintenance of tradition ("below average uncertainty avoidance" (22)) means that the privileged women who are well connected to the traditional power structure by virtue of class (e.g., nobility involved in government and the military) or wealth (e.g., the Chinese business families) are most likely to succeed. The middle-class women who are dependent on educational attainment for entry into managerial positions and on individual ability for advancement are at a disadvantage. Thus, the picture is rosier for some women than for others.

Some see the concepts of *ibu* (mother) and *priyayi* (a cultural concept containing elements of social class and refinement) give elite woman access to power (11). However, the concept of power in Javanese terms is different from the concept of power in the West. Javanese power is an ascribed attribute. One does not get power by striving for it. As a member of the nonelite, one is automatically excluded. The concept of *priyayi* thus appears to have more strength than the concept of *ibu* when it comes to a woman's career.

Although there are no employment policies that overtly discriminate against women, there is evidence that employers' attitudes do serve to exclude them. Protective labor laws (e.g., maternity and menstruation leaves) may be used as justifications for not hiring women. Employment advertisements frequently specify gender (51). Stereotypical images of women in management such as "Men are better decision-makers/emotionally more stable/intellectually superior," or "Women are more interested in husbands and children" that are occasionally found in popular business periodicals reflect and reinforce prejudicial attitudes (17;47).

Despite the gloomy picture painted here, there is room for optimism. Some positive forces are facilitating women's movement into management – namely that the pool of educated women is increasing and that the most highly educated women are the most likely to work and to seek challenging jobs. The traditionally strong economic role of women in influential ethnic groups, such as the Javanese and the Chinese, further supports this movement. It is reinforced by importing recent Western cultural values emphasizing managerial roles for women. The role models presented by strong women leaders and highlighted in the popular press contribute toward changing attitudes, despite the fact that they often give mixed signals concerning the desirability of pursuing career goals. Women's organizations are a ready vehicle for bringing about change. Already experienced in promoting concerns such as marriage-law changes, education, and maternal and child health, some are beginning to turn their attention to employment issues.

The optimism is also based partly on the Javanese cultural background. Indonesia, in contrast to many other countries, does not sharply distinguish between the public and private spheres of life. Women are not restricted to the private sphere and thus have more access to power (11).

An important element of power comes from the juxtaposition of binary pairs, such as elder–younger, male–female, and married–not-yet-married, with the first being more powerful or having more authority than the second. (The status of widowed or divorced women, however, is not as clear (35).)

Gender distinctions are not deeply embedded in Javanese culture. There is little labeling, at least among the Javanese, the most populous ethnic group, of characteristics as masculine or feminine, as is commonly done in the West. Ascribed class differences are more important and characteristics are either *halus* (smooth, refined) or *kasar* (crude, rough), with neither being the exclusive province of either sex. Srikandi, the active, energetic, generous, go-getting wife of Arjuna in the *wayang* stories of the Ramayana, is an honored type of woman for the Javanese (12). Although equal treatment of women and men has not yet been realized in occupations or careers in Indonesia, the worth and potential of women and girls are rated on a par with those of men and boys, even in very traditional parts of the country (see (12)).

Whereas many observers of the Indonesian scene have commented on the economic independence, freedom of movement, and overall self-reliance of the Javanese woman, it was generally the lower-class woman who worked outside the home. In the past, the higher-class husband's role was to fully support the family, with the wife's income from work outside the home reflecting badly on her status and that of her husband (58). These traditional attitudes are slowly changing, especially among the younger generation, where women are gaining more education and where economic pressures are making the wife's income important for the family to maintain a decent standard of living.

The Indonesian economy is growing at the rate of 5 to 6 percent a year, and as spates of deregulation open up more sectors, the need for managers is growing rapidly, thereby bringing opportunity for women as well as men. Sectors like banking, where the demand for trained managers is great, will not be too concerned with whether they hire women or men managers – at least for entry- to mid-level management positions.

As long as the Indonesian economy continues to grow, the obstacles are not insurmountable and the number of women in mid- to top-level management positions should continue to increase. In line with one recent article, which maintains that "though the present number of Asian women managers is small, it is nonetheless significant, considering that only ten years ago there were only a handful of them" (4:18), the same can be said for Indonesian women managers in particular. Indonesian women managers are under-represented at present, but their numbers are increasing and, given the social and economic climate, the trend should continue.

Notes

1 All figures are drawn from the 1980 census unless otherwise noted.
2 In reality, just a few ethnic groups are dominant, because of history and numerical strength. In particular, the Javanese account for over 60 percent of the total population. The island of Java cradles the national capital, Jakarta, which was also the Dutch colonial

seat of power, under the name Batavia. Jakarta is the largest city in Indonesia. In 1980, it had over six million residents and accounted for nearly 20 percent of the total urban population (26). As the Indonesian government is highly centralized and exerts a strong influence on the private sector, Jakarta is also the economic center of the nation. Traditional Javanese political structure reinforces this centralization of power. The precolonial Hinduized kingdoms focused on the sultan, who represented the center of both spiritual and political power. The Javanese nobility, or *priyayi*, formed the core of the revolutionary movement and have been extremely influential in all spheres of national life ever since.

3 It should be noted, however, that the Indonesian government has succeeded in steadily reducing this rate through its widespread family-planning program, with projections of 1.6 percent for the period 1985 to 1990 and 1.9 percent for the period 2010 to 2015 (39).

4 After the Dutch colonial government took over the Dutch East India Company (VOC) in the nineteenth century, it introduced the "cultivation system" (*cultuurstelsel*), a deliberate policy of forced cultivation of a narrow range of export crops (sugar, tea, coffee, indigo, and rubber). Liberal reforms in the colonial motherland during the late nineteenth and early twentieth centuries replaced the cultivation system with direct taxation and led to a plethora of private and government plantations using coolie labor. Indigenous manufacturing was not encouraged, since the Dutch saw Indonesia as a viable market for their infant manufacturing sector. Indonesia gained its independence from the Dutch after World War II, following the Japanese occupation. See Geertz (1963*b*) for a detailed analysis of this policy and its economic effects; see White (1973) for an excellent review of Dutch economic policy in Indonesia.

5 See Wertheim (1956), Furnivall (1939), Boeke (1946, 1953), and Schrieke (1955) for classic treatments of the social and economic conditions under Dutch colonialism.

6 This attitude stemmed from the "golden age" of Javanese history and from the traditional Hindu caste system, in which traders held lower status than noblemen, scholars, and warriors. The inland, Hinduized kingdoms ruled by virtue of their control over the fertile rice paddies of upland Java; trade was conducted at the periphery, through the small, northern, coastal sultanates, which eventually converted to Islam and rose to dominate Java just as the Dutch took control. See also Geertz (1963*a*) for a discussion of the contrasting values of the *priyayi* (princes) and those engaged in business (peddlers).

7 Use of Bahasa Indonesia, the national language, rather than Chinese, is common; until recently it was illegal to post signs using Chinese characters. Many Chinese Indonesians have assumed Javanese or Indonesian names; they are no longer enumerated as a distinct ethnic group in official data collection.

8 For instance, Mohammed Hatta, a key leader of the Indonesian revolution and the nation's first vice president, studied economics – and, incidentally, revolution – in the colonial motherland.

9 During the 1950s and 1960s, a Ph.D. in economics – preferably from the University of California at Berkeley – was the ticket to success, particularly for those who guided the nation's economic growth through the series of five-year development plans. An MBA degree is now becoming the talisman, as Indonesia's economy faces further challenges to growth.

10 Pancasila, the "Five Principles," was inserted in the 1945 constitution. See Sutoyo (1985:28–31) for examples of the debate about Indonesian management development. Pancasila does not have direct significance for women in management. It was promulgated at a time when all people in power were men. The attitude of the government is still paternalistic. The 1988 Guidelines for State Policy stipulate that "in the implementation of development, women are equal partners with men, having the same rights, responsibili-

ties and opportunities," but adds "in accordance with the nature, self-esteem, and dignity of women"and then outlines roles and programs that have more to do with the family than careers. A document specifically making recommendations based on this, in its industrial and trade section, concentrates on employment opportunities for women in home-based industries and as street vendors and small entrepreneurs ("The Role of Women in Nation Building: Policies and Programmes of the Repelita V" n.d., mimeo).

11 Dewey (1962), Jay (1969), Stoler (1977), and Geertz (1961) have published some significant studies.

12 Rather, ethnicity is inferred by provincial birthplace. This is generally an accurate assumption for indigenous Indonesians but does not work for identifying the Chinese, most of whom have been born in Indonesia and are assimilated, speaking only Indonesian. Panglaykim and Palmer (1970) and Wilmott (1960), describing successful Chinese firms, show how a wife assisted her husband in the store, took over for him while he was on business trips, and trained her son to take over after she was widowed. While her son was young, she gave active control of the business to a brother. Another woman relative supported the family business by investing capital.

13 Some selected articles, among numerous writings on this topic, are those by Douglas (1980), Willner (1980), KOWANI (1980), and Ismail (1959).

14 Female labor force participation rates in the following discussion are age-standardized rates unless otherwise noted.

15 With few exceptions, members of each one of the three hundred diverse ethnic groups in Indonesia tend to embrace the same religion. Javanese are almost universally Moslem. Other dominant groups from the outer islands are Christians; Balinese are Hindu; Chinese are usually Buddhist, Confucian, or Christian. Among the Javanese, the strength of Islamic beliefs varies widely, however, with one important group professing orthodoxy and a large majority adhering to a less strict version tempered by Hinduism (Islam *abangan*, or nominal Islam).

16 Some popular articles in the Indonesian media have discussed women managers briefly (e.g., Hawkins (1971), and *Manajemen* (n.d.)); and several studies of educated Indonesian women touch peripherally on the issue (e.g., Rahardjo and Hull (1984), Stoler (1977), Rahardjo (1975), Kumar (1980), Kartini (1976), Papanek (1979a), M. Oey (1980), and H. Papanek (1979b).

17 This section is based on data from the unweighed sample population subset of SUPAS II (second phase of the Indonesian Central Bureau of Statistics' three-stage 1976 Intercensal Survey (25)), which is composed of 26,112 men and 9,541 women aged ten and over who were working during the year before the survey and who were living in urban areas. Similarly detailed occupational data have not been published for the 1980 census or subsequent labor force surveys. Therefore, the 1976 data, though somewhat out of date, are the best available for this type of analysis. The Indonesian Central Bureau of Statistics generously made the SUPAS II computer tape available to the East-West Centre's Population Institute (EWPI) for this and other analyses. More detailed information on occupational classification and distribution in Indonesia can be obtained by writing to Virginia Crockett-Tellei.

18 Educated women were defined as high school, university, and academy graduates aged fifteen and over. The education variable used here is a composite of two questions: "level currently or last attended" and "highest class ever/currently attended." Based on these questions, five levels of education, ranging from "never attended" to "high school and above," are tabulated. Unfortunately, for the purpose of this analysis of elite women, the higher levels of education were not tabulated separately in the EWPI printouts. As the

review of labor force participation rates shows, there are important differences in work patterns between women who are high school graduates and those who have completed university education.

19 All the information in this section is taken from "Indonesia Country Report" in *Women Managers in Business Organizations* (3), an unpublished report of the Asian Institute of Management. The individual country reports were not published in the final textbook *Corporate Women Managers in Southeast Asia*.

20 The survey was sent to over 300 respondents, 76 of whom were women. At the time of writing, the responses are still coming in, so only preliminary tabulations have been made.

21 Note that the total group of civil servants discussed in Logsdon's study is broader than the government administrators defined in the SUPAS data set, and includes nonadministrative categories such as elementary school teachers. Indonesian government rankings are complicated, being a mix of *golongan* (entry-level positions based on education) and echelon (structural positions, the top three of which are managerial). There are four *golongan* in ascending order I–IV, and five echelon in descending order V–I, I being highest. A person needs to be in *golongan* III or IV to have a chance of entering a structural position.

22 Hofstede's attitudinal survey of Indonesian employees of a multinational corporation identified several work-related values that he uses to describe typical Indonesian organizational behavior: 1. Characterized by patron–client relationships ("strongly collectivist"); 2. hierarchical and paternalistic, with ascribed instead of achieved status ("high-power distance"); 3. highly tolerant of uncertainty, able to "muddle through" unstructured situations by negotiation, valuing mystical predictions and maintenance of tradition, and fatalistic ("below average uncertainty avoidance"); and 4. characterized by low social acceptance of assertive and competitive behavior and by disapproval of ego motives ("slightly below average masculinity").

References

(1) Arroyo, Jesusa T. (1986) *Case History: Christine Effendi*. Unpublished case study as part of CIDA sponsored research project on women managers in business organizations of Southeast Asia, Asian Institute of Management.

(2) Arroyo, Jesusa T. (1987) *Case History: Shanti Poesposoetjipto*. Unpublished case study as part of CIDA sponsored research project on women managers in business organizations of Southeast Asia, Asian Institute of Management.

(3) Asian Institute of Management (1989) "Indonesia Country Report," in *Women Managers in Business Organizations*. Unpublished report. Manila: Asian Institute of Management.

(4) "Asian Women – Have They Arrived?" (1990) *World Executive Digest* (June):18.

(5) Boeke, J. H. (1946) *The Evolution of the Netherlands Indies Economy*. New York: Netherlands and Netherlands Indies Council, Institute of Pacific Relations.

(6) Boeke, J. H. (1953) *Economics and Economic Policy of Dual Societies*. New York: International Secretariat, Institute of Pacific Relations.

(7) *Buku Alamat Pejabat Negara* (1984), 13th edn. [*Book of Addresses of State Functionaries of the Republic of Indonesia*]. Jakarta: B. P. Alda.

(8) Chandler, G. (1985) "Wanita Pedagang di Pasar Desa Di Jawa" ["Rural Market Women in Java"], *Prisma* 14(10):50–58.

(9) Crissman, L. W. (1977) "A Discussion of Ethnicity and Its Relation to Commerce,"

Southeast Asian Journal of Social Science 5(102):96–110.

(10) Dewey, A. (1962) *Peasant Marketing in Java.* New York: The Free Press.

(11) Djajadiningrat-Nieuwenhuis, Madelon (1987) "Ibuism and Priyayization: Path to Power?" in Locher-Scholten, Elsbeth (ed.), *Indonesian Women in Focus.* Dordrecht, Holland: Foris Publications.

(12) Douglas, S. A. (1980) "Women in Indonesian Politics: The Myth of Functional Interest," in S. A. Chipp and J. J. Green (eds.), *Asian Women in Transition*, pp. 152–181. University Park, Penn.: Pennsylvania State University Press.

(13) Furnivall, J. S. (1939) *Netherlands India: A Study of Plural Economy.* New York: Cambridge University Press.

(14) Geertz, H. (1961) *The Javanese Family: A Study of Kinship and Socialization.* New York: The Free Press.

(15) Geertz, C. (1963a) *Peddlers and Princes: Social Change and Economic Modernization in Two Indonesian Towns.* Chicago: University of Chicago Press.

(16) Geertz, C. (1963b) *Agricultural Involution: The Process of Ecological Change in Indonesia.* Berkeley: University of California Press.

(17) Hatta, H. (1984) "Wanita Dan Manajemen: Masalah Kualitas dan Kesempatan" ["Women and Management: A Problem of Quality and Opportunity"], *Eksekutif* (December):30–32, 83.

(18) Hawkins, E. D. (1971) "Labor in Developing Countries: Indonesia," in B. Glassburner (ed.), *The Economy of Indonesia: Selected Readings*, pp. 196–250. Ithaca, N.Y.: Cornell University Press.

(19) Hoffarth, Victoria B. (ed.) (1989a) *Corporate Women Managers in Southeast Asia.* Manila: Asian Institute of Management.

(20) Hoffarth, Victoria Bantug (1989b) "Corporate Women – And the Men in Their Lives," *World Executive's Digest* (January):10–16.

(21) Hoffarth, Victoria Bantug, and Almario, E. Soriano (1988) "Getting to Know the Women Managers of Southeast Asia," *The Asian Manager* (April):17–21.

(22) Hofstede, G. (1979) *Cultural Pitfalls for Dutch Expatriates in Indonesia*, 2ed edn. Deventer: Twinjnstra Gudde International.

(23) Hull, Valerie J. (1979) "A Woman's Place . . . : Social Class Variations in Women's Work Patterns in a Javanese Village," Working Paper Series, No. 21. Jakarta: Population Studies Centre, Gadjah Mada University.

(24) Hull, Valerie J. (1982) "Women in Java's Rural Middle Class: Progress or Regress?" in Penny Van Esterik (ed.), *Women of Southeast Asia*, Occasional Paper No. 9, pp. 100–123. Northern Illinois University, Center for Southeast Asian Studies.

(25) Indonesia, Biro Pusat Statistik [Central Bureau of Statistics] (1976) *1976 Intercensal Population Survey: Indonesian Labor Force*, Technical Report Series, Monograph 2. Jakarta: Biro Pusat Statistik.

(26) Indonesia, Biro Pusat Statistik [Central Bureau of Statistics] (1982) *Population of Indonesia: Results of the 1980 Population Census*, Series S, Number 2. Jakarta: Biro Pusat Statistik.

(27) *Indonesia 1989: An Official Handbook.* Jakarta: Department of Information.

(28) Ismail (1959) "Women's Organizations in Indonesia," *Asian Review* 55:303–308.

(29) Jay, R. (1969) *Javanese Villagers: Social Relations in Rural Modjokuto.* Cambridge, Mass.: MIT Press.

(30) Jones, G. W. (1977) "Factors Affecting Labour Force Participation of Females in Jakarta," *Journal of the Malaysian Economic Association* 14(2):71–93.

(31) *Kabinet Pembangunan V Berserta Buku Alamat Pejabat Indonesia 1990*, 19th edn.

[*Book of Addresses of State Functionaries of the Republic of Indonesia*]. Jakarta: B. P. Alda.

(32) Kartini, R. A. (1976) *Letters of a Javanese Princess* (translated by Agnes Louise Symmers). Kuala Lumpur: Oxford University Press.

(33) Kongres Wanita Indonesia (KOWANI) [Indonesian Women's Congress] (1980) *The Tale of Women in Development: The Indonesian Experience.* Jakarta: KOWANI.

(34) Kumar (1980) "Javanese Court Society and Politics in the Late Eighteenth Century: The Record of a Lady Soldier," Part I: "The Religious, Social and Economic Life of the Court," *Indonesia*, No. 29, pp. 1–46.

(35) Locher-Scholten, Elsbeth, and Niehof, Anke (1987) "Introduction," in Elsbeth Locher-Scholten (ed.), *Indonesian Women in Focus.* Dordrecht, Holland: Foris Publications.

(36) Logsdon, Martha G. (1985) "Women Civil Servants in Indonesia: Some Preliminary Observations," *Prisma the Indonesian Indicator*, 37 (September):77–87.

(37) McGee, T. (1978) "An Invitation to the 'Ball': Dress Formal or Informal?" in P. J. Rimmer, D. W. Drakakis-Smith, and T. G. McGee (eds.), *Food, Shelter and Transport in Southeast Asia and the Pacific*, pp. 3–27. Publication HG/12, Research School of Pacific Studies. Canberra: Australian National University.

(38) *Manajamen: Majalah Para Manajer dan Eksekutif Indonesia* [*Management: The Magazine for Indonesian Managers and Executives*] (n.d.) Published by LPPM.

(39) Morrison, C. E. (ed.) (1987) *Asia-Pacific Report, 1987–88: Trends, Issues, Challenges.* Honolulu: East-West Centre.

(40) National Development Information Office (n.d.) *Indonesia: A Profile*, p. 3. Jakarta: National Development Information Office.

(41) *National Labor Force Survey* (1987). Jakarta: SAKERNAS.

(42) Oey, M. (1980) "Issues in the Labor Force Participation of Female Migrants in Indonesian Cities." Paper presented for the Intermediate Cities in Asia meeting, East-West Population Institute, Honolulu, Hawaii, 16–28 July.

(43) Panglaykim, J. (1977) *Indonesian's Economic and Business Relations with ASEAN and Japan.* Jakarta: Yayasan Proklamasi, Centre for Strategic and International Studies.

(44) Panglaykim, J., and Palmer, I. (1970) "Study of Entrepreneurship in Developing Countries: The Development of One Chinese Concern in Indonesia," *Journal of Southeast Asian Studies* 1(1):85–95.

(45) Papanek, H. (1979a) "Development Planning for Women: The Implications of Women's Work," in J. Rounaq and H. Papanek (eds.), *Women and Development: Perspectives from South and Southeast Asia*, pp. 171–201. Dacca: Bangladesh Institute of Law and International Affairs.

(46) Papanek, H. (1979b) "Implications of Development for Women in Indonesia: Selected Research and Policy Issues." Paper presented at the Eighth Annual Conference on Indonesian Studies, Centre for South and Southeast Asia Studies, University of California, Berkeley, 2–5 August.

(47) "Pilihan Kita: Indira Wati, Kelana Yang Panjang" (1984) ["Our Choice: Indira Wati, the Far Wanderer"], *Eksekutif*, (February):43–47.

(48) "Pilihan Kita: Marlene Setiyadi, Saya Manusia Kerja" (1983) ["Our Choice: Marlene Setiyadi, I'm a Working Person"], *Eksekutif* (February):43–47.

(49) Price, Susanna (1983) "Rich Woman, Poor Woman: Occupation Differences in a Textile Producing Village in Central Java," in Lenore Manderson (ed.), *Women's Work and Women's Roles.* Canberra: The Australian National University.

(50) Rahardjo, Y. (1975) "Beberapa Dilemma Wanita Bekerdja" ["Some Dilemmas of Working Women"], *Prisma* 5(October):45–51.

(51) Rahardjo, J., and Hull, V. (1984) "Employment Patterns of Educated Women in Indonesian Cities," in G. W. Jones (ed.), *Women in the Urban and Industrial Workforce: South and Southeast Asia*, pp. 101–126. Development Studies Centre Monograph No. 33. Canberra: The Australian National University.

(52) Richter, Linda K. (1991) "Exploring Theories of Female Leadership in South and Southeast Asia," *Pacific Affairs* (Winter):524–540.

(53) Schrieke, B. (1955) *Indonesian Sociological Studies: Selected Writings* (2 vols.) Bandung, Indonesia: "Sumur Bandung".

(54) Schwarz, Adam (1990) "Free and Uneasy: Perils of Excess Threaten Indonesia's Liberalized Banks," *Far Eastern Economic Review* 20(December):50–53.

(55) Sethuraman, S. V. (1976) *Jakarta: Urban Development and Employment*. Geneva: International Labour Office.

(56) Sihombing, C. (1984*a*) "Retnowati Abdulgani: Bertahan Sambil Maju" ["Retnowati Abdulgani: Progress through Perseverance"], *Eksekutif* (December):18–24.

(57) Sihombing, C. (1984*b*) "Embrio MBA Indonesia" ["The Embryo Indonesian MBA"], *Eksekutif* (December):48–62.

(58) *Situational Analysis of Children and Women in Indonesia* (December 1988) Government of Indonesia/UNICEF.

(59) Soewondo, N. (1968) *Kedudukan Wanita Dalam Hukum Dan Masyarakat* [*The Position of Women in Law and Society*]. Jakarta: Timun Mas NV.

(60) *Standard Trade and Industry Directory of Indonesia* (1991) 11th edn. *List of Important Functonaries and Addresses*, Vol. 2.

(61) Stoler, A. (1977) "Class Structure and Female Autonomy in Rural Java," in Wellesley Editorial Committee (eds.), *Women and National Development: The Complexities of Change*, pp.74–92. Chicago: University of Chicago Press.

(62) Sullivan, Norma (1983) "Indonesian Women in Development: State Theory and Urban Kampung Practice," in Lenore Manderson (ed.), *Women's Work and Women's Roles*. Canberra: The Australian National University.

(63) Sutoyo, H. (1985) "Management Philosophy, Culture and Education in Indonesia" *Majalah Management & Usahawan Indonesia* (September–October):41–44.

(64) Tjiptoherijanto, Prijono (1989) "Economic Role of Women in Indonesia." Mimeographed. Faculty of Economics, University of Indonesia.

(65) Wertheim, W. F. (1956) *Indonesian Society in Transition: A Study of Social Change*. The Hague: W. Van Hoeve.

(66) White, B. (1973) "Demand for Labor and Population Growth in Colonial Java," *Human Ecology* 1(3):217–235.

(67) Williams, L. (1952) "Chinese Entrepreneurs in Indonesia," *Explorations in Entrepreneurial History* 5(1).

(68) Willmott, D. E. (1960) *The Chinese of Semarang: A Changing Minority Community in Indonesia*. Ithaca, N.Y.: Cornell University Press.

(69) Willner, A. R. (1980) "Expanding Women's Horizons in Indonesia: Toward Maximum Equality with Minimum Conflict," in S. A. Chipp and J. J. Green (eds.), *Asian Women in Transition*, pp. 182–190. University Park, Penn.: Pennsylvania State University Press.

(70) *Women Managers in Southeast Asia: Directory* (1990) (3 volumes). Women for Women (Asia) Foundation Inc.

(71) Woodcroft-Lee, Carlien Patricia (1983). "Separate but Equal: Indonesian Muslim

Perceptions of the Roles of Women," in Lenore Manderson (ed.), *Women's Work and Women's Roles*. Canberra: The Australian National University.

(72) "World Bank Highlights Strong Private-Sector Response to Economic Reforms" (1991) *Indonesia Development News* 14(5):2.

5 JAPAN

Women Managers in Japan

Patricia G. Steinhoff and Kazuko Tanaka

At first glance, it would seem that the topic of women managers in Japan could be handled in one sentence: there are none. In fact, there are women in managerial positions in Japan, but finding them requires careful examination of Japan's employment patterns, promotion policies, and economic structure, all of which are now changing. In this update of our 1988 review of the status of women managers (27) we shall attempt first to locate the women managers in Japan, and then to explore who they are and how they achieved their present positions. Finally, we shall assess the future prospects for increased participation of women in Japanese management, taking into consideration the impact of the 1986 equal employment opportunity law and other forces that are changing Japanese society.

The Available Talent Pool: Training and Culture

On the basis of objective, universalistic criteria, Japan possesses an enormous pool of well-educated women with work experience from which managerial talent could potentially be drawn. Japan has had universal, coeducational, primary education for a century. Since the end of World War II, educational levels for both sexes have risen steadily until at present, about 94 percent of all young people complete high school, and more than one-third go on to higher education. This represents a considerably higher rate of high school completion than that in the United States, and a comparable rate of postsecondary education. Although women appear to be equal to men in overall rates of higher education, in 1990 about 60 percent of the women receiving higher education went to two-year institutions, as compared to less than 5 percent of men (15).

Japan has had a relatively high proportion of women in the labor market since at least the early part of this century. The main shift from the early part of the century to the 1970s was the steady movement of working women from the status of family worker to wage earner (30). In 1990, women constituted 41 percent of the labor force. The transition from family worker to wage earner continues, and by 1990 only 17 percent of women in the labor force were still counted as paid or unpaid family workers (36).

Less than a century ago, Japan's economy was overwhelmingly agricultural, and women worked alongside men in the fields. As family workers, Japanese women were heavily involved in small-scale commercial and manufacturing enterprises, as well as in agriculture. In the early stages of industrialization, young women were sent by their families to work in the textile industry and other light industries; they formed the absolute majority of factory workers through the 1920s (24). Later, as men were drawn into military service, women were heavily utilized in the war economy that propelled Japan to a higher level of industrialization during the 1930s and 1940s. Even in the prewar period, small numbers of women with relatively high high levels of education also worked in various kinds of white-collar occupations.

Virtually all young women in contemporary Japan join the labor force after they complete their schooling. They work for several years until marriage and often continue until their first pregnancy. Until very recently, nearly three-quarters of all Japanese women married between the ages of twenty and 27, and the overwhelming majority of married women became mothers within a few years. Only in the late 1980s have significant numbers of women begun to delay marriage past their late twenties (33). Compared with most other countries, Japan has shown astonishing uniformity in the age range within which marriage and parenthood take place (1;6). Family planning is also practiced very widely, resulting in a low rate of births outside of marriage and an average number of children per family that by 1990 had dropped well below replacement to 1.53 (2;6;25;26).

As postwar Japan developed into a major industrial power during the 1960s, the nonworking wife became a status symbol of economic success. What had once been a luxury of elite women was now within reach of the middle class. A cultural ideal arose of the middle-class, white-collar salaried man, working in a large company, whose wife devoted all her time to her home and the rearing of her children. Such women were expected to utilize their education and skills in managing the home and were given substantial control over the household finances (34). As middle-class status spread to the permanent, salaried, blue-collar worker's family, so did the status symbol of the full-time housewife who did not work outside the home.

Initially, there may have been some long-term economic advantage to this arrangement, in that the full-time mother closely supervised the education of elementary school children and thus gave them an edge in the meritocratic educational system that determines the social status of the next generation. As the educational competition intensified, however, families shifted to outside tutors and commercial cram schools, and the mother's role was reduced to providing emotional support and encouragement to the studying child.

Despite its importance as a cultural image, the ideal of the nonworking wife has never represented an actual life-style for the hundreds of thousands of women who participate in the operation of family businesses. In addition, during the 1960s and 1970s, it became common for housewives to do piecework at home in order to supplement the family income while sustaining the image of the nonworking housewife. Since the mid-1970s, married women have been returning to the labor force more openly; and, at present, half of all married women work outside the home (28;36).

Married women who return to the labor force after a break in employment are usually employed in lower-status positions than they occupied before marriage. Such women are generally classified as part-time workers. The classification is not based precisely on hours worked, but implies that they work slightly fewer hours than regular employees. The primary distinction is that part-time workers usually have no employment security, no opportunity for advancement, and no fringe benefits, as opposed to the "permanent" or "regular" workers who enjoy all of these advantages. Using the more precise definition of those who work 35 hours or less per week, about 15 percent of all employees and 28 percent of all women employees would fall into the part-time category. In the past 25 years, the number of part-time workers has tripled to 7,220,000 and their proportion of the total labor force has more than doubled. The trend is much stronger for women, who by 1990 constituted 69 percent of all nonagricultural part-time workers. The number of women part-time workers (5,010,000) is six times what it was 25 years ago, and their share of the female labor force has almost tripled (36).

Japan has a double-peaked (M) distribution of female employment by age and marital status, with the overwhelming majority of young, unmarried women in the labor force, a drop in female labor force participation during the early years of marriage and childbearing, and a gradual return to the labor force of growing numbers of older, married women. The bottom of the M has gradually been rising, but is still much lower than in the United States. Because of this demographic pattern of women's labor force participation, coupled with the reality that most women cannot return to the same type of job they left, relatively few women remain in a career track long enough to attain a management-level position in a large corporation.

Employment and Promotion in Large Organizations

The barriers against placing women in managerial positions in large companies stem not only from family ideals in the larger society but also from the strictures of the permanent employment system, another cultural ideal that finds its major expression in large corporations. In both the public and the private sectors, large organizations in Japan hire entry-level white-collar employees and expect to retain them until retirement at about age 60. Incoming permanent, white-collar employees are generally employed fresh out of school, with no previous work experience. Management-track employees normally have four-year college degrees but no specialized graduate training. New employees are given considerable in-company training during their first year on the job. Thereafter, they are moved around to various parts of the company to develop their knowledge and skills; and they receive continuing in-service training over the years.

Most companies would prefer to send an employee for graduate training, if it becomes necessary, rather than hire someone who already has obtained it independently. The company grooms employees within an internal labor market of managerial positions by providing a wide range of internal career-development opportunities. To a certain extent, all career employees in a hiring-year cohort receive the same opportunities, but specific assignments are made on the basis of the company's view of each individual's potential.

Large Japanese bureaucracies, both corporate and governmental, have a relatively standarized rank structure of administrative levels. All persons at the rank of section head (*kachō*) or above are considered to be managers who participate in decision making. Management studies sometimes also include the subsection-head level (*kakarichō*), the first supervisory-level position, from which appointments to section head are made.

Virtually all promotions are internal, and they are carefully graded by seniority. After about eight years of service, all permanent employees who entered the company in the same year become eligible for promotion; all attain the rank of *kakarichō* or subsection head, although some are placed in more important posts than others. Most will eventually receive a second promotion in rank to *kachō* or section head, about five to six years later. Only a small proportion of these will later become *buchō*, or division heads. Even fewer will be named plant managers (*kōjōchō*) or branch managers (*shitenchō*). Traditionally, appointments of the highest ranked corporate officers have been given to people near or even past the formal retirement age. Such promotions were usually managed so that those from the same age cohort and rank who were not promoted would retire from their posts at the same time. Consequently, rank and seniority coincided at the top of the corporate ladder. Recently, however, a few large corporations have appointed somewhat younger presidents, in their late forties or early fifties, as the seniority principle begins to give way to merit considerations in a highly competitive external business environment.

The Japanese system of organization and management features a narrow span of control, with an average of five to fifteen people under one direct supervisor at each level. The consequent abundance of supervisory positions, plus the practice of foisting excess managers off onto lower-ranked subsidiaries, makes it possible to provide sufficient positions in the main administrative ranks for the entire age cohort of permanent managerial class employees.

Virtually all employees are rotated within their companies at about three-year intervals to broaden their experience. At a single rank level, assignments can vary considerably in the amount of responsibility and opportunity they provide. Thus, the actual managerial responsibility a person is given may not be reflected in formal rank or even in compensation, which is heavily determined by rank and seniority. At the same time, the range of experience employees accumulate and the opportunities to develop and display their skills weigh heavily in their future placement in a developing managerial career.

The seniority-based promotion system creates an attractive and predictable management career track for permanent employees. It is precisely this package that makes entry-level white-collar positions in large corporations and government among the most prized commodities in Japanese society. This, in turn, fuels incredible competition for entry into the relatively small number of elite universities from which the major corporate employers and the national government hire their permanent employees.

In the private sector, virtually all of those who acquire these coveted entry-level positions, with their guaranteed promotion ladders, are men. These secure promotion opportunities are preserved, however, primarily by hiring large numbers of educated women to fill positions at the bottom of the employment pyramid at the white-collar rank of ordinary employee.

Young, single women are hired with the expectation that they will "retire" into marriage and motherhood within a few years without being promoted to a higher rank. Because the company does not intend to promote these women, they often have lower educational levels (high school, or two-year rather than four-year degrees) or come from lower-ranked four-year colleges than do the men employed by the same company. The forced retirement of women employees is often helped along by management urging young, white-collar employees to marry at the appropriate age, preferably to an eligible person in the same company. When two employees marry, nepotism rules are invoked; and, of course, the wife is the one who retires. Although it is against the law to force a woman to retire because of marriage or pregnancy, avoiding nepotism is considered a legitimate reason. Social pressures effectively eliminate most of the remaining young women from the white-collar managerial pool soon after they marry.

Until recently, women have generally cooperated with this system. Families traditionally have encouraged women to get the type and level of education that will equip them to marry managers, rather than to become managers themselves. Although the competition for university entrance is open and meritocratic, women still do not compete in great numbers for entry into the elite coeducational institutions. When they do enter, they tend not to go into the "male" disciplines of economics, law, and engineering, from which companies are more likely to hire future managers. Yet there are some eligible women with the same qualifications as the men, and in some cases they are hired for entry-level positions in large corporations. The number of such women has been gradually increasing, though they still constitute a small proportion of their age cohort.

Japanese Management Culture and Women

Much has been made of Japan's unique managerial culture as another barrier to women. Japanese white-collar employees are expected to work long hours and to be available until late at night when there are special work demands. Women members of a work group are also expected to stay late when the work requires it. They may make excuses to leave early, which the men could never do, but this is considered evidence of their weaker commitment to the company. Legal restrictions on women's night work have been lightened under the 1986 equal employment opportunity law, and thus can no longer be used as a reason to exclude women from managerial positions.

Japanese managerial style also mixes work and play to a greater degree than is found in other countries. Co-workers are expected to socialize regularly after work, which often means bar-hopping until late at night. Managers take their subordinates drinking in order to break down the status barriers and permit employees to speak more freely about problems at work and at home. Some women are accepted as full co-workers and invited to join in these activities. Although evening socializing in small restaurants and bars remains heavily male-oriented, it is quite possible nowadays for women to participate as part of the group.

The problem thus is not so much an absolute sex barrier as it is a matter of time commitment and personal style. A married woman with home and family responsibilities in the evening would be very hard-pressed to meet these work demands. A single woman or one whose husband had similar work hours could do so more easily. A mother with young children at home could maintain such a managerial lifestyle only if she had resident childcare. Many women are not comfortable with the evening socializing at male-oriented bars that is required of Japanese managers; some men do not like it either, which also affects their careers.

Another important aspect of Japanese managerial culture is a consensus-oriented decision-making style that aims to avoid conflict after the decision is made by anticipating resistance and negotiating compromises beforehand. This avoidance of conflict encourages a managerial style based on teamwork, and favors leaders who listen and are sensitive to the feelings of others. Ironically, the qualities required of good Japanese male managers are the same qualities that are often held in American management research to be female characteristics disadvantageous to success. (In fact, when Japanese managers complain that they have difficulty finding American men who can fit into their overseas operations, the authors have recommended that they try American women.) There is thus no inherent reason why Japanese women would have difficulty handling the decision-making aspects of management in Japan, given similar opportunities to develop their skills in the work group. Even in the home, Japanese women are expected to be competent managers and good negotiators, using a similar style of consensus decision making.

Utilization of Women: Large Firms in the Private Sector

The equal employment opportunity law that went into effect in April 1986 is intended to improve the promotion opportunities of women employees. Unfortunately, it has weak enforcement provisions and does not effectively address the problem of differential hiring. It has, however, prompted some new research on the actual status of women in large organizations. We will first utilize this research to analyze the placement of women managers within the Japanese economic structure and then try to assess the emerging effects of the law itself.

In 1979, as part of the background research for the forthcoming equal employment opportunity law, a cabinet-level commission surveyed all companies listed on the stock exchange and special corporations in the three major urban centers of Tokyo, Osaka, and Nagoya that were capitalized at over 500 million yen or about $4 million[1] (20). The 1,497 companies surveyed had an average workforce of 3,321 and an average of 242 persons in decision-making positions.

The study found that women constituted about one-quarter (23 percent) of the workforce in these large companies but only 0.3 percent of those in decision-making positions. Nine-tenths (90 percent) of the companies had no women at all in decision-making positions, and most of the remainder (8 percent of the total) had only one or two women in such positions. Fewer than one percent (0.7 percent) of the companies had ten or more women in decision-making positions (20).

In the entire sample of 1,497 companies, employing almost five million people, the study was able to identify fewer than a thousand women in managerial positions. Two-thirds of the 996 women managers identified by the study (67 percent) were at the section-head (*kachō*) level, 7 percent were department heads (*buchō*), and only 1.6 percent were corporate officers (20).

In a companion study conducted in 1981, the same cabinet-level commission surveyed women in decision-making positions in associations, organizations, unions, and cooperatives, all institutions that fell outside the purview of the earlier study of joint-stock corporations. Of these institutions, 85 percent had no women in decision-making positions and only 5 percent had more than one woman (21). Women made up 40 percent of the workforce, but only 0.5 percent of management in these organizations, an even greater disparity than in corporations listed on the stock exchange (21).

Some small changes were visible even as the equal employment opportunity law went into effect in April, 1986. A 1986 survey of 321 large firms by the Labor Administration Research Institute found that 80 percent professed to treat men and women equally with regard to promotion and that the larger the firm, the greater the support for women's promotion opportunities (13). This is a substantial increase from a 1984 study by the Women's Bureau, in which only 56 percent of companies reported that they offered promotion opportunities to women (35). In the 1986 Labor Administration Research Institute study, however, only 1.2 percent of the companies surveyed had any women above the rank of division manager (*buchō*). Just 4.1 percent of the companies had women up to the level of division manager, but about one-fifth (22 percent) had women in positions up to section head (*kachō*), and slightly more (23 percent) had women in the lowest-level supervisory position, subsection head (*kakarichō*) (13).

An update of the 1979 Prime Minister's Office study was commissioned by the Ministry of Labor three years after enactment of the Equal Employment Opportunity Law. One-quarter of the companies reported having women in decision-making positions in 1989, 2.4 times the number in 1979. However, two-thirds of these companies had filled less than 1 percent of their decision-making positions with women (37).

In a 1989 update of its 1984 study, the Women's Bureau surveyed 7,000 companies with 30 or more employees three years after the Equal Employment Opportunity Law had taken effect. In the largest companies, the study found that 12 percent of companies with more than 5,000 workers and 6.7 percent of those with 1,000 to 4,999 workers had women at the *buchō*, or division-head, level. At the *kachō*, or section-head, level, the rates were 45 percent for companies with over 5,000 workers and 25 percent for those with 1,000 to 4,999 workers. At the level of *kakarichō*, the first supervisory level which represents the pool from which decision-making personnel will be selected in the future, 72 percent of companies with 5,000 or more workers and 52 percent of companies with 1,000 to 4,999 workers reported having women managers (16).

These figures are a remarkable improvement over the situation reported in 1984. They all refer, however, to the percentage of companies that report having any women at all in their managerial ranks. The actual percentage of women in these positions remains miniscule. According to the national wage census for 1989, in companies employing 1,000 or more persons, only 0.36 percent of division heads (buchō) and 0.13 percent of section heads (kachō) were women, but women held 3.6 percent of the kakarichō or subsection-head positions. By the most generous measure, women occupied only 2.2 percent of managerial positions in companies with 1,000 or more employees (17).

A major mechanism for blocking women from the promotion ladder is to exclude them from transfers to branch offices or posts far away from their homes, which means they are unable to acquire the range of experience needed for promotion to a managerial position. About two-thirds of the firms surveyed by the Labor Administration Research Institute in 1986 excluded women from long-distance transfers as a matter of policy, and most intended to continue excluding them after the equal employment opportunity law went into effect (13). The 1989 Women's Bureau survey explored the actual extent of job transfers. Among companies that had transferred employees to distant locations during the previous year, only 12 percent had transferred any women (16).

Because of the very orderly, seniority-based internal training and promotion system within large Japanese corporations, placing large numbers of women in managerial positions quickly would not be possible, even if the companies were truly committed to doing so. In the absence of such commitment, it is not surprising that the process is slow and that many structural barriers remain in place. Since the companies must groom young women for future internal promotion, it will be a very long time before women are well represented in Japanese corporate management.

Utilization of Women: The Public Sector

The situation of women in the public sector is similar to that in the private sector. Local, prefectural, and national levels of government all hire permanent white-collar employees directly out of school. Like private corporations, they hire both men and women but expect to retain the men until retirement in their mid-fifties and to lose many of the women within a few years. Government, however, is not as free as the private sector to discriminate against women, because the laws governing the hiring and promotion of public employees provide some protection.

Women schoolteachers, for example, routinely work until the mandatory retirement age, even if they marry and have children. Many are promoted to grade-level or subject supervisor, and some achieve the rank of principal. Women have traditionally been more prevalent at the elementary school level, with men predominating in the relatively high prestige position of high school teacher. The number of women high school teachers has been increasing, but it is not clear to what extent this signals a rise in status for women rather than a degrading of the status level of the position of high school teacher.

Even in the regular administrative areas of the public sector, it is now difficult for government not to hire women for permanent positions if they have competitive qualifications. Once hired, they have at least a claim to equal treatment, although they may not receive it. The numbers are still small, but there are women in managerial positions at all three levels of government. At the national government level, only 1.1 percent of managers at the *buchō* level and 0.6 percent at the *kachō* level are women. The overall representation of women in all supervisory and decision-making positions is 0.7 percent, about the same as in 1985. At the prefectural level, the percentages are twice as high at 1.4 percent overall. The city level is slightly higher (1.9 percent) (22). These figures reflect the public sector's resistance to hiring women for the upper career tracks in past years. As in the private sector, it will take many years before young women work their way up to managerial positions in government in any substantial numbers.

In our earlier study, we found that women had more opportunity to be promoted to managerial positions in the public sector than in large private corporations (27). It now appears that the relative opportunity for women in large corporations and government has been reversed since passage of the equal employment opportunity law in 1986. The percentage of women in managerial positions in corporate bureaucracies is now about three times that of the national government, and 1.5 times that of prefectural governments. The corporate sector is also incomparably larger, so the absolute number of women in corporate management (19,100) is immensely greater than the 57 managerial women in the national government and their 146 counterparts at the prefectural level nationwide.

Enterprise Scale in the Japanese Economy

Clearly women managers are rare in the corporate world, and even less visible in government. To stop at this point, however, would seriously distort the actual situation of women managers in Japan. In fact, there are women in managerial positions just about everywhere in Japan, except in large corporations. Generally, the smaller the firm, the greater the presence of women in management. To get a proper perspective on the situation, the overall pattern of firm size in Japan must be examined in more detail.

In general, Japanese firms are much smaller than their American counterparts. Instead of having one giant corporation under central control, with a proliferation of corporate divisions, the Japanese tend to have smaller separate companies interlocked in tight networks by economic and social ties. The overall group of companies may be as large as a giant American conglomerate but it is actually made up of many, sometimes several hundred, legally separate companies, ranging in size from large corporations listed on the stock exchange, down to tiny firms employing fewer than five people. In manufacturing, the firms are linked through subcontracting relationships; in service and merchandising, they are linked in distribution networks. In addition to these vertical product-related ties, corporate diversification is often undertaken through the formation of either horizontal or vertical relationships between companies, with interlocking directorates and cross-holding of stock. Through these complex links, large companies are frequently members of a corporate group or subsidiaries of other firms, whereas very small companies tend to be independently owned and operated firms that are economically dependent on certain other large firms.

The definition of a large company varies by industry: 300 employees and capitalization at 100 million yen ($800,000) in manufacturing; 100 or more employees and capitalization at 30 million yen ($240,000) in wholesale firms; and 50 employees and capitalization at 10 million yen ($80,000) in retail enterprises.[2] Even with these rather generous definitions, only 0.6 percent of all Japanese corporations meet the definition of a large company. The overwhelming majority of firms (99 percent) are small or medium sized, and together they employ 81 percent of all private-sector employees in the Japanese labor force. About three-quarters of all working women are employed in small or medium-sized enterprises (4;19). The apparent under-representation of women overall in small and medium-sized companies is due to the hiring by large companies of great numbers of young, unmarried women whose access to managerial career opportunities is extremely limited.

It is not surprising that women in managerial positions are most often found in independently owned small and medium-sized enterprises, but the percentage of women managers in smaller firms goes far beyond what would be expected from the distribution of the labor force alone. The 1989 Women's Bureau study found that the largest firms were most likely to report having one or more women at each managerial rank. However, the actual percentage of managerial positions held by women was inversely related to the size of the firm. This was true at all managerial rank levels.

For *kakarichō*, the lowest managerial level, the range was from 11.8 percent women in companies with less than 100 employees to 2.2 percent in companies with more than 5,000 employees. Hence, the probability that a *kakarichō* position will be filled by a woman is five times greater in the smallest firms than it is in the largest.

At the first decision-making level of *kachō*, 6 percent were women in firms with less than 100 employees, but only 0.6 percent of all *kachō* were women in firms with 5,000 or more employees, making the probability of finding a woman as *kachō* ten times greater in the smallest firms.

At the division-head level, 3 percent of all *buchō* in companies with less than 100 employees, but only 0.1 percent of all *buchō* in companies with more than 5,000 employees are women, making it 30 times more likely that a *buchō* will be a woman in the smallest firms (16).

These figures reveal a profoundly different level of opportunity for women managers in small firms. It is impossible to evaluate the actual job content and degree of independent managerial responsibility involved in such positions, but there is probably as much variability in job content within the largest firms as there is between the largest and smallest companies overall.

For most managers, the ultimate level of success is to be the president and chief executive officer of the company, although the significance of this title also varies considerably with the company's size and internal organization. Nearly 2.5 million

Japanese women run their own (nonagricultural) businesses, most of which have fewer than five employees (36). These figures also include women who work independently.

The number of women serving as presidents of companies has been increasing rapidly in recent years. In 1986, there were 25,447 women presidents of companies, but by 1990 there were 39,058, an increase of more than 50 percent in four years (31;32).

Komatsu, who conducted a study of women company presidents, sees three factors behind the rapid increase. The first is the general changes that are pushing women out of the home and into the public sphere, such as smaller family size, reduced household work, and women's recognition that they can do what used to be defined as men's work. Second, the structural problems involved in penetrating the existing corporate system force women to go around the system and act on their own. Third, leisure and volunteer activities associated with the new affluent Japanese life-style are giving rise to new types of enterprises that women can develop (11;12).

The most common types of enterprises run by a woman president in 1989 were companies that retail women's or children's clothing (2,229). Real estate rental agencies (1,690) were second, followed by retail kimono and bedding stores (1,080). Fourth were road construction companies (1,052), with inns and hotels fifth (1,022). Restaurants (899) outranked bars and cabarets (843). The remaining three types in the top ten were barber and beauty shops (737), retail fuel companies (686), and real estate sales firms (668). The 1989 annual income of the top 100 companies with woman presidents ranged from one of Japan's largest publishing companies, with net earnings of $111.5 million, down to a retail food company earning under $0.6 million (in 1989 dollars, calculated at 140 yen to the dollar) (32). These figures for the top 100 companies with a woman president suggest that the overwhelming majority of companies headed by women are quite small.

At the most common enterprise level in Japan, the small business employing less than five persons, the participation of women in management is most visible and significant. A 1983 study of 37 small retail businesses in a single commercial neighborhood found women heavily involved in running nearly all of the shops, but in varying capacities.[3] Some shops were owned and run by women whose husbands worked as salaried employees elsewhere. A few women had inherited a business, including one daughter-in-law who had been brought into the family to take over her mother-in-law's shop. The majority were family businesses run jointly by husband and wife, often with each spouse running a branch store in a different neighborhood. In the few businesses large enough to have non-family employees, the wife was the major supervisor and decision-maker in daily operations.

The uneven distribution of women managers throughout the Japanese economy also results in their being differentially visible to women and men of different social positions. Women of all social classes are most likely to interact with women managers either through commercial transactions or as part-time employees of smaller firms. Men who work in small or medium-sized firms and handle interfirm business relations with other small companies are far more likely to interact with woman managers than are male white-collar workers and managers in large firms, who may meet women managers only as the owners of the bars and restaurants they frequent after work. Hence, the men with the power to open the doors to management positions for women in large firms are the least likely to notice the managerial potential of women outside the home.

Background and Characteristics of Women Managers

The Prime Minister's Office studies of women in decision-making positions in large corporations provide the most extensive data on the backgrounds of these nearly invisible women managers (20;21). The educational levels of women managers were surprisingly low for contemporary Japan: about one-third had only a middle school education, and another third, a high school education. Only 17 percent had four-year college degrees, and fewer than 1 percent had graduate degrees. Their average age was 50 years, with about two-thirds of the women in decision-making positions in large corporations being unmarried. They had worked for the same company for an average of 29 years (20).

The women who attained managerial positions in large corporations prior to the equal employment opportunity law clearly did not do so through the white-collar employee route that is now the norm for men in such companies. These women managers may have begun their careers in traditionally women's occupations, such as a nurse or a telephone operator, or in businesses connected with women's apparel, from which it is possible to rise to mid-level supervisory positions. Another possibility is that some large companies in domestic product areas may have grown from small and medium-sized enterprises during the past three decades, carrying along a few of their long-term women employees in the process. Even companies with a predominantly female clientele and labor force, however, remain overwhelmingly male in management (23).

A second conclusion that may be drawn from these findings is that women who have achieved managerial rank in large corporations have done so after long service to the company, largely at the expense of marriage and motherhood. This is consistent with the inference that women in management may be located primarily in traditionally women's occupations. In contrast to the usual pattern of women's employment in large companies, such occupations provide an alternative to the long-term economic security of marriage and eventually reward the competent and experienced unmarried employee with some opportunity for promotion. The general absence of married women with children among the ranks of corporate management also attests to the barriers in management culture discussed earlier.

A questionnaire study conducted for the Japanese Association of Women Executives (JAWE) included 66 women in positions ranging from section chief to corporate officer (29). Over half the women in the study were from corporations having more than 1,000 employees. Two-thirds were college graduates, and another 13 percent were junior college graduates. The average age of the managers was 45. Slightly over one-half of the women were married, and the great majority of those

(86 percent) had children. Three-quarters reported that their husbands were quite cooperative about their work (29).

These results differ considerably from the Prime Minister's Office surveys. The JAWE study sample included relatively more women with high managerial rank, and their mean age was younger; but it also included managers in smaller companies. The differences may be an artifact of sampling differences, or they may point to future trends.

Several other recent studies of women managers in small and medium-sized companies report results similar to those of the JAWE study (4;5;7;12;14). The picture that emerges from these studies is that women managers are generally not highly educated, although college training seems increasingly to be the norm. Among women who work their way up from employee to managerial status, those with appropriate professional qualifications can be promoted to central managerial positions, but women without qualifications rarely rise higher than chief of a secretarial or accounting section.

Women managers in small and medium-sized enterprises are more likely to be married and have children, although the possibility of combined roles may be increasing in larger firms as well. Women in management appear to come from families that encourage women to study and work. A substantial minority have working mothers as role models. Their fathers tend to be in professional or managerial occupations that offer role models for their daughters and also possibly the capital to help some daughters realize their ambition of starting their own companies.

Career Paths of Women Managers

Studies using life history interviewing methods, found a variety of career patterns among Japanese women managers (14;18). This supports the view that women achieve managerial positions by working around the dominant male career pattern, rather than by competing within it. American studies have also found that women often take routes different from men to reach the same managerial positions.

The JAWE study did not trace career paths directly, but the survey results provide some indication of women managers' experiences and attitudes. Although only about half reported that becoming a manager had been an important goal for them, the overwhelming majority (87 percent) found it advantageous to be one. About a third of the women managers had decided while they were still students that they would continue working rather than quit when they married. Another 17 percent decided soon after they began work, but 29 percent decided only after they had discovered how interesting the work was. Over 90 percent had decided before they married or had a child that they would continue working after these life changes occurred (29). The findings suggest that the women achieved managerial status because of special ability and circumstances, unlike most Japanese men, who are directed toward such careers from childhood.

Over two-thirds reported that there were many people available to help them in their careers, suggesting that these women had been able to acquire a network of sponsors and allies just as male managers do (29). The women managers in the JAWE study believed that there was no difference in ability between female and male managers, but that women were at a disadvantage in the world of business. They agreed overwhelmingly that being able to handle male–female relations effectively was an essential skill for women managers. In the Japanese context this skill includes avoiding status confrontations with men. Interviews with twelve very successful women company presidents revealed that the women used a variety of gender-based strategies, including adopting a very deferential, nonaggressive posture when dealing with men and using a maternal managerial style toward employees of both sexes (14). However, women in positions of authority in large bureaucracies, particularly government officials, appear freer to adopt an authoritative style that transcends traditional gender roles (14). Businesswomen in small and medium-sized companies must use gender strategies because they lack the protection of a rigid, formal bureaucracy.

Almost half of the women managers in the JAWE survey had changed jobs at some point in the past. Furthermore, only half said they were willing to relocate geographically if their job required it (29). Their unwillingness to make internal transfers coincides with the general policy of large companies not to transfer women, but the record suggests that these women may have resolved the problem in the past by changing jobs. Such flexibility about leaving an employer works to women's disadvantage in the largest companies but may open opportunities for them in smaller firms that can utilize their experience and business contacts.

If effective career strategies for women within larger corporations remain murky, the picture is somewhat clearer and easier to evaluate for women who are actually running or heading smaller firms. The heads of Japanese companies are customarily divided into three types: founders, relatives of founders, and employees who have worked their way up. This categorization reflects the traditional family-enterprise orientation of Japanese society. Founders are generally characterized as dynamic and aggressive entrepreneurs who maintain firm personal control over the enterprise; successors tend to rely more heavily on staff; and employees who work their way up tend to have a more bureaucratic, team-oriented, managerial style.

A Keiō research group found that each of these three categories required further specification in order to reflect the actual career paths of women who inherited family businesses or began their own, with prior managerial experience ranging from zero to many years of full partnership (4;7). Older women were more likely to have been thrust into a managerial role by circumstances such as widowhood, whereas young women were more likely to have achieved it by the accumulation of relevant experiences. The study also found that women company presidents placed more value on realization of their ideals and self-actualization than on social and monetary success. They were, therefore, more likely to maintain their enterprise at an appropriate size with a good rate of profit, rather than risk expansion (7). The sample of very successful women company presidents referred to earlier also eschewed heavy risk taking (14). Most had succeeded by finding a niche in some aspect of communication services and by gradually acquiring a reputation by word of mouth. They believed they were not as free as men to take risks, because if they failed it would reflect badly on them as women managers. In addition, they felt a strong responsibility toward their employees that also deterred risky business decisions.

The Keiō study found that women company presidents were not necessarily supportive of increased opportunity for other women. Many women presidents in their late fifties or older did not treat female and male employees equally, and they often imposed the same constraints on their women employees as the large corporations do. Regardless of age, women company presidents made extensive use of middle-aged, part-time women workers (7).

Most women founders said they would appoint women to managerial posts exactly as they would appoint men, and would consider appointing a woman to succeed them (10). Successors, on the other hand, said they would consider appointing women only to certain areas of work. Attitudes toward managerial posts for women also varied sharply by industry, with support for women's advancement being more common among presidents of service and retail businesses, and more negative attitudes found among those in manufacturing. Opinion was also sharply divided by age, with younger women presidents favoring managerial opportunities for women, and women over 55 being sharply opposed (10).

Although the distinction in attitudes between founders and successors could be interpreted as an indication that attitudes toward women in management become more discriminatory as a company matures, generational differences must be taken into account, since in both studies women successors tended to be older than women founders. Women under 50 who were educated in the postwar era have fundamentally different attitudes toward women's achievement from those over 50; and these attitudes are less likely to change as these women grow older, or as the companies they manage mature. It seems highly unlikely that the next generation of women successors will be as conservative as the present one.

However, there still seems to be a bias toward male succession in family businesses, reflecting the strong patrilineal tradition in Japan. Lebra reports that none of the women presidents in her study had designated a daughter as successor (14). Those with sons generally hoped the son would take over the business, whereas those with only daughters hoped their sons-in-law might do so. One, with a business that required a female head, had designated her daughter-in-law as the successor to keep the business in the family of her son (14).

Prospects for the Future

There is some indication that large companies are beginning to offer more promotion opportunities to women. In a 1985 study by the Japan Manpower Administration Research Institute, primarily of companies listed on the stock exchange, 64 percent of the companies said they would promote women college graduates if they had the same abilities as men. The larger the company, the greater the professed support for promotion of qualified women. When asked what they thought of the current trend for women to work for a longer period of time, 84 percent of the companies said it was acceptable if the woman was strongly motivated; but only 6 percent of the companies found the trend desirable (8).

The distinction implied here between broad support for the unusually motivated career women and continuing resistance to offering career opportunities to all women is reflected in the general response of large corporations to the equal employment opportunity law of 1986. Charged with formulating a response to the new law, a committee of the Kantō Managers Association (a major association of corporate managers in the greater Tokyo area) said it was not economically feasible for companies to offer management training opportunities to all women employees. Instead, they suggested that companies create a two-track system that would offer promotion opportunities to highly qualified and motivated women but leave intact the existing system of high turnover position for most women (9).

Evidence from the first few years under the new law suggests that companies have done just that, requiring women to commit themselves at the time of hiring either to a traditional track with good benefits but no promotion opportunities or to a career track with more rigorous standards and opportunities ostensibly equivalent to those offered to male permanent employees. Under present interpretations of the law, this approach is not illegal. In both the public and private sectors, entry-level hiring is explicitly organized into closed career tracks, with differing entry requirements and promotion potential. For women, the issue may well become one of initial commitment and aspiration, since there are structural barriers to moving from a lower to a higher track. These structural barriers are of course not as absolute as they appear to be. When it is in a company's interest to get around them, it will figure out a way to do so without altering the basic pattern, in the inimitable Japanese fashion.

At the moment, however, there is no great interest in doing so. The equal employment opportunity law lacks an enforcement mechanism except for "administrative guidance," which can be a powerful force in Japanese society if the ministry in charge of administering the law has the will and the resources to use it. There is no indication yet that the Japanese government intends to press companies to change their practices fundamentally in order to provide women equal access to promotion opportunities. Government ministries themselves have very few women in decision-making positions, despite the fact that laws regarding equal treatment of employees are stronger in the public sector. Most companies will probably be able to continue to use mechanisms such as restricted job assignments and multiple tracks to limit women's eligibility for promotion, as long as they can show token compliance by promoting a few exceptional women.

There is some evidence that male employees of large companies are becoming more accepting of women managers. A 1989 survey of married male employees of large companies in Tokyo and Osaka by Japan's largest bank, Daiichi Kangyō, found that more than three-quarters thought gender was irrelevant if a person had managerial ability and temperament. Whereas only 13 percent of the men surveyed looked forward enthusiastically to having women managers, another 45 percent had more mildly positive attitudes. Another 29 percent indicated that they were not conscious of gender differences, which may also be interpreted as a favorable response. These attitudes have little practical application at present, since less than one-fifth of the respondents had any women managers at their workplaces (3).

Overall, the studies reviewed here suggest that opportunities for women in management are likely to increase in the future, but not as rapidly in the large corporations from which women are still largely excluded. For a very limited number of unusually qualified women, opportunities will grow in large bureaucracies as well. Although the numbers remain small, it appears that large corporations are now expanding promotion opportunities for women faster than is the case in the public sector.

For Japanese women with good foreign language skills, there may be more opportunity for advancement in foreign companies. Such companies are at a disadvantage in the Japanese labor market, and provide a small secondary labor market for individuals with good personal qualifications who have been excluded from the main white-collar labor market that, as noted earlier, concentrates on new graduates of Japanese universities. Women and men with foreign educational credentials or prior work experience often find their credentials are more highly valued by foreign corporations. This segment of the Japanese economy, however, remains relatively small.

Small and medium-sized enterprises, in which three-quarters of all women are employed, represent a dynamic growth area for women with managerial ambitions. Because there is greater job mobility in these smaller-scale enterprises, there may be considerable movement into such firms by women with previous experience in large corporations. This group would include both women who leave to start their own firms and women who are hired by existing firms because of their skills and experience.

As more educated women with work experience either remain in the labor force through the childbearing years or return after only a few years' absence, cultural images of the working married woman are likely to change, as they have elsewhere. Yet resistance to such change remains quite strong. The Daiichi Kangyō Bank survey found that less than 10 percent of married businessmen felt women should continue working without any change after they married. The majority (58 percent) thought women should work as long as it did not interfere with their household responsibilities.

There were substantial variations by age, with men in their fifties most likely to feel that women should quit work entirely after marriage. Although men in their twenties were least likely to think women ought to quit their jobs, they were the most likely (71 percent) to believe that women's continuation of work ought to be contingent on their ability to fulfill household responsibilities at the same time (3).

Less than half the men surveyed actually had working wives, and the great majority of those wives only worked part-time. Three-quarters of the men felt that married women's primary responsibility was to their household and children but that it was acceptable for women to go out into society if they had extra time. This response was moderately consistent across age categories, with older men more likely to think that women should not go out into society at all. These attitudes suggest that businessmen are likely to view managerial careers for women as suitable only for those who remain unmarried.

A study of blue-collar women documents the pressures that the management of a large women's lingerie company used to discourage woman factory workers from working until retirement and suggests that similar strategies were used by the company to remove women in sales and white-collar positions (23). These strategies were all premised on the company's view, despite its position as a major employer of women, that women belonged at home taking care of their husbands and children (23).

Despite such male resistance, the middle-class status symbol of a nonworking wife, a relatively recent postwar addition to Japanese culture, already shows signs of decline, with half of all married women currently in the labor force. Moreover, Japan is gradually developing the infrastructure of services such as daycare, supermarkets, convenience foods, and cleaning services that make it possible for women to combine work and household responsibilities. Japanese men still have one of the world's lowest rates of participation in household work, and it will probably take a generation of men raised by working mothers to change this situation appreciably. In the meantime, providing domestic services for working married women constitutes one more area of business opportunity for other women entrepreneurs.

At the same time, a small but growing number of young women in Japan are simply rejecting the traditional package entirely, preferring to keep working and remain single past the customary age of marriage and childbearing (33). If this trend continues, companies may find themselves with more experienced female employees who will not quit gracefully and more male managerial employees who cannot find suitable stay-at-home wives to support the demanding corporate life-style. Indeed, most large companies already transfer male managers arbitrarily to distant locations, without consideration for family requirements such as the wife's job or the children's schooling. As a result the manager frequently goes alone to his distant post and makes occasional visits home, which suggests that Japanese male managers can function without wives if they have to.

Gender roles are very much in transition in Japan, and the messages women receive are mixed. The owners of small family businesses in Japan now encourage their sons to get a higher education and to move into the more prestigious world of the white-collar "salaryman." Fewer expect their children to take over the family firm, with its traditional pattern of participation by the wife. The same families also envision their daughters as the nonworking wives of salaried employees. Thus, the middle-class pattern of the white-collar salaryman with his nonworking wife remains a cultural ideal of upward mobility for the children of small-business families, although most of them will not make it into the largest and most prestigious companies.

There is also increasing evidence that nonworking, middle-class housewives who are married to successful salarymen now encourage their daughters to prepare for careers outside the home. It is not at all clear, however, whether these same mothers are rearing their sons to accommodate a wife with a career. To the extent that the Japanese corporate world continues to freeze women out of managerial positions and to expect that a male manager will have a nonworking wife as a personal support system, these differing parental encouragements point toward both domestic and workplace conflict in the future.

Much of this potential for conflict is likely to be defused, however, by the dynamism and fluidity of the small and medium-sized enterprise sector. Despite long-standing predictions, this sector does not seem to be decreasing in size or significance in the Japanese economy. It is in fact a large part of the secret of Japan's economic success. Moreover, despite the elitism of the Japanese education system and large corporations, a great deal of talent still flows into small and medium-sized enterprises. If that is the sector that accommodates women's growing career aspirations, still more talent will find its way there.

If we look only at the existing structure of Japanese employment practices and the prevailing attitudes toward the utilization of women in management, we can predict only gradual, long-term improvement, particularly in large companies. However, in the near future, the major factor in opening up managerial opportunities for women will not be changes in laws and attitudes so much as the sheer demand for skilled employees in a strong economy with a severe, long-term labor shortage due to low birthrates combined with highly restrictive immigration policies. As companies are unable to meet their managerial requirements with sufficient numbers of Japanese men, they will turn to qualified Japanese women rather than hire foreigners.

The impact of the long-term labor shortage has been slowly working its way up from the bottom of the Japanese employment structure over the past two decades, despite minor fluctuations. The movement of married women into part-time employment reflects the abandonment of lower-level positions by men, first in small and medium-sized companies and then in the large companies as well. The greater representation of women in managerial positions in small and medium-sized companies is also in part a reflection of the inability of smaller firms to attract male managerial talent in a tight labor market. It now appears that the shortage is beginning to affect even the large companies and may make them more receptive to the promotion of particularly talented women.

The labor shortage will not only increase employment opportunities for women in large companies but will at the same time lead to changes in the way large companies utilize their managerial employees. The companies assume that women are unwilling or unable to meet the high time and energy commitments the current mangerial system demands, but young men are also increasingly reluctant to pay the price. As the companies reduce working hours, social demands, and arbitrary transfers in order to keep their male managers, they will also be creating a more favorable working environment for women. Thus Japan appears to be at a turning point, with several factors converging to change both the opportunity structure and the work environment for women in management.

Notes

The authors wish to thank Fumiko Tsukada for research assistance, and the Japan Endowment Fund, a gift of the Japanese government to the University of Hawaii, for making that assistance possible.

1 This figure is based on an exchange rate of 125 yen to the dollar, the average rate in 1992. This exchange rate will be used throughout the paper, but caution is advised in interpreting

the results. The exchange rate reflects the weakness of the dollar and does not have equivalent meaning in dollar value within the domestic Japanese economy. Furthermore, these figures do not translate directly into American corporate equivalents, since Japanese companies are organized into smaller independent units, and derive less of their operating capital from the sale of stock than do their American counterparts. The data reported here appear to include most of the large, publicly held corporations in Japan.

2 Some of the key studies were based on even more restrictive definitions, such as companies listed on the major stock exchanges. To provide rough correspondence with these studies, in the previous section we have reported figures for companies with 1,000 or more employees, rather than the much broader category of large corporation as it is defined officially.

3 These findings are based on unpublished data gathered by Patricia G. Steinhoff during 1983.

References

(1) Brinton, M. (1988) "The Social-Institutional Bases of Gender Stratification: Japan as an Illustrative Case," *American Journal of Sociology* 94(2):300–334.

(2) Coleman, S. (1992) *Family Planning in Japanese Society: Traditional Birth Control in a Modern Urban Culture*, 2nd edn. Princeton, N.J.: Princeton University Press.

(3) Daiichi Kangyō Bank (1989) *Bijinesuman ga Miru "Josei Pawā"* [*Businessmen's Views of "Women's Power"*]. Tokyo: Daiichi Kangyō Bank.

(4) Hara, H., Muramatsu, Y., and Minami, C. (eds.) (1987) *Chūshō Kigyō no Joseitachi* [*Women in Small and Medium-Sized Enterprises*]. International Association for Women's Studies, Subcommittee on Women in Small and Medium-Sized Enterprises. Tokyo: Miraisha.

(5) Hirano, T. (1981) "Josei no Shokugyō Keisei to Kankyō" ["The Structure and Circumstances of Women's Work"], *Musashino Joshidaigaku Kiyo* 16:59–74.

(6) Hodge, R., and Ogawa, N. (1991) *Fertility Change in Contemporary Japan.* Chicago: University of Chicago Press.

(7) Iwao, S., Hara, H., and Muramatsu, Y. (1982) "Chūshōkigyō ni okeru Josei Keieisha no Seichōreki Seikatsu Keieikan – Tōnai 42 sha (42 mei) no Mensetsuchōsa ni motozuku Jireikenkyū" ["The Career, Living Conditions, and Management Attitudes of Women Managers in Small and Medium-Sized Enterprises – Research Based on Interviews with 42 Companies (42 Persons) in Tokyo"], *Soshiki Kōdō Kenkyū* 9:1–120.

(8) Japan Manpower Administration Research Institute (1986) *Shōrai Arubeki Jinji Kanri o Kangaeru tame no Kiso Chōsa 1985* [*1985 Research for Consideration of Desirable Manpower Management in the Future*]. Tokyo: Japan Manpower Administration Research Institute.

(9) Kantō Managers Association (1986) "Danjo Koyō Kikai Kintō Hō to Korekara no Koyōkanri no Hōkō" ["The Equal Employment Opportunity Law and the Future Direction of Employee Management"]. Tokyo: Kantō Managers Association.

(10) Komatsu, M. (1984) "Joseikeieisha no Ningenzō – Sogyōsha no Seishindojō o Saguru" ["A Human Picture of Women Managers – Searching for the Spirit of the Founders"]. *Josei no tame no Esso Kenkyū shōreiseido Kenkyū Hōkokushū* [*Research Report of Esso-Sponsored Research Fund for Women*] 3:3–6. Tokyo: Esso Oil Company.

(11) Komatsu, M. (1986) "Joseishachō wa Kigyō Shakai o kō kaeru" ["Women Presidents – How They Are Changing Industry and Society"]. *Shūkan Diamond*, February 11, pp. 82–87.

(12) Komatsu, Makiko (ed.) (1988) *Josei Keieisha no Jidai* [*The Era of Woman Company*

Presidents]. Kyoto: Minerva Shobō.

(13) Labor Administration Research Institute (1986) *Danjo Koyō Kikai Kintō Hō ni taisuru Kigyō no Taiō Jokyō o Miru* [*A Look at How Enterprises Have Responded to the Equal Employment Opportunity Law*]. Tokyo: Labor Administration Research Institute.

(14) Lebra, Takie Sugiyama (1992) "Gender and Culture in the Japanese Political Economy: Self-Portrayals of Prominent Businesswomen," in Shumpei Kuon and Henry Rosovsky (eds.), *The Political Economy of Japan*, Volume 3; *Cultural and Social Dynamics*, pp. 364–419. Stanford, Calif.: Stanford University Press.

(15) Ministry of Education (1991) *Gakkō Kihon Chōsa* [*Basic Research on Education*]. Tokyo: Printing Office, Ministry of Finance.

(16) Ministry of Labor, Women's Bureau (1990) *Joshi Koyōkanri Kihon Chōsa* [*Basic Research on the Employment Management of Women*], Fujin Chōsa Shiryō [Women's Research Materials] No. 14. Tokyo: Ministry of Labor.

(17) Nihon Horei Kyokai (1989) *Chingin Sensasu* [*Wage Census*]. Tokyo: Nihon Horei Kyokai.

(18) Nohata, M. (1986) "Joseiyakushokusha no Career Keiseikatei to Sokushin Shoyoin" ["Factors and Process of Career Formation of Managerial Women"], *Shakaigaku Hyoron* 34:438–456.

(19) Prime Minister's Office, Bureau of Statistics (1986) *Jigyōsho Tōkei* [*Workplace Statistics*]. Tokyo: Prime Minister's Office.

(20) Prime Minister's Office, Women's Section (1979) *Fujin no Hōshinkettei Sankajōkyō Chōsa Hōkokusho* [*Report of Research on the Conditions of Women's Participation in Decision Making*]. Tokyo: Prime Minister's Office.

(21) Prime Minister's Office, Women's Section (1981) *Fujin no Hoshinkettei Sankajōkyō Chōsa Hōkokusho (Kaisha igai no Hōjin, Hōjin de nai dantai)* [*Report of Research on the Conditions of Women's Participation in Decision Making (Corporations Other Than Companies, and Unincorporated Associations)*]. Tokyo: Prime Minister's Office.

(22) Prime Minister's Office, Women's Section (1990) *Fujin no Seisakukettei Sanka o Sokushinsuru Tokubetsu Katsudō Kankei Shiryō* [*Materials on Special Activities to Promote Women's Participation in Policy-making*]. Tokyo: Prime Minister's Office.

(23) Roberts, G. (forthcoming) *Standing on the Line: Women, Work and Family in Contemporary Japan*. Honolulu: University of Hawaii Press.

(24) Saxonhouse, G. (1976) "Country Girls and Communication among Competitors in the Japanese Cotton-Spinning Industry," in H. Patrick (ed.), *Japanese Industrialization and Its Social Consequences*. Berkeley: University of California Press.

(25) Statistics Department, Ministry of Health and Welfare (1990) *Heisei Gannen Jinkodōtai Tōkei Gaisu no Gaikyō* [*Summary of Population Growth Statistics for 1989*]. Tokyo: Ministry of Health and Welfare.

(26) Steinhoff, P. (1992) "Foreword," in S. Coleman, *Family Planning in Japanese Society: Traditional Birth Control in a Modern Urban Culture*, 2nd edn. Princeton, N.J.: Princeton University Press.

(27) Steinhoff, P., and Tanaka, K. (1988) "Women Managers in Japan," in N. Adler and D. Izraeli (eds.), *Women in Management Worldwide*. Armonk, N.Y.: M. E. Sharpe.

(28) Sugawara, M. (1985) "Josei Kanrishoku no Hikari to Kage" ["Light and Shadows of Women Managers"], in H. Hara and A. Sugiyama (eds.), *Hataraku Onnatachi no Jidai* [*Working Women's Era*]. Tokyo: Nihon Hōsōshuppankyōkai.

(29) Takagi, H., and Nakamura, N. (1986) *Joseikanrishoku no Yaruki to Noryoku soshite Shinshutsu* [*Women Managers' Desires, Talent, and Advancement*]. Tokyo: Japanese Association of Women Executives.

(30) Tanaka, Kazuko (1976) "Female Labor Force Participation in Japan." Unpublished paper. Honolulu: University of Hawaii.

(31) Teikoku Data Bank (1986) *Josei Shachō no Rankingu 100sha* [*The 100 Top Ranking Companies with Woman Presidents*]. Tokyo: Teikoku Data Bank.

(32) Teikoku Data Bank (1990) *Josei Shachō no Rankingu 100sha* [*The 100 Top Ranking Companies with Woman Presidents*]. Tokyo: Teikoku Data Bank.

(33) Tsuya, N., and Mason, K. (1992) "Changing Gender Roles and Below-Replacement Fertility in Japan." IUSSP Seminar on Gender and Family Change in Industrialized Countries, Rome, Italy.

(34) Vogel, E. (1968) *Japan's New Middle Class*. Berkeley: University of California Press.

(35) Women's Bureau (1984) *Joshi Rōdōsha no Koyōkanri ni Kansuru Chōsa* [*Research on Employment Management of Women Workers*]. Tokyo: Women's Bureau.

(36) Women's Bureau (1991) *Fujin Rōdō no Jitsujō* [*The Actual Condition of Women Workers*]. Tokyo: Printing Office, Ministry of Finance.

(37) Women's Work Foundation (1990) *Joshi Kanrishoku Chōsakekka Hōkokusho* [*Report on Results of a Survey on Women Managers*]. Tokyo: Women's Work Foundation.

6

MALAYSIA

Women Managers in Malaysia: Their Mobility and Challenges

Norma Mansor

Malaysia, situated in Southeast Asia, is made up of thirteen states, the eleven of peninsular Malaysia together with Sabah and Sarawak, which are separated from peninsular Malaysia by the South China Sea. It is a relatively small country: 329,758 square kilometers. The population of 17.8 million is of mixed ethnic origin (10). The Malays of peninsular Malaysia together with the indigenous groups from Sabah and Sarawak (who are officially considered one ethnic group and are referred to as *bumiputra*, or "sons of the soil") make up 62 percent of the population. The Chinese (30 percent) form the second largest ethnic group, followed by the Indians (8 percent).[1]

The official religion of the country is Islam, adhered to by approximately 50 percent of the population. The remainder are Christians, Buddhists, Hindus, Taoist, and Sikhs. Malaysia is a secular state in that the system of government, economy, and education is not governed by any religious doctrine. Although all citizens must abide by the federal law, the Muslims also adhere to the Muslim syariah law for all family matters (8). In everyday life, the religious value system is practiced along with local tradition and customs.

Malaysia achieved independence from the British in 1957 and has since been a constitutional monarchy based on the British model. Every five years, the rulers of the nine sultanates elect one of their own as head of state (known as the Yang DiPertuan Agung), who is basically a symbolic supreme ruler. In those states in which there is no hereditary ruler, a governor, appointed by the Yang DiPertuan Agung, heads the state. The governors do not participate in the election of the Yang DiPertuan Agung.

Malaysia's political system is also based on a parliamentary democracy. The Malaysian Parliament comprises the Dewan Negara (Senate) and the Dewan Rakyat (House of Representatives). The legislative assemblies of the thirteen states each elect two of the Dewan Negara's 69 senators, with the rest being appointed by the Yang DiPertuan Agung, on the recommendation of the prime minister and the Dewan Rakyat. Each of the 177 elected members in the Dewan Rakyat represents a single-member territorial constituency and serves a five-year term or until the parliament is dissolved. The current government is basically made up of the same component parties that existed in 1957. The National Front is an alliance of eight political parties. There are two main opposition parties, the Democratic Action Party (DAP) and the Pan Islam Party (PAS). Politically, change has been incremental, with few radical changes occurring either within parties or among them. Also, domestic and foreign policies have remained relatively consistent.

The law in Malaysia grants equality to women and men. According to the Constitution, "All persons are equal before the law and entitled to the equal protection of the law." The Employment Act of 1955 regulates the conditions of work for all employees and the Act specifically defines "employee" to include women. Whereas the law contains protective clauses limiting the night work, shift work, and underground work of women, it also provides for exceptions.

Women employees enjoy the same benefits as their male counterparts under the 1951 Employees' Provident Fund Ordinance, the Pensions Act, and the 1952 Workmen's Compensation Act. In addition, women are given 60 days' paid maternity leave.[2] The employer pays this benefit only to employed women with fewer than five surviving children.[3] Before the amendment in 1984, the limitation was for three surviving children, after which the woman had to take a leave of absence without pay to have more children.[4] Women in government service and in statutory bodies are entitled to only 42 days' maternity leave.[5] In terms of wages, however, they receive equal pay, which is not the case in the private sector. In Malaysia, there is no minimum wage legislation, which places women at a disadvantage since women have been concentrated in low-wage and labor-intensive industries. Women receive 74 to 79 percent of the hourly wages paid to male workers. In addition, the Income Tax Act of 1967 aggregates a wife's income with that of her husband.[6] However, since the beginning of 1991, a wife is entitled to have her income assessed separately for tax purposes when the tax file is in her own name. In most cases, however, tax files remain in the husband's name.

Malaysia is a society in transition from a traditional to a modern society, with local customs and traditions giving way and education playing a more prominent role in determining a person's life opportunities. Educated individuals are needed to meet the demands and requirements of the fast-expanding economy. The government uses the educational system as a vehicle for achieving long-range economic goals. Therefore, education for all is very much encouraged by the government. The Constitution prohibits discrimination in education on the grounds of religion, race, descent, or even the place of birth, but not gender. Although educational opportunities and facilities are available for all, some parents still do not see the necessity of sending their daughters for higher education. When resources are limited, families give sons priority and preference in gaining an education. Among the Chinese and Indian populations, women have been discriminated against in educational opportunities at higher levels because of the belief that once a daughter gets married, she no longer serves her own family but rather her husband's family. Therefore, families believe that it is not worth investing in a daughter's schooling as it is seen as far more important for her to learn how to be a good wife than to get an education. Malay girls were discouraged from going to school for reasons of modesty, except among the Malay societies in the states of Kelantan and Negeri Sembilan, where female children are very much desired.

Kelantan is a unique case as far as women are concerned. In Kelantan, the woman is generally the dominant person in the household. She is the decision-maker regarding family matters, including financial and place of domicile decisions. Many Kelantan women are the breadwinners of their families. Men perform the more strenuous jobs of farming and fishing, while many women engage in the more lucrative small businesses. Women dominate the business scene in Kelantan. The dominant position of Kelantan women in the family economy, however, is not reflected in the big corporations and government organizations based in Kelantan, where women paradoxically do not hold managerial positions.

Another unique case is Negeri Sembilan, a matrilineal society in which the tradition of *adat perpatih* gives women the right to inherit wealth. In Negeri Sembilan, a female child is greatly desired by parents, since wealth that is passed on to her remains in the family. However, this tradition does not give women power over men (as it does in Kelantan) (2). In terms of the gender division of power and authority, the situation in Negeri Sembilan is similar to that of women in the rest of Malay society.

Women's opportunities have been shaped by wide economic interests. The Sixth Malaysia Plan includes a special chapter on women in development (9). In 1976, the prime minister's department had set up the National Advisory Council on the Integration of Women in Development, with the mission to translate the United Nations world plan on women in development into a national Malaysian context. In 1983, the Secretariat for Women's Affairs (HAWA) was established to monitor and evaluate services for women provided by the public and private sectors (8). In 1987, the Malaysian Women Development Institute (IKWAM), which promotes the development of women in various fields, was established. This organization offers courses, services, and training designed to encourage women to establish themselves in both the public and private sectors. It is the only organization funded by the private sector (e.g., through membership subscription and fund-raising activities), as well as by government and nongovernment organizations. All of these organizations, together with academia (the KANITA project of the University of Science, the HAWA project of the University of Malaya, and the Women Studies Unit of the University of Agriculture), contribute to the growing literature on women's studies, covering various themes on women in development as well as women and family welfare.

Although there are many studies being conducted on women, there is a scarcity of empirical data on women entrepreneurs and managers in either business or nonprofit organizations (8). This scarcity is largely due to the absence of time-series data prior to 1970. Also, the role of women as key decision-makers in corporations and businesses is a relatively recent, and as yet unresearched, phenomenon.

In the Second Malaysia Plan, a structural shift in the economy switched the focus from the agricultural sector to the industrial sector (7). Manufacturing, especially in export-oriented industries, became especially important as Malaysia's efforts to industrialize began to focus on exports in the late 1960s.

Women's participation in the productive sector in Malaysia started long before the modernization of the economy, as women had been working side by side with men in the agrarian economy. During the precolonial era, women engaged in paddy planting and fishing. In both, there was a gender division of labor. In paddy cultivation, women were given lighter tasks, such as seeding, weeding, reaping, and winnowing; in fishing, women mended and braided the nets and sorted, dried, processed, and sold the fish caught by the men. On the east coast, particularly in Kelantan, women produce handwoven textiles that are sold in both local and foreign markets; they also became established vendors in the marketplaces. Thus, women have always contributed to the country's economy. During the colonial era, however, women's participation in the paid labor market declined, and they were confined to household tasks. Those in the labor market were employed primarily in labor-intensive jobs. Their contributions were assessed at a lower level than men's, and they were paid lower wages (3).

Malaysia is still an agrarian society, with 31 percent of the population engaged in agriculture, 16 percent in the industrial sector, and the remainder employed in the public as well as the private sectors as professionals, managers, and clerical and manual workers. As agricultural work was mechanized, the men (but not the women) were educated and trained to use the new technologies. Moreover, men were also given responsibility to handle the more important functions of receiving subsidies, marketing the product, and functioning as a liaison with extension officers.

The arrival of multinationals in Malaysia in the 1970s created job opportunities for women in the cities. Women's migration to the cities was encouraged. By the 1970s, about 90 percent of the garment workers and 57 percent of the textile workers were women.

In 1986, 46 percent of the women aged fifteen to 64 and 85 percent of the men were in the labor force. Because a large portion of Malaysian women are unpaid workers in family businesses or on family farms, they make up only about one-third of the total employed, even though two-thirds of them contribute to economic development. Women in the rural areas, where employment is more akin to a cottage industry model, combine childcare responsibilities with employment. Urban

Table 6.1 Labor force participation rates of women by age group, Malaysia 1957, 1970, 1980, 1986

Age group	1957 (%)	1970 (%)	1980 (%)	1986 (%)
15–64	30.8	36.3	39.3	46.4
15–19	27.9	33.0	33.5	32.2
20–24	31.2	41.9	54.0	58.8
25–29	27.7	45.5	44.6	50.4
30–34	30.5	39.0	40.5	47.9
35–39	34.2	40.0	42.7	49.4
40–44	35.3	40.0	43.8	51.6
45–49	36.3	40.7	41.4	50.8
50–54	33.7	36.6	36.5	44.0
55–59	29.4	29.2	30.8	34.8
60–64	22.3	23.7	25.0	25.9

Malaysia achieved independence in 1957.

Source: The Labour Force Survey Report, 1957, 1970, 1980–1988. Kuala Lumpur: Department of Statistics.

Table 6.2   Labor force aged ten and over by industry in peninsular Malaysia (1957, 1970, and 1980)

	1957 (%)	1970 (%)	1980 (%)
Primary Sector	78.4	59.7	43.7
Agriculture & Fishing	76.6	58.9	43.3
Mining & Quarrying	1.8	0.8	0.4
Secondary Sector	5.3	9.0	19.7
Manufacturing	4.3	8.5	18.6
Construction	1.0	0.5	1.1
Tertiary Sector	16.3	31.3	36.6
Utilities	0.1	0.1	—
Commerce	3.6	5.8	11.7
Transport and communication	0.3	0.5	0.7
Services	11.7	16.4	21.8
Activities undefined	0.6	8.5	2.4
Total	100.0	100.0	100.0

Source: Population Census Report, 1957, 1970, 1980–1988. Kuala Lumpur: Department of Statistics.

women who choose to raise a family must often stop working due to the lack of proper and affordable childcare services. The decline in labor force participation rates of women between the ages of 25 and 35 can be explained by the fact that neither public nor private employers systematically provide childcare. Recently many women have entered the informal sector (i.e., petty trading), which allows them to combine their domestic duties with paid work.

Several factors encouraged women's involvement in employment. First, with the launching of the new economic policy in 1970, Malaysia embarked on a program of vigorous economic development. With its Sixth Malaysia Plan, 1991–1995, the government took an active role both directly and indirectly in the economic sector to promote growth and equality (9). The new economic policy allowed rural *bumiputra* women to make a transition from the rural economy to modern sector paid employment (see Table 6.2).

Second, rapid industrialization in the 1970s, especially with the sudden rush of foreign investors and the establishment of manufacturing companies, created many new job opportunities for women, particularly in labor-intensive industries. Subsequently, this increase in jobs created a demand for managerial and administrative personnel. In fact, in the late 1970s and 1980s, the shortage of personnel for management positions acted to encourage women's participation.

Third, easy and equal access to education at every level, primary, secondary, and tertiary, resulted in more women obtaining the skills and knowledge necessary for entering into male-dominated realms. Education also influenced women's attitudes towards taking advantage of options other than those traditionally available to them (namely, marriage and childbearing). Between 1965 and 1990, the proportion of women among students of secondary, postsecondary, and university-level education increased significantly (see Table 6.3).

Table 6.3 Percentage of female students according to level and stream of education (1970, 1980, and 1990)

	1970 (%)	1980 (%)	1990 (%)
Level of Education			
Primary	46.8	48.6	48.6
Secondary	40.6	47.6	50.5
Pre-university	42.6	45.5	59.3
University	29.1	35.5	44.3
Colleges			
Polytechnics	13.2	21.5	25.2
*Teacher Training Institutions	41.9	48.3	56.1
*MARA Institute of Technology	32.4	42.9	45.8
*Tunku Abdul Rahman College	23.5	33.9	37.2
Stream: Secondary and Tertiary Level			
Arts	47.4	61.0	64.8
Science	24.5	36.3	44.7
Vocational	24.2	30.4	22.0
Technical	4.3	27.1	35.9

Pre-university is a two-year course that is a prerequiste for entering universities in Malaysia. Institutions in the other category (*) offer professional diplomas.

Source: The Sixth Malaysia Plan (1991–1995) Kuala Lumpur: National Printing Department.

Women's areas of specialization also expanded to include economics, business administration, law, accounting, and engineering – all fields that men had once dominated. The percentage of women enrolled in the technical stream rose from a mere 4 percent in 1970 to 36 percent in 1990.

Fourth, the introduction of effective birth control methods enabled women to plan their families and thus to enter into full-time employment and build their careers. The establishment of the National Family Planning Board in the 1970s was an attempt to educate women about their options on family-related issues. The birth rate declined from 46 births per thousand in 1957 to 29 births per thousand in 1988.

Women in Administration and Management

With few exceptions, Malaysian culture still adheres strongly to traditional values that prescribe a clear distinction between women's and men's roles. As described earlier, the two exceptions are the people in the moderately developed state of Negeri Sembilan, who practice *adat perpatih*, and in Kelantan. Except in Kelantan, the man is generally perceived to be the breadwinner of the family. A woman's work is secondary and her income is considered supplementary to the man's. The stereotypical view of women as home and family oriented and not career-minded, continues to make employers reluctant to employ or to promote women. Although these attitudes are slowly changing, the traditional belief that women are unable to hold leadership positions remains strong.

Women's voluntary organizations established in the postindependence period, including the National Council of Women's Organizations, provide pressure groups for change. These voluntary organizations also include the women's branches of local political parties, which echo their main party's issues as well as encouraging women to participate in public life. Women's political organizations – such as the women's sections of the United Malay National Organization (UMNO), the Malaysia Chinese Association (MAC), and the Malaysia Indian Association (MIC) – contributed greatly to obtaining women's votes for their respective parties. Within the parties, however, women are still relegated to supporting roles as mere campaigners and voters. In the 1960s and 1970s, the government appointed two women in succession to the post of Minister of Welfare. To date, there have been two women ministers, three deputy ministers, and several women senators and state legislative members, but the proportion of women in these bodies has never been greater than 2 percent.

Few women are in top management positions. In Malaysia in 1990, only 0.6 percent of the employed women were managers, compared to 2.8 percent of the men (11). Most women managers hold lower management positions, with only a very small percentage in middle management. In top management, the number of women remains extremely small.

There is less gender discrimination in the public sector than in the private sector. Women in the public sector have more equal opportunity for training and skill enhancement up to middle management. In Malaysia, there seems to be a common pattern in women's progression up the organizational ladder. Women proceed into lower and middle management in a fairly orderly fashion, but few are then promoted any higher. The prospects for advancement into senior management are very slim. In 1988, women accounted for less than 2 percent of company directors and for only 32 of the 1,990 directors of companies listed on the Kuala Lumpur stock exchange.

Women in the public sector have been heavily concentrated in the fields of teaching and nursing, professions traditionally considered suitable for women. However, in the last two decades, women have gradually moved into engineering, law, and architecture – professions previously closed to women. These professions were considered too "masculine" and therefore unsuitable for women. In spite of this progress, the number of women entering these fields is minimal. In practice, Malaysia still restricts women to a few professions. Women are relatively better represented in fields such as personnel, human resource management, public relations, and training. A small percentage of women work in finance or as managers of factory production or operations (1).

The Socioeconomic Background of Corporate Women Managers

Several studies on women in Malaysia today suggest that women's success is partly due to family support and connections. In 1987, the Women Managers' Association of Malaysia compiled a directory of women managers in Malaysia. The target group was women managers in public and private organizations, women entrepreneurs, and women academics who teach management. A review of the *Directory of Women*

Managers in Malaysia shows that the majority come from affluent or middle-income families (1). Opportunities for Malaysian women, especially from lower-income families, to enter management are still very slim. This situation changed somewhat in the 1980s as a result of the Malaysian government's strong investment in education during the 1970s, following its introduction of the new economic policy. An increased effort to improve the overall education system and to give more scholarships created better opportunities for women from lower-income and rural families to enter the corporate sector (although town schools continued to have better facilities than rural schools). In addition, improved information systems created an awareness of career opportunities among a wider circle of women.

A large proportion of women executives were educated abroad, primarily in England, the United States, and Australia. Government bodies and foundations sponsored most of these women, based on their academic achievements during high school. Parents, or at least fathers, of these women managers have higher educational achievements than the population at large. The fathers, as well as some mothers (who themselves were civil servants, businesspeople, teachers, or professionals), recognized the importance of education for their daughters over the time-honored tradition of strictly preparing daughters to become good wives and mothers. These parents sent their daughters to schools to be educated and trained. However, unlike the women executives, the younger women who occupy lower and middle management positions come from more varied backgrounds, including from families in which the parents have little formal education and work in the agricultural sector. The women executives often cite hard work and determination as the factors contributing to their success. Numerous studies show that women have to struggle more than men to achieve the same opportunities and positions. As one successful woman executive stated, "I was promoted to head this department because my male colleague resigned, but only after I headed the department for six months; then the CEO finally consulted me on important issues." She added, "Mind you, I have to continuously prove myself worthy of his trust."

Management and Style

Women managers in Malaysia are as motivated, visionary, and committed to their jobs as their male counterparts. Most, however, have worked hard and often harder than their male counterparts to attain a management position. They have made sacrifices in their personal or family lives and, like men, many have put their careers first. Given the same opportunities, they are no less capable. Women managers are assertive and firm in decision making. To quote one woman manager, "I may not shout or bang the table when work is not up to the quality I expected, but I certainly make it clear that it was not acceptable. . . . On one occasion, I rejected a proposal three times until he [a male subordinate] produced the best work I have ever seen."

The same manager who is demanding of her subordinates also cares for their well-being and the well-being of their families. She involves herself in department sports and visits her subordinates' homes during festive seasons. She regards her subordinates not merely as co-workers but also as friends and as part of her family.

A Malaysian woman manager is as soft-spoken as the average Malaysian woman, but more self-confident. Malaysian women managers appear to approach decision making differently from their male counterparts. They tend to be more cautious. Most male managers feel confident enough to decide before having all the facts and considering all possible angles. Women managers feel more comfortable deciding after processing all the relevant information and facts. A possible reason for this difference is the women's fear of making mistakes. Since the percentage of women in high positions is marginal compared to men, their failure would be more visible.

Problems and Obstacles

In the past, Malaysian women faced difficulties becoming managers. In recent years, the situation has improved somewhat. However, contemporary women managers still find it difficult to get their employers to give them positions of greater responsibility. Three major barriers to career success confronting women managers in Malaysia are the conflict between their careers and family responsibilities, employers' stereotypical attitudes, and the lack of strategic career planning among women executives.

Conflict between career and family responsibilities

About 95 percent of the Malaysian women managers surveyed in the *Women Managers in Southeast Asia* (1) study were between 30 and 40 years old, married, and with one or two children. Given that the minimum requirement for an executive position is a university degree or equivalent, most women managers had graduated from university in their early twenties. Many of the women, however, hold a master's degree. At graduation, these women face the job/family dilemma. Some solve the conflict by using family support or domestic help for childcare. Since the 1980s, however, extended families started to disintegrate. Proper child-care services and domestic help are not readily available and are affordable only by those earning higher incomes. Moreover, it is uncommon in Malaysian society for a husband to manage the household while his wife works. Some women managers indicated that their husbands help with the children and other domestic chores, while many expressed disappointment at their husbands' uncooperative attitude towards housework. The pattern of career advancement in Malaysia requires a woman to progress during her early years in the workplace – precisely the years of childbearing and primary childcare needs. If a woman chooses to delay her career progress, it becomes more difficult for her to be promoted after her early thirties. A large number of women, therefore, ignore promotion opportunities, opting to maintain the position they currently have rather than intensifying family conflict or their own feelings of guilt regarding their children (12).

Employers' stereotypical attitudes

Prejudice and stereotyping of women are still prevalent among Malaysians. The most recent reason employers use for their failure to promote women is women's geographical immobility. When employers offer women more responsible positions involving job rotation from department to department in various branches of the organization, they claim the women are reluctant to accept since it would mean leaving their families or their comfortable living arrangements. Consequently, employers tend to relegate women to relatively subordinate positions. However, if employers were really committed to providing equal promotional opportunities to women, they would develop job exchange programs in which the husband and wife could move together, regardless of whether they work for the same or different organizations.

Employers also argue that many women do not have the right qualifications or skills to hold top management positions. Many also believe that women's upbringings are not congruent with organizational interests. Apparently, even the few women executives are not treated as equals, as most men do not know how to deal with women either as colleagues or as superiors. For some men, it is not so much prejudice as confusion that makes them either ignore women or merely tolerate them in the workplace.

Male employers' other stereotypical views are that women are emotional and overly sensitive. Employers claim they are wary of commenting or giving direct feedback to women executives concerning their performance, because they fear an embarrassing emotional reaction. Due to this fear, the job performance of many women is not adequately evaluated. As a result, many women remain unaware of both their true potential and their current inadequacies. This lack of feedback adversely affects their professional growth. However, the negative reaction to criticism, if there is any, is not gender specific, but rather a cultural phenomenon of Eastern societies in which direct open communication is not as appreciated as it is in Western societies (5).

Lack of strategic career planning

A third barrier to career success is the lack of career planning among women. Most Malaysian women commit themselves to their careers relatively late in life, usually in their thirties. When first joining the employment market, women tend to accept whatever position employers offer them, without giving much thought to whether it is what they really want. Although this is also true among men during times of unemployment, men generally start to visualize their future careers, choose particular college courses, and acquire suitable training and skill enhancement at an earlier stage in their lives than do women. As a result, women rarely enter the field of their greatest interest or get jobs that utilize their special talents.

Career progress often requires the creation of "power bases" within the organization to advance one's career. This aspect of career planning, which enhances a manager's ability to control organizational outcomes, is relatively unfamiliar to most women. Women neither understand nor feel the need to build networks with those in positions of power either within or outside the organization. Similarly, women rarely discuss their futures in an organization. Most women in Malaysia view their hard work and job competence as the top priority. They frequently fail to realize the importance of other factors for their career success. Moreover, being "too good" in a specific expertise often results in them becoming "indispensable," and thus severely limits women's potential promotion beyond their particular specialities.

Although many factors are pressuring Malaysian organizations to change their policies towards women, change within the corporate sector is slow in coming. Impatient with the slow progress, many women are leaving their companies to look for better opportunities in other organizations. Unfortunately, this choice can also work against the women since Malaysian society is more personal than is Western society. Trust and confidence are built not solely on a person's capability but also on her or his long-term acquaintance and personal support. Employees must prove themselves – demonstrate good performance, including the ability to handle problems – before the organization will entrust them with greater responsibility. To succeed, a person must understand the organization. Switching jobs works against women when the employer, aware of her "unstable" work history, loses interest in promoting her or other women.

The three barriers discussed here are certainly lower today than they were in the past. At the same time, however, women's search for management opportunities has become even more difficult in the 1990s since the recession has made the job market much more competitive.

Conclusion and Reflection

Women's participation in management in Malaysia started in the 1970s when the country was undergoing a transition from an agrarian to a more industrialized economy. However, there are still many barriers to overcome. Stereotypical attitudes in both the society at large and work organizations remain strong barriers inhibiting women's progress. Religious and cultural norms contribute to limiting women's activities. Several teachings based on interpretations of certain Islamic groups discourage women from playing an active part in worldly affairs, and especially in taking leading roles in organizations with men.

The British education system in Malaysia also reinforced gender segregation, as boys were educated in vocational training while girls studied home economics in secondary school. The new curriculum in both primary and secondary schools reflects recent efforts to change the system. The introduction of commerce and accounting into the secondary curriculum is a positive step towards abolishing gender roles. Education could be used as a tool to erase traditionally restrictive attitudes and prejudices that encourage and propagate gender differences. Since the workplace is also discriminatory, to succeed in their careers women must try to overcome such obstacles as the reluctance of male employers to recruit women, uncooperative male peers, male-oriented working conditions, and the lack of women role models.

Although the process has been slow, women have broken down some barriers that prohibited them from entering certain careers. As women have managed to obtain the necessary qualifications and skills, some have begun to enter male-dominated fields. However, the majority of Malaysian women in the corporate sector remain in human resource management, personnel management, public relations, and training – areas that are viewed as an extension of women's traditional occupations in teaching and nursing. Although few women hold positions in production, marketing, and sales, an increasing number are entering finance.

The recruitment base for women managers has expanded. Whereas most managers still come from a relatively better socioeconomic background than the average Malaysian woman, increasingly women from modest rural backgrounds are joining the managerial workforce. The new economic policy, along with Malaysia's general national economic progress, has benefited many women, but not as much as it has benefited men. By contrast, the economic slow down in the 1980s adversely affected women more than men. In the future, however, considering the shortage of qualified men and the availability of unutilized, qualified women, Malaysian organizations may have no choice but to open their doors to women.[7] So far, many women have proven that they are just as capable (and in some cases more capable) of holding senior positions as men. They have thereby forced many organizations to promote them. However, to take advantage of women as a resource, organizations need to become more flexible in their rules, review their employment policies, and, in general, employ qualified women on more equitable terms.

There are signs that in the future Malaysian women will face bigger problems in performing their dual professional and private life roles. The extended family, a major source of child support, is eroding, and domestic help is becoming more expensive. However, given that Malaysia desires national economic progress, balancing career and family demands should not be viewed as solely a woman's problem, but rather as the nation's problem. Whether this will happen remains an open question.

Notes

1 Calculated by the writer based on the data in the *Malaysian Statistics Yearbook* (1990).
2 Section 37 (1)(a), Employment Act 1955.
3 Section 37 (1)(c), Employment Act 1955.
4 Employment (Amendment) Act, 1984, Act A610.
5 Chapter C General Order Malaysian Government, Kuala Lumpur, 1989.
6 Section 45 (2), Income Tax Amendment Act 1978, Act A 429.
7 Nowadays, the girls, apparently, perform better than the boys in schools.

References

(1) *Directory of Women Managers in Southeast Asia* (1990) Vol. 1, 2, and 3. Kuala Lumpur: WOW-Malaysia.
(2) Kassim, Azizah (1985) *Women and Society*. Kuala Lumpur: Pelanduk Publications.
(3) Kaur, Amarjit (1990) "An Historical Analysis of Women's Economic Participation in Development." Paper presented in the colloquium on Women and Development in Malaysia – Implications for Planning and Population Dynamics, Population Studies Unit, FEA, University of Malaya, Kuala Lumpur.
(4) *Labour Force Survey Report, 1957, 1970 and 1980–1988*. Kuala Lumpur: Department of Statistics.

(5) Pascale, Richard Tanner, and Athos, Anthony (1981) *The Art of Japanese Management*. New York: Simon & Schuster.

(6) *Population Census Report 1957, 1970, and 1980*. Kuala Lumpur: Department of Statistics.

(7) *Second Malaysia Plan* (1971–1975) Kuala Lumpur: National Printing Department.

(8) Sieh Lee, Mei Ling; Lang, Chin Ting; Pharg, Siew Nooi; and Mansor, Norma (1991) *Women Managers Of Malaysia*. Kuala Lumpur: Faculty of Economics & Administration, University Malaysia.

(9) *Sixth Malaysia Plan* (1991–1995) Kuala Lumpur: National Printing Department.

(10) *Statistics Yearbook* (1990) Kuala Lumpur: Department of Statistics.

(11) Yahya, Siti Rohani (1990) "The Development Process and Women's Labour Force Participation – A Macro Level Analysis of Patterns and Trends 1957–1987." Paper presented at the colloquium on Women and Development in Malaysia – Implications for Planning and Population Dynamics, The Population Studies Unit, FEA, University of Malaya, Kuala Lumpur.

(12) *Women Managers in Southeast Asia* (1990). Kuala Lumpur: Women for Women Foundation (Asia) Inc.

7

PEOPLE'S REPUBLIC OF CHINA

Managerial Women in the People's Republic of China: The Long March Continues

Karen Korabik

Background

Historical, political, and social context

Over the last 40 years, sweeping social, political, and economic changes have taken place in the People's Republic of China. Although China has the world's oldest continuous civilization, until 1949 it was still a feudal society, isolated from the outside world and characterized by poverty, illiteracy, and premature mortality. During the 1950s and 1960s, in an attempt to eradicate these conditions through modernization, the Communist government instituted a variety of policies aimed at land reform (collectivization) and the abolition of private ownership and of class and gender inequities.

To further the latter aim, the All-China Women's Federation – an umbrella organization operating at the national, provincial, and local levels – was founded in 1949. It was given the mandate of overseeing those policies targeted specifically at improving the conditions for women. These were intended to break down Confucian traditions of male superiority, which had kept women in subservient roles and had resulted in a social system that was patriarchal, patrilocal, and patrilineal in nature (26). Laws were passed to ensure women's political, cultural, economic, and social equality (18). Women's economic emancipation was to be brought about through their participation in production (25); through reforms in the marriage laws that eliminated concubinage, polygamy, child betrothal, bride prices, and arranged marriages; through making status and property settlements more equitable; and through allowing greater access to divorce (10;13).

During the Cultural Revolution (which began in the mid-1960s) a shift toward radical leftist thinking occurred. There was great scepticism about intellectual achievement; and foreign ideas and the professions, including management, were devalued. Formal management education literally ceased to exist and those who were professionals or who had foreign sympathies were sent to the countryside to engage in manual labor.

With the ascent of Deng Xiaoping to national leadership in 1976, the situation changed once again. Deng instituted a program of reforms designed to quickly bring about modernization so that China could compete in the world economy. These included decentralizing planning and decision making; instituting the responsibility system, which emphasizes individual accountability for production; encouraging private enterprise; and increasing technological development, often in partnership with foreign collaborators (18). Because the government saw management as helping to further their agenda, management is currently viewed as a high-status occupation (13).

Today's China is a society with mixed feudal, socialist, and autocratic features (3). Despite its current openness to Western ideas, China remains a collectivistic culture (18). Concepts such as privacy and freedom therefore do not have the same meaning in China that they do in the West (24). The Communist party continues to have a pervasive influence on the lives of everyday citizens (11). The winds of social change have slowed somewhat due to the government's response to the demonstrations in Tienanmen Square in June 1989.

The All-China Women's Federation has continued its fight to improve women's status. Current issues of concern include equal access to education, training, and employment; equal pay for equal work; workplace benefits and protections (e.g., daycare, maternity leave); and population control (8). Recently, however, the government's focus has shifted away from women's development as a national priority. Instead, officials have instituted a "trickle down theory," whereby they assume that women, as well as other groups, will benefit from the reforms that benefit society as a whole (13;18).

It is now clear that the attempt to achieve equality through the economic emancipation of women has met with only limited success (5;25). Although there has been a long-standing constitutional commitment to sexual equality, the Chinese Communist party has neither successfully eliminated the remnants of feudal thinking nor implemented a viable feminist theory (25). Belief in male superiority continues despite radical social reorganization and constant ideological crusades aimed at abolishing it. Stereotyped views about the nature of women and men are still ubiquitous and often serve to perpetuate discrimination and keep women in inferior positions (30).

Chinese women do not share power equally with men. They are vastly underrepresented in key government positions (19;26). Their opportunities for leadership occur primarily within the context of the All-China Women's Federation, an organization that is subordinate to the government and its directives (6;19). Such women-centered organizations may do much to improve women's welfare, but they do little to redistribute power and resources from men to women.[1] Changes, however, have slowly been taking place and it should be realized that, "A legacy which is more than 1,000 years old cannot be changed overnight" (22:36).

Geography and demography

An understanding of the situation existing in China today must necessarily include some discussion of its geography and demography. China is the third largest country in the world and has nearly one-quarter of the world's population (11). However, per capita income is low and 80 percent of the citizens are peasants, with the rural areas being underdeveloped compared to the cities (18).

The massive population means that there is an overly abundant supply of labor which is exacerbated by the labor force reorganization taking place as a consequence of modernization. This situation is detrimental to women. Women constitute 64 percent of all surplus labor (12) and, therefore, they remain more likely to be unemployed or under-employed than men (5;13).

The government is attempting to halt population growth and decrease over-crowding through enforced birth control and the one-child family policy. The consequences of such policies on women's lives are often dramatic. The one-child family policy, for example, appears to have led to increased violence against women, with rates of female infanticide and the abuse and/or divorce of women who bear daughters having risen due to the strong cultural preference for male offspring. On the other hand, however, the policy also has reduced the amount of time women must spend on activities related to mothering and this has freed them to take on other roles in society (6;19).

Conducting research on women managers in China

We have little direct knowledge about women managers in the People's Republic of China. There are several reasons for this. During the Cultural Revolution, social science research fell into disfavor, and China closed its doors to foreigners. There-fore, until recently, it was culturally unacceptable for Chinese scholars to carry out such research on women managers, and impossible for Westerners to obtain permis-sion to do so (18).

In addition, current conditions in China often affect the quality of information that researchers can obtain (27). The vastness of the country makes getting a geographically diverse sample impractical. Nonrepresentative sampling is the rule because access to managers is frequently controlled by the government. Moreover, managers' awareness that their answers may be scrutinized by persons associated with the government affects their responses. For example, during my first trip to China in 1985, personnel from the All-China Women's Federation were always present during the interviews my research team conducted with Chinese women managers (16). Similarly, another foreign researcher reports that all the envelopes that were returned to him containing completed questionnaires looked like they had been opened (20).

Foreigners conducting research in China also encounter difficulties due to lan-guage and cultural barriers (27). Western concepts and research methods are often not meaningful in the Chinese context (1). Furthermore, the researchers' own cultural bias always affects the choice of research methodology and the manner in which data are interpreted (10).

Given these problems, it is not surprising that so few scholars have conducted studies on Chinese women managers. The picture that emerges from the existing research, however, is remarkably consistent (11;15;16;17;20;21). Moreover, it is also consistent with information from research carried out by Chinese and foreign scholars using a variety of different methodologies on other topics in the People's Republic of China (e.g., research on Chinese women in general and on Chinese women in the workforce) both before and after June 1989.

The Role of Women Managers

Although exact figures are hard to obtain, it appears that "In university teaching, in scientific research, in medicine, in management, the percentages of Chinese women employed are higher than in the United States" (26:12). Despite equal opportunity laws, however, male managers still far outnumber women managers in China. Partly, this appears to be due to several factors that put Chinese women at a disadvantage in their preparedness for managerial positions when compared with their male counterparts.

These same factors also act to restrict women's career progress once they have become managers. For instance, there is considerable evidence of women's exclusion from top-level positions. Chinese women managers thus appear to confront a "glass ceiling" similar to that encountered by their sisters in other parts of the world. As one woman accurately described, "Many women take part in the management of industry and enterprises compared to in the past. . . . Women hold posts as factory production managers, workshop directors, [and] chief accountants, although they still account for only a small percentage compared to men. . . . But, the higher the post, the fewer the women" (16). My own research supports these contentions. In some locations, women held almost all the management positions and in others women leaders were practically nonexistent, but there were always fewer women at the top than at lower levels (16).

A discussion of the primary factors affecting women's access to managerial jobs and their advancement into positions of authority follows, beginning with cultural stereotypes.

Cultural stereotypes

Gender-role stereotypes are prevalent in China and hinder women's preparation for managerial roles as well as their opportunities for promotion. Cultural stereotypes, which are transmitted through socialization, influence not only the characteristics that women themselves embody, but also the attitudes that others hold about them.

Women's socialization   Many Chinese women have been socialized to be shy and unassertive (13;30). Such socialization does not adequately equip them to undertake positions of leadership or to take the risks necessary for entrepreneurial activities (5).

Women's self-confidence is also often undermined by their acceptance of the Confucian adage that "it is a virtue if a woman has no ability" (30:37). Thus, scholars note the pervasiveness of a female inferiority complex (9). Such scholars have chronicled the negative effects on women's sense of effectiveness that result from the societal perception that "men are more able" (13). As an article in *Women of China* notes, the tendency of many women to internalize their culture's beliefs about their inferiority diminishes their motivation to achieve (29).

In an attempt to eradicate this feeling of inferiority, the All-China Women's Federation waged a campaign promoting development of the "four selfs" (i.e., self-esteem, self-respect, self-possession, and self-strengthening) among women, especially those in rural areas (13). Such campaigns, however, focus on changing the women themselves instead of focusing on changing the societal attitudes that perpetuate discrimination against women.[2] Consequently, the success of such campaigns is certainly not assured. Although the government has tried for many years to ensure that women are portrayed favorably and nonstereotypically in the media (26), a study of the images of women in contemporary Chinese fiction found that employed women are nearly always depicted as subordinate to men and that women's assertiveness is deemed unacceptable (7).

Attitudes toward women leaders   In China negative attitudes about women leaders abound. Many women and men believe that women bosses are unfair, disorganized, narrow-minded, and hard to work with compared to men (27). A survey of attitudes toward Chinese women managers revealed that "there remains much resistance to women leaders among the less educated" (20). This resistance seems to be particularly true in rural areas where (according to the Confucian principle that women should be obedient to their fathers, husbands, and sons) it is still perceived as culturally inappropriate for women to hold leadership positions in relation to men (13;16). Thus, it is considered acceptable for women to be leaders only as long as they do not hold positions of authority over men (e.g., in women's organizations, those with a labor force made up primarily of women, or when there are not enough qualified or suitable men) (13).

Such attitudes hamper women managers' opportunities for advancement. As one woman manager claimed, "The feudal influence means that some men . . . are reluctant to promote women" (16). And, as another elaborated, "The same criteria for promotion are used for men and women . . . [but] it is more difficult for women to attain these criteria" (16).

Restricted opportunities

Chinese women's restricted access to recruitment pools (such as the Communist party), educational and training opportunities, and certain types of jobs also impedes their chances both of becoming managers and of advancing through the managerial ranks. Such restricted opportunities put women at a clear disadvantage compared to their male colleagues.

Communist party membership   In China, access to managerial positions may be conferred as a reward for party loyalty (11). Because 86 percent of party members are men, this route into management has been less available to women than to men (11).

Women have more problems becoming party members than do men. One reason for this difficulty is that membership is generally granted only after a lengthy period of observation by local officials. Women are more likely than men to change their place of residence upon marriage, thus interrupting the observation process (13).

Moreover, another common precursor of party membership is service in the army, traditionally a male bastion (6).

Women's restricted access to party membership serves not only to limit their access to managerial positions but also to promotions. Although 18 percent of women managers feel that the fastest route to the top has been through party channels, only 9 percent had actually entered management in this way (11). Unfortunately, no comparable figures exist for men.

Education and training   Women's lack of education and training may also hamper their opportunities for promotion once they have become managers. Based on feudal traditions, Chinese women have been less likely than men to be educated. Before liberation, 90 percent of Chinese women were illiterate or semiliterate (9). As recently as 1982, illiteracy was still far more prevalent among women than men, including those under the age of 40 (9).

However, the percentage of educated women in China has been rapidly increasing. In 1983, there were nine times as many women in college as had attended in 1949 (9). Yet, women still constituted only 40 percent of those in high school, 36 percent of those in vocational schools, and 27 percent of those in college (9).

The smaller number of women in colleges compared to men is partly due to discrimination. Because women are perceived to be less competent than men, universities require women to achieve higher scores than men on university entrance examinations (5;9;30). Moreover, the number of women is restricted in certain specialties (e.g., petroleum, navigation, geology, and metallurgy) (9). Women therefore face more difficulty than men in obtaining the same educational qualifications. As a consequence, women are more limited in the types of jobs for which they can obtain training (13). Far fewer female (0.6 percent) than male (7.7 percent) managers therefore have any postuniversity education (11).

In an attempt to overcome this obstacle, many women managers are currently enrolled in makeup classes to raise their educational levels or to acquire management training or scientific and technical expertise (11;16;17). For example, one study found that 78 percent of the women managers had taken general management courses to supplement their formal education (11). There is some evidence, however, that women managers may have less access than their male counterparts to such advanced training (16).

Job segregation   A factor that further restricts the career opportunities of Chinese women is their segregation into certain types of occupations. Despite the saying, "women are in all realms, women cross all bounds," Chinese women and men seldom do the same jobs. For example, in a brewery, the men operated the bottling machines and the women did the quality control work (15). Similarly, in a tablecloth factory, the men ironed while the women folded and packed the tableclothes (15). In an oil depot, the men filled the kerosene cans, while the women carried them (6).

The Chinese view such disparities as justified based on the belief that women and men differ in their talents and inclinations (19). However, until recently, the state allocated work assignments, with individuals often assigned to jobs without much consideration for either their personal interests or abilities (32). Although today's policies supposedly allow women to have more voice in selecting their vocations, the extent to which their choices are actually accommodated is unclear. Only about 30 percent of nurses, for example, expressed a preference for the nursing profession (12).

One reason that job segregation is so prevalent is that job assignments are often made in line with prevailing gender-role stereotypes. Because women are believed to be more attentive, patient, dexterous, and gentle than men (5), it is thought to be more "natural" for them to hold certain positions, such as those of teacher, nurse, and old age home attendant. Most Chinese women work in jobs consistent with the feminine stereotype (e.g., weaving, handicrafts, women's health care) (5;13;21).

Such job segregation often has serious consequences. Because women and men do not do the same work, they do not get the same pay (5;21). So, as in North America, an inverse relationship exists between the percentage of women in a profession and the wages it pays (12). Therefore, despite equal pay laws, Chinese women earn only about 72 to 74 percent of what men earn (10;27).

More central to the focus of this chapter, however, is the manner in which job segregation impedes women's entry into managerial positions. Due to government-controlled job allocation, Chinese women have little likelihood of selecting management as their vocation. Moreover, because one of the main avenues into management is through technical expertise (11;21), the segregation of women into nontechnical fields limits their opportunities to become managers.

Most Chinese women who are currently managers have backgrounds in science, accounting, politics, or engineering (11;16;21). In China, however, women are not encouraged to pursue careers in these fields, and far fewer Chinese women than men work in these specialties. For example, women account for only 2 percent of the enrollment in university engineering programs (21). Similarly, women represent only one-third of all technical and scientific jobholders and only one out of every ten advanced researchers in science and technology. Therefore, women are less likely than men to have the type of technical expertise that would facilitate their entrance into managerial roles.

Under the new economic reforms, the government is placing less emphasis on heavy industry (i.e., the production of machinery) and more on light manufacturing (i.e., of consumer goods) and services. This change should expand women's opportunities because these are areas in which women employees have typically been clustered (6). However, because these jobs do not emphasize technical skills, they may lack the potential to foster the movement of women into management beyond the level of first-line supervisors (21).

By contrast, the increasingly complex nature of organizations which has resulted from industrial development may increase opportunities for women with nontechnical backgrounds (e.g., education) to enter managerial roles. Women with such backgrounds tend to be concentrated in those stereotypically female managerial specialties, such as personnel (21), that are created as organizations get bigger and more differentiated. However, as in other parts of the world, these are not positions that put women in line for promotion to top-level positions. Thus, job segregation not only impedes women's chances of becoming managers, but it also limits their chances to advance after having attained entry-level managerial positions.

Discrimination

Job recruitment and assignment   There is clear evidence of discrimination against women in managerial recruitment and job assignment (16;30). As one woman manager claimed, "in recruiting, preference is often given to men because of some doubt . . . about women's potential" (20:8).

The government has attempted to deal with discrimination against women in jobs requiring managerial skills by regulating hiring practices and setting quotas (5). In addition, it has established policies and procedures to deal with sex discrimination in the workplace when it occurs (17). The efficacy of such measures is, however, uncertain.

Workplace protections   In China the physiological differences between women and men have been used as a justification for providing women with certain privileges in the workplace. For example, women are entitled to rest periods during menstruation, pregnancy, and breast-feeding and to maternity leave during confinement. These protections provide a form of reverse discrimination in that they give women benefits not given to men. However, these supposed benefits actually work as a double-edged sword since employers often see women as less desirable and productive employees as a result of them (5;12;26). Thus, even though employers are not supposed to discriminate against women based on the benefits they receive, they often do (28). For example, recent surveys show that over two-thirds of work units prefer men to women employees and that 80 to 90 percent of women college graduates have difficulties in securing work assignments (17).

Workplace practices   Certain discriminatory workplace practices may also impede women managers' chances of making it to the top. One way such discrimination is manifested is in the requirement that women retire at an earlier age (60 years) than men (65 years). Although the reason usually given for this is a biological one – namely, menopause – this practice actually serves several social functions. Women who retire early free up places in the workforce for their daughters or daughters-in-law who are "waiting for work" (the Chinese euphemism for being unemployed) (13). Moreover, they become available to do the domestic work in their sons' and/or daughters' households. Women's early retirement age, however, truncates their career advancement, and may prevent them from reaching senior management levels.

Access to men's networks and women role models

Women managers in China, like their counterparts in other countries, are often excluded from male networks (13). Such networks provide men, but not women, with the connections and influence (*guanxi*) that they need for entry into management positions, as well as for election or appointment to top management positions. Women's lack of access to such networks makes it difficult for them to effectively run entrepreneurial enterprises except on a small scale, where they are not dependent on men to make needed outside arrangements for marketing and supply procurement (13).

Traditionally, China's huge government bureaucracy, which was not open to women because of their subservient status, provided the source of men's networks. Today, such networks are more likely to be drawn from the army or Communist party, where women are under-represented compared to men.

One way that Chinese women have dealt with their exclusion from men's networks is by forming their own associations. The All-China Women's Federation is a prime example of such an organization. It has provided a significant source of female role models as well as a training ground for developing women's leadership skills (5). It has not, however, been consistently effective because it often suffers from a lack of both political clout and material resources and its leaders have not always approached issues from a feminist perspective (13). Still, such women's groups are important in "translating the individual experience of oppression into a collective consciousness. They act as mediators between their members and other social institutions and organizations, and attempt to legitimize and institutionalize women's participation in political decision-making bodies" (4:62).

Recently, several organizations aimed specifically at providing women managers with their own networks (for example, the China Women Managers' Association) have been formed by women managers who had previously participated in leadership training courses sponsored by the All-China Women's Federation. These organizations, although they have the backing of the All-China Women's Federation and the government, function independently of them (17).

Such organizations provide women managers with training and support by creating an opportunity for them to exchange information and share their experiences with one another. In addition, such organizations lobby to end discrimination in the workplace and popularize the achievements of successful women entrepreneurs who then act as role models for other women (17).

China culturally accepts the notion that one should be a model of good behavior for others. For example, the Chinese are exhorted to be model workers or model husbands. Therefore, it is not surprising that Chinese women leaders consider being a role model for other women to be one of their most important functions (23). Most women managers whom I interviewed spoke about having had mentors who helped their careers and about acting as a mentors to other women (16). Thus, although Chinese women managers lack integration into men's networks, they appear to have ample access to female networks and role models.

The dual burden

In China, almost all women face a dual burden in that society expects them to have families as well as participate in production (2). Thus, the vast majority of women managers are married and have children (11;15;16). Managerial women have an average of 1.2 children, with women under 35 years of age being much more likely, due to government restrictions, to have only one child (11;16).

Although the situation is beginning to change, it is still customary in China for wives' positions to be lower in prestige than those of their husbands (17). This certainly appears to be the case among managers. All the women managers I interviewed had husbands with jobs equal to or higher in status than their own. Correspondingly, male managers for whom data are available have wives with lower status jobs than their own (16). Similarly in another study, all the women managers had husbands who were more educated than they were, and all the male managers except for one had wives who were less educated than they were (11).

In China, a patriarchal division of labor, in which household tasks are delegated to women, still exists, with women's domestic roles viewed as equal to or more important than their careers (2). Working women thus have the dual responsibilities of engaging in paid work and maintaining the home (21).

Although the government encourages men to be "model husbands" and most husbands do provide their wives with moral support (16), they rarely do an equal share of the housework (21). Women workers consequently spend an average of 3.7 hours per day on household chores compared to 2.2 hours per day for men (31). This additional burden puts women managers at a disadvantage compared to their male colleagues.

Surprisingly, Chinese women managers do not appear to suffer very much work–family conflict (16). This may be because they are able to delegate many domestic responsibilities to others. Due to the traditional close-knit family structure, grandmothers often assist with childcare and domestic work (14). In addition, the government provides working women with many support services in the areas of childcare and meal preparation (14). Daycare is widely, if not universally, available (10;12). Most workplaces have on-site daycare, with some accepting children as young as four months old. These factors ease the domestic burden of Chinese women managers, thereby allowing them more time to concentrate on their careers.

Conclusions and Predictions for the Future

Many factors act as stumbling blocks to the advancement of Chinese women managers. One is the oversupply of labor, which creates greater competition with men for more desirable jobs. Another is the discrimination against women in job allocation and in access to education and technical training. A third is women's virtual exclusion from men's networks and male-dominated power structures.

Each of these factors reinforces the segregation of women into traditionally female roles that restrict their access to high-level managerial positions. Moreover, they perpetuate detrimental stereotypes about women managers and result in negative attitudes that women often internalize and that serve to decrease women's motivation to achieve. Such stereotypes cause doubts about women's competence. Such doubts result in fewer women being promoted to top positions. Similarly, such doubts force the women who do make it into management to work harder than men to prove their ability.

Stereotypes in China are particularly insidious because no research exists to show them to be inaccurate. Many Chinese therefore believe them to represent the "true" nature of women and men. Government campaigns to eradicate such stereotypes have been largely ineffective, and their consequences are often not redressed because they are not viewed as discriminatory. Thus, despite many laws intended to insure equality in the workplace, Chinese women managers are still at a disadvantage compared to men.

In spite of the factors hindering advancement, women managers in China appear to have ample access to women's networks and role models. In addition, although they still manage the bulk of the domestic responsibilities, most have the support of their families, and many government provided services and workplace protections.

Recent political and economic changes in China will probably both help and hinder the progress of women managers. Although the changes are opening up new economic opportunities for women, they will do nothing to counteract the inequitable treatment that women often encounter in the workforce nor will they facilitate women's ascendance into top-level positions.

The increased emphasis on marketplace competitiveness may result in women losing some of the special privileges they now enjoy – for example, workplace protections and daycare centers – as these benefits will be seen as costly and as resulting in lower profit margins (28). Women may, however, be less in need of such benefits in the future since they relate primarily to their maternal roles, roles that are playing a less important part in women's lives with the predominance of single-child families. On the other hand, the problem of eldercare may become significant for women because changing family structures mean that fewer daughters will be available to share the burden of looking after aging parents. Another change that is not likely to benefit women managers is the trend away from multigeneration families living together, thereby eliminating live-in grandmothers, who now constitute a plentiful source of free domestic labor.

As one woman manager noted, "China's economic changes impose new demands on managers, and women will have to improve themselves in order to be able to cope with these changes" (16). Many women managers are now doing so by acquiring advanced education and training. The government must assure, however, that their access to such training is not limited and that they receive the support they need to be able to take advantage of the opportunities afforded them.

The most significant social changes to affect Chinese women's lives, however, may result from the one-child family policy. Because families want the best for their only child, parents of girls are apt to become powerful advocates for their daughters' rights to equal access to education and high-paying jobs (18). This should help end many discriminatory practices that now exist. Moreover, as more women become educated and highly trained, it will be harder for people to sustain negative attitudes about women's competence. It is likely, therefore, that some of the detrimental gender-role stereotypes that now exist will slowly be eroded.

In the short term, however, the situation may not be easy for those women who are competent and highly trained. In the workplace, they will probably experience resistance from those who believe that male leadership prerogatives should not be questioned (13). Likewise, within the family, marital conflicts may arise if both the wife and husband are career-minded. Such conflicts are exacerbated when the government assigns spouses to work in different locations, as is frequently the case. Moreover, societal expectations that husbands should be higher in status than their wives mean that highly educated, professional women may have trouble finding husbands (17). Given the current stigma attached to being an unmarried woman in China, this predicament is not insignificant.

It will probably be many years before Chinese women managers truly have the opportunity to "hold up half the sky." In the meantime, their "long march" toward full equality with men continues.

Notes

I would like to gratefully acknowledge the help and support I received from my delegation leader, Gloria Levin, and my translator, Wei Bowen, and to thank Oded Shenkar for his comments on a previous draft of this manuscript.

1 D. Izraeli, personal communication, November 15, 1991.
2 D. Izraeli, personal communication, November 15, 1991.

References

(1) Adler, N. J.; Campbell, N.; and Laurent, A. (1989) "In Search of Appropriate Methodology: From Outside the People's Republic of China Looking In," *Journal of International Business Studies* 20:61–74.

(2) Bear, R. M. (1986) "The 'Superwoman' Syndrome, Chinese Style: Effects on Home and Family." Paper presented at the annual meeting of the American Psychological Association, August, Washington, D.C.

(3) Cao, X. (1987) "Lives of My Contemporaries: Women of China," *US-China Review* (January/February):19–22.

(4) Croll, E. (1978) "Rural China: Segregation to Solidarity," in P. Caplan and J. M. Bujra (eds.), *Women United, Women Divided: Cross-Cultural Perspectives on Female Solidarity.* London: Tavistock Publications.

(5) Croll, E. (1983) *Chinese Women Since Mao.* Armonk, N.Y.: M. E. Sharpe.

(6) Dalsimer, M. (1985) "New China, Old Values," *The Women's Review of Books* (2):3–5.

(7) Eber, I. (1976) "Images of Women in Recent Chinese Fiction: Do Women Hold Up Half the Sky?" *Signs* 2 (Fall):24–34.

(8) Gilmartin, C. (1984) "Recent Developments in Research about Women in the PRC," *Republican China* 10 (November):57–66.

(9) Hao, K., and Zhou, Y. (1985) "Growth of Women's Education," *Women of China* (April):2–3.

(10) Hare-Mustin, R. T., and Hare, S. E. (1986) "Family Change and the Concept of Motherhood in China," *Journal of Family Issues* 7:67–82.

(11) Hildebrandt, H. W., and Liu, J. (1991) *Female Chinese Managers: Their Role in China Enterprises*. Unpublished manuscript.

(12) Johnston, N. E., and Roberts, G. S. (1991) *Thankless Tasks and Scarce Incentives: The Work and Life Experiences of Chinese Nurses*. Unpublished manuscript.

(13) Judd, E. R. (1990) "'Men Are More Able': Rural Chinese Women's Conceptions of Gender and Agency," *Pacific Affairs* 63:40–61.

(14) Kane, P. (1976) "How Women Hold Up Half the Sky," *People* 3:15–17.

(15) Korabik, K. (1987) "Women at Work in China: The Struggle for Equality in a Changing Society," *Resources for Feminist Research* 16:33–34.

(16) Korabik, K. (1992) "Women Hold Up Half the Sky: The Status of Managerial Women in China," in W. Wedley (ed.), *Advances in Chinese Industrial Studies*, (Vol. 3), pp. 197–211. Greenwich, Conn.: JAI Press.

(17) Korabik, K. (1993) "Women Managers in the People's Republic of China: Changing Roles in Changing Times," *Applied Psychology: An International Review* 42:353–363.

(18) Levin, G. (1986) "Context for Understanding the Psychology of Women in Today's China." Paper presented at the annual meeting of the American Psychological Association, August, Washington, D.C.

(19) Lu, X. (1984) "China: Feudal Attitudes, Party Control, and Half the Sky," in R. Morgan (ed.), *Sisterhood Is Global: The International Women's Movement Anthology*. Garden City, N.Y.: Anchor Books.

(20) Mathison, D. L. (1988) "A Comparative Study of Attitudes toward Women Managers in 5 Asian Nations: A Preliminary Report." Paper presented at the annual meeting of the Academy of Management, August, Anaheim, Calif.

(21) Nisonoff, L. (1983) "China: Sex-Segregation in Job Placements . . . ," *Workplace Democracy* 10(4):5–10.

(22) Schwarcz, V. (1981) "Ruminations of a Feminist in China," *Quest* 5:27–40.

(23) Sheridan, M. (1976) "Young Women Leaders in China," *Signs* 2 (Fall):59–88.

(24) Sidel, R., and Sidel, V. W. (1981) "Revolutionary Optimism: Models for Commitment to Community from Other Societies," in J. M. Joffee and G. A. Albee (eds.), *Prevention through Political Action and Social Change*. University Press of NE.

(25) Stacey, J. (1983) *Patriarchy and Socialist Revolution in China*. Berkeley: University of California Press.

(26) Tien, J. S. (1986) "A Long and Winding Road: Chinese Women and Judith Stacey's *Patriarchy and Socialist Revolution in China*," *US-China Review* 10(2):10–12.

(27) Wolf, M. (1985) *Revolution Postponed: Women in Contemporary China*. Palo Alto, Calif.: Stanford University Press.

(28) "Women Say Prejudice Still Exists," (1987) *China Daily*, December 26, p. 3.

(29) "Women's Vocational Education," (1985) *Women of China* (January):3–4.

(30) Xi, L. (1985) "Are Women Intellectually Inferior to Men?" *Women of China* (January):37.

(31) Xia, W. (1989) "Changes in the Position of Women in Urban Families," *Women of China* (October):11–13.

(32) Zhang, L. (1989) "Women Become 'Surplus'," *Women of China* (March):1–2.

8

SINGAPORE

Women Executives in a Newly Industrialized Economy: The Singapore Scenario

Audrey Chan and Jean Lee

As nations industrialize and modern life-styles acquire popularity, policy-makers are directing more attention to women's legal rights and their economic contributions to contemporary society. Singapore, as one of the most rapidly developing newly industrialized countries in the Pacific Basin, presents a special case of women participating in an expanding economy. This chapter describes the changing roles of women in the Singapore economy. Societal and institutional factors that have helped and hindered women in joining the managerial ranks are examined, and strategies for their future career success are suggested.

Singapore's population consists mainly of immigrants and descendants of immigrants from the world's two major agrarian societies: China and India. The great majority of early migrants to Southeast Asia (the Nanyang) during the nineteenth and early twentieth centuries were men. They came in search of opportunities to earn a living for themselves and the families they left back home. The majority of these early migrants had no initial plans to settle in the region.

In 1836, only 7,229 women lived in Singapore, whereas the male population had reached 22,755. Up to the 1920s, only a very small number of women migrated to the Nanyang, in part due to the ban the Chinese government placed on women's emigration. More women began to arrive in the late 1920s and 1930s. Singapore's passage of the Aliens Ordinance in 1933, which regulated aliens' admission to the island by imposing a more expensive passage for men, facilitated this change. Women from Canton and other parts of China came by the shipload, many to work as domestic servants. Others were kidnapped and sold to brothels as prostitutes. Whatever their position, they belonged to the generation imbued with a strong work ethic that they applied to "pursuing material gain" (14:2–7).

Changing Roles of Women in the Singapore Economy

Women's participation in Singapore's economy may best be understood in terms of three chronological stages: Stage 1 – Lifting legal barriers; Stage 2 – Economic growth bringing women into the labor force; and Stage 3 – New opportunities for women managers.

Stage 1: 1959–1965 – Lifting legal barriers

In 1959, after Singapore became a self-governing state within the Federation of Malaysia, the governing People's Action Party (PAP) began to use the liberation of women as a prelude to liberating the country politically. The emancipation of Singaporean women was endorsed through passage of the Women's Charter in 1961, a monogamous marriage law; the legitimization of married women's right to engage in trade and professions; and the implementation from 1965 on of equal pay for equal work in the civil service (7).

Unfortunately, postwar Singapore was burdened with a high rate of unemployment and social instability. Few job opportunities were available. Consequently, there were few women in full-time paid jobs. Between 1957 and 1966, the women's labor force participation rate increased only marginally from 19 percent to 21 percent (4). Significant changes in the rate of women's participation did not occur until the late 1960s.

Stage 2: 1966–1978 – Economic growth brings women into the labor force

Singapore's separation from Malaysia in 1965 marked a new era for the nation's economic development. Deprived of a resource-rich hinterland for its *entrepôt* trade, Singapore moved quickly to develop a new strategy emphasizing the export of labor-intensive manufactured goods. The government was highly committed to creating an environment and building an infrastructure that would attract labor-intensive multinational corporate investment. This development strategy proved successful, partly due to its appropriate timing. During the late 1960s and early 1970s, the world economy was booming, and multinational firms searched for cheap labor and low-cost facilities for their assembly production. From 1960 to 1980, Singapore experienced an annual growth rate of 9.2 percent in gross domestic product (GDP) and 13.3 percent in total trade. A diversified economic structure, based on manufacturing, trade, finance, and transportation activities, was also established (21). During this period, the demand for labor grew at an annual rate of 6 percent. Increases in women and foreign workers contributed significantly to meeting this rapidly expanding labor demand.

With economic prosperity creating new job opportunities for women, the proportion of working women increased from 21 percent of the workforce in 1966 to 32 percent in 1974 (10). However, the majority were employed in low-income jobs. In 1970, 31 percent of the female workforce was employed in labor-intensive manufacturing industries, working predominantly as electronics and textile workers. The second major job category for women was commerce and trade, employing up to 19 percent of the female workforce, most of whom worked as secretaries, clerks, sales representatives, or service personnel (5). The third dominant sector was professional and technical, accounting for 14 percent of all employed women. Most woman professionals were teachers and nurses, but increasing numbers became lawyers and doctors (15).

Despite the increase in women workers, labor shortages persisted in a number of sectors of the economy. Consequently, Singapore pursued a selective policy of admitting foreign workers, mainly from the Association of Southeast Asian Nations (ASEAN) countries, for jobs in the manufacturing and construction industries. Between 1970 and 1980, the citizen and noncitizen labor forces increased by 55 and 47 percent respectively (26). Foreign labor contributed greatly to the expansion of Singapore's economy as well as forming a hedge against massive layoffs of Singaporeans during the recession in the mid-1980s.

Stage 3: 1979 to the present – New opportunities for women managers

In 1979, the government launched a second Industrial Revolution to restructure the economy from low-wage, low-capital business activities to investment in high value-added and skill-intensive activities. This new economic development strategy was introduced to counteract the competitive challenge of other countries in the region that are richly endowed with natural resources and cheap labor. To accomplish this mission, the government offered private investors attractive financial incentives, such as tax relief and special grants for industrial automation, wide-scale adoption of information technology, and a massive effort in human resource development (HRD). The ambitious HRD policy provided Singapore's women with a golden opportunity to upgrade themselves for professional jobs.

The new economic plan, although well envisioned, encountered a temporary setback during the initial period, due partly to a global recession in the early 1980s and partly to the adoption of some fiscal policies that had unfortunate consequences. For example, a three-year wage correction policy in 1979 to 1981 forced the national wage bill up by 20 percent annually. The result was diminished business competitiveness. As a consequence, the average 8.5 percent growth in real GDP in the years from 1980 to 1984 took an unprecedented dip to minus 1.6 percent in 1985, followed by a marginal improvement to 1.8 percent growth in 1986. A series of retroactive and quick adjustments in fiscal and other government policies succeeded in pushing Singapore's economy back to health, with a 9 percent annual growth in GDP from 1987 to 1991.

The biggest achievement of the economic restructuring was the creation of an upgraded labor force equipped with greater skills and productivity for more value-added operations. In 1991, about 53 percent of the workforce had at least secondary qualification. The *World Competitiveness Report 1990* ranked Singapore as the most competitive country in a group of ten newly industrializing economies. Industrial efficiency and human resources were two of the five categories in which Singapore emerged as top among the ten nations. *BERI Quality of Workforce Index 1990* also ranked Singapore as the top nation among ten economies – the five principal OECD countries (Germany, Japan, Sweden, Switzerland, United Kingdom); the United States; and the four newly industrialized Asian economies (Hong Kong, South Korea, Taiwan, and Singapore). Among the eighteen assessment criteria, Singapore earned the highest score in areas such as relative productivity, company support for education and training, quality of trained workforce, absenteeism, and workforce organization and practices.

Singaporean women have benefited greatly in this upgrading effort. Between 1981 and 1991, the rate of women's participation grew from 45 percent to 51 percent, particularly among women aged 35 to 45 years. The proportion of women among professional and technical workers increased from 38 percent to 40 percent, and women's representation among the administrative and managerial workers also expanded from 15 percent to 16 percent (24;25).

The labor shortage, which contributed to more women participating in the workforce, is expected to increase in the coming decades. In the 1970s, the rapid industrialization of Singapore resulted in almost full employment. During most of the 1980s, the unemployment rate remained low at around 2 percent. Also over the past decades, economic progress, improvements in health care, and rapid urbanization resulted in dramatic demographic changes in Singapore, including delayed marriage, a decline in the birthrate, and extended life expectancy. The 1990 statistics on marriage and divorce showed that more Singaporeans are postponing marriage until their late twenties, with the average age of the groom and bride reaching 29 and 26 respectively, around two years older than the newlyweds of a decade ago. For graduates, the average age for marriage was 31 for grooms and 28 for brides. With delayed marriages comes delayed childbirth. The average age of Singaporean women having their first child also rose, from 26 in 1985 to 28 in 1990 (31;34).

The 1990 population census of Singapore reported a total population of 3 million, of which 90 percent were Singapore residents (citizens and permanent residents). In the prior decade, the resident population grew at an annual rate of only 1.7 percent, an unfavorable rate in comparison with the higher 2.4 percent growth rate in new permanent residents. As the proportion of the population below fifteen years of age declined and the adult and elderly segment simultaneously grew, the median age of the resident population rose from 24 years in 1980 to 30 years in 1990 (6). These demographic transitions will significantly affect the composition of Singapore's labor supply.

To overcome the shortage of human resources and reduce Singapore's long-term reliance on foreign workers, the government launched a major campaign to attract economically inactive Singaporean women, estimated to number around 600,000 in 1991, back into the labor force. The labor statistics for 1991 indicate that 75 percent of those who have left the labor force for less than a year were women, and, of these, 84 percent were married. Household duties were cited by 44 percent of those leaving as the major reason for quitting their jobs.

Singapore is not a signatory to the three United Nations conventions that call for equality of the sexes in employment opportunities, in renumeration for work of equal value, and in institutional treatment in all forms (29). Yet, following the recommendations proposed by a national task force (23), substantive improvements could be observed in quality childcare services, flexible work scheduling, special work incentives, training and retraining programs, and in societal attitudes toward career women. This official endorsement of women participating in the workforce reinforced a growing trend among dual-career families in Singapore. More wives now pursue their own careers, not only for personal fulfillment, but also to meet the higher family expectations of home ownership, material comfort, and children's education (27). On the whole, efforts aimed at attracting women back into the labor force have reaped encouraging results.

Women Managers in Singapore

An emerging profile

Whereas the proportion of women among legislators, administrators, and managers has improved only marginally, the total number of women administrators and managers has grown from 8,644 to 22,580 within the past decade. The majority of these women managers are Chinese and relatively younger than their male counterparts: 62 percent of the woman managers compared to 47 percent of their male counterparts are between twenty and 39 years old. Sixty-four percent of the women managers are married. However, the percentage of singles among women executives (27 percent) is more than twice that among men (12 percent) (24;25).

By 1991, most women managers were employed in the growing sectors or sunrise industries such as commerce (51 percent); finance, insurance, real estate and business services (18 percent); manufacturing (14 percent); and community, social, and personal services (9 percent). Among the women executives, 38 percent are employers, the majority of whom owned jewelery firms, boutiques, travel or employment agencies, or fashion and food companies. Women owners are also increasingly represented in a few traditionally male-dominated industries such as shipping, publishing, and computer systems (27). By 1981, only 536 women managers earned S$3,000 (US$1,850) or more per month, forming 6 percent of the management population in this top-income category. By 1991, 7,397 women managers earned at least S$3,000 a month, accounting for approximately 12 percent of the managers in this top echelon of wage earners (24;25).

A growing corps

What has contributed to the large increase in the number of Singapore's women managers during the past decade? Three factors appear most important: economic conditions, women's improved educational attainment, and rising living costs coupled with changing social expectations.

Economic conditions The second Industrial Revolution, launched in 1979, aimed to push Singapore out of labor-intensive industries towards more sophisticated, knowledge-intensive technological industries and highly skilled "brain" services. The government strongly believes that Singapore's competitive future lies in its export of value-added goods and services. It has identified finance, insurance, real estate, computers and information processing, transportation, communication, biotechnology, medical healthcare, management consultancy, and other personal services as sunrise sectors. Indeed, in the 1980s, these sectors registered the fastest growth rates in terms of their contribution to GDP (11). The growth of these industries provided new

Table 8.1   Distribution of employed women by industry

Industry	1981 Women as a percentage of all employed women	1991 Women as a percentage of all employed women
Agriculture, hunting, forestry, fishing	0.8	–
Mining and quarrying	0.1	–
Manufacturing	38.5	31.3
Electricity, water, and gas	0.3	–
Construction	1.3	1.4
Commerce	23.1	22.7
Transport, storage, and communication	5.4	5.7
Financing, insurance, real estate	9.8	13.2
Community, social, and personal services	20.7	25.4
Activities not adequately defined	0.0	0.3
Total	100.0	100.0

Sources: *Report on the Labour Force Survey of Singapore* (1981) p. 39; *Report on the Labour Force Survey of Singapore* (1991) p. 40. Singapore: Research and Statistics Division, Ministry of Labour.

employment opportunities for Singaporean women (see Table 8.1). These new opportunities, in turn, led to a marked shift in the employment pattern of women from manufacturing to financial and business services as well as to community, social, and personal services. These growth industries have become the largest employers of women managers.

Women's improved educational attainment   In the 1970s and early 1980s, two government policies facilitated Singaporean women's entry into management: first, the introduction of compulsory military service of 2.5 years for all men citizens delayed their entry into the labor force; and second, the adoption of new university admission criteria from 1980 to 1984, that gave greater weight to language achievement, inadvertently discouraged male applicants, who traditionally have had more difficulty with language studies. These two factors resulted in a sharp increase in the proportion of women university students, from 44 percent in 1980–1981 to 55 percent in 1983–1984 (16). The government subsequently revised university admission criteria to halt the unanticipated consequences of the new language policy.

Labor statistics have consistently shown that women's labor force participation increases with education and is much higher for women who have obtained at least a secondary level education. In 1991, over 80 percent of the university educated women were in the labor force. Women workers, in general, are better educated than their male counterparts, with approximately 60 percent of the employed women compared to 48 percent of employed men holding at least secondary qualifications (25).

The establishment of a second full university in 1991, the Nanyang Technological University, and the expansion and upgrading of polytechnic diploma courses provide women with more opportunity to undertake tertiary education. Upon graduation, most women have had ample job opportunities due to the booming economy. Many women managers in their thirties and forties claim that "we are the first generation of Singapore women to benefit from greater parental awareness of the importance of education" (1). Between 1981 and 1991, the proportion of economically active women with tertiary education more than doubled (from 2.7 percent to 6.4 percent). In a society committed to meritocracy and with only 7 percent of its working population completing tertiary education, a university degree virtually guarantees a solid start to one's career.

Rising living costs and changing social expectations   In the second half of the 1980s, the Singapore government deregulated the economy to ensure industrial adaptability and national competitiveness in a rapidly changing global economy. According to plan, the government privatized selected statutory boards, government-owned companies, and most of Singapore's public hospitals. In 1990, the new government, headed by Goh Chok Tong, assumed leadership and pledged to achieve an even higher standard of living for all Singaporeans. The government is directing special efforts at developing human talents, considered the most precious resource of the nation. Besides the design of a new population policy to bring about higher birthrates, the government is also determined to upgrade living quality in Singapore and to strengthen people's national identity. Both tactics are designed to attract foreign talent to Singapore and to minimize the outflow of residents (17).

Recently, the government established independent schools that promise students a lower student–teacher ratio and better facilities for an enriched school life. In addition, the government developed plans to upgrade public housing and support for more arts, sports, and recreational activities. All of these are attempts to enrich the personal and social life of Singapore's residents. They provide the increasingly affluent population with the possibility of pursuing better material comforts and quality social services, albeit at a higher price. Besides granting financial subsidies to the needy and economically disadvantaged, the government encourages all residents, women and men, to upgrade themselves professionally and to participate in productive work for individual as well as national gain. The increasing participation of women in the labor force, especially those who have benefited from tertiary education, is in part the consequence of such developments.

Remaining Barriers

Numerous factors, internally perceived or externally fostered, inhibit women's career progress in management. This section first describes corporate barriers to women's career advancement, including gender stereotyping, work discrimination, and inadequate networking. Then it discusses a number of social developments in Singapore that physically or psychologically constrain women's total commitment to their careers.

Corporate barriers to career advancement

Gender stereotyping   Several social and cultural factors prevent women from competing equally with men for managerial positions. Gender stereotyping is one of the more prominent career barriers. Perlita Tiro, a private consultant specializing in executive-search, reports some of the common reservations that employers express about hiring women managers (33:19); these include that companies:

- Consider married women unsuitable for jobs that require frequent travel;
- Only reluctantly hire women to head departments staffed by men;
- Seldom recruit women managers from outside, but rather prefer to promote women who have a proven track record within the organization;
- Hesitate to employ women to supervise plants, shipyards, or construction sites, all places that they label as "off limits" to women;
- Often doubt women (and especially working mothers) will take their careers seriously and be willing or able to work the long hours necessary to succeed;
- Fear that women will have more difficulty gaining customers' trust and respect.

A study of 31 female and 22 male managers revealed that occupational gender segregation remains extensive in Singapore, with more women hired in the service sector than in other sectors and in support functions than in line positions (9). Among the male managers, 36 percent had women superiors. Interestingly, whereas all of these men held either neutral or favorable attitudes toward their women peers and subordinates, 23 percent of them expressed unfavorable impressions of their women superiors, attributing to the women bosses such behaviors as pettiness, an inability to confront or take risks, and being overly calculating.

Work discrimination   One direct consequence of such gender stereotyping is work discrimination. Graduate employment surveys of recent years have revealed unfair company policies against women university graduates. In general, women graduates wait longer to secure their first job, receive fewer job offers within the first six months after graduation, receive lower pay, and are less satisfied with their starting salary than men graduating the same year. Both the 1984 and 1990 Graduate Employment Surveys showed that women graduates, despite similar qualifications, continued to draw salaries almost one-quarter lower than their male contemporaries (18;19).

Table 8.2 compares the time needed for women and men graduates to secure their first job in 1975, 1984, and 1990. Each of these three years was characterized by a drastic slowdown in Singapore's economy. These data substantiate a common claim that equal opportunity for women can only be truly tested in hard times when employers are likely to become more discriminating. Prejudice often results initially in slower career progress for women.

A study interviewing twenty women executives found that, on average, the women required between eight to ten years to reach senior management, compared

Table 8.2 Working women graduates's waiting time for their first job

Time taken to find first job	Percentage of total graduates		
	1975	*1984*	*1990*
No wait	–	51.4	–
Less than 1 month	51.5	44.2	37.8
1 to 3 months	–	48.8	48.0
3 to 6 months	71.9	68.4	64.6
Over 6 months	100.0	68.7	64.4
Not stated	20.0	–	–
Not applicable (self-employed or further study)	–	56.1	–
Percentage total	55.1	54.0	51.8

Sources: 1984 Graduate Employment Survey (1985) Appendix Table 3 and Appendix Table 4. Singapore: National University of Singapore; Pang, Eng Fong and Sean, Linda (1975) *A Report on the 1975 Employment Survey of University of Singapore Graduates*; Singapore: National University of Singapore. *1990 NUS and NTI Graduate Employment Survey* (1991) Appendix Table 1. Singapore: National University of Singapore.

to about five years for men (1). Most of these women executives anticipated that it will take another generation before women become common in the board-room.

Besides having to climb a more circuitous path to reach the top, women managers also generally receive lower salaries. Table 8.3 shows the percentage of women in each salary category. Although the past decade saw an increasing representation of women managers in the higher-income groups, women still fare unfavorably compared with their male counterparts in take-home pay. Gender differences in job choice, functional affiliation, and level of management may partially explain this earnings gap. However, employers' reported reluctance to increase women employees' job responsibilities and to provide them with proper training and advancement opportunities is an equally likely explanation (23).

Inadequate networking   Social attitudes and structures unwelcoming to women managers in many organizations – such as their exclusion from the real power networks, insufficient help from superiors or co-workers, and unfavorable attitudes toward women's assertiveness – further inhibit women managers from realizing their potential. Moreover, cultural values restrain women managers from entertaining their business associates in private clubs or on the golf course, places well known among the Singaporeans as congenial for establishing networks and "learning through the grapevine." Without a supportive working climate, women managers, not surprisingly, work mainly for financial independence, better material comforts for their family, pleasure from job accomplishment, and self-worth. The women seldom see their job as a stepping-stone to advancement and power. One senior bank manager, a mother of two, stated it clearly: "The status, perks, and power are not worth the sacrifices and hassle" (1).

Table 8.3   Women executives by gross monthly salary

Gross monthly salary	Percentage of all executives in salary range	
(Singapore dollar)	*1981*	*1991**
Under $400	48.0	23.1
$400–$599	17.4	33.6
$600–$799	19.5	21.2
$800–$999	23.5	19.9
$1000–$1499	16.4	17.0
$1500–$1999	14.9	15.8
$2000–$2499	9.7	17.4
$2500–$2999	4.8	18.3
Over $3000	5.9	12.4
Percentage total	14.7	15.6

* The 1991 Report grouped legislators, administrators, and managers into one category as executives, while in the 1981 report, "executives" included only administrative, managerial, and executive workers.

Source: Report on the Labour Force Survey (1981) and *Report on the Labour Force Survey* (1991).

Social constraints and psychological hurdles

A number of developments heighten work–family conflicts and dampen the efforts of career women to establish themselves in the corporate world. Emerging social issues that physically and psychologically limit womens' careers include a new population policy, difficulty in locating a suitable marital partner, the rising number of divorces and single-parent families, and the increasing burden of physically caring for aging parents and relatives (27).

New population policy   In 1987, the Singapore government announced a new population policy encouraging couples to have three or more children if they could afford to. This represents a national attempt to halt the declining birthrate and the shrinking of the productive workforce. To achieve a target population of four million, the government introduced monetary incentives, such as enhanced tax relief for working mothers. This progressive, per-child tax relief of 5, 15, 20, or 25 percent is given to the first four children of working mothers who have obtained at least three General Certificates of Education ordinary level passes, or the equivalent, in one sitting. The tax rebate is calculated as a percentage of the mother's earned income. In addition, the government offers a rebate for the levy paid to hire a foreign maid as well as a childcare subsidy of $100 per child per month.

Taking the lead, the government initiated additional work-related incentives for women civil servants, such as leave without pay of up to four years for the third child, optional part-time employment for women with children below age six, and off-the-record paid leave to attend to sick children. After implementation, the policy apparently produced some impact on the aspiring parents. Singapore's birthrate rebounded from a historic low of 1.4 percent in 1986 to 2 percent in 1988 (17). In 1991, 8,937 women had their third child, and another 2,949 had their fourth or subsequent child. This was 28 percent and 33 percent more than the respective birthrates in 1987, when the policy was first announced (34).

Although these incentives and support measures make the financial burden of childrearing more manageable, they also "reinforce a notion that childcare is largely the responsibility of mothers and indirectly causes employers and fellow employees to view working mothers as a financial (and operational) liability and may subsequently adversely affect the working mother's job opportunities and career prospects" (27:42).

Moreover, the policy creates additional burdens for working mothers trying to maintain an acceptable balance between their family and career life. Most of the 354 married professional women in Singapore surveyed for one study reported that they experienced moderate levels of work–family conflicts (2). These professional women listed parental demands and inadequate support from their husband as the factors contributing to job–parent and job–spouse conflicts. These conflicts, in turn, reduced their life satisfaction and adversely affected their work quality.

In another survey, which studied 95 dual-earner families in Singapore, the working wives reported a significantly higher level of burnout than did their husbands (3). Moreover, burnout for wives was related to both work and family, whereas burnout for husbands appeared to be mainly work-related. The women identified role ambiguity, work schedule inflexibility, quality of spouse support, and job–parent conflict as important factors contributing to their burnout. Socialization that prescribes "women's primary allegiance to the family" may explain the higher burnout rate among working wives as they engage in paid employment in addition to fulfilling their culturally mandated role of caring for their families (3). In Singapore, alternative arrangements to alleviate women's work load include the help of relatives or the employment of domestic help, most frequently foreign maids from the Philippines, Indonesia, Malaysia, or mainland China. Even with the availability of such assistance, many high-earning women feel they should bear the primary responsibility for the care and socialization of their children. Most working women believe that nonemployed women are better mothers than those who work and that women should be willing to sacrifice their careers for a number of years to bring up their children properly (8;10).

The high demands made on children's performance further expands the mother's role in Singapore. The local bilingual education system is highly competitive. Streaming, a method for placing students into different classes according to their academic performance, occurs early in grade four. Mothers often play a more active role than fathers in helping to push their very young children to gain a "head start." They assist their children with homework, hire private tutors for core academic subjects, and enroll their children in piano, art, swimming, ballet, and other extracurricular classes. Parents who can afford to travel will go abroad with their children during school vacations. In paying the "pioneer's price" of balancing career and family responsibilities, many working mothers have to "put in incredibly long hours, give up almost all leisure and personal time, and feel guilty for not getting everything done in time" (30:8). Over half of Singapore's women managers surveyed in an Asian Institute of Management study considered that the dearest price they had to pay for their career success was in the quality of relationships or time spent with their husbands and children (12). Personally, they had to compromise with less time for leisure and sports, as well as for other responsibilities unrelated to their job. Some 13 percent of the women managers even felt that they had missed the chance to marry because of job obligations (12).

Difficulty in locating a suitable marital partner   Higher educational and career aspirations may have made it more difficult for women professionals and managers in Singapore to locate compatible marital partners. Statistics show that from 1975 to 1991, the number of brides aged over 30 increased from 5.8 to 15 percent of all brides. The 1990 population statistics also indicate that more people aged twenty to 44, both men and women, are single; but for those aged 35 to 44 years, the increase in singles is more significant for women than men. In the past decade, the proportion of single women rose from 9 to 14 percent for those aged 35 to 39 years and from 6 to 11 percent for those aged 40 to 44 years (6).

Delayed marriages may partially explain such marital developments. However, the problem of involuntary single status, especially for women with higher educational attainment, may also be caused by a deeply rooted cultural value in which Singaporean men prefer to marry women who are academically and professionally their inferior. Similarly, few highly educated Singaporean women are willing to marry men of lower status than themselves. For example, in 1991, 76 percent of the college-educated women who married chose men of comparable or higher educational attainment, whereas only 55 percent of male university graduates married women of comparable educational status. The tendency for Singapore's women managers to marry men with at least the same level of education was also reported in the Asian Institute of Management's study (12). Despite the "matchmaking" efforts of the government-sponsored Social Development Unit, one inevitable emerging phenomenon in Singapore appears to be the increasing number of single women. As predicted by the Population Planning Unit, between 15 and 20 percent of Singapore women will remain single all their lives.

Failure to locate suitable marital partners may be contributing to the emergence of culturally "deviant" behavior, such as couples cohabiting without marrying each other or putting off marriage registration until they are ready to have children (34). There are also isolated incidents of financially independent women experimenting with single parenthood. For the majority of women professionals, efforts to locate potential marital partners may become an important agenda in the early stages of their careers, even at the expense of their career progress.

Single parent families and aging parents   Marital breakup grew markedly in Singapore during the past decade, from 1,025 divorces in 1978 to 4,419 in 1991. Sixty percent of the divorces were petitioned by women. Couples between the ages of 25 and 34 were at highest risk of divorce, with 40 percent of divorces occurring prior to the tenth year of marriage (20).

The problem of separation is aggravated when one party then has to head a family with young children. In Singapore, there are approximately 13,000 single parents, the vast majority of whom are women with school-aged children between six and sixteen. Many single mothers turn to parents, siblings, and other relatives for financial assistance, advice, and help with housework and childcare. However, in some families the women do not seek help or such help is not available. In other families, relatives shy away from divorcees, unwed mothers and even widows to avoid the social stigma. In other families, help is unavailable due to family conflicts. In still other families, the single parent refuses to accept help out of a sense of pride or a fear of losing face or losing control of childrearing. In addition to parenting worries, single parents must cope with legal problems, loneliness, and the financial burden of being the sole breadwinner. At present, 21 percent, or around 2,800 working women with secondary education or above, are single parents. Depending on the individual woman's achievement needs and determination to succeed, single parenthood can serve either as a stumbling block or as a special incentive to her career advancement (32).

Singapore, though modernized, continues to be based on Asian cultural values, including the belief that it is the family's responsibility to care for the young and the ailing elderly. Due to delayed marriage and an extended life span, many people in their thirties to fifties have joined the "sandwich" generation, looking after their aging parents as well as their own children. At present, 9 percent of the population is over 65 years old: over 92 percent of them are physically healthy. It is projected, however, that with the current population growth rate, one-quarter of the population will be above 60 years old by the year 2030.

As more working adults in Singapore care for their sick and aging parents, reports of financial, physical, and emotional stress increase. Providing help with daily activities, such as dressing, feeding, walking, and bathing the sick and elderly, and providing total nursing care for the bedridden, continue to be considered the duties of women, whether or not they have a career. The caring daughter, whether single or married, often has to change her life-style to meet the needs of the ailing elderly by keeping her social activities to a minimum. For those who can afford to hire a caregiver, the emotional turmoil remains, with sadness, anger, frustration, and depression common sentiments. Placing their parents in nursing homes or daycare centers burdens women not only financially but also with a strong sense of guilt and anxiety, since such arrangements generally conflict with traditional Asian cultural expectations of filial piety (13).

To cope with these diverse social constraints and corporate barriers, women managers and executives must learn to understand their physical and emotional limits and to seek help from their spouse, relatives, friends, or professionals. The division of family responsibilities based on gender needs to be redefined. Women managers and executives need to make special efforts to identify their career goals, to develop achievable career paths, and to establish proper support networks for personal and professional growth.

At the societal level, several women's associations are taking a more active role in generating public awareness of women's contribution to the Singapore economy and of the problems inherent in occupational and societal stereotyping of women. The Singapore Association of Women Lawyers (SAWL), for example, has compiled a number of booklets that discuss the rights of single and married women – including their property rights, marriage and citizenship rights, and punishments for sex offenses – as well as the labor laws affecting women employees (28). The newly formed Association of Women for Action and Research (AWARE) took one further step by launching research projects and holding forums covering important aspects of women's lives and experiences such as careers, portrayal in the media, legal status and sexual harassment.

The government, for its part, is increasing its assistance. Besides promoting and sponsoring quality childcare and urging employers to adopt flexible work schedules, the ruling party established a women's chapter to address societal problems faced by women and to promote the involvement of more professional women in public affairs. Granting legal status to foreign husbands of Singapore women and their offspring and awarding women civil servants the right to equal benefits are other goals that have yet to be achieved.

Conclusion and Future Scenario

A future scenario for women managers in Singapore may include the following developments:

- A gradual increase in women managers in all sectors of the economy due to women's increasing enrolment in university and colleges.
- More women administrators recruited into the public sector and sunrise industries. Women, however, will continue to occupy positions in the predominately female niches of these industries.
- A disproportionate number of women managers will continue to be single. However, with improved childcare services and the introduction of more flexible work schedules, more career mothers will assume managerial positions in the years to come.
- The traditional role of women as family-bound will continue to cause work–family conflicts among women managers.
- Barriers to mobility for women will persist in companies with predominantly male-dominated power structures as well as in traditional industrial sectors such as manufacturing, construction, marine industries, and oil refining.
- Besides working hard and persevering, women who formulate clear career goals and develop strategies to achieve them, who risk assuming line responsibility, and who actively solicit mentorship from executives will fare better in reaching senior management than their more traditional sisters.

References

(1) Arasu, Siva and Ooi, Suzanne (1984) "Women Who Have Risen High," *The Sunday Times*, November 4, p. 19.

(2) Aryee, Samuel (1992) "Antecedents and Outcomes of Work-Family Conflict among Married Professional Women: Evidence from Singapore," *Human Relations* 45(8):813–837.

(3) Aryee, Samuel (in press) "An Empirical Examination of Work and Non-Work Stresses as Determinants of Burnout in Dual-Earner Families," *Human Relations*.

(4) *Census of Population* (1967) Singapore: Department of Statistics.

(5) *Census of Population* (1970) Singapore: Department of Statistics.

(6) *Census of Population* (1990) Singapore: Department of Statistics.

(7) Chan, Heng Chee (1975) "Notes on the Mobilization of Women into the Economy and Politics of Singapore." Occasional paper, Institute of Southeast Asian Studies, Singapore.

(8) Chew, Anna (1984) "A Background Paper on Married Women in the Workforce," in *National Employers' Symposium on Working Parents: Work and Family Responsibilities – The Role of Employers*. Organized jointly by the American Business Council; The British Business Association; The German Business Group; The Japanese Chamber of Commerce & Industry, Singapore; The Singapore Federation of Chambers of Commerce & Industry; The Singapore Manufacturers' Association; and the Singapore National Employers Federation, Singapore, October 1–2.

(9) Chua, Eng Kian, et al. (1990) The Executive Women – Issues in Focus. Unpublished BBAIII student project, National University of Singapore.

(10) Deyo, Frederic C. and Chen, Peter S. J. (1976) *Female Labour Force Participation and Earnings in Singapore*. Bangkok: Clearing House for Social Development in Asia.

(11) *Economic Development of Singapore, 1960–1990* (1991) Singapore: Economic Development Board.

(12) *Getting to Know the ASEAN Women Managers* (1987) (Study funded by Canadian International Development Agency). Manila: Asian Institute of Management Press, March.

(13) Kong, Lisa (1992) "Caring Is Hard to Do," *The Straits Times*, March 14, p. 8.

(14) Lebra, Joyce, and Paulson, Joy (1980) *Chinese Women in Southeast Asia*. Singapore: Times Books International.

(15) Lim, Linda Y. C. (1982) *Women in the Singapore Economy*. Singapore: National University of Singapore, Economic Research Centre.

(16) *National University of Singapore Annual Reports* (1980/81–1983/84).

(17) *The Next Lap* (1991) The Government of Singapore.

(18) *1984 Graduate Employment Survey* (1985) Singapore: National University of Singapore, July.

(19) *1990 NUS and NTI Graduate Employment Survey* (1991) Singapore: National University of Singapore, June.

(20) *1991 Statistics on Marriages and Divorces* (1992) Singapore: Department of Statistics.

(21) Pang, Eng Fong (1982) *Education, Manpower and Development in Singapore*. Singapore University Press.

(22) Pang, Eng Fong and Sean, Linda (1975) *A Report on the 1975 Employment Survey of University of Singapore Graduates*. Singapore: National University of Singapore, December.

(23) *Report of Task Force on Female Participation in the Labour Force* (1985) Singapore: National Productivity Council Committee on Productivity in the Manufacturing Sector, January.

(24) *Report on the Labour Force Survey of Singapore* (1981) Singapore: Research and Statistics Division, Ministry of Labour.

(25) *Report on the Labour Force Survey of Singapore* (1991) Singapore: Research and Statistics

Division, Ministry of Labour.

(26) Saw, Swee Hock (1984) *Labour Force Projections for Singapore 1980–2070*. Research Notes and Discussions Paper No. 47, Institute of Southeast Asian Studies.

(27) *SCWO Salutes Singapore Women 1980–1990* (1991) Singapore: The Singapore Council of Women's Organizations (SCWO) Publication.

(28) The Singapore Association of Women Lawyers (SAWL) (1986) *The Legal Status of Singapore Women*. Singapore: Singapore Association of Women Lawyers.

(29) *The Singapore Women* (1988) Singapore: The Association of Women for Action and Research (AWARE) Publication.

(30) Singson, Evelyn R. (1985) "Women in Executive Positions." Paper presented at the Congress on Women in Decision Making, The Singapore Business and Professional Women's Association, September 22–23.

(31) *The Straits Times* (1992) "For Whom the Bells Toll," May 4, p. 7.

(32) *The Straits Times* (1992) "The Family to the Rescue," March 31, p. 2.

(33) Tan, A. (1984) "Women Urged to Take High-Tech Road," *The Straits Times*, November 12, p. 19.

(34) Yohanna, Abdullah (1992) "Singles Pairing But Not Marrying," *The Straits Times*, March 29, p. 41.

9 TAIWAN

Women Managers in Taiwan

Wei-yuan Cheng and Lung-li Liao

Taiwan is a prosperous island. It has an international reputation for its export of manufactured goods – from light manufactured goods to relatively high technological products. In the past four decades, Taiwan has transformed itself from a predominantly agricultural society to a highly industrialized society. Between 1955 and 1990, employment in industry rose from 18 percent to 41 percent of the labor force, and employment in agriculture dropped from 54 percent to 13 percent (see Table 9.1). During that period, Taiwan's population growth rate dropped from 3.8 percent to a mere 1.1 percent. Economic growth has been impressive, with an annual per capita increase from less than US$100 in the 1950s to more than US$7,000 at the end of the 1980s, while income distribution has been kept relatively equal by the world standards (37).

Taiwan's economic success is shared by three other countries in East Asia – Hong Kong, Singapore, and South Korea. Together these four are called the East Asian NICs (newly industrialized countries) and also East Asia's "four little dragons." People in the "four little dragons" share a similar oriental work ethic, labeled the "Confucian ethic" since it promotes "individual and family sobriety, a high value on education, a desire for accomplishment in various skills . . . and seriousness about tasks, job, family, and obligations" (25:121).

The NICs also share a similar economic strategy, referred to as "export-oriented industrialization," that is based on exporting light manufactured goods to stimulate fast economic growth under strong government guidance (1).[1] Exporting industries have a common characteristic: they employ a large quantity of cheap labor, mostly young women, especially in the two major exporting industries – textiles and electronic assembly.[2] In mid-1973, for example, women constituted 79 percent of the total workers in the textile industry and 66 percent in the electronic industry (21). In the three export processing zones, over 80 percent of workers were women (16). It would be accurate to say that the economic success of the East Asian NICs is based on cheap female labor. Small and medium-sized family enterprises account for the major share of export value. Although men head most of these enterprises, women secretaries who are fluent in a foreign language are in charge of communicating with foreign importers. Many women managers therefore began their careers as secretaries in such firms.

In the traditional Chinese society of Taiwan, a woman's primary role is in the

Table 9.1 Selective economic indicators for Taiwan, 1955–1988 (percentages)

Year	Employment by industries				Women in labor force (5)	GNP growth rate (6)	Population growth rate (7)
	Agriculture (1)	Industry (2)	Manufacturing* (3)	Tertiary (4)			
1955	53.6	18.0	(13.2)	28.4	**	8.6	3.8
1965	46.5	22.3	(16.3)	31.2	33.1	7.7	3.0
1975	30.4	34.9	(27.5)	34.7	39.3	4.3	1.9
1985	17.5	41.4	(33.5)	41.4	43.0	5.2	1.3
1990	12.9	40.9	(32.0)	46.3	44.5	4.1	1.1

* Manufacturing is the largest part of the industry.
** Figure not available.

Sources: 1. CEPD (1991) *Taiwan Statistical Data Book*. Taipei: CEPD.
2. DGBAS and CEPD (1990) *Report of the Manpower Utilization Survey*. Taipei.

family. The great majority of women who work outside the family, do so primarily to supplement family income and not to pursue a career. The proportion of women in management is small – approximately 8 percent – and has increased very slowly over the last decade. Nonetheless, the issue has recently become a popular topic for discussion. Interest was stimulated by a best-selling book entitled *Nü-Qiang-Ren* (*Strongwoman*) written by the woman novelist Zhu Qiujuan, who was herself a manager (44). Following the publication of her book, Taiwan's popular business and women's magazines reported interviews with many top women executives. Apart from anecdotal stories, there is little systematic information about women managers, and a number of studies of career women include women managers. However, from these sources, we can begin to construct a mosaic of the women managers in Taiwan. After a brief introduction to Taiwan, we describe the processes by which women gain access to managerial positions. We then turn to a microlevel description of four aspects of women managers' lives: their early socialization, the challenges posed by being a woman in a man's world, women's relations with colleagues, and the influences of and on family life.

Introduction to Taiwan

Taiwan is located off the southeast coast of China. Though only 13,855 square miles in area, it has a population of twenty million. Until the large Chinese immigration in the seventeenth century, Taiwan was sparsely populated, primarily with aboriginal tribes of Malay origin. China ceded Taiwan to Japan in 1895, after China's defeat in the Sino-Japanese War. Taiwan was restored to China in 1945, after World War II. In 1949, the Nationalist Chinese government-in-exile retreated to Taiwan after being defeated in a bloody four-year civil war during the Chinese Communist Revolution. The Nationalist Chinese government still nominally claims to be the sole legitimate government of China. Taiwan's rigid position on this issue has led to her diplomatic isolation and made Taiwan an international pariah as country after country established diplomatic relations with the People's Republic of China. The United States withdrew official recognition from Taiwan in 1978, but maintains a semiofficial relationship with the island state.

The Taiwan government has only recently adopted more flexible policies regarding China. It now allows Taiwan residents to visit mainland China and takes no action against businesses that trade and invest on the Chinese mainland. Although Taiwan is the world's thirteenth largest trading nation, it lacks international standing (2). It is neither a member of the GATT nor a member of the United Nations, and it maintains formal diplomatic relations with only two major nations in the world – South Africa and South Korea. It sent athletes to participate in the 1984 and 1988 Olympic Games under the banner of Chinese Taipei. Taiwan is a member of the Asian Development Bank, where, at its annual meetings, Taiwan's delegates sit behind the nameplate "Taipei, China." Taiwan's businesspeople carry their suitcases around the world regardless of the obstacles resulting from the country's diplomatic isolation and without the ordinary diplomatic protection enjoyed by most businesspeople of other countries. Over half of Taiwan's exports, however, are marketed through large-scale Japanese trading companies.

Diplomatic isolation does not discourage Taiwan's businesspeople nor does it seem to hinder Taiwan's economic growth. The growth has been based on three major factors: export-oriented government economic policies (19); American aid (24); and the culture, which includes a permissive folk religion that encourages economic endeavor, aggressive businesspeople, and an efficient literate labor force motivated by the Confucian ethics of hard work and achievement (said to be equivalent to the Western world's Protestant ethic) (25). A basis of legitimacy for Taiwan is its ability to provide a better standard of living than that provided by mainland China. Therefore, in order to provide jobs for the growing population, the government pushed forward an intensive industrialization program. From the 1950s through the 1970s, the government provided handsome financial incentives for investors and exporters, depressed agriculture prices and wages, and maintained a well-disciplined labor force by controlling labor unions. The United States provided huge amounts of economic aid to Taiwan. Before it terminated its aid in 1965, the United States sent a total of $1.4 billion to the small island. The amount was equivalent to about 6.4 percent of Taiwan's GNP over the period (24:38).

Government policy has changed gradually since 1980. It has relaxed its control over the market and labor unions and reduced its subsidies to exporters. One reason for the economic liberalization is pressure from the United States government for Taiwan to reduce its trade surplus. In addition, the government is reducing its political control. Economic prosperity has created a well-educated middle class and a favorable climate for political liberation and democratization. In creating democracy, Taiwan still lags behind her two neighboring countries, South Korea and the Philippines. Most people on Taiwan, however, are politically conservative. They treasure their economic gains and fear that rapid democratization might destabilize the economy and the society. Furthmore, Taiwanese export-oriented entrepreneurs, who face rising wages, the appreciation of Taiwan's currency, and shrinking profit margins, have moved their labor-intensive factories to mainland China and other Southeast Asian countries. Those remaining in Taiwan employ illegal foreign workers in increasing numbers, claiming that young Taiwanese workers are losing the traditional Confucian ethic of work. They base their claim on the fact that few young workers are willing to take low-paid labor jobs. Although the unemployment rate in Taiwan remains low, moving businesses overseas and hiring foreign workers in Taiwan's labor-intensive industries are depressing wages and may also lead to the displacement of indigenous workers, especially older women and men.

Thus the societal environment in which Taiwan's women managers were raised can be characterized as a politically authoritarian society with a mixed economy in which people enjoy the freedom to conduct business, especially with foreign countries.

Socioeconomic Factors Contributing to the Emergence of Women Managers

Open and merit-oriented education and examination system

Social interaction in China is shaped by networks of personal relations, or connections, called *guanxi* (22;23). The government bureaucracy is no exception. Promotion is based on *guanxi* (who you know and thus trust), as well as on candidates' performance. A universalistic merit-oriented system based on open examinations thus operates in parallel with the parochial *guanxi* in the government bureaucracy. Since the seventh century, the Chinese imperial courts have used the examination system as one of the means to recruit new blood into their administrations and to buy off the literati (41). The Chinese myth is that everyone can succeed through education (or, actually, through examination). A typical story tells of a peasant boy who studied very hard for more than ten years, won top ranking in a series of government exams from the county level through the national level, and eventually became a high-ranking government official. Once a person becomes a high-ranking official, other family members can benefit from connections with that person. Because the whole family and extended kinship group have an interest in it, the open and fair examination system is considered almost sacred in the Chinese society.

Although open examinations provide those without connections with a way to cross the threshold into officialdom, they *do not* give equal opportunity for promotion. There is a long history of competition and conflict between those who acquire a position on the basis of merit and those who make it on the basis of *guanxi*. The latter are referred to as "black" officials (*hei guan*). Only a few years ago, the press severely criticized the appointment of "black" officials.

Taiwan uses the examination system in areas other than government bureaucracy, including the admission of new students into schools and new employees into large, private firms. Because decent jobs require a university diploma, Taiwanese parents place great importance on their children's education.[3] Initially, parents only emphasized sons' education but later included daughters when education for girls was expanded, especially among middle-class families that could afford to educate

Table 9.2   Women as a proportion of all graduates earning bachelor's and master's degrees in business and social sciences and passing high civil service examinations

Year	Bachelor's degree (%)	Master's degree (%)	High civil service exam	
			%	Number
1960	36.6	*	1.3	3
1970	41.5	10.6	9.1	35
1980	45.4	15.4	26.7	456
1988	60.4	30.4	37.6	631

* Figure not available.

Sources: Ministry of Education, Republic of China (1961–1992) *Educational Statistics*. Taipei; Ministry of Examination and Recruitment, Republic of China (1961–1992) *Kao Xun Tong Qui [Examination and Recruitment Statistics]*. Taipei.

both daughters and sons. All universities, four-year colleges, and public senior high schools – which are more prestigious than private high schools – recruit freshmen through a system of joint examinations that the government administrates or supervises.

In 1988, 9.2 percent of women and 9.7 percent of men between the ages of twenty and 24 had a four-year college education (34). College students, especially those in national universities (which are more prestigious than private universities), come from the more economically advantaged families, either because their families can afford the costs associated with passing the highly competitive exams (cram schools, tutors, etc.) or simply because these families provide their children with better learning environments, allowing them to concentrate on preparing for the exams.

The exam system furthers educational disparity. Students from advantaged families are over-represented in national universities, where they pay lower tuition and fees (about US$750 for the academic year 1991–1992); conversely, students from disadvantaged families are over-represented in private universities, where they pay higher tuition and fees (about US$2,500). The government mandates the ceiling cost, thus limiting the competitiveness of the private institutions and preventing them from becoming schools for the wealthy only.

Women are concentrated in the humanities and social sciences. In 1988, 60 percent of graduates with bachelor's degrees and 30 percent of those with master's degrees in business and social sciences were women (see Table 9.2). According to the joint-entrance exam system, students are required to choose one of the three major fields *before* taking the exam – namely, the humanities and social sciences; engineering and the physical sciences; and the biological sciences. Business schools are classified as part of the humanities and social sciences and invariably recruit a large proportion of women. Graduates in this field provide the major recruitment pool for managers in public and private service sectors. Employment opportunities in the service sector have expanded rapidly in recent years. Women college graduates have an advantage over their male counterparts, who are required to do two years of military service following college. When a male graduate is released from military service, many of his women classmates have already had two years of experience in the job market while some have already earned a master's degree.

College women have a high commitment to the labor market. In a survey of 733 female and 871 male students from sixteen universities in Taiwan, only 29 percent of the women planned not to work full-time after graduation, 57 percent intended to continue working regardless of marriage or having children, and only 22 percent intended to discontinue working after marriage or while they had school-age children (43).

Women's entry into public service management has been greatly enhanced by the rules of access to universities. The government holds annual service examinations, that are administrated by a special branch of government outside the ordinary executive, judicial, and legislative branches. The establishment of the special examination branch, the Examination Yuan, indicates the importance given to open and impartial examination, free from intervention or any connection, for recruiting government employees. Since the majority of government services recruit from the pool of social science majors (public administration, political science, business) and most graduates in these majors are women (see Table 9.2), women have been joining government services in increasing numbers. In 1983, women constituted 31 percent of Taiwan's civil servants (12). Among those who passed the high civil service examination (gao-kao),[4] women constituted just over 1 percent in 1960, 9 percent in 1970, 27 percent in 1980, and 38 percent in 1988.

The high civil service examination qualifies a person for a government managerial position; it does not, however, guarantee the person such a position. In fact, most women who pass high civil service exams are routed to nonmanagerial positions for reasons well documented in the Western gender-studies literature (18;26;27). In some government agencies, such as the postal service, public health administration, and national financial institutions, top executives do promote women to managerial positions, probably because there are few equally qualified male candidates. For years, the Police Academy has recruited women cadets. A married woman police officer now commands a country police station, with a force of 30 police officers (30). However, women constitute only a small proportion of high-level managers, even though there are two women among the eighteen cabinet ministers (Economic Planning and Development and Health Administration). In 1986, women constituted 3.6 percent of all those in senior positions in the central government administration, 11 percent of those in middle-level positions, and over 70 percent of those in junior-level positions. Of the latter group, 58 percent were overqualified for their jobs (13). This situation may be explained, in part, by the fact that seniority governs promotion in the civil service, and women with adequate credentials for senior positions are relatively new. Discrimination against women also explains the situation.[5]

Industrialization and the expansion of the service sector

The export-oriented industrialization that led to expansion of the manufacturing sector employed large numbers of unskilled women workers. It did not, however, lead to women's promotion into managerial positions. Women's entry into management was brought about more by the expansion of the service sectors – government services, finance, trade, advertising, mass media – which recruit graduates from the humanities and social sciences, where women dominate. Taiwan has no equal employment law requiring employers to hire a certain number of women. Qualified women candidates are recruited to managerial jobs from an open and merit-oriented education and examination system, which generally does not discriminate against women. Women are hired or promoted on the basis of merit, although, in most cases, they must outperform men to get the same positions.

Two developments encouraged the hiring of women as managers. First, rapid economic expansion since the 1970s created a demand for managers. There were more managerial positions than qualified men could fill and the demand "spilled over" to women employees or applicants. Second, expansion of the service sector created "new demand" for managers. Many new positions were considered especially suitable for well-educated women. These new managerial positions are generally in such areas as personnel (to handle women workers), advertising, mass media, and research and development.

Women are also attracted to other professions in which discrimination has become less significant, such as law, computing, international trade, and architecture. The demand for professionals increased considerably over the past two decades, and with it the proportion of women professionals has also increased (see Table 9.3). Women used their education to create inroads into the professions. This, however, is not the case in management. In 1990, over 41 percent of professionals were women, but only 9 percent of managers were women; approximately 8,000 women were classified as in "administrative and managerial occupations."[6]

The most visible senior women executives are disproportionally found in multinational corporations (MNCs). Most foreign companies owned by overseas Chinese and Japanese are small firms where connections, *guanxi*, are important, but most Western companies are large MNCs that consider performance more important than connections. These Western MNCs recruit and promote employees based primarily on objective criteria and, therefore, discriminate less in recruiting and promoting women employees. Western MNCs and banks provide managerial opportunities for women managers, especially in finance, R & D, and personnel (15).

Table 9.3 Professional and managerial personnel in Taiwan (unit: 1,000 people)

	Professional Personnel			Managerial Personnel		
Year	Men (number) (1)	Women (number) (2)	Women (%) (3)	Men (number) (4)	Women (number) (5)	Women (%) (6)
1979	223	125	35.9	50	3	5.7
1983	250	156	38.4	71	6	7.8
1990	376	270	41.8	76	8	9.5

Source: DGBAS and CEPD (1990) *Report on the Manpower Utilization Survey*. Taipei.

A View of Women Managers' Lives

In this section, we will discuss three aspects of women managers' lives: their professional challenges, their relationships with male colleagues, and their family responsibilities. Since so few studies have focused directly on women managers, the reported characteristics are only tentative and therefore possibly stereotypical.

Professional challenges

Facing negative stereotypes   Even when organizations promote women on their merits, they face resistance to their leadership and need to overcome stereotypes about women in positions of authority. Few studies have investigated how men view women managers, even though stereotypes abound. An example of an extremely negative stereotype is that expressed by a professor who commented that women managers play multiple roles inappropriately: they play the wife's role with inadequate tenderness, the mother's role with inadequate kindness, and the supervisor's role with excessive emotionalism (3). Similarly, according to a report from the personnel administration of the Examination Yuan (13), many government agencies will not accept women high civil service exam credential holders assigned to them by the personnel administration, contending that women civil servants lack the capabilities for working independently, designing plans, drawing up proposals, and analyzing situations. Furthermore, they believe that women civil servants' level of concentration and motivation to work deteriorates after they get married. The report concluded that after marriage, women civil servants are only capable of routine work and not of taking major responsibilities (13). The news report presenting this situation did not mention that the administration would take any action to solve the problem.

Such stereotypical beliefs about women make it difficult for them to gain recognition of their authority. According to a survey of women managers conducted by the students of the Ming Chuan Junior Business College for Women, women managers complain about their lack of credibility in the eyes of their colleagues and superiors and their difficulty in exerting authority over male subordinates (4). According to the same survey, work and performance pressure for women managers is considerable (4). In a 1988 study, however, high-ranking women executives indicated that once they made it to a high executive position they no longer experienced either gender-related performance pressures or the need to prove themselves (38). By contrast, positive stereotypes work in women's favor. For example, because they perceive women to have good social and coordinating skills, organizations promote women into managerial positions to serve as coordinators between higher managers and workers (36).

Honor and duty   Financial improprieties and corruption are widespread among businesspeople and government officials in Taiwan. In a recent example, 80 vocational school principals were suspected of taking bribes from textbook dealers (39). Corruption, however, is not perceived to be a particularly serious problem in Taiwan. People generally hold a "that's the way it goes" attitude, even though conventional Confucian thought emphasizes virtue and uprightness in vocational life (41;42). Conventional wisdom considers the moral failure of emperors (their corruption and, in many cases, their concupiscence) to be the major cause of the downfall of dynasties.

The Taiwan government often reminds its civil servants of the importance of uprightness in business conduct, declaring uprightness to be more important than competence for important political appointments. Although it seems that no one takes the above statements seriously, an official or manager with political enemies must act carefully so as not to be caught or trapped by his or her enemies. In addition to performance, being perceived as honorable and of high moral stature by colleagues and clients is more important for women than for men to ensure job security (15). Thus women managers emphasize principles of upright and proper conduct and guard their reputation more carefully than do their male counterparts.[7]

Unfulfilled high expectations   As women, female managers are under pressure to show that they can perform better than their male colleagues. However, since women managers often fail to receive full recognition of their authority, they are frequently frustrated by their own poor performance as leaders. They often try to achieve high group performance and to make organizational changes, neither of which is easy to achieve. These disappointments lead many women to feel a lack of achievement and may explain why, compared with other career women, women managers' overall job satisfaction is low. Only 61 percent of women managers report feeling satisfied with their work, the lowest proportion, after social work, among the ten occupations studied (8). When asked why they were not satisfied, 35 percent of women managers mentioned "lack of achievement" (highest among the ten occupations), 21 percent indicated "dissatisfaction with my performance as leader" (second only to head nurses), and 27 percent mentioned unequal treatment (not including pay) (highest among the ten occupations). Women managers have an easier time with younger male subordinates, who tend to be more accepting of the women's leadership. Younger male subordinates can relate to their women superiors as elder sisters, thus justifying their subordination to a woman (38). In the family, a woman's authority increases with age.

Playing it safe in politics   Most women managers neither have a feminist consciousness nor participate in current social movements. Because they do not think they personally can change the status quo, they support or at least conform to it (38). A woman director of a Taipei municipal bureau warned women managers in an interview that speaking out about male–female equality could trigger antipathy (40). A survey of women's voluntary associations discovered that over half were only semiofficial organizations and most were inactive (8). Radical women's groups do exist, but they attract only a small number of followers. Of 540 career women, 60 percent noted that there was no need for new women's movements, whereas only 19 percent mentioned that a movement for women's and men's equality was needed in the next ten years. These businesswomen's attitudes were similar to those expressed by career women in other occupations (8).

Relationship with male colleagues

Women managers do not have an easy time adjusting to the male managers' world. Although they have good academic backgrounds, women managers lack role models. They must continually adjust and learn the norms of their managerial roles by trial and error (40). The gender-segregated school system keeps most teenage girls and boys apart in school. They attend separate junior and senior high schools or gender-segregated classes. Dating is discouraged, if not prohibited. It is considered a distraction from their preparation for the joint-entrance exams for senior high school and university.

Deprivation of ordinary interaction with the opposite sex during the formative years introduces additional tension in the relationship between women and men managers. The culture, which keeps women and men in separate worlds, also hinders businesswomen and businessmen from interacting in professional and business relationships. "Men can be very buddy-buddy and can go to a club and have a drink, but I never do that," reported a woman computer sales manager (29). The feeling of lacking close ties with male colleagues is typical. Since women and men have different life experiences, they have few topics in common. When male strangers first meet, their military experience becomes the most popular opening topic of conversation. When women strangers first meet, they also have no difficulty finding common interests. However, there is no common topic when a woman manager finds herself the only woman among a group of male managers. Many women managers do not like the sexual joking men take part in at informal gatherings.

Women managers are also excluded from the "wine houses" (playboy-style restaurants), where Taiwan businessmen often go to facilitate doing business with clients. Under the influence of fine alcohol and the flattery of attractive bar girls, businessmen become uninhibited and let their barriers down (even if only in pretense), thus developing a buddy-buddy relationship (even if only superficially). In this way, they develop special *guanxi*. Women managers find it difficult to join such men's parties. The "wine houses" serve male customers exclusively; women managers are not welcome.

The same barrier occurs in universities. An engineering professor complained that her male colleagues liked to chat with her but never invited her to join their applied research projects and consulting work, thus limiting her influence in industry (20). Men managers play golf together, drink together, and join the same clubs to improve their personal ties and form alliances during their leisure time. In contrast, women managers spend their leisure time with their family (36). However, the lack of close *guanxi* also frees the women from involvement in corporate corruption, committed by colleagues with "close ties" and mutual trust.

The drinking subculture of the Taiwanese business world excludes women in another way as well. In both the private and public sectors, to "bottoms up" with a top leader is an honor and to "bottoms up" with your boss is a responsibility. After a heavy dose of alcohol, subordinates express, with dramatic displays of emotion, their great loyalty to their bosses. Because they are, presumably, partially drunk and unrestrained, their behavior is considered to be a sincere expression of their loyalty. The ability to "bottoms up" with one's boss is a necessary condition to succeeding in the Taiwanese bureaucracy (31).

Although women managers are not accustomed to Taiwan's drinking subculture and some may feel uneasy about it, many are also flexible, active, vigorous, and unrestrained extroverts, who can "bottoms up" without hesitation at business parties and can take sexual joking with ease. For those women managers whose daily work consists of dealing with people, being able to adapt to the drinking subculture facilitates their career. This kind of woman is labeled a "manlike woman" (*nu zhong zhang-fu*) or a "heroine" (*nu zhong hao-jie*). Women managers whose main responsibility is dealing with technical matters may be able to avoid this drinking subculture.

Family responsibilities

The traditional Chinese culture, which still exerts a strong influence on roles and relations of women and men in Taiwan, emphasizes women's roles and responsibilities in the family. The traditional Chinese saying that the "husband masters affairs outside of the family and wife masters affairs inside" (*nan zhu nei nü zhu wai*) is still the rule for the division of labor between husbands and wives, including working wives. This tradition discourages many highly educated women with managerial potential from pursuing careers and encourages them to choose occupations that require minimum interference with their family responsibilities. In one study, 85 percent of women managers agreed with the statement that "between the family and the career, the family is more important" (8:33). That a disproportionate number of women managers, especially the more senior among them, is not married is, therefore, not surprising.

One study asked 540 career women to suggest research topics on women's studies that reflected their greatest concerns (8). Fifty-eight percent of the women chose the conflict between their work and family responsibilities – that is, "how to take care of the family and have a job at the same time." Taking care of the family means different things to different working women, but most frequently includes childcare, housework, and dealing with both husbands and in-laws.

A low birthrate lessens the family burden of many well-educated career women (see Table 9.1). In 1989, women with a four-year college education had an average of only 1.75 children (35). Women managers usually hire tutors to supervise their young children's homework and send the children to expensive "cram" schools to improve their academic performance. Even with this support, the women still feel they cannot give their children adequate time. The lack of time to share and to communicate with their children arouses feelings of guilt among a large proportion of women managers (4;9;38). Frustration is especially great when children become sick, because women must usually interrupt their business to take care of the sick child and may also feel that the lack of maternal attention somehow helped to bring about the illness.[8]

Housework is a problem for women managers in the early period of their marriage and career. However, once they achieve a managerial income, they are able to hire a housemaid (quite often an illegal Filipina immigrant) to take care of housework, including the cooking (6). The proportion of career women concerned about the burden of housework among ten occupations is the second smallest among business managers (18 percent) and highest among head nurses (33 percent) (8). Forty-five percent of women managers report that they are not the major housekeepers of the family, while among head nurses the percentage was 33 (8). Women managers who still took major responsibility for housework explained their traditional choice in a number of ways (8). Some reported that they were dedicated to housework and were proud of their ability to meet its demands by planning and working efficiently. Others said that they did not trust their husband's capabilities in doing the housework and preferred to do the work themselves. In a traditional family, the wife opens the door and welcomes her husband as he returns from work. Since many women managers are still working when their husbands return home, their husbands must open the door themselves. Such husbands are called "key-carrying husbands" (yue-shi zhang-fu), and their children are called "key-carrying children" (yue-shi-erl) (28).

For many women managers, freeing themselves from some of the housework, getting recognition from their husbands and mothers-in-law for the value of their work and career, and simply getting their husbands to agree to take care of themselves has been a long and difficult challenge (38). Even when women can hire housemaids, other family responsibilities remain, such as taking care of children and the elderly. In-laws and husbands exert psychological pressure on women to perform their traditional family roles. One women manager reported that her mother-in-law still expected her to do the housework, just as if she were a full-time housewife. One way some women managers found to solve the "in-law problem" was to establish a separate home.

Even men who support their wives in a career usually consider their own work more important (38). Women managers who enjoy high status in the office often return to a subordinate position at home. As daughters-in-law and wives in the traditional male-centered Chinese society, they are supposed to obey their mother-in-law and husband. When women managers climb to senior positions, their work status spills over into family life, and their husbands' status at home is threatened. Some women turn their earning power into power at home. For example, they may use it to seal the complaining mouth of a traditionally authoritarian mother-in-law. Their income often makes it possible for the couple to buy a home. In Taiwan, owning a house is the goal of every family. Given the high price of apartments in metropolitan areas, a double income is essential in enabling working families to acquire even a low-priced apartment.[9]

While the wife's income solves some problems, it creates others. How to share the couple's income can become a heated issue. Many working women consider their income their own, to be used themselves ("my income is mine"), yet they still control their husbands' incomes ("your income is mine"). Their husbands may feel that their wives should share the economic burdens of the family ("your income is ours") (10). In a study of 396 married career women, 44 percent used the majority of their income at their own discretion (10). In Taiwan, employers transfer salaries monthly to employees' saving accounts, and account cards are in the employed wives' purses. Low-ranking salarymen receive a daily allowance from their wife for bus tickets and a pack of cigarettes (they carry lunch boxes).

The common practice for upper middle-class husbands is different. They accumulate their private savings by keeping (or hiding) their extra income (a common practice among women in traditional Chinese society in which the husband controlled the family income). However, according to the civil code in Taiwan, all property acquired during the duration of a marriage belongs to the husband. If a wife wants to keep her own property, the couple has to sign an agreement, authorized by a notary public; a legal action few couples bother to take. Divorce leaves the working wife without such an agreement in an unfavorable situation. Because of their high incomes, many high-ranking women executives have gone to notaries to separate their property from their husbands', so that their husbands have no claim to an equal share of it. If the couple has signed such an agreement, the husband does not have to take responsibility for his wife's debts.

The divorce rate in Taiwan is rising rapidly. The approximate divorce rate (number of divorces per thousand of population) was 0.8 in 1980 and 1.3 in 1989 (35), an increase of 63 percent in ten years. University-educated women have a higher divorce rate than less educated women. The higher rate, however, does not mean that the marriages of better-educated couples are less stable. When the marriage goes wrong, the better-educated wife may seek divorce; the less-educated wife, with poor legal knowledge, just runs away. Although the divorce rate in Taiwan is rising, it is still low compared with that in the United States.

Single women managers have difficulty finding suitable mates and often remain single (4;6). Most men prefer pretty women to smart women, and many men do not like women who are "too rational" (38). All married high-ranking women executives in one study had married in their twenties, before they achieved high career success (38).

Summary

Although the number of managerial women in Taiwan remains small, they are highly visible and more important than their numbers would indicate. The prominence of women managers is promoted both by popular magazines and by the few academic surveys focusing on this small minority.

The proportion of middle-management women in government services is definitely growing. Overall, however, few women become managers. Most highly educated women become professionals. Even when they are equally qualified, most women managers do not receive managerial positions when they compete with men. Especially when organizations promote managers on the basis of performance, women attain managerial positions primarily from the "spilled over" category (when there is no qualified man to fill the position) or the "new demand" category (when the position is often best filled by a woman in the eyes of the employer –

for example, as a personnel officer whose job it is to handle women factory workers).

Despite the prevalent influence of traditional cultural norms – which define the home as the woman's responsibility and woman's rightful place as being in the home – improved opportunities for advancement pull qualified women away from their traditional familial responsibilities. The tradition of free access to examinations and the subsequent use of examination outcomes for job entrance and advancement opens doors to women who are both qualified and highly motivated to achieve managerial positions. Because performance is considered more important in fields such as advertising and insurance and in traditional MNCs, gender has less influence; women thus have new opportunities to succeed in their careers.

Notes

We would like to thank Professor Dafna Izraeli for providing instructive comments on and patiently polishing earlier drafts and Professor Anthony Y. T. Wu for correcting grammar mistakes in the first draft.

1 See Amsden (1979) and Gold (1986) for Taiwan's postwar history. The Taiwan economic miracle is under criticism recently because the income gap between the higher- and lower-income groups has widened since 1980 (see Cheng (1990) for a comprehensive literature review).

2 These export industries thus promote women's labor participation. Women's labor force participation rate rose from 33 percent in 1965 to 45.8 percent in 1988 (see Table 9.1). For married women with children under the age of six the labor force participation rate was 44.6 percent in 1989. For women over the age of fifteen, the figure is even higher than for the overall women's labor participation rate. The lower overall rate is due to the lower participation rate for teenage girls, who mostly remain in schools. The labor participation rate for teenage girls was 52.7 percent in 1965, but it was only 27.4 percent in 1989 due to increasing educational opportunities for them (DGBAS and CEPD, 1990).

3 Taiwan's primary and secondary education systems put great emphasis on grades and examinations. They ignore the needs of those students whose grades fall below average and who are unlikely to pass entrance exams for senior high schools or junior colleges.

4 There are two levels of civil service examinations in Taiwan, the high examination (gao-kao) for middle-managerial or equivalent positions and the ordinary examination (pu-kao) for low-ranking and first-line managerial positions. A bachelor's degree is required for taking the high exam.

5 The increasing proportion of women in government service worried Premier Yu Kuo-hua who was reported to have told the legislative body that the government should encourage more male college students to major in the humanities and the social sciences (China Times, 1984). Women professors reported that they were not discriminated against in terms of promotion, salaries, and recruitment (see Hsu, 1988).

6 Since women managers are scarce in the sampling survey, their estimated number in the population is subject to sampling error, which could be large because the sample size of women managers is so small. It is too difficult to draw any conclusions about the fluctuation in the number of women in management in Taiwan at the present time. The number of women managers could be exaggerated since many women hold only nominal managerial positions in the numerous family enterprises in Taiwan. One of the reasons for

appointing women to nominal managerial positions is that in the event of a business misdemeanor being found to have occurred in such a company, the nominal manager (in most cases the wife) would take the legal responsibility and thus allow the actual manager (the husband) to continue to conduct business without interruption.

7 Corruption is not unusual among male managers, but it is rare among women managers. We suspect that the reason might be that women carry less financial burden than do men. For instance, many male managers need extra money to spend on their extramarital extravagances (a subculture of the oriental businessman), whereas women managers rarely do.

8 These feelings are shared by people in occupations that require long working hours and thus deprive them of family life, such as professional soldiers, policemen, sailors, and even researchers.

9 In the early 1980s, to purchase an apartment in suburban Taipei cost about 120 times the average monthly pay of a school teacher or white-collar worker. In the late 1980s, the cost jumped to 200 times. A popular saying states, "Marrying a good wife [i.e., with at least moderate earning power] can save a man ten years' hard work." In the 1990s, ten years is turning out to be twenty or even 30 years.

References

(1) Amsden, Alice H. (1979) "Taiwan's Economic History: A Case of Etatisme and a Challenge to Dependence Theory," *Modern China* 5:341–380.

(2) Baum, Julian (1991) "Taiwan: In Search of Recognition," *Far Eastern Economic Review*, 18 July, p. 26.

(3) *Central Daily News* [*Zhong Yang Ri Bao*] (1985) "Bien-qian-zhong De Nan-xing Zhuo-tan Pien-feng" ["Distortion of the Panel Discussion on Changing Males"], 14 December:6.

(4) *Central Daily News* [*Zhong Yang Ri Bao*] (1986) "Jin-guan She-hui Bien-qian Guan-nien Kai-min, Nü-xing Zhu-guan Mien-lin Ya-li Nai-da" ["Regardless of Social Change and Progressive Ideas in Society, Women Managers Are Still under Great Pressure"], 8 March:3.

(5) CEPD (Council for Economic Planning and Development, Republic of China) (1991) *Taiwan Statistical Data Book*. Taipei: CEPD.

(6) Chen Xiaojun, et al. (1985) "Nian-qing Zhuo-yue" ["Young and Excellency"], *Women's Magazine* [*Fu Nü Zha Zhi*] (October):13–34.

(7) Cheng, Wei-yuan (1990) "Economic Dependency and the Development of Taiwan: Cross-Sectional and Longitudinal Analyses," in J. D. Miley, L. Rappoport, and T. Ting (eds.), *Change and Development in Taiwan*, pp. 78–112. Manhattan, Kans.: Transformations.

(8) Cheng, Wei-yuan, and Liao, Lung-li (1985a) *Tui-bien Zhong De Tai-wan Fu-nü* [*Changing Women in Taiwan*]. Taipei: Ta Yang.

(9) Cheng, Wei-yuan, and Liao, Lung-li (1985b) "Tai-wan Zhi-ye Fu-nü Dui Jia-ting Yu Zhi-ye Shuang Zuong Ya-li De Fan-yin" ["Responses of Taiwanese Career Women to Cross-Pressure from Family and Occupation"], *Chinese [Taiwan] Journal of Mental Hygiene* 2(2):43–51.

(10) Cheng, Wei-yuan, and Liao, Lung-li (1985c) "Ni-de, Wuo-de, Wuo-men-de: Tai-wan Yi-huen Zhi-ye Fu-Nü Dui Gong-zhuo Sou-de De Zhi-pei" ["Yours, Ours, and Mine: How Married Career Women in Taiwan Share Their Income with Their Husbands"], in *Fu-nü Zhai Kuo-jia Fa-zhan Kuo-cheng Zhong De Jiao-she Yen-tao-hui Lun-wen Ji* [*Conference on the Role of Women in the National Development Process in Taiwan Proceed-*

ings], pp. 391–417. Taipei: Population Studies Center, National Taiwan University.

(11) *China Times* [*Zong Guo Shi Bao*] (1983) "Guo-zhen Qing-guo Bu-ran Shu-mei" ["Indeed, Women Are as Competent as Men"], 10 December:7 [Northern Region Edition].

(12) *China Times* [*Zong Guo Shi Bao*] (1984) "Gong-jiau Ren-yuan Yin-shen-yang-shuai" ["Females Outnumber Males in Civil Services and Public Schools"], 3 October:3.

(13) *China Times* [*Zong Guo Shi Bao*] (1986) "Nü-xing Zha-bie Dai-yu?" ["Female Sex Discrimination?"], 25 August:3.

(14) DGBAS and CEPD (Directorate-General of Budget, Accounting and Statistics and Council for Economic Planning and Development) (1990) *Report on the Manpower Utilization Survey, Taiwan Area, Republic of China, 1989.* Taipei.

(15) Di Yin, Shun Manpin, and Li She (1984) "Ta-men Zhen Shi Nü-qiang-ren Ma?" ["Are They Really Strongwomen?"], *Commonwealth* [*Tian Xia*] (December):16–27.

(16) Galenson, Walter (1979) "The Labor Force, Wages, and Living Standards," in W. Galenson (ed.), *Economic Growth and Structural Change in Taiwan*, pp. 384–447. Ithaca: Cornell University Press.

(17) Gold, Thomas Baron (1986) *State and Society in the Taiwan Miracle.* Armonk, N.Y.: M. E. Sharpe.

(18) Hennig, Margaret, and Jardim, Anne (1977) *The Managerial Woman.* Garden City, N.Y.: Anchor Press.

(19) Ho, Samuel (1978) *Economic Development of Taiwan, 1860–1970.* New Haven: Yale University Press.

(20) Hsu Tsung-kuo (1988) "Kou-luei Da-xue Nü-jiau-shi De Gong-Zhuo Shen-ho Shu-zhi" ["Quality of Worklife among Academic Women in Taiwan"], *Fa Shan Xue Bao* 22:177–213.

(21) Huang, Fu-san (1977) *Nü-gon yu Taiwan Gon-ye Hua* [*Women Workers and the Industrialization in Postwar Taiwan*]. Taipei: Cowboy Publishing Company.

(22) Hwang, Kwang-kuo (1987) "Face and Favor: The Chinese Power Game," *American Journal of Sociology* 92:944–977.

(23) Hwang, Kwang-kuo (1990) "Modernization of the Chinese Family Business," *International Journal of Psychology* 25:593–618.

(24) Jacoby, Neil H. (1966) *U.S. Aid to Taiwan.* New York: Praeger.

(25) Kahn, Herman (1979) *World Economic Development: 1979 and Beyond.* New York: Free Press.

(26) Kanter, Rosabeth Moss (1977a) "Some Effects of Proportions on Group Life: Skewed Sex Ratios and Responses to Token Women," *American Journal of Sociology* 82:965–990.

(27) Kanter, Rosabeth Moss (1977b) *Men and Women of the Corporation.* New York: Basic Books.

(28) Lin Shiuyin (1985) "Gia You Yue-shi Zhang-fu" ["Having A Key-Carrying Husband at Home"], *Women's Magazine* [*Fu Lü Zha Zhi*] (August):21–23.

(29) Lo, Dolly Tai-lan (ed.) (1985) *Images of the Phoenix: Interview with Career Women in Taiwan.* Taipei: Awakening Magazine.

(30) *Ming Shen Bao* (1990) "Guo-luei Sou-wei Nü-xing Fen-zhu-so Zhang: Zhai Xiufan" ["First Female Head of Police Station: Zhai Xiufan"], July 11, p. 22.

(31) *Ming Shen Bao* (1991) "He-giou Wen-hua Dai Gai-gin" ["Drinking Culture Needs Improvement"], August 4, p. 15.

(32) Ministry of Education, Republic of China (1961–1992) *Educational Statistics.* Taipei.

(33) Ministry of Examination and Recruitment, Republic of China (1961–1992) *Kao Xun Tong Qui* [*Examination and Recruitment Statistics*]. Taipei.

(34) Ministry of the Interior, Republic of China (1989) *1988 Taiwan Fukien Demographic Fact Book*. Taipei.

(35) Ministry of the Interior, Republic of China (1990) *Taiwan Demographic Quarterly* (March).

(36) Peng Huaizhen (1982) "Nü-zhu-guan De Xin-lu-li-chen" ["Mental Process of Women Managers"], *China Times Magazine* [*Shi-Bao Zha-Zhi*], March 7–13:31–5.

(37) Ranis, Gustav (1978) "Equity with Growth in Taiwan: How 'Special" Is the 'Special Case'?" *World Development* 6:397–409.

(38) Tang, Wen-huei (1988) "Gao-zhi-ye Chen-jiu Fu-nü De Gia-ting Yu Shi-ye: Yi Gong-shang Qi-ye Nü-xing Jing-li-ren Wei-li" ["The Families and Careers of High Achieving Women: Cases of High Women Business Executives"]. Master's thesis, Graduate Institute of Sociology, National Taiwan University.

(39) *United Daily News* [*Nien He Bao*] (1991) "Xiao-yuan Tan-du-an Uan-cheng Diao-cha" ["Investigation for Campus Corruption Completed"], August 17:i.

(40) Wang Mei (1986) "Nü-qiang-ren Shi Pei-Jiao?" ["Do Strong Women Play Supporting Roles?"], *Leader* [*Tong Ling*] (February):14–24.

(41) Weber, Max (1951) *The Religion of China*. New York: Free Press.

(42) Yang, Martin M. C. (1971) *Chinese Social Structure*. Taipei: The National Book Company.

(43) Yeh Shaokuo (1986) *Da-xue-shen De Nü-xing Jiao-she Tai-du Yu Xiang-guan Yin-shu Yen-jiu* [*Attitudes of Female University Students toward Female Roles and Related Attributes*]. Taipei: Women's Research Program, Population Studies Center, National Taiwan University.

(44) Zhu Qiujuan (1984) *Nü-qiang-ren* [*Strongwoman*]. Taipei: Central Daily News.

THAILAND

Women in Management in Thailand

Sununta Siengthai and Orose Leelakulthanit

Thailand is still basically an agricultural society, with over 60 percent of the labor force engaged in activities related to agriculture. Thai women have traditionally worked side by side with their men as unpaid family labor in the rice fields and performed other activities related to agriculture. Since the 1980s, Thailand has been undergoing rapid industrialization. The agricultural sector is declining both in terms of GDP and employment, as women and men join the new industrial labor force (see Table 10.1). The process involves the growth of management and the emergence of a new hierarchy of skills and occupations that differs for women and men. This chapter focuses on women's role in management in Thailand. We first present a brief description of the cultural context and current economic conditions. We then discuss the status of women in Thailand with respect to their labor force participation and the factors influencing their representation in management. We emphasize educational attainment, as it is one of the significant factors opening up new opportunities for women as managers in Thailand. The chapter concludes with a series of policy recommendations.

Brief Description of Thailand

The Kingdom of Thailand, formerly known as Siam, covers an area of approximately 200,000 square miles (or 300,000 square kilometers) and is situated in the center of continental Southeast Asia. Shaped like an axe, it is roughly equivalent in size to Spain. Thailand is bordered to the southeast by Cambodia; to the east and northeast by Laos; to the west, north, and northwest by Burma; and to the south by the Andaman Sea, Malaysia, and the Gulf of Siam. The national language is Thai. Most Thais speak one of the Thai dialects, with the exception of the hill tribes in the northernmost provinces and the Muslims in the southernmost provinces. Previously an absolute monarchy, Thailand became a constitutional monarchy in 1932, with a strong centralized government administered by a council of ministers. The present king, His Majesty Bhumibol Adulyadej (Rama IX), acceded to the throne in 1946.

Cultural influences on women's roles in society

The dominant religion, Thervāda Buddhism, has had a profound and pervasive influence over the Thai culture, traditions, and way of life. Over 95 percent of the

Table 10.1 Employed women and men by economic branch in 1980 and 1988
(in thousands)

Economic branch	1980		1988	
	Men (%)	Women (%)	Men (%)	Women (%)
Agriculture	8,048	7,893	10,296	9,279
(includes forestry, hunting, fishing)	(67.8)	(74.1)	(65.5)	(67.5)
Manufacturing	1,036	752	1,346	1,114
	(8.7)	(7.1)	(8.6)	(8.1)
Commerce	881	1,034	1,344	1,552
	(7.4)	(9.7)	(8.6)	(11.3)
Services	1,017	869	1,417	1,598
	(8.6)	(8.2)	(9.0)	(11.6)
Other	882	107	1,314	199
	(7.4)	(1.0)	(8.4)	(1.5)
Total	11,866	10,657	15,718	13,745
	(100)	(100)	(100)	(100)

Source: *Labor Force Survey* (1989) Round 1. Bangkok: National Statistical Office.

population is Buddhist; and Buddhism is an integral part of national life. Other religions practiced in Thailand include Christianity, Confucianism, and Islam.

Traditional Thai culture requires women to be under the strict supervision of their parents and to marry men chosen for them by their parents. According to tradition, a "good wife" is one who obeys and serves her husband unfailingly in all matters and who looks after the children and other household responsibilities without complaining (14).

Thirty years ago, it was rare to see women in the business world. Traditionally, their roles confined them to caring for the home and children. Upper-class women managed all household affairs, including family expenditures. Among poor families, in which both the wife and husband worked outside the home, husbands usually looked after financial matters. Today's higher living standards and the subsequent need for women to supplement their husband's income has encouraged women to join the labor market.

Until recently, the Thai pattern of occupational specialization was patterned on a division of labor based on gender, with more women specializing in "economic-type" activities and more men specializing in "political-type" activities (4). This pattern is historically consistent and pervasive throughout Thai society, with its origins tracing back to the influence of Theravāda Buddhism. The pattern is as follows: in keeping with socioreligious norms, men aspire to become monks, an arduous undertaking at which only a small proportion succeed. Alternatively, men seek status through activity in politics, a sphere valued by Buddhism. The polity derives its status from its association with the king, whom the Thais believe to be a reincarnation of the Buddha. Economic roles are relatively unappealing to Thai Buddhist men because they represent worldly attachment, and as such pose a threat to men in their accumulation of merit. Thai women, on the other hand, are more open to economic activity since "if women 'sin' it is only to be expected and the consequences are less severe" (4:182). In addition, government regulations have barred women from important government occupations, such as becoming a district officer and, until recently, a judge in any other than juvenile courts (10). The primary rationale given has been the concern for women's safety, since these positions require traveling throughout the country.

Buddhism does not define women's roles differently from those of men, but it does specify the relationships among six groups of people of different status: parents–child, husband–wife–children, teacher–student, friend–friend, master–servant (employee), and monk–devotee (Buddhists). Thus, other than in social status there is no specification of gender differences. In Buddhism, mind is neither male nor female. Buddhism encourages everyone, no matter which gender, social status, occupation, education, ethnicity, or age, to learn and to practice *dharma* (the Buddha's teachings) so that they can attain enlightenment. Mind is the leader in *dharma* practice, not the physical body, which is used metaphorically as a place to practice. In the Buddha's time, there were four groups of people who were regarded as supporting elements for Buddhism to stand the test of time. These were male monks (*bhikshu*), female monks (*bhikshunī*), male supporters who led mundane lives (*ubāsaka*), and female supporters who also led mundane lives with their families (*ubāsikā*). Whereas the monkhood does not officially exclude women, women at the time of the Lord Buddha could not stand the test of the 227 restrictions on mundane practices required for monkhood. Although a few old women were ordained as monks in the Buddha's time, since then women have not been ordained as monks (*bhiksunī*). Thai Buddhists believe that many women achieved enlightenment during the Buddha's time and that this is still possible today. Although viewing women as second-class citizens is foreign to Buddhism, it is, nevertheless, rooted in Thai folk tradition. Even though over 90 percent of the Thai population is Buddhist, women still play less important roles in the public sphere than do men (5).

Performance of the Thai economy

In the past three decades, agriculture's share of Thailand's gross domestic product (GDP) has declined, whereas the service sector's share has increased. However, due in part to the country's relatively productive agricultural sector, industrialization in Thailand proceeded more slowly than it has in other economically developing countries, where greater population and land pressures pushed people to urban centers. Employment data indicate that the service industries absorbed most of the employees lost from agriculture. Manufacturing's share of the total labor force has remained almost unchanged at under 10 percent.

Between 1978 and 1988, the Thai economy underwent a rapid structural transformation. With the industrial sector providing the major stimulus, the GDP grew at an average annual rate of just over 6 percent. Reinforced by a large inflow of foreign capital, manufactured exports increased dramatically. The textile, leather, metal products, and machinery industries expanded at a rapid rate. In 1988, the Thai economy performed well beyond the expectations of many observers, achieving the most rapid growth in over two decades. Indeed, 1988 could well be regarded as a watershed year, as Thailand became a newly industrialized economy. Both the rapid expansion of exports, which currently constitute more than 30 percent of the GDP, and the accelerated investment are expected to continue. Proportionately in descending order, more men tend to be employers in agriculture, manufacturing, commerce, and construction; whereas more women tend to be employers in agriculture, services, commerce, and manufacturing.

In the past, the manufacturing sector concentrated primarily on consumer goods and the processing of primary products, with the contribution of intermediate and capital goods to manufacturing output remaining rather small. Continued rapid growth of labor-intensive industries, such as textiles and clothing, is expected to increase demand for women entrants into the labor force; most, however, are expected to be assigned to routine, semiskilled, poorly paid jobs, with few opportunities for promotion beyond the level of first-line supervisor.

As the industrialization process continues, larger operations are replacing home or cottage industries. Foreign investment is rising, both in the form of foreign-owned operations and joint ventures with Thai partners. Between 1980 and 1988, the share of foreign direct investment in gross, fixed capital formation increased from 2 percent to more than 7 percent, with foreign businesses tending to be large and aimed primarily at exporting (3).

Large firms generally require their professional managers to have either higher education or prior experience in business administration. Such firms occasionally provide on-the-job training but usually only as a supplement to prior education and experience. Thus, women can enter the managerial recruitment pool for large firms either by obtaining a formal business administration education, a route that is equally accessible to both women and men, or by acquiring actual management experience, which is more difficult for women to obtain. In comparison to Japanese firms, the majority of Thai firms do not invest in on-the-job training and very rarely invest in training women.

Women in Development: A Policy Perspective

The development of women as a human resource was included as part of national planning for the first time in the Fourth Development Plan (1977–1981). The plan observed that boys had greater educational opportunities than girls and that women were discriminated against in employment, career advancement, and wages. It proposed a number of remedial measures, including nonformal education and training, especially in rural areas, equality of employment conditions in government service, and legal reform and enforcement. The national budget for education, however, remained low compared to the monies allocated for other sectors. For the first time in 1992, the national budget proposed to allocate a larger share for education than in the past and even a little more than that proposed for the Ministry of Defense.

In the fifth national five-year plan (1982–1988), the government identified women as one of the special target groups and specified certain groups of women to receive specific benefits, mainly those in vocational training, education, and health.

These plans reflect the concerns of women's groups and organizations. The Long-Term Women's Development Plan (1982–2001), designed to underlie subsequent five-year development plans, is more far-reaching and ambitious. It offers an array of indicators to measure women's development, which the fifth five-year plan lacked. However, the government has not implemented many of the recommendations, and therefore the targets have not yet been reached.

Women in the Labor Force

Women's participation in the civilian labor force has always been high and stable. Women constitute half of the Thai population and 41 percent of employed Thais (8). The rapid economic expansion in the 1970s encouraged an increasing number of Thais to join the labor force, resulting in an annual growth rate of 2.3 percent in the 1970s. In the 1980s, the male labor force grew at a slightly faster rate than the female labor force, thus the proportion of women among the total number employed declined slightly from 47.3 percent to 46.7 percent.

Currently, Thai women are shifting from providing unpaid work within the family to serving as paid workers in urban labor markets. The shift is motivated primarily by women's needs to earn supplementary income for their families. In spite of their increasing role in the economy, Thai women still face many problems. These include limited job opportunities, a lack of job security, work discrimination, fewer chances for promotion, and family disharmony (14). Family responsibilities are not shared equally or adequately by men. Although some families can afford housemaids or part-time helpers, the majority cannot. However, women use other backup support, such as delegating some household responsibilities to their children. Social values and gender role expectations that require women to take charge of the household remain strong, and most women accept them without either questioning or demanding change.

Employers prefer unmarried women, especially for routine blue-collar jobs which require manual dexterity and pay low wages. They justify reserving better-paying jobs for men by claiming that women are neither as physically suited for such employment nor as geographically mobile. In times of economic recession, employers usually lay off women first, claiming that men are breadwinners and therefore should continue to hold a job (17). Employers pay women less than men for work of the same nature and quality (14;15;19). In addition, given the dual responsibilities of the home and workplace, women employees often lack adequate time to supplement their work with additional study and training. They consequently have little chance to move up the career ladder. Of the total number of employed women, only 5.8 percent hold managerial or professional positions, compared to 23.6 percent of the total number of employed men, thus showing the extent to which Thai women are under-represented in management (8).

Growing competition from men has diminished the opportunities for women who want to engage in professional or managerial careers in business. As family firms modernize and seek professional managers, the mere fact that a woman or man is a family member no longer entitles her or him to become a manager. In contrast to earlier times, when inheriting positions was the practice, female and male siblings today have to acquire both relevant education and experience in order to qualify for managerial positions in family enterprises. Because more men than women are attracted to the more lucrative private sector, men more frequently acquire the relevant managerial training.

The rapid expansion of government services during the 1960s and 1970s opened new employment opportunities for women. Public services required educated people to fill clerical, professional, and technical jobs. Competition was less severe for government positions, where selection is based on more formal measures of merit. In 1985, 46 percent of the 716,131 civil servants were women. Over 30 percent of women civil servants were classified as senior officials (2). Currently, the majority of those taking civil service examinations and gaining appointments are women. There is a clear trend toward women moving selectively into government and men into private business.

Factors Influencing the Scarcity of Women Managers

Thai women who become managers are generally well respected and successful in their work. Why then, are there so few Thai women managers? A worldwide study of women in management suggests that the barriers to women entering the executive suite are both structural and psychological (1). The structural barriers include legal, educational, cultural, social, and historical factors. The major psychological factors influencing the scarcity of women managers in Thailand include cultural and societal attitudes toward women, education, legislation, top management's perception of women, and women's own self-perceptions (16).

Cultural and societal attitudes toward women and their education

Thai women are still expected to be supportive of men, dependent on them, and subservient to them; to yield to the wishes of others, as well as to care for others' needs before their own (16). Many firms believe that women employees are more obedient, less rebellious, and more willing to work for less pay than men. They regard men as having higher social status and greater authority. Men traditionally gained power through the monkhood, political positions, the military, and high government service, all of which have been closed to women (4). Men retain these positions almost exclusively today. However, the growing importance of education and wealth as avenues of status attainment is improving women's ability to compete with men on a more equal basis.

At one time, Thailand's Buddhist monasteries were virtually the only source of semipublic education in the country, with only a very small portion of the population, mostly men, receiving any formal education. By the early 1900s, it was clear that educational facilities had to be drastically improved if Thailand was to modernize. Responsibility for education was transferred to the national government. Hundreds of young male Thais were sent to study in Europe as a stopgap measure while the government passed laws to reorganize and improve the entire school system along Western lines. However, the govenment did not enforce the laws until after the 1932 revolution, when it introduced four-year compulsory free education for all girls and boys between the ages of seven and fourteen. Since 1970, compulsory education has expanded to seven years. Today, the literacy rate for the country as a whole is almost 90 percent for men and 75 percent for women.

In 1970, more male than female students attended secondary school and university. Many Thais still held the traditional belief that women did not need to be highly educated because they would soon get married and have to take care of their family and household chores. In 1973, at the secondary level, 44 percent of the students were girls; and at the university level, 43 percent (12). However, by 1985 the gender gap had closed at the secondary school level and narrowed at the university level (13). Education is the most important avenue for women's entry into management. It is more important for women than for men, because men have more access to alternative routes. For example, among women managers employed by municipalities, 78 percent have higher education, 15 percent have secondary school education, and 8 percent have a primary school education or less. Among male managers, 61 percent have higher education, 13 percent have a secondary school education, and 25 percent have primary school education or less. Education is making women more competitive in today's job market.

Marital status is not a significant factor in determining whether a woman becomes a manager. Most women in Thailand continue to live in extended families; and married women still get considerable support from their parents and relatives, including help with childcare from parents, grandparents, sisters, and relatives. Although the nuclear family is gradually replacing the extended family, domestic help is available and widely used by married working women, releasing them from many household chores. Thus, women managers and would-be managers can significantly reduce their childcare workload, so that, among the educated, raising children does not present a major obstacle to pursuing a management career.

Legislation

The Thai constitution states that all people are equal before the law, a provision that has been used to repeal several laws discriminating against women. Although the Women Lawyers' Association has actively worked to bring about legal reform, some laws still do not grant women equality, such as those barring women from certain civil service positions and from entering the military and police academies (18). The Civil Service Act of 1934 provides that the head of a department may declare a ministerial regulation prohibiting women from doing certain jobs if the nature of the work is considered unsuitable for them. Moreover, enforcement of antidiscriminatory employment laws remains lax.

Men have always dominated the political arena in Thailand (18). Women's participation at the local and national level has remained insignificant. At the local level in 1988, only 6 percent (36 out of 6,599) of elected *kamnan*, or district heads, and 7 percent (385 out of 34,945) of elected *phu-yai bahn*, or village heads, were women. Since the first elections at the national level in 1933, few members of the House of Representatives have been women. In 1988, only 2.8 percent of House members and 1.9 percent of the appointed senators were women.

Women helping themselves

Many women's professional organizations support women's advancement. For example, the National Council of Women of Thailand acts as a central organization for exchanging information and ideas among women's associations and organizations in Thailand. It has 106 member organizations and over 500,000 individual members. Other associations include Friends of Women's World Banking Association in Thailand, Business and Professional Women's Association of Thailand, the Thai Association of University Women, and the Thai Medical Association. All these associations aim to promote women's status. For instance, the Women Lawyers' Association of Thailand, which was first established in 1947, has as its objective the promotion of women's legal education and women as legal professionals. A major objective of the Friends of Women's World Banking Association of Thailand is to promote small businesses for women. The association provides information on how to run small businesses and guarantees loans made by financial institutions to women for self-employment activities. Likewise, the Business and Professional Women's Association of Thailand focuses on organizing social welfare and developmental activities for women (11).

Top management's perception of women

Senior executives often doubt women's ability to combine the roles of wife, mother, and executive. They typically view women as weak, indecisive, emotional, dependent, and less productive than men and, therefore, only suited for domestic roles. These attitudes underlie executives' discrimination against women in the corporate arena. In addition to facing discrimination in acquiring jobs, women receive lower pay and fewer opportunities to prove their capabilities. The average wage of women in the private sector is about two-thirds that of men (7). In addition, women at the lower corporate levels are less likely to be assigned challenging jobs and have fewer opportunities for realizing both their potential and actual abilities. For example, in a study of life satisfaction, 103 nonmanagerial/nonprofessional Thai women reported being less satisfied with opportunities to prove their abilities than were comparable men (9).

Self-perception of women

On one hand, it is the rare woman in Thailand who does not believe that she is at least equal to her husband or to any other man. On the other hand, Thai women often internalize the popular stereotype of themselves as dependent, passive, and emotional – self-concepts that may obstruct their advancement in the occupational world. In a study evaluating women employees' managerial competence – including their ability to supervise, coordinate, show initiative, act cleverly, and handle crisis situations – very few of the 225 managers surveyed believed that women had the requisite managerial competencies (14).[1] However, women holding supervisory positions in finance or commerce evaluated themselves as having equal or more ability to coordinate than men, while estimating their initiative and cleverness less highly. In a slightly confusing result, the women supervisors described women as less able to handle crises than men, while simultaneously believing that women's tolerance for pressure was equal to or greater than that of men.

All surveyed women, including supervisors, reported having fewer opportunities for career advancement than men (14). Likewise, all women, except those in finance or commerce, believed that women with high work status are given less social recognition than men. These attitudes discourage women from developing stronger achievement motivation and from working toward achieving higher work status. A study found that women and men generally hold similar values and attitudes. Women, however, tend to emphasize love, family, and mutual help, whereas men tend to emphasize achievement, knowledge seeking, freedom, and equality (6).

Rapid economic development in the last two decades has brought an impressive increase in the number of managers, including women managers. Between 1974 and 1989, Thailand's GNP grew from 271,002 million to 1,752,574 million baht (approximately US$10,840 million to US$70,103 million) at current market prices, and the number of managers increased from some 15,000 to almost 160,000. The rate of increase of women managers was faster than that of male managers, so that the proportion of women among all managers grew from an average of 10 percent for the period 1971 to 1976 to over 20 percent after 1985. By 1989, approximately 28,300 women and 125,900 men were classified as managers (8).

The number of Thai women in management will probably continue to grow, provided the Thai economy continues to expand. Economic growth would increase the need for managers to run the new and growing businesses. Women should gain a greater share of managerial positions, given the increasing number of women motivated and educated appropriately for management and expecting to capitalize on their investment. However, economic growth is not assured. The 1991 oil crisis, caused by the disputes between Iraq and Kuwait, affected the Thai economy as well as the world economy. Then, in February 1991, Thailand experienced a *coup d'état* that created turmoil and caused a slowing of economic growth. However, in the general election held on September 13, 1992, fifteen out of the 360 members of parliament elected to the House of Representatives were women, the highest number ever. The stability of this newly elected government should enhance Thailand's economic growth.

Policy Recommendations

The Thai economy as a whole will not be competitive if it does not fully and effectively utilize all its human resources, regardless of gender. Thai women are a potential human resource, and they can contribute to the social and economic development of the country, provided current obstacles are overcome. To this end, we propose the following policy recommendations:

First, Thai women need to realize their own potential for contributing not only to their families but also to the economic and social development of the nation. To fully use their untapped potential, Thai women must take more initiative and be more active and enthusiastic in their self-development, work, and society.

Second, employers need to recognize Thai women's potential and eliminate inequality in hiring practices and wages. Many managers argue against promoting women because of limitations placed on women traveling away from home, thus preventing them from taking assignments elsewhere in the country. However, if the infrastructure and transportation systems are improved and if the family division of labor becomes more equitable, these limitations would be mitigated and managers would be less able to make such claims. Government investment in improving the infrastructure and transportation systems would not only increase labor mobility across the country for all employees, and particularly for women, but it would also enhance economic growth.

Third, entrepreneurship for Thai women should be promoted. The Thai government should grant special assistance to women entrepreneurs, such as long-term, low-interest loans, with flexible collateral requirements, accompanied by training and consulting services.

Fourth, the government should remove legal inequities between women and men. Such policy level changes in the legal structure would signal increased opportunities for women to realize their potential.

Fifth, the government should provide more training and retraining programs for women returning to the workforce after a period of childcare. Similarly, it should sponsor management training programs designed for women's needs at the managerial and administrative levels.

Sixth, organizations should implement policies to help women combine their dual roles of mother and manager (or manager-to-be). This recommendation is crucial for the nation to grow in a healthy manner. Until men share responsibility with women for nurturing and supporting their children spiritually, socially, and ethically, organizations must provide women with facilities to help them save time in other nonwork-related activities. These facilities would allow them to work and to spend quality time with their children. Needed policies include maternal leave with pay for longer than 60 days (similar to the leave taken by men for national service), flexible working hours, work assignments in the home, quality nurseries in industrial communities, childcare centers at the workplace, and incentives for quality kindergartens and primary schools in each business community, sponsored or run by the private sector.

The implementation of such policies and programs will enable women to play a more significant role in business and politics, for they have much to contribute and their voices should be heard.

Notes

We thank the NIDA Research Promotion Committee for partial funding. Thanks are also extended to Nancy J. Adler and Dafna N. Izraeli for their suggestions and comments. The responsibility for any remaining errors, however, is ours alone.

1 The survey included 25 selected enterprises, including four electronic/electrical firms, seven textile/garment firms, and fourteen commerce/banking and finance institutions.

References

(1) Adler, Nancy J., and Izraeli, Dafna N. (eds.) (1988) *Women in Management Worldwide.* Armonk, N.Y.: M. E. Sharpe.
(2) Civil Service Commission (1985) *Survey Report of the Civil Servants.* Bangkok: Research Division, Office of the Prime Minister.
(3) ESCAP (1991) *Industrial Restructuring in Asia and the Pacific in Particular with a View to Strengthening Regional Co-operation.* Bangkok: United Nations Publications.
(4) Kirsch, Thomas A. (1975) "Economy, Policy, and Religion," in William G. Skinner and Thomas A. Kirsch (eds.), *Change and Persistence in Thai Society: Essays in Honor of Lauriston Sharp*, pp. 172–196. Ithaca, N.Y.: Cornell University Press.
(5) Komin, Suntaree (1979) "Opportunities and Training for Women," in *Selected Socioeconomic and Demographic Characteristics of Thai Women: Country Report on Income-Generating Skills for Women in Asia.* Bangkok: Research Center, the National Institute of Development Administration.
(6) Komin, Suntaree, and Smuckarn, Sanit (1979) *Values and the Thai Value System: Tools and Measurements.* Bangkok: Research Center, National Institute of Development Administration.
(7) *Labor Force Survey* (1988) Round 3. Bangkok: National Statistical Office.
(8) *Labor Force Survey* (1989) Round 1. Bangkok: National Statistical Office.
(9) Leelakulthanit, Orose (1989) *Measuring Life Satisfaction in Thailand: A Marketing Perspective.* Unpublished Ph.D. dissertation, Indiana University.
(10) Meesook, Kanittha (1980) "The Economic Role of Thai Women," in *Aspects of Thai Woman Today*, pp. 7–28. Bangkok: Thailand National Commission on Women's Affairs, World Conference of the United Nations Decade for Women.
(11) National Committee for International Cooperation (1987) *Directory of Personnel and Organizations Concerned with Women's Development in Thailand.* Bangkok: National Commission on Women's Affairs.
(12) National Education Council (1973) *Educational Statistics of Thailand 1967–1971.* Bangkok: Office of the Prime Minister.
(13) National Statistical Office (1985) *Report on Education Statistics.* Bangkok.
(14) Raviwongse, Vichitr, et al. (1987) *Strengthening of Employers' Initiatives in Favour of a Better Integration of Women in Economic and Social Development.* Bangkok: Thammasat University.
(15) Siengthai, Sununta (1986) *Male-Female Earnings Differentials in Urban Labour Markets.* Paper prepared for the IIRA/WG/WDFM workshop at the 7th International Industrial Relations Association (IIRA) Congress, September 1–5, 1986, Hamburg.
(16) Sukumolnant, Somsri (1989) *Women in Development.* Bangkok: Mae Kam Pang Publisher.

(17) Task Force on Long-Range Women's Development (1983) *Long-Range Women's Development Plan (1982–2001)*. Bangkok: Kurusapa Printing.
(18) Thomson, Suteera; Sopchokchai, Orapin; and Charoen-Rajapark, Daranee (1988) "Thai Women in National Development," *TDRI Quarterly Newsletter*, pp. 12–17. Bangkok: Thailand Development Research Institute.
(19) Tonguthai, Pawadee (1986) *Women and Work in Thailand and the Philippines*. Bangkok: Faculty of Economics, Thammasat University.

PART III

EUROPE

11 FINLAND

Women Managers, the Challenge to Management? The Case of Finland

Eva Hänninen-Salmelin and Tuulikki Petäjäniemi

Introduction

Finland introduced universal suffrage in 1906, the first country in Europe to do so. Yet, despite women's early start in gaining a legitimate presence in the public sphere, they remain highly under-represented in management.

Finland, a republic with a parliamentary system of government and a market economy, belonged to Sweden until 1809 and then, as an autonomous Grand Duchy, to Russia. Finland achieved independence from Russia in 1917. In terms of its values, laws, and governing institutions, Finland belongs to the Nordic democracies (Denmark, Finland, Iceland, Norway, and Sweden). Its historical tradition and cultural heritage are characterized by the Protestant work ethic, political democracy, and a conscious attempt to build a welfare state. Finnish culture emphasizes individuality and economic independence, such that Finns consider it natural that every person should be able to support herself or himself. Finnish society is small and homogeneous, with a total population of five million people, a low birthrate, a low rate of immigration, and a relatively high standard of living. In 1986, the average life expectancy for women was 79 years, and for men, 70 years (36).

Finland shared in the economic expansion that took place in most countries in the 1960s and 1970s. With the expansion of industry, the structure of the labor force underwent rapid changes, with the number of employees in the agricultural sector decreasing and the number in the service sector increasing. By 1990, 8 percent of the labor force worked in agriculture (women 6 percent, men 10 percent), 31 percent in industry (women 17 percent, men 43 percent) and 61 percent in services (women 76 percent, men 47 percent) (10).

Education and the Labor Market

Education is highly valued in Finland and has always played an important role in providing access to public life (25). Among students in universities and vocational schools, women outnumber men. For instance, in the twenty- to 24-year-old age group, 17 percent of women study in vocational schools and 12 percent in universities, compared to 12 percent and 10 percent respectively for men (8). In 1988, women received 55 percent of the degrees granted by vocational schools and 54 percent of those granted by universities. These numbers contrast with those prior to the Second World War, when women constituted approximately 40 percent of all students matriculating. In the 1950s, women constituted 40 percent of all new students enrolling in universities. By 1972, the proportion of women among students studying for university degrees had already reached 52 percent (6).

Women constitute 48 percent of the Finnish labor force and the majority of wage earners (7). Of all OECD (Organization for Economic Cooperation and Development) countries, only Denmark and Sweden surpass Finland in women's participation in paid employment. In 1990, 64 percent of women aged fifteen to 64 participated in the labor force (10).

Finnish women have a long history of participation in the labor force. In 1890, in Helsinki, about 39 percent of all working-age women were in paid employment. By 1900, this figure had grown to 55 percent (22). In the whole country, 32 percent of women in the nonagricultural population participated in the labor force in 1900, and 39 percent did so in 1920 (17).

Women's entry into paid employment was not the outcome of an emancipatory struggle, but rather the consequence of public policies that took shape as early as the late nineteenth century (24). For a long time, Finland remained an agrarian society, with capitalism appearing simultaneously in agriculture and industry. Wood processing, the most important industry, was based in the countryside and relied on the same labor force as did agriculture. The need for a mobile female and male labor force was seen as necessary. From the 1850s onwards, the old regulations on trades and occupations were abolished. Between the 1860s and 1890s, a communication network was built, popular education and occupational training were established, central and local government machinery was expanded, and banking and commercial enterprises were established in the private sector. Finland's economy also needed women's labor in the service sector. From the employers' point of view, women offered an advantage over men in that they could pay women less than men. The proportion of women in the industrial labor force before the First World War was higher in Finland than in the other Nordic countries (24).

The great majority of women (89 percent) currently work in full-time jobs, that is jobs of 35 hours or more per week. The official Finnish work week is five days. Compared to the other Nordic countries, Finland's small percentage of women part-timers is unique. In the other Nordic countries, women's participation in the labor market is high, but 30 to 40 percent work only part-time (36). Part-time employment has not been considered as a means of either increasing the equality between women and men in the Finnish labor market or pulling women into employment.

A high proportion of mothers with small children entered the labor market in the late 1960s and 1970s. Women rarely quit their jobs because of marriage or motherhood. In 1989, 78 percent of mothers with preschool children were employed, and the large majority of them worked full-time (10).

The occupational structure of the labor market is segmented along gender lines (Figure 11.1). Segregation appears stable and so general that women and men

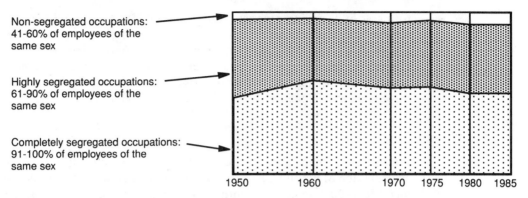

Non-segregated occupations:
41-60% of employees of the
same sex

Highly segregated occupations:
61-90% of employees of the
same sex

Completely segregated occupations:
91-100% of employees of the
same sex

1950   1960   1970   1975   1980   1985

Figure 11.1.   Distribution of employed men and women in nonsegregated, highly segregated, and completely segregated occupations from 1950 to 1985.

rarely compete for the same jobs (3;16). Only 2 of 10 women work in occupations in which women comprise a balanced 40 to 60 percent of employees, and these occupations represent only 7 percent of all occupations and professions (3). Journalism and architecture are two examples of nonsegregated professions.

During the 1970s, Finland, like all Nordic countries, set up a national agency to tackle equality questions. Women in political parties (especially in the left-wing parties), supported by women's organizations and the women's movement, demanded that the government institutionalize equality policies. The United Nations' Decade of Women, 1975–1985, created an impact that cannot be overlooked. By increasing information about women, the United Nations made women's contributions to society more apparent. Moreover, the economic boom, which produced a greater demand for women in the workforce, provided an additional incentive for creating equality legislation as well as plans for increasing equality in all areas of life (14).

Finland abolished all formal discrimination in laws and statutes. In 1987, the government passed the Equality Act, which requires that employers encourage both women and men to apply for vacancies, create equal opportunities for promotion for women and men, and develop working conditions suitable to both female and male employees. Employers have consequently become more sensitive to equality in their job announcements, advertisements, and reports. Although equality is publicly and generally accepted, in practice many difficulties remain. For example, the Equality Act provides no strong penalties for noncompliance. People who have suffered inequitable treatment must conduct their own case and prove that they have been subjected to discrimination. Overall, Finland's Equality Act seems to have had more impact on women's attitudes, making women more conscious of their rights, than it has had as an instrument for advancing women into management positions.

Equality of opportunity has not yet been achieved. The labor market remains gender-segregated, and inequalities in women's and men's wages and salaries still exist. Although a public agreement exists regarding the goal of equality, willingness to invest in achieving it varies, and disagreements concerning the best means to achieve the goal continue. Inconsistencies among the implementators of the Equality Act and other acts concerning labor market regulations still prevail.[1] Finland is currently revising the Act and has started a job re-evaluation process to determine the qualifications for and value of different types of work (specifically in three large municipalities: Espoo, Tampere, and Helsinki).

Family policies

Finland bases many social benefits on citizenship rather than employment. For example, the Maternity Leave Act of 1963 covers all women regardless of employment. In 1992, families were entitled to a total of 281 days' parental leave, with 80 percent compensation based on the last taxable wage or salary. The government pays a minimum allowance to students and persons with no taxable income. Since 1978, fathers have been entitled to six to twelve days' paternal leave with full pay at the time of a child's birth. Today, the 281 days are shared as follows: the first twelve days either parent may take; only the mother may take the next 93 days; and the following 170 days may be shared, with payment made to the parent who provides primary childcare. The remaining six days are for fathers only. Social security finances the system based on contributions paid by the state, employers, and employees.

Fathers' interest in paternal leave (twelve days) has increased slowly. In 1978, 12 percent of eligible fathers took advantage of the opportunity; in 1987, 35 percent; and in 1990, about 40 percent. Only 3 percent of eligible fathers used all 170 days available to them. The men taking paternal leave tended to be younger and better educated than other fathers.

Either parent may take three days' leave per year without losing pay to care for a sick child under ten years of age. For older children, the parent's sick leave is without pay. In most families, the mother usually takes these child-related leaves.

Finland provides childcare services for all children from the age of one. Under the Day Care Act (1972 and revised in 1982), every municipality in Finland must arrange daycare services for children under three years of age. The Allowance for Home Care for Children Act (1985) gives parents the option between home care and daycare.

As a rule, municipal daycare centers are open from 7 A.M. to 6 P.M., and provide meals for the children. Some even stay open for children whose parents work evening or night shifts. As an alternative, either parent may stay home, without loss of job, to take care of a child until age three. In 1989, 24 percent of eligible women and only 0.3 percent of eligible men used this right.

The proportion of nontraditional families – including both childless married couples and women living alone with a child or children – has increased (Table 11.1). The average family size in 1987 had decreased to 3.1 persons from 3.7 persons in 1960. By 1989, families had an average of only 1.7 children, compared with 2.3 in 1960 (10).

Among managers, more women than men live in nontraditional families. More

Table 11.1   Composition of Finnish families in 1970, 1980, 1987, and 1990

Type of family	1970 (%)	1980 (%)	1987 (%)	1990 (%)
Married couple without children	23.0	25.0	28.0	26.9
Cohabitants without children	*	*	*	9.1
Married couples and cohabitants with children	64.0	60.0	57.0	51.6
Single mothers with children	12.0	13.0	13.0	10.6
Single fathers with children	1.7	1.9	2.0	1.8
Number of families	1,134,778	1,218,392	1,243,976	1,364,312

* Data unavailable.

Source: *Information Booklet*, Central Statistical Office of Finland, 1991 and 1992.

women managers are either unmarried, divorced, or widowed (1;4;29;30;34). Despite the widespread availability of public childcare services, educated and professional women report having problems combining family and work (1;26;30). They find it difficult to coordinate the demands of private life (i.e., schedules for daycare and schools) and worklife (such as meetings and travel outside regular working hours).

However, women managers also view the family as having a positive effect on their work. Responsibility for children and family taught them how to work with a wide variety of different people in the workplace (1). Viewing the family as a resource for management is becoming one of the new themes in the study of work and management. Women and men in various interview and survey studies have pointed to the significance and diverse influence of the family on the career, for instance as mediators between private life and worklife.

Career Channels and Career Mobility

Women accounted for 41 percent of the upper-level white-collar employees in 1990. The proportion of women among senior officials and executives (such as CEOs, presidents, managing directors, mayors, and directors of state institutions) increased from 13 percent in 1980 to 21 percent in 1990. In 1990, of all economically active women (excluding entrepreneurs), only 1.5 percent were employed in management as compared with 6 percent of all economically active men (10). A major barrier to women's promotion is their absence from leadership recruitment pools (5). Based on their education and work experience, Finnish women qualify for access to the recruitment pools from which managers are promoted. However, not until recently have recruitment channels in business, such as head-hunting agencies, consultancies, and recruitment firms, paid attention to women as potential managers. Women manager's visibility in the flow of regular business information will increase organizations' interest in competent women and therefore women's credibility as potential managerial and executive recruits.

Table 11.2 Women managers in various institutions in Finland

Institutions/Organizations Area	Number of women	Percentage of women
Women members of parliament (1991)	77	38.5
Women ministers of government (1991)	7	41
Women managers in ministries (1989)	67	16.4
Women members on the boards and councils of the 100 largest private firms (1990)	81	5.8
Women managing directors of private firms (1991)	3,800	15.3
Women in banking (1988)		
– upper management	222	12
– middle management	2,027	45

Source: Databank on women in management, the International Women's Management Institute, Tampere; see also references (23), (31), (32); S. Hajba (1990) *Naiset suuryritys ten hallintoeiimissä* [*Women as non-executive directors in the board room of large firms*]. Turku: Publications of the Turku School of Economics and Business Administration.

Women and men generally work in different economic branches and occupations. Women managers are concentrated more in the public sector and men in the private sector. The managerial labor market is further segmented both vertically and horizontally along gender lines. Women more often work as managers in smaller or medium-sized firms (34), while men are managers in larger organizations. Women managers occupy lower levels in the organizational hierarchy, with men filling the topmost levels.

In the following section, we will focus on senior women managers as leaders in politics, central administration, business organizations, nonprofit organizations and as entrepreneurs. Table 11.2 illustrates the distribution of women leaders in different spheres of society.

Women Leaders in Politics: Parliament and Government

In most European countries, more women have advanced to leadership in the political than the economic sphere (15). In the Scandinavian countries, women's participation at the national and local levels of the political system has increased significantly since the 1960s and early 1970s (32). In Denmark, Finland, Norway, and Sweden, the number of women in parliament grew from 16 to 22 percent in the early 1970s, and from 30 to 39 percent by the late 1980s or early 1990s (32).

A number of factors explain women's achievements in the political sphere, such as representation, the election of individuals, and women's activities in society. A clear connection exists between proportional elections and women's representation (32). The Finnish electoral system involves proportional representation in multi-member constituencies. Each constituency elects a number of representatives (ranging from one to 30) based on population. However, candidates' places on the party list are not preestablished. Therefore, voters can vote for any candidate on the list. Individual representatives are then chosen from the party list in order of popularity (based on the number of votes each individual receives). Parties are represented in parliament according to the total number of votes their candidates receive in each constituency. Experience has shown that it is essential to have many women among the candidates; where there have been more women, more women have been elected. There is no quota system for women in the major parties, but in 1990 the Left Union party required a minimum of 40 percent of either gender in its decision-making bodies.

Women's success in parliamentary elections has influenced their appointment as government ministers. Each political party takes into consideration the fact that many women politicians receive among the greatest number of votes. In the current government, seven of the seventeen ministers are women. Their portfolios include justice, social affairs and health, education, environment, housing, culture, and defense. The minister of defense also holds responsibility for matters related to equality. The women ministers provide role models for other women in a variety of ways. For instance, the minister of justice completed her LL.D. dissertation while in office. Similarly, the minister of social affairs and health, with the largest share of the state budget of Finland under her control, gave birth to a daughter and then continued filling her responsibilities as minister, while her husband assumed responsibility for childcare.

Women and men differ in the issues they promote once elected as members of parliament. A study on parliamentary motions revealed that between 1907 and 1977 women proposed proportionately more motions than men on issues related to social policy, such as family, health, alcohol, housing and social security, education, culture, the environment, and consumer policy (28). Men put forward proportionately more motions on issues related to foreign policy, defense, crime and police, and development of administrative and political systems.

Women have expanded political discourse by introducing new issues on the political agenda. They have also strived to create new ways of doing political work. For example, women politicians and women's interest groups in Finland and Norway were instrumental in establishing equal rights committees on the local level. These committees introduced new issues and made novel proposals, such as equal pay for women employees in local government and alternative scheduling of meeting times. Issues of common interest to women, including concern for children, the sick, and the handicapped, unite women politicians across the political spectrum (27). The impact of these committees on the decision-making processes, however, has been limited due to their lack of permanent staff and financial resources.

Women Managers in Public Administration

Candidates with law degrees traditionally filled senior civil service positions as well as many other high-level offices. In the 1970s, the regulations requiring a formal law degree for senior posts were gradually canceled, and the predominance of lawyers consequently decreased. Today one-third of the highest civil servants and managers in the central administration (i.e., the ministries) hold a law degree.

The number of women among holders of a law degree has increased over the last few decades. Women made up 6.2 percent of people holding a law degree in 1960,

20 percent in 1982, and 28 percent in 1990. The great majority of women with law degrees are employed as public sector lawyers or judges (19;26). A study of the careers of 25 female and 25 male senior civil service officials found that although both the women and men managers held university degrees, the women were slightly more educated than the men (30;31).

Women give a number of reasons for selecting a career in the civil service. First, they consider a position in public administration to offer more security than an equivalent position in the private sector. Second, women appreciate the regular and often shorter working hours in the public sector that make combining paid and family work easier. Third, women value the equal pay and the better career opportunities and pension. The state pension policy has been more advanced than its equivalent in the private sector. The reasons men gave for selecting a career in civil service focused on their previous work experience and education, in particular, holding a degree in law, engineering, or forestry.

The factors women see as most important in helping them advance in state administration include their own competence, possessing requisite qualifications, pressure applied by the women's movement, and the equality law. Many also feel that the women's movement has raised awareness about women's invisibility in decision-making processes.

The top of the hierarchy (department head and above) includes only a few token women.[2] However, by 1990, at the bureau head level in ministries, women occupied 16 percent of the positions; and among senior civil servants in all the ministries, they accounted for 37 percent. Women are well represented in the pool from which persons are recruited for higher positions (30).

Among the barriers to advancement, women mention recruitment practices, nomination procedures, and the "old boy" tradition. The "old boy" tradition refers to the distribution of information, contact opportunities, and recommendations primarily shared among certain men. Women managers remain "invisible," even to their male colleagues, and are left outside this informal social communication network. The government nominates senior position holders, often on the basis of political party interests. Some women report having few contacts among top politicians. It should be noted that men also cited the politicization of the senior civil service nominations as a barrier to promotion.

Women Entrepreneurs

Entrepreneurship among women has a long and interesting history in Finland. As far back as the late 1700s, the widows of businessmen ran their late husbands' businesses in such fields as shipping, export, transportation, and restaurants (18). Among 350,000 entrepreneurs (including farmers) in 1990, 35 percent were women (10). The proportion of women entrepreneurs in various key economic sectors in 1989 was as follows: service sector, 40 percent; farming and forestry, 36 percent; and industry and construction, 14 percent. The majority of women entrepreneurs (71 percent in 1985) are self-employed or employ less than ten people (37).

As reported in many studies in Sweden (33), the United Kingdom (12), and Finland, the number of women entrepreneurs has increased during the last five years. Between 1980 and 1985, there were about 12,000 new women entrepreneurs in Finland. These newcomers have created businesses in areas such as public relations, communications, law, and other business-related services.

Finnish women entrepreneurs established The Federation of Women Entrepreneurs as early as 1945 to identify and to lobby for the interests of businesswomen. As of 1991, the Federation had 7,500 members. Women entrepreneurs also often belong to the Federation of Entrepreneurs, which has 93,000 member enterprises, 20 percent of them owned by women.

A study by the Federation of Women Entrepreneurs reports that the barriers for women entrepreneurs include conflicts between work and family roles, lack of credibility with banks, and lack of husbands' support (37). Women who had worked in business for less than five years also mentioned having too few social contacts and information channels in business life.

Women Business Managers

Little research exists on women managers in business organizations. A study of women and men upper-level managers holding business school degrees found that middle-sized or small companies were more likely to employ women managers (46 percent of women compared to 15 percent of men) while large companies were more likely to employ men (44 percent of men compared to 18 percent of women) (34;35).[3] Gender-based salary differences are considerable: 75 percent of women managers earned less than FiM15,000 (US$3,000) per month, compared to only 34 percent of men managers. Only 9 percent of women managers, compared to 35 percent of the men managers, belong in the highest salary category. Such pay discrepancies are partly explained by firm size and the high level of gender-based job segregation, both horizontally and vertically (35).

Both women and men say that the most important determinants of career success are related to their own resources, abilities, and performance (34). Over 95 percent of women and men cite "personal properties, hard work, own merit, own activity" as salient. They also consider support from upper management and their spouses as well as participation in training as important, but to a lesser degree. Few managers cite networking or support from outside factors, such as unions, other family members, or community organizations, as relevant. The greatest gender difference is that the majority of men, but only a minority of women, believe that their gender is a positive factor for career advancement: 84 percent of Finnish men consider "being a man" an advantage, while only 19 percent of Finnish women consider "being a woman" to be an advantage.

The industrial structure of the largest firms partly explains women's low representation or complete absence from senior executive positions in private business organizations. These large firms operate primarily in forestry, paper and pulp, metal, and shipbuilding, industries in which the few women that can be found work only in small and medium-sized firms. Although the proportion of women among the potential applicants for these industries has increased, the impact of gender-segregated education still exists. For example, the proportion of women among those with an academic degree in forestry has only increased from 1.6 percent in 1960 to 9 percent in 1990 (2;21). Women engineers are entering these industries in various ways – sometimes as board members and sometimes as directors of specific areas, such as research, strategic planning, or marketing – but these positions have so far not led them to senior positions in general management.

In banking, the labor force is dominated by women. Women constituted about 80 percent of bankers in 1987, compared to 58 percent in Sweden and 56 percent in Norway. About 90 percent (26,630) of the women and only 42 percent of the men, however, held operational level jobs (e.g., accountants). Men, by contrast, held positions as branch managers, lawyers, marketing managers, and chief executives. The proportion of women among supervisors increased from 40 percent in 1981 to 45 percent in 1987, and among managers from 7.4 percent to 11.8 percent (23).

The Union Bank of Finland, one of the largest banks in Finland, exemplifies the gender-based structure of the managerial hierarchy. In 1991, women constituted 27 percent of the managers (306 women), of whom 53 percent were assistant managers, 13 percent branch managers, 2 percent heads of divisions and assistants to general managers (hierarchically just under the board of directors), and the remainder were heads of sections and advisory units.

Women in Nonprofit Organizations

Many women's voluntary organizations and associations, each with its own aims and objectives, operate in Finland. Several have been innovators in such social affairs fields as municipal "homecare" (an occupation requiring a high level of training), health, nutrition, and the environment. Others have become experts in the political decision-making process. These groups mobilize voters, train women politicians, become involved in nominating candidates for national and local elections, and articulate new issues. Although others have called upon them for their expertise and they have contributed to the political decision-making process, women's organizations in the Nordic countries have little direct political influence (13).

In recent years, the long-standing and more traditional women's organizations have become active in advancing women's interests in society by cooperating across organizational lines. An example of such cooperation was the "one hundred women to parliament" campaign during the 1991 election. Many women's organizations provided a forum for candidates to speak about their programs. The campaign encouraged women and women's organizations to openly discuss the candidates and their issues. It empowered women as voters and as candidates and was perceived favorably among men. No studies exist yet documenting the impact of the campaign or of other unconventional methods used to advance women in public life, such as personal support, discussion groups with women politicians, and cooperation among women across organizational and party lines.

The contact network, known as the corporate system in the Nordic countries, consists of public *ad hoc* and permanent committees, boards, and councils. These committees and boards function at the intersection between the state, organized interests (such as federations of employers, employees, producers, and business organizations), and technical experts for the purpose of forming agreements and resolving conflicts (20). Organizations themselves recommend individuals as members of the *ad hoc* and permanent committees, commissions, and councils. The national central ministries or government also often nominate members. Members of these committees and boards become recognized as strategic elite individuals, who are in a position to obtain information from and disseminate information to each other.

The number of women representing the organized interests of women managers, and associations among these strategic elite individuals, is small, because few women hold decision-making or executive positions in economic organizations. The main actors of Finland's corporate system are the central administration, universities (of technologies), and economic organizations – all arenas in which women's representation in high-ranking positions has remained limited (20). Although women have a place in the labor market, albeit a gender-segregated labor market, they share little of the control of that market. Given this reality, it is not surprising that women have formed their own organizations that are not linked in any way to the central corporate networks (20).

In the 1980s, women managers, entrepreneurs, and professionals started empowering themselves by building urban networks to exchange relevant business and work information, form new contacts, develop new ways of working together, organize seminars and conferences to disseminate new research and create new opportunities. Some networks are open to anyone who is interested, others are by invitation or member recommendation only.

In 1988, a group of Finnish women managers, entrepreneurs, trade union leaders, senior civil servants, politicians, and academicians set up a nonprofit organization called the International Women's Management Institute. The idea behind the Institute was to open a public dialogue on the question of women in management. The purpose of the Institute was and is to promote a leadership culture by encouraging and supporting women to use their skills and opportunities to develop their work environments. The Institute provides information on women in management, consultancies, and training. It also follows developments and research on professions and entrepreneurship. The Institute is financed partly by its revenues and membership dues, and partly by support from the Ministry of Trade and Industry. The Ministry of Labor finances the special Service Center for Women Entrepreneurs project administrated by the Institute in 1989–1992.

To date, little systematic information is available about many of the existing networks. One of the functions of the International Women's Management Institute is to create and develop networks, such as the regional network of women managers in the Pirkanmaa district, which includes managers, entrepreneurs, and networks of women and men trainers. The Institute provides a link between the existing networks of women managers and entrepreneurs, while also cooperating with the women economists' network and the Finnish members of the European Women's Management Development network.

Women Managers: The Challenge to Management

Many similar factors influenced the progress made by Finnish women as decision-makers in parliament, as civil servants in central administration, as entrepreneurs, and as managers in business. These include women's historically long and continuous labor force involvement, political rights advancements, public policy support, women's high level of education and training, and women's own initiative and activities. These factors have empowered women as citizens to engage in diverse activities. As a result, the number of qualified women working in business, administration, and politics, in the positions from which private and public organizations select managers has expanded.

The substantial increase in women entering managerial positions during the past ten years has taken place primarily in industries dominated by women. For example, in 1992, a woman economist was appointed chief executive of the Bank of Finland. In a highly segregated labor market, few women managers work in male-dominated sectors and occupations. Segregation creates barriers to upward mobility and thus contributes to women's exclusion from positions on boards of directors, reduced nominations to chief executive offices in multibranch business organizations, and selection onto important corporate committees.

Women managers have established their own networks to overcome their isolation in the men's world. Women's networks have served as a forum for informal communication, support, and mentorship, as well as serving as a counterbalance to men's groups and clubs. However, women's networks do not provide an arena in which women managers can demonstrate their ability to achieve business results. For that, more women need to join powerful corporate networks and apply for senior executive positions.

Although women managers do not constitute a homogeneous group, there are indications that women are making unique contributions to management. Studies comparing women and men managers have found women managers' strength to be in their leadership style. The studies found that Finnish women tend to encourage employees to use their abilities, and to cut through bureaucratic red tape. To a greater extent than men, they do this by facilitating informal contacts between leaders and workers, introducing new working methods and training, disseminating information, and taking workers' views into consideration. In these approaches, Finnish women are challenging some of men's more traditional definitions of managerial culture, a culture which seems to have become dehumanized.

Many women managers in Finland seem to act like ambassadors who have been entrusted with certain discretionary powers and freedoms, but only within one organization, not between institutions. To diversify the management culture of the whole society, a "critical mass" (approximately 15 to 40 percent) of women managers is needed at each level of business and public administration, the same number of women as are currently in national and local politics.

Notes

1 The purpose of the Act on Equality between Women and Men, which was passed in 1987, is to combat discrimination on the basis of gender, to promote equality between women and men, and, to this end, to improve the status of women, specifically in their worklives.

2 The Finnish central administration, which combines ministerial departments and central boards, has fewer than 10,000 employees, whereas the total personnel in state employment was 210,000 in 1989. The minister, as the political leader of each ministry, has a staff consisting of a permanent chief, directors of central boards, heads of departments, and heads of bureaus.

3 The sample was picked from the register of members of SEFE (an occupational cooperation and training organization for those graduating from different business schools in Finland). The sample covered all female upper-level managers, top managers (213 in all, or 9 percent) and a systematic sample of 10 percent of all male upper-level and top managers in SEFE's register.

References

(1) Aitta, U. (1988) *Miesten ja naisten tasa-arvon toteutuminen akavalaisessa työelämässä [Implication of Equality among Men and Women in the Trade Union of Academic People].* Helsinki: Akava. Grafitex Oy.

(2) Akavalaiset [The Trade Union of Academic People] (1991). See also (34).

(3) Anttalainen, M. L. (1986) *Sukupuolen mukaan jakautuneet työmarkkinat Pohjoismaissa [Gender Segregated Labor Markets in Nordic Countries].* Tasa-arvoasiain neuvottelukunta [Equality Council] mimeo-graphy, Helsinki.

(4) Asplund, G. (1986) *Uran luominen. Miehet, naiset ja johtajuus [Creating Career Women, Men and Leadership].* Helsinki: Kustannusosakeyhtiö Tammi.

(5) Berthoin Antal, A., and Izraeli, D. N. (1993) "Women Managers from a Global Perspective: Women Managers in Their International Homelands and as Expatriates," in E. A. Fagenson (ed.), *Women in Management: Trends, Issues and Challenges in Management Diversity, Women and Work*, Vol 4. Newbury Park, Calif.: Sage.

(6) Central Statistical Office (1988) *Pojat ja tytöt koulussa 1987. [Boys and girls at school in 1987].* Education and Research 7. Helsinki: Central Statistical Office.

(7) Central Statistical Office (1989) *Labor Statistics.* Helsinki: Central Statistical Office.

(8) Central Statistical Office (1990) *Koulutus ja tutkimus [Education and Research].* Helsinki: Central Statistical Office.

(9) Central Statistical Office (1991a) *Information Booklet.* Helsinki: Central Statistical Office.

(10) Central Statistical Office (1991b) *Labor Research Statistics.* Helsinki: Central Statistical Office.

(11) Central Statistical Office (1992) *Information Booklet.* Helsinki: Central Statistical Office.

(12) Coffee, R., and Scase, R. (1985) *Women in Charge: The Experiences of Female Entrepreneurs.* London: George Allen & Unwin.

(13) Dahlerup, D., and Gulli, B. (1985) "Women's Organizations in the Nordic Countries: Lack of Force or Counterforce?" in E. Haavio-Mannila et al. (eds.), *Unfinished Democracy: Women in Nordic Politics.* Elmsford, N.Y.: Pergamon Press.

(14) Eduards, M.; Halsaa, B.; and Skjeie, H. (1985) "Equality: How Equal?" in E. Haavio-Mannila et al. (eds.), *Unfinished Democracy: Women in Nordic Politics.* Elmsford, N.Y.: Pergamon Press.

(15) Epstein, C. F., and Coser, R. L. (eds.) (1981) *Access to Power*. London: George Allen & Unwin.

(16) Haavio-Mannila, E. (1990) "Men's Work and Women's Work" in M. Manninen and P. Setälä (eds.), *The Lady with the Bow: The Story of Finnish Women*. Helsinki: Otava Publishing Company Ltd.

(17) Haavio-Mannila, E., and Kari, K. (1980) *Changes in the Life Pattern of Families in Nordic Countries*. Yearbook of Population Research in Finland XVII. Helsinki: The Population Research Institute.

(18) Hajba, S. (1988). *Naisyrittäjä menneiltä vuosisadoilta [Women Entrepreneurs of Past Centuries]*. Turku: Turun Kauppakorkeakoulun julkaisuja Sarja A:2.

(19) Hänninen-Salmelin, E. (1991) *Naisjuristit muuttuvassa työympäristössä [Women Lawyers in Changing Work Environment]*. Suomen Lakimiesliitto – Finlands Jurist förbund r.y. [Association of Lawyers in Finland]. Jyväskylä, Finland: Gummerus Oy.

(20) Hernes, H. M., and Hänninen-Salmelin, E. (1985) "Women in the Corporate System," in E. Haavio-Mannila et al. (eds.), *Unfinished Democracy: Women in Nordic Politics*. Elmsford, N.Y.: Pergamon Press.

(21) Ihalainen, R. (1987) *Nainen metsänhoitajana [Woman as a Forester in Finland]*. Folia forestelia 698. Helsinki: Institutum Forestale Fennia, Metsäntutkimuslaitos.

(22) Jallinoja, R. (1983) *Suomen Naisliikkeen taistelukaudet [The Campaign Periods of the Finnish Women's Movement]*. Porvoo, Finland: WSOY.

(23) *Pankkialan tasa-arvotyöryhmän raportti* (1988) [*Report of the working group on equality in banking*]. Helsinki.

(24) Pohls, M. (1990) "Women's Work in Finland 1870–1940," in M. Manninen and P. Setälä (eds.), *The Lady with the Bow: The Story of Finnish Women*. Helsinki: Otava Publishing Company.

(25) Rantalaiho, L. (1986) *Vocation: Woman*. The National Council of Women in Finland. Tampere, Finland: Aaltospaino.

(26) Silius, H. (1989) "I Athenas järnbur. Kvinnliga juristers arbete och ställning i dagens Finland" ["Athena's Irongate. Work and Position of the Women Lawyers in Finland Today"], in H. Silius (ed.), *Kvinnor i mansdominerade yrken [Women in Male-Dominated Professions]*. Åbo, Finland: Publikationer från Institutet för kvinnoforskning vid Åbo Akademi.

(27) Sinkkonen, S. (1985) "Women in Local Politics," in E. Haavio-Mannila et al. (eds.), *Unfinished Democracy: Women in Nordic Politics*. Elmsford, N.Y.: Pergamon Press.

(28) Sinkkonen, S. and Haavio-Mannila, E. (1981) "The Impact of the Women's Movement and the Legislative Activity of Women's MPs on Social Development," in M. Rendel (ed.) *Women, Power, and Political Systems*, 195–215. London: Croom Helm.

(29) Sinkkonen, S., and Hänninen, E. (1978) *Organizational Type, Women's Careers and Administrative and Political Involvement*. Grenoble, France: European Consortium for Political Research.

(30) Sinkkonen, S., and Hänninen-Salmelin, E. (1989) "Nais-ja miesjohtajien uran kehityksestä valtion hallinnossa ja sitä määräävistä tekijöistä" ["Career Development and Its Determinants of Women and Men Managers in Central Administration"], *Hallinnon tutkimus [Administrative Studies]* 1:24–52.

(31) Sinkkonen, S., and Hänninen-Salmelin, E. (1991) "Women in Public Administration in Finland," in J. H. Bayes (ed.), *Women and Public Administration: International Perspectives*. Women & Politics, Vol. 11, No. 4. New York: The Haworth Press.

(32) Skard, T., and Haavio-Mannila, E. (1985) "Women in Parliament," in E. Haavio-Mannila et al. (eds.), *Unfinished Democracy: Women in Nordic Politics*. Elmsford, N.Y.:

Pergamon Press.
(33) Sundin, E., and Homqvist, C. (1989) *Kvinnor som företagare* [*Women as Entrepreneurs*]. Malmö, Sweden: Liber.
(34) Vanhala, S. (1986) *Liikkeenjohtajien uraan vaikuttavat tekijät* [*Factors Influencing Business Careers*]. Helsinki: Helsingin Kauppakorkeakoulun julkaisuja D-80.
(35) Vanhala, S. (1987) Woman Manager and Managerial Career Markets: A Comparison of Male and Female Business Managers in Finland. Paper prepared for Den 14. Nordiska Sociologkongressen: Norden, Sociologin och världssamhållet [The Nordic Congress of Sociology: Nordic countries, Sociology and Society of the World], Tampere, August 21–23.
(36) "Women and Men in the Nordic Countries" (1988) *Facts on Equal Opportunities*. Copenhagen: Nordic Council of Ministers.
(37) *Yrittäjänaisten jäsentutkimus* [*helmi – maaliskuu*] (1989) Yrittäjänaisten Keskusliittory [Member survey of the Federation of Women Entrepreneurs]. Taloustutkimus Oy, February–March.

12 FRANCE

Women Managers in France

Evelyne Serdjénian

This chapter reviews the development of French women in management over the last fifteen years and relates their situation to that of women more generally. It identifies five cultural and social phenomena that allow women, and more specifically women graduates, to enter the job market and remain in it while still fulfilling the duties of motherhood: male–female role changes; the French system of crèches and nursery schools; the increasing number of girls in secondary and higher education; the European and French equality legislation; and the increasing demand for skilled employees. The chapter shows the relative advantages and limitations of these factors in explaining why most women remain in a situation of compromise between tradition and equality, in the workplace as well as at home.

After reviewing the categories of French women managers, whose numbers increased by more than 800 percent during the last 35 years (twice the rate of men), we identify two alternative types of managerial careers for women – namely, as assistants to men or as pioneers in positions traditionally held by men – along with intermediate strategies of compromise. We view compromise specifically as a woman's strategy that aims to make realistic choices in situations of inequality between women and men in the workplace, coupled with the difficulty of balancing work and homelife.

A lack of positive action on the part of companies and political parties along with a lack of pressure on behalf of women explains the perpetuation of the glass ceiling. The chapter concludes that for most women managers, equality of women and men is only a declaration and does not yet exist in top positions in management or politics. Thus France is, in fact, an unbalanced democracy.

Introduction to the French Environment

The proportion of women in the total labor force remained remarkably constant, at around 35 percent, from the beginning of the twentieth century until the French cultural revolution of 1968. Since the mid-1970s, however, two million women were added to the labor force, compared to the addition of only 143,000 men. By 1991, the proportion of women increased to 43 percent (11). Fifty-six percent of women aged fifteen to 64 are in the labor market. Women's participation rate varies with age. It is greatest among those who are 25 to 49 years old, 72 percent of whom are in the labor force (14).

In 1988, 52 percent of working women were employed in services, 35 percent in agriculture, and 24 percent in industry. The unemployment rate in March 1992 was 8 percent for men, 13 percent for women, and 26 percent for women between fifteen and 24 years old (10).

The attitude toward women's employment changed radically following the cultural revolution of 1968. At that time the traditional division of labor within the family came under public criticism, especially among the middle-class urban population which had weaker ties to Catholic patterns of life. Young women began wanting to have the same careers as men. Also, the consumer society did not give much choice to many couples who had to earn a double income in order to buy the many products offered to them. In spite of this evolution, salaried women in 1990 still spent two hours more per day than salaried men in family and domestic work (five versus three hours).

Career and Motherhood in France

The great majority of French women have full-time jobs. France has the lowest rate of part-time women workers in all of Western Europe: 24 percent, which is an increase from 16 percent in 1982. Employment, since 1975, is continuous, even after the birth of children.

The birthrate is low – namely, 1.8 children; and only 24 percent of mothers have more than two children. In 1989, 28 percent of the births were to unwed parents (as compared to 45 percent in Denmark and 23 percent in the United Kingdom), but 16 percent of marriages occurred after a child's birth. In 1990, 32 percent of marriages ended in divorce, with the divorce rate having tripled since 1968 (4).

Continuous and full-time employment is made possible by the French system of subsidized crèches (daycare centers) and nursery schools, which accept all children between the ages of two and three without charge (except for the cost of lunch). The schooltime schedule is synchronized with work hours. School hours are usually from 8:30 to 11:30 A.M., with the possibility of lunch at school if both parents are employed, and then from 1:30 to 4:30 P.M., plus a *garderie* (baby-sitting service) until 6:00 P.M. There are not enough crèches for all children between three months and three years old, so parents of young children may take either a parental leave of absence for a maximum of two years or a part-time job. The French system is among the best for allowing both parents to combine a professional career and childcare (6).

The law grants women sixteen to eighteen weeks of paid maternity leave, with guaranteed re-employment. An employer may not fire a woman on the grounds of pregnancy.

Imbalances Between Women and Men

Since the mid-1960s, the number of women graduating from the second cycle of secondary education has exceeded the number of men graduating. Of the 1989 cohort, 46 percent of the girls and 36 percent of the boys passed the *baccalaureat*, the exam which allows them to register at university. Men are more likely to attend vocational high schools, while women are more likely to remain in academic high schools, which normally lead to university studies and white-collar jobs.

At university, women constitute just over half the students. Until recently, women students constituted a minority in the economic, scientific, technical, and other disciplines that are the most valued for high-paid careers (3;9). In 1990, only 20 percent of the students in engineering schools were women (about 10 percent in the best schools), but in business schools 50 percent were women (with 40 percent in the top schools), which is a significant increase over the last fifteen years (2). In economics, 42 percent were women.

Since 1981, the minister of women's rights has supported women's entry into nontraditional jobs, but with limited success. In 1987, women made up only 37 percent of the participants in professional training programs, public administration not included (11).

In 1987, full-time women workers, on average, earned 24 percent less than did men; and this salary discrepancy reached 30 percent for managers with comparable full-time working contracts. We can assume the 6 percent difference between 24 percent and 30 percent is because fewer women work in top managerial positions, where the highest salaries and most demanding time schedules are found.

The Legal Environment

Women managers in France benefit from a long tradition of women working in the labor force, including legal protection for maternity and a school system based on a full-day schedule – both of which date back to the beginning of the century. The status of working women was bolstered three times during this century: first, during the First World War, when women demonstrated their ability to replace men in activities related to the economy; second, following the Second World War, with the passing of the equality rights principle in the constitution; and third, in the 1970s and 1980s, when equal opportunity legislation was passed.

Since 1983, an employer may not discriminate on the basis of gender. For example, the employer cannot refuse fathers a leave of absence for a child's illness if such a leave is available to mothers. The equal opportunity law passed in 1983 was expanded in 1987 to include women employed in small businesses. The law requires that each company employing more than 50 people present an annual report to its work council and union representatives, providing a comparison of the employment situation and training of women and men. The report must include a statement describing what was done during the previous year to improve the situation for women; explanations must be provided if objectives have not been achieved. The report must also set objectives and define a plan of action for the following year.

To finance part of the action plan, a contract for professional equality may be signed with the Professional Equality Government Agency. However, by the beginning of 1992, only 25 contracts had been signed. An evaluation of the effects of the law, made in 1988 and 1989, concluded that most companies preferred not receiving financial support rather than undertaking positive action for women under government control. In fact, a number of corporations had introduced equal opportunity programs without government support. The clause in the 1983 law that made implementing change programs depend heavily on unions negotiating voluntarily with management on behalf of women curtailed its potential success; unions initiated few of the 25 contracts. During the 1980s, union power was on the decline. In addition, French unions (right-wing and left-wing) are no less sexist than are French employers. No training program accompanied the legislation.

Equal opportunity legislation was initiated by the conservative party, approved by each of the subsequent governments, and encouraged by the European Community Commission. Whatever its political tendency, each subsequent government has recognized the necessity of employment equality for bringing more skilled employees into the workforce. Measures shown to work against women in the labor market have been minimized. An exception is the taxation system, which still treats husbands' and wives' income as a single income, thereby forcing couples into a higher tax bracket (5).

A secretary of state for the women's condition was first instated in 1974 by the conservative government. The first socialist government of the fifth republic transformed it into a Ministry of Women's Rights in 1981. In 1986, it was reduced to a secretary of state with no specific budget, and in 1993 to a simple department.

Defining Women Managers

In French employment statistics, the term closest to the word "manager" is *cadre*. A *cadre* is not necessarily a hierarchical superior responsible for the work of subordinates. She or he may be a staff professional or may hold a consulting position. The term refers more to a level of organizational status than to a job category with specific task responsibilities. It applies to an employee with a university degree representing four or five years of study (the equivalent of a master's degree) or to an employee who has climbed the ladder and acquired a *cadre* position through her or his work and continuing educational experience.[1] The position is governed by specific work regulations and includes pension retirement plans. Official statistics concerning French *cadres* include job categories such as secondary school teachers, lawyers, journalists, and artists.

Statistics on women managers

Among the *cadre* populations provided by French statistics (see Table 12.1), we consider as managers only those working in a business or administrative environment. To make the French statistics comparable with U.S. data, we include some "intermediate professions" in which people work in administrative and business environments, although in positions inferior to the *cadres*. In France, the people in "intermediate professions" usually have a two-year university degree and often

Table 12.1   The *cadre* categories (1989)

Cadre occupations and job sectors*	Women	% women per category
Public sector administration	55,354	24
Administration and sales	156,565	25
Engineers and technicians	49,400	10

*Excluding secondary school teachers, scientists, independent or non-salaried positions, journalists, artists.

Source: INSEE (1989) *Enquête sur l'emploi* [*Employment Inquiry*]. Paris: INSEE.

Table 12.2   The "intermediate professions" (1989)

"Intermediate professions" and job sectors*	Women	% women per category
Corporate administration and sales	507,642	44
Technicians	78,919	10
Department managers	36,613	7
Public sector administration	189,452	51

*Excluding primary school teachers and health and social workers.

Source: INSEE (1989) *Enquête sur l'emploi* [*Employment Inquiry*]. Paris: INSEE.

become *cadres* after five to ten years of professional experience, provided they meet the requisite qualifications for a *cadre* job (see Table 12.2).

Women managers among thirteen types of functions

The distribution of women managers (*cadres* only) in the thirteen branches of activity defined by the Association for Managers' Employment (APEC) shows that in 1989 20 percent of women were employed in marketing and sales and 18 percent in administration, but in both categories the proportion of women is decreasing (see Table 12.3). Women are moving to other fields – to newly defined functions such as communication and information systems. Although the proportion of women in corporate management is small (less than 3 percent), it is on the rise (1).

Women make up more than 30 percent of the *cadre* managers and professionals in the following subcategories:

Product promotion and sales	Urban planning and architecture
Import–export	Socioeconomic studies
Sales administration	Patents
Real estate	Chemistry

The proportionate increase in women managers during the last 35 years was twice that of the total managerial population. For instance, the number of women managers grew from 76,400 in 1954 to 640,000 in 1989 (an increase of 838 percent), whereas the total *cadre* population grew from 553,700 to 2,286,000 (an increase of 412 percent).

Table 12.3 Women and men managers by function (1989)

Function	Women (%)	Men (%)	Women as % of total
Corporate management	2.9	6.6	13.6
Manufacturing, construction	2.2	10.7	6.8
Manufacturing support services	2.4	8.5	8.9
Research, development	7.9	12.9	17.7
Marketing, sales	19.9	27.1	20.4
Bank, insurance, real estate, tourism, transportation	4.0	4.4	24.3
Administration	18.4	6.1	51.2
Finance, accounting, control	8.6	5.7	34.6
Information systems	7.8	9.7	22.1
Personnel, education	7.7	2.7	50.2
Communication	8.7	1.8	62.3
Medical, social, culture	6.3	2.4	48.1
Others	2.8	1.4	41.6
Total	100.0	100.0	25.9

Source: Hélène Alexandre (1990), *Les femmes cadres* [*Women Managers*]. Paris: APEC.

Women Managers' Motivations and Attitudes

The remainder of the chapter describes a study, conducted between 1975 and 1984, of women and men in a large computer company (16).[2] The study allows us to observe the relationship between women's and men's experience in similar professional positions, and provides a blueprint for the future. In 1975, women *cadres*, or managers, represented 5 percent of the managerial population in the company (see Table 12.4).

The purpose of the study was to identify women's specific career difficulties in order to build a positive action program for the 3,500 women (350 of them managers) employed by the company. The 3,500 women participated in an opinion survey. In addition, 20 percent of the women managers participated in interviews or workshops organized according to job categories and locations. The average age of

Table 12.4 Women managers' positions

Position	1975 Women	1975 Women as % of total	1984 Women	1984 Women as % of total
Sales representative	23	2	145	10
System engineer	82	7	257	14
Administrative—personnel and communication	245	6	611	9
Total	350	5	1013	10*

*By 1991, 14 percent.

Source: Author's collected data, 1975–1984.

the women managers was 34 (35 for the nonmanagers). Of the managers, 64 percent had a university diploma, and 76 percent described their studies as useful for their present activities. Compared to 59 percent of the men managers, 62 percent of the women managers had more than seven years of seniority in the company.

All the women reported that they worked for both financial reasons and professional interest. For the most part, they were satisfied with their jobs, but they perceived their careers to be more uncertain than those of the men due to the sexist attitudes of some managers.

The women managers disliked remarks and compliments concerning their physical appearance and comments emphasizing how their behavior differed from men's model of professional behavior. In the workplace, women managers wanted to be recognized for their abilities. The French language allows a job title to indicate the gender of the person holding the job, but most women managers chose to use the masculine form rather than the feminine form of their professional title, especially on their visiting cards, in spite of a government circular (March 11, 1986) concerning the feminization of job, function, grade, and title names. For example *directeur* was used instead of *directrice* and *secretaire général* instead of *secretaire générale*. The great majority believed the masculine title gave them more credibility and power. Few of them were conscious of their role in creating new models.

Among the 47 percent of women managers with children, 49 percent had only one child, 41 percent two, 9 percent had three; 42 percent had at least one child less than three years old (three being the entrance age into the French school system). The women managers were more likely than their nonmanager counterparts to be unmarried and to not have children.

The women managers disliked men stressing their views on women's maternal responsibilities; the women felt that making reference to their "feminine" characteristics was a method men used to remind women of the traditional gender hierarchy. In contrast to low-skilled women, the women managers objected to protective legislation and specific measures for mothers, such as paid days of absence to care for a sick child. They feared that such considerations would reinforce the usual clichés concerning the working women's lack of availability and would therefore become another obstacle to their career development. Women managers, who as a group had fewer children than other women in the company, preferred asking for more community support in educating their children and greater participation from the father in domestic duties.

Table 12.5 Women's family status (1975)

Status	Women managers (%)	Women nonmanagers (%)
Married without children	15	15
Married with children	38	49
Nonmarried without children	38	24
Nonmarried with children	9	11

Source: Author's collected data, 1975–1984 (More recent data not available.)

Table 12.6   Comparison of views held by women staff experts and decision-makers

Issues	Women staff experts (assistants, specialists)	Women decision-makers (project or people managers)
Career strategy/family responsibilities	Want less demanding positions after maternity	Remain in time consuming and stressful jobs
Business values	Reject competitive values	Accept competition
Existence of sexist attitudes	Are somewhat conscious of them	Become conscious of them only after some years of experience
How seen by colleagues	Are seen as friends	Are seen as competitors
Willingness to change the rules	Want part-time or reduced time job; respect working time regulation	Support existing traditional work rules
Affirmative action	See it as positive – a means to get another career chance	See it as a negative, except when they are refused a promotion
Membership in women's associations	Are members	Are not members; are more interested in business-oriented associations

Source: Author's collected data, 1975–1984.

Career Strategies

As a result of this study, we found that most women managers used one of two contrasting career strategies. Either they used the more traditional route of serving as an assistant to a male decision-maker, usually as staff expert, or the less traditional route of a line position, which brought them into more direct competition with men in positions of power (see Table 12.6). Regardless of which strategy they used, most women, at some stage in their careers, made compromises to diminish the stress in their private or professional lives.

Women staff experts

The role of staff expert, a subordinate support role in which women assist men in their decisions, but do not directly participate in the decision-making process, avoids the struggle for power, so costly to women in terms of wasted emotion and energy. This career strategy, in which women do not manage subordinates and have limited responsibilities and workloads, characterizes women with staff positions in personnel, as specialists in recruitment and education, in communication departments, as administrators in the sales support functions, as scientists in laboratories, and in administrative and technical support functions in plants. The majority of women managers in the company held these type of positions.

To support their decision to fill these subordinate positions, some of the women maintained they had rejected the traditional "masculine" game of career competition and search for power and instead advocated what they described as a "feminine morality" based on respect for the individual and on cooperation (12). Some used this view as a justification for remaining in subordinate positions in a highly competitive career environment.

Women decision makers

In the company we studied, a career in sales was a prerequisite for promotion onto the board of directors or into senior management. Until the mid-1970s, the company had only men sales representatives: thus not being able to get sales experience was a serious obstacle to women's career development. After the directors adopted an equal opportunity policy in 1976, the situation improved for women. With women by then constituting half of MBA students, more were able to get into sales positions.

The women assuming power positions that had traditionally been held by men tended to be younger and have less formal education in such fields as finance and legal services, marketing, and sales than their male counterparts. During their thirties, this new generation of women managers made significant progress up through the hierarchy, with many gaining exposure to various company constituencies, including customers, bankers, purchasers, unionists, employees, and public administrators.

The women succeeded as managers when they acquired the experience needed to be promoted into senior management, and when they avoided making compromises in their professional careers, such as choosing to care for a child or accommodate a husband's assignment. Most women managers in our study who received their first senior management position in their thirties had had a child before taking their first managerial position, thus making it easier for them to take the three to four months of paid leave of absence (six months' leave for the third child). None who had attained the position of director, and practically none in second-line positions, had had any additional children.

Most of the women believed that they could fashion the same type of career as a man by working as much as a man did. They were aware, however, of having some difficulties in their relationships with peers, subordinates, and customers and acknowledged that it took them more time to be accepted by those around them than it did for a man.

Most of the women in top management positions believed they had been chosen more for their loyalty to the existing management system than for their entrepreneurial spirit. Few of the women managers had ever belonged to a women's association and most did not consider themselves feminists. They objected to special regulations to advance women. They believed they could improve their position only by fitting into the existing system, which they did not intend to change. The women saw men managers as being in a better position than women to take positive actions in favor of women's employment, and some of the men did so.

Making compromises

Many of the women managers made compromises at different stages in their life to meet family demands, to reduce work pressure, or to perform in line with their own business values. For example, in not choosing technical studies, they avoided working in industrial areas far from the cities where they lived or managing plant workers with shift schedules. Choosing to become a manager in a staff function allowed them to work fewer hours than was necessary in a line position.

A *cadre* may expect to work 50 hours a week, and a director about 60, even though the legal work week is 38.5 hours (with five weeks of vacation and about ten days' holiday). Women who chose jobs with no regular overtime had significantly more time to devote to housekeeping and children's education than did those who were required to work overtime. Being in a less essential position in the organization, they could more easily stay home when children were ill, and more readily obtain a part-time job, thereby balancing career and family demands with less stress. Not having line responsibility, they also avoided conflict with subordinates over company priorities and interests.

After a few years of work experience, some women wanted an easier professional life for a limited period of time. Especially after the birth of a child or after their husbands had received a significant promotion, some women were tempted to seek a less demanding managerial job that would allow them to perform their traditional role – duties they found important to fulfill. Their own managers rarely pointed out the long-term negative consequences of such a decision on their future career.

When women managers make compromises in their careers, they may lose their credibility as potential candidates for senior positions. Their actions signal that they are less committed; and, as a result, management often decides to promote a man who has not made an equivalent compromise, arguing that he will be more available and motivated.

Obstacles to Equality

In the workplace

Equal opportunity careers depend on more than diplomas, abilities, and ambitions. They require health, self-confidence, management support, professional acceptance, job opportunities at key moments, and training opportunities. Even when women make the same career decisions as men, they rarely receive the same career opportunities.

A career with high management potential demands geographical mobility; but dual-career couples have difficulty arranging a succession of regional and international assignments. As it is not unusual to move eight times in the course of a career, executives who wish to promote a woman into senior management must make specific career arrangements for her, such as giving her a short assignment without requiring the family to move instead of a three-year assignment. Unfortunately, most companies are unwilling to make such arrangements. Beyond practical considerations, some board members continue to reject the principle of professional equality, often times because their own private lives are built around traditionally differentiated women's and men's roles.

Being a manager includes having to work long hours, travel, make difficult decisions, motivate people, and achieve high objectives – most often with limited resources and strong business competitors. For women managers, it also often

means fighting within their own company to establish a reputation as a leader –
since women are rarely spontaneously seen as leaders, avoiding or responding
appropriately to sexist criticisms, motivating employees to accept and execute their
decisions, and sometimes hiding their family problems. Women frequently have
more difficulty than men getting access to information necessary to make wise
career decisions. Although it is important for women to understand the organization's career criteria, few companies in France provide such information through
either equal opportunity managers or assertiveness courses.[3]

Whereas marriage often signals equilibrium and ambition for men, it frequently
signifies the risk of competing commitments for women. Women reassure their
colleagues that they will still give sufficient time and energy to the company. When
women managers marry and have children, they must create a secure family environment – a supportive husband, a strong home organization, good community
childcare services or available grandparents, and healthy children. It is no wonder
that only a small proportion of women ever succeed at both professional and family
roles.

Some French companies have built temporary affirmative action programs, such
as training courses for women in specific job categories, but few have introduced
equal opportunity policies that include annual action plans in all areas: recruitment,
training, career planning, and promotion.

In the marriage

The traditional family model – that requires women who marry men of the same
social-professional class to hold jobs of inferior status to those of their husbands –
did not fit the women managers in our study: 39 percent earned a higher salary than
their husbands and 32 percent an equivalent salary. For those whose husband's
position was inferior, the usual pattern of the husband returning from his office later
than his wife, bringing home files for work after dinner and during weekends,
inviting business partners home, making business trips, and attending distant seminars, was not only changed but reversed. For some couples, this situation caused
stress. Women avoided talking about their jobs, and couples masked the salary
disparities by not discussing them:

> We never speak about our jobs and earnings; for some years, the difference between
> our two incomes has been increasing, he doesn't feel good about it, he never
> mentions it.

> I travel, he doesn't; he never has anything to say about his working day; therefore in our
> relationship, talk about work is taboo; whereas I have indeed an interesting job, he
> speaks of it as only worth the salary it provides. I feel frustrated because he doesn't
> recognize me for what I am.

Among the couples in which the wife was more successful, some preserved the
marriage by sustaining a myth of the husband's superiority.

When the husband was an executive, the wife often reduced her involvement in
the labor market or stopped working altogether. In our study, 56 percent of the

wives of men managers, but only 5 percent of the husbands of women managers, did not do paid work. In France, most couples will not accept separation as a viable option and will rarely agree to live in different cities. Society exerts strong pressures on women to curtail their careers, especially with the potential gain afforded by reducing joint income taxes. When a woman chooses to lower her career profile, her family's social status is rarely diminished, since status is determined primarily by the husband's standing. The quality of life of the family often improves since the wife has more time available for household and children's needs. Women who accept this arrangement usually embrace traditional family values and gain more leisure time for themselves.

In the French welfare society, most skilled women do not feel guilty for contributing less than they could to the economy, and, in the 1990s, some even felt good about making a job available for an unemployed person. The prestige of being a woman executive is usually not enough to compensate for other sacrifices. Quality of life, health, and self-accomplishment through cultural activities and sports compete with work for women's commitment. Women managers often have jobs in which their self-fulfillment is limited. In addition, many of them are not independent enough to value equality in marriage.

Many men managers prefer a lower family income over sharing housework. Women managers thus have a smaller pool of potential husbands from which to choose. Many French women feel more limited by their husbands' traditional attitudes than by the lack of available childcare.

In our study, marital stability was greater when the division of labor matched the expectations of both the husband and wife. One woman manager, whose expectations of equality in marriage were not met, expressed her disappointment as follows: "Being a woman, I'd like my husband to encourage me to do what really matters to me instead of using my little leisure time to do administrative paperwork or clean the house. We women have too many opportunities to do what is not essential for us."

Most women managers hire a domestic helper; but, since a full-time domestic helper is an expensive solution, most couples (even those with young children) must do some house work when they return home in the evening. Even when home duties are shared, many women managers express the need for more commitment from their husbands; some would like their husbands to demonstrate real interest in their professional development instead of showing apathy or rivalry: "Sharing home duties is not enough, one should also understand the professional problems of the other and encourage him or her to understand what is really important."

The marriage often becomes more vulnerable when the woman's professional achievements are equal or superior to those of her husband, when she becomes economically independent, and when work becomes an important source of her satisfaction. Most women managers in our study enjoyed the excitement of business, while at the same time experiencing difficulties in the relationship with their husband. Most women managers saw their jobs as a source of self-fulfillment, and wanted to continue in their positions of responsibility.

Equality in Theory

Women managers in France have full formal equality. Legislation guarantees equal treatment and equal professional opportunities; and, since 1983, it prohibits direct as well as indirect discrimination. The parental benefits within employment are satisfactory, as is the system of care for young children through the free national public education system. French social policy definitely allows women managers to raise children and pursue a career at the same time. Although the proportion of women in management has increased, there are still very few women in senior positions on executive committees and boards, and few women share in the political power.

In 1993, French political arenas remain dominated by men. Laws are made by a parliament in which 94 percent of the members are men, with women constituting 6 percent of the representatives in the Chambre des députés and 5 percent of those in the Sénat. Both right- and left-wing parties are reluctant to put women in positions in which they could be elected and replace a man. The three main political parties only presented 6 to 9 percent women on their lists for the 1993 legislative elections (8). In the new right-wing government, laws are executed by a government (headed by Edouard Balladur) in which only three (15 percent) of the ministers are women. One of the three, Simone Weil, is Minister of State. The dismissal of the Prime Minister Edith Cresson (1991–1992), mostly due to her lack of communication skills, seriously set back women as it was stereotypically, although not openly, regarded as proof of women's political incompetence in senior positions.

French political parties, like French corporations, restrict women's progress in their own ranks and they do not impose quotas on themselves. At the local level, women represent about 20 percent of the city council members and 4.5 percent of the mayors.

The feminist liberation movement, which was made up largely of intellectuals on the fringes of the salaried world, had focused on assessing the differences between women and men and not on salary and professional equality. A large majority of women rejected the image of women promoted by this group and, in doing so, they rejected feminism. To declare yourself a feminist is still not acceptable in France, nor is the feminist movement a significant political force. Women's consensus concerning the abortion law cannot be taken as indicative of the existence of an organized feminist movement in France. France had and still has women opinion leaders, such as philosopher Simone de Beauvoir, lawyer Gisèle Halimi, psychoanalyst and publisher Antoinette Fouque, politicians Marcelle Devaud, Simone Weil, and Yvette Roudy, and women journalists, including Françoise Giroud. However, they do not mobilize large groups of women employees and workers around professional issues; work equality interests women less than abortion and human rights.

However, as a reaction to the mere 6 percent women among the Chambre des députés representatives, compared to the 10 to 33 percent in most European countries, parity is becoming a better mobilization issue and is uniting women's associations in common action programs which could go beyond presenting studies and expressing right- and left-wing moral support in congresses and meetings. In 1982, the Conseil constitutionnel repealed a law which specified that there should be no more than 75 percent of the same sex on lists of candidates for the city council elections. Following this, groups within the women's movement are now proposing a revision of the Constitution to give a better balance between women and men in all elections, 50:50 being the ideal proportion. The Green party has parity in its statutes, "wherever it is possible," and put forward equal numbers of women and men in its list of candidates for the European Parliament in 1984 and 1989. Michel Rocard, head of the Socialist party, has committed himself to presenting a 50:50 ratio of women to men on his list of candidates for the European Parliament elections of 1994.

The unions have resisted taking on women's issues. They claim that women's liberation will come at the same time as workers' liberation and therefore requires no special attention. Most political parties, as well as the unions, still have a women's caucus or a woman representative for women's issues, but they have very little influence on the choice of candidates. The CFDT (Confederation française democratique du travail) union, headed by a woman, Nicole Notat, is an exception as it has become one of the most creative in solving unemployment and work–family compatibility problems by putting both parents on an equal basis (13).

There are no organizations in France comparable to the Coalition of Labor Union Women in America to promote professional issues or to the American League of Women Voters and the National Women's Political Caucus to support women's political views and candidates. There are associations of women managers in Paris and some other large cities that are based on type of job, origin of diploma, or level of responsibility. Their purpose is primarily social networking. Newly created associations, however, include the exchange of business opportunities in their goals. Associations gathered in the French Coordination of the European Women's lobby are now mostly preoccupied by the parity issue and receive support from the European Commission (7).

Effects of Economic Changes on Equality

Following the economic recession, the increased need for skilled and adaptable employees should have a positive effect on hiring women graduates and should expand opportunities for women managers. At the same time, the current 11 percent unemployment rate could lead to reduced work time for all, thus making managerial work more compatible with family life. However, it is unlikely that any government in the foreseeable future will choose to face the consequences of a completely restructured work schedule, especially with its effects on the cost of employment for companies and on the salary levels and retirement pensions for individuals. Current economic conditions do not favor change, except for encouraging more part-time jobs and parental leave for women and for increasing taxation rates. Increased economic competition and personnel cutbacks will require managers and executives to work even longer hours than before to achieve more demanding professional objectives.

Women managers seeking opportunities to change jobs, especially from administration and personnel to line management, will need to spend additional time and energy in retraining programs. Some companies have promoted women to executive positions. Some of these women, however, have been chosen for their conformity to senior management values and therefore have not contributed to the advancement of other women in the organization. Most women managers who reach senior positions often adapt their behavior to men's expectations to win their trust and confidence and in so doing frequently reduce their support for other women. Difficult economic conditions and a highly competitive environment with pressures to reduce costs may not be conducive to implementing affirmative action programs. Companies' needs for the best possible managers will favor highly qualified women; but to succeed, these women will most likely have to accept even more difficult working conditions.

Notes

I wish to express my sincere gratitude to the Centre national d'information et de documentation sur les femmes (CNIDF) and to the Institut national de la statistique et des études économiques (INSEE) for the help of their documentalists. I owe a special debt to the Association pour l'emploi des cadres (APEC) and to Hélène Alexandre who agreed to discuss her latest findings. On the other side of the Atlantic, it is my pleasure to thank Rose Coser and Cynthia Epstein for the support and helpful views they gave me when I started a comparative inquiry on women and men employees of a large corporation in France. My appreciation of the chances for equality of women in management has been considerably enlarged thanks to a German Marshall fund fellowship and Wider Opportunities for Women, which permitted me, in 1987, to interview more than 100 political, university, and corporate persons in the United States.

1 *Cadres* are distinguished by the fact that they are electors in a specific group or "college" which votes for the different personnel representatives in the organizations. They also have specific pension funds to which they and their employers contribute; those pension funds are in addition to the general social security pension to which they are entitled at the age of 60 to 65. The *cadres* enjoy a privileged status. For example, some corporations still have a separate restaurant for them, which provides better service than the non-*cadres'* cafeteria. *Cadres* are generally not required to punch in since their pay is determined by the results they achieve and by the level of their responsibilities, not by the number of hours they work in the firm.
2 The study was based on interviews with 224 women and men in various job categories, fourteen workshops concerning careers and working conditions, and an opinion survey among 3,500 women (350 *cadres*) and a sample of 500 men in comparable job categories. See Serdjénian (1988).
3 See Serdjénian (1987) and Serdjénian (1990) for examples of positive action programs in 100 European companies.

References

(1) Alexandre, Hélène (1990) *Les femmes cadres*. Paris: APEC.
(2) Baudelot, Christian and Establet, Roger (1992) *Allez les filles*. Paris: Seuil.

(3) Bedaria, C. and Helfter, C. (1990) "Filles: la fausse róussite scolaire," in *Le monde de l'éducation*, Paris.

(4) Capul, Jean-Yves (1993) "La France et sa population," in *Cahiers français N°259*, La documentation française, Paris.

(5) Conseil économique et social (1984) *Le statut matrimonial et ses conséquences juridiques, fiscales et sociales*, Journal officiel de la république française, Paris.

(6) Dumon, Wilfried (1992) *Les politiques familiales nationales des états membres de la communauté européenne en 1991.* Brussels: ECC.

(7) ECC (1991) "Equal Opportunity between Women and Men," *Social Europe* 3/91. Brussels: ECC.

(8) Gaspard, Françoise (1993) *Elections législatives mars 1993-Etude parité.* Paris: CNFF.

(9) INSEE (1989) "Les emplois du temps des Français," *Economie et statistique N°223.* Paris: INSEE.

(10) INSEE (1989, 1991, 1992) *Enquête sur l'emploi* [*Employment Inquiry*]. Paris: INSEE.

(11) INSEE (1991) *Les femmes. Droits des femmes.* Paris: INSEE.

(12) Laufer, Jacqueline (1982) *La féminité neutralisée? Les femmes cadres dans l'entreprise.* Paris: Flammarion.

(13) Ouin, Béatrice (1990) *Femmes: Clés pour l'égalité.* Paris: CFDT Editions.

(14) Prondzynski, Isabelle (1989) "Les femmes en chiffres," in *Les cahiers de femmes d'Europe N°30.* Brussels: ECC.

(15) Serdjénian, Evelyne (1987) *Les femmes et l'égalité professionnelle – Des moyens d'action* [*Women's Equal Opportunity – Action Tools*]. Paris: INSEP Editions.

(16) Serdjénian, Evelyne (1988) *L'égalité des chances ou les enjeux de la mixité* [*Equal Opportunity and the Mixity Challenge*]. Paris: Editions d'organisation.

(17) Serdjénian, Evelyne (1990) *12 European Programs for Equal Opportunity.* Brussels: ECC.

13 GERMANY

Women in Management in Germany: East, West, and Reunited

Ariane Berthoin Antal and Camilla Krebsbach-Gnath

Several significant changes have occurred in the political and economic landscape surrounding women in management in Germany since we wrote the first review of their situation in the mid-1980s (3). First of all, women managers have become established as a target group of attention in the media, politics, and business community. Individual women are frequently profiled in business journals, for example; topics such as dual-career couples are making an appearance; and a growing number of conferences and seminars focus on women in management.

Second, a variety of measures designed to implement equal opportunity have been introduced at various levels of government and business during the past few years. Equal opportunity officers and action plans, both voluntary and mandatory, have been put into place.

Third, the task of describing and explaining the situation of women managers and their future outlook in Germany has taken on several new dimensions since October 3, 1990, the date of the unification of East and West Germany.[1] Most simply, the size of the workforce expanded significantly when the approximately seventeen million citizens of East Germany were united with the 61 million people living in West Germany. The increase in the size of the pool of human resources is bound to have an impact on the opportunities for women in management in Germany. If we want to shape the future and improve the opportunities for women in management, it is essential to gain a better understanding of the past. What can we learn by comparing the effects of the policies pursued in the two systems? The opening of East Germany allows a closer analysis of the living and working conditions of women in that system and of the factors promoting or hindering their entrance and promotion in management. A preliminary assessment of the facts and myths relating to women in management in both systems lays the groundwork for gauging what they might be facing together in the upcoming years and what policies are needed to improve their prospects.

Background

Women's labor force participation and management representation

The situation in West Germany 1980–1989 In 1987, women made up 39 percent of the workforce in West Germany; that is, 10.1 million women, or 47 percent of women between the ages of fifteen and 65 (8). However, their representation in management does not even closely correspond to their participation in the labor force. The absence of women managers went largely unnoticed until the mid-1980s, before which time no articles specifically on "women in management" had been published. During the last five years, public interest in this topic has definitely increased in West German media and politics, and several popular business books have focused on it (6;12). Not surprisingly, the facts are not changing as quickly as interest is growing: women managers remain few and far between in West Germany, compared with the United States.

The data remain scant, but the message is well illustrated in Figure 13.1. According to a study conducted in 1988 of 45,000 companies with more than 20 employees and with a cash flow of at least DM2 million, 5.9 percent of top managers and 7.8 percent of managers at the next level were women (19).[2] Another study noted that women accounted for only 0.7 percent of manag-ing board members in public companies (*Aktiengesellschaften*) in West Germany in 1988, and 0.3 percent of supervisory board members (19).[3] Companies owned by women appear to be more likely to have women in management positions. According to a study conducted by the Association of (West German) Women Business Owners in 1989, women held 10 percent of the upper management positions in women-owned companies (21).

The situation in East Germany until 1989 The representation of women in positions of responsibility in economic, academic, and political organizations was considerably greater in East Germany than in West Germany. In East Germany, women held about one-third of all management positions in the 1980s (29). As impressive as this statistic is, however, it needs to be examined more closely. First, as leading East German sociologists now point out, "the fact that most of these were positions with low status and little money in lower management was not mentioned" by the former regime, which preferred to publicize this statistic as one of its "success stories" (27:5). Second, 30 percent of management positions is less impressive when one considers that 91 percent of women of working age were in the labor market (30). "The percentage of women in management positions does not at all reflect the broad potential of qualified women in the labor force" observed the first major critical study of the situation of women published by the East German Minister for Women's Affairs after the "peaceful revolution of 1989" (39:94 [our translation]).

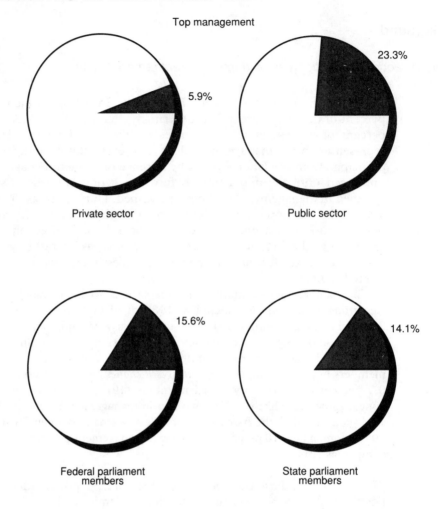

Top management

Private sector   5.9%

Public sector   23.3%

Federal parliament members   15.6%

State parliament members   14.1%

Source: Adapted from C. Demmer (1988) "Was Frauen fordern – Wie Frauen fördern?" ["What Women Demand – How to Promote Women"], in C. Demmer (ed.), *Women in Management: From Reserve Forces to the Reserve of Talents*, p. 27. Wiesbaden: Gabler Verlag.

Figure 13.1   Women in management and politics in West Germany: The gap

Distribution of women in management according to sector in West and East Germany

Common to both Germanies is a high degree of gender-specific segmentation of the labor market. Almost 70 percent of working women in West Germany are concentrated in ten (out of 400) occupational categories (8). Women account for 86

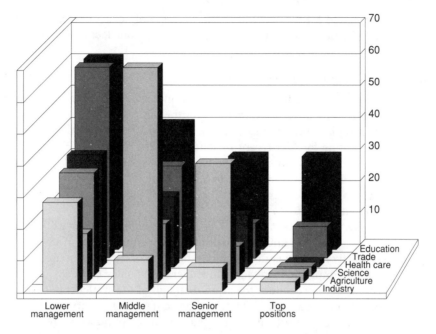

Source: Adapted from G. Winkler (ed.) (1990) *Frauen Report '90 [Report on Women '90]* Report to the Beaufiragte des Ministerrates für die Gleichstellung von Frauen und Männern, Dr Marina Beyer, p. 94. Berlin: Verlag die Wirtschaft.

Figure 13.2 Women in management in East Germany, 1989 (%)

percent of people employed in the health services (excluding medical doctors and pharmacists), 79 percent of people in the social services, 62 percent of people employed in retail, and 48 percent of teachers. In East Germany, women represented 92 percent of people employed in the social services, 83 percent of those in health-related occupations, 77 percent in education, 72 percent in retailing, and 69 percent in postal and telephone services. They remained a minority in industry, the trades, construction, agriculture and forestry, and the transportation sector (29).

Women in both systems tended to have a better chance of obtaining a management position in those sectors of the economy in which they are strongly represented. In East Germany, for example, women held almost two-thirds of management positions in education, health care, and trade; in light industry and in services, 40 to 50 percent of all managers were women; and in transportation and local government, women held 25 percent of the management positions. On the other hand, in heavy industry, construction, and science, women remained a rarity in the management ranks. As noted above, however, "women are mostly employed in lower and middle management positions; in top positions they are still the exception" (39:95 [our translation]). In education, for example, where women accounted for 80 percent of employees, only one-quarter of East German schools were headed by a woman. In academia, only one lecturer in seven and one professor in nineteen was a woman (27:5).

Education and training in West Germany

The levels of education and vocational training achieved by women have risen significantly in West Germany over the past two decades. The system of vocational training is much more extensive in Germany than in the Anglo-Saxon countries, accounting for 60 percent of school leavers. Between 1970 and 1985, the percentage of working women who completed vocational training rose from 38 to 65 (compared with 65 percent to 77 percent for men during the same period). Similarly, women accounted for 41 percent of university students in 1987 (up from 33 percent in 1970).

The low representation of women in management is still often attributed to the courses of study and occupations that young women choose. Some 54 percent of young women are concentrated in only ten of the 380 potential training occupations – for example, hairdresser, office clerk, and sales clerk (8). At the university level, young women account for more than half of the students in the arts, languages, and sports, in contrast to their low representation in engineering – namely 11 percent (8). It is significant, however, that the most popular degree for both women and men is economics and that women now also account for almost 40 percent of law students (8). Both economics and law degrees lead into management in Germany, where there have been no MBA programs until very recently (17).

The increase in the number of women university graduates and their expansion into areas more suited to management careers in the public and private sectors give reason to hope that the younger generations of women will achieve higher ranks than their mothers. However, two notes of caution are in order. First, higher education is no guarantee of employment, let alone access to management positions. In fact, women university graduates in West Germany have higher unemployment rates than do male graduates: women represent 25 percent of the working population with a university degree, yet they account for 45 percent of those unemployed graduates (8).

Education and training, particularly when obtained outside the company, play a limited role in promotion decisions, especially into upper management. Research has shown that German companies rely predominantly on in-firm training (18). This implies that if selection procedures filter women out in early career stages, they will not participate in training programs that are specifically designed as a basis for promotion.

It has been shown that the weight placed on professional qualification is inversely related to position in the hierarchy: that is, that the higher the position, the less significance the organization attaches to such "objective" criteria. The factors that receive more weight in promotion decisions for senior management positions are both less objective and more often based on traditional male career patterns. In effect, therefore, they discriminate against women. Among the factors listed in one study for promotion into upper-level management were professional competence, effectiveness, professional experience, length of experience, time with the company, commitment to the job, and professional and regional mobility (18). To the extent that "objective" factors and qualifications, such as education and training that women can consciously acquire, play a lesser role in decision making, other sociopsychological and systemic factors assume increasing importance and create less easily surmountable barriers to career development for women (see (4)).

Education and training in East Germany

In East Germany, too, the levels of education and vocational training achieved by women increased steadily over the past decades. The official statistics of the former German Democratic Republic showed that by the 1980s no difference existed between the education and vocational training levels achieved by women and men. Some 86 percent of working women had completed vocational training, and women accounted for 54 percent of university and college graduates (32). However, a closer look indicates that the problem of gender-specific segmentation occurred in the education and training courses in East Germany, albeit in different areas. Although women made up 51 percent of students in mathematics and the natural sciences, they were concentrated in the fields of chemistry, biology, psychology, and pharmacy, rather than in engineering and physics (32). Nevertheless, women accounted for 25 percent of students in technical courses and 66 percent of those in economics (39), so that their under-representation in management positions cannot easily be attributed to educational and training levels in these fields either. Significantly more East German women than men worked in jobs below their level of qualification (39).

Women entrepreneurs

A major difference between the management options open to women in East and West Germany has been the opportunity to run one's own business. In 1987, 5.7 percent of working women in West Germany were entrepreneurs, as compared to 10.3 percent of men (8). It is estimated that in the 1980s women created one-third of all new West German companies (1).

East Germany's planned economy did include a very small private sector, but the state tightly controlled it, so the concept of "entrepreneurship" is difficult to apply. Some 5.4 percent of the East German labor force worked in the private sector, with 1.8 percent of working women in 1989 either self-employed or working in family-owned companies (not including agriculture) (36). In other words, whereas in West Germany women could choose to set up their own business either early in their careers, or later if they felt limited by the restrictions to their career development in large organizations, entrepreneurship was not a serious option for women in East Germany.

The income issue

Another characteristic common to both systems is women's lower average income. In both East and West Germany, women earn about one-third less than men do (30;35). This gap is generally attributed to "structural" reasons: women are in lower-paying sectors and jobs, and they work fewer hours.[4] The existence of other reasons, specifically the unequal value society attaches to the work done by women and by men, is only gradually coming to the fore. Largely as a result of pressure from the European Community, the issue of "comparable worth" is now being raised in West Germany (8).

Studies in West Germany now show that even the small number of women who are in the elite class of "management" do not receive the same pay as their male counterparts. Their salaries are roughly 20 percent lower than those of comparable male managers (15). A review conducted by a major German personnel consultancy, Kienbaum, revealed that in 1988 the average pay differential between men and women top managers was DM84,500 per year, at the next level DM27,500, and at the third level DM18,000 (19). The income gap persists and increases with the level in the hierarchy and the size of the firm. Unfortunately, research has only just begun to document such differentials and has not yet progressed to examine how the gap is maintained.

Women in management – and their children

A significant difference between women in management in East and West Germany is in their family situation. The birth of children still has a major impact on work patterns of women in West Germany, where almost 60 percent of 25- to 35-year-olds with children leave the labor market at least temporarily (8). A primary reason, as the official federal government report points out, is that "working life is still organized today as though workers had no family responsibilities or household to take care of" (8:43). Only four out of ten women in middle management in West Germany are mothers – and they usually have only one child; by contrast, almost all their male colleagues are married and have an average of two children (33).

In East Germany, 94 percent of women with children remained in the labor force (14). No statistical evidence exists indicating that the women managers were less likely to have children than other women. As will be discussed in a later section, the much broader availability of childcare in East Germany was a significant factor in enabling women to combine work and family responsibilities. However, studies now indicate that in East Germany, career decisions for women were also made "according to their family situation, not according to their professional achievements" (39:96). In this system, too, the fact that women maintained the primary responsibility for children – particularly when the children were ill and needed a parent at home – represented a barrier to women's advancement in organizations (28).

Policies and Legislation Affecting Women in Management

Constitutional guarantee of equal rights

The constitutions of both the Federal Republic of Germany and the former German Democratic Republic include articles specifically recognizing the equal rights of women and men. However, as the preceding review of available data shows, neither state has achieved equality in practice.

There are two particularly significant differences between the two societies in this respect that influence the career development of women. First, the constitutional "right to work" in East Germany was not essentially a question of choice; in practice it was actually a "requirement to work." The labor needs of the economy were so high that the state could not afford *not* to have women working. A second significant difference between the two states is that the regime in East Germany did not anchor the "right of free speech" in its constitution nor practice it in reality. Critical voices could not be raised. A women's movement that was vocal and effective in placing the issue of inequality on the table and getting it integrated into political party agendas did not emerge in East Germany. Only now, after the opening of the wall, can East German sociologists publish the observation that "the equality of women was treated as achieved in the official GDR propaganda, the women's question was seen as resolved" (26:10 [our translation]).

The subject of inequality between the sexes was taboo and no women's movement developed to break this taboo (see, for example, (22)). As a leading East German sociologist noted, "the placement of taboos on problems on the one hand and the dissemination of success stories on the other blocked the development of critical awareness, of a women's consciousness in the GDR" (29:8 [our translation]). In other words, the GDR's masking of the inequality that existed, in spite of the political proclamation of equality in the constitution, was so effective that even women remained unaware of it and therefore unable to generate change.

New West German equal opportunity legislation and positions[5]

Probably the most important change for the career opportunities of women in West Germany in the past decade has been the introduction of laws mandating equal opportunity and the creation of equal opportunity positions throughout the public administration. The European Court found that the articles in the *Grundgesetz* (constitution of the Federal Republic of Germany) were not specific enough to assure women their rights. Having been prompted by the European Communities, West Germany took the first step in 1980, which required all member states to ensure that their legislation provided for the equal treatment of women and men at work. Since then, cases have been brought before the courts in Germany and in the European Communities, giving the law more bite by ensuring that the compensation given in cases of discrimination will become too expensive for employers to take lightly.

Whether Germany needs stronger legislation that would apply not only to the public sector but also to the private sector is controversial and its constitutionality is questioned. The Christian Democratic party, which dominates the coalition at the federal level and controls the government of several states, shares the view of the employers' organizations that mandatory measures, specifically those including quotas, are unacceptable.[6] As a result, the federal government has restricted itself to programs to be implemented within its own ranks and to elaborating a variety of recommendations and voluntary guidelines. The effectiveness of such voluntary programs is limited, as becomes particularly evident in international comparisons (2).

The need for strong measures in the public administration is obvious, since women are no better represented in the management ranks there than in the private sector in Germany (16). In 1986, the federal government passed mandatory guidelines on the occupational promotion of women in the federal administration. Since then, public authorities at various levels have introduced similar policy measures. They cover measures to increase the recruitment, promotion, and further training of women as well as measures designed to balance work and family responsibilities (e.g., part-time work). It is significant, however, that although these guidelines are mandatory, they do not include sanctions; the effect, therefore, remains limited.

One of the key elements in the policy provisions at this time is the requirement that all government agencies identify a person or a group as the equal opportunity "officer," whose job it is to monitor developments in the organization that affect women and to encourage change. Unfortunately, the government has not always given these "officers" the support and authority they needed. Although the actual changes have been limited and slow, the attention paid to the issue has revealed the manifold hurdles to women in management and has provided a solid basis for working out concrete solutions (7). The improvements, however, remain meager. Not much more can be claimed, even by the official report of the federal government, than that "the proportion of women recruited increasingly corresponds to the proportion of women applicants" (8:41 [our translation]).

An analysis of advertisements for management positions illustrates well the hurdles that remain in the absence of strong legislation. Despite the existence of a law requiring nonsexist job advertising, firms in Germany reveal their preference for male managers in advertisements directed to men. In the public sector, 94 percent of management openings are neutrally formulated; but in the private sector, 95 percent of advertisements for top management positions use the masculine noun form (31).[7] In other words, since no effective sanctions exist, current equal opportunity legislation is not even strong enough to mandate nonsexist advertising for openings, which might encourage a higher number of women applicants.

East German parental leave and childcare provisions

The issue that has received the most attention as a hurdle for women in management is the difficulty of combining family and career responsibilities. For this reason, it is useful to look at the support provided by the state as a framework within which companies, women, and men make career decisions.

Over the course of the past decades, the extensive provisions for childcare in East Germany have served as a reference point for women in West Germany. East Germany introduced several measures in 1976 specifically to help women combine family and work responsibilities: one year's paid leave – with a guaranteed job on return – after the birth of the second child (extended to the first child in 1986), one "household day" per month for women with children, and the right to four weeks of paid leave to care for sick children (extended by two weeks for each additional child).

The provision of childcare for working mothers was more extensive in East Germany than in any other country in the world. In large cities, almost 100 percent of parents needing childcare for infants and preschool children could obtain it at no cost, and 82 percent needing after-school care for school children could find it (22).

Children, in other words, were not permitted to stand in the way of East German women's ability to work. These provisions proved especially important given that almost 20 percent of mothers were single parents.

A further factor to keep in mind when assessing the benefits provided to working mothers is that running a household under the conditions of the East German socialist economy was an extremely time-consuming and difficult task, since goods and services were hard to come by. The case of East Germany shows that providing childcare is but one – albeit a key one – of the factors needed to enable people to balance home and work responsibilities.

West German parental leave and childcare provisions

The difficulties involved in combining a career with a family have also received a great deal of public attention in West Germany. Although the provision of childcare by the state and by some employers is more extensive in West Germany than in the United States, it is still by no means sufficient. Only 2 percent of infants born in West Germany can find a place in a crèche, so women have to make informal arrangements, often with relatives. Families can place some 78 percent of three- to six-year-olds in nursery schools, although significant regional variations exist.

The school hours are probably the most problematic factor for working women in West Germany. Unlike schools in the United States and most other European countries, most primary schools in West Germany open only four to five hours in the morning, and hours can vary from day to day, thus making it very difficult for women to work full-time. West Germany provides for only 4 percent of six- to ten-year-old children who need after-school care (11:22).

Since the negative birthrate gave rise to demographic concerns in West Germany (as well as in East Germany), the government has introduced increasingly generous provisions in the past few years to encourage women to have children. Beyond the fourteen-week paid maternity leave (six weeks before and eight weeks after the birth of a child), the government introduced parental leave in 1986, which currently allows either parent to take an eighteen-month leave. During this period, the parent is entitled to a state-paid allowance, which is calculated according to income. Some 97 percent of those eligible take the parental leave – but in 98.5 percent of the cases, the mother, not the father, takes the leave; and of the fathers who do take it, 70 percent were unemployed prior to doing so (11). There are plans to extend the leave to two years and eventually three years, "reflecting a widespread view that children should be in full-time parental care up to age three" (11:14).

This attitude regarding the role of the mother in raising children represents one of the most significant barriers to equal opportunity in management careers in West Germany. As long as mothers, fathers, and employers continue to share this assumption about the conditions for the healthy growth of small children, it will remain extremely difficult for women of childbearing age to have equal access to career opportunities. West Germany still has a long way to go before realizing the hope expressed by the president of the German Employers' Association, Klaus Murmann, that "when [men] take their father role to be as important as their work, the world of work will change" (25:262 [our translation]). Such a change in attitude to fatherhood would mean a change in the distribution of the family responsibilities between women and men and would most probably lead to a change in the way paid work is organized and scheduled. Both kinds of changes would make it easier for women to pursue management careers.

West German corporate policies and programs

With this framework of labor legislation and social policies in mind, what are companies doing about the number and role of women in management? Companies in West Germany are in a quandary. Business leaders such as the late Heinz Nixdorf express concern that "the increased participation of women in the labor force has meant that tens of thousands of children are not born each year" (25:262 [our translation]). As a leading business magazine pointed out, this implies a shortage of future consumers, employees, and supporters of pension plans (25). Companies, however, are experiencing an immediate lack of skilled workers and recognize that they cannot afford to waste the potential that women represent today.

Alexander Geck, a top manager at Esso in Germany, admitted that "we can no longer afford to have competent women leave the company only because they cannot combine their careers and their family" (38:73 [our translation]). These combined concerns – together with a substantial amount of pressure through the media and political channels – has led companies to introduce policies to identify, develop, and keep qualified women, particularly those with management potential.

One approach that German companies are taking is to introduce voluntary equal opportunity programs. In 1984, the Federal Ministry for Youth, Family and Health requested one of the authors of this chapter to develop guidelines for companies interested in recruiting, developing, and promoting more women, and the resulting booklet has been widely distributed in the German business community (24).

Other bodies, such as employers' associations, have since developed similar tools (9). Although they remain a minority, a growing number of companies have nominated a person or group responsible for equal opportunities. In many cases, however, these "officers" still do not have the necessary staff support and political backing in the organization to make significant changes. Studies that seriously assess the extent and impact of these policy instruments and agents have not been conducted.

A second more recent development is the conclusion of company-level agreements between employers with the workers' representatives on parental leave and return plans. The purpose of these plans is to allow employees to take a longer leave than that granted by law and to attract the employee back by guaranteeing an equivalent job on her or his return. Most major West German corporations have not only extended the parental leave (e.g., to seven years for the first child, with the possibility of an additional three years after the birth of more children), but they have added provisions for the parent to keep in touch with colleagues and changes at the workplace through seminars and holiday work.

These agreements appear very progressive at first glance, but they are already being looked at sceptically since it is unclear whether women – who are the overwhelming majority of applicants to date – will really be able to return to comparable jobs (see (5)). More significantly, such plans will prove to be a mixed blessing if men do not take the leave, thereby making recruiting women appear to be an even greater "risk" for a department, because the parental leave is so much longer than the maternity leave. If management feels that it has done enough to help women balance work and children by "giving them leave not to work," the very existence of these agreements may hinder experiments with other programs and organizational changes that would do more to facilitate combining work and childrearing.

Outlook

Drawing on a comparison of the experiences and achievements in the two Germanies, what might the future of women in management look like in the united Germany by the end of the decade?

Can we count on economic demand?

The greatest promoter of women throughout the economy is very simple: economic need. When organizations are desperate for labor, they definitely hire women; and when the deficit is in the management ranks, they apparently hire women for managerial positions too. Economic need, however, is not a stable condition, and the history of West Germany's market economy shows that the unemployment of women rises disproportionately during economic downturns.

From the perspective of the need for labor, the current situation in reunited Germany is very unbalanced. The East German labor force suffers from exceptionally high unemployment levels, estimated to have reached almost 50 percent of the labor force by the end of 1991. East German women represent over 60 percent of the unemployed, and anecdotal evidence indicates that women who held management positions in East Germany were laid off faster than their male colleagues. On the other hand, unemployment is dropping in West Germany and there is a great concern about the estimated deficit of 50,000 people with managerial potential that is predicted to grow to 500,000 by the end of the century (20;34).

What are the implications of the labor market situation for East and West German women managers? For slightly different reasons, the outlook does not appear to be good for either, especially if policy is based only on a perception of the "urgent need for labor." The concern about the projected deficit of managers in West Germany that was identified in the second half of the 1980s became one of the most important factors leading companies to reassess their recruitment and personnel development policies in order to try to attract and keep qualified women. Will the reunited Germany maintain this momentum? The high levels of unemployment among men in East Germany will certainly have an impact on companies' perception of the need for women managers. It is likely that the demographic shift afforded by the opening of the wall and resulting expanded pool of men to draw from will make the specter of unfilled management positions fade and will drain away the sense of urgency that had stimulated West German companies' search for women managers.

There are various projections for how long it will take to revive the economy in the former East Germany, but most experts expect a significant turnaround to have been achieved by the end of the century. It is unlikely that East German women will automatically regain their position in the labor market, because re-entering the labor market after a period of unemployment will be particularly difficult given the extensive retraining needed to adapt to the needs and standards of Western industrialized companies. East Germans who fail to move into training and employment now risk being unable to catch up later. Since the Communist planned economy made re-entry automatic, it is difficult for workers from that system to realize how high the cost of not fighting for a job in the current system might well be. Considering how central a part paid work has played in their lives, it is unlikely that many East German women are choosing to leave the labor market willingly. Rather, the well-established mechanisms whereby men tend to hire, keep, and promote other men appear to be functioning effectively during this period of transition.

Need for legislation

In both Germanies, the existence of a constitutional right to equal opportunity has not sufficed for women to achieve that right, particularly when it is applied to access to power and resources in the form of management responsibilities. As the president of the German Bundestag, Rita Süssmuth, pointed out, "A glance at history documents that women have never received their rights voluntarily, they have always had to fight to claim them" (37). She added, "This is still true, and for this reason women should and must continue to fight for the necessary changes in our societal structures, because when we stop fighting, we cannot move anything any more" (37 [our translation]). This statement is especially true about getting men to share power.

One of the most disturbing aspects of the transition to a reunited Germany has been the rapidity with which the legislated achievements of East Germany have been dissolved[8] and the ease with which managers sent to operate in East Germany have overlooked the equal opportunity practices that had become established in West German organizations. In the turbulence of transforming East German companies to operate in a market economy and of adapting East Germany's public administration to the West German system, personnel decisions have been made without applying the advertising or consultation procedures that had become standard operating procedure in West Germany. The mandatory government guidelines for equal opportunity in public administration, discussed earlier, have not been enforced in the process of reorganizing East German administrations. As a result, there has been a significant gender bias in the decisions to keep, fire, or recruit staff in both the public and private sectors, and that bias will have far-reaching consequences.

Clearly, stronger legislation must be fought for if change is to be achieved and a significantly higher number of women managers are to be found in Germany by the end of the century. Organizations and individual managers must be required to set reasonable targets in this area, just as they do for other management tasks, and then they must be held accountable for achieving these goals. Serious consequences need to follow when women are not adequately represented in management and in the training programs and seminars considered essential for career development.

Infrastructure and underlying values

The review of the experiences of women in management in East and West Germany in the past decades and past months shows that neither great economic need nor legislation alone can guarantee that women will gain access to significant numbers of positions of authority in Germany's economic, political, and societal systems. International comparative studies of women in management lead to the same conclusion (2). What more needs to be taken into consideration?

Providing childcare is an essential, but not sufficient, precondition for managing the dual responsibilities of children and a career. Although the East German state introduced sweeping childcare provisions to enable its women to work, it did nothing to change the structure of work; nor was there an opportunity for East Germans to question the basic assumptions about the roles of women and men in the home and in childrearing. In both Germanies, jobs, particularly those leading to and in management, remain tailored to the person (generally a man) who can devote almost unlimited time to the work, leaving other responsibilities for life in the hands of another (usually a woman). In both Germanies, women have traditionally carried – and continue to carry – the major responsibility for housekeeping and childcare. Time-budget studies indicate that in both systems women spend significantly more hours at these tasks than do their partners (39).

Parallel to seeking legislation and ensuring its implementation, much more attention must be paid in the upcoming years to developing numerous flanking measures designed to change organizations from the inside. German organizations need new forms of structuring and distributing work that provide paid employment as well as changing the "household/family" organization.

A glimmer of hope: A new constellation of forces for change

There is reason to hope that change can be achieved through the combined energy of a constellation of forces in Germany during the present decade. First, a source of energy for the struggles to come will probably be found in the women of former East Germany. The things that they had come to see as their birthright – such as the right to work and the right to childcare – are being swept away during the transition to a reunited Germany. If East German women can link forces with the women in West Germany, who have already learned to fight for their rights in the hard way, their combined energy could achieve the changes needed in society. Active networking of women in management in East and West is already underway in such organizations as the European Women's Management Development Network.

A second factor that might well add fuel to this process is the rapprochement currently occurring between women seeking change from within the establishment and those seeking change from the fringes. The issue of women in management received no attention at the outset from feminist scholars, and women managers were simply rejected out of hand by most members of the critical women's movement in West Germany during the 1970s. Similarly, few women managers had any interest in the women's movement. Since the mid-1980s, however, there is increasing recognition on the part of all concerned that they have more in common than meets the eye, and attempts to learn from one another are being launched in seminars and through the literature.

A third source of pressure on organizations to change may well come from men. Although, unfortunately, international comparative surveys indicate that men's attitudes about the childrearing role of women remain particularly conservative in Germany (10), other attitudinal surveys show that a small but growing number of men are looking more critically at the traditional German work ethic and seeking more meaningful activities, both at work and in their leisure time (23). It is hoped that more male managers will follow in the footsteps of the few pioneers who are choosing to work part-time or take parental leave and thereby break the stereotypical molds of successful managerial careers.

A final factor promoting change in management decisions on personnel and organization policies may be found in the increasing debate about the need for new management styles and structures. Project management, as a flexible and nonhierarchical structure, and cooperative and holistic management styles are receiving increasing attention in the popular management literature and at corporate seminars.[9] In an experimental atmosphere in which companies become open to a variety of new ideas, recruiting and promoting women in management in Germany may not appear to be such a crazy idea after all.

Notes

The authors would like to thank Dafna Izraeli, Maria Oppen, and Donna Wood for valuable comments on an earlier draft of this article.

1 We will use the terms East Germany and West Germany in this text, although the political terms applicable until 1990 were German Democratic Republic and Federal Republic of Germany, respectively. Since unification the former territory of East Germany is referred to as the "new federal states."

2 It is important to note that all such statistical data are of questionable value since there is no explicit definition of "manager" on which to base surveys in Germany. Respondents and analysts apply their own definitions, thereby essentially precluding verification, comparisons between companies, and longitudinal analysis.

3 German corporations have a two-tiered board structure: the management board and the supervisory board above it.

4 Although in West Germany this refers to part-time work, East German women did not have that option. They did, however, tend to work significantly less overtime than their male colleagues and therefore did not receive bonuses (Winkler, 1990).

5 As critics point out, the "women's policy" of the former East German regime was essentially limited to "family policy" (Merkel, 1990, p. 60). For this reason, this section does not provide a comparison between policies in East and West Germany as do the other sections of this chapter.

6 The resistance to applying quotas to the recruitment and promotion of women until the current imbalance is corrected is interesting to observe in a system that allows for both explicit quotas for other groupings (e.g., party affiliation and labor representation) and for

"hidden" quotas that tend to favor men in a range of occupations and hierarchical levels.

7 There is no gender-neutral term for "manager" or "supervisor" in German. The commonly used form (reflecting reality) is masculine; adding the feminine ending must be a conscious decision (e.g., *Leiter* and *Leiterin, Meister* and *Meisterin*).

8 The one legislative achievement of East Germany that received special attention was the abortion law, which is much more flexible in East Germany than in West Germany. For a transition period, this is the only law that has been permitted to remain different between the two parts of reunited Germany.

9 One of the elements that is raised in this discussion in Germany as well as in other countries is the potential match between women's leadership qualities and the features needed for management in the future. As attractive as this argument may appear at first, it contains the seeds of further stereotyping. Significantly more research would need to be done before solid arguments can be presented on this matter. Existing research is of limited use since it has been conducted almost exclusively in the United States, either in laboratory-like settings or in large male-dominated organizations. Insights from experiences in other countries and in women-only or women-dominated organizations are needed for this discussion.

References

(1) Assig, Dorothea (1989) "Women, Entrepreneurship and a Sense of Adventure," *EWMD News* 19 (Spring):4–5.

(2) Berthoin Antal, Ariane, and Izraeli, Dafna (1993) "Women in Management: An International Comparison," in E. A. Fagenson (ed.), *Women in Management: Trends, Perspectives, Challenges in Managerial Diversity*. Newbury Park, Calif.: Sage Publications.

(3) Berthoin Antal, Ariane, and Krebsbach-Gnath, Camilla (1986) "Working Women Abroad: West Germany," *Equal Opportunities International*, 5(1):26–30.

(4) Berthoin Antal, Ariane, and Krebsbach-Gnath, Camilla (1986–87) "Women in Management: Still Plenty of Unused Resources in the Federal Republic of Germany," *International Studies of Management and Organization* (Fall–Winter):133–151.

(5) Biallo, Horst (1990) "Ungedeckte Wechsel" ["Uncovered Bills"], *Wirtschaftswoche* 21:52–54.

(6) Bischoff, Sonja (1990) *Frauen zwischen Macht und Mann: Männer in der Defensive. Führungskräfte in Zeiten des Umbruchs* [*Women between Power and Men: Men on the Defensive. Managers in Time of Change*]. Reinbeck bei Hamburg: Rowohlt.

(7) Bulmahn, Edelgard, et al. (1990) *Frauenförderung in der kommunalen Verwaltung* [*Promoting Women in Local Administration*]. Gesprächskreis Frauenpolitik, Forschungsinstitut Friedrich Ebert Stiftung.

(8) Bundesministerium für Jugend, Familie, Frauen und Gesundheit [BMJFFG] (1989) *Frauen in der Bundesrepublik Deutschland* [*Women in the Federal Republic of Germany*]. Bonn: BMJFFG.

(9) Busch, Carola, et al. (1990) *Betriebliche Frauenförderung* [*Promoting Women in Companies*]. Frankfurt am Main: Vereinigung der hessischen Unternehmerverbände.

(10) Commission of the European Communities (1987) *Women and Men of Europe in 1987*. Women of Europe, Supplement 26, Brussels.

(11) Commission of the European Communities (1990) *Childcare in the European Communities 1985–1990*, 31.

(12) Demmer, Christine (ed.) (1988) *Frauen ins Management. Von der Reservearmee zur Begabungsreserve* [*Women in Management: From Reserve Forces to the Reserve of Talents*].

Wiesbaden: Gabler Verlag.

(13) Demmer, Christine (1988) "Was Frauen fordern – Wie Frauen fördern?" ["What Women Demand – How to Promote Women"], in C. Demmer (ed.), *Frauen ins Management: Von der Reservearmee zur Begabungsreserve* [*Women in Management: From Reserve Forces to the Reserve of Talents*], pp. 9–28. Wiesbaden: Gabler Verlag.

(14) Deutsches Institut für Wirtschaftsforschung [DIW] (1990) "Vereintes Deutschland – geteilte Frauengesellschaft? Erwerbsbeteiligung und Kinderzahl in beiden Teilen Deutschlands" ["United Germany – Divided Women's Society? Labor Force Participation and Number of Children in Both Parts of Germany"], *Wochenbericht* 41/90 (October):575–582.

(15) "Frauen im Management: selten, tuchtig, unterbezahlt" ["Women in Management: Scarce, Qualified, and Underpaid"] (1985), *Wirtschaftswoche*, Vol. 18.

(16) Friesen, Juliane von (1989) *Bericht der Kommission Gleichberechtigung und Gleichstellung von Frauen und Männern in Beruf, Politik und Gesellschaft* [*Report of the Commission on Equal Opportunity for Women and Men in Jobs, Politics and Society*]. Düsseldorf: Deutscher Juristinnenbund.

(17) Handy, Charles (1987) *The Making of Managers: A Report on Management Education, Training and Development in the U.S.A., West Germany, France, Japan and the U.K.* London: Manpower Series Commission, National Economic Development Council, and the British Institute of Management.

(18) Hegelheimer, Barbara (1982) *In-Firm Training and Career Prospects for Women in the Federal Republic of Germany*. Berlin: CEDEFOP.

(19) Hochstätter, Dietrich, with Schunke, Marion (1989) "Cherchez la Femme" ["Recruiting Women"], *Wirtschaftswoche* 9:46–61.

(20) Hofer, P.; Weidig, I.; and Wolff, H. (1989) *Arbeitslandschaft bis 2010 nach Umfang und Tätigkeitsprofilen* [*Work until 2010: Scope and Job Profiles*]. Nuremberg: Prognos AG.

(21) Hübner, Eva (1989) Untitled statement published in *Forum: Frauen in Führungspositionen* [*Women in Managerial Positions*]. Proceedings of the Social Democratic Party of North Rhine-Westfalia, Düsseldorf, November 27, pp. 18–19.

(22) Jaeckel, Monika (1990) "Frauen in beiden Teilen Deutschlands: Fremd und Selbstwahrnehmungen," ["Women in Both Parts of Germany: How They Perceive Themselves"], in Michael Haller (ed.), *Rita Sussmuth und Helga Schubert. Gehen die Frauen in die Knie?* [*Are Women Giving Up?*], pp. 9–44. Zurich: Pendo Verlag.

(23) Klippstein, Michael von, and Strümpel, Burkhard (1985) *Gewandelte Werte – Erstarrte Strukturen: Wie die Burger Wirtschaft und Arbeit erleben* [*Changed Values – Ossified Structures: How People Experience the Economy and Work*]. Bonn: Verlag Neue Gesellschaft.

(24) Krebsbach-Gnath, Camilla, and Schmid-Jörg, Ina (1985) *Leitfaden zur Frauenförderung in Betrieben: Die Durchsetzung der Gleichberechtigung als Chance für die Personalpolitik* [*Guideline for the Promotion of Women in Companies: Equal Opportunity as the Chance for Personnel Policy*]. Bonn: Der Bundesminister für Jugend, Familie und Gesundheit.

(25) "Mehr Familiensinn" ["More Family Minded"] (1989), *Capital* 9:258–268.

(26) Meier, Uta (1990*a*) "Nachdem die Panzerschranke geöffnet sind . . ." ["After the vaults have been opened"], *DJI Bulletin, Deutsches Jugendinstitut* 15 (June):7–12.

(27) Meier, Uta (1990*b*) "Women at Work: The German Democratic Republic," *EWMD News* 25 (Autumn):5–6.

(28) Merkel, Ina (1990) "Frauenpolitische Strategien der DDR" ["Political Strategies for Women in the GDR"], in Sabine Gensior, Friederike Maier, and Gabriele Winter (eds.), *Soziale Lage und Arbeit von Frauen in der DDR* [*The Social Situation and Work of*

Women in the GDR], pp. 56–70. Working paper 1990–6, Arbeitskreis Sozial-wissenschaftliche Arbeitsmarktforschung (SAMF), Universität Gesamthochschule, Paderborn.

(29) Nickel, Hildegard Maria (1990) "Zur sozialen Lage von Frauen in der DDR," in Sabine Gensior, Friederike Maier, and Gabriele Winter (eds.), *Soziale Lage und Arbeit von Frauen in der DDR* [*The Social Situation and Work of Women in the GDR*]. Working paper 1990–6, Arbeitskreis Sozialwissenschaftliche Arbeitsmarkt Forschung (SAMF), Universität-Gesamthochschule, Paderborn.

(30) Nickel, Hildegard Maria (1991) "Geschlechterverhältnis in der Wende?" ["The Change in the Gender Relations?"], in *Frauen in den neuen Bundeslandern. Ruckzug in die Familie oder Aufbruch zur Gleichstellung in Beruf und Familie?* [*Women in the New Federal States: Retreat to Family or Start for Equal Opportunity in Work and Family*], pp. 5–16. Gesprachskreis Frauenpolitik, No. 2. Bonn: Friedrich Ebert Stiftung.

(31) "Offerten nur für Männer" ["Offers Only for Men"] (1990), *Management Wissen* 11:8.

(32) Radtke, Heidrun (1989) "Der Einsatz von Frauen in verantwortlichen Funktionen von Wissenschaft und Technik – Möglichkeiten und Grenzen" ["The Employment of Women in Managerial Functions in Science and Technology"]. Unpublished paper, Akademie der Wissenschaften der DDR, Institut für Soziologie und Sozialpolitik, May 15.

(33) Ridder-Melchers, Ilse (1989) "Rahmenbedingungen fur Frauen in Führungspositionen – Situation, Bedarf, Tendenzen" ["Conditions for Women in Managerial Positions – Situations, Requirements, and Tendencies"], in *Forum: Frauen in Führungspositionen*. Proceedings of the Social Democratic Party of North Rhine-Westfalia, Düsseldorf, November 27, pp. 14–17.

(34) Rotkirch, C. von and Weidig, I. (1985) *Die Zukunft der Arbeitslandschaft. Zum Arbeitskräftebedarf nach Umfang und Tätigkeit bis zum Jahr 2000* [*The Future of Work. Manpower Requirements in Scope and Activity Until the Year 2000*]. Nuremberg: Prognos AG.

(35) Schmidt, Renate (1991) "Neue Rechte für Frauen in Gesamtdeutschland" ["New Rights for Women in Unified Germany"], in *Nach der Vereinigung Deutschlands: Frauen fordern ihr Recht* [*After Unification: Women Demand Their Rights*], pp. 1–10. Gesprächskreis Frauenpolitik, No. 2. Bonn: Friedrich Ebert Stiftung.

(36) Statistisches Amt der DDR (ed.) (1990) *Statistisches Jahrbuch der DDR 1990* [*Statistical Yearbook of the GDR 1990*]. Berlin: Rudolf Haufe Verlag.

(37) Süssmuth, Rita (1989) *Kämpfen und Bewegen Frauenreden* [*Fighting and Moving: Addresses to Women*]. Freiburg: Herder Verlag.

(38) Weimer, Sybille (1991) "Mit Mutti ins Büro" ["With Mommy in the Office"], *Journal für die Frau* 15:73–76.

(39) Winkler, Gunnar (ed.) (1990) *Frauenreport '90* [*Report on Women '90*]. Report to the Beauftragte des Ministerrates für die Gleichstellung von Frauen und Männern, Dr. Marina Beyer. Berlin: Verlag die Wirtschaft.

14

GREAT BRITAIN

The Scenario for Women Managers in Britain in the 1990s

Valerie Hammond and Viki Holton

In 1918, Nancy Astor took her seat in Westminster as the first woman member of Parliament in Britain. It is ironic that after the vigorous suffragette campaigns for "votes for women," the first woman to win a seat in the House of Commons was an American. British women followed, but by the late 1980s they still held only 6 percent of the seats. By then, Margaret Thatcher was prime minister. However, no other woman was ever a member of her cabinet, a matter that caused comment. When John Major became prime minister in November 1990, he was also roundly criticized for not appointing women to his cabinet, a situation he remedied after the 1992 election by appointing two women, Gillian Shepherd and Virginia Bottomley as ministers of state for employment and health, respectively, and four others to junior ministerial positions. The fact that public opinion was expressed strongly is an indication of the change occurring in Britain. Increasingly, there is an expectation that women will hold top positions.

Similar trends exist in other professions. Mary Harris Smith was allowed membership in the Institute of Chartered Accountants in 1920, 29 years after her initial application; but it was not until the 1990s that the number of women enrolling as members of the institute reached more than 10 percent. Accounting is an important field for women to conquer, because within British commercial life accountancy is recognized as a route to the board. In 1991, Kathleen O'Donovan, a partner in the firm Ernst and Young, achieved significant publicity on her appointment as finance director of BTR, one of Britain's most profitable companies. At the age of 34, she not only became one of the very few women to reach such a high boardroom position in a top British company but also one the youngest executive directors of either gender.

In law, that most traditional of professions in Britain, where current debate focuses on whether to stop wearing wigs and gowns, change can also be detected. Until 1919, women were barred from entering the legal profession; and, although this situation has changed, the legacy is that by the end of the 1980s women still only accounted for 4 percent of the professional judiciary. Among lay magistrates, the numbers are more evenly matched. Law has become an increasingly attractive subject for women to study and one at which women students excel. In 1987, more women than men passed the final solicitors' examinations, more women passed at their first attempt, and more women received higher class degrees than did men (11). However, fewer women go on to become barristers or judges and more drop out of law practice. Some use their law studies as a route to senior management. The most obvious example here is Yvette Newbold, company secretary of Hanson Plc, a major Anglo-American conglomerate. She is also a nonexecutive director of British Telecom, governor of London Business School, and a member of the Royal Commission on Criminal Justice.

As the saying goes, however, a few swallows do not make a summer. Has the situation really improved? Are more women entering and being retained in management? What is the outlook? As has already been demonstrated, most of the twentieth century has seen a slow pace of change with regard to the role of women in management. Although the United Kingdom ratified both the United Nations International Covenant on Civil and Political Rights and the UN International Convention on the Elimination of All Forms of Discrimination against Women, and, on joining the European Community, signed the Treaty of Rome, which states that "each member state shall during the first stage ensure and subsequently maintain the application of the principle that men and women should receive equal pay for equal work" (Article 119), national legislation has been slow and has given minimal support to these rights. The Sex Discrimination Act of 1975 forbids sex discrimination, direct or indirect, in a wide range of activities, including employment and education. Whether employers – or government ministers – fully appreciated their legal obligations, however, remains doubtful. Although discrimination has been challenged in the courts, the process is bruising and the awards in the most part have been derisory.

Few women have sought to bring about change through the courts, though it remains true that some of the more significant advances have come about in this way. For example, Helen Marshall, a National Health Service dietician who did not want to retire at 60, challenged the rules about women's pensionable age through the British courts and then in the European Court of Human Justice before winning her case. It forced the government to amend the Sex Discrimination Act in 1987 to require all employers to have equal retirement ages for women and men (7). In 1992, Alison Halford, who, as an assistant chief constable, was one of Britain's most senior women police officers, alleged that her employers had persistently (eight times) and over a number of years discriminated against her promotion to chief constable. This highly publicized case was eventually settled out of court. Almost immediately, two other women were appointed to the rank of assistant chief constable, appointments that Alison Halford believes were influenced by her case.

Women have lobbied vigorously for changes in fiscal arrangements, and it is only since April, 1991, that married women have been allowed to elect to be taxed separately from their husband. Until 1991, the wife's income was treated as part of her husband's income as far as taxes were concerned. Tax returns were sent to the husband, as were demands and refunds.

Women have also fought for tax concessions with regard to the cost of childcare. In 1990, for the first time, the government granted tax allowances for childcare, if provided by the employer – that is, workplace nurseries or employer-sponsored places. Previously the tax rules considered employer-provided nurseries as benefits in kind; and, like cars and private health plans, employees paid a tax on childcare services. The new allowance does not include privately organized nursery provision, although the government may yet widen the benefit to include more types of nurseries.

Beyond the question of tax allowances is the more vexing issue of the availability of affordable childcare. With membership in the European Community and, even more, with the advent of the single market, it has become increasingly common to compare the situation in Britain with that of other Community countries and to use the European Commission, European Parliament, and other institutions to create pressure for change. Comparisons on childcare show that Britain's provision is poor, lagging behind all other member states apart from Portugal, where, in any case, women's employment rates are lower (2).

Women in the Workforce

Despite the difficulties, the number of working women in Britain has increased, both in actual numbers and in terms of their proportion of the labor market (see Table 14.1). In 1984, just over 9.5 million women, or 41 percent of the workforce excluding those on government-training programs, were employed. By spring 1991, women accounted for over eleven million employees, and their share of the employed workforce had risen to 44 percent (18). In spite of recessionary times and increasing unemployment, women are expected to maintain and even to increase their share of the workforce in light of the demographic decrease in young people and the increasing competition for highly skilled, competent people.

Part-time work continues to be important to British women, perhaps reflecting the previously mentioned paucity of childcare. In 1991, 44 percent of employed women regarded their jobs as part-time (hours were unspecified); this figure had decreased slightly from 45 percent in 1984. A government survey carried out in 1991 found that 68 percent of those women who worked part-time did not want a full-time job, and, for married women, this figure rose to 75 percent (18). The definition of part-time varies enormously. For some purposes, it is eight hours per week; for others, up to 30 hours. These circumstances give rise to different possibilities for work to be split or shared. In one example, the chief executive position of a National Health Service Trust hospital is shared by two married women enabling them to continue their careers through their childrearing years in a situation in

Table 14.1   Women in the British workforce

Women in workforce	1984	1991
Total women in the workforce	9,500,000	11,000,000
Women as percentage of workforce	41.4%	43.7%
Women working part-time as a percentage of all women working	43.9%	44.6%

Source: Naylor, M. and Purdie, E. (1992) "Results of the 1991 Labour Force Survey," *Employment Gazette* (April). London: HMSO.

which a single job holder would typically work 60 to 70 hours per week. For some, each part of this shared job would constitute a full-time position, but these women regard it as a satisfactory part-time position.

Women's Work

Women and men continue to be employed in different occupations and sectors. Women form the majority only in clerical and secretarial work and in sales and personal service occupations. However, by spring 1991, 28 percent of all working women held a managerial or professional job (8).

Women's opportunity for a career in management depends heavily on the industry sector. The Equal Opportunity Commission showed that in 1989 the large majority of women managers (some 250,000) were employed in retail distribution, followed by hotel and catering, with less than 100,000 women managers. Banking and finance, medical and other health services, and food, drink, and tobacco each employed less than 50,000; electronics and engineering employed far fewer. However, women in Britain are increasingly entering management in non-traditional sectors, such as manufacturing, insurance, and banking. Statistics from Midland Bank, one of the five clearing banks in the United Kingdom, show that women now make up 19 percent of its management; and at Imperial Chemical Industries (ICI), the major pharmaceuticals and chemical company, in 1992, women represented one-third of the annual graduate intake, the future management resource.

Changes in the way the government compiles data make it impossible to compare the present situation with that for earlier years. In 1980, the occupational groups were reclassified, but data continued to be reported under the earlier system, thereby allowing us to make comparisons with previous years. In 1991, comparative data were no longer available by gender. The data were only presented in the new form, which had the effect of increasing the size of management and professional occupational groups by 25 percent. For example, the New Earnings Survey for 1975 and 1986 (see Table 14.2) shows women to represent 11 percent and 17 percent, respectively, of all employees in management, professional, and supporting administrative occupations (19). The 1991 data for these categories include, in addition, those associated with professional and technical occupations, with a total of 38 percent women. While the figures are not comparable, the sharp increase nonetheless suggests that there has been a substantial growth in the proportion of women managers and those doing related work.

The above figures reveal nothing about today's employment of women at different levels of management. The government has so far not made such data available, although the 1991 census may be revealing. An estimate by the National Economic Development Office put the percentage of women holding senior and middle management positions at only 4 percent and those holding senior executive positions at a mere 1 to 2 percent (12).

A survey by the British Institute of Management found that the number of companies employing women executives increased from 49 percent in 1986 to 64

Table 14.2   Women in management and related occupations

Category	Women as percentage of all employees in category		
	1975	1986	1991
General management	9.7	10.4	—
Managerial positions excluding general management	10.9	16.4	—
Professional and related supporting management and administrative positions	12.0	20.3	—
Managers and administrators	—	—	30.6
Professional occupations	—	—	38.3
Associate professional and technical occupations	—	—	49.3
Total, all management and related occupations	11.3	17.4	37.9

Source: *New Earnings Survey 1975*, Part E, Table 138; *New Earnings Survey 1986*, Part E, Table 138. London: HMSO; Naylor, M. and Purdie, E. (1992) "Results of the 1991 Labour Force Survey," *Employment Gazette*, (April). London: HMSO.

percent in 1990. The survey also found that the proportion of women directors grew in the same period from 4 percent to 8 percent (20).

Getting to the Top

We can possibly best glimpse the seriousness of women's career intentions through their membership in the relevant functional institutions, where entrance depends on professional examination (see Table 14.3). The memberships show some remarkable increases over a seven- to eight-year time span and indicate that in some functional areas, such as personnel management (HRM) and marketing, women are making their presence felt. In other, generally less woman-friendly occupations, such as engineering and information technology, women have responded by setting up their own professional organizations. For example, the Women's Engineering Society has 700 members. Although not itself an examining body, its members are qualified engineers. In a different kind of initiative, the Women into Information Technology Foundation was established with assistance from the government and information technology companies to encourage women's progress in this industry.

These organizations provide support and training for members and serve as a lobbying group on behalf of women's interests. Among the considerable achievements of the Law Society's Women's Association are the annual refresher courses they organize to help women returning to practice after a career break. The association also persuaded the Law Society to reduce subscription rates for all non-practicing members who wished to remain in contact with the profession. In other professions, women have formed a new association outside the traditional professional institution, such as Women in Management or Women in Banking, providing services, meetings, and skill-training specifically for their members.

Table 14.3 Women's membership in selected management and professional institutions

Professional institution	Total members	Women	Women (%)	Date
Bankers, Institute of	111,381	21,370	19.2	1986
	110,813	27,399	25.0	1992
Building, Chartered Institute of	27,297	192	0.7	1985
	33,229	545	1.6	1992
Certified Accountants, Association of	28,309	2,831	10.0	1986
	23,912	2,823	11.8	1992
Chartered Accountants of England and Wales, Institute of	82,135	5,716	7.0	1985
	97,720	11,757	12.0	1992
Chemical Engineers, Institute of	16,796	822	5.0	1985
	20,000	2,000	10.0	1992
Computer Society, British	35,000	N/A	10.0	1992
Directors, Institute of	N/A	N/A	2.0	1987
	40,432	2,602	6.5	1992
Health Service Management, Institute of	5,909	2,298	38.8	1986
	7,000	N/A	50.0	1992
Hotel, Catering and Institutional Management Association	22,944	10,957	47.8	1986
	23,000	N/A	50.0	1992
Law Society, The (Solicitors) with practicing certificate without certificate	44,837	6,262	14.0	1984
	57,000	14,000	24.5	1992
	12,000	4,000	33.3	1992
Management, British Institute of	74,268	2,407	3.2	1986
	75,000	N/A	11.5	1992
Marketing, Chartered Institute of	20,633	1,207	5.8	1986
	20,700	4,000	19.3	1992
Personnel Management, Institute of	26,266	10,758	41.8	1986
	50,104	30,124	60.0	1992

Source: Authors' direct inquiry with each institution.

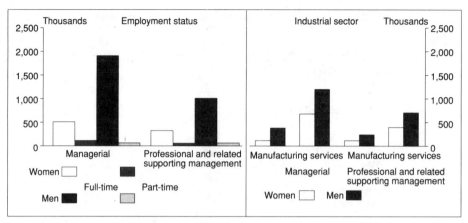

Source: Equal Opportunities Commission (1991b) *Women and Men in Britain 1991*. Manchester: Equal Opportunities Commission.

Figure 14.1   Women in management in selected industries

Networks for women operate across most functions and sectors, locally and internationally. To increase their strength, there are now "networks of networks" – an approach that brings increased lobbying power, and sometimes funding, from the government and the European Community. Indeed one government minister, Baroness Denton, who is herself an experienced networker with a long career in industry, has set up a forum expressly to raise the profile and possibility of women for senior roles.

If membership in the Institute of Directors is an indicator, the proportion of women at the most senior levels in both the public and private sector remains very small. There are no woman chief executives among Britain's top 100 companies, as listed in *The Times 1000* (1), and a 1989 report found that among members of company boards in the 200 largest industrial companies in the United Kingdom, only 21 had women board members (15). In total, 24 women were appointed, but the majority, eighteen, were either part-time or nonexecutive directors. Several of the appointed women had a family connection to the company or a title – that of lady or baroness. Women often hold appointments on boards of a number of companies belonging to the same group or with firms in similar sectors.

The paucity of women board members may be due to the way in which British industry defines appropriate experience. ProNed, a not-for-profit organization sponsored by the Confederation of British Industry, the British Institute of Management, and a number of companies, aims to promote the appointment of independent nonexecutive directors by stressing the benefit of an external perspective on corporate affairs. ProNed is involved in approximately 10 percent of all nonexecutive directorships offered in Britain and keeps a register of suitable candidates to match with the criteria that companies supply. The majority of requests stipulate that candidates must have board experience of a public limited company. As indicated, only a small minority of British women currently have this background, so it is not surprising that among some 600 names on ProNed's register only 50 belong to women. Unless such criteria are reconsidered, it would seem that the chances of seeing many more women on the boards of British companies is still a long way off.

Attention has focused over recent years on ways to increase the number of women at the top. Campaigning bodies have encouraged women to take up senior and public appointments and, at the same time, they have persuaded companies and public bodies to open their doors to women. The 300 Group, which celebrated its tenth anniversary in 1990, campaigns for women to stand for election to Parliament. Its aim is for women to hold 50 percent of all 650 places in the House of Commons. In 1992, there were just 60 women, 9 percent, in the House.

Since 1983, the Government Cabinet Office has published information on the number of women appointed by government ministers and departments to sit on statutory and advisory boards and other public bodies. In 1987, the Women's National Commission, the official body of advisers to the government on women's matters, achieved a major step by gaining agreement that details of some 50,000 public appointments should be published for the first time. Figures for 1985 showed that, on average, women received 18.5 percent of the appointments, with some departments being more open to women, ranging from 3.2 percent of appointments in the Ministry of Agriculture, Fisheries, and Food to 31 percent of those made by the Home Office. By 1989, there was a marked improvement. On average, women received 23 percent of the appointments – varying from a low of 5 percent again in the Ministry of Agriculture, Fisheries, and Food to 43 percent awarded by the Cabinet Office itself – although this figure includes appointments to the all female Women's National Commission (25;26).

On the other side of the negotiating table, and despite the general decline in trade union membership, the number of women members of trade unions is increasing. In 1992, three million out of the total 8.6 million members in the Trades Union Congress (TUC) were women. Yet, it is still a relatively new phenomenon to see a women at the head of a trade union. Diana Warwick of the Association of University Teachers became the first woman union leader in 1983; and in 1989, the number of women heads, or general secretaries as they are known, rose from six to twelve. It may be significant that in 1992 both Diana Warwick and Brenda Dean, another very high-profile and highly regarded leader, gave up their union posts – the former took up a nonunion role and the latter resigned, following a merger in which she lost the top position. Statistics have generally shown that women are less likely than men to attend conferences, to represent their local union branches, or to sit on working committees. Statistics published by the European Trade Union Institute for 1986 show that women made up 33 percent of the membership of the TUC, but only 18 percent of the union executives and 15 percent of the conference delegates (6).

Education, Qualifications, and Training

The last decade has been a period of major educational reform in Britain, a process that is continuing, with new forms of qualification and an increased emphasis on educational achievement. In 1989, women accounted for 56 percent of all enrolments in further education (predegree programs). Sixty-one percent followed short courses of less than one year, and 45 percent took programs of two or more years. Women accounted for a major expansion in the provision of evening study; men are more likely to get day-release from work to study, whereas women are more likely to study on their "own" time.

Business administration was the most popular subject in further education, accounting for 20 percent of all enrolments, and 72 percent of these students were women. At 9 percent, women were grossly under-represented in engineering and technology courses, and at 2 percent they were scarcely present in architecture, building, and planning. There is also a marked difference between women and men in the type of qualification gained, with women opting for commercial, professional, or academic qualifications while men tend to gain craft or other qualifications that permit access to management diplomas and beyond (5).

More women are also investing in higher education. In 1987, women achieved 45 percent of all first degrees awarded and 37 percent of all postgraduate degrees (22). In 1988, women represented 49 percent of the graduate-level business and administration students. Subjects included business and management studies, accountancy, and financial management (24).

Subjects studied at university, however, do not necessarily limit career choices. In 1989, 59 percent of women graduates went directly into employment, while 21 percent continued their education or training. The figures for men were similar. For women, 30 percent took jobs in commerce, 20 percent in the public sector, and 18 percent in industry. The situation for men differed, with 41 percent going into industry (4).

Overall, there has been a trend for graduate employment away from the public sector and toward industry and commerce. The decline in competition in the public sector may account for more women finding jobs in that sector. The Civil Service (the administrative arm of the government), in particular, has widened its recruitment approach to broaden its intake to include more women.

In 1984, the Civil Service surveyed equal opportunities for women within the service. Among their recommendations were specific courses to help women prepare for careers in middle management and nonresidential training to encourage women and men with domestic commitments to attend. Women's participation in training was monitored from 1984 to 1987. Although women accounted for roughly half the 389,000 people attending departmental training, significantly fewer women attended external or senior-level courses, 27 percent of 50,000 and 31 percent of 18,000, respectively. While the recommendations to help women gain access to more training may have helped improve women's representation, the very act of monitoring women's progress has kept it as a priority issue (9).

Based on functional specialization in 1989, women's first job was most likely to be in personnel, health, or social work. More than 20 percent of new graduates chose these fields. Finance and legal work were also popular; and marketing, administration, and science and engineering each attracted 10 percent of the new women graduates. Men's first choice, made by more than 30 percent, was scientific or engineering work (4).

There have been some innovative ways to encourage girls to identify with new subject areas and career choices. Recent figures for chemical engineering, traditionally a male-dominated subject, show that the proportion of women undergraduates is growing faster than in any other engineering subject. In 1980, only 8 percent of chemical engineering graduates were women; in 1989, this figure had increased to 26 percent (23). Among the reasons for this increase that the Chemical Engineers Professional Institute identified were the university summer schools run exclusively for women, which have made chemistry more available to them.

Qualifications specifically for management are in a state of flux in the United Kingdom. Views are divided about the value of providing a national qualification that would charter managers. More universities and business schools have introduced MBA (master of business administration) programs and other new management studies, and some companies have developed in-company MBA programs for their employees in conjunction with a university. Although there is lively debate about the value of the MBA degree, it provides professionals and managers with a "high-flier" appointment after completion. The Association of MBAs estimates that the proportion of women graduates has increased to around 20 to 25 percent. In 1992, there were 5,500 MBA graduates in the United Kingdom.

Earnings and Benefits

Since the implementation of the Equal Pay Act in 1975, women's salaries have improved. In 1970, women generally earned less than 65 percent of men's salaries, compared with 74 percent in 1987. A 1990 study of pay in the City of London, the heart of British business, revealed that men hold more than four in every five of the highest paid jobs and almost all of those positions paying £70,000 (US$144,857) and above. Only in the newer areas of business such as investment banking do women earn more than their male colleagues when matched by age (27).

The pay gap is partly explained by the fact that women are much more likely to be in lower-grade, lower-paid occupations than men. Civil Service data illustrate this: 75 percent of clerical assistants are women, the lowest paid grade in the Civil Service; 37 percent of executive officers are women (the entry grade for management); while at the top, women hold only 5 percent of the 1,000 posts of the four most senior grades (13;14).

Other factors contributing to the pay gap are that women managers have less seniority and are rewarded at a lower rate. For example, a regular national salary survey for the British Institute of Management (BIM), based on the experiences of over 400 companies with more than 21,000 executives, revealed that women are, on the average, seven years younger and have seven years' less service with their current companies (20). The pay survey of women in the City of London found a clear age-related factor in that salaries for women and men diverged during their mid-twenties and the gap increased with age (27). For the first time in recent years, the BIM survey found that women averaged a lower pay increase during the year, 9.8 percent, compared with 11.7 percent for men. At the managerial level, women earned only 3 percent less than men, but at the director level the gap was 33 percent (20).

Women Managers and Their Families

One of the major changes in Britain has been the number of company initiatives regarding family issues, such as flexible working arrangements, childcare benefits, and provision for dual careers, and the corresponding amount of interest these initiatives have generated in the British national press and business journals.

Organizations have found that many women who take maternity leave do not return to the company. Companies' recognition of this expensive waste of talent, combined with the looming specter of a dwindling number of young people over the next ten to twenty years, has helped focus companies' efforts on improving ways to recruit and retain women. Notwithstanding these efforts, research suggests that companies are slow in providing practical or financial help to get mothers back to work (3).

The overall number of companies active in creating "family friendly" organizations remains small; and the majority are the larger, blue-chip, multinational organizations. A 1989 survey by one national newspaper found that the majority of leading British companies considered childcare to be mostly a matter for the parents to organize for themselves. Fewer than one-quarter of the companies offered any practical or financial help to encourage mothers to return to work. Only six companies of the 100 surveyed provided workplace nurseries, with nine more considering offering them. The biggest growth area was in providing less expensive options: fourteen companies had launched job-sharing programs, 22 had instituted career-break programs, and nearly one-third of those surveyed offered flexible working hours (3).

There are signs that such benefits are important to all employees. The Royal Society of Chemistry published a survey of its members in 1989 stating that whereas 90 percent were not offered childcare facilities at work, 70 percent of the women and 39 percent of the men felt that such a benefit would be "desirable" or "highly desirable." Similarly, only one-third of all members were offered flexible working hours. However, among those under 35, 85 percent of women and 74 percent of men said that such flexibility would be advantageous (21).

Childcare services have been introduced primarily by companies with a large women labor force, such as the major banks and retail companies. Pioneering work by the Midland Bank involved setting up a chain of nurseries, often in partnership with other companies throughout the country. Grand Metropolitan funded half the costs of its first workplace nursery. The company talked with its women managers about ways in which it could help them combine work and family responsibilities. Although 30 percent of Grand Metropolitan's managers are women, the proportion holding more senior positions is considerably smaller, a fact that made the company decide to look at ways to improve the representation of women.

In 1989, Luncheon Vouchers launched an initiative to help employees who are also parents. Employers can make a monthly contribution to the cost of childcare in the form of vouchers that are offered to employees. It is an area of slow growth; for instance, after one year, only eighteen organizations had registered, covering 300 employees.

Initiatives for Equal Opportunity

Companies (particularly those in banking) in which there has been strong competition for competent new managers are looking to women as a potential resource. They have introduced career development programs specifically for women employees that frequently involve participation in "women only" courses at an early stage, active support and encouragement for the women to attain appropriate qualifications, and career guidance and counseling. Such firms encourage women to manage their own careers and demonstrate their commitment through the introduction of career-break and re-entry schemes.

One of the first companies to institute such a program was the National Westminster Bank, which since 1982 has offered career breaks of up to five years to women managers who wish to take time out to bring up their children. During their time out, the Bank requires the women to participate in training to keep up to date with banking practices and to work for at least two weeks a year. Provided these conditions are met, the Bank guarantees the women a management position at their previous level when they return to work. Similar plans have been introduced in other major financial institutions, although some have been broader and allowed all women and men staff members at any level within the company to take advantage of a career break.

In 1989, ICI became the first manufacturing organization to launch a career-break plan. Offered at managers' discretion, this program provides for the care of children or older dependents. Over 10 percent of ICI's UK workforce of 50,000 are women. The company was reacting to a situation in which one-third of the women who take maternity leave do not return to work with ICI, a figure that is even higher in other organizations. Some companies clearly see the business sense and economic advantage in helping to increase the number of valued employees who will return to work after a few years away.

A survey of over 2,000 organizations in different sectors found that larger organizations and those employing a high proportion of women were more likely to offer help to women to combine work and family responsibilities. However, the assistance offered was often minimal. Just over one-quarter of firms surveyed offered one or more benefits such as optional part-time work, flexitime, and job sharing. More costly benefits to implement, such as career breaks and childcare assistance, remain much rarer and were offered by only 4 percent of the companies surveyed (17).

Opportunity 2000

At the end of 1990, seventeen chief executives and directors of leading companies, working as part of the "Business in the Community" target team under the leadership of Lady Elspeth Howe, a redoubtable worker for women, were charged with improving women's economic development. Business in the Community is an initiative of the Prince of Wales that aims to foster corporate involvement in resolving local and national issues and concerns. It operates through task forces of the most senior businesspeople, who guarantee their commitment and energy for a given period of time while, of course, continuing to run their own businesses. This particular target team resulted in the national business-led campaign "Opportunity 2000."

The Business in the Community target team working on women's economic development had already implemented a number of initiatives – namely, training for women, assistance to enable women to set up businesses on their own, guidance on employer-provided childcare, and so on. As the target team of chief executives and directors reviewed progress, they became perplexed about why change seemed so slow in increasing the number of women progressing to the top of the organization.

The team commissioned an investigation to discover why legislation and other actions appeared to be having only a limited effect. The resulting study collected experience from employers and from advisory and regulatory groups in the United Kingdom, Europe, and the United States, Canada, and Australia (10). Taking a cultural perspective and building on earlier work, the team simultaneously followed two lines of inquiry: first, it reviewed the processes firms experienced as successful in bringing about organizational change, and second, it reviewed the processes employers used to implement equal opportunity.

Changing organization cultures

The target team studied some 150 documented cases of major organizational change of many different kinds. Analysis showed that in cases of successful change, a number of factors were invariably present, some elements more strongly than others but always interlinked to promote and sustain the change. These critical success factors can be grouped conveniently under four broad headings: commitment to the change as demonstrated by the board or senior management team; behaviors that reflect and promote the desired goals; broadly shared ownership; and investment – both financial and in terms of time (see Figure 14.2).

The major drivers for change were the commitment of the people at the top, together with strong and pressing business reasons for change. The combination of these two factors seemed to be most significant in protecting the change against fluctuating market conditions and ensuring broad participation. The time factor was important since, even in a very supportive environment, cultural change takes years rather than months. In the fast-moving business world, where firms frequently amend their priorities, the risk that change will not be maintained is high unless it is linked to business strategy. At the same time, a high-level champion, with responsibility for board commitment and power to orchestrate actions through all interest groups, appeared essential.

Along with the necessary training and communication to sustain the culture change, firms paid close attention to the link with business strategy, to setting goals for achievement, and to establishing systems to reward desired behavior. Line managers were actively involved. Communications about the change typically ex-

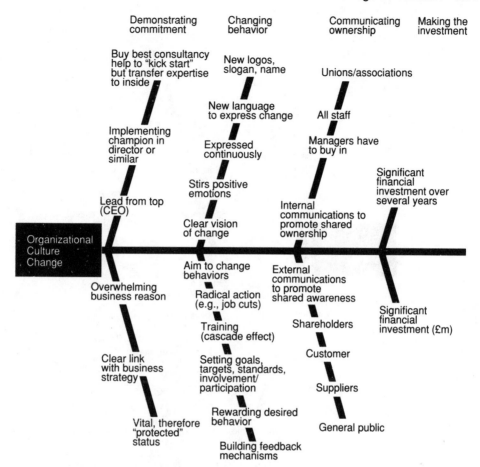

Source: V. Hammond and V. Holton (1991) *A Balanced Workforce: Achieving Cultural Change for Women, a Comparative Study.* Berkhamsted, UK: Ashridge Management Research Group.

Figure 14.2   Organization culture change

tended beyond staff to other stakeholders – that is, shareholders, customers, suppliers, the media, and the general public. The push-pull effect that was created served to explain the rationale for the change, thereby gaining wider support for it, and at the same time encouraging staff to meet the expectations of the wider group of stakeholders.

Implementing equal opportunities

Learning from the literature was combined with field work in British and American corporations to build a picture of how the implementation of equal opportunity is typically handled (see Figure 14.3). The resulting structure is similar to that for other types of organizational change. It includes the same key elements:

Source: V. Hammond and V. Holton (1991) *A Balanced Workforce: Achieving Cultural Change for Women, a Comparative Study*. Berkhamsted, UK: Ashridge Management Research Group.

Figure 14.3 Implementing equal opportunities

commitment, behavior, ownership, and investment. These elements, however, differ in the specific content and scale of activities.

In less successful cases of implementing equal opportunity, commitment equated to "endorsement" rather than active long-term involvement by top management. Any link with business strategy was incidental; line managers tended to regard equality of opportunity as being in direct competition with their attainment of strategic goals. Champions for equal opportunity tended to have responsibility but little power.

In the United Kingdom, but not generally elsewhere, the idea of setting targets for achieving and monitoring progress was unacceptable. Managers confused targets and goals with quotas and positive discrimination. The latter are both illegal in the United Kingdom. Confusion may have contributed to inaction, since even in those British organizations that had monitoring systems in place, little was done with the available information.

Attempts to change behavior were limited almost entirely to training for women, with little effort to amend the content or style of training more generally. American companies typically used payment systems and promotion criteria to support behavioral change, while Scandinavians opted for family-friendly policies. Neither was typically used in the United Kingdom.

Communication tended to focus on policy, asking "what" but not "why." The media were and are active in publicizing the situation for women, but there was little company-initiated comment. Companies in the United Kingdom did not, as they do in France, record the training and progress of women and men in their annual reports. When the issue arose at annual general meetings, it was because a shareholder, often a woman, asked a question. There was little concept of shared ownership, and the development of women was perceived to be at the expense of men and, by inference, not in the best interests of the company.

This last point seems to be linked to the scale of the investment, which in the United Kingdom tended to be minute. The equal opportunity position was rarely filled by a senior appointment. The work was more typically part-time, of low priority, and with little or no budget – the first place to make a cut.

Organization change and equal opportunity

The differences between the two situations, companies who have successfully introduced equal opportunity and those that have been less successful, demonstrated vividly that the United Kingdom had not tackled equal opportunity in a way in which the necessary cultural and structural changes could be sustained. In contrast, in organizations that had succeeded in achieving a significant redistribution of opportunity for women, there was a clear match with the culture change model. Successful implementors were drawing many elements of their approach from an explicit or implicit understanding of the need to change their organizational culture. They recognized the need to maintain complex and interlocking measures over long periods of time.

The business case

Chief executives in the target team placed a strong emphasis on identifying the business case for equal opportunity. Research elicited six major business reasons for a strong commitment to implementing equal opportunities (10):

Customer/market orientation
Favored employer
Reduction in costs
Increase in productivity
Increase in creativity and innovation
Belief in the development of all individuals

The customer/market orientation was by far the most common reason for implementing equal opportunity policies cited by companies, with examples from several sectors but, particularly, those firms with products or services for which women make the buying decisions. Those firms in fierce competition for key staff commonly mentioned wanting to be seen as a "favored employer," still an important factor even in a recession. Those quoting cost reduction had usually experienced high turnover, especially among trained staff.

Firms citing the advantage of increased productivity and creativity are interesting because they focus on augmented performance when work teams are diverse rather than homogenous. Finally, for a minority of organizations studied, belief in fostering all their talent was a sufficient reason for developing opportunities for women.

The Opportunity 2000 Approach

Linked to an appropriate business reason, the following four key required elements were developed from the culture change model for Opportunity 2000:

Demonstrating commitment
Changing behavior
Building ownership
Making the investment

Each element has its own set of actions; and, where needed, advice is available together with tools and techniques. All four elements are designed for use by each of the three levels: chief executive/board, human resource management, and line managers.

The Opportunity 2000 campaign is an independent initiative led by employers for employers. It is steered by the needs and demands of the members. Organizations becoming members of Opportunity 2000 do so because they see some value to themselves in the campaign. They assess their current situation against the model, using specially designed diagnostic questionnaires, and then set their own quantitative or qualitative goals. In practice, they set input goals – the actions they will take to increase the number of women recruited, promoted, returning from career breaks – or output goals – the actual numbers they expect in specified grades in a given time.

Membership in Opportunity 2000 was seventeen when the firms began their work in 1990 but expanded to 61 by the first launch by prime minister John Major in October 1991 and doubled again by the "second wave" launch in April 1992. The members, major private and public sector organizations, employ approximately 20 percent of the UK workforce. The campaign had 220 members by the end of 1992 and will continue to grow through the coming years.

Membership in Opportunity 2000 is voluntary but requires payment of a fee related to the number of employees. Opportunity 2000 requires members to make three commitments: first, to set their goals for increasing opportunities for women; second, to publish these goals; and third, to regularly monitor and report on progress. In return, the organizations have access to information and assistance and become part of a community dedicated to sharing and learning from their experience.

Implications for women managers

Opportunity 2000 is probably the most encouraging initiative in recent years for all women, but particularly for managers. It is the first national initiative of its kind. It has an extremely high profile as the media constantly comments on its progress, or lack thereof, and thereby keeps it in the public eye. Significantly, the national press now reports on these matters on the business as well as on the life-style pages. The planned phasing of new waves of members as well as well-publicized reviews of their progress will help maintain the high profile.

Most organizations have chosen women managers as one of their "marker" occupations to monitor the effect of their actions and to measure progress towards the goals they have set. Some member organizations have used the campaign to relaunch or refocus their activities with regard to women's development. Others have used it to start such measures. In all of them, the campaign's emphasis on board involvement as well as involvement by personnel/HRM and line managers has meant that women's development is being considered, often for the first time, at the highest level.

Almost all members of Opportunity 2000, including those who are reducing staff, can produce evidence of increased flexibility, increased training and development opportunities, and the investigation if not the actual provision of help with childcare and other forms of support. Some organizations have gone on to expand the scope of their initiative to cover other groups including ethnic minorities and people with disabilities.

The effect of Opportunity 2000, has not been limited to its member organizations. Many organizations that decide for one reason or another not to join, are nevertheless influenced. It is a typically British solution, based in the community and enjoying government approval. However, it is too early to say how effective it will ultimately be.

Summary and Conclusions

Recent forecasts of the economy in Britain have highlighted the increased dependence that companies will have on women well into the twenty-first century. It forecasts that there will be greater need for managers, professionals, and associated staff and that women will generally represent an increasing proportion of that workforce (16). It remains to be seen whether initiatives such as Opportunity 2000 will enable the number of women managers to reach a self-sustaining critical mass. Women managers have made strides forward in the last decade. Perhaps with many companies waking up to the necessity of retaining all good employees, more will also learn to use the full potential of their women as managers in order to benefit both the corporate and the national economies.

References

(1) Allen, M. (1991) *The Times 1000: 1991–1992*. London: Times Books.
(2) Commission of the European Communities (1990) *Employment in Europe 1990*. Luxem-

bourg: Office for Official Publications of the European Communities.

(3) *Daily Telegraph* (Newspaper) (1989) "Survey of Britain's Leading 100 Companies," London, 6 October.

(4) Department of Education and Science (1991*a*) "First Destination of Graduates," *Statistical Bulletin* (June). London: Her Majesty's Stationery Office.

(5) Department of Education and Science (1991*b*) *Statistical Bulletin* (July). London: Her Majesty's Stationery Office.

(6) Equal Opportunities Commission (1988) *Women and Men in Britain 1987*. Manchester: Equal Opportunities Commission.

(7) Equal Opportunities Commission (1991*a*) *Annual Report 1990*. London: Her Majesty's Stationery Office.

(8) Equal Opportunities Commission (1991*b*) *Women and Men in Britain 1991*. Manchester: Equal Opportunities Commission.

(9) *Equal Opportunities for Women in the Civil Service: Progress Report 1984–87* (1988) London: Her Majesty's Stationery Office.

(10) Hammond, V., and Holton, V. (1991) *A Balanced Workforce: Achieving Cultural Change for Women, a Comparative Study*. Berkhamsted, UK: Ashridge Management Research Group.

(11) Hansard Society (1990) *The Report of the Hansard Society Commission on Women at the Top*. London: The Hansard Society.

(12) Hirsh, W., and Jackson, C. (1990) *Women into Management: Issues Influencing the Entry of Women into Managerial Jobs*. Brighton, UK: Institute of Manpower Studies.

(13) HM Treasury (1976) *Civil Service Statistics*. London: Her Majesty's Stationery Office.

(14) HM Treasury (1987) *Civil Service Statistics*. London: Her Majesty's Stationery Office.

(15) Holton, V., and Rabbetts, J. (1989) *Pow(d)er in the Board Room*. Berkhamsted, UK: Ashridge Management Research Group.

(16) Institute of Employment Research (1990) *Review of the Economy and Employment 1988/9*. Warwick, UK: Institute of Employment Research.

(17) Metcalf, H. (1990) *Retaining Women Employees: Measures to Counteract Labour Shortage*. Brighton, UK: Institute of Manpower Studies.

(18) Naylor, M., and Purdie, E. (1992) "Results of the 1991 Labour Force Survey," *Employment Gazette* (April). London: Her Majesty's Stationery Office.

(19) *New Earnings Survey 1975*, Part E, Table 138 and *New Earnings Survey 1986*, Part E, Table 138. London: Her Majesty's Stationery Office.

(20) Remuneration Economics (1991) *1990 Salary Survey*. Corby, UK: British Institute of Management.

(21) Royal Society of Chemistry (1989) *Employment and Attitudes of Men and Women Members*. London: The Royal Society of Chemistry.

(22) "Social Trends" (1990) *Education*, Vol. 20. London: Her Majesty's Stationery Office.

(23) *The Times* (1990) "The Woman's Place," London, 7 June.

(24) Universities Central Council (1989) *26th Report 1987–88, Students and Staff and University Statistics 1984–5*, Vol. 1, Table 1. London: Her Majesty's Stationery Office.

(25) Women's National Commission (1987) *Women into Public Appointments*. London: Women's National Commission.

(26) Women's National Commission (1990) *Women into Public Appointments*. London: Women's National Commission.

(27) Wren, Executive Jonathan (1990) *Women's Pay in the City*. London: Jonathan Wren Executive.

15

POLAND

Women Managers in Poland: In Transition from Communism to Democracy

Renata Siemienska

This chapter examines women's access to managerial positions in Poland at a time of systemic political and economic change. It focuses primarily on women in local leadership positions in two time periods: the Communist period in the 1980s and the period following the first partially free elections since World War II, in June 1989, which brought the demise of the ruling Communist party (the Polish United Workers Party).

The increase in the number of university-educated women in the labor force had a moderate effect on the number of women in higher managerial positions after World War II. Thus, women's under-representation in higher positions in some sectors has been due not to a lack of qualified women, but rather to decisions made by the Communist government concerning when and how many women they would hire at any given time. In addition, compared to men, women were appointed or elected to positions that gave them less control over the distribution of resources. In the post-Communist period, even fewer women are being elected to parliament than in the earlier period when a quota system existed. More women, however, are being appointed to managerial positions at the local level.

Poland Prior to World War II

Poland regained independence in 1918 and became a republic after nearly 150 years of partitioned existence under foreign rule by Russia, Austria, and Prussia. In 1939, Poland was an economically underdeveloped agricultural country with a low level of urbanization. In 1931, only 25 percent of the total population were urbanites (7). Twenty-three percent were illiterate, with illiteracy higher among women (28 percent) than men (18 percent) (14).

Poland was a mosaic of diverse ethnic cultures and religions, including Roman Catholics, Greek-Catholics, Greek Orthodox, Protestants, and Jews. Roman Catholicism, however, was hegemonic and held a special place in the cultural and psychological makeup of the Poles. Poland's geopolitical location lent special importance to her ties to the Roman Catholic church.

Although women's roles varied by class, Polish women were among the first in Europe to be enfranchised, in 1918. However, prior to the Communist regime, women had little political representation. In the late 1930s, only 2 percent of the lower chamber and 5 percent of the upper chamber of the Polish parliament were women (7).

Poland under the Communist Regime

Political structure and leaders

The Communist system was established in Poland after World War II, as it was in other Eastern European countries. The system was highly centralized, with the center located at the confluence of the highest organs of the Communist party – the Polish United Workers Party (PUWP) and state structures. It had final authority, derived from the supremacy of state power and the hegemonic position of the Communist party. The party urged the United Peasant Party (UPP), made up of farmers, and the Democratic Party (DP), composed primarily of crafts people and small producers, to cooperate with it. The constitution defined the PUWP as the dominant party. Following a period of reform (1972–1975), the commune became the basic administrative unit. The leading role of the PUWP was reflected in both institutional structures and personnel policies. Most high-ranking officials in all areas of public life were PUWP members. Local bodies had very limited prerogatives. They were subordinated to higher-level party authorities. Local party units provided ideological and political "guidance" and played a control function *vis-à-vis* elected self-government organs and their staffs.

Following World War II, Poland, like other Communist countries, went through a period of struggle for power, followed by intensive industrialization and then economic modernization. During the first period, the PUWP fought for dominance in the political arena. Loyalty to the party was the chief criterion for leadership. Little or no attention was paid to such candidate qualifications as education, skills, or job experience. Active membership in the wartime Communist party, the resistance movement, or an army unit that had fought alongside the Soviet Army during World War II, were the overriding criteria for access to the new positions of influence. Having a working-class or peasant background also became an asset. These criteria continued to be strongly emphasized in the industrialization period that followed the consolidation of the PUWP's power in the early 1950s.

When the political situation stabilized, priorities shifted to socioeconomic development. Criteria for leader selection began to shift, with more emphasis placed on professional qualifications. Specialists recruited to decision-making positions and those already in positions of leadership were encouraged to acquire more education and new skills.

A limited number of *cadres*, who rotated among positions, filled leadership posts at the local level. People already holding leadership positions were on the roster of the "reserve cadre" (members of the so-called nomenclature) and were among the first to be considered for vacant leadership positions. In Poland, this was called the "job merry-go-round." When the crisis of August 1980, occurred, many protested that people who failed in one job were simply moved to another (9).

This recruitment system hindered the active participation of women in politics.

Fewer women than men had been members of the Communist party before World War II, fewer had fought during the war in underground military forces that were connected with the re-establishment of the Communist party in 1943, and fewer had joined the Communist party or other parties cooperating with it following World War II (15).

Women's promotion to leadership positions also depended on the political center's assessment of the need for women at each level. Women's promotion to leadership positions in most cases was centrally decided and was generally determined by a quota system that provided for representation of women, as it did for representation of young people and other recognized social and political groups. Political interests shaped these decisions, with the number of each group that would be made members of political bodies at particular levels changing with changes in political views. When the political center was threatened or when there was no special interest in increasing women's presence in leadership positions, the number of women promoted decreased.

For example, in the Stalinist years between 1950 and 1955, a number of conditions combined that proved favorable for women's promotion. These included an ideological emphasis on social equality, the assertion of Communist party control after having crushed the political opposition, and a shortage of available male labor. Women constituted 22 percent of the total leaders promoted at that time, more than in any other period. The fairly high proportion of women promoted under Edward Gierek's rule (First Secretary of the PUWP from 1971 to 1980), 17 percent, can be explained by the relatively low level of political tension at the time, combined with the rapidly rising standard of living, and the need for women's labor to advance state plans for modernizing the economy.

In the 1970s, the number of women promoted into leadership positions at the local level was almost twice that in the early 1980s (1;15;23). The sixth period national congress of the PUWP held in the 1970s declared that "Women should be more often selected to managerial and supervisory posts provided their personal traits, professional knowledge, and moral standards can guarantee their responsible work in leadership positions."

Fewer women were promoted between 1956 and 1970 (6 percent) when political tensions were high, following the crisis of 1956 (referred to as "Polish October"). In the 1960s, economic stagnation meant that there was no special need to attract women into the labor force, as studies of the Kalisz and Siedlce provinces have shown (23). Studies conducted in the turbulent period of the 1980s showed a 35 percent decline in working women in local leadership after the end of the 1970s, when the proportion of women working was around 20 percent (15). In other words, at any given time the political and economic interests of the Communist party, in large measure, determined the vicissitudes of women's promotion opportunities. In practice, Poles had no commitment to gender equality; and, as resistance to the party grew, women's opportunities declined. At times of political struggle, the number of women in local leadership decreased. Party survival, and not representation, was the key concern of politicians. The lowest number of women (3 percent) promoted to managerial and supervisory positions at local levels was in 1982, the first year after the imposition of martial law.

Under the Communist regime, there were three women's organizations: the Polish Women's League (the main organization), the Circles of Rural Women, and the Association of Women in Cooperatives. These organizations played an intermediary role between the PUWP and women. They helped mobilize women to participate in realizing goals set up by the PUWP and the government. Thus the Communist party created and co-opted the women's organizations that existed. Such organizations served to facilitate the process of manipulating and mobilizating women to implement economic and political goals formulated by the Communist party. These women's organizations also provided a springboard for the promotion of a few women into mainstream politics, where they neither played significant roles nor represented women's interests (15;17). The Communist party did not permit independent women's organizations. Moreover, frequent political and economic crises (in 1956, 1968, 1970, and 1980) united people around common problems, dividing society into "we" (average people) and "them" (the authorities), rather than along gender lines.

Socioeconomic status of women in postwar Poland

The 1952 constitution proclaimed the equality of women and men as citizens. In reality, however, women's status differed significantly from that of men. The highly centralized political system and state ownership of the means of production (with the exception of agriculture and small handicraft concerns) enabled governmental control over labor force participation and distribution (11). The government determined the pay structure in the large public sector and created different jobs and employment opportunities for women and men. Greater individual job choice existed in the professions.

Government, family, and employment policies were guided primarily by the needs of the economy. During periods of economic expansion, when male labor was in short supply, the government expanded childcare and other facilities to encourage women's labor force participation (15). The government manipulated media messages to support its current interests. For example, at times of economic expansion the government lauded women for pursuing professional careers, whereas at other times they glorified women for following the more traditional roles of mother and housewife (3).

Education Following World War II, school enrolment increased rapidly, with education targeted especially for women (see Table 15.1). By the 1960s, women often chose to stay in school longer than men. Since the beginning of the 1980s, women have accounted for more than half of the students in university-level institutions (4). Notwithstanding women's longer schooling, their education has been less clearly oriented to the job market. Women received training for lower-paying jobs. In Poland, as in most Communist countries, jobs demanding a university education belonged to this fairly low-paid group. As shown in Table 15.2, higher education for women did not result in desegregation of the labor market, except in a few professions such as medicine and agriculture. Until 1985, the government enforced a quota of 50 percent women in medicine and

Table 15.1 Education of women of fifteen years old and above who have completed more than primary school

Field of education	Percentage of women among total high school and university graduates	
	1978	1988
Technology/Engineering	23.7	25.6
Agriculture	50.0	50.6
Economy	76.2	81.0
Law/Administration	35.8	39.7
Humanities	60.8	60.5
Math/Natural Sciences	61.0	60.6
Teaching	78.6	80.1
Medicine	83.3	85.9
Hotel Management	90.0	89.8
General	71.3	74.9
Others	53.3	58.7
Total	46.5	48.1

Source: Kobieta w Polsce [*Women in Poland*] (1990), p. 19. Warsaw: Central Statistical Office.

agriculture, regardless of the proportion of women candidates, supposedly to avoid the overfeminization of these professions. They defended the limits set on women's entry based on the need for such professionals in small towns versus

Table 15.2 Women in the labor force as a percentage of total employed in particular branches of the Polish national economy

Economic branch	Percentage of women employed among total in particular branch		
	1955	1979	1989
Industry	30.2	39.0	37.2
Construction	12.4	19.4	20.0
Agriculture	20.5	27.0	27.8
Forestry	6.4	19.6	18.5
Transportation/Communication	15.2	25.9	24.4
Trade	51.4	71.6	69.7
Municipal economy and services	31.1	32.8	25.7
Housing			42.8
Science/Development			48.3
Education	56.6	69.9	76.5
Culture/Art			61.0
Health service/Social welfare	76.7	78.5	81.4
Sports/Recreation			55.3
Public administration/Justice system	38.8	60.7	64.4
Finance/Insurance	57.0	83.4	84.5

Sources: Calculated on the basis of *Statistical Yearbook* (1990) Warsaw: Central Statistical Office, 1975, p. 53 for 1955, 1980, p. 59 for 1979; *Kobieta w Polsce* [*Woman in Poland*] (1990) Warsaw: Central Statistical Office, pp. 50–51 for 1989.

women's supposed preference for working in urban centers. In other fields, the gender of candidates for admission to universities was not taken into account. Compared with women, men more often selected three-year vocational secondary schools that enabled them to become qualified workers in a relatively short period of time and thereby quickly obtain relatively well-paid jobs (14).

With the emergence of Communist regimes in Eastern European countries, new concepts of women's and men's roles were introduced that, especially at the beginning, were radically different from traditional concepts. As part of the concept of a presumably gender-neutral, Marxist "new man," women and men were presented as citizens capable of participating to the same extent and in the same manner in the construction of the economic foundation of the new system. In reality, the occupational structure that evolved under Communist rule was highly gender-segregated. Finance, insurance, education, culture, art, and trade became female-dominated fields. In 1989, women made up 71 to 84 percent of these fields. Eighty percent of those employed in health service and social welfare were women. In traditionally male fields, such as industry, construction, and farming, the increase in women's participation among all employees did not exceed 10 percent. The structure of women's employment became stabilized, and from 1979 to 1989 practically no change occurred. In the early 1970s, women constituted over 40 percent of the labor force; and by 1989, almost 47 percent.

Under Communist rule, the Roman Catholic church continued to play an important role in shaping social relations in Poland. It enjoyed strong support from the Polish people. With the extermination of the Jewish population during World War II and territorial changes after World War II, Catholics came to constitute about 90 percent of the Polish population. Poles viewed the Roman Catholic church not only as a religion, but also as a national institution, supporting the Polish nation's efforts to restore Polish independence from Communism.

Women at senior administrative levels

Women have been essentially absent at the highest administrative levels (ministers and deputy ministers). In 1987, only one minister was a woman, and only two were undersecretaries of state. There were more women among directors and, in particular, among deputy directors of departments, and decidedly more women working as chief specialist and division head, both of which are more directly based on academic training. However, as shown in Table 15.3, women remained a minority in these positions. By 1985, women constituted 18 percent (29 among 533) of directors, 10 percent (76 among 733) of the deputy directors of departments, 27 percent (628 among 2,284) of the chief specialists, and 40 percent (220 among 550) of the ministry heads of divisions (19).

Between 1944 and 1979, only thirteen women held positions as top state authorities, whether as members of the Presidium of the National People's Council, the State Council, the Cabinet, or as chairpersons of permanent or extraordinary commissions of the Seym (parliament) and the Presidium of the Seym (8). The political background of these women is instructive. Eight were PUWP members,

Table 15.3   Women in positions of authority (1987)

Position of authority	Number of women
Central Committee of the Polish United Workers Party:	35
Political bureau member	1
Deputy of political bureau member	1
Members of Central Control and Audit Commission	21
Secretaries of PUWP provincial committees	4
Presidents of Voievodship Control and Audit Commission PUWP	2
Deputies of CC PUWP divisions head	1
Parliament members	93
State Council member	1
State Tribunal	3
Local authorities heads/Ciechanow, Chelm, Ostroleka	3
Ministries and central cooperative unions:	
Minister	1
Undersecretary of state	2
Vice-presidents of National Union of Farmers, farming organizations, etc.	1
Directors of departments	29
Vice-directors of departments	76
Chief specialists	628
Heads of divisions	220
Advisors	13
Local offices:	
Deputy heads of provinces	6
City presidents	9
Heads of city – communes	28
Heads of Communes	82
Diplomatic Service:	
Ambassador	1
Essential employees in embassies	17

Source: Siemienska, R. (1990) *Plec, zawod, polityka* [*Gender, Occupation, Politics*]. Warsaw: University of Warsaw Press.

attaining the positions of deputy members of the Central Committee of PUWP. Three of the women were simultaneously long-standing presidents of the Women's League. One each was a member of the Polish Workers Party, the United Peasant Party, and the Democratic Party, and two were nonparty members. All thirteen were deputies to the Seym, with six presiding over Seym commissions. Their presence in the Seym, however, was always limited to peripheral economic sectors, such as light industry and cooperatives, whereas economic priority traditionally emphasized heavy industry.

Women's failure to make a significant breakthrough into political leadership contrasts with their success in such feminized sectors as the judiciary and education, where women held from 32 to 68 percent of the managerial positions (see Table 15.4). Few women, however, became full professors in Polish universities. In the academic year 1987–1988, women represented only 13 percent (489 among 3,712) of the professors (20). Similarly, among the 188 directors of state administration in Warsaw and 200 in twelve *voivodeship* (provincial) cities selected at random, only 12 percent were women (5).

Table 15.4 Women in managerial positions in selected sectors of the national economy (1987)

Sectors of national economy	Percent of women	Number of women
Judiciary		
Voivodeship[a] courts of law president		2
Voivodeship courts of law vice-president		5
Local courts of law president		29
Local courts of law vice-president		67
		103
Total judges	54.5	2,666
Public Prosecutor's Office		
Voivodeship level[b] deputy public prosecutors	5	
Regional public prosecutors	11	
Deputy regional public prosecutors[c]	81	
		97
Total public prosecutors	32.4	2,962
Education and Learning		
Headmistresses and deputies of primary and secondary schools	67.8	32,139
Total primary and secondary education	81.0	423,000
Health Service		
Voivodeship doctors		7
Directors of district unit of health protection		34
Directors of voivodeship hospitals		5
		46
Total health service workers	80.3	672,600
Higher-Level Education[d]		
Rectors		1
Prorectors		6
Deans		20
Deputy deans		42
Directors of institutes		49
		118
Total higher-level education	33.1	17,634
Polish Academy of Science:		
Full members	3.0	6
Correspondent members	1.5	2
Directors of institutes	8.5	4
Deputies of directors of institutes	*	21
Total academy of science		33

* Data unavailable

[a] *Voivodeship* is the name of an administrative unit (province).
[b] There are 49 voivodeship public prosecutor's offices/*Statistical Yearbook* 1986, p. 512.
[c] There are 301 regional public prosecutor's offices/*Statistical Yearbook* 1986, p. 512.
[d] In 1985–1986 there were 92 schools of higher learning, universities, polytechnics, etc.

Source: Siemienska, R. (1990) *Plec, zawod, polityka* [*Gender, Occupation, Politics*]. Warsaw: University of Warsaw Press.

Membership of political organizations

Women's increased membership in the Communist party after 1960 did not greatly improve their representation in senior positions. Women's party membership rose consistently, particularly in the 1960s when the percentage of women in the PUWP rose by 50 percent, in the UPP by more than 100 percent, and in the DP by about 70 percent. In the next twenty years, women's membership in each of these organizations increased by only 5 to 6 percent. In the late 1980s, it reached about 30 percent in the PUWP and UPP and about 33 percent in the DP (17). However, the proportion of women in decision-making bodies of all political parties remained less than half of the total female membership. Women were less active than men in the same level positions and less often worked as activists in the PUWP appara-tus, youth organizations, voluntary workers' militia, trade unions, and workers' councils. Compared with men, women were often more active in organizations that were politically less important, such as the Front of National Unity. The increase in women's political party membership paralleled their increase in the professions rather than simply following their increase in education (15).

The multidimensional crisis at the beginning of the 1980s included demands for women's rights. For example, the Gdansk and Szczecin agreements of late August and early September 1980 contained demands exclusively concerning women, such as a three-year paid maternity leave. From the early 1970s until 1980, women were entitled to a three-month paid maternity leave and an optional two-year unpaid leave with a guarantee of the same job when they returned to work. The Inter-Factory Strike Committee recommended a three-year maternity leave with an allowance equaling a woman's pay in the first year of leave and half her pay in the second year, as well as a guaranteed number of places in nurseries and kindergartens for the children of working women. It also recommended raising nurses' wages and providing apartments for single nurses. The first two proposals were designed to create the conditions under which women would better be able to fulfill their traditional role. The latter two focused on a professional group, nurses, consisting almost exclusively of women. In 1982, the government introduced a four-month paid maternity leave and an additional option of a three-year paid parental leave, usually taken by the mother. The agreements contained no clauses specifying women's increased participation in political or workplace decisions.

Although women made up almost half the membership of the newly created independent trade union "Solidarity," they were rarely elected to office. In the election of delegates to the First National Solidarity Congress in 1981, no women delegates were chosen in sixteen out of 41 local elections. In all, women constituted only 7 percent (63) of the delegates (12;13).

Women in local authorities in the 1980s

In 1983 and 1984, studies were conducted on the functioning of the local authori-ties in the Kalisz and Siedlce *voivodeships* (provinces) (23). Among the 564 top members of the local authorities (282 from each voivodeship), only 13 percent were women (15). The research combined elected heads of local councils, local party

Table 15.5 Social background of women and men local leaders in Kalisz and Siedlec *voivodeships* (1983–1984)

Profession/area of employment of the respondent's father	Men (n = 493) %	Women (n = 70) %
Specialists of political and social activities, army and militia employees	6.9	2.9
Employees in trade, transport, communication, banking, industry, farming, forestry	13.0	10.0
Employees in education and learning, lawyers, economists, engineers, technicians	6.1	5.7
Other nonmanual workers	4.3	5.7
Workers	18.7	14.3
Farmers	41.4	47.1
Craftspeople, small manufacturers	5.9	7.1
No data	3.7	7.2

Source: Siemienska, R. (1990) *Plec, zawod, polityka* [*Gender, Occupation, Politics*], p. 208. Warsaw: University of Warsaw Press.

committees, and appointed heads of local offices into a single category because the system was such that those allegedly elected were in fact appointed. The studies found that since twice as many women (36 percent) as men were born in the place where they currently worked, fewer women than men were employed in provinces to which they were officially transferred (43 percent of men versus 21 percent of women). This suggests that either women were less mobile than men, which is a career constraint (2;6), or, alternatively, that women were offered job transfers less frequently than men, perhaps because women are assigned to lower-level positions in organizations.

As shown in Table 15.5, the social background of women and men leaders was similar, even though their professional careers differed. One-third of the women began as office workers, with a significant, but decidedly smaller, number beginning as teachers and technicians. By contrast, more men began as manual workers, teachers, and instructors of cultural activities. The latter was usually associated with the activities of a political party.

The proportion of women employed as top civil servants in local administration was higher than that of men. Although many women officially occupied relatively high positions, in fact they had much less responsibility for influencing local matters (see Table 15.6). Women tended to work in institutions that had little influence on the allocation and distribution of resources. For example, in the PUWP, women were much more likely than men to occupy the less influential positions of deputies. Women were virtually never the heads of divisions of provincial offices. Moreover, women stayed longer in the same position than did men. This fact is not surprising since the PUWP authorities changed people (usually men) more often in the higher positions. When new politicians took office at the top, they usually preferred to have their "own" people, whom they could trust, as subordinates. As a result of this pattern, women, who generally occupied less influential positions than men, were more convinced than their male counterparts that after five years they would remain in the same position. Men, almost twice

Table 15.6   Jobs of local leaders in Kalisz and Siedlec *voivodeships* (1983–1984)

Sector	Men (n = 493) %	Women (n = 70) %
Administration	35.3	47.1
PUWP party	26.8	14.3
Youth organizations	2.4	2.9
United Peasants' party	1.6	1.4
Democratic party	1.8	–
Production/directors of industrial enterprises, farming collectives	6.7	1.4
Municipalities, housing cooperatives	7.1	11.4
Trade	1.8	1.4
Courts of justice, public prosecutor's office	2.2	–
Militia, army	2.4	–
Local authorities, PMNR[a]	1.4	1.4
Education	2.2	1.4
Other	6.9	14.4
No data	1.4	2.9

[a] PMNR, or Patriotic Movement of National Rebirth, was created after the introduction of martial law on December 13, 1981. The main goal of this organization was to gather citizens, irrespective of their organizational affiliation, around the program of overcoming the crisis proposed by the Communist party.

Source: Siemienska, R. (1990) *Plec, zawod, polityka* [*Gender, Occupation, Politics*], p. 212. Warsaw: University of Warsaw Press.

as frequently as women, stated that they did not know what they would be doing in five years' time (1;15).

One of the most common reasons given to explain why women advanced at a slower pace than men is the limited amount of time and energy that women can devote to professional work, primarily because they must combine professional duties with family duties. Although generally true, the problem is more complicated in Poland. Women, burdened with various conflicting duties, often refrain from investing the effort that would ensure promotion.

A related impediment to women's advancement was their more limited access to higher education once on the job. Men, more often than women, continued to raise

Table 15.7   Education level of local leaders in Kalisz and Siedlce *voievodships* (1983–1984)

Education level	Men Beginning work career (%)	Men at present (%)	Women Beginning work career (%)	Women at present (%)
Primary	10.0	1.7	7.4	3.0
Basic vocational	9.4	1.3	4.4	–
Secondary vocational	31.0	16.5	33.8	24.3
General secondary	17.3	2.6	23.5	12.1
Post-high school courses	7.3	8.3	7.4	9.1
University	25.0	69.6	23.5	51.5

Source: Siemienska, R. (1990) *Plec, zawod, polityka* [*Gender, Occupation, Politics*], p. 215. Warsaw: University of Warsaw Press.

their educational level during their careers. At the beginning of their professional careers, women were, on average, slightly better educated than men (see Table 15.7). By 1984, however, almost 70 percent of the men had acquired university-level education, compared to only 52 percent of the women. It is impossible to conclude whether this gender difference in human capital accumulation was caused by women's more burdensome social roles, by women's lower incentive to get more education due to their lower likelihood of promotion, or by superiors less frequently encouraging women than men to further their education.

Gender as a factor shaping social and political awareness of local leaders

The Kalisz and Siedlce *voivodeship* studies discussed earlier revealed few and rather weak gender differences in the attitudes and perceptions of local leaders, after accounting for personality traits and background variables. The studies, however, found that women had weaker feelings of political efficacy than did men. They felt less alienated from members of the communities in which they worked, but felt slightly more alienated from other members of the managerial staff to which they belonged (16). This finding suggests that even on the local level, where more women were present, women were more likely to feel like strangers among political leaders. Despite the fact that women had lower positions, they felt they lacked autonomy. Gender significantly differentiated women's and men's perceptions of the conflict-forming role of social differences. Men more often than women believed that differences in access to power could be a source of conflict. Women tended to deny the existence of conflicts. Local leaders demonstrated the same tendency when describing conflicts between church and state; only 16 percent of women versus 22 percent of men believed that such conflicts existed in the early 1980s. The overall similarity in women and men managers' attitudes may have resulted from the selection process. Since women were elected or appointed based on similar criteria to men, perhaps they were in fact selected because they shared the views of their male colleagues (15).

Transition to Democracy in Poland

Political and economic changes

The crisis at the beginning of the 1980s in Poland was not only an economic crisis but also a political and moral crisis. The independent trade union Solidarity had a membership of about ten million Poles. Many factors indicated widespread political malaise. In public opinion surveys, Poles lacked confidence in existing institutions, and representatives of opposing parties, and even some members of the Communist party criticized the existing order. The introduction of martial law in 1981, with its restrictions on personal freedoms, wetted popular demand for the democratization of government, greater citizens' influence on decision making, and economic reforms.

Poland's economic system, which had reformed too slowly and inefficiently, totally broke down at the end of the 1980s. This breakdown was accompanied by growing social dissatisfaction, which led to widespread strikes. They were stopped in the spring of 1988, when the Catholic church and Lech Walesa, then president of the illegal Solidarity union, intervened. The government promised Walesa that talks would be undertaken on the status of the political opposition in Poland, as well as on general political and economic policy.

In the winter of 1989, negotiations were held between representatives of the ruling Communist party (PUWP) with their allies and the opposition led by Solidarity, with the Catholic church in the role of observer. The talks resulted in an agreement on the legalization of Solidarity, thus creating conditions for political pluralism and for conducting partially free elections for parliament in June 1989. A specified number of the seats in the Seym (lower chamber of parliament) were reserved for the PUWP, the parties in the government coalition, and the organizations of secular Catholics. The result was an overwhelming electoral success for the Citizens' Committees (at the time, the advisory political body created by their leader, Lech Walesa). In September 1989, the long-time advisor to Walesa, Catholic intellectual Mazowiecki, formed a coalition government.

The political changes opened the way for major additional political and economic reforms, designed to transform the Polish political system from totalitarianism to democracy and the Polish economy from centrally planned and controlled to market-oriented. Local governments were granted greater autonomy. The elections to local councils held May 27, 1990 were the first fully free elections in Polish postwar history. The Communist party had been dissolved a few months earlier. Its descendants did not play an important role in the Polish political arena. Solidarity, as a trade union, and the Citizens' Committees, as its political branches, were the most powerful political forces at the time of the elections.

The new government replaced a number of people in managerial positions. The process began after the creation of the first government led by a non-Communist prime minister. The new government replaced a large number of senior local bureaucrats, most of whom had been Communist party members, with those who had been politically in opposition during the Communist regime.

The change in the political system did not improve the political status of women. Women played almost no visibly active role in the changes taking place at the end of the 1980s. In 1989, women were absent among negotiators of the "round table" (17). The only woman on the side of the government, a university professor, decidedly renounced any association with women's problems. In the partially free elections in June 1989, when the Communist party was defeated, only 62 women (13 percent) were elected to the lower chamber of the parliament (the Seym) and only six (6 percent) were elected to the higher chamber (the Senate). These women members represented fewer women than under the Communist system, when women constituted over 20 percent of the members of parliament.

In the first free elections to the local self-government held in May 1990, women constituted only 11 percent among those elected. The tendency not to elect women became visible again in the next parliamentary elections in 1991. Forty-two women (9 percent) were elected to the lower chamber, even fewer than in 1989, and eight (8 percent) to the higher chamber of the parliament.

In the first government dominated by non-Communists created in September 1989, there was only one woman minister. In the second and third governments formed in the 1990s, there were none. In the fourth government, created in 1992, a woman was made prime minister – the first in Polish history. Women constitute ten of the 229 members of the government and 2 percent of the 98 heads and deputy heads of provinces. The proportion of women managers in each of the ministries is associated with the proportion employed in the ministry. For example, the largest proportion of women managers work in the ministries of Health and Social Protection, Work and Social Policy, and Culture and Arts, where they constitute 58 percent, 47 percent, and 41 percent, respectively, of the managerial labor force. The smallest proportions of women managers work in the Ministry of Transportation (none), Foreign Affairs (6 percent), and Foreign Economic Co-operation (9 percent). Women have greatest access to managerial positions in the professions in which a large proportion of those employed are women.

Very few women are visible in political life as representatives of political parties, organizations, or trade unions. The Catholic church, which has always played a powerful role in Poland and which emerged from Communist rule as a central power, is a major force in the current move to return women to more traditional roles as full-time homemakers and mothers. Under the leadership of the Catholic church, political parties are attempting to introduce legislation to make abortion – available since 1956 – more difficult if not virtually impossible to obtain and to limit access to both contraceptives and divorce. Since March 1993, abortions are highly restricted. They cannot be performed for social reasons.

The change in the economic system created new problems and made the situation for women especially difficult. Women have more often been victims of the change than have men. Women constitute about 52 percent of the unemployed and have greater difficulty getting new jobs. Jobs offered do not coincide with women's skills; most are for manual workers. The decreasing availability of subsidized childcare services has further narrowed women's employment options. More women must now stay home to care for children, rather than being able to pursue careers. In addition, following a decrease of 20 percent in real earnings during the last three years, many families simply cannot afford the cost of childcare services. Consequently, there is the ironic situation of a shortage in available services, with those that do exist not being used to full capacity. Women's lack of previous managerial experience (women were rarely managers in state companies), and their resulting lack of social connections that could facilitate entering the new private sector, make it particularly difficult for women to start their own businesses (18). In other words, the new period of greater political democracy and the move to a freer market economy struck a damaging blow to women's political and economic positions.

Women in the local authorities in the early 1990s

The situation at the local political level is not dissimilar to that at the national level. In spring 1991, a national study was conducted of members of the local authorities in randomly selected medium-sized cities by the Institute of Sociology, University of Warsaw. Its purpose was to create a profile of the new leaders in local governments. The study included 686 persons: 162 (24 percent) women and 524 (76

Table 15.8   Positions of local leaders (1991)

Positions	Women %	Men %
	n = 84	n = 141
Administrators	51	27
Mayor	2.4	6.3
Deputy mayor	6.1	5.6
Secretary in mayor's office	14.6	3.3
Treasury officer in mayor's office	11.6	1.3
Department director in mayor's office	16.5	6.8
	n = 40	n = 201
Councillors	25	38
Local council chairperson	3.0	6.3
Local council deputy chairperson	3.7	7.4
Local council chairperson of committee	11.0	10.6
	n = 38	n = 182
Politicians (Chairperson of local committees)	24	35
Solidarity	0.6	5.5
Citizen's committee	4.3	4.8
Political parties	11.6	15.5
Deputy, senator of the parliament	6.7	4.3
Total number	162	524

Source: Unpublished data; author's calculations.

percent) men. Leaders were identified on the basis of positions held and public reputation. The groups compared were administrators (people holding managerial positions in mayors' offices), politicians (chairpersons of the local committees of political parties, Citizen's Committees, and Solidarity) and people elected to the local councils. Priests and businesspeople were excluded from the analysis because there were no women among them.

The distribution of women and men among the three major positions differed significantly (see Table 15.8). Over half the women were administrators, and about one-quarter were elected members and politicians. Among the men, the distribution was more even, with the largest group being elected officials. Administrators have far less political clout than do either elected officials or politicians; women's under-representation in this category, therefore, means that their potential impact on the system and their ability to influence the future promotion of women is more limited. Moreover, women's influence is small, as in the past, because women are more likely to occupy deputy positions and positions of directors of departments in mayors' offices. Over 70 percent of the local leaders were new in their positions and were appointed or elected since the beginning of 1990, compared with 19 percent first appointed between 1982 and 1989; and only about 10 percent were appointed earlier than 1982. More men than women were new to their positions: about 10 percent more in each of the analyzed groups (administrators, politicians, councillors).

The political changes in the 1990s, as expected, brought more local people into local leadership than previously. The majority were born in the community where they now live, or at least in the same province. This, however, is less the case for local politicians and councillors, who more often than the local administrators were born in other parts of the country. The pattern is even stronger among women than men.

In all the categories of local leaders, women are more than 20 percent more likely to be unmarried or divorced. A similar pattern has been identified for most other countries. However, the majority of female local leaders are married, with single women constituting a rather small fraction of the leader population.

The local leaders of the 1990s are, on average, less educated than their predecessors in the early 1980s: 67 percent of the local leaders have a university education, compared with about 80 percent in the 1980s. Politicians of both genders are less well-educated, with only half having a university education. The level of education is higher among local administrators and local councillors. Among administrators, men more often than women have completed university education (82 percent versus 64 percent). Among the councillors, the reverse is true; 80 percent of women and 61 percent of men are university educated. Differences in the educational pattern can be explained as follows: women administrators hold lower positions than do men, positions that rarely demand a university education. By contrast, women competing in elections to become councillors have to have more "educational capital" than men to make them competitive in the eyes of voters.

Women and men university graduates who become managers specialize in different fields. For example, the largest group of men administrators has a diploma in a

Table 15.9 Education of local leaders in 1991

Education level	Administrators Women %	Men %	Politicians Women %	Men %	Councillors Women %	Men %	Total %
Primary	1	–	5	3	5	–	2
Basic, vocational	–	–	2	7	–	5	4
Uncompleted secondary	–	–	2	4	–	1	1
Secondary, vocational	21	8	13	15	2	20	15
General secondary	8	2	18	5	2	3	5
Post-high school courses	7	5	8	11	10	9	8
University	63	82	52	55	80	61	64
No data	–	3	–	–	1	1	1
Field of university education							
Teaching	2	2	33	13	24	9	9
Law/Administration	27	15	–	12	6	7	12
Other humanities	3	5	22	15	13	6	8
Economy	34	12	11	8	15	10	13
Engineering	26	57	16	32	18	41	39
Math and computers	–	–	–	–	–	–	–
Medicine	–	–	–	5	21	7	5
Agriculture	7	7	5	11	–	10	8
Other	1	2	13	4	3	10	6

Source: Unpublished data; author's calculations.

technical field (57 percent), followed by law and administration (16 percent), and economics (12 percent). Among women administrators, the largest group gained their diploma in economics (34 percent), followed by law and administration (27 percent), and technical fields (27 percent) (see Table 15.9). Professional expertise is becoming an increasingly important route for women to enter politics. Women are usually appointed to positions in the lower levels of the political structure on the basis of their professional qualifications. Given the strong prejudice against women as leaders and decision-makers, women succeed far less frequently in achieving positions when they compete against men in public elections (22).

Political affiliation of local leaders

The new policy encourages selecting administrators on a basis other than political affiliation, especially for lower-level positions. This policy appears to work in favor of women. Membership in political organizations played a less significant role in 1991 than it did under Communist rule: 33 percent of the local leaders were not currently members of any political organization, nor had they ever been. The majority of the local leaders (56 percent) had never been members of a political party or political association prior to their election. Sixty-seven percent were currently connected with some political party or trade union such as Solidarity or Individual Farmers' Solidarity.

Among administrators, there were no differences in women's and men's former political party membership. However, among politicians and councillors, a greater proportion of women than men had not been organizationally active in the past. This fact suggests that more women than before are moving into local leadership positions. Among former Communist party members, men indicated a stronger orientation to the left, and women were more aligned to the right and center – a finding that requires further study (Table 15.10).

Generally, party policy at the local level reflects that of the national level. Women at the local level appear to be more stable in their jobs than men, probably because they hold less politically sensitive positions and consequently also have less political

Table 15.10 Relationship between past political membership and left–right orientation of local leaders (1991)

	Membership of political parties under Communist regime											
	Administrators				Politicians				Councillors			
	Women		Men		Women		Men		Women		Men	
Current political orientation	Yes (%)	No (%)	Yes (%)	No (%)	Yes (%)	No (%)	Yes (%)	No (%)	Yes (%)	No (%)	Yes (%)	No (%)
Left	8	7	18	3	40	5	26	10	22	3	22	8
Center	64	64	56	60	54	60	42	42	66	70	50	50
Right	21	29	26	37	6	26	32	46	11	18	27	38
No data	7	—	—	—	–	7	—	2	1	9	1	4

Source: Unpublished data; author's calculations.

Left: 1 to 4 on 10 point scale; Center: 5 and 6; Right: 7 to 10.

clout. The growing women's lobby in Poland is expected to create pressure on politicians to pay more attention to women's appointments to managerial positions in the future.

Role of the women's lobby in promoting women to decision-making positions

In the early 1980s, students at Warsaw University created the first feminist group under Communist rule (10). Gradually people not associated with the university also joined. Its purpose was to become acquainted with the ideas and ideals of the feminist movement in Western countries. Its main aim, therefore, was developing women's consciousness. The appearance of feminist groups in the 1980s was part of a wider process of awakening social awareness and the emergence of a variety of illegal, politically oriented organizations. The feminist groups were small, operating mainly in big cities and among communities of students and the intelligentsia. Feminist organizing increased in 1989 in opposition to a church and government proposal to make abortion illegal. Ultimately, the explicit conflict was seemingly resolved; since March 1993, abortion can be performed only under special circumstances. However, for the Catholic church, the new law is too liberal, and for many political parties and groups, it is too restrictive.

Some women's organizations have a wider agenda than merely to fight the restrictive antiabortion law, and assist women looking for jobs or wishing to start new businesses as well as helping those already in business to form supportive networks. These organizations did not participate in the campaign preceding the May 1990 elections to local governments. They became visible in the political arena just prior to the first free elections to the parliament in October 1991. Women of different political orientations attempted to become candidates for various political parties. They also created their own women's list of candidates. Only one small women's group (the Women's Alliance against Life Difficulties) won a seat in the Seym.

Another initiative was carried out by the governmental Office of Women's and Family Affairs. The Forum (a network of 30 women's groups and organizations of different political orientations) was created in the spring of 1990 to give opportunities to their representatives to meet, to exchange views, and to formulate their demands regarding women's issues. The organizations established under the Communist regime were also invited to participate in the meetings. These organizations had become very weak after the change of the political system. Women deputies organized a Women's Parliamentary Circle in the spring of 1991. The purpose of the Circle is to unite women deputies across political party lines to serve as a women's lobby within the parliament. Following the parliamentary elections in 1991, one-third of the women deputies and senators joined the club.

Women are becoming increasingly aware of the need to unite in order to preserve their rights, especially in the face of strong conservative political forces attempting to undermine their status and autonomy and make their situation even worse than it had been previously. The dominant tendency has been for many women activists to cooperate on a basis of temporary (as well as more stable) alliances while preserving independence of the respective groups and associations. This form of cooperation appears to be the most promising. The growing number of contacts with Western women's organizations may result in the creation of an international women's lobby that could help to defend women's interests in particular countries and to make women's promotion to decision-making positions one of the tests of the process of democratization now taking place.

References

(1) Bartkowski, J. (1990) *Kariery dzialaczy lokalnych* [*Careers of Local Leaders*]. Warsaw: Institute of Sociology, University of Warsaw.

(2) Chapman, J. (1985) "The Impact of Women's Movement on the Political Orientations of Local Politicians." Paper presented at the XIII Congress of the Inter-Political Science Association, Paris.

(3) Jasinska, A., and Siemienska, R. (1983) "The Socialist Personality: A Case Study of Poland," *International Journal of Sociology* 13(1) (Spring):1–84.

(4) *Kobieta w Polsce* [*Woman in Poland*] (1990). Warsaw: Central Statistical Office.

(5) "Kurier Podlaski," (1987) quoted after "Zycie Warszawy," June 12.

(6) Lovenduski, J. (1986) *Women and European Politics: Contemporary Feminism and Public Policy*. Amherst: University of Massachusetts Press.

(7) Maly Rocznik Statystyczny (1939) *Small Statistical Yearbook 1939*. Warsaw: Glowny Urzad Statystyczny.

(8) Moldawa, L. (1979) *Naczelne wladze panstwowe 1944–1979, Sklad osobowy i podstawy prawne organizacji i funkcjonowania wedlug stanu na dzien 30.09.1979* [*Central Authorities 1944–1979. A Personal Structure and Legislative Basis of Organization and Functioning on Sept. 30, 1979*]. Warsaw: University of Warsaw.

(9) Siemienska, R. (1983) "Local Party Leaders in Poland," *International-Political Science Review* 4(1):127–136.

(10) Siemienska, R. (1985a) "Women's Political Participation and the 1980 Crisis in Poland," *International-Political Science Review* 6(3):332–346.

(11) Siemienska, R. (1985b) "Women, Work and Gender Equality in Poland: Reality and Its Social Perception," in Sharon L. Wolchik and Alfred G. Meyer (eds.), *Women, State and Party in Eastern Europe*, pp. 344–361. Durham, N.C.: Duke University Press.

(12) Siemienska, R. (1986) "Women and Social Movements in Poland," *Women and Politics* 6(7):13–41.

(13) Siemienska, R. (1989a) "Women and Solidarity in Poland in the Early 1980s," in Y. Cohen, *Women and Counter Power*, pp. 33–45. Montreal/New York: Black Rose Books.

(14) Siemienska, R. (1989b) "Poland," in Gail P. Kelly, *World Handbook of Women's Education*, pp. 323–347. Westport, Conn.: Greenwood Press.

(15) Siemienska, R. (1990) *Plec, zawod, polityka. Kobiety w zyciu publicznym w Polsce* [*Gender, Occupation, Politics. Women's Participation in Public Life in Poland*]. Warsaw: Institute of Sociology, University of Warsaw Press.

(16) Siemienska, R. (1991a) "Popular Demands and Local Leadership Responses in Periods of Economic Retreat in Poland," in A. Farazmand, *Handbook of Comparative and Development Public Administration*, pp. 155–167. New York: Marcel Dekker, Inc.

(17) Siemienska, R. (1991b) "Polish Women and Polish Politics Since World War II," *Journal of Women's History* 3(1):108–125.

(18) Siemienska, R. (1992) "Women in the Period of Systemic Changes in Poland." Paper

presented at the Conference on Equality between Women and Men in a Changing Europe, Council of Europe, Poznan, Poland.

(19) *Statistical Yearbook* (1986) Warsaw: Central Statistical Office.

(20) *Statistical Yearbook* (1988) Warsaw: Central Statistical Office.

(21) *Statistical Yearbook* (1990) Warsaw: Central Statistical Office.

(22) Vianello, M., and Siemienska, R., et al. (1990) *Gender Inequality: A Comparative Study of Discrimination and Participation.* London: Sage.

(23) Wiatr, J. J. (ed.) (1987) *Wladza lokalna w warunkach kryzysu* [*Local Government in the Conditions of the Crisis*]. Warsaw: Institute of Sociology, University of Warsaw Press.

16

FORMER SOVIET UNION

Women Managers in the Former USSR: A Case of "Too Much Equality"?

Sheila M. Puffer

Imagine a country in which women are granted equal rights with men under the constitution, have excellent professional and technical postsecondary education, make up half the labor force, and are revered as the standard-bearers of the country's moral and social values. Furthermore, imagine that this country was founded on the basis of a grand social design, whereby women were to be full participants in all aspects of society and a department of women's affairs, headed by an influential and respected woman, was established to implement this policy. Who could ask for a better country for women to enter the management profession and to assume positions of power and responsibility in society?

The former Union of Soviet Socialist Republics fits the description of the country described above. With all these advantages supposedly granted to them, Soviet women have been touted for years by their government officials as being "the very happiest women in the world" (26:139). Yet, the typical Soviet woman will tell you that these conditions have brought her little happiness. The myth that they have done so existed only in the propaganda of Soviet officialdom for the past 70 years. The reality experienced by the vast majority of Soviet women in their personal and professional lives remained far different. Whereas the state officially proclaimed women's equality, many women complained, "We have *too much* equality" (7:201–202). This ironic statement reflects women's dissatisfaction with having to fulfill society's expectations that they should work as well as assume primary responsibility for home and family. An additional source of frustration for women aspiring to influential managerial positions was that their careers were often blocked in spite of the fact that they possessed the requisite educational background and motivation.

Background

Duality of women's roles

This chapter discusses the reality experienced by Soviet women aspiring to or currently occupying managerial positions. As a result of the policy of *glasnost'*, or openness, in the past several years, the role of women in Soviet society has become the subject of much debate. One position maintains that women should have increased power and visibility at work, which would result in greater numbers of women in management. The opposing view holds that women should devote more time to their nurturing role in the home and reduce their participation in the workforce (4). During his tenure as president of the USSR, Mikhail Gorbachev publicly advocated both positions. At one point he acknowledged the important role of women in rebuilding society. This position reflected the official policy that granted equality to women in society and the workplace under the USSR Constitution (Articles 34 and 35 of chapter 6 of the Constitution of 1977, as amended on December 20, 1989). Gorbachev said, "Further democratization of society, which is the pivot and guarantor of *perestroika* (restructuring), is impossible without enhancing the role of women, without women's active and specific involvement, and without their commitment to all our reforming efforts. I am convinced that women's role in our society will steadily grow" (9:117).

At the same time, Gorbachev supported the idea of returning women to their traditional role of raising a family. He referred to "the question of what we should do to make it possible for women to return to their purely womanly mission" (9:117). He reaffirmed this position in a letter to the USSR Supreme Soviet in April 1990, the result of which was the creation of high-level government committees on the affairs of women, family, motherhood, and the protection of children (10).

Women in the USSR have clearly not advanced into managerial positions to the full extent of their training and abilities. The many factors responsible for this situation are rooted in the dual roles that society expects women to fulfill. This "double burden" has existed since the beginning of the Soviet state. The first constitution of 1918 "recognized work as a duty of every citizen of the republic" and included the statement, "He who does not work shall not eat" (18:41). At the same time, women's roles as wife, mother, and homemaker were officially hailed as critical to the moral and social development of Soviet society.

Alla Aleksandrovna Karnauhova, a professor of American literature at Irkutsk University in Siberia expressed the conservative view of women in managerial roles. She claimed that it is unnatural, and virtually impossible, for a woman to be an effective manager as well as a good wife and mother. She reasoned,

> When a woman assumes a high post it becomes the foundation of her life. The husband and the family just don't exist, she loses her femininity, she becomes domineering and bossy, no one likes this! She loses what has been assigned to her by nature. If she has a child, she doesn't take care of him; we call such children half-orphans. Yes, woman must lead, but if she assumes masculine qualities she loses her essence. . . . Of course, women must *try* to participate in the work collective while retaining their femininity. . . . But this is a very complex problem, not to lose our womanliness. . . . The men working under a woman executive may look on her as noble, but to the women working under her, she becomes a monstrous nonwoman (7:201–202).

This view posits a basic contradiction between leadership and femininity. Implicit in Karnauhova's remarks is that the debate about the duality of women's roles masks a more fundamental reason for the lack of complete access by women to managerial careers. After all, many women have found ways to accommodate their jobs and domestic responsibilities and are accustomed to working long hours in both spheres. A key phenomenon underlying this debate is very likely the reluctance of men to relinquish their monopoly on power and control and to share it with women.

Overview of this chapter

These dual pressures on women are a recurrent theme in writings about women in the former USSR (4;23;27;43). The origins of these pressures and their impact on women's access to managerial positions are the focus of this chapter. To put this discussion in context, the chapter first presents some background information on the former USSR as well as an overview of statistics on women in the labor force. A more detailed look at the dual roles of women follows this background material. Then follows an analysis of the factors affecting Soviet women's access to managerial positions, based on the framework developed by Adler and Izraeli in *Women in Management Worldwide* (1). Adler and Izraeli concluded that seven factors had an effect on women in management to varying degrees in the countries represented in their earlier book. These factors are: the perception of management as a masculine domain, cultural constraints on women's roles, women's roles in family life, the stage of the country's economic development, social policy, access to higher education, and organizational context (1). The chapter concludes with an assessment of the prospects for women in managerial positions.

Background on the former USSR

The USSR was established after the Communists, inspired by Marxist doctrine and led by Vladimir Lenin, seized power during the Russian Revolution of 1917. Following the civil war of 1918–1921 the new Soviet state was formed, composed of the nations that had been formerly part of the Russian empire. With the annexation of the three Baltic republics of Latvia, Lithuania, and Estonia during World War II, the USSR consisted of fifteen republics and had a population in 1990 of approximately 280 million. The republics, which are diverse in terms of economic development, culture, and religion, range from the Central Asian republics, in which the Moslem religion and Eastern philosophy prevail, to the Slavic republics, in which Christianity and European thought predominate. The goal of the Communists was to transform this multicultural population into the "new Soviet man" and thus to build a society in which the individual was subordinate to the common good, and the state would direct every facet of people's lives. The Communists attempted to achieve this goal through a repressive dictatorship and totalitarian state. In 1985, President Mikhail Gorbachev initiated a break with the past through his policies of *glasnost'* (openness) and *perestroika* (restructuring). These policies, which triggered the end of the Communist dictatorship and marked the beginning of a politically free society and a market-based economy, culminated in December 1991 in the dissolution of the USSR and the independence of its republics. The world continues to witness extraordinary political, economic, and social changes in the republics of the former USSR. These epoch-making changes will take years to reach their ultimate conclusions.

It is important to keep in perspective the applicability of the information included in this chapter, written at a time of turmoil and uncertainty, to these changing conditions. The statistics on labor force participation, education, and the like, refer to the diverse population in the fifteen republics of the former USSR in the 1980s. However, a wide disparity exists throughout the various republics regarding the role of women in society and in the workplace. For example, in the Central Asian republics, few women hold managerial positions compared with the number in other republics. The information about managerial and professional women refers primarily to the European republics of the former USSR. The concluding comments about prospects for the future will therefore be confined to women managers in the Russian Federation.

Women in the labor force

Women's participation in the labor force in the former Soviet Union is strong in numbers but weak in status and influence. Before the Communists took power in 1917, women constituted 10 percent of the workforce and were employed predominantly as manual laborers in factories and agriculture. Lenin advocated that women should have greater opportunities in the labor force and appointed Aleksandra Kollontai to head the department of women's affairs. By 1922, women's participation in the workforce had increased to 25 percent (11). Today virtually all women (92 percent) of working age (sixteen to 54) in the former Soviet republics are employed or in school (36;40). Since 1970, women have constituted more than half (51 percent) of the workforce. Women currently hold one-tenth (11 percent) of top management positions (44).

According to Communist ideology, there was no occupational or wage discrimination in the USSR. One of the fundamental principles of Communist doctrine, which until very recently governed all official aspects of Soviet life, is embodied in the phrase, "From each according to his abilities, to each according to his labor." Legislation mandating equal pay for equal work came into effect shortly after the Russian Revolution of 1917. In reality, however, occupational and wage discrimination against women remained widespread. The majority of women work in the most poorly paid sectors of the economy and in positions with the lowest wages and the most dangerous conditions. Nearly 20 percent of working women work on the evening and night shifts in the Russian republic, and women perform 58 percent of manual labor in industry (38). Women accept hazardous jobs out of economic necessity. Jobs in hazardous conditions, such as those in the chemical industry, which is considered a "female" industry, pay more than jobs in other "female" sectors but not enough to attract male workers.

Women are concentrated in lower-paying industries. This structural differentiation can be traced to the first five-year plan initiated in 1928. To promote industrialization of the country, Communist party officials decided to pay higher wages in sectors of the economy that were central to promoting industrialization, such as industrial production, transportation, and construction. In analyzing the available statistics on women's occupational status and wages, these sectors were still found to pay wages that exceed the national average and also have the lowest concentration of women (12). In 1984 in industry, transportation, and construction, the average wage exceeded the national average by 11, 17, and 24 percent, respectively. Conversely, in the public health, education, retail trade, and restaurant sectors, where women are predominantly employed, wages were lower than the national average by 29, 23, and 21 percent.

Similar wage differentials for women and men were reported in Taganrog, an industrial city on the Sea of Azov (12). Overall, women's earnings were 70 percent of men's in the late 1960s, a figure which remained unchanged in the late 1970s. Among specialists (i.e., professionals), women engineers typically earned 15 to 20 percent less than their male counterparts. Researchers attributed this disparity to two factors. First, women are concentrated in sectors of the economy that pay less well. Second, during the formative years of work experience, which provide the foundation for career advancement, many women reduce their participation in the labor force to raise children.

Studies of the machine-building industry in Leningrad in 1970 and 1977 found that 69 percent of engineering and technical workers who performed skilled intellectual work (e.g., engineers, economists, engineer-mechanics) were women (12). The percentage of women performing highly skilled scientific and technical work was 62 percent, yet only 6.3 percent of managers in this field (from section chief to enterprise manager) were women (12). A 1970s study of engineers in Leningrad found women lagging three years behind men in promotion to the position of group leader (14). While this inequality has again been attributed to interruptions in women's careers due to childbearing, the study fails to report comparisons between women with and without children. That other factors also play a part certainly remains plausible.

This phenomenon of feminization of the labor force at the rank-and-file level is also evident in the sectors of the economy typically considered "female." For example, in public education, 81 percent of the teachers in grades one through ten are women, yet only 41 percent of the principals in elementary schools (up to the eighth grade) and only 36 percent of those in secondary schools are women (45).

The managerial job

Working as a manager in the former Soviet republics is a very demanding job. One study found that plant managers and other senior executives usually work 50 percent longer than the standard work day (a total of twelve hours), and managers at other levels work 25 percent longer (a total of ten hours) (22). Many managers joke that they work an eight-hour day – from 8 A.M. to 8 P.M. (33). Managers are responsible not only for the work organization but also for meeting many of the social needs of employees, including housing, childcare, food, and cultural enrichment.

Managerial work can also be frustrating. Under the Communist regime, managers were pressured to meet plans established by the central authorities and were often denied the requisite resources. Managers had little latitude to negotiate with higher authorities and were held accountable for results without having the authority to make policy decisions. It is little wonder that many people, women and men alike, declined management positions because they often paid less than nonmanagerial jobs and brought more headaches. Such people would rather earn extra money working overtime in their regular nonmanagerial job or in a second job, often in the growing private sector, where they could earn many times the salary paid in state organizations. To these people, the perks of a managerial position, such as prestige and preferred access to goods and services, were not worth the effort.

Under the Communist regime a mandatory qualification for promotion to management was membership in good standing in the Communist party. Individuals who planned managerial careers typically became involved in party activities at an early age. They would join the Young Communist League (Komsomol) as teenagers, and in their twenties would become party members. Virtually all managers were party members, but it was not essential for professionals in nonmanagerial positions to be members. Preparation for senior managerial positions often included experience in an important role in the party organization away from the workplace (33). Traditionally, however, women held few party leadership positions, although they did have a presence at the local level (36). This absence was the subject of debate in the 1970s. It frequently was attributed to a "certain psychological barrier" that took the following form: "On the one hand, a number of leaders are afraid to entrust women with responsible positions; and on the other, women themselves demonstrate timidity, doubting their strength and refusing, under various pretexts, a promotion to leadership positions" (30:44). Insufficient experience in Communist party activity therefore hindered women's advancement into management. Early in their careers, women may have viewed party membership as unnecessary because they assumed they were oriented toward a professional rather than a managerial career.

No longer is the Communist party the official ruling force in the independent Soviet republics. However, the vestiges of the Communist party will continue to have a negative impact on women for some time because the personal relationships developed among former party members will still be relied upon for doing business, and women have remained largely excluded from this network.

Women managers: Where they are, what they do

The distribution of women in managerial and professional positions in industry in the former USSR is presented in Table 16.1. In professional and technical positions, women are concentrated at the bottom levels. They virtually monopolize the professional staff positions of bookkeeper (94 percent women), engineer economist and economist (89 percent) (economist includes a broader type of administrative work than the American definition, as well as the specific profession of economist), rate-setter specialists (85 percent) (those setting and measuring standards of output), technicians (84 percent), and chief and senior accountant (77 percent). These staff positions are not directly related to production and therefore are less influential and less likely to lead to top management positions.

With respect to managerial positions, the greatest concentration of women managers is in services or staff positions. The majority of women managers work in staff departments (39 percent are women). The more prestigious managerial staff positions in design bureaux and the like have far fewer women managers (16

Table 16.1 Percentage of women in managerial and professional positions in industrial enterprises (1983)

Position	Percentage of women
Presidents of production associations and independent enterprises	11
Vice presidents of production associations and independent enterprises (except chief engineers)	8
Chief engineers and their deputies	9
Senior staff managers and their deputies[a]	13
Shop managers (*tsech*) and their deputies	12
Shift managers, section managers (*uchastok*), department managers in shops (*tsechovye laboratorii*) and their deputies	18
Managers of design bureaus, technology and project departments, bureaus and groups in plant administration and shops and their deputies	16
Managers of other production departments, services, bureaux and groups in plant administration,[b] in shops, and central and shop units (*laboratorii*) and their deputies	32
Managers of nonproduction departments, bureaux, and groups in plant administration[c] and their deputies	39
Engineers performing all types of industrial-production work[d]	58
Technicians of all types[e]	84
Engineer economists and economists	89
Forepersons	30
Rate-setter engineers, rate-setter technicians, and rate-setters	85
Chief and senior accountants	77
Bookkeepers	94

[a] Head designer, chief technologist, head of mechanical services, chief economist, etc. (except line managers reporting directly to the plant manager)
[b] E.g., mechanical and electrical services, shipping, planning, labor and compensation, etc.
[c] Financial, purchasing and distribution, personnel, etc.
[d] Except engineer economists and engineer rate-setters
[e] Except rate-setter technicians

Source: *Zhenshchiny i Deti v SSSR* (1985) [*Women and Children in the USSR*], p. 30. Moscow: Finansy i Statistika.

percent). In line management, women's participation is also greatest at the lowest levels, namely as first-line supervisors or forepersons (30 percent) and managers of production departments and services (32 percent). Only about half as many women work at the next managerial level – namely shift managers and department managers in shops and laboratories (18 percent). Shop managers and their deputies form the next step up the ladder, and women managers constitute only 12 percent of this group. The representation of women in top management positions is similarly small. Eleven percent of presidents of industrial enterprises are women, a percentage that also applies to women members of the top management team (vice president, 8 percent, chief engineer and deputies, 9 percent, and senior staff manager and deputies, 13 percent).

Overall the concentration of women in professional and managerial positions in the nonproduction sphere, and predominantly at lower hierarchical levels, indicates that women exercise little power in organizations despite their impressive numbers and educational qualifications.

Literature on women in management

Although women managers have actively participated in the Soviet economy since the early years following the Russian Revolution of 1917, little has been written about them. Some observers believe that the topic has not been addressed because management is traditionally viewed as a male profession (19). This belief suggests that women have been ignored because they are considered an aberration in management. Another compelling explanation is that, before *perestroika* and *glasnost'* took hold in the mid-1980s, the Soviet government perpetuated the myth that women fully exercised rights and opportunities in equal measure with men. The Communist party viewed any negative information about the role of women as nonessential and even damaging to the image of the egalitarian Communist state. Until the mid-1980s, most statistics and results of sociological surveys were considered classified information (9;21).

The fact that women are, in reality, treated as second-class citizens has become a matter of public discussion only in the last few years. In a candid, live interview on ABC television on September 5, 1991, President Gorbachev admitted that Soviet women live under very difficult conditions, have been discriminated against in career opportunities, and remain scarce in high-level positions (39). He added that society will improve when it eliminates inequality and gives women greater opportunities to develop. Interviewed on the same program, Boris Yeltsin, president of the Russian Federation, echoed Gorbachev's remarks.

The information reported in this chapter comes from a variety of time periods and sources, and consequently requires careful interpretation. Some data and opinions may have been contrived to reflect the Communist party line, the "official" version of events that people felt compelled to report in order to avoid reprisals. Other information may reflect totally candid and brutally honest opinions as a result of people exercising their newly granted freedom of speech under the policy of *glasnost'*. However, because people are currently living in a transition period, it is not always clear whether they are responding according to the rules of the old or new system.

Factors Affecting Soviet Women's Access to Managerial Positions

Perception of management as a masculine domain

Unquestionably, management has been considered a masculine domain in the former USSR, official Communist dogma of equality of women and men to the contrary. The extent to which women managers are held in ill-regard has come to light in two recent studies (19;46). The studies, which surveyed both women and men, resulted in very similar images of women managers. Not only did society portray women managers in an unflattering stereotype, but it also made them the butt of jokes spread by women and men alike, and even by women managers themselves (46).

This prejudice against women in professional roles is long-standing. In the 1970s, studies reported that Russian women have less initiative and creativity than men and are, therefore, believed to be less suited for managerial positions (31). In 1976, a woman captured the sentiment of the 1970s in a letter she wrote in response to a newspaper article about the recruitment and training of industrial executives, "For some reason it seems taken for granted that an executive is a man" (25:10).

The findings of two scholars, Komarov and Zhuplev, stand in marked contrast to the idealized image of working women portrayed in many official state publications (19; 46).[1] The remarks expressed by many of those responding in these studies would be labeled as blatant sexism and unsubstantiated stereotyping in the West. However, Soviets may not see their remarks in this light. They may feel that *glasnost'* gives them the right to express opinions regardless of their social appropriateness or basis in fact. They may also be unaware that their opinions consist of perceptions rather than fact or that they are unconsciously blaming women for problems that society as a whole has created.

Komarov conducted his study through interviews, questionnaires, and conversations with an unspecified number of men and women but provided no information about their backgrounds, an ommission that puts his findings in question (19). Zhuplev's sample consisted of 124 respondents, employed in six organizations located primarily in Moscow (46). The majority were managers (52 percent), the remainder held nonmanagerial professional positions. Women constituted 58 percent of the respondents.

Both Komarov and Zhuplev took the position that gender differences exist in performing managerial work. In the words of Komarov, "The music of management is the same for everyone. But a man and a woman will play it differently" (19:53). Both investigators claimed that there is an identifiable female managerial style. They structured their survey questions to accentuate the differences between women and men managers, and respondents provided vivid descriptions of the differences they perceived (19). These attitudes are consistent with the complementary contribution model of assumed differences between women and men managers, as opposed to the equity model of assumed similarity (1). The fundamental issue underlying the complementary contribution model is whether women's differences are considered a constraint or a valuable asset. The responses to Komarov's and Zhuplev's surveys reflect both views and therefore create contradictions. For example, femininity, physical attractiveness, and sensuality are seen as both assets and liabilities. Similarly, they report different expectations of what behaviors constitute competence and professionalism in women and men managers. The general tone of their remarks, however, is one of labeling women managers with sexist stereotypes. Even the positive attributes associated with women managers come across as patronizing. The presumed lack of certain positive attributes in many men is equally patronizing to men. Some findings from the two surveys follow. It is important to keep in mind that the surveys contain many stereotypical questions, which may have contributed to respondents constructing stereotypical answers. Research observing the managerial behavior of women and men is sorely needed to determine actual similarities and differences.

Perceived characteristics of the ideal woman manager Based on his interview data, Komarov concluded that women and men consider the ideal woman manager to possess the following three sets of qualities: first, femininity, physical attractiveness, and charm; second, competence and professionalism; and third, the ability to deal with people (19).

Respondents rated femininity, physical attractiveness, and charm as the top priority. They disliked sloppiness and excessive makeup and jewelry. Furthermore, some men lamented that there are too few beautiful women managers. Komarov offered the following explanation:

> I think it is difficult for a very beautiful woman to be a manager. Beauty, as one might guess, requires a great deal of time and effort, as well as many admirers and amusements. A beautiful woman, if the author's observations have not deceived him, lives for her beauty, and for this reason remains a woman, ever a woman, in all respects. A businesswoman, it seems to me, is likable rather than beautiful, and is a manager who is also a woman rather than a woman who is also a manager (19:54).

The second most important set of qualities in a woman manager, according to Komarov's survey, includes competence and professionalism. However, there are different expectations of what constitute competence and professionalism for a woman manager than for a man. Whereas aloofness, brevity, and sternness are considered normal in male managers, in women they are perceived as callousness. Both the men and women surveyed by Komarov seemed to want women managers to possess a series of traits, such as kindness and strictness, femininity and efficiency, calmness and exactingness, and gentleness and a strong will. Even in decision making, Komarov concluded, people have different expectations of women and men managers. From a man, they expect decision making accompanied by understanding; from a woman, they expect understanding first, followed by a decision.

Komarov's respondents put in third place the ability of women managers to deal with people (19). Komarov claimed that women and men differ in the ways they interact with subordinates (19:80). Men pay little attention to how their managerial style affects the women managers who report to them. In contrast, women managers show more sensitivity to the effect they have on subordinates and more willingness to change their style. According to Komarov, women managers ask themselves, "Why should I maintain a style that people condemn?"

Respondents in Zhuplev's study developed a similar list of characteristics of successful woman managers: "kindness, humaneness, and charm; the ability to be trusted in personal contacts with business partners and subordinates (one respondent called it 'a family approach to management'); and determination combined with exactingness and practicality." A half-dozen respondents also mentioned two additional factors: the ability to work hard without resorting to alcohol and the ability for a woman to manage like a man (46).

Komarov argued that women are superior to men in four managerial skills: flexibility in using different approaches to completing a task; thoroughness in checking the facts with various sources; intuition in decision making; and personal stress management (19). It is ironic that, despite widespread discrimination against women in high status positions, many women and men perceive the quality of women's work to be superior to that of men. Soviet women are sometimes called "our Japanese," because of their strong work ethic (7:35). In general, women are believed to be more responsible, more accurate, and more conscientious than men. Such qualities make women prized employees at lower levels, but do not give them access to positions of power because of the various barriers discussed in this chapter. To illustrate, consider the claims of the chief editor of a Moscow publishing house: "If I have to choose between a man or a woman for a middle-level editorial position, in nine cases out of ten I'll choose the woman. How much more careful, responsible, punctual, neat, conscientious, they are in their work!" (7:35).

A female managerial style?   According to these findings, some people believe there is an identifiable female managerial style. In some sense, this view fits the complementary contribution model of different, but equally valuable, contributions of women and men (1). However, people appear merely to be paying lip service to the notion of valuing equally women's contributions. For one thing, women remain poorly represented in top management. Second, most women and men in Zhuplev's survey claimed they preferred to work for a man[2] and expressed negative feelings toward potentially increasing the number of women managers in the country (46).[3]

Cultural constraints

The cultural constraints on women's access to managerial positions can be traced far back in Russian history. Elvira Novikova, a prominent feminist and historian, contended that the Soviet media juxtaposed two stereotypes of women that are deeply rooted in Russian culture:

> They've taken two basic images of women in our folklore – the Cinderella sweetie pie who sacrifices her life to family, and *Baba Yaga*, the wise independent witch who lives alone in the forest and is doomed to solitude. They ask us, "Who do you want to be, Cinderella or *Baba Yaga*?" The honey who must run around bringing man his slippers . . . that's the woman they're all pressing us to be, even after seventy years of our being fully employed in the workforce! (7:88–89)

These deep-seated images pull Soviet women in opposite directions, but the traditional woman's role seems to be especially strong and serves as a brake on women's wholehearted launching into managerial careers. "The dominant theme in the current literature [on sex roles] is that women should 'choose' between work or family. However, genuine choice is hindered by stereotypical ideas about women's natural role, and by considerable psychological pressure to choose a family" (4:208).

The traditional female role is a central theme of Russian culture and is found in nineteenth-century literature. The literary phrase "women's suffering as redemptive force" (7:39) depicted women as

> . . . priestess and redeemer, the chief repository of virtue in the form of agape. . . . The desire for a woman savior is expressed in a constant adulation of the ethical strengths of the good woman and the refusal to consider the virtues of male heroism. Male

identity is perceived as precarious, contingent, existing only in the ethereal world of ideas rather than rooted in the "real" world. Woman, on the other hand, is regarded as the essence of stability, of life, of growth, of *lichnost'* (individuality) itself. She is "whole" (*tsel'naia*), while man is neurotic, torn. (13:230–231)

Once a year, on March 8, women are celebrated in recognition of International Women's Day. On this occasion, the cultural traditions pertaining to women become evident. For example, the newspaper *Rossiiskaia Gazeta* wrote: "Thank you for being near us, not losing faith in us, and for generously sharing with us the truths of life" (35).

Many women admit that their "tradition of heroic self-sacrifice is a form of power play, a way of retaining their aura and their status" (7:39). This attitude was also evident in comments made by a variety of professional women interviewed on the eve of International Women's Day in 1992. Galina Nagornaya, a 35-year-old economist asserted, "The men are right to have a holiday for us because they know we're the real leaders. We set things straight" (5:11). I recently talked with several young women students at Moscow State University who also agreed with this view. This cultural norm may help explain why some women sacrifice a promising managerial career for the sake of their family or to maintain harmonious relations with male colleagues.

There are two points of view about women and work. On the one hand, some women would be happy to work less because they have been subjected to a decade of gender-role socialization on what it means to be a woman. "Many women agree that their full participation in the workforce has had negative consequences for the family, children, and themselves and seem happy to accept the notion that they are the repositories of a set of innate, traditionally feminine personality traits, however much at odds this is with their lived experience" (4:212).

On the other hand, according to surveys conducted in the 1970s, some professional women oppose reduced work hours and part-time work. For example, some research scientists who were surveyed feared that society would expect them to be as productive in their own careers as full-time professionals but at reduced pay. Similarly, professionals in industry feared that their career advancement would be jeopardized by reduced work hours (27:17).

Women's role in family life

Not only are Soviet women expected to work, but they are also held responsible for managing the household. Soviet women have long lamented the "second shift" or "double burden", which has even become the subject of fiction. In the novella, *A Week Like Any Other (Nedelia Kak Nedelia)*, Natalia Baranskaia portrayed, in diary form, a week in the life of a talented young woman overburdened in her attempts to balance a promising career as a research scientist with her duties as a wife and mother (6). The story became immensely popular when it was published in 1969, and many women identified with the angry sentiments expressed in it.

The situation has failed to improve. A 1985 survey of 51,000 households found that women spend on average two to three times longer on household chores than men and have 1.5 times less free time. On a typical work day, women spend nearly seven hours on chores, whereas men spend less than two hours (41:68–69). This is in addition to putting in a full day at work. On weekends, the time that women spend on household chores is even greater. Women typically spend several hours a day standing in line to buy food and other essentials. They wash clothes and dishes by hand because of the shortage of household appliances and sew clothes for themselves and family members because of poor quality or overpriced apparel in stores.

Many women feel overwhelmed by the double burden of work and family, and the demands can lead to chronic fatigue. A television producer in Riga, Latvia, who was married with two young children complained: "I come home, I'm exhausted. I feel lonely because I'm so exhausted that I can't and don't want to love anyone, I only want to rest, they all just bother me, all my womanly instincts have been drained out of me. . . . I'm too tired to love!" (7:39).

This woman's situation is not atypical. Fatigue was a common complaint among the women in the Ivanovo study, who rated how they felt at the end of the work day. Although half of the women (48 percent) felt fine, one-third felt poorly, and 18 percent felt too tired to do anything once they got home (29).

So much ado is made about family responsibilities that one would assume that women had many children. Yet, few women in the European republics have more than one child. Cramped living quarters, scarce childcare facilities, divorce rates approaching 50 percent in urban areas of the Russian republic, and the emphasis on work are some of the factors accounting for the small numbers of children (32). Since children do not appear to represent an inordinate portion of the family responsibilities, it is important to examine the uneven distribution of household tasks between spouses as a more likely source of the woman's "burden."

Several reasons have been suggested for the imbalance between women's and men's family responsibilities. They all revolve around power relations between women and men. One view is that men are superior to women and should be indulged and pampered at home. This special treatment is to compensate for the emasculation of men as a result of serfdom in tsarist times and powerlessness in their jobs in modern times due to the centralization of decision making and authority under the Communist regime. In addition, because of the great loss of life in World War II, many women who were fortunate enough to have husbands wanted to make life easier for them. An opposing explanation for the excessive family responsibilities women perform is that women are superior to men and they manifest their superiority by taking on more tasks. Yet another possible explanation is the high incidence of alcoholism among men, a condition that makes many men appear weak and unreliable in the eyes of women.

There is little question that the heavy commitment of time to household and family responsibilities has interfered with many women's career advancement for at least two reasons. First, women take courses only half as often as men. Of those who take courses, less than 2 percent of women with children go to out-of-town locations to study (34). This factor can become a serious drawback since the best management development programs are generally offered in large cities, and promising managers from around the country attend for several weeks or even months.

Second, women's family responsibilities make it difficult for them to adopt the demanding schedules of typical managers.

Many women, despite their complaints about overwork and the double shift of job and domestic responsibilities, accept their lot and do not actively try to change the status quo. A St. Petersburg school teacher gave little hope for the development of a women's movement to address these issues. She reasoned, "We simply don't have enough energy left to have friendships outside of the workplace, we have no time to pick up the phone and communicate our grief and weariness to a sister soul. In such solitude, with such a heavy professional and domestic work load, how do you expect us to fight for women's rights as you do in Chicago?" (7:38).

In recent conversations with several women students at Moscow State University, I learned that they are pessimistic about the prospect of change in the distribution of family responsibilities. They said that their young male acquaintances have the attitude that household chores and childrearing are a woman's responsibility. The women students doubted that these men would change their attitudes very easily. Nevertheless, women have different ways of reducing their own burden – some cease working, others forego a family, and others find more efficient ways of fulfilling both roles.

Economic development of the republics

The republics of the former USSR are currently in a state of economic chaos. This crisis presents threats and opportunities for both women and men. The threats for women are manifold. One prediction is that, as a result of restructuring the economy, approximately sixteen million people will lose their jobs, nearly all of them (fifteen million) women (24). Women will be hardest hit for two reasons. First, the jobs to be eliminated and replaced by technology are primarily in manual labor, a sector in which women predominate. Presumably, the managers of these women, who are often women themselves, will also lose their jobs. Second, some people, including some leading economists, believe that women are not full contributors in the workforce. The argument is that they cannot be relied upon because their family obligations cause them to be absent from work and prevent them from taking courses to improve their skills (8). The best thing, according to some economists concerned about improving the economy, is to phase women out of the workforce by shortening their work day and improving maternity leave benefits. Cuts in state-run childcare are also forcing some women to stay home with their children.

Such measures, however, fail to take into account the rampant inflation in the republics. With wages rapidly losing their buying power, it is imperative to have more than one wage earner in the family. Consequently, women may be forced to remain in the workforce and seek well-paying jobs. However, this does not necessarily mean a managerial job. As discussed earlier, many people decline managerial positions in favor of other jobs that pay more money and require less responsibility. A counter-argument, however, is that if there is less competition for managerial jobs, women should have a greater opportunity to be appointed to these positions.

On the positive side, the restructuring of the economy and the emergence of the private sector are creating new job opportunities for enterprising individuals. Greater opportunities for women exist within specific organizational contexts.

Social policy

Two fundamental social issues have had a major impact on women's roles and their decision to pursue management positions. One was the Soviet central government's concern about the low birthrate in the European republics in comparison with the Central Asian republics. The authorities were concerned for two reasons. First, they argued that more children would be needed who could later join the labor force and support the growing number of retired people—a belief consistent with official Communist ideology that the major function of the family was to provide a labor force for industry (42). Second, the central authorities gave the appearance of wanting to keep the European population dominant. Given that the birthrate is lowest in areas in which women constitute a greater proportion of the labor force, some demographers warn that a population decline is likely unless women spend less time working.

The second major social issue affecting women is the patriarchal view that women must fulfill their natural role of mother and nurturer and leave the responsibility of providing materially for the family to men. Adherents to this view attribute the decline in moral values in society and the breakup of the family to women's neglect of their most important role. (Note that it goes without saying that a more likely cause of moral decline was the social policies implemented by the communist regime itself.)

Social legislation suggested to address these issues included raising the status of motherhood, replacing the image of the emancipated working woman with that of the happy family characterized by distinct female and male roles, exempting mothers with more than two children from working, encouraging longer postnatal leave and more part-time work, and changing child custody rules to discourage women from seeking divorce (4).

To popularize this view of women's roles, the Soviet government developed a two-year course called "The Ethics and Psychology of Family Life" that they required all students to take in the ninth and tenth grades of high school (4). They introduced the course in 1984 in the European republics for two hours per week throughout the school year. The curriculum included emphasizing the importance of the family as the basic cell of socialist society, the reverence of motherhood as women's "great mission," and the need to return to traditional gender roles, in which men are the breadwinners and women, although equal, put home and family before their jobs. The course was not offered in the Central Asian republics, presumably to avoid encouraging a higher birthrate there. Reactions to the course were mixed but generally unfavorable. Teachers were not well trained, students were bored and found the material far removed from their immediate concerns, and the topic of sex education was completely ignored (4).

Another social policy that may potentially restrict women's access to managerial positions is, ironically, the newly implemented legislation on maternity leave. Women are legally guaranteed their jobs for three years after having a baby.

Although this policy is laudable, it also has a negative side. The women who are adversely affected by this policy are those seeking their first job, including recent college graduates interested in pursuing a managerial career. Many employers consider recent women graduates a bad investment because they assume that these women will become pregnant and then take maternity leave; employers are, therefore, reluctant to hire them.

Finally, the policy, enforced for decades under the Communist regime, of appointing token women to positions of prestige and high visibility often caused the public to view women's abilities with skepticism. Some women, such as Ekaterina Furtseva whom Krushchev appointed to the Politburo, and Valentina Tereshkova who was selected as the first woman cosmonaut, were touted as examples of equality in a socialist society. However, in these and other cases, the authorities deliberately chose unqualified women and denied them significant power. As a result, competent women had difficulty being taken seriously, and people often assumed that a woman in a high position did not obtain it on the basis of merit.

Access to higher education

Overall, women obtain a higher level of education than men, and yet employers continue to under-utilize women's education in the workplace. Women with the same education and jobs as men at the time of entry into the workforce often receive lower pay and are promoted less frequently to senior positions. Women represent 60 percent of workers, both blue- and white-collar, who have a specialized secondary or postsecondary education. However, this level of education is not reflected in the type of work women perform. Specifically, 48 percent of men with postsecondary education hold managerial positions at various levels. The corresponding figure for women with the same education level is 7 percent (40).

People gain access to management training in two ways. The traditional way is for a superior to nominate them. This method can create a bottleneck for women. The superior must recognize their seriousness in pursuing a managerial career and their ability to be an effective manager. The immediate superior is more likely to know women subordinates' abilities. This first-hand knowledge may prevent the superior from reacting stereotypically to them. Yet, the superior may also experience pressure from male superiors or subordinates who prefer that men receive training instead. The second method to gain access to managerial training is for employees to apply to management programs independently and to pay their own way. An increasing number of women are currently taking advantage of this opportunity, particularly those interested in entrepreneurship and the market economy. For example, the School of Management founded in 1990 at Moscow State University (MGU) has a number of women enrolled in its programs. In the two-year full-time MBA program, 40 percent of the students (twelve out of 30) are women. In the advanced management program for entrepreneurs, women constitute 20 percent of the participants. Of the middle managers from a state-owned enterprise enrolled in an MGU management program, one-third are women. Two women are among the five full-time international business students currently studying in the United States under the sponsorship of an American charitable foundation. Finally, in MGU's executive management program, less than 2 percent of the participants are women.

According to the deputy director of MGU's School of Management, Aleksandr Naumov, this distribution of women participating in management training programs is typical of management institutes in the Moscow area.[4] These data show that women have fairly good access to management training at the entry and middle management levels, but remain highly restricted from training programs at the executive level. Moreover, women are virtually absent among managers sent abroad for training. Of the numerous groups of executives that undertook training in the United States in the last three years, I know of only one group that included women managers.

Several factors account for the minimal representation of women in executive management programs. First is the stereotype that management is a male profession. This constitutes the most serious impediment to women's access to the executive ranks. Second, almost all the gatekeepers to executive positions are men, who are unaccustomed to considering that their women subordinates might want managerial responsibilities. Third, the nature of the executive's job, with its long hours and travel, may be considered by women and men alike as too onerous for women with heavy family responsibilities. Finally, executive programs, especially those offered in the West, provide the perks of foreign travel and knowledge of the market economy. Since officials want a return on their investment in sending executives abroad, they may feel that men are a safer bet than women for all the reasons cited above.

A promising development in management training is the recent formation of businesswomen's clubs, including the Association of Moscow Business Women and the club Vera. These organizations offer management training programs for their members. In addition, a monthly column appearing throughout 1991 in the magazine *Soviet Woman* offered advice on how women could start their own businesses.

Organizational context

The dissolution of the Soviet state, concomitant fall of the Communist regime, and dismantling of the centrally planned economic mechanism are creating unprecedented opportunities for enterprising and achievement-oriented women and men to start their own businesses. Privatization of the economy began on a small scale in 1983, when Estonia legalized enterprises run by family members. Since then thousands of private enterprises or cooperatives have been formed, a number of them by women. A 1990 survey found 14 percent of the 586 owners of private businesses (cooperators) in ten large cities were women (16:27).

Cooperatives, which are private enterprises ranging in size from a few employees to many thousand, offer greater autonomy and flexible working conditions than state-owned enterprises. Salaries are much better, and pay is directly linked to performance, ability, and initiative—rather than connections and gender. Because cooperatives are a new organizational form and relatively free from state control, they provide an organizational context more hospitable to women than state-owned organizations (7). Women have expressed more positive attitudes toward cooperatives than have men (7:195).

Women have begun to create cooperatives in traditionally female economic sectors and in previously nonexistent niches. Women's cooperatives are characterized by low capital investment and small size. Anthony Jones, a Western expert on Soviet cooperatives, recently told me about several cooperatives he encountered that were founded and managed by women. All were well-educated professionals who had connections that enabled them to get the resources they needed. For example, a Moscow sociologist founded a for-profit journal of small business, another woman started a management consulting business with her husband, and a third became a "business facilitator," serving as an intermediary between foreigners and nationals and between suppliers and customers. In the Komi region, a group of women started a clothing factory, and a teacher founded a business school for teenagers. In Moscow, a former journalism professor with connections to the Komsomol (the former Communist youth league) founded a monthly magazine for teenagers called *Business and Culture*.

A serious drawback to working in a cooperative is that people who operate private businesses often face violence and bribery from the criminal element (mafia), which deters women, as well as men, from starting their own businesses. Private business operators often need police protection, security guards, and sometimes bodyguards.

As the free-market economy becomes established in the former Soviet republics, the term "cooperative," which is a holdover from the *perestroika* era, is being replaced simply by the term "private enterprise." Regardless of what they are called, and in spite of the hazards, cooperatives, or private enterprises, offer a new opportunity for women to prove themselves in an organizational context that is less likely to exhibit the gender-role stereotyping found in traditional state-owned organizations.

Prospects for Women in Management in the Former USSR

Surveys conducted over the past few years show that many Soviet women want to continue working and that a sizable number seek advancement up the managerial ladder. According to one survey, 60 percent of women said they would continue working even if their husbands earned the sum of what they both currently earned (28:48). This response reminds us of similar sentiments expressed in the 1970s, when 75 to 80 percent of women surveyed reported that they would continue working even if they no longer needed the income. The proportion was higher for white-collar than blue-collar workers (15:73). These findings suggest that work satisfies many women's intrinsic needs for personal growth and development, rather than simply providing a source of economic sustenance. Work may also satisfy many women's need to become economically independent from their husbands.

Women managers in the Ivanovo region, where the textile industry predominates and the majority of employees are women, also cited the intrinsic satisfaction of work. Two-thirds of Ivanovo's surveyed women managers liked their jobs (29). Those who sought career advancement reported that they did so to earn more money and improve their living standards (57 percent), to make decisions about bigger issues (54 percent), and to gain more rights and opportunities at work (25 percent). However, three-quarters of those surveyed did not foresee any opportunities for career advancement, and 88 percent did not want a promotion. Why was there so little opportunity for career advancement? The dearth of promotional opportunities may be due to the small size of the textile plants, thus limiting the number of hierarchical levels and promotion opportunities.[5] Alternatively, perhaps the textile plants discriminated against women in promotion decisions or women were not as well qualified as men. The fact that 88 percent of the women managers did not want a promotion is more difficult to explain than the simple lack of career advancement opportunities. The women may not want the stress or the prospect of earning less money as a manager. Similarly, they may feel a promotion is unobtainable or that it might upset the power balance with their husbands.

Work was not the only priority of professional women in the former USSR. Surveys by Soviet sociologists have found that 90 percent of professional women polled rated equally the importance of their professional and familial roles (28:48). Surveys also showed that many women wanted to combine both sets of responsibilities and sought more respect for their efforts at home and at work (3). The view commonly expressed by professional women is summarized as follows:

> We're equally oriented toward family and career and that's our tragedy, we want to write our thesis but we also feel we should be making *pirozhki* [turnovers]. Most of us end up compromising one or the other, or both. . . . We've been brainwashed with the notion that our state has done everything for us to reconcile the two roles, but the state hasn't begun to provide for us (7:90).

These remarks leave little doubt that many Soviet women take their professional careers seriously. However, as described above, many barriers stand in their way. A few years ago, the Center for the Professional Development of Sociologists in the USSR conducted a survey to determine managers' perceptions of barriers to women's advancement into managerial positions (2). The sample consisted of 1,725 managers at various hierarchical levels in 103 large industrial enterprises in the USSR. Managers gave their opinions about women in general, rather than describing their own experiences. The factor cited most frequently as a barrier to women in management (by 62 percent of those surveyed) was women's family and domestic obligations. Other factors suggested by respondents included that management is a male profession (28 percent), that women lack the necessary qualities to be a manager (19 percent), and that women are not sufficiently active themselves in pursuing managerial careers (15 percent).

Based on the results of opinion surveys as well as the analysis presented in this chapter, action clearly needs to be taken on five fronts if women are to become more prominent in managerial positions in the republics of the former USSR. First, an infrastructure of social services needs to be created to help women cope with the responsibilities of childcare and household tasks. This measure includes the provision of a greater number of reliable childcare centers and medical facilities, development of the retail sector to reduce shopping time, and production of a wide range of labor-saving home appliances. Second, a mass educational campaign needs to be conducted to eradicate gender-role stereotypes, including eliminating those stereotypes of women that were introduced in the high school curriculum in the 1980s.

Third, a concerted effort must be made to train women for managerial positions at all hierarchical levels and to integrate them into the networks of power and decision making. Fourth, the nature of the managerial job needs to be re-examined. Management would be more accessible to women if firms and managerial practices became more efficient, thereby resulting in a reduction of managers' work hours. Fifth, women need to organize and create pressure groups to gain greater control over the rules of the game in organizations.

To succeed in management currently requires that women in the former USSR assume the persona of "superwoman." As described earlier, these women face a multitude of obstacles in their pursuit of a managerial career. At home, they must juggle family responsibilities frequently without the benefit of adequate childcare, household conveniences, or a supportive husband. At work, organizations often subject them to wage discrimination and gender-role stereotyping. As many American professional women discovered in the 1980s, the pressures of being a "superwoman" can lead to burnout and disillusionment. It has also been recognized in the West that women alone lack the power to change this situation. Rather, fundamental changes in society must be effected through government and corporate policies as well as education.

Virtually every aspect of life in the republics of the former USSR is currently undergoing scrutiny and is ripe for reform. Bright spots exist for women managers in private businesses and management training programs. However, it is a utopian dream to think that the conditions for women in management will improve in the near future to any significant extent. Attention to other higher priority economic and social issues, competition for scarce jobs, and the existence of deep-seated stereotypes about women make such improvements unlikely in the short run. For instance, in 1992 women constituted 70 percent of the workers who were laid off, with two-thirds of these women having university degrees. In addition, by early 1993 women earned only 40 percent of the amount men earned, down from nearly 70 percent (17). Influential women, such as Liudmilla Bezlepkina, who in 1990 was the deputy minister of the State Committee of the USSR for Labor and Social Issues, recognize men's reluctance to share power with women as a major obstacle. The following incident, recounted vividly by Bezlepkina, illustrates how strongly some men in high-level positions feel about retaining power; the incident suggests that power sharing with women will not occur overnight:

> Recently one colleague asked another in my presence: "Could a woman become the chairman of our committee?" And he responded: "Never." I was surprised: "Why?" He said: "A chairman knows neither day nor night, holidays or days off." "But women are different and those who would consent to this post know about all its delights," I objected. My colleagues shook their heads and smiled indulgently: "No, a woman can't be, can't be and that's that" (20:5).

Notes

This chapter contains information on political, economic, social, and cultural conditions, both as they existed prior to the dissolution of the USSR in 1991, as well as the way they have subsequently evolved during the transition to a more democratic society and a market-oriented economy.

I am grateful to the editors, Nancy J. Adler and Dafna N. Izraeli, for their many insightful comments that helped strengthen this chapter. I also express my appreciation to Aleksandr Naumov, deputy director of the School of Management at Moscow State University, and Anthony Jones of Northeastern University for useful background information and comments.

1 The 124 respondents in Zhuplev's study were from the following organizations: 33 participants in a management development program at the Marxism-Leninism University of the Communist Party, 28 employees in the Russian Federation Ministry of Culture in Moscow, seventeen employees at Khimiia (Chemistry) Press, twenty editors and administrators of regional and city newspapers, and 26 managers of bookstores. With respect to age, 23 percent were under 30, 45 percent were 31 to 40, 23 percent were 41 to 50, and 9 percent were over age 50.

2 Respondents, regardless of their gender, expressed an overwhelming preference for a male manager: 81 percent preferred a man, 6 percent preferred a woman, 8 percent were indifferent, and the remaining 5 percent could not say. Interestingly, not a single respondent from the Communist party management program preferred a woman manager (the sample was 70 percent male). The preference for women managers in the two samples of predominantly women respondents was not much higher: 6 percent of respondents from Khimiia Press (the sample was 96 percent female), and 17 percent of bookstore managers (the sample was 85 percent female) preferred a woman manager. These findings correspond with those in Panov's study (1987). He found that 75 percent of women managers he surveyed in the Ivanov region considered men to be better managers and 61 percent answered that male managers treated them with respect, thus the respondents went to men for advice and help. These results are similar to an earlier study in which even among highly educated professionals in the sciences, both men and women strongly preferred men in supervisory roles (Shubkin and Kotchetov, 1968). One reason offered for why women sometimes prefer a male manager is that they have had an unpleasant experience with a woman manager (Komarov, 1989). However, male superiors can also be problematic for women. Komarov (1989: [1992 English translation of Chapter 3, p. 66]) found that "women, for example, especially do not trust affectedly gallant male managers – that is, those who are courteous and attentive around other people but, one-on-one are offensive and cynical." Some male superiors have also engaged in sexual harassment (Korobkov and Franklin, 1991).

3 Zhuplev (1988) found that 71 percent of respondents viewed the potential increase in the number of women managers negatively, and 6 percent, positively.

4 Personal communication with Aleksandr Naumov, October 1991.

5 I thank Aleksandr Naumov for this observation.

References

(1) Adler, N., and Izraeli, D. (eds.) (1988) *Women in Management Worldwide*. Armonk, N.Y.: M. E. Sharpe.

(2) Andreenkova, N. (1987) "Kakim byt' rukovoditeliu" ["How to Be a Manager"], *Argumenty i Fakty [Arguments and Facts]* 32.

(3) Antonov, A. I., and Medkov, V. M. (1982) "Usloviia Zhizni Sem'i s Det'mi i

Reproduktivnaia Motivatsiia v Krupneishom Gorode" ["Living Conditions for Families with Children and Reproductive Motivation in Large Cities"], in *Urbanizatsiia i Demografcheskie Protsessy* [*Urbanization and Demographic Processes*], p. 83. Moscow.

(4) Attwood, L. (1990) *The New Soviet Man and Woman: Sex-Role Socialization in the USSR*. Bloomington: Indiana University Press.

(5) Auerbach, J. G. (1992) "A Tribute to Russia's Babushki," *The Boston Sunday Globe*, March 8, p. 11.

(6) Baranskaia, N. (1974) "A Week Like Any Other," *The Massachusetts Review* (Autumn): Originally published in Russian in 1969 as "Nedelia Kak Nedelia," *Novy Mir* 11:23–55.

(7) du Plessix Gray, F. (1989) *Soviet Women: Walking the Tightrope*. New York: Doubleday.

(8) Egorova, I. A. (1990) Speech in *Izvestiia*, June 30.

(9) Gorbachev, M. S. (1987) *Perestroika: New Thinking for Our Country and the World*. New York: Harper and Row.

(10) Gorbachev, M. S. (1990) "Poslanie Prezidenta SSSR Verkhovnomu Sovetu SSSR" ["Letter from the President of the USSR to the Supreme Soviet of the USSR"], *Rabotnitsa* 5:2.

(11) Grigorieva, N. (1990) "Zhenshchiny Vskryvaiut 'Paket'" ["Women Open the 'Package'"], *Rabotnitsa* 5:6–7.

(12) Gruzdeva, E. B., and Chertikhina, E. S. (1988) "The Occupational Status and Wages of Women in the USSR," *Soviet Review* 29(1):55–69. Originally published in 1986 as "Professional'naia zaniatost' zhenshchin v SSSR i oplata ikh truda," *Rabochii Klass i Sovremennyi Mir* 3:57–67.

(13) Hubbs, J. (1988) *Mother Russia: The Feminine Myth in Russian Culture*. Bloomington: Indiana University Press.

(14) Iadov, V. A. (1977) *Sotsial'no-Psikhologicheskii Portret Inzhinera: Po Materialam Obsledovaniia Inzhinerov Leningradskikh Proektno-Konstruktorskikh Organizatsii* [*A Sociopsychological Portrait of Engineers: Results of a Study of Engineers of Leningrad Project Design Organizations*], pp. 78–81, Moscow.

(15) Iankova, Z. A. (1975) "Razvitie Lichnosti Zhenshchiny v Sovetskom Obshchestve" ["The Development of the Female Personality in Soviet Society"], *Sotsiologicheskoe Issledovanie* [*Sociological Research*] 4:43.

(16) Jones, A., and Moskoff, W. (1991) *Ko-ops: The Rebirth of Entrepreneurship in the Soviet Union*. Bloomington: Indiana University Press.

(17) Kaplan, F. (1993) "Second-Class Citizens – and Then Some," *The Boston Sunday Globe*, March 7, p. 1.

(18) Kiezun, W. (1991) *Management in Socialist Countries: USSR and Central Europe*. Berlin: de Gruyter.

(19) Komarov, E. I. (1989) *Zhenshchina-Rukovoditel'* [*The Woman Manager*]. Moscow: Moskovskii Rabochii. An English translation of Chapter 3, *Kachestva i Stil' Zhenskogo Rukovodstva* [*The Qualities and Style of the Woman Manager*], was published in 1992 as "The Woman Manager" in S. M. Puffer (ed.), *The Russian Management Revolution: Preparing Managers for the Market Economy*, pp. 52–76. Armonk, N.Y.: M. E. Sharpe.

(20) Kopeiko, V. (1991) "Destruction of a Stereotype, or a Monologue of a Woman about the Woman," *Soviet Woman* 1:4–5.

(21) Korobkov, A. V., and Franklin, G. (1991) "Male/Female Issues in the Soviet Union: Focus on Sexual Harassment." Paper presented at the Academy of Management Meetings, Miami, Florida.

(22) Korotaeva, G. A., and Chichkanov, V. P. (1981) "Organizatsiia Truda Rukovoditelia" ["The Organization of Managerial Work"], *EKO* 8:140.

(23) Lapidus, G. W. (1978) *Women in Soviet Society: Equality, Development, and Social Change*. Berkeley: University of California Press.

(24) Lebedeva, M. (1988) "Poka Muzhchiny Govoryat . . ." ["While the Men Are Talking . . ."], *Izvestiia*, October 23, p. 6.

(25) *Literaturnaia Gazeta* (1976) [*Literary Newspaper*], September 15, p. 10.

(26) Mamonova, T. (1989) *Essays on Sexism in Soviet Culture*. New York: Pergamon Press.

(27) Moses, J. C. (1983) *The Politics of Women & Work in the Soviet Union & the United States: Alternative Work Schedules & Sex Discrimination*. Berkeley: University of California, Institute of International Studies.

(28) Novikova, E. E. (1985) *Zhenshchina v Razvitom Sotsialisticheskom Obshchestve* [*Women in Advanced Socialist Society*]. Moscow: Mysl'.

(29) Panov, A. I. (1987) in S. N. Krasavchenko (ed.), *Perestroika i Rukovoditel* [*Perestroika and the Manager*]. Moscow: Ekonomika.

(30) *Partiinaia Zhizn'* (1975) [*Party Life*] 16:44.

(31) Pavlova, M. (1971) *Literaturnaia Gazeta* [*Literary Newspaper*], September 22.

(32) Perevedentsev, V. (1985) "Interview with Perevedentsev," *New York Times*, August 25, p. 8.

(33) Puffer, S. M. and Ozira, V. I. (1990) "Hiring and Firing Managers," in P. R. Lawrence and C. A. Vlachoutsicos (eds.), *Behind the Factory Walls: Decision Making in Soviet and US Enterprises*. Boston: Harvard Business School Press.

(34) Pukhova, Z. (1987) "Ravnye Prava, Ravnoe Uchastie" ["Equal Rights, Equal Participation"], *Kommunist* 10.

(35) *Rossiiskaia Gazeta* (1992) [Russian Newspaper], March 7.

(36) Sanjian, A. S. (1991) "Social Problems, Political Issues: Marriage and Divorce in the USSR," *Soviet Studies* 43(4):629–649.

(37) Shubkin, V. N., and Kotchetov, G. M. (1968) "Rukovoditel', Kollega, Podchinennyi" ["Managers, Peers, and Subordinates"], *Sotsial'nye Issledovaniia* [*Social Research*] 2: 143–155.

(38) Sukhoruchenkova, G. F. (1987) "Rubezhi Zhenskogo Truda" ["Boundaries of Women's Work"], *EKO*, 2:28–37.

(39) Town Meeting with Mikhail Gorbachev and Boris Yeltsin (1991), ABC Television Network, New York, September 5.

(40) Vaneyeva, N. (1991) "Politics and Business: Any Chance for Women?," *Soviet Life* (March): 16–17.

(41) *Vestnik Statistiki* (1986) [*Statistical Review*], Moscow, pp. 68–69.

(42) Yuriev, M. (1991) "The Family: On the Eve of the 'Year of the Family,'" *Soviet Woman* 2:23.

(43) Zakharova, N.; Posadskaya, A.; and Rimashevskaya, N. (1989) "Kak My Reshaem Zhenskii Vopros" ["How We Are Solving the Woman Question"] *Kommunist* 4:56–60.

(44) *Zhenshchiny i Deti v SSSR* (1985) [*Women and Children in the USSR*], p. 30. Moscow: Finansy i Statistika.

(45) *Zhenshchiny v SSSR* (1985) [*Women in the USSR*], p. 14. Moscow: Finansy i Statistika.

(46) Zhuplev, A. V. (1988) "Zhenshchina-Rukovoditel': V Zerkale Mnenii i Problem" ["The Woman Manager: In the Mirror of Opinions and Issues"], in V. A. Arkhipov (ed.), *Kak i Kem Upravliat': Opyt, Problemy, Mneniia* [*How and Whom to Manage: Experience, Issues, and Opinions*], pp. 206–229. Moscow: Moskovskii Rabochii.

17 FORMER YUGOSLAVIA

Women in Management: The Case of the Former Yugoslavia

Bogdan Kavčič

Although Yugoslavia's legislation and official ideology assured the equality of women and men in all respects, in practice the evidence suggests that women remain subordinate to men in the overall structure of social power in general and in enterprise management in particular. Women are generally under-represented in management, with their under-representation especially pronounced at the higher levels where power is more concentrated. While this chapter provides data and some explanations for this situation, more detailed studies of the qualitative aspects of women's participation in management are needed.

Introduction

The socioeconomic and political system of what was Yugoslavia has undergone substantial change in recent years, especially since 1989. In fact, Yugoslavia has been in crisis since 1979, when numerous signs of economic recession started to appear (economic stagnation, inflation, drops in production, decreases in living standard, inability of the state to repay foreign loans, etc.). The crisis encompassed all spheres of society, not just the economy. The previous system, called "socialist self-management," introduced after World War II and practiced for more than four decades, proved incapable of ensuring further development of the country. Following a decade of discussions considering what action to take, the government decided in 1989 to introduce substantial change in the entire system. Initial changes, once introduced, required further and more profound changes. The result of all these processes has been that, since 1992, Yugoslavia ceased to exist as one state. Yugoslavia had in fact already disintegrated in 1991, as one republic after another declared its independence: first Slovenia, then Croatia, Bosnia and Hercegovina, and then Macedonia. The new "Yugoslavia," formed in 1992, is composed only of Serbia (with two previously autonomous provinces, Vojvodina and Kosovo) and Montenegro.

Recent societal changes

Abandoning of the one-party political system in favor of a multiparty system was among the most important changes recently introduced. In 1990, the first multiparty elections were held in Yugoslavia, first in Slovenia and Croatia and later in the other republics. The Communist party lost its dominant position in three of the six republics.

The system of ownership of the means of production has also changed. The so-called social ownership system proved economically inefficient. The Enterprise Act, passed in 1989, recognized different forms of ownership of the means of production as able to compete equally in the market.[1] However, one year later, it became evident that previously socially owned property needed to be legally transformed either into private or state property.[2] As late as 1992, methods for most efficiently transforming this property into private property were still under discussion.

In the system of self-management of work organizations, labor was the only legal participant in management. Officially, all workers (all employees) participated directly in the decision-making processes on all important issues through the self-management bodies of the enterprise. Only now is ownership being recognized as the legitimate basis for managing an enterprise. Thus the system of management is becoming more similar to that in Western European economies. This shift is requiring fundamental changes in the organizational structure of enterprise management. Whether and how to arrange for workers' participation in the decision-making processes within enterprises is still hotly debated.

Another major change is that, under the previous system, both the organizational structure and the mode of organization were prescribed by law, whereas now, enterprises have complete freedom to determine their internal structures and modes of organization. The final major change is the beginning of domestic market competition, with success in the market becoming the decisive criterion for a company's success and survival. At the same time, exposure to international competition is also increasing.

Although these changes are certainly significant, they are only a beginning and are far from complete. Slovenia and Croatia have openly declared their intention to completely break from the previous socialist social system and embrace a new system more similar to the social systems of Western societies. Bosnia, Hercegovina, and Macedonia are also following this pattern, but at a slower pace. Serbia and Montenegro are maintaining the old system, introducing only insubstantial changes. These changes and the political disintegration of Yugoslavia have been accompanied by intense conflict among some of the republics (especially between Croatia and Serbia, and more recently between Bosnia, Hercegovina, and Serbia). The Serbs declared their intention to establish a new state – The Great Serbia – under the slogan "Where the Serbs live, there is Serbia." This declaration caused civil war first in Croatia (between Serbs and Croats) and then in Bosnia and Hercegovina (between Serbs, Croats, and Muslims). In one year, (spring 1992–spring 1993) the war in Bosnia and Hercegovina took more than 200,000 lives, most of them civilian inhabitants, and forced more than one million residents to flee their homes (from among a total population, in 1981, of 4.1 million).

Historically, Yugoslavia has never been a homogeneous state. According to a well-known anecdote, Yugoslavia is one state, with two alphabets, three religions, five main nations, 22 national minorities, and six republics. Roughly it can be divided into the north (Slovenia, Croatia, and Vojvodina) and south (the rest). The north, is far more economically developed and, in the past, was under Western European economic, cultural, and political influence; the south is less developed and historically evolved under the influence of the Turkish Empire. The attempts of the central government over the last 45 years to diminish the economic, cultural, and other differences among the republics have not succeeded; in fact, the opposite has occurred: the differences have grown. For example, the ratio of per capita GNP between the most developed republic, Slovenia, and the least developed, Kosovo, was 1:10. The unemployment rate in Slovenia was 1.8 percent in 1987 compared to 53 percent in Kosovo (9). These differences in levels of development are the main cause of the present conflict.

This chapter describes women managers in a Yugoslav social situation that is in transition. For all parts composing the state, the term Yugoslavia stood for a common history during the last 45 years. Even though the past has a strong influence on the present, Yugoslavia, as it was, will never exist again. While initial changes have already occurred, changing the whole social system will require much more time.

Consequences of societal changes on women

The consequences of these changes on the position of women in society are still unclear. However, it appears that in the near future women will have fewer opportunities in management than have been available to them in the recent past. The following indicators support this prediction.

First, the current ruling coalition of political parties in Slovenia is ideologically more conservative than the previous one. The Christian Democratic party, the strongest party in the after-free-elections ruling coalition, strongly supports more traditional Catholic norms concerning women's role in society. They stress family life as being a more important sphere for women than it was before. They are demanding that abortion be made illegal again. Moreover, fewer women are represented in the new power structure than before, when the quota system was in place.

Second, unemployment is growing very rapidly, and competition for the remaining jobs has become intense. In Slovenia, for example, between 1990 and 1992 unemployment grew from 3 percent to over 12 percent; in Kosovo, it already exceeds 50 percent. Women, together with the young, the disabled, and other politically weaker groups, have become over-represented among the unemployed. Further cutbacks for economic reasons are expected in public services, a sector that employs the majority of women, including professional workers such as those in health, education, and cultural activities.

Third, subsidies for childcare facilities are diminishing while prices are rising. Families with lower incomes can no longer afford childcare services; consequently more mothers will stay home. A mother at home means not only cutting costs for childcare but also for many other expenses as well.

The following discussion about women in management is based on information collected during the era of self-management and is therefore valid strictly for that system. However, the present is largely determined by the past, and thus forms the real basis for future development. The following section reviews the formal position of Yugoslav women under the self-management system in the light of the nation-wide legal and official norms of equality. Subsequent sections present the reflection of these norms on employment rates, educational structures, types of work performed, membership in important self-management decision-making bodies in enterprises, and directly on the position of women managers themselves. The descriptions indicate whether the comments apply to all of the former Yugoslavia or only to Slovenia.

Legal and Official Status of Women in the Socialist Self-Management Society

As in most modern states, Yugoslavia declared women to be legally equal to men in all respects. This basic principle of equality was stated in all legal enactments concerning women after World War II. The federal constitution of 1974, for example, states that "Citizens shall be equal in their rights and duties regardless of nationality, race, sex, religion, education, or social status. All shall be equal before the law." Each individual's freedom was declared to be limited only by the freedom of another individual.

Yugoslavia also adopted all resolutions of the United Nations and most conventions of The International Labor Office concerning the social and economic status of women. The conventions of the ILO are binding in Yugoslavia and implemented by the courts (1). Yugoslavia also enacted special protective legislation for mothers and children, including prohibiting night work, work by children under fifteen years old, and work by mothers and young workers under eighteen years old in heavy work conditions, as well as providing special provisions for health care and special bonuses for children.[3]

Socialist ideology also officially supported the equality of women and men. The Communist party endeavored to create social conditions for implementating equality. Social equality for women was declared and to a large extent also practised during the national liberation war (World War II), in which women participated on an equal footing with men in the armed struggle. In the postwar development of Yugoslavia, society considered women important.

Yugoslav social, political, and economic structures developed in keeping with Marxist theory, according to which ownership of the means of production was considered the most important source of social inequality. Similar to the situation in other socialist countries, the means of production were first taken over by the state. With the introduction of self-management in 1950, the means of production were declared to be socially owned property. During the period of self-management, labor was considered the focal point of the whole social organization and therefore determined the social position of every individual, whereas the importance of assets was overlooked. Employment became the basis for citizens' entitlement to most social rights. On the basis of their employment, citizens were entitled to receive social benefits, such as health and pension insurance, special bonuses for children, a societally- or company-owned apartment, and use of societally owned vacation facilities. The state limited private ownership of the means of production to small trade and handicraft shops and to small farms and small firms in other industries. The number of workers an owner could employ in such small businesses was, until recently, limited to five.

Equal employment opportunities were expected to give women both full economic independence from men and also full access to public life. The question of women's social equality was treated not as a special "women's question" but as an issue to be addressed by society as a whole. According to the quota system, the number of women members of all elected decision-making bodies had to be proportional to the total number of women employees in the enterprise. This measure was designed to guarantee women's influence on decision making in enterprises as well as government. All other special women's political and social organizations were declared unnecessary and were eliminated. Despite the quota system, women did not achieve equality either in the real structure of social power or in their representation in management. There is no simple explanation for this result. Many different variables must be taken into account; some of the most important are discussed here.

Women and Employment

In the postwar period, the percentage of women in the year-round, full-time workforce increased steadily from 25 percent in 1954, to 34 percent in 1974, and to 40 percent in 1989 (9;11). In Slovenia, the most economically developed republic, the percentage of women in the total labor force was already 41 percent in 1970 and grew to 46 percent in 1989 (11). Women who were unpaid family and farm workers as well as full-time homemakers were officially classified as not employed and therefore were not entitled to receive the social benefits granted to employees. Until a decade ago, such "unemployed" women were not covered by health or pension insurance and, therefore, not entitled to paid maternity leave. They did not receive child allowances; could not get credit to buy an apartment or to build a house; and could not get bank loans to buy home appliances.

Unlike the case in other Communist countries, obligatory employment of all adult citizens never existed in Yugoslavia. The pressure to be employed was predominantly economic.

Access to employment, the nature of the job, and the wages earned were strongly linked to education. Therefore, the level of formal education was probably the single most significant determinant of an individual's social and economic position. The higher the level of formal education, the greater the probability of getting a job. The level of education also largely determined which job a person got. Senior management positions, for example, required a university education. Formal educational level was also one of the most important factors determining an individual's wage or salary. In addition, more highly educated people tended to be more accepting, at least overtly, of the idea of gender equality.

Of course, a number of additional variables influenced the relationship between educational level and social position, including the region or republic the individual came from. The level of unemployment differed substantially among the republics. Between the end of the 1960s and the end of the 1980s, only Slovenia could boast of an almost fully employed workforce (with registered unemployment a mere 2 and

3 percent); the unemployment rate in all other republics remained much higher.

Similarly in wages, large differences existed not only among the republics but also among firms operating within the same republic. Workers with only a public school education could earn more working for one firm than employees with a university degree earned working for another firm. These cases, however, were the exception.

During this period, Yugoslav society became highly politicized. In some places, it was important to be a member of the Communist party to get employment or a higher position; in other places, having influential relatives was important. Yugoslavia has traditionally been one of the least developed, agricultural countries in Europe. In 1939, over 75 percent of the population worked in agriculture; in 1981, the figure was still nearly 20 percent. Agricultural populations have traditionally been less educated than their urban counterparts. Similarly, women have traditionally been less educated than men. In 1939, for example, about 40 percent of Yugoslavia's population over age ten were illiterate. Among women, approximately 56 percent were illiterate, and in the least developed regions, women's illiteracy was over 90 percent (12). By 1981, the overall illiteracy rate had fallen to 9.5 percent, with 4 percent of men and 15 percent of women illiterate (8). Illiteracy was the lowest among the younger generations: 2.1 percent among ten- to nineteen-year-olds (with women higher at 2.9 percent), but still a high 40 percent among those over 40 years old (with women again higher at 50 percent).

The gender gap in school enrolment decreased gradually and remains large only at the postgraduate level. In 1987, girls constituted 48 percent of primary and secondary school students and made up the same proportion in college and university education (9). Greater gender equality in education improved women's opportunities in the labor market, including enhancing the type of job and wage they received, especially for senior management positions where higher education is required. The effects of increased education, however, appear relatively slowly, with noticeable changes only occurring now among the younger generation. The rise in unemployment in recent years has again changed this trend. At present, the largest group among the unemployed are those just completing their schooling (including those with university degrees) and looking for their first job.

Historically, not all types of work requiring the same level of education were equally accessible to women. Women became over-represented in most routine manual assembly line jobs and in general clerical positions. By contrast, women remained under-represented in management, in top-level professional positions, and to a lesser extent in research and development. Similarly, women became over-represented in the weakest branches of industry, those areas in which the economic conditions (including the average wage) ranked below the average. See Table 17.1 for examples of these "women's branches," which include areas such as textiles and education.

Membership in the Workers' Councils

The Yugoslav system of self-management, in fact, constituted a dual system of management. One part consisted of self-management, in which, according to the

Table 17.1   Type of work performed by women in Yugoslavia (1986)

Type of work performed	Women as percentage of total workforce*
Individual manual work	33.0
Linked-up manual work	58.8
Machine work	40.4
Clerical work (administration)	58.0
Professional work (staff)	44.2
Management (all levels)	14.8
Research and development	32.6

*The percentage of women among all employed personnel in Yugoslavia is 38.6 percent.

Source: *Statistical Yearbook of Yugoslavia* (1988) p. 155. Belgrade: Savremena administracija.

principle of social ownership, workers had the right and duty to manage their own enterprises. All employees participated equally in making managerial decisions, especially those of a strategic nature. Workers ran self-managed firms directly through participation at workers' assemblies (consisting of all employees) or through referenda, and managed the firms indirectly through representatives elected to workers' councils. The workers' assemblies met infrequently. However, since such meetings were too big to be efficient, and because they took place during working hours and were thus too expensive, the operative decision-making body became the workers' council. The workers' council usually consisted of ten to 30 elected delegates, with each division of an organization having its own representative.

The second part was the organization of work, which followed the traditional hierarchical pattern of relations between superior and subordinate. In this traditional (Tayloristic) organization of work, the conventional values concerning the position and role of women have been preserved.

The constitution required that the membership structure of the workers' councils correspond to that of the general body of employees. This requirement meant that the number of women, younger workers, and production workers elected had to approximate their proportion in the enterprise. Notwithstanding, the proportion of women in the workers' councils has remained stable over the last few decades (at around 30 percent) even though the number of women in the labor force has increased in the last twenty years (see Table 17.2).

The quota system assured women's presence in elected bodies, but it did not give them real access to power. A relatively small number of women filled the influential role of chairperson. In this respect, the situation in the workers' councils was similar to that in both the government and the ruling political party. A quota system ensured that women were represented among the members of basic decision-making bodies, although they were always under-represented. Moreover, women remained highly under-represented in executive bodies and other more influential posts. For example, in the League of Communists, the ruling party until 1990, only 27 percent of the members were women; in the Central Committee in 1985, only 14 percent were women; and not a single woman was a member of the presidency

Table 17.2   Proportion of women among members of workers' councils in Yugoslavia

Year	Percentage of women among all members of workers' councils	Percentage of women in labor force
1970	31.0	31.6
1976	26.5	34.6
1981	30.5	38.6
1989	30.3	39.7

Sources: *Statistical Yearbook of Yugoslavia* (1989) p. 96. Belgrade: Savremena administracija; *Statistical Yearbook of Yugoslavia* (1990) p. 122. Belgrade: Savremena administracija.

(consisting of eight members) of the Central Committee (6). After 1953, no special party-sponsored women's organizations existed. The "woman question" was treated as part of the general program for development.

A gap remained between the declared policy and practice, between ideology and reality. In the newly established democracy, in which the gender quota has been eliminated, women have been pushed to the margins of political life. Political pressure on the ruling party for equal representation of women does not exist any more. The machinery of workers' self-management has been eliminated. In addition, at this time, women do not have any organizations with sufficient social power to assure equal representation in decision-making bodies. The newly formed women's organizations are weak and not active in the sphere of work (except for the Association of Women Managers). Instead, they focus on family life, the protection of battered women and children, and similar aspects of life. The feminist movement in Yugoslavia has no real social influence.

Women in Management

The theory behind the concept of self-management was that all workers participate equally in managing their organizations. Jobs were supposedly differentiated by technical responsibility, but not by their influence on management decisions. Managers, in theory, had only to execute the managerial decisions made by the workers. In practice, however, the situation worked quite differently. Research shows that, as in other industrialized countries, the real power in the vast majority of work organizations remained in the hands of senior management (4).

How was the position of manager filled in a self-managed firm? By law, all vacant positions had to be publicly announced, together with the qualifications required of candidates (including education, training, and practical experience). Until the beginning of the 1980s, requirements for top managers (the two most senior levels) included "moral-political qualifications". Political organizations in the firm – including the trade union, the Communist party, and the youth organization – assessed each candidate in this respect. Whereas membership in the Communist party was a desired "qualification," it was neither a requisite nor a sufficient condition. About 70 percent of managers were members of the party. Applicants both from within the organization and from outside were invited to apply. A commission of the workers' council or the workers' council itself selected from among the candidates. Candidates from inside the firm were usually favored, at least for lower-level management positions. Salary was not a strong motive for becoming a manager.

In industrial enterprises, only 6.4 percent of managers were women in 1987. The proportion of women among the senior managers varied with the size and level of the organizational unit (see Table 17.3). Few women became managers of a basic organization, which corresponds approximately to a profit center, a strategic business unit, or a division of a larger company. Basic organizations performed predominantly production functions, and their managers were typically technical experts. The number of women was slightly higher in work organizations that correspond to enterprises. Women managers were virtually nonexistent as heads of composite organizations, those larger companies composed of a number of relatively independent enterprises. This organizational structure applied to all economic sectors, including public services, until the new legislation was passed in 1989.

Women were clearly under-represented among senior managers in all types of organizations. The more senior the management level, the fewer women were represented. This reflects a more general pattern – namely, that women are less represented at higher hierarchical levels than at lower levels.

One study conducted only in Slovenia (the most developed republic in the former Yugoslavia) of 40 women managers in business organizations found the following patterns. First, the majority of women managers were between 30 and 50 years old (82 percent), married, and had, on average, two children. Most were economics graduates. Sixty-five percent were members of the Communist party, and 92 percent were trade union members.

Second, 65 percent of the women managers had been invited by the management of their firm to compete for specific managerial positions, with only 17 percent competing for the positions on their own initiative. If no candidate applied for a publicly announced, vacant managerial position, management usually invited candidates from both inside and outside the firm to do so.

Third, women managers' main motives for accepting managerial jobs included the challenge of achieving good results and success, the desire to use their knowledge, and the stimulation gained by working in a managerial environment. Only 5 percent mentioned the financial motive of receiving a higher salary. (At the time when the research was conducted, the wage differential between the lowest paid

Table 17.3   Proportion of women among all managers of industrial enterprises in Yugoslavia (1987)

Organizational level	Percentage of women among managers
Basic organizations	4.9
Work organizations	8.5
Composite organizations	0.8

Source: *Statistical Yearbook of Yugoslavia* (1989) p. 124. Belgrade: Savremena administracija.

worker – usually a cleaner – and the top manager was slight, varying from 1:5 to 1:8.)

Fourth, the main reason stated for not accepting a managerial position was prior obligations in private life in general and in the family in particular.

Fifth, the majority of women managers held lower-level management positions, with only 10 percent being senior managers. Even in factories, where more than 80 percent of the employees were women, managers at all levels were usually men.

Sixth, 55 percent of women managers were very well accepted by their male colleagues, with only a few (2.5 percent) claiming to be poorly received. Eighty-two percent received support from their family and relatives.

Seventh, the vast majority (68 percent) believed discrimination against women did not exist in their organizations. At the same time, however, 80 percent expressed the opinion that performing a managerial role is much easier for a man than a woman (3).

These responses come from a select group of successful women managers and therefore may not represent women managers as a whole. Their responses indicate that there are many hindrances and very little motivation for women to become managers. The obstacles are both objective and subjective. To explain why these women managers succeeded, it would be helpful to know the extent to which they felt they had to accept or adopt "male ways of thinking and acting."

Family Life

The failure of the old regime to significantly alter gender inequality in family life had direct implications for working women. Housekeeping and childcare demands were only slightly reduced (partly by public services and partly by husbands). Social institutions, which were supposed to free women, did not meet many of their needs. Childcare facilities were constructed mainly in towns, and covered only approximately one-quarter of the children in the below-seven-year age group. Until recently, placing a new child in childcare was difficult. Special priority lists gave an advantage to those with lower incomes and lower-level positions.

Although one meal was provided at work and children received lunch at school (mainly in the towns), other meals had to be cooked at home. Women also had many other household duties. Social institutions could not fully replace the work done by the wife or other family members in the household. The alternative solution – namely, sharing household work between the husband and wife – was rarely practised in Yugoslav families. Traditional beliefs regarding the woman's responsibility for housekeeping still persist in family life.

A combination of incentives drove women to work full-time even when their children were small. One salary was just not sufficient for a family to reach and maintain a desired standard of living, or for the lowest-paid families to survive; the woman's salary improved the family's budget. From the 1960s on, Yugoslav society showed more signs of becoming consumer-oriented. However, only those who were employed enjoyed a number of state benefits, such as health and pension insurance, paid holidays, opportunities for further training paid for by the company, receipt of an apartment or credit to build a house or buy an apartment, and special allowances for children. Thus, economic as well as personal reasons pushed women into the labor force. Women wanted the greater financial benefits given to employees, especially since they were socially and economically unrecognized when performing only housework. Given these conditions, very few women stayed home after childbirth.

The result was that the employed Yugoslav woman performed two full-time jobs: one at her workplace and the other at home. The majority of Yugoslav families also cultivate some land, frequently bringing an additional obligation to the woman. This traditional and strongly rooted gender division of labor in the home, coupled with pressures to accept paid employment outside the home, created a double load of work for women.

The managerial role requires a full day's work. The usual working hours in Yugoslav factories are from 6 A.M. to 2 P.M.; but managers, especially those at senior levels, often continue working until 8 P.M. It is not surprising, therefore, that women managers cited physical fatigue and a lack of time as the most important reasons for not accepting managerial positions (3).

Maternity leave and raising children interrupt the normal career development path of many young women. Maternity leave in Yugoslavia is one year for each child. Mothers with young children frequently miss work to take care of sick children. Fathers may also take leave because of a child's illness, but few fathers do so. Young families sometimes use alternative options for childcare. Childcare facilities, however, close in the afternoon and evening, and hiring housemaids is too expensive for most people. Moreover, the majority of urban families are first generation townspeople, whose parents live in the countryside and therefore can only help out occasionally. Strong social norms continue to assert that a mother's most important duty is to be with her children.

Women, thus, have little time left to advance professionally. Mothers can only start building a professional career after their children are eight to ten years old. For mothers who are single parents, the possibilities for a professional or managerial career are even more limited (3).

Beliefs about Women

Structural inequalities are reflected and supported by a system of beliefs about women that obstruct women's opportunities for managerial roles. Traditional stereotypes regarding women as inefficient and not competent in politics and management are used to support and justify women's exclusion from positions of authority. When there are two equally qualified candidates for an important managerial or political position – one woman and one man – the male candidate will, as a rule, be chosen. Negative stereotypes of women in Yugoslavia, such as those listed below, hinder their progress (7):

Women are less self-confident than men;
Women are less successful in making public speeches;
Women are more interested in practical matters (schooling, medical care); they prefer to spend more time on housekeeping and taking care of others.

It is still widely believed that women are simply not suited for managerial positions. Furthermore, many male subordinates still view obeying the orders of a woman boss as offensive.

The current economic and political developments in Yugoslavia do not favor women. In contrast to the previously declared policy of equal opportunity, the emerging ideologies and policies reinforce traditional patriarchal beliefs and structures, thus endangering the small gains women had made in the world of management.

Notes

1 In the first phase of transition to a market economy in the former Yugoslavia, it has been assumed that it is enough to allow free competition of private and socially owned enterprises in the market to transform the whole economy. Until this law, public and only very small private enterprises (up to ten employees) were allowed to compete.

2 Social property was officially declared as the property of everybody (of all the citizens) and of nobody at the same time. All the enterprises were in social property: they were managed by the employees (but not owned by them) in the name of society but on the account of the employees (this system was labeled "self-management"). Social property was the necessary basis for the system of self-management. In other words, social property has no permanent addressee. It can be used only by those working within it. On the contrary, state property is the type of property which is owned and managed by the state.

3 Heavy work conditions are: working in high temperatures, high humidity, high noise and/ or vibrations, etc. What is "high" is defined by special regulations.

References

(1) Bubnov-Skoberne, A. (1975) "Mednarodna ureditev pravnega položaja delavk" ["International Regulation of the Legal Status of Women Workers"], in *Ženske v združenem delu I.del*, pp. 7–22. Ljubljana: Institut za delo.

(2) *Constitution of the Socialist Federal Republic of Yugoslavia* (1974).

(3) Kanjuo, A. (1989) "Žene – vodilne delavke v gospodarstvu Slovenije" ["Women – Leading workers in the Economy of Slovenia"]. Ljubljana: Jugoslovanski center za teorijo in prakso samoupravljanja: Edvard Kardelj.

(4) Kavčič, B. (1987) *Sociologija dela [Sociology of Labor]*. Ljubljana: Delavska enotnost.

(5) *Letopis SR Slovenije za leto 1989* (1989) [*Statistical Yearbook of S(ocialist) R(epublic) of Slovenia*]. Ljubljana: Zavod za statistiko.

(6) Petrović, J. A. (1986) "Zene u SK danas" ["Women in the Alliance of Communists"], *Žena* 44(4):2–13.

(7) Rener, T. (1987) *Socialni vidiki procesa politične emancipacije žensk [Social Aspects of the Process of Political Emancipation of Women]*. Ljubljana: Faculty of Sociology, Political Science and Journalism.

(8) *Statistički godišnjak Jugoslavije (SGJ) 1980* (1980) [*Statistical Yearbook of Yugoslavia*]. Belgrade: Savremena administracija.

(9) *Statistički godišnjak Jugoslavije (SGJ) 1988* (1988) [*Statistical Yearbook of Yugoslavia*]. Belgrade: Savremena administracija.

(10) *Statistički godišnjak Jugoslavije (SGJ) 1989* (1989) [*Statistical Yearbook of Yugoslavia*]. Belgrade: Savremena administracija.

(11) *Statistički godišnjak Jugoslavije (SGJ) 1990* (1990) [*Statistical Yearbook of Yugoslavia*]. Belgrade: Savremena administracija.

(12) Tomšič, V. (1980) *Women in the Development of Socialist Self-Managing Yugoslavia*. Belgrade: Jugoslovenska stvarnost.

PART IV

MIDDLE EAST/AFRICA

18

ISRAEL

Outsiders in the Promised Land: Women Managers in Israel

Dafna N. Izraeli

Emerging Interest in Women in Management

In November 1982, the Israel Management Center, a not-for-profit organization, sponsored a conference on women in management. This was the first time the issue of women's under-representation in management had been raised in a public forum in Israel. During the years since, growing numbers of women each year participated in the training courses and seminars for women managers, would-be managers, and entrepreneurs that have mushroomed across the country. The Senior Women Managers' Forum, established in 1986 within the Israel Management Center, provides networking opportunities for its members. A bimonthly magazine for career women, which began appearing in the late 1980s, highlights the successful achievements of individual women. Despite the increase in the level of activity of women in management, women remain under-represented in the management of Israeli corporations and government institutions, and the prospect for significant change is not encouraging.

In 1991, women constituted 40 percent of the total employed labor force and 16 percent of the managers and administrators in Israel.[1] This under-representation is remarkable considering the fact that women constituted 40 percent of scientific and academic employees, including 50 percent of pharmacists, 33 percent of physicians, and 27 percent of lawyers (9). Furthermore, although the absolute number of women managers has increased threefold in recent years, the occupational gender segregation has not changed significantly. Of the 79,400 managers and administrators in 1991, 12,400 were women, compared to 50,000 and 4,100, respectively, in 1977. Between 1977 and 1991, women as a percentage of all employees grew by 6 percent, whereas women as a percentage of all managers and administrators grew by 8 percent.

Until the end of the 1980s, no one seemed particularly concerned by women's lack of participation in the power centers of the economy. The low priority given to women's access to senior positions is reflected in the responses of almost 1,000 Israeli university students who rated the importance of fifteen current social issues as social problems in Israel. The men rated "discrimination against women in promotion" second to the lowest in terms of importance as a social problem, slightly higher than inequality between the sexes and kidnapping, which tied for lowest scores. Women rated the issue relatively higher, but significantly lower than crime, traffic accidents, religious coercion, and violence against women (24;25). Violence against women arouses considerably more public indignation and organized activity than does women's under-representation in management.

In the last two decades, Israeli women entered managerial positions in those economic branches in which structural changes in the occupation and favorable market conditions created new opportunities and decreased the level of competition among men for the same positions. Women, however, did not succeed in breaking through the glass ceiling to senior management positions, and they remain significantly under-represented even at the lower levels of the managerial hierarchy.

This chapter analyzes women's under-utilization in management in the context of processes that support men's power and authority in Israeli society. The chapter is divided into four sections: the first section analyzes three of the developments that created favorable conditions for women's entry into management from the late 1960s on – namely, the growth in the female labor pool, management's entry into academe, and the differentiation of managerial specializations. The second section focuses on some of the major barriers to women's advancement within management and emphasizes three contextual factors that are particular to Israel – state domination of the economy, the importance of political and military networks in the selection and assignment of managers, and the family-centered culture. The third section presents the outcomes of these developments and processes, and charts both women's gains in management and differences in women's and men's earnings. The fourth section analyzes how the articulation of women's interests within the centralized political structure shapes women's responses to their limited opportunities. This last section also describes current activities for change.

The Israeli Context

Israel, established as a state in 1948, bears the imprint of its early beginnings. Young Zionist pioneers, driven by the vision of a Jewish homeland reconstructed on principles of social justice and equality, established Israel's institutional infrastructure. The pioneers came during the early decades of this century, mainly from Eastern Europe, most without parents and in peer groups of single women and men, although women were a small minority. The women pioneers, who expected to be equal partners with the men, were disappointed by their exclusion from the valued activities of nation building. Beginning in 1914, they struggled within the Labor Zionist movement for the opportunity to do "men's work," such as building houses, paving roads, and farming the land.

Women legitimated their demands for a share of the scarce jobs based on their right to contribute to the creation of the new society. The rhetoric of motives was couched in communal rather than individualistic terms – appropriate to the hegemonic collective ideology prevalent until the 1960s. It was an ideology not of personal entitlements but of social obligations, not of equal opportunity for individual advancement but of commitment to a collective (21). The term *career* was a pejorative term, implying that the individual put her or his personal success above the needs of the collective; and the term *careeristit* (career-oriented woman) aroused even greater disdain than *careerist* (career-oriented man). In later decades, the collectivist ideology, although much weakened, continued to inhibit women from making claims for individual and professional advancement. The strongly Jewish nature of Israel and the continuing military hostility on its borders had similar effects but for other reasons.

The majority of Israel's population of five million, are first- or second-generation Jewish immigrants, most of whom fled from persecution or the fear of antisemitism in other countries. In 1990 and 1991 alone, Israel absorbed over 375,000 new immigrants, close to 350,000 of them from the former Soviet Union. The population of Israel is segmented into a number of socially significant ethnic groupings. The deepest division is national – between Israeli Jews (82 percent of the population) and Israeli Arabs. This division overlaps with that of religion, between Jews on the one hand and Moslems, Christians, and Druse on the other. Almost all non-Jews are Arabs.

The major division among Jews is based on country of origin. Immigrants and their offspring from the more traditional, economically less-developed Moslem countries of North Africa and the Middle East, who constitute about half the Jewish population, are known as Easterners. Immigrants and their offspring from the more modern, industrialized Christian countries of Europe and North and South America are known as Westerners. Westerners, Easterners, and non-Jews are organized into a system of ethnic stratification and "a tripartite ethnic order, with European-American Jews on top, Asian-African Jews in the middle and Arabs [Moslems, 13.9 percent; Christians, 2.4 percent; and Druse, 1.7 percent] on the bottom" (39:653).

The majority of the managers, both among women and men, are Westerners or second-generation, Israeli-born individuals. Both first- and second-generation Easterners as well as Arabs remain under-represented in management. Eastern women are not more under-represented than Eastern men. The number of Arab women managers is so small that only a blank appears in the appropriate space on the labor force tables of the Central Bureau of Statistics.

Setting the Stage for Women's Entry into Management

During the 1970s, numerous developments contributed to setting the stage for women's entry into management. These included the importation and dissemination of feminist ideas through the activities of the feminist movement and the activities surrounding the Prime Minister's Commission on the Status of Women, which was established as part of the United Nations Decade on Women (1975–1985). This section, however, focuses on the three structural developments that crystallized toward the end of the 1960s and became especially important for bringing women into management: the increase in the number of women in the labor pool, management's entry into academe, and the differentiation of managerial specializations.

Growth in the female labor pool

During the 1970s and to a lesser extent the 1980s, women joined the labor force in increasing numbers, in some years contributing 70 percent to the net increase. Women's entry into the labor force increased their presence in the labor pools from which organizations select entry-level managers. Women came in response to the demand for more workers, stemming primarily from the expansion of financial, public, and community services following the 1967 war (41).

The founding and expansion of organizations, especially in finance and business services, increased the number of middle-level management positions. The organization of public and community services, which employ large numbers of women in the semiprofessions, such as teaching, nursing and social work, became somewhat more decentralized, introducing new supervisory and administrative positions. Although Arab men from the administered territories met the need for additional unskilled labor, there remained a shortage of qualified men to fill the new administrative and professional positions.

At the same time, a number of factors reduced the growth rate of the Jewish male civilian labor force. The expansion of the professional army and the extension of compulsory military service from two to three years (and for women from eighteen months to two years) siphoned off potential labor. The increase in university attendance extended the moratorium on labor force participation. Similarly, the aging of the population and the relative geographical immobility of the Israeli labor force, resulting from the nontransferability of social benefits, such as accumulated vacation rights and compensation pay (a constraint recently mitigated), further curtailed the pool of available male labor. Successful experiences with women in positions of responsibility reinforced employers' readiness to hire them.

The proportion of women managers is greatest in economic branches in which women constitute the majority of those employed and in which task continuity is greatest. Task continuity reflects the extent to which those in managerial positions are drawn from and have the same skills as those at the base of the organizational hierarchy (30). High task continuity tends to be more characteristic of professional organizations, where entry-level positions require academic accreditation. Although women's availability in recruitment pools makes their promotion possible, a strong link between the lower and upper levels of the hierarchy makes it more probable.

For example, in education services, where school principals and supervisors were traditionally promoted from the ranks of teachers and where women constitute the great majority of the teachers, the proportion of women managers is especially high. In 1982, women constituted more than 75 percent of those employed in education services and 45 percent of the managers (20).[2] Similarly, in health and welfare services, where task continuity is considerable, women constituted over 75 percent of those employed and 30 percent of the managers. In industry, where task discontinuity is the norm, since managers are not recruited from industrial workers, women constituted 25 percent of the labor force and only 7 percent of the managers in 1982.

The continuity of a task hierarchy is frequently less the result of the inherent task requirements at the top than it is the outcome of power struggles over the definition of acceptable qualifications for higher-level positions. For example, until the mid-1970s, heads of social welfare agencies were usually recruited from pools other than social workers, the latter being predominantly women. These employment pools included school principals, youth movement leaders, and party functionaries, who at the time were predominantly men. Pressure from the social workers' union resulted in social work training becoming a necessary requirement for promotion, thus increasing the task continuity of the occupation and the proportion of women managers in health and welfare services (20). In contrast, the education services hierarchy has become somewhat less task continuous in recent years. Seeking job options for retiring officers, *Zevet*, the retired officers' association, in conjunction with the Ministry of Education, sponsors a special course for academically trained retiring military officers to acquire a teacher's certificate in one year, followed by qualification for school management in another year. Since 1988, about 25 retiring officers annually have completed the management training, with an annual average of one woman participant. The women moving up the educational hierarchy must now compete with a growing number of retiring military officers pulled into the system at the managerial level.

Although the availability of women in the labor pool and task continuity of the hierarchy contribute to women's entry into managerial positions, these factors are insufficient to ensure women's upward mobility within management. Task continuity in the social and community services branches of the public sector characterizes the link only up to the middle level of the hierarchy. The link between middle-level management and more senior positions is highly task discontinuous. Access to senior-level positions requires other qualifications, including belonging to the appropriate social networks.

Management's entry into academe

Until the 1960s, the overriding importance attributed to political considerations in the assignment of people to positions of power discouraged the development of a group of skilled managers. The Mapai (Labor) party, which was the dominant political force in the country from the mid-1930s until 1977, sought to consolidate its political control of the economy through a policy of strategic selection and placement of personnel in the public and labor-owned sectors of the economy. Political appointment extended to middle and even lower levels of management (13). Active women party members, who were few to begin with, tended to be routed to managerial positions through the women's sector – namely, the party-affiliated women's organizations and their network of social services (19).

At the end of the 1960s, a number of factors reduced the intrusion of politics in the economy. After two decades in power, the Labor party had less interest in mediating job placement. At the same time, business came under pressure from international competition to emphasize market criteria, including greater recognition of the technical requirements of management. Increased demand for technically qualified managers tightened the link between various sectors of the economy and the educational system. Management as an occupation entered academe and university training came to be regarded as necessary cultural capital, especially for newcomers to the field. Training in any tangentially related discipline became an asset; the demand was not necessarily for a degree in management but rather for proof of relevant higher education.

These processes were accompanied by the rapid expansion of the universities. The first MBA program was established at the Hebrew University in the early 1960s. The Faculty of Management at Tel Aviv University was established in 1966. Today, all six Israeli universities grant graduate degrees in management. Some have undergraduate programs as well, and there are a number of institutions with diploma-granting programs.

Between 1961 and 1990, the number of university students increased sevenfold, from 10,836 to 71,900; concurrently the proportion of women recipients of first degrees rose from 25 percent to 51 percent. In 1990, women constituted 51 percent of all university students; 51 percent of the students in the social sciences, which includes business and administration; 43 percent of the students in law; 44 percent in mathematics, statistics, computers, and the sciences; and 16 percent in engineering and architecture.

The entry of management into academe and the new focus on professional knowledge and expertise provided women with a legitimate basis for their managerial authority. The universities supplied credentials of competence and authority based on expertise, which increasingly became required capital for entry into management. In both the public and private sectors, employers structured opportunities for managers, such as free time for attending lectures and tuition to gain academic accreditation. In 1991, 60 percent of the women managers and 55 percent of the men managers had thirteen or more years of education, compared to only 37 percent and 27 percent, respectively, in 1981. While the gender difference reflects the greater importance of accreditation for women than for men, the decreasing gender gap may reflect the greater opportunities employers provide their male managers to get advanced training and higher education.

Differentiation of managerial specializations

The development of a cadre of skilled managers was impeded by an overall government policy that subsidized enterprises regardless of their productivity, emphasizing instead their function as providers of work for new immigrants (13). By the mid-1960s, the economy had integrated the nearly doubled labor force into productive employment (31). The military victory of 1967 marked the end of a two-year recession that had stimulated a search for foreign markets and a greater awareness of the need for technically skilled managers to compete effectively in foreign markets (35;41). These trends plus the introduction of more advanced technologies were among the developments that encouraged greater occupational differentiation in management – an increase in staff functions and new managerial specializations.

In the 1960s, most managers with university training were either engineers (particularly in industry) or economists (particularly in public administration). When Barad and Weinshall looked for a sample of women for their pioneering study of women managers, they selected them from the lists of women graduates in engineering and economics on the assumption that these graduates were most likely to be in the managerial recruitment pool (6). Engineering remains an important avenue to senior management in industry; and the small proportion of women in engineering may explain their absence in more senior positions, especially in the high-tech industrial sector.[3] During the 1970s, demand accelerated for managers in such areas as marketing, finance, computers and information technology, legal services, public relations, organizational development, and human resources – many of which being relatively new specializations with as yet no clear gender label nor institutionalized status sequences.

The new specializations drew potential candidates from a wide catchment area that contained a high proportion of women, including university graduates in law, economics and other social sciences, labor studies, and business administration (20). Computers provided another new area receptive to women, whose early entry was assisted by opportunities for computer training given to women assigned for compulsory military service to the computer center since the early 1970s. A number of women "army graduates" today head software and computer services companies. More generally, the Israeli military has had a significant impact on women's civilian occupations (18).

In sum, the rapid expansion of staff specializations and the greater consideration given to technical qualifications supported women's entry into managerial positions. The pressures for increasing market competitiveness of firms and technical meritocracy in management, however, were offset by other pressures that worked to women's disadvantage, including those that sustained and at times strengthened the patronage system along with the lack of attention given to economic and technical efficiency. Three such processes are state control of the economy, the importance of political and military networks in the selection and assignment of managers, and the family-centered culture.

Barriers to Women's Promotion within Management

State control of the economy

Compared to other Western democracies, Israel has a more centralized, state-regulated economy with a high level of government intervention in economic life (13). The economy is divided into three sectors: the private sector, composed of privately owned firms, including those operating on the stock exchange; the Histadrut (worker-owned) sector, composed of the collective settlements as well as a variety of economic enterprises; and the government sector, which is the largest employer in the country, employing some 29 percent of the labor force, and comprising mainly the public services, numerous state-owned enterprises, and the military (1). Of the 100 largest industrial firms in Israel, 43 are owned by the private sector, 33 by the Histadrut sector, 21 by the government sector, and three by foreign investors (1). Both the private and the Histadrut sectors are heavily dependent on the state as the major regulator of economic investment (14). The government "also affects business profits through the use of differentiated rates of exchange, granting licenses and by a very wide net of subsidies . . ." (1:183).

Since the establishment of the state in 1948, the primary goals of Israel's economic policy and investments were the reconstruction of the Jewish homeland, immigrant absorption, and military security. National, political, and social goals rather than strictly economic growth and efficiency determined Israel's priorities in settling the border areas, decreasing Israel's dependence on other countries for strategic goods and services, and sustaining full employment as a buffer against unrest and demoralization. Market considerations, such as competitiveness and profitability, were secondary considerations, when they were considered at all. This strategy was possible because of the continuous flow of foreign capital into the country from sources such as German reparations, United States aid, and gifts from Jewish communities around the world. "The concentration of all these resources in the hands of the state made it the great repository of capital and the major regulator of the direction of investments in the economy" (14:215).

The ability of economically inefficient firms to claim government support on the basis of social and political considerations was dysfunctional for the development of professional and market-oriented managers. The secondary importance attributed to market forces retarded the development of professionalism among managers, which elsewhere provided an impetus for women's entry. Up to the present, few firms have instituted career paths or effective management assessment and evaluation mechanisms, frequently found to be more important for women than for men (32). In this environment, firms could afford to discriminate against quality and to overlook women's potential.

Importance of political networks

The lack of market competition, the considerable monopolization and cartelization of the economy, and the patron–client quality of the relationship between the state and economic firms also influenced the requisite qualities of senior managers.

> The Israeli political economy is patterned the same way in each and every economic branch: resource allocation to individuals by the government is made essential to be successful. Moreover, those who do not get concessions and exemptions, not [to] mention . . . licenses, cannot enter the market. In such a system, economic considerations of efficiency or optimal resource allocation have little significance. To be successful in such a system, one has to be "one of us" and able to put pressure on the government. Those firms (and economic sectors) with strong political backing would be able to be more successful. . . (1:243–244).

In such a system, managerial candidates with good connections (known locally as *protecstia*) had special advantages. Women rarely had the opportunity to develop such connections. For example, the successful careers in the private sector of former employees of the Budget Department of the Ministry of Finance are well known. However, the Budget Department has always been closed to all but token women. The politicization of elite recruitment created a further barrier for women, who, both as individuals (with a few remarkable exceptions) and as an interest group, lacked political clout (4).

In the public and Histadrut sectors, access to senior management positions has always been strongly influenced by political considerations. From the mid-1930s until the elections of 1977, the Labor party dominated the political institutions, including the Histadrut, where elected party representatives filled key positions. The party's control over access to economic opportunity and jobs was an important political resource, which it used to establish its power (3). Whereas grass roots patronage declined over time, the politicization of the top echelons, which had tapered off by the end of the 1960s and early 1970s, got a new lease on life after 1977, when the right-wing Likud party took over from Labor as the ruling party, and intensified further after the Likud's re-election in 1981. It received a further boost during the tenure of the "national unity government" (1984–1988). At this time, the Likud and Labor alignment made formal agreements on how to "divide the spoils" concerning appointments to senior government posts (17). The new Likud government, in power for the first time, used the patronage system to establish its party faithful in managerial positions of the various institutions of Israeli society. This process was again reproduced when the Labor coalition returned to power after fifteen years following the 1992 election. For example, in December 1992, the Labor minister of police made 75 new senior appointments – not one of them going to a woman (37). Women did not benefit from the new appointments despite the fact that they constitute approximately 15 percent of the police force, the largest proportion of women police officers in any country in the world, and in certain departments women fill a significant number of the middle-level staff positions.[4] The patronage system worked to the advantage of only a handful of women who were either members of, or well-connected to, the centers of political power.

Importance of military networks

A uniquely Israeli phenomenon is the influence of the military in almost every area of private and public life and the widespread overlapping of the military and all other elite networks, including political, managerial, cultural, intellectual, and even artistic networks. Men's access to high positions in the military, especially the prestigious air force, opens doors to senior positions in many other arenas, and assures their monopolization of the power structure.

The Israeli military defines experience in a combat role as a prerequisite for access to the great majority of senior-level military positions. In turn, experience as an officer, especially in a combat unit, is considered valuable training for management; and senior officers are an important recruitment pool for managers in many sectors of the economy. Combat officers at all levels, whether in the professional army or the reserves, continue to expand their networks in the civilian society through contacts with civilians doing reserve duty. It is not uncommon for a 28-year-old officer to have a 35-year-old bank manager under his command, while both are doing their annual compulsory reserve service. Later the younger man is in a good position to ask the older man for help in his career.

Legislation prohibits women from assuming combat roles, thus virtually closing women's access to the more senior military positions and consequently to roles and contacts with the highest potential postmilitary trade-in value. Furthermore, with only rare exceptions, women do not serve in the reserves. The military elite, in turn, adds to women's deprivation of opportunity by reproducing a culture that emphasizes role modeling and personal identification as key elements in the transformation of citizen to (male) soldier. It implicitly, and sometimes even explicitly, views masculinity as a component for identification with the role. For example, in a November 1992 meeting with the chief of military personnel, a delegation intent on opening positions such as chief of military education to women argued that such positions did not require combat training and experience.[5] The chief personnel officer disagreed emphatically, insisting that the most important educator was the soldier's immediate commander and that the chief educational officer had to be a role model with whom the (male) commanders could identify. In his view, this required that the chief personnel officer be a man.

In 1954, Chief of Staff Moshe Dayan drew up a plan to facilitate the retirement of army officers at the age of 40 and bribed reluctant "pensioners" with the top jobs in society.

> Dayan's concept had far-reaching influence on Israeli society. His "double life" plan let loose into civilian life forty-year-old ex-officers – talented, ambitious, vital men at the height of their powers. The economy began wooing these pensioners with offers of top-level positions, so much so that the profile of Israeli society assumed an increasingly military character (Shabtai Teveth as quoted in 36:67).

Initially drawn into the public and semipublic sector after 1973, officers were increasingly recruited to economic enterprises of the private sector as well (42). The diffusion of military personnel throughout the managerial elite was reinforced subsequently. Those who were already in brought in other officers with whom they shared a leadership culture and whose loyalty and support were unquestionable.[6] For example, the following headline appeared in a 1988 Tel Aviv newspaper: "One more than in the General Chief of Staff: 22 senior reserve officers fill senior positions in the municipality. Lahat [mayor of Tel Aviv and a senior reserve army officer] chooses most of them" (2:15).

The military facilitated officers' transition to the civilian market with preretirement opportunities to acquire university accreditation. The training provided both marketable expertise and a resocialization experience in preparation for civilian organizational life. In 1979, the army established an employment office for retiring officers that provides services such as job search and referrals and exerts considerable moral pressure on employers to give preference to military retirees.

Having been an officer increases the likelihood of a woman getting a managerial job (16). As a mechanism for producing managers, however, the system works most effectively for men. The majority of women officers are assigned to the women's corps, where they fill social service jobs, or to administrative and professional positions in the general army. As noncombat officers, they play secondary roles by definition (7). Furthermore, the military does not expose them to the same intensive training and experience believed to contribute to developing the special leadership skills and authoritative personality of the Israeli officer, which again sets a ceiling on women's upward mobility within the military.

Women's exclusion from the core activities of military life and from the locales in which these are carried out severely limits women's opportunities for visibility; for establishing connections with the "old boy" network so instrumental for postarmy positioning; for becoming effective bearers of one of the most valued national symbols – combat duty; and for moving up into the senior ranks that provide training, experience, and social capital, highly valued in the civilian market.[7] A negligible number of women achieve the ranks that provide men access to senior management positions. With the exception of the commander of the Women's Corps, there are no women in the two ranks just below chief of staff and only about a dozen women in the rank just below that.

The few exceptions, however, are instructive. Most had nontraditional military career paths. For example, the most senior woman in banking is a retired officer who joined the professional army following compulsory military training and simultaneously completed her degree in economics. She rose to the positions of deputy to the financial advisor to the General Chief of Staff and deputy head of the Department of Budgets in the Ministry of Defense with the rank of colonel. She then served as commander of the Women's Corps. Upon retiring to civilian life in the mid-1970s, she became a senior manager in a large bank and within three years of retiring became general manager of one of its subsidiaries. A second example, the most senior woman in hospital administration, who is the assistant director of a large civilian municipal medical center, had a prior career as a military medical officer. She was brought to her civilian job by her superior in the military, the former chief physician of the medical corps, who, upon retiring, became director general of the municipal medical center.

Family-centeredness as a disincentive for management

Israel is a family-centered society. In 1991, over 95 percent of women by the age of 40 were married; the average number of children per family was 2.8; the divorce rate was 24 percent (up from 10 percent in 1975). Only 1.3 percent of the births were from never-married women, with the majority being desired births to women in their thirties. Parents as well as children value family life; the Friday evening Sabbath meal and national holidays are normally celebrated within the family setting. Although both women and men value family life, greater and less flexible time demands are made on women than on men. Women more than men are expected "to be available" to their family, especially when children come home from school or from after-school activities and when spouses return from work.

Israel's family-centered society operates as a disincentive for women to seek management positions and as a disincentive for employers to promote them to such positions. It encourages women to seek other, less-demanding career paths and results in employers preferring men managers, whose availability for long working hours is not in question.

In Israel, marriage and motherhood are social imperatives; women do not have a real choice between having children or a career. Israel has more publicly funded *in vitro* fertilization (IVF) clinics per capita than any other country in the world, but it invests relatively very little in contraceptive research and family planning (27).

Employed mothers in Israel use a number of strategies to fit paid work in with family life (22), all of them inappropriate for getting promoted to management. They gravitate to part-time jobs and to jobs synchronized with the children's school schedules, such as teaching. Similarly, they seek positions that have flexible working hours, such as nursing and social work, or postpone taking on more responsible positions until after their children are grown. Only 53 percent of married, divorced, or widowed women administrators and managers have children at home under age fourteen, compared to 65 percent of academic and professional workers and 72 percent of other professional and technical workers. Even within the professions, women tend to concentrate in specializations or locales that permit control over time. For example, with the exception of pediatrics, 83 percent of women doctors specialized in fields rated by independent judges as high on permitting time control, compared to 38 percent of men doctors (43). Fixed and relatively short working hours are among the major attractions of government service, where women constitute 73 percent of the pharmacists and 68 percent of the lawyers, compared to 50 percent and 27 percent, respectively, in the labor force (11).

Compared to alternative career options, management, as it is organized in Israel, has none of the characteristics that facilitate a woman's juggling her multiple roles. Employers are resistant to hiring managers on a part-time basis, in contrast to employers' readiness to hire women part-time in other professions. In 1991, only 22 percent of women administrators and managers worked part-time (up to 34 hours a week), compared to 49 percent of scientific and academic professionals and 50 percent of other professionals. Salaried women managers worked an average of 41 hours a week, compared to 33 hours for scientific and academic professionals and 32 hours for other professionals. The proportion of scientific and academic as well as other professional employees working part-time increased over the last decade, but the proportion of part-time managers remained stable. Managers generally have more discretion to determine their work schedules than do lower-level workers, but their workload is also less predictable and more likely to expand beyond official work hours. Working overtime, furthermore, has important symbolic value; it is a visible expression of one's commitment to the organization and consequently one's entitlement to further promotions.

The managerial role also produces "responsibility overload" – namely, strain that is experienced as a result of having to cope with two jobs, in both of which the person has major responsibility for the performance of others over whom she or he has limited control. The married woman is also manager in her own home. She need not produce all the goods and services herself but she is accountable for them. It is this quality of responsibility in managerial and family work that makes psychological compartmentalization difficult, creates a sense of overload, and has made managerial jobs less appealing to married women than alternative professional routes. This sentiment is captured in the oft-repeated response to the question "Do you want to become a manager?" – namely, "What do I need it for?" The implication is that the perceived costs of being a manager are greater than the foreseeable benefits.

The new generation of women managers differs in several important respects from the previous one, and the differences between them reflect emerging trends among educated urban women in general. There are indications that younger women are changing the relative salience of family and work in their lives. In contrast to the older generation, which tailored work involvement to fit the demands of family, a growing number of young women, especially among the more educated, are modifying their family plans to fit their career aspirations (22).

They are delaying marriage, having fewer children (5), and planning their families more rationally (33). In 1988, women of twenty to 24 years of age had a 22 percent greater probability of being never-married than in 1968; and women between 25 and 29, a 68 percent greater probability. In 1988, 53 percent of twenty- to 24-year-old women and 19 percent of the 25- to 29-year-olds were never-married, compared to 43 percent and 11 percent, respectively, in 1968. The mean age at first marriage for the total population of ever-married women in 1983 was 23, and the average number of children was 3.4. In contrast, among women with sixteen years and more of schooling, it was 26 years and 2.0 children, respectively. As we have already seen, more women are making long-term investments in higher education, accumulating human capital, and adopting a career perspective to their work.

Whereas the previous generation of women managers most likely began their work careers as entry-level clerical workers, without plans for becoming managers, and worked their way up slowly, the newer generation is more likely to enter the organization after completing a first and increasingly more often a second university degree, with a clearer vision of wanting to move up the hierarchy. They are more overtly, personally ambitious women – a position made respectable by the weakening of the collective ideology in Israeli society and the growing individualism (21). The rising divorce rate may be both a symptom and a consequence of these developments.

Despite these shifts of emphasis, Israeli women still view themselves as responsible for managing family life, which they interpret as being physically available for their children at important hours during the day. The informal arrangements of management intrude on the hours mothers reserve for their families. For example, the following story, told to me by a signing officer in one of Israel's large financial institutions of what she called the bank's "afternoon culture," is typical of stories I heard from many women middle managers.

> At headquarters, the offices of the department line both sides of a long corridor. In the rooms on the right sit the managers – all men. In the rooms on the left sit the secretaries – all women. A female assistant also sits on the right as does the man who delivers the mail and runs errands. During the day the managers are in their offices speaking on the phone and dictating letters to their secretaries. At 3 p.m. the offices on the left empty out, only the secretary on duty remains. Then the managers come out of their offices and visit one another. That's also when all the meetings are held. I get called to headquarters about once a week and make a special point never to miss a meeting because I know that is when the really important information is exchanged. After the official meeting is over, most managers linger on and gossip or give one another tips on issues of current interest. They rarely leave the office before six in the evening. That's the ritual of the afternoon culture of the managers at headquarters.

Another woman who was passed over for a senior position in the bank described to me what she felt was a typical problem for women: "When the business of the [evening] meeting was over and I felt I had contributed my maximum and that staying on was a waste of my time, I got itchy, stood up and left for home. The men stayed on and chatted and that's when the cliques formed. I just didn't understand that at the time." I asked whether, had she understood that, she would have stayed with the men. "No," she said. "At that stage in the day, home was more important. I wanted to put my children to bed." "What about women whose children are grown?" I asked. "It wouldn't matter. Even when my children are 17 and 18, I want to be home for dinner, to at least have one meal together."

The Situation Today

Charting the gains

The major gains for women during the past two decades were their entry into lower-level managerial positions and, for a few, their promotion to middle-level positions. They are more severely under-represented in the private sector than in the public sector, where they are concentrated in public and community services. They are more severely under-represented in line than in staff positions, which generally carry less authority and have lower promotion ceilings. With few exceptions, women did not break through the glass ceiling that divides lower- and middle-level managers from senior management and the centers of organizational power.

Systematic data on the proportion of women managers at different levels are not available, but the following indicators support the above argument. Beginning with government service, where the gains are more impressive, women constitute 51 percent of the employed but only 20 percent of those in the top five grades (middle- and senior-level management) of the professional hierarchy and 11 percent of the administrative hierarchy (12). As everywhere, the higher the grade, the smaller the proportion of women.

In a survey of senior managers of large private, public, and Histadrut sector organizations (over 300 employees), for which "a special effort was made to reach women managers," only three of the 236 respondents (2.8 percent) were women (8:2). In 1990, women constituted 5.5 percent (49 of 885) of the members of the boards of directors of state-owned enterprises (28).

Women make up only some 3 percent of the members of the Israel Management Center.[8] Of the 250 members of the Senior Women Managers' Forum, only twenty could be classified as senior managers in terms of the size of the unit they manage or their control of resources and the wider impact of their policy decisions. The remainder are middle managers in large organizations or heads of very small firms.

The phenomenon of family connections, of being "the wife or daughter of" as an alternative mobility route for women into senior management has not been studied in Israel. A preliminary examination suggests that if such a phenomenon exists, it is still in an embryonic stage. Of the 300 firm-level members of the Continuing Generation Club within the Israel Manufacturers' Association, the managerial offspring and/or their spouses (up to age 45 years) of owner-managers of Israel's industrial firms, only three are women.

Assessing the gains, the general picture that emerges is that although the number of women in influential managerial positions is minute, it is greater than it was a decade ago; and women managers are dispersed, albeit unevenly, across many different fields of management. What the data do not reveal is the growing awareness among women that they are not solely responsible for their failure to reach more senior managerial positions. For example, a woman member of the Continuing Generation Club of the Manufacturers' Association told me, "We're only three women out of 300 in the club, and there were only four women among the 500 people who attended the annual meeting of the association last summer. There's something wrong with that and I want to find out what it is."

Earnings gap

In Israel, as elsewhere, women managers earn less than men managers, even when we compare the salaries on a per-hour basis of women and men with the same amount of education, training, and seniority. Researchers agree that a sizeable proportion of the difference between women's and men's earnings and opportunity is the result of discrimination (12;29;40). Earnings inequality is greater in those cases in which the controls over employers' inclination to discriminate are less effective. For example, the gender gap in managers' earnings is smaller in the public sector than in the private sector. Public sector earnings are open to the scrutiny of the comptroller general, thus limiting employers' ability to make "irregular" payments that are more often extended to men. Information about promotion opportunities are more readily available in the public sector. Although notice of an opening must be posted and candidates invited to apply, managerial positions may be tailored to fit specific individuals already preselected. Comparing women's full-time earnings in the top ten percentile of women's earnings with those of men in the top ten percentile of men's earnings reveals that men's earnings in the public sector are approximately 25 percent more than women's earnings; and men's earnings in the private sector are about double those of women (15). The sector difference in the gender gap in earnings reflects women's greater success in gaining access to higher level positions in the public than in the private sector. Furthermore, the income range in the top ten percentile in the private sector is much greater than in the public sector, which allows for greater income variance in the private sector and perhaps for greater discrimination. For example, the average earnings of the top ten percentile in the public sector were NIS6,885 a month (NIS2.8, or new Israeli shekels, equaled US$1 in 1993), whereas for the top 1 percent, the earnings were NIS10,178. In the financial sector, the figures were NIS12,314 and NIS23,470, respectively (15).

A study of gender wage differentials in government service, found that although women were more educated than men and had almost the same seniority, women in managerial grades earned 30 percent per hour less, on the average, than did men in the same grade (12). Moreover, comparing gender differences in 1988 with those in 1978, showed that the gender gap had *increased* from 21 percent to 30 percent.

The increase can be explained as resulting from the decentralization of the distribution of fringe benefits, such as overtime pay, car and travel allowances, and telephone allowances, which constitute a sizeable portion of take-home pay (12). In contrast to the basic wage still negotiated at the industry level, part of the fringe benefits are negotiated at the local level between the individual employee and the employer. In the 1980s, the weight of fringe benefits in gross earnings increased and their allocation was decentralized, thereby granting local heads of organizational units greater discretion over their distribution. The decline in centralized control and the increase in managerial discretion contributed to men receiving a greater share, thus increasing the gender gap in earnings at all levels of the hierarchy.

In interviews I conducted over the last five years, women offered some of the following explanations for their lower earnings than men with similar qualifications:

Discrimination at entry   In both the public and the private sector, the salary assigned to a job is on a sliding scale and adjusted to the qualifications of the candidate. Women in Israel receive lower entry-level salaries than equivalently qualified men, suggesting that gender is an implicit qualification (29). Consequently, even when promotion opportunities are equal, which they are not, the gender-based earnings gap is retained.

Accumulated disadvantage   Women who rise from within the organization often have greater difficulty shaking off their initial lower status and claiming perks and privileges than those who enter the organization at a managerial level. For example, women managers who advance within the same organization from low-level clerical jobs frequently continued to be devalued as if they were still clerical workers. One bank personnel manager explained that one of the women managers in the bank continued to perform some of the clerical tasks that had been her responsibility in her previous position. "Her performing those tasks colored the way top management valued her current job. Had a man continued to do additional tasks as she did, he would probably have demanded and received extra pay for doing so."

Blocked opportunity   Many women believed that despite their impressive performance and credentials, they were overlooked in favor of less qualified men. Had they been men, they would have been promoted. Others believed that if a man were doing the same job, it would be upgraded to a higher rank.

Limited access to information   The women complained that they had difficulty getting information about new openings, especially in other organizations. Such information circulates within social networks to which fewer women than men have access for reasons already discussed.

Devalued entitlement   The women who were promoted to a job previously held by a man did not always get all the perks, such as a company car and general travel allowance, granted to their male predecessor. Executives seemed to believe that men were entitled to more benefits than women.

Lack of support   The women managers who encountered discrimination hesitated to complain, believing that they had no one to back them. As will be shown further on, this was not an invalid assumption.

Women's Responses

The articulation of women's interests

The political strategies open to advocates of gender equality and their chances for success were influenced by the corporate structure of interest articulation in Israel. The centralist statist tendencies at the beginning of statehood gave way to a tripartite corporatism – state, Histadrut, and private sector – "in which government and various social and economic interest groups make an effort to reach an acceptable policy through bargaining and compromise" (17:154).

> [In general], a corporatist structure results in co-optation of women's demands for equal employment opportunities because feminists working within the male-dominated system tend to win concessions on issues like childcare and pregnancy leave, rather than on "bread and butter issues" like affirmative action. . . . In pluralist systems, where they are unconstrained by the necessity to work through the intermediation of existing groups such as parties and unions, feminists enjoy greater autonomy in the choice of tactics (10:487).

From the prestate period, the women's caucus within the dominant Labor party and the women's organization affiliated with the Histadrut (currently called the Naamat) were co-opted by the Labor party, limiting their ability to make demands for the greater representation of women in positions of power.

The promise of gender equality had been included in Israel's Declaration of Independence in 1948, one of the earliest constitutional documents to include gender as a group classification for the purposes of equal social and political rights (34). Its inclusion reflected the egalitarian ideology of the socialist pioneers and the political influence of women's interest groups in the prestate period (19). The impact of the egalitarian ideology, however, was counteracted by the Labor party's co-opting of the affiliated women's organizations and their consequent inability to put women's interests above those of the party. Within the labor coalition, the small group of influential women were divided internally along party factions, which put pressure on them to display loyalty to their respective male patrons and to put faction interests over women's interests. Factional competition further weakened women's motivation and ability to unite on behalf of claims to greater women's representation in the varied institutions of the state-controlled and Histadrut-owned economies. In the 1970s, women gained token representation within the Histadrut Trade Union Department, but never within its economic enterprises.

The women's organization associated with the Labor party (the Naamat) and the Histadrut provided its women members with promotion opportunities within the network of childcare, occupational schools, and other social services that it sponsors and administers. These positions within the "women's sector" were presented to women as an alternative route to leadership. In actuality, the women's leadership reserved access to the few positions open to women on the ruling bodies of the party and the Histadrut to themselves, thus preventing entry of other women who would pose a competitive threat to them.

The corporatist mode of interest articulation, which made women's organizations so dependent on the ruling groups, discouraged the establishment of independent women's organizations and severely limited the ability of new organizations, such as the feminist movement, to mobilize resources without paying the price of co-optation. An important breakthrough in this respect was the impressive rise to public visibility and influence of the Israel Women's Network, a liberal-feminist political organization established in the mid-1980s, whose activities in Israel are almost totally financed by non-Israeli sources. Not dependent on party factions for its survival, the Israel Women's Network has been a major force in developing women's leadership within the different political parties and uniting women's organizations and party caucuses around women's issues, across party lines. Five of the eleven women elected to the Knesset in 1992 had been active members of the Israel Women's Network.

Israeli women were more successful in creating a support structure for encouraging women's labor force participation, including high quality childcare, than they have been in institutionalizing affirmative action and creating greater equality of opportunity. For example, the Social Security Act passed in the early 1950s provides twelve weeks of paid maternity leave (never extended since) and job security for pregnant women and new mothers. Collective labor agreements permitted mothers of small children employed in the public or Histadrut sectors to work a shorter day at the employer's expense. They also provide equal prorated benefits for all part-time workers, including security of tenure, vacations, sick leave, and worker compensation, a policy that benefits women in particular but does not facilitate their advancement in their careers.

In Sweden, corporatist social democracy enabled the state to play a key role in changing traditional views of women as mothers first and "in reversing market forces that, for example, place women in the lower paying categories of occupations" (38:296). In Israel, the government was more receptive to paternalistic policies that protected employed women from market exploitation than they were to egalitarian policies that would change the gender imbalance in the labor market. Family-friendly work norms and public policies contribute to a supportive work environment for women while also contributing to employers' viewing all women as candidates for "the mommy track" instead of for promotion into the executive suite (22).

Women's employment and legislation

From the 1980s on, lobbying by women's groups supported by members of the Knesset produced a wave of what could be considered equal opportunity measures. Protective legislation, which 25 years earlier had been considered a significant accomplishment, came to be viewed as a barrier to women's opportunities. The change in strategy, however, was pragmatic, taking women's needs into consideration, rather than being based strictly on the principle of absolute equality. For example, the prohibition against women's night work (more honored in the exception than the rule) was repealed, but women retained the right to refuse to work the night shift. Compulsory retirement age, previously governed by collective labor agreements, was equalized at 65, up from 60 for women, but women retained the right to retire at 60 if the current collective agreement permitted. Advancing the retirement age was especially important for women managers, who often lagged behind men in their climb up the managerial hierarchy.

Benefits related to maternal leave were changed to parental benefits. However, the right of mothers with small children to work a shorter day, granted by collective agreement, was not extended to fathers. In 1992, a Tax Ordinance Amendment defined the higher-income spouse instead of the husband as the family representative for tax purposes. Whereas the amendment has little practical significance, it symbolizes public readiness to redefine relations within the family in accordance with the changing reality. (In Israel either spouse may request that his or her income be calculated separately for tax purposes.)

The Equal Employment Opportunity Law passed in 1988 made discrimination on the basis of either gender or family status in job advertising, hiring, training, promotion, and firing illegal. It also defined sexual harassment as discrimination and allowed, in specified circumstances, for the burden of proof that there had been no discrimination to be put on the employer. The Equal Opportunity in Employment Law (1988), however, did not include affirmative action in its definition of equality, nor did it provide for enforcement agencies to implement its principles in the courts (34).

Furthermore, neither the courts nor the labor unions have proven effective in combating gender inequality.[9] Few cases of gender discrimination have been heard by the courts (four before the 1988 law and about fifteen since). In the great majority of instances, workers' committees either did not support or openly opposed the woman plaintiff. During the 1980s, judges in the labor courts were not supportive of the discrimination claims that women did file. Women, for their part, are not accustomed to bringing discrimination complaints to court and were reluctant to do so. From the perspective of the plaintiff, the procedure is cumbersome, costly, time-consuming, and often brings about harassment by the employer and union representatives, along with criticism from fellow employees. Due to the difficulty in proving discrimination, the outcome is dubious.

The case of the women flight attendants against El-Al airlines, in the courts since 1988, is a case in point.[10] Twenty-one senior women flight attendants employed by El-Al airlines demanded the right to participate in the preparatory training given to employees prior to being assigned as station managers to foreign countries – training that previously the company had denied them on various technical pretenses. El-Al's 28 men flight attendants appealed to the court and demanded to be joined as defendants, claiming that granting the women access to the training would damage the men's opportunities for promotion. The registrar of the labor court and the regional labor court had denied the men flight attendants the right to become defendants in this case; the national labor court granted that right.[11] With the assistance of the court, the men of El Al united across class lines to counter the women's claim to equal opportunity for advancement to managerial positions.

Women on behalf of women

Until the late 1980s, the activities promoting women's advancement in management were premised on the assumption that the environment was benign and that women had to change and learn what men know (23). Women were led to believe that they had to be helped to become more assertive in order to take advantage of the opportunities that presumably existed for them. These assumptions were incorporated in the courses and seminars first offered to women managers in the mid-1980s that provided assertiveness training and basic managerial skills, but rarely feminist consciousness raising.

In the early 1990s, women's groups took new initiatives that went beyond activities aimed at changing women and sought ways to make "the system" work for women as it does for men. More women are becoming aware that competence and motivation may be necessary for a woman to get ahead, but they are not sufficient. Women, like men, need sponsors. The current major thrust of women's organizations' activities is to enhance women's representation on boards of directors of state, Histadrut, and public companies. They are taking advantage of a recent legislative amendment to the Companies' Act requiring all companies registered on the stock exchange (about 400 in January 1993) to include among their board members at least two members as representatives of the public at large. A campaign has started to secure some of these positions for women. In 1993, women's organizations were instrumental in the passing of an amendment to the State-Owned Enterprises Law, requiring "that in the composition of their Boards of Directors suitable representation be given to both sexes" and that "wherever possible, the minister in charge should appoint to the Board representatives of the sex that is not suitably represented."

The leaders of the Naamat – the women's organization associated with the Histadrut – the Israel Women's Network, and the Women's Senior Management Forum are using their organizational clout as well as their personal connections with men in positions of power to get women appointed as board members. In addition, they are working through the women in "pivotal positions," those with access to the men who select board members. For example, a number of women have already been referred to boards by the newly appointed director of the Association of Companies Registered on the Stock Exchange, who is also a member of the Women's Senior Management Forum. As Zohar Karti, founding chair of the Forum explained to me, "We are using 'the new girls' network' to sponsor one another and other women."

The main target of the new women's initiative is not the senior managerial positions responsible for the daily operations of organizations – the positions with real power – but instead positions on the boards of directors, which usually have far less power than managers, that meet from time to time and reward incumbents with status and the opportunity to make good connections.[12] The women's choice of target is pragmatic. In a sponsored system, where boards are made up of representatives of interest groups and constituencies, women in Israel can legitimately demand representation for women as an interest group. Furthermore, positions on boards of directors are also easier targets for women's groups than are management positions since information about board openings is more readily available and requisite qualifications more easily met. As one woman activist stated:

> I can't know what kind of person would fit a specific managerial job – that requires meeting specific technical requirements and matching personalities so that people can work together on a daily basis. I know who would make a good board member – someone who knows how to make sense of a balance sheet, has good judgment, and some experience in the industry.

Will this new strategy bring the outsiders into the promised land and women managers into the executive suite? There is room for an optimistic scenario. As board members, women can get visibility and provide role models for other women and examples for men of women's suitability for senior positions. They could influence appointments to senior managerial positions, ensure that firms do not discriminate against women, and use their connections on the boards to advance other women. Will they do so? As token members on all-male boards, it is unlikely. Under pressure to prove themselves worthy of board membership, isolated from the support of other women, and having to cultivate men's support to remain on the board, these women are unlikely to be able to replicate themselves and sponsor additional women. Unlike male sponsors who open doors for their protégés to move up, the women who become board members will likely remain protégées, dependent on male patrons. The pessimistic scenario is more convincing. In the next decade, Israel's women managers are likely to remain under-represented and under-utilized, and undermined by the probable emergence of a larger cadre of Golda Meirs to sustain the myth that the system is not exclusionary and that women who are truly competent and strongly motivated can make it to the top. In actuality, women will most likely remain outsiders in the promised land.

Notes

I gladly acknowledge my debt of gratitude to Judith Lorber for her insightful critique and skillful editing of this paper, and to Hava Etzioni-Halevy for her helpful comments.

1 Unless otherwise specified, all the statistics reported in this chapter were taken from the relevant yearly volume of the *Statistical Abstract of Israel* or the *Labor Force Survey*, both published by the Central Bureau of Statistics, Jerusalem. All figures were rounded to the closest percent.
2 The 1982 data reported here are based on a broader definition of managers than used by the Central Bureau of Statistics and also include school principals and school supervisors, supervising clerks and inspectors in transport and communication services, working proprietors in retail, wholesale, and the trades and in lodging and catering services.
3 I thank Binyamin Phillips for pointing out to me the role played by personal networks even in the high-tech industrial sector, in which many new firms were established by individuals who had studied together at the Technion, Israel Institute of Technology.
4 Personal communication, Menachem Amir.
5 The author was present at the meeting.

6 The tighter labor market for managerial positions in recent years has made it more difficult for retired officers to find employment.

7 Judith Lorber (1984) describes similar personalized characteristics in the medical profession.

8 An examination of the membership lists of the various management forums affiliated with the Israel Management Center revealed the following. Of some 1,700 members of boards of directors, less than 2 percent (29) were women. Of these, 23 were directors of public sector or Histadrut organizations, the majority of whom were political appointees, and only six were directors of private sector organizations. Of the 100 members of the Senior Marketing Managers's Forum, five were women, compared to none a decade ago, when not one of the women who applied was senior enough to qualify for membership. Of the members of the Financial and Stock Brokerage Managers, 10 percent were women. Of the 549 members of the Personnel Managers Forum, 15 percent were women. Of the 240 members of the Managers of Public Sector Welfare Departments, 36 percent were women. (The data on the various forums of the Israel Management Center were taken from their lists and do not include all managers in that category in Israel.)

9 The union represents all employees, including managers, except for those managers engaged under individual contract. In the public sector personal contracts are limited to the most senior levels.

10 Personal communication, Francis Raday.

11 The national labor court argued that this was a public interest case and a constitutional issue where civil rule procedures that usually made it difficult to join a defendant did not apply. The case is still in court.

12 The women's organization associated with the Histadrut sponsored a training course for 80 women preparing them to fill positions as members on boards of directors. The Women's Senior Management Forum affiliated with the Israel Management Center, in cooperation with the Israel Women's Network, is preparing a data bank of women qualified to serve as board members to make available to appropriate firms.

References

(1) Aharoni, Yair (1991) *The Israeli Economy: Dreams and Realities*. London/New York: Routledge.

(2) Avnieli, Anat (1988) "One More Than in the General Chief of Staff," *Ha'ir*, September 16, p. 15.

(3) Azmon, Yael (1985) "Urban Patronage in Israel," in Eric Cohen, Moshe Lissak and Uri Almagor (eds.), *Comparative Social Dynamics*. Boulder, Colo.: Westview Press.

(4) Azmon, Yael, and Izraeli, Dafna N. (1993) "Women in Israel: A Sociological Perspective," in Yael Azmon and Dafna N. Izraeli (eds.), *Women in Israel: Studies of Israeli Society*. New Brunswick, N.J.: Rutgers University, Transaction Books.

(5) Bakki, Roberto (1986) "The Demographic Crisis of the Jewish People," *Ha'aretz*, June 1.

(6) Barad, Miriam, and Weinshall, Theodore D. (1967) "Women as Managers in Israel," in *Public Administration in Israel and Abroad*, pp. 78–87. Jerusalem: Israel Institute of Public Administration.

(7) Bar-Yosef, Rivka, and Padan-Eisenstark, Dorit (1977) "Role System Under Stress: Sex Roles in War," *Social Problems* 25:135–145.

(8) Caspi, Amnon (1987) "A Profile of the Israeli Senior Manager," *Nihul* (December): 7–12.

(9) Central Bureau of Statistics (1991) *Labor Force Survey 1989*. Special Series No. 894. Jerusalem: Central Bureau of Statistics.

(10) Charles, Maria (1992) "Cross National Variation in Occupational Sex-Segregation," *American Sociological Review* 57:483–502.

(11) Civil Service (1990) *Annual Report* No. 40. Jerusalem: Ministry of Finance.

(12) Efroni, Linda (1989) *Women in Government Service: A Comparison 1979–1988*. Jerusalem: Civil Service, Training and Education Service.

(13) Eisenstadt, Shmuel N. (1967) *Israeli Society*. London: Weidenfeld and Nicolson.

(14) Eisenstadt, Shmuel N. (1985) *The Transformation of Israeli Society*. Boulder, Colo.: Westview Press.

(15) Gabai, Yoram, and Lifshitz, Yehudit (1992) "Wages, Taxes and the Costs of Labor in Financial Institutions and Government," *Rivon Le'kalkala* (April):591–599.

(16) Har-Gad, Y. (1984) "The Status of Women in Managerial Positions in Israel." Master's thesis, Faculty of Management, Tel Aviv University.

(17) Horowitz, Dan, and Lissak, Moshe (1989) *Trouble in Utopia: The Overburdened Polity of Israel*. Albany, N.Y.: SUNY Press.

(18) Izraeli, Dafna N. (1979) "Sex Structure of Occupations: The Israeli Experience," *Sociology of Work and Occupations* 6(4):404–442.

(19) Izraeli, Dafna N. (1981) "The Zionist Woman's Movement in Palestine: 1911–1927," *Signs: Journal of Women in Society and Culture* 7:87–114.

(20) Izraeli, Dafna N. (1988) "Women's Movement into Management in Israel," in Nancy J. Adler and Dafna N. Izraeli (eds.), *Women in Management Worldwide*, pp. 186–212. Armonk, N.Y.: M. E. Sharpe.

(21) Izraeli, Dafna N. (1991) "Women and Work: From Collective to Career," in Barbara Swirski and Marilyn P. Safir (eds.), *Calling the Equality Bluff: Women in Israel*, pp. 165–177. New York: Pergamon Press.

(22) Izraeli, Dafna N. (1992) "Culture, Policy and Women in Dual-Earner Families in Israel," in Suzan Lewis, Dafna N. Izraeli, and Helen Hootsmans (eds.), *Dual Earner Families: International Perspectives*. London: Sage.

(23) Izraeli, Dafna N., and Adler, Nancy J. (1994) "Competitive Frontiers: Women Managers in a Global Economy," in Nancy J. Adler and Dafna N. Izraeli (eds.), *Competitive Frontiers: Women Managers in a Global Economy*, pp. 1–21. Cambridge (USA)/Oxford, (England): Blackwell Publishers.

(24) Izraeli, Dafna N., and Tabory, Ephraim (1986) "The Perception of the Status of Women in Israel as a Social Problem," *Sex Roles: A Journal of Research* 14:663–678.

(25) Izraeli, Dafna N., and Tabory, Ephraim (1988) "The Political Context of Feminist Attitudes in Israel," *Gender and Society* 2:463–481.

(26) Lorber, Judith (1984) *Women Physicians: Careers, Status and Power*. New York: Tavistock Publications.

(27) Marantz, Felice (1992) "The Flip Side of Fertility," *Jerusalem Report*, November 5, p. 20.

(28) Ministry of Finance (1990) *Report on State-Owned Enterprises*. Jerusalem: State-Owned Enterprises Authority.

(29) Moore, Dahlia (1992) *Labor Market Segmentation and Its Implications: Inequality, Deprivation and Entitlement*. New York: Garland Publishing.

(30) Offe, Carl (1976) *Industry and Inequality* (translated by J. Wickham). London: Edward Arnold.

(31) Patinkin, Dan (1969) "The Progress toward Economic Independence," in Shmuel N. Eisenstadt, Rivka Bar-Yosef, and Chaim Adler (eds.), *Integration and Development in*

Israel, pp. 93–106. Jerusalem: Israel Universities Press.

(32) Pazy, Asya (1987) "Sex Differences in Responsiveness to Organizational Career Management," *Human Resource Management* 26:243–256.

(33) Peres, Yochanan, and Katz, Ruth (1984) *The Working Mother and Her Family*. Tel Aviv: Modi'in Ezrachi, Ltd., Institute of Research.

(34) Raday, Frances (1991) "Women Work and the Law," in Barbara Swirski and Marilyn P. Safir (eds.), *Calling the Equality Bluff*. New York: Pergamon Press.

(35) Radom, M. (1967) *Management Development in Israel*. The Israel Management Center and the Department of Industry and Management Engineering of the Technion, Israel Institute of Technology.

(36) Rein, Natalie (1979) *Daughters of Rachel: Women in Israel*. New York: Penguin Books.

(37) Ringel-Hoffman, Ariella (1993) "What Kind of Police Force?" *Yediot Ahronot*, January 1.

(38) Ruggie, Mary (1984) *The State and the Working Woman: A Comparative Study of Britain and Sweden*. Princeton, N.J.: Princeton University Press.

(39) Semyonov, Moshe, and Tyree, Andrea (1981) "Community Segregation and the Costs of Ethnic Subordination," *Social Forces* 59:649–666.

(40) Shenhav, Yehouda A., and Haberfeld, Yitchak (1988) "Scientists in Organizations: Discrimination Processes in an Internal Labor Market," *Sociological Quarterly* 29:451–462.

(41) Weinshall, Theodore D. (1976) "The Industrialization of a Rapidly Developing Country – Israel," in Robert Dubin (ed.), *Handbook of Work, Organization and Society*, pp. 949–989. Chicago: Rand McNally.

(42) Yariv, D. (1980) "Integration of Zahal Officers (Pensioners) into the Civilian Economy and Continuity between the Military Career and the Civilian Career." Master's thesis, Faculty of Management, Tel Aviv University.

(43) Zimmer, Hana, and Halperin, Nilli (1978) "The Distribution of Women among Medical Specialties in Israel." Unpublished seminar paper, Department of Labor Studies, Tel Aviv University.

19

SOUTH AFRICA

South African Women: Changing Career Patterns

Ronel Erwee

While South African managerial women are advancing slowly up corporate career ladders, many other women are also moving into nontraditional careers, such as entrepreneurship. Their career advancement has been enhanced by removing discriminatory clauses regarding race and gender in labor legislation and by creating a greater willingness on the part of companies to invest in women. By establishing multiracial women's groups, women are coordinating their efforts to abolish societal and organizational barriers to career growth and to enhance women's overall quality of life.

Despite the fact that the South African economy is the strongest among all African economies (27), its growth rate remains lower than that of its European trading partners. A primary reason has been the relatively low level of productivity caused primarily by a lack of "productivity consciousness" (an awareness of the economic necessity to increase output), insufficient education and training, and inadequate management skills. The latter is of particular relevance to women.

South Africa suffers from a critical shortage of high-level human resources (21;22). The ratio of executives to lower-level workers is 1:52, compared to a ratio of 1:15 in most economically developed countries. The ratio is a function, in part, of the particular type of industries in South Africa and how they are managed. There is great pressure on managers and professional groups to create job opportunities; and, as a result of the rapid growth of unskilled workers, this pressure will increase. The chronic shortage of executives is exacerbated by the racial and sexual segregation of authority. The white minority, which controls both economic and political power, constitutes only 17 percent of the population; yet the majority of executives are white males. There is growing recognition among companies, however, that women and men of all races must be trained to provide a cadre of future executives.

During the 1980s, companies allocated significant funding to training potential managers of all races and the government encouraged these efforts with generous concessions. Companies complain that too little new managerial talent has emerged from their training efforts – particularly among black managers (both women and men) over the past ten years. By blaming the disadvantaged groups for their own failure, companies try to shift attention away from their discriminatory employment policies and practices that have limited the effectiveness of the training efforts.

Despite the increase in women employees during the past decade, companies claim that they lack suitably qualified women to promote to managerial positions. This scarcity of potential women managers results from multiple factors, including labor legislation, employment practices in companies, lack of encouragement, and inadequate career guidance.

The slow rate of change in education, employment, and training patterns stands in stark contrast to the rapid changes in sociopolitical realities since February 2, 1990 – the date the government announced Nelson Mandela's release and its decision to scrap apartheid legislation. The outcome of negotiations currently taking place between various racial groups will affect the distribution of power and wealth, which, in turn, will have an impact on the racial segregation of authority and the careers of black managers, both women and men.

Because it is beyond the scope of the present discussion to describe all the sociopolitical changes currently taking place in South Africa, this chapter focuses on three issues: participation trends among women of all races in management and related occupations, problems facing women aspiring to managerial careers, and recommendations for better utilization of women's power in South Africa.

Employment Trends

Many companies, in starting black advancement programs during the 1980s, ignored the 1987 National Manpower Commission report which documented that while white men formed the largest source of high-level manpower (HLM) in 1985, white women formed the second largest source, black women the third largest source, and black men only the fourth largest source (see (5)). South African companies chose to skip the second and third largest sources of high-level manpower – white and black women – and focused their attention on promoting black men.

Women made up 36 percent of the economically active population in 1985 and increased to 4.1 million women or 41 percent of the workforce by 1991. When companies consider women, they can no longer assume that they are dealing with an insignificant portion of the economically active population whose demands for workplace reform they can ignore or slight.

While varying by racial group, all group's participation rates increased markedly between 1985 and 1991: 44 percent of colored women (women of mixed race) were economically active in 1991, up from 41 percent in 1985; 41 percent of blacks were economically active, up from 36 percent in 1985; 40 percent of whites were economically active, up from 36 percent in 1985; and 33 percent of Asian women were economically active, up from 28 percent in 1985 (5). Figure 19.1 shows the projected participation rates for women in 1995 by age and racial group (30).

Black and white women enter the workforce at a younger age than do Asian and colored women. White women enter the labor force after completing school or tertiary education. A small portion of white women leave the workforce between the ages of twenty and 30 to raise children, but the majority, especially the more

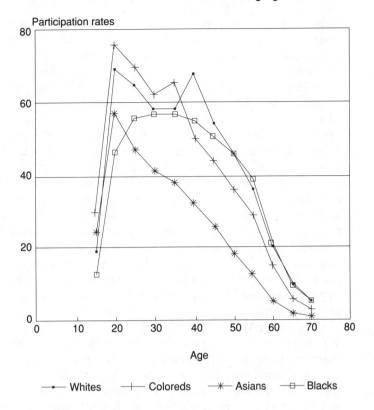

Source: HSRC estimates (1991).

Figure 19.1   Projected participation rates of women by age and racial group in 1995

educated, never leave the workforce. There is an increase between the ages of 30 and 40, as women who previously left to raise children re-enter the workforce. White women in the age group 30 to 50 therefore form a significant and consistent source of experienced employees.

The effect of the 1991 to 1993 recession can be seen primarily on the participation rates of black women which are generally lower in most age groups than similar rates in 1985. It is estimated that in 1995, black women will enter the workforce a few years younger than previously, but with many still filling unskilled, clerical, or sales positions. Due to their escalating divorce rate, black women will be forced to remain in the workforce for a longer period of time to support their extended families.

Asian women remain the most traditional group. They stay in the job market until marriage or the birth of their first child and then leave the workforce to be supported by their husband or to work in a family business. In 1985, colored women's participation rates resembled those of Asian women, but the 1995 estimates show a pattern more similar to that of white women.

Current recruitment policies take into account the 1991 census data, showing that women now constitute 40 percent of graduates with bachelor's degrees (up from 30 percent in 1985), 25 percent of graduates with master's degrees (up from 17 percent in 1985), and 23 percent of doctorates (up from 14 percent in 1985). More white women graduate from high school than their white male counterparts (654,380 women versus 608,965 men), whereas the opposite still applies to black, Asian, and colored graduates (5). Although more black men graduate from high school than black women (441,901 men versus 410,496 women), more black women obtain a bachelor's degree than black men (105,955 women; 81,235 men).

Only 10 percent of the white labor force and 1 percent of the black labor force have academic degrees. This low level of education is one of South Africa's most crucial problems. Organizations usually select managers from the most highly educated employees; that is, those with tertiary education. Such a small pool of potential managers is characteristic of an economically developing country. The danger inherent in this low level of education is that since the number of educated employees is insufficient, companies will select less educated individuals for managerial positions.

Most South African managers have not risen to senior positions through obtaining higher education qualifications, but instead either through the seniority system based on an uninterrupted career; through overt and covert types of job reservation (which reserved certain career paths for white males); or as a result of prejudice against minority groups. As the level of education of the workforce increases and becomes a more important criterion for entry and promotion, and as cultural and legislative barriers disappear, women should have more opportunities for managerial careers.

Some companies argue that the vocational choices of women university graduates and high school graduates do not suit their organizational needs. In reality, women's career patterns are changing dramatically in the direction of companies' expressed needs. Women have increased their representation in the following nontraditional occupations: engineering, engineering technicians, and architects (now 6 percent); natural sciences (30 percent); humanities (35 percent); other professional, semiprofessional, and technical occupations (23 percent); transport, delivery, and communications (6 percent); protective services (8 percent); farming (26 percent); artisans and apprentices (5 percent); production supervisors, miners, and related workers (22 percent) (5).

Despite the focus on black men's promotion, women have also managed to begin climbing corporate career ladders. Women constitute 20 percent of all managers, executives, and administrators (up from 17 percent in 1985). In this occupational category, women constitute 14 percent of all managers in the government sector (2,263 women managers out of a total of 16,448 managers); in the private sector they constitute 19 percent (51,703 women managers out of a total of 270,630 managers). Women hold 43 percent of all administrative (i.e., junior management and supervisory) positions (5,994 women out of a total of 13,679 people). The total

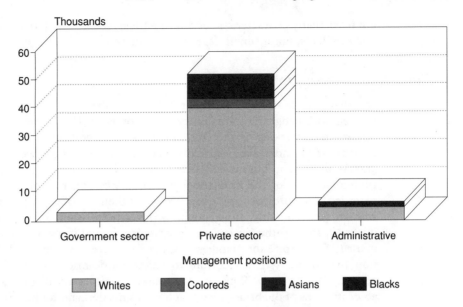

Source: Central Statistical Services (1992) *SA Labour Statistics*. Pretoria: Central Statistical Services.

Figure 19.2   South African women of all races in management positions (1992)

number of managers and administrators (women and men of all races), as defined by the Central Statistical Services (6) is 300,757. As shown in Figure 19.2, the private sector employs many more women managers than does the government sector. The proportion of colored and Asian women managers remains much lower in all sectors than their white and black managerial counterparts. White women represent 19 percent of all white managers, colored women represent 24 percent of all colored managers, Asian women 14 percent of all Asian managers, and black women 26 percent of all black managers. The most significant increase in women managers since 1985 occurred among blacks, as women constituted only 16.5 percent of black managers at that stage.

The persistent low numbers of women among South African managers, despite the women's higher educational qualifications, high economic participation rates, and changing career choices confirms the need for the government to extend equal opportunity programs to women of all races. An interesting new trend is that a few companies have started to poach the highly trained, but under-utilized, women managers from firms with a reputation for neglecting, or not supporting, their women employees.

Women managers worldwide face a host of problems in becoming managers and in moving up the ranks to senior positions. Many of the problems faced by American women managers (1;13;17;18) are also common among South African women managers of all races. This chapter therefore focuses on those salient issues which are particularly characteristic of South African society; including cultural and societal problems, employment legislation, and employment policies.

Cultural and Societal Problems

In 1984, the Matrimonial Property Act abolished one of the major barriers to women advancing, the status of married women as legal minors. One of the most important provisions of the Act, the husband's control over his wife's right to negotiate and undertake contractual agreements, was abolished for white, colored, and Asian women, but not for black women. The latter group is still subject to the traditional laws of the nine tribal groups, according to which black women are regarded as subordinate to men regardless of their age or educational status. A black woman, consequently, must obtain written permission from a man (her father, husband, son, brother-in-law, or other male relative) if she wishes to enter employment (24). Despite the changes that black culture is undergoing due to urbanization, the Lobola system, according to which a bride-price must be paid to the bride's parents, still operates. This practice makes a successful black woman "unaffordable" in terms of the bride-price that her parents demand for her. When a successful career woman becomes a member of another family through marriage, her in-laws, according to tradition, may veto her decisions about career advancement. Various male tribal leaders have resisted abolishing this type of power.

Like black men, black women who gain access to managerial careers face additional problems related to belonging to a discriminated group. Black male managers can be described as "marginal men" who are "partially accepted and partially rejected by the white world in which they are expected to perform; they face the psychological burden of not knowing where they stand; they cannot take the knowledge they require for practical competence in routine performance for granted" (15:102). The male manager "faces discrimination on a social level and encouragement to be individualistic while at the same time being constantly reminded of his ethnic background" (15:102). These problems, generalized from a study of men, apply to black women managers as well. Black women, however, may have developed strengths that help them cope with their marginality better than their male counterparts (24).

Tradition also remains a powerful barrier for Asian women in South Africa. Permission and approval of fathers, husbands, or other guardians is still necessary for Indian women "to step outside the family for any reason" (5:41). Family opposition in part explains Asian women's virtual absence from executive positions in even the more traditional women's niches such as welfare, educational, political, and labor organizations.

Employment Legislation

The debate about equal employment opportunity and affirmative action has taken a new direction with the tabling of the Promotion of Equal Opportunities Bill and the Abolition of Discrimination Bill on February 19, 1993. These bills are based on clause 33 of the proposed Charter of Fundamental Human Rights which focuses on "women and equal rights." The fact that women will constitute 54 percent of eligible voters in the next general election demonstrates their potential political clout and explains why this legislation was tabled before the general election in 1994.

The Abolition of Discrimination Draft Bill deals mainly with the elimination of discriminatory clauses in existing laws, for example, the abolition of discriminatory provisions relating to the automatic dismissal of women as a result of marriage or pregnancy. The Bill stresses the concepts of freedom of choice and the right to work which are specifically applied to underground work and other high-risk jobs, as well as work during pregnancy. The latter amendment does not yet provide for a "job-back guarantee"; nor does it make any provision for either maternity leave or for remunerating a woman employee during such a leave.

Many women find the decision not to address the discrimination against married women – namely, taxation, unfair medical and pension schemes, and subsidies – in the Abolition of Discrimination against Women Draft Bill, unacceptable. The legally unfounded concept of "breadwinner" leads to great unfairness and flies in the face of the principle of equal remuneration for equal work (6).

The Promotion of Equal Opportunities Draft Bill currently prohibits discrimination on the basis of gender, marital status, and pregnancy. The Bill includes the principle of equal remuneration for equal work. It prohibits all discrimination by employers, prospective employers, employment agencies, partnerships, registered associations, occupational controlling bodies, or educational institutions. It formulates a broad definition of sexual harassment and deems it to be an unfair labor practice.

The Minister of Justice envisages establishing an Equal Opportunities Commission. The Women's Bureau Working Group suggested that such a Commission should: (a) inquire into complaints, and, whenever possible, effect conciliation; (b) carry out investigations relating to contravention of the Act; (c) undertake research and educational programs to promote the purposes of the Act; (d) consult with various organizations to ascertain means of improving services and conditions affecting areas that are subject to contravention of the Act; (e) investigate requests for exemptions from the Act; (f) examine other Acts to determine whether they are inconsistent with the purposes of this Act; (g) research additional grounds for discrimination; and (h) advise the minister as to all of the above (11). The Commission may also, after consultation and with the approval of organizations striving for equality and equal opportunity between women and men, draft a code of conduct. The latter law also includes sections that can be described as "positive action" measures, for example, allowing single-sex schools and supporting developmental training.

Although these bills seemingly support an equal opportunity paradigm, the process of drafting the bills as well as some of the content reflect the inherent paternalistic mindset of the judiciary. Very little consultation took place with women's organizations, employer or employee organizations, or political parties during the drafting process.

Employment Policies

Women have become legal equals in the workplace during the past few years. However, employers do not always implement the positive changes in the legislation. Some employers still practice discriminatory employment measures in hiring, placement, and remuneration.

South Africa does not have institutions like the British Equal Opportunities Commission, which can prosecute companies who transgress laws or can counsel companies to adhere to legal requirements, or legislation like the Australian Affirmative Action Act, which requires companies to report annually on their progress in implementing affirmative action programs. However, industrial courts do exist that deal with cases presented by trade union members concerning the Labour Relations Act. No women to date, however, have presented cases in the industrial courts concerning companies' hiring, placement, or remuneration practices.

Training policies

Companies do recognize the special needs of minority groups and have developed programs that include special training, mentorship, supervisory development, and career counseling. Programs for "black advancement" are in vogue and are being conducted by 66 percent of surveyed companies (8). The beneficiaries are primarily black men, thus confirming the belief that race is seen as a more important variable than gender in South Africa.

In most companies, women are not recognized as a special group entitled to special programs or as high-level human resources with potential to be promoted into senior management. For example, surveys in 1982 and 1984 regarding employment conditions in companies employing professional women showed that the companies provided women with inadequate career planning, insufficient access to training programs, and few promotional opportunities, as well as being guilty of providing unequal fringe benefits to women and men (8).

Companies offer very few programs specially for women. For example, a recent survey of the career development practices in 58 manufacturing, financial, and consulting companies found that only one-third (34 percent) offer supervisory training and even fewer provide career management programs for women (8). Women, therefore, have restricted access to supervisory and managerial training, which further restricts their upward mobility.

Reward structures

Salary surveys indicate pay differentials by race and sex. The anomalies between women's and men's salaries (as well as blacks' and whites' salaries) are a consequence of industry-level and individual-level factors, as well as factors both internal and external to the organization (2). Factors such as the economic climate, type of industry, and level of competition in the industry influence the company's ability to pay certain salaries. To a certain extent, wage differences between women and men may reflect gender differences in human capital, such as education, continuity of job experience, labor market continuity, absenteeism, or turnover. Tables 19.1 and

Table 19.1   Women's pay as a percentage of white men's pay (1984, 1988, 1990)

	Paterson band[a]					
	C Lower junior management professional persons			C Upper department heads		
	1984	1988	1990	1984	1988	1990
White men	100	100	100	100	100	100
White women	79	91	100	96	92	98
Asian women	74	74	84	79	80	84
Black women	NA	65	70	NA	69	70
Colored women	60	77	73	NA	NA	70

[a] The Paterson system is an internationally known job evaluation system with the "C band" indicating the level of decision making. Annual salaries of full-time personnel of all large South African companies participating in these annual salary surveys are being compared.

NA means data not available, no women in the category.

Source: Brehm, N. (1989) "Women and Pay," *Institute of Personnel Management Journal* (March): 20–21.

19.2 present women's and men's salaries for supervisory personnel and departmental managers.

Table 19.1 illustrates the differences in pay between white women and men of all races in a representative sample of large companies.[1] The pay gap between white women and men of all race groups (in supervisory and departmental manager positions) narrowed considerably between 1984 and 1990. Women have moved into job levels previously held only by men (e.g., supervisory levels) in which they receive salaries closer to those of their male counterparts than to the lower salaries paid in "traditionally female" jobs (2).

Table 19.2   Women's pay as a percentage of men's pay by race groups (1988)

	Paterson band[a]	
	C Lower junior management professional persons	C Upper department heads
White men	100	100
White women	91	92
Asian men	100	100
Asian women	93	91
Black men	100	100
Black women	104	94
Colored men	100	100
Colored women	95	NA

[a] The Paterson system is an internationally known job evaluation system with the "C band" indicating the level of decision making. Annual salaries of full-time personnel of all large South African companies participating in these annual salary surveys are being compared.

NA means data not available, no women in the category.

Source: Brehm, N. (1989) "Women and Pay," *Institute of Personnel Management Journal* (March): 20–21.

The differences in salaries between white women and white men have caused much less of a problem and have been more easily rectified than the differences in salaries between the races within each occupational category. Caution is needed, however, in interpreting the trends since responding companies tend to provide information about white men's salary scales and then simply state that pay parity exists.[2] Feedback from women professionals confirms that pay parity exists at all levels, but that the problem of achieving promotion into senior management, and thus receiving the higher salaries, remains difficult.

When pay is compared by race (see Table 19.2), women in all races fare reasonably well in comparison to their male counterparts in supervisory and departmental positions. The interesting exception is black women in supervisory positions whose salaries are higher than those of black men. In these cases, black women moved into jobs that were previously viewed as "white female" jobs (2). The black women started their jobs at a lower pay level than that received by white women, but at pay levels higher than those traditionally offered to blacks, including black men.

These reward structures illustrate that blacks as a racial group have been more successful in getting themselves defined as a group in need of special support than have women as a gender group, so that black women do better as *blacks* than as *women*. Black women, therefore, have even more to gain by breaking through the racial impasse than the gender impasse. Where privilege is so strongly associated with race, white women are perceived to be part of the privileged class and, therefore, may have difficulty in getting the support they need.

Benefits

Maternity leave offered by the majority of companies usually adheres to the stipulations of the Basic Conditions of Employment Act. Section 17 of the Act states that "no employer shall require or permit any female employee to work during the period commencing four weeks prior to the expected date of her confinement and ending eight weeks after the date of her confinement" (12). This section does not clearly protect an employee from dismissal as a result of her pregnancy and does not place employers under obligation to pay their employees who are on an obligatory maternity leave.

A few companies are moving beyond meeting the minimum legal requirements in an innovative way. For example, Nestlé, a Swiss multinational company, grants all women employees four months' maternity leave at 78 percent of their salary, with an option for an additional three months' unpaid leave, with continued medical aid and pension benefits, and with a guarantee of the same job or one at a similar level on their return (23). These provisions imply that a woman manager will not forego her level of seniority or benefits. Such benefits, however, are still the exception.

Another problem facing managerial mothers is the acute shortage of crèches and daycare facilities (3). Black women managers in particular face great hardships. In the traditional extended family system that operated in black society, the care of relatives' children was a part of any family's responsibilities. The extended family system, however, has disintegrated in urban communities. Moreover, because of the high cost, very few companies make daycare facilities available. Daycare centers are provided primarily by local communities; and such government agencies do not take the per capita income of the family into account when setting their fees. In the Asian community, the extended family system still operates to a greater extent; while white women managers have access both to relatively more crèches and to the possibility of employing black domestic workers.

Company training policies, reward structures, and benefits are among the factors that contribute to women's lack of promotion into positions of power. An example of how few women there are in executive positions is provided by a small sample of award-winning companies selected for their favorable treatment of women (29). As shown in Table 19.3, property companies, educational institutions, and travel agencies have the highest percentages of women at the executive level. The general situation for South African women, even in these award-winning companies, is reflected in the low percentages of women at the executive level in retail companies, banks, computer companies, utilites, and manufacturing companies.

Table 19.3   Gold Award[a] nominees (1988): Percentage of women and men employees (of all races) at three organizational levels

	Level		
Organization	*Executive*	*Senior personnel*	*General personnel*
Utility company			
Men	100	95	95
Women	0	5	5
Manufacturing petroleum			
Men	100	90	93
Women	0	10	7
Travel agency			
Men	64	38	22
Women	36	62	78
Computer company			
Men	91	85	36
Women	9	15	64
Retail; food			
Men	90	54	38
Women	10	46	61
Bank			
Men	92	66	32
Women	8	34	67
Educational institution			
Men	60	40	33
Women	40	60	67
Property company			
Men	50	55	62
Women	50	45	38

[a] The Gold Awards were created by the South African Federation of Business and Professional Women and are presented to companies in recognition of their fair employment practices.

Source: South African Federation of Business and Professional Women (1988) *Gold Award: Report on the Competition*. Johannesburg: SAFBPW.

Psychological Impact of Cultural Norms

Stereotypes

In the South African culture (as in most other cultures), women are expected to give priority to their traditional roles as a wife and mother, with such qualities as subservience, supportiveness, and submissiveness being highly valued. Career women, therefore, often find themselves in conflict. Those qualities that make them "acceptable" in traditional terms can undermine their self-confidence and make them unable to be assertive in ways needed to succeed in a managerial career.

The stereotypes that some male managers hold regarding women's capabilities can create self-fulfilling prophecies. Failures of minority members at the workplace are often due to their internalized poor self-esteem. One researcher states, "The stigmatised internalise their own stigmatisation by overconforming" (20:4). If women internalize the negative stereotypes, they may under-perform, which may in turn confirm men's stereotypes of women and perpetuate discriminatory practices.

Attitudes of white male managers

The ways in which individuals relate to each other in a work situation are, to some extent, related to the ways in which they perceive each other. Researchers investigated the attitudes of 103 white English-speaking male managers toward the upward mobility of women and contrasted them with prior research regarding their attitudes toward the promotion of blacks (14). They found that although white male managers accept the principle of equal opportunity, agree that women can acquire managerial skills, and believe that women's contributions should be valued, some question women's ability to compete on equal terms with men. Approximately one-third of the male managers hold one or more of the following beliefs: women are less objective, less aggressive, less capable of contributing to organizational goals, less ambitious, less self-confident, and less capable of learning mathematical and mechanical skills than their male counterparts. One in three male managers attribute women's lack of career advancement mainly to women's own internal dispositions, thus completely discounting the effects of situational factors.

Researchers found that only one-third of the surveyed companies' senior management is committed to developing and advancing women and only 12 percent support affirmative action for women (14). Furthermore, the researchers found that there is no clarity on the affirmative action policies applied to women of different races:

> The ... [senior managers] have not seriously contemplated the position of black women in present day South Africa. Alternatively, they could perceive black women as a group to be classified with black men and feel that affirmative action should be practised in relation to this group but not towards white women who, it may be tacitly assumed, can progress without any affirmative steps being taken (14:23).

Career orientations of women

In contrast to the perceptions of male managers, many business and professional women describe themselves as "career women" who take their careers seriously, formulate long-term career goals, and would continue with their career even if there was no financial need to do so (7). Interest in pursuing managerial careers was examined for 95 career women, including personnel specialists, marketing managers, engineers, and general managers (10). The Career Orientations Inventory was used to understand the "career anchors" of the various occupational groups (25).[3] The most dominant career anchor was "service," indicating that the women's primary concern was "to achieve some value – making the world a better place in which to live; helping others" (25:14).

The next most important cluster of career anchors for the women managers in most of the occupational categories was "managerial competence," "variety," and "security." The relatively high score on the "managerial competence" career anchor seems to indicate that these women aspire to become more upwardly mobile within their organization. In general, managerially anchored people want high levels of responsibility, leadership opportunities, and challenging and integrative work (25). Such managers measure themselves by their income level and expect to be highly paid. They view the most important form of recognition as promotion to a position of greater responsibility and insist on promotions based on merit.

Accepting the Challenges

Despite the barriers, there are many forces in South African society and strengths within the women managers themselves that can assist them in overcoming the obstacles to advancing in a managerial career. By identifying and using these forces constructively, individual women can advance in their managerial careers.

Companies' social responsibility

Organizations that have adopted a positive policy of nondiscrimination provide a constructive force for change. In 1983, of the 400 United States multinational corporations operating in South Africa, 146 were signatories to the Sullivan Code. A human rights activist, Reverend Leon Sullivan instituted a code with the aim of ending racial discrimination in American companies operating in South Africa (27). These 146 foreign multinationals made a substantial and direct contribution toward providing employees with equal opportunities to secure quality education and community facilities, adequate housing, unrestricted union organizations, and the freedom to relocate where jobs exist.

The Sullivan Code, which focused on improving the employment conditions of black workers, had a direct positive influence on the upward mobility of black women. White women have also benefited indirectly as companies eliminated discriminatory personnel policies. The Sullivan Code was dropped in 1991 due to the sociopolitical and legislative changes in South Africa supporting black advancement.

Creating mentors

Several South African companies are debating whether an official management-sponsored mentor system would be applicable in their organizations. Some support the idea of a mentor system for most South African organizations, whereby potential managers can be assigned a mentor (16). However, male managers are often reluctant to function as mentors to women because this role is unfamiliar to them. Mentoring is often underrated as a personnel development technique, and women mentors are scarce. Furthermore, the male model of mentorship does not appear to be totally applicable to women. Moreover, women managers may be just as reluctant as men to function as mentors to other women, but for different reasons (26;32). Women's reluctance is due mainly to the small number of women in senior management positions (see Table 19.3) and to their own feelings of insecurity. Insecurity exists because of a lack of guidance in mentoring, time pressures, and the fear that they may be penalized if they associate with unacceptable protégées.

The mass media's portrayal of role models in the broader South African society can substitute, in part, for mentors within a particular organization. In the past, black, colored, and Asian women had few role models. Currently, business magazines such as *Black Enterprise, Tribute,* and *Leadership* profile women business owners, political leaders, and community developers. The oldest and most eminent financial journal published a lead article on "Women in Business" for the first time in its history in September 1990. The proportion of women leaders of all races in the *Who's Who in Business* is steadily increasing.

Women's networks

Another trend that has emerged is white women becoming more involved with enhancing the quality of life for women of all races. This development has led to the formation of groups such as the Women's Bureau of South Africa, Women for Peace, and the Women's Legal Status Committee. Members of organizations such as these work together across racial lines to promote cross-cultural understanding and to help identify and solve problems common to all women. These women believe that being a woman transcends racial divisions. Several business and professional women's clubs have organized seminars on career guidance and advancement at which women of all races share strategies for advancing. The re-emergence of the African National Congress's women's group is creating a new dynamic as this group contemplates cooperation or competition with the other women's groups and with individual women.

The South African Federation of Business and Professional Women (SAFBPW) has been part of the International Federation of Business and Professional Women for 40 years. It does not regard itself as a feminist group, but rather focuses on providing seminars on business topics for its members, expanding members' local and international business networks, and striving for equal opportunities and status for women in the economic, civil, and political arenas. The SAFBPW has created the unique Gold Award. This award is one of the most prestigious recognitions of fair employment practices in the country. To be considered, companies must be nominated by their women employees. Companies become finalists for the award if they: appoint women to senior management positions in nontraditional areas; provide absolute parity in salary and all fringe benefits; are leaders in innovative benefit policies such as extended maternity leave and daycare for employees' children; nominate all deserving candidates for supervisory and management training; and base promotions on merit while providing career development plans.

The SAFBPW Gold Award was launched in 1981. The number of participating companies has increased consistently; approximately 60 companies are nominated nationwide annually. An independent panel of judges selects five finalists annually to be honored, from which the winner is chosen. Since 1981, the winners have included Nestlé, Arthur Anderson Consulting, Gilbeys Distillers, Thomas Cook Rennies Travel, Murray and Roberts Construction, the Carlton Hotel, Pick and Pay Retailers, Anglo Alpha Cement Manufacturers, Southern Life Assurers, and the Fedsure Group. Nestlé, Arthur Anderson Consulting, and Thomas Cook Rennies Travel are non-South African multinationals, while the other companies are South African owned. As the media coverage of the award increases annually, the largest South African companies are starting to compete with each other to be nominated for the award. Their women staff members are using this competition for the Gold Award to ensure changes in personnel policies before their companies are nominated. The SAFBPW monitors the positive changes in equal opportunity policies among entrants; and, therefore, the judging criteria have become more stringent over the past decade.

The only network for women who are senior executives or recognized leaders in their fields is the Executive Women's Club. Membership is by invitation only and usually does not exceed 300 members. The aims are: to monitor and advance the interests of women executives; to promote the personal development of members; to promote the development of members' managerial skills; and to provide a forum for the interchange of ideas and experience among women executives. The club nominates a "businesswoman of the year" and provides grants to younger businesswomen to study for advanced business degrees. Some club members have joined international networks such at the European Women's Management Development Network and the Women in Management division of the American Academy of Management. This group neither regards itself as a feminist group nor conducts any political lobbying.

Career workshops

In response to women's interest in careers, the Women's Bureau of South Africa formed a career counseling work group, which developed training courses and workshops aimed at equipping women to meet higher-level professional and managerial job demands and to develop entrepreneurial and industrial skills. This group also developed vocational and career counseling methods to meet the needs of individual women and of companies (31;32).

Since 1989, the Graduate School of Management of the University of Pretoria has been the only institution to offer an annual "Women as Executives" program for women managers who are climbing the corporate ladder. The program is presented in two three-day modules, spaced two months apart. Between the two modules, participants investigate leadership, power, mentorship, and networking in their own companies and present their findings for peer review during the second module. They have identified three problems that are especially relevant to women: First, companies lack participative management, and women therefore have little input into decision making. Second, whereas women use expert power, they frequently neglect other power bases. And third, while participation in mentorship programs should be voluntary, women need to pay more attention to developing professional networks.

The majority of women executives participating in the program are between 30 and 39 years old. Most are married (56 percent), with the rest either never-married (21 percent) or divorced (23 percent). More than half of the women have no children (54 percent). Many are personnel or training managers (32 percent), while others are financial managers, marketing managers, general managers, corporate communicators, administrators, and researchers. Most women executives hold a bachelor's or higher degree. Whereas the women executives participating in the program are sponsored by their companies, they must take leave to participate.

With more women of all races seeking opportunities for self-development, some are now choosing entrepreneurship as a career. In 1984, about 70 percent of small businesses owned by blacks were run by women (27). Although many of these businesses are family concerns that women manage while their husbands work elsewhere, more black women are now managing their own shops. Since its inception in 1980, the Small Business Development Corporation (SBDC) claims to have created or maintained 350,000 jobs by financing small enterprises for all racial groups. The SBDC estimates that 25 percent of its clients in 1990 were woman entrepreneurs of all races (28).

South African women entrepreneurs are creating jobs for others as well. Among previous candidates for the Small Businesswoman of the Year Award, 54 percent of the 200 women usually employed no more than one other person when they started their ventures, while 46 percent employed between one and six people. After approximately four years, only 46 percent still employed only one to six people. Thirty-two percent already provided work for seven to twenty people, and 22 percent employed more than twenty people. These women entrepreneurs felt proud of their job creation and the training they provided their personnel (28).

Future Trends

In South Africa, the growing recognition of the shortages in qualified managerial and professional personnel augurs well for women aspiring to managerial careers, as this will create more opportunities for them. Although the numbers of white, black, Asian, and colored women who have moved into management remain relatively small, the trends are encouraging.

According to management policy regarding equal opportunity, South African companies may be classified into three categories (9). Companies in the first category have not yet taken note of the elimination of discriminatory clauses in the 1983 labor legislation. Managers in such firms act on their stereotypical views of women as workers and do not perceive creating equal opportunity as a relevant issue. The second category consists of firms who comply with the new labor legislation, are aware of women as a high-level resource, provide women with limited access to supervisory and management training, and advocate equality in pay and benefits. The majority of South African companies fall into this second category. The third category consists of companies who have been nominated by their women employees for the SAFBPW's Gold Award and have instituted equal opportunity for women and men of all races.

Many changes in South African society support women's advancement, such as the removal of discriminatory clauses in labor legislation, changes in the legal status of women, and the greater availability of educational opportunities. There is a greater awareness in multinational and South African companies of the aspirations and strengths of women and men of all races as well as of the problems related to their advancement. Barriers, such as unequal access to training, must still be overcome; however, women are campaigning against these unfair practices. More women are taking the initiative, such as in planning their own career development and in managing their own small businesses. These innovative women are becoming role models for other women. No less important is the greater readiness of women to support the career aspirations of women in general and to assist in their realization.

Notes

This chapter has been substantially updated since it first appeared in *Women in Management Worldwide* (1). The author wishes to thank Professor Dafna Izraeli for her valuable comments on an earlier draft of this article.

1 Confirmation of published figures by interview on August 29, 1991, with N. Brehm.
2 Confirmation of published figures by interview on August 29, 1991, with N. Brehm.
3 A career anchor is the occupational self-concept that an individual develops based on her or his self-perceived abilities, needs, attitudes, and values.

References

(1) Adler, N. J., and Izraeli, D. N. (1988) *Women in Management Worldwide*. Armonk, N.Y.: M. E. Sharpe.
(2) Brehm, N. (1989) "Women and Pay," *Institute of Personnel Management Journal* (March):20–21.
(3) Bryant, W. (1990) "Child Care Options for Employers," *Institute of Personnel Management Journal* (August):17–21.
(4) Buchwan, D. (1984) "Woman and Special Indian Problems," in *Women's Bureau Congress Report*, pp. 1–63. Pretoria.
(5) Central Statistical Services (1992) *SA Labour Statistics*. Pretoria: Central Statistical Services.
(6) Delport, E. (1993) Comments on the Abolition of Discrimination Draft Bill. Research report for the Women's Bureau, pp. 1–11, Pretoria.
(7) Erwee, R. (1984) "Creative Career Development," *RSA 2000* 6(1):12–20.
(8) Erwee, R. (1988) "Career Development Strategies in Organisations: Current Practices and Future Scenarios." Unpublished research report, University of Pretoria.
(9) Erwee, R. (1989) "Beyond the Foundations of Female Advancement," *Institute of Personnel Management Journal* (March):4–9.
(10) Erwee, R. (1990) "Career Anchor Profiles of a Sample of Business and Professional

Women," *SA Journal for Industrial Psychology* 16(2):5–12.

(11) Erwee, R. (1993) "Women's Bureau Working Group: Comments on the Promotion of Equal Opportunities Draft Bill." Research report for the Women's Bureau, pp. 1–35, Pretoria.

(12) Gon, S., Trollip, A. T., and Wendland, W. (1988) "Maternity Rights and Benefits under South African Law," *Industrial Relations Journal* (4th Quarter):57–63.

(13) Hennig, M., and Jardim, A. (1979) *The Managerial Woman*. London: Pan Books.

(14) Human, L., and Allie, F. (1989) "Attitudes of White English-Speaking Male Managers to the Advancement of Women in Business," *Institute of Personnel Management Journal* (March):22–24.

(15) Human, L., and Hofmeyr, K. (1984) "Black Managers in a White World: Strategy Formulation," *South African Journal of Business Management* 15(2):96–104.

(16) Human, L., and Hofmeyr, K. (1985) *Black Managers in South African Organisations*. Cape Town: Juta.

(17) Josefowitz, N. (1980) *Paths to Power*. Reading, Mass.: Addison-Wesley.

(18) Kanter, R. M. (1977) *Men and Women of the Corporation*. New York: Basic Books.

(19) Mkalipe, P. (1984) "Black Women in the Labour Market," *RSA 2000* 6(1):8–11.

(20) Moodley, K. (1986) "Multiculturalism in the Workplace of the Future." Paper presented at the End-of-the-Decade for Women Conference, Women's Bureau of South Africa, Johannesburg, September 4.

(21) National Manpower Commission (1986) "The Training and Development of Managers in the RSA, 1983/84 – A Factual Survey," pp. 1–89. Pretoria: National Manpower Commission and National Training Board.

(22) National Manpower Commission (1987) "High-Level and Middle-Level Manpower in South Africa: Recent Developments," pp. 1–75. Pretoria: National Manpower Commission.

(23) Newton, C. (1989) "Firm Favourites," *Femina* (October):82–83.

(24) Prekel, T. (1989) "The Quiet Contributors: Black Women at Work," *Institute of Personnel Management Journal* (March):10–14.

(25) Schein, E. (1987) "Individuals and Careers," in J. W. Lorsch (ed.), *Handbook of Organizational Behavior*. Englewood Cliffs, N.J.: Prentice-Hall.

(26) Schmikl, E. D. (1984) "Developing Tomorrow's Managers Today: An Examination of Superior/Subordinate Relationships," *South African Journal of Business Management* 15(2):109–115.

(27) Schomer, H. (1983) "South Africa: Beyond Fair Employment," *Harvard Business Review* (June):145–156.

(28) Small Business Development Corporation (SBDC) (1990) "Small Business Week," supplement to *Finansies en Tegniek* (October):1–23.

(29) South African Federation of Business and Professional Women (1988) *Gold Award: Report on the Competition*. Johannesburg: SAFBPW.

(30) Van der Walt, S. (1991) Participation Rates by Age Group: Women in 1985. Faxed communication. Pretoria: Human Sciences Research Council.

(31) Van Rooyen, J. (1984) "Developing the Female Labour Force of South Africa: A Challenge," *RSA 2000* 6(1):21–26.

(32) Van Rooyen, J. (1989) "Women and Organisational Power," *Institute of Personnel Management Journal* (March):16–19.

20 TANZANIA

Women Managers in the Tanzanian Civil Service

Wendy Hollway and Laeticia Mukurasi

Background

Tanzania is located on the coast of East Africa, just below the equator and covers 945,000 square kilometers; a considerably larger area than any European country and one-tenth the size of the United States. Tanzania is an agrarian country, with 86 percent of the labor force engaged in agriculture in 1980, and most people living in rural areas. Agriculture contributes 45 percent of the GDP (6;13). Women make up 51 percent of Tanzania's population of 23 million. Over 70 percent of the women are engaged in small cash crop and food crop production, and they produce 70 percent of all the food in Tanzania (9). Average annual per capita income is approximately US$280, which means that Tanzania rates among the poorest nations in the world (2). Compared to other economically developing countries, however, Tanzania has relatively small income differentials between rich and poor and a good record on health and education.

Tanzania is a former British colony and attained its political independence in 1961, when Tanganyika joined with Zanzibar. There are more than 120 ethnic groups in Tanzania, united by one national language, Kiswahili. The population is approximately half Christian and half Moslem. Unlike many sub-Saharan African countries, stable government has not been jeopardized by ethnic conflict.

During the colonial period, the emphasis on production of raw materials for British industry led to the establishment of large-scale plantations for the production of cotton, coffee, and sisal. Women were employed seasonally as casual laborers on the plantations. In addition, financial institutions were established, as well as an infrastructure geared to facilitate Britain's easy access to raw materials. At the time of independence, a rudimentary type of industrialization existed, based on an import substitution strategy and including initial processing of raw materials for exports. These industries tended to be capital-intensive and were predominantly foreign-owned (12).

Unequal access to education and to jobs in the industrial sector led to inequalities between women and men in employment in the newly emerging economic enterprises. The women's illiteracy rate is estimated to be above 60 percent, although it is considerably lower among the younger age groups, where girls have benefited from the government's policy of free access to education for all children. Between 1961 and 1981, the proportion of girls among school graduates increased from 11 percent to 29 percent and of women among college graduates from less than 2 percent to 15 percent (15). More girls than boys, however, drop out of school in response to their families' demands for their labor and due to the traditionally greater value attributed to boys' education.

In the Arusha Declaration of 1967, the government announced its policy of socialism and self-reliance and nationalized the major means of production. The public sector was intended to play a leading role in the development process. The government's recognition that human resources are the major source of economic development was important in encouraging the employment of educated women. It provided women with legitimate grounds for claiming equal treatment, in contrast to their prior exclusion on the grounds of gender.

Nationalization and state ownership of the means of production failed, however, to bring about the envisaged industrialization of the economy. In 1976, the government promulgated the Basic Industrialisation Strategy (BIS), which aimed at achieving self-reliance through establishing domestic-based heavy industry. The strategy failed to achieve its goals; and in 1982, Tanzania, then in a deep economic recession, negotiated with the World Bank and the International Monetary Fund for funding. Consistent with structural adjustment policies being pursued by these banks in the 1980s, they required Tanzania to cut public spending drastically, with social expenditures such as health becoming the major victim. As in most developing countries undergoing structural adjustment, these cuts had a disproportionately negative effect on women (1).

The private sector continued to exist alongside the public sector. Although the number of *parastatals* (publicly owned companies) grew from 67 at the time of nationalization in 1967 to more than 400 in 1990, the private sector accounted for more than 70 percent of the industrial value-added ratio in 1979.[1] The proportion of women employed in the nonagricultural sector, although rising, remains very small. In the decade up to 1980, the proportion nearly doubled from 9 percent to 16 percent. More recent figures are not available, but we can assume that this trend is continuing. Of this number, the finance sector accounts for 22 percent; services, 20 percent; and manufacturing, 11 percent (2). As elsewhere, most trained women are concentrated in teaching, nursing, and clerical occupations.

Women in Management

The growth of the public service sector, both the civil service and *parastatal* companies, created new opportunities for women, especially in positions of responsibility. In 1980, women constituted 20 percent of all employees in high- and middle-level positions (15), although their proportion in the highest echelons remained very small (see Table 20.1). Since 1988, the number of women ministers declined from twenty to three. It is possible that the larger number was influenced by the International Decade for Women.

When Tanzania announced its policy of socialism and self-reliance in 1967, it

Table 20.1   Women and men in leadership positions (1988)

	Number of women and men	Percentage of women
Government ministers	20	25.0
Deputy ministers	10	0.0
Regional commissioners	25	0.0
Principal secretaries	21	5.0
Area commissioners	190	12.0
Chairs of boards	450	0.2
Managing directors	40	0.0
General managers	410	0.2
Directors	74	2.7
Commissioners	24	0.0
Ambassadors	57	1.7

Source: Mukurasi, L. (1988) *Report for Workshop on Women Leaders in Tanzania.*

included women's emancipation and the achievement of equality between women and men as ingredients for achieving its goals. The president declared, "If we want our country to make full and quick progress now, it is essential that our women live in terms of full equality with their fellow citizens who are men" (11).

The government enacted legislation and issued a number of policy directives aimed at eliminating discrimination against women in employment.[2] For example, a civil service standing order, applicable also to the *parastatal* sector, provides that "all employment will be open to women who are suitably qualified, and there will be no difference between the salary and other terms of service of men and women officers of equivalent qualifications and experience" (14).

On giving birth to a child, all mothers regardless of marital status are entitled to 56 days' leave paid by the employer, in addition to 28 days of annual leave. The 56 days of maternity leave can be taken only once every three years. The government also directed that all fringe benefits, such as housing, leave allowance, transport entitlements, and medical benefits, apply to women in their capacity as employees and not as wives or dependents of men. Finally, women are forbidden to work night shifts and in the mines. The fact that employers must cover costs of benefits such as maternity leave may act as a disincentive for those in the private sector to employ women.

Efforts to identify and train women in management are very recent. The Institute of Development Management (IDM), a government-sponsored institution, and the Eastern and Southern African Management Institute (ESAMI), which is based in Tanzania but covers all the countries of southern Africa and has the regional governments' support, have organized workshops, carried out research, and developed training packages for women managers.

In 1988, the Institute of Development Management organized a workshop for women leaders in Tanzania, attended by government ministers, women heads of institutions, and women in other levels of management (7). In 1990, aid agencies[3] jointly funded research that was carried out in Tanzania, among other countries, to investigate the reasons why such a small number of women hold senior positions (8). The purpose of the research was to provide information for the design of specialized training packages at management training institutions. Also in 1990, the British Overseas Development Administration funded the research reported here (5).[4]

Little information is available about the position of women in the private sector. Government control of the public sector, and particularly of the civil service, has led to more women being employed at managerial and professional levels there than in the private sector.

Despite a rapidly expanding private sector, the public sector remains the major employer of professionals and managers. University graduates do not choose their jobs but are assigned to them. Women are usually placed in stereotypically women's fields, notably education, health, and personnel management. Fewer women trained in public administration are posted in *parastatals* than in the civil service.

Senior posts in the Tanzanian civil service are filled by presidential appointment and very few women surmount this barrier. The few who qualify are rarely selected. For most women, disadvantages accumulated over life seriously curtail their opportunities for career development, so that few women become sufficiently qualified, competent, and experienced to be included in the recruitment pool for senior positions. Relations between women and men in marriage and at work indicate some of the constraints that women managers face.

Married Life

Educated women commonly marry soon after graduating from university (typically in their mid-twenties) and start a family almost immediately. Professional women have smaller families than their mothers did, but two to five children is still standard. With no available nursery facilities, working women rely heavily on either their mother or, more frequently, on a "housegirl," who is often a relative who comes to live with the family. In a low-wage economy, housegirls are paid less than unskilled men; and a family member may earn little more than her keep. The civil service provides for either parent to take time off to care for a sick child; however, it is extremely unusual for a man to do so. Most men feel that doing so would reflect badly on their masculinity. Despite the fact that most educated women come from privileged families, the vast majority must work because the family's financial viability depends on it. Nonetheless, the domestic division of labor remains unchanged and virtually unchallenged. As one husband described the situation:

> Let me admit, the bulk of domestic chores are done by my wife, because she has more time (this man's wife was a teacher). At the same time, I believe it is one of her duties. Yes, one of her duties [laughs]. I do help when it is necessary, for example, when she falls sick. I do some cooking, special foods. And occasionally washing and ironing (5).

Women often interpret support from a husband in terms of lack of hindrance: "Support from my husband. What kind of support? If you mean that he has never hindered me from coming to the office, then right. That is the type of support I get" (5).

The husband is still presumed to have control over his wife's movements, even when these are required for her job or necessary for her career advancement. Until recently women were required to have their husbands' permission to go for further training, a custom upheld by male decision-makers. We came across many cases of women who had never been allowed to go for training, since it would involve being away from home. The following case of a senior and experienced officer presents an extreme example of the more insidious but day-to-day ways in which husbands' behavior can spoil the chances for women's equal treatment and in doing so probably poison the climate for other women as well:

Once I was required to go to two different districts in my region to do some work. As usual my boss informed me in advance and, knowing the type of husband I have, I decided not to ask him [for] permission, but to tell him that I was leaving my station for the districts on an official duty. When I told him about this, he kept quiet. The next day I went to my office and got my imprest [expenses money paid in advance] ready for the trip. At this time, my husband had been dismissed from his job and he was just at home. When I got back home, I gave him the money from the imprest so that he could purchase provisions when I was away. The next day I left in a ministry Landrover. When I was in the meeting, I received a call from my boss asking me if everything was fine when I left home. Since I had no worries about this, I answered in the affirmative, only to be told that my husband had gone to the office to inquire about my whereabouts, claiming that he had not seen me for two days. I became furious and told my boss not to take any note until I came back. As if this embarassment was not enough, after two days my husband went again to my boss and told him that he wanted me back, otherwise he would take a legal action against me. Being terrified, my boss dispatched another (junior) officer to meet me so that I could come back. I came back to find my boss worn stiff. From that day on they have never tried to give me assignments outside my station (5).

A boss who has encountered this kind of problem is loathe to take further risks. Given the tendency of male officers to generalize from single cases to all women, this sort of story, which circulates energetically through the networks, begins to provide a rationale for men who have financial or other reasons for not allocating traveling jobs to women. Other examples came up in interviews, for example:

One man used to tell his wife which route to take home. Another used to phone her up three or four times a day. X's husband used to deliver her to the office and pick her up. She was not allowed to get a lift. Then he bought her a car and she was forbidden to give anyone a lift (5).

These stories served to rationalize male bosses' preferences for allocating traveling to other men as a favor, since considerable financial benefits were associated with it. A woman community development officer told us, "I work under a man who

I can see puts personal interests first. Our work should involve traveling, but no women are normally allowed to travel. No one asks if you are available" (5).

Some women have developed tactics for challenging their male bosses' assumption that women require their husband's permission to travel: "He would ask if I had permission from my husband. I'd always tell him I had permission from my boss, and I don't ask permission from my husband, because he's not my boss in my job."

This woman's husband never complained about her traveling, but, as she pointed out:

> I've never given him cause for alarm. I'm very particular before I travel. If I know well in advance, I try to put my house in order. If I'm going to travel, I never give him surprises. So I try as much as possible to respect him as the head of the household. Sometimes it's difficult to satisfy these African men, you might do a little thing . . . and so I try and be extremely careful (5).

This woman implies that African men are more possessive of their wives than men elsewhere. In fact, the pattern varies greatly in different parts of Africa. Certainly many Tanzanian women perceive Western women as being more liberated from patriarchal control; but they do not have direct experience of the different, more covert, forms of control that still influence women's relations with men in the West. In Tanzania, patriarchal authority is a complex product of cultural practices that predate colonial domination and the effect of first Muslim and then Christian influences. It seems that the strong patriarchal tradition which gives men control over their wives and daughters transcends the effects of religious differences on gender relations in Tanzania.

Women at Work: Sexual Harassment

The professional women to whom we talked would dearly have liked for sexuality to have nothing to do with work. In fact, it makes life difficult for them in several ways. First, as we have shown, the husband's behavior, often the result of almost obsessive sexual jealousy, limits the woman's freedom of movement in ways that seriously impinge on her job. If the woman is not married, her freedom of movement is policed in a less direct way by assumptions about proper and improper behavior. Second, most of the women we talked to reported being sexually harassed. Third, regardless of how they behave, their success will provoke rumors that it was achieved through sleeping with some man in a powerful position.

The following response of a married man exemplifies a common attitude toward sexual harassment:

> *Researcher*: How would you react if an attractive woman started to work in your department?
> *Manager*: I would seduce her and what we agree is our affair and has nothing to do with work.

Implicit in this statement are three commonly held assumptions: first, it is perfectly natural that he should wish to seduce her; an attractive woman is automatically considered an object of a man's sexual attentions. Second, she has a free choice as to whether they have a sexual relationship or not; his power over her does not enter into his consideration. Third, sex is separable from work. Each of these assumptions is problematic for women and serves to legitimate sexual harassment.

When men harass women, the women almost always are junior to them, thus ones over whom the men have power. Every case reported to us fell into this category. As a senior woman manager explained, "I'm very comfortable with junior male officers because it's very rare they'll suspect a senior woman of running around with junior males. It's not common. But it's very common for male officers to go with junior female officers. So they can only suspect me with senior male officers."

A woman's power in the organization depends not only on her place in the hierarchy but also on her husband's status. For example, one woman described a time of family crisis when her husband lost his job: "Maybe that is also the time I was exposed to sexual harassment because people more senior . . . took advantage of that and thought I should give in because of my problems. I said no. . . . during that time I got a lot of sexual harassment [from] a lot of very senior people, in political positions, because they thought I would say, 'Now [that] I'm helpless, I'll go with them'" (5).

From this statement we can infer that women may be protected from sexual harassment if they have a powerful husband. We asked one man whether a man would try to seduce a woman who was the wife of a senior officer. The answer was threefold: one, "Not unless she was willing" (thus implying that in other cases, a woman's willingness is irrelevant); two, "One has to think twice," and three, "Only young girls are vulnerable."

Older women, especially if they are senior, generally experience less sexual harassment. One senior woman was quite relaxed about the subject: "I've had colleagues [make sexual advances]. I've always been very open with men. I've said I'm not interested; and I've made a joke with them. I've said, 'If I want to have some funny business, I'll go with a man who is higher than me. What benefit would I draw [from having relations] with a colleague?'" (5). Even in jest, the power relations are clear. The premise of the joke is that women consent to sex with superiors because they get benefits.

However, senior women are also subject to rumors about their sexual liaisons. Indeed, their visibility and the resentment many men feel about women's success make it virtually inevitable that rumors circulate. The common thread running through these rumors is that women have slept their way to their present position. As one senior man put it, "By lying horizontally, they rise vertically."

All that is required for a rumor to spread is the development of a friendly professional relationship between a woman and a man.

Once I heard a nasty rumour about myself – that my boyfriend was the minister of —. My work involved looking after this man and arranging various things for him when he came in [to the office]. He was nice, we used to talk. If he said, "Let's go for a beer" [I went]. I think I gave people reasons to think that I was running with that man, but I have never done it (5).

For junior women, sexual harassment is a constant hazard. As one man expressed it, "In principle a woman can refuse without repercussions, but in practice she cannot." The repercussions can easily affect a woman's career. In the civil service, only junior women such as secretaries are directly dependent on their departmental bosses for jobs. The secretaries' cases are the only ones to be recognized as a problem by senior management.

At management levels, women in the civil service are not directly dependent on their bosses for jobs and promotions. Nonetheless, senior women depend on their bosses for favorable appraisals, which affect their promotion prospects. The informal network at senior levels ensures that one man's grudge can turn into a woman's bad work reputation in the central office. One (unmarried) woman said that she had reason to believe that she received one transfer without promotion because her boss resented her refusal to have a sexual relationship. Another boss bore no grudges:

> This thing has been occurring throughout my career, but I've always told my bosses that if you want us to work as a team, let us not have a relationship, because, whatever we say, people won't believe that a decision has been made professionally. So let's only be friends. If I want to have a relationship, I'll look around. There's plenty of people who I'm not working with. This is what I told Mr – and he accepted it.

Men commonly use their power to pressure women to have a sexual relationship and this behavior presumably feeds into husbands' jealousies and results in husbands policing their wives' actions. The double standard is the norm; according to it, women do not engage in free sexual behavior. The "sexual revolution" never reached Tanzania. Any social relationship between a woman and a man ignites assumptions that sex is at its base. As a result, all contact between women and their male bosses or peers is deemed to be risky for women. (Male subordinates are a separate issue.) Consequently the limits imposed on women in their informal work relations are strict: "If you go to the hotel, they think you are a prostitute." Women are expected to return straight home after work and to socialize only in their husband's company. Bosses may fear asking women to work late or on weekends because of the minority of husbands who will object. One woman director explained that if she needed to ask one of her women subordinates to stay late, she sent a note in advance to the woman's husband. Of course men who are uncomfortable with having women in positions equal to theirs will use their nonavailability for late or weekend work as a reason for stopping all women from moving into jobs where they might be required to work late. Thus one man with responsibility for recruitment said, "We have not tried to recruit women because [a woman] might have problems in the field, for example, with her domestic responsibilities."

Women have authority within the organization, based on expertise and position; men, however, still tend to relate to women first as women – that is, as inferior. This dilemma produces the common situation in which women managers find their formal authority undermined. One woman manager gave the following example: "I once went for special duties in the region and left written "handing-over" notes for my male colleague on what was supposed to be covered while I was out. When I came back, everything was untouched. When I inquired, he said that he did not touch anything because he will not take instructions from a woman."

Women had to resist being positioned as other than a professional manager. Women's authority is challenged by being regarded not only as sex objects but also as maternal figures, as indicated in the following statement by a woman manager: "A lady is supposed to act like a mother. She's supposed to be kinder. 'Mama please' . . . I tell male officers, 'Don't call me mama. I'm not mama, I'm Mrs. —. I'm not here as a woman, I'm here as an officer.' If they don't get what they want, they'll say 'She's not a woman, not a motherly-like woman.'"

Networking

Restrictions on their informal socializing after work hours, even with women colleagues, were experienced by every woman we interviewed:

> Being an African society, there's limited movement for women in association just for the sake of it. If I want to meet a woman friend, there's no way I can nip out of my house and just meet her unexpectedly, like my husband can. Just after taking a shower "OK, I'm going out to meet my friends," simple as that. There's no way I can do that and I do think that meeting friends in social clubs is very relevant to your career, exchanging ideas and so on (5).

Unmarried women, although not limited in their movements by a husband, are constrained by gossip: "Networking for women like me who are single is not easy, because people might misunderstand you." Married women also feared being misunderstood, in particular by their husbands: "I do not see why I should push it [networking], particularly because I do not like such things to interfere with my relationship with my husband." In the case of either a married or an unmarried woman, there is the danger that the boss and his wife would assume a sexual motive:

> I know of a man who actually networks seriously by taking gifts to the boss to get recognised. Men do it and women cannot do that because there'll be misunderstanding from the boss and from the wife of the boss. The boss would think you wanted a relationship . . . and the wife would be scared, if you're not a friend of the wife's. But if the subordinate was a man, the wife would not be shocked. She would think they were discussing office things (5).

Prevalent norms of behavior for women seriously restrict women managers' ability to join informal networks and consequently to gain visibility, credibility, and access to information. One woman civil servant who occupied a job at the same level as her husband (which is not a rare occurrence) explained:

> In our society, if you're a female officer, you have to think twice before going to a pub. [If I went] with my husband it was OK, but we thought it was best for me to stay at home. My husband had a lot of interaction. Yes, he was always going off to the pub

with the boys. What they said about me when they were out, I never knew; whatever plans they made outside, I never knew. I relied on the information my husband brought back home. Sometimes I got it. Sometimes he would keep it to himself (5).

The following is another example of women's reliance on their husbands for networking. One senior woman and her husband occasionally socialize with his friends who do not work in the civil service: "Sometimes when I go out with my husband, I sit with his group; but even then, there are some things I can benefit a lot from, just sitting listening. There [is] lots of gossip – things about this ministry which I personally don't know, yet it's where I work."

The meeting places that matter most when it comes to visibility and influence are distinctly masculine, as shown in this example given by a woman manager:

It is hard [to network]. That is why some of us are never remembered when promotions are being discussed. There is a club for civil servants called the Leaders' Club. But it is a beer club where people drink alcohol and eat roasted meat. It is not customary for Tanzanian women to go to a club just to drink beer and eat meat. It would be a good club if it [were] designed to cater [to] families. You could then go there as a family. But the way it is designed it is a pub. Women here do not go to pubs. I do not frequent [it] but the few times I have been there the main activity [was] drinking (5).

In the Tanzanian public sector, informal contacts are all the more important because of the small size of the professional class, in which everybody assumes they know everybody else, and if they do not, that person must be a nobody. Who knows whom is governed by family, school, party membership, residence, and, to some extent, ethnic group.

It is commonly said that neither women nor men get far without a "godfather." The "godfather" provides support, which can range from corrupt financial influence and influence in return for sex to overcoming errors of omission, commission, and unfair treatment resulting from a malfunctioning bureaucracy. Women and men who lack informal ties to men of influence remain vulnerable and liable to being rendered invisible.

Middle-level women managers can use several sources to mobilize support at work, including their husband's influence, appeals to members of their ethnic group, and school friends; for example,

The fact that I was married to the regional party boss was important. I was promoted as a result of my husband's position. Then when we moved, my husband was no longer a regional party boss, without the power, but with the contacts previously made. I was promoted. My boss was a man. He was capable of listening to me. I took initiative on a lot of things and I always got his approval. He was also my husband's friend (5).

By the time women are in a senior position, particularly if they work in the capital, they have direct access to influence through their own working relationships.

The one thing I've solicited for is training. Being in Dar es Salaam made it easier. I used to go to Utumishi [the central offices] almost every day. When you are senior you can drop in, you can complain and answer them back. If I was out in the regions, I wouldn't know them. People used to be scared of Utumishi. I was so senior by then that I knew everyone. I've developed a lot of contacts. I was invited to almost all the official parties. By that time, my husband was more relaxed [about my independent socializing] (5).

In this account, three factors converge to promote the woman executive's influence: being senior, being in the capital, and her husband's accepting attitude to her independent socializing as she got older and more senior and once he earned more than she did.

Women and Men in the Organization

Most women we interviewed had been obliged to move when their husband's job changed. Although the moves were often to the detriment of their own careers, they accepted the inevitability of having to move: "I was not bitter at having to move because of my husband's posting, because I believed that I had to make the sacrifice." The government as the main employer believes this to be the case as well. Generally, when they transfer a man, they expect the wife to follow, no matter what her qualifications or job position. If she is a government employee, they will eventually find her another position, but its appropriateness is usually compromised by the circumstances.

Women claimed that they were not given equal access to training. In Tanzania, as in most other ex-colonies in the Third World, training occupies a critical place in career opportunities. Until the mid-1960s, very few Africans had access to education or training, and all senior job occupants were white. A shortage of skilled personnel still exists; and in the race for training opportunities, women are losing out.

Women who managed to get training usually took the initiative themselves and used their informal influence to gain access. Frequently, however, women lack information about available opportunities, as expressed by one woman: "We do not know if there is a training program here. In fact, we think there is no training program here. We see people go for training but nothing happens to us."

A pronounced lack of performance criteria for promotion and a lack of feedback on performance are common. Several women pointed out that they were judged on isolated incidents related to their domestic commitments, rather than on their actual job performance. As voiced by one woman:

I am not satisfied with the way I have progressed . . . in 1972 I perceived that some moves were being made to prevent me from ever being promoted. Junior officers were recommended for promotion and I got to know about them. When I knew, I began to look for the reasons. I approached the Civil Service Commission and they said that reasons were not given but my name was not submitted for consideration. So I requested them to look into the matter. Luckily they followed up [on] the matter and I was promoted (5).

The Civil Service Commission has responsibility for dealing with such complaints, which is an important safeguard. However, they do not always deal with complaints satisfactorily.

Promotion in the civil service depends on a person receiving three satisfactory annual performance appraisals. The appraisal form specifies that "it is the duty of the assessor to inform the person being assessed of the outcome of the appraisal." Yet we did not hear of a single case in which the boss had given the woman feedback on what was contained in her appraisal. Most women even assumed that appraisals were "completely confidential." The actual administration of the performance appraisal system is haphazard. Forms are often not issued, or not filled in, or not returned and processed for three successive years. Most women understand that promotion depends more on the informal system than on performance appraisals: "A boss can lift the telephone and talk to another boss and say anything he wants about you, which is not recorded" (5).

> There are haphazard modes of promotion. A person may recommend his friend, his brother, or a person who is really hard working, which means promotion in the civil service is not necessarily based on an employee's performance. Even when one is promoted, one is never sure on which grounds one has been promoted (5).

One senior woman, when asked about her boss's qualifications, said, "The report I have is that he failed all the requisite administration exams. When they were designing the scheme of service, they did not incorporate the requirement to pass exams, so he was brought here" (5).

The move to presidential appointment is often achieved by networking, nepotism, and corruption. Most women felt that as long as the formal system is so comprehensively undermined by informal influence, men will have a wide margin of advantage in obtaining top positions in the civil service.

Change Strategies

Present conditions for improvement of women managers' opportunities in the Tanzanian civil service are favorable. Aid agencies who fund the vast majority of employee training are anxious to improve their record on training women.[5] This international aid climate, combined with the internal political climate, is such that senior policy-makers are under pressure to demonstrate that women are not discriminated against. Moreover, a woman minister heads the Civil Service Department, which is responsible for the personnel function throughout the civil service and beyond into the *parastatal* sector. The minister has been in a sufficiently strong position to challenge the climate of the civil service and to influence some key appointments; for example, the director of training, is now a woman.

Questions of strategy remain unclear, however, to the women involved. To what extent does women's advancement in management depend on bureaucratic reform? What are the advantages and disadvantages of quota policies? Could Western-style affirmative action work? Should women strive to become part of men's informal networks? How effective can women's networks be and what form should they take? The newly established Women's Unit in the Civil Service Department would benefit by knowing answers to these questions in order to argue for appropriate terms of reference and resources and to devise a strategy for fair advancement opportunities for women.

The Women's Unit was established in response to pressures on the civil service to demonstrate opposition to discrimination against women employees. However, resistance to these pressures may help to account for the form that this unit has taken so far. It does not have an independent budget, and its brief is restricted to policy. The Women's Unit is expected, for example, to make changes in rules and regulations to ensure that there are no remaining asymmetries in the way that female and male employees are treated. However, in an organization in which implementation, rather than policy, is the problem, the unit risks being irrelevant, especially in a directorate whose senior members are unsympathetic to its purpose. It is easy to render such a unit ineffectual by appointing a woman as head who has neither the qualifications, experience, connections, nor independence necessary to challenge the status quo.

What should the main strategies of a strengthened unit be? First, there is clearly a case for reforming the bureaucracy; for example, an improved performance appraisal system, clear job schedules, and job orientation would enhance the position of women managers.

The history of equal opportunity in the West can be seen as an attempt to improve the fairness of bureaucratic procedures within a legal and policy framework (4).[6] No such measures exist in Tanzanian law. It would be easy to recommend that the Tanzanian government put into place a combination of equal opportunity measures as part of its wider agenda of reforming the public sector bureaucracy. However, while desirable, it is unlikely to be effective in practice. Widespread bureaucratic malfunction has led to a dominant informal culture, premised on patriarchal traditions, that is inimical to women's interests.

The Western women-in-management literature has emphasized the importance of women's entry into informal networks and that individual women's tactics must include networking if they are to achieve promotion. However, women's equal access to these networks in Tanzania is not a viable policy, at least in the short term, primarily because the informal networks are tainted with a reputation for corruption and nepotism. One senior woman even suggested that the importance of networking should be reduced rather than stressed as a means for women enhancing their opportunities: "The way society looks at networking is with a great deal of suspicion. If one of your tasks is to create an enabling environment for women, then you should be careful that the issue of networking does not become the dominating factor, that people must meet in clubs" (5).

The strength of the networking model is that it recognizes that the exercise of power is not limited to formal channels and formal statutes. Its weakness is that it supports the view that women must change to fit in; that women's exclusion is *their* problem. It does not address the way that women managers are subjected to power relations, which continuously undermine their authority and influence and threaten their career progress. In Tanzania, men's networks are exclusive, nepotistic, and often corrupt. Alternatively, women's networks have the potential to be different.

A women's network has been established in a few ministries of the civil service by a handful of fairly senior women managers in Dar es Salaam, who know each other personally. The success of the network so far has been patchy and its perpetuation depends on the few women who are prepared to spend the time and effort to organize it. Support from the Women's Unit might help to strengthen and legitimate this initiative. Linked to the Women's Unit, such a network could provide women with both formal and informal aspects of organizational influence, a combination that to date has been problematic for women managers.

Notes

1 Later figures are not available.
2 The law provided for enforcement through the Civil Service Commission in the case of civil servants and the Standing Committee on Parastatal Organization and the Industrial Court in case of employees in the *parastatal* sector.
3 It was funded by the United Nations Development Program, the Educational Development Institute of the World Bank, the International Labor Organization, the Commonwealth Secretariat, and others.
4 The research was conducted with a research team from the Tanzanian civil service. We defined a manager as anyone who entered the service starting at GS3, which is the grade where graduates enter. It was recognized that many women at this level would not hold managerial responsibilities, but also that they would be likely to do so in the future. The main focus of the research was to obtain accounts of their experiences from women managers. This was done through in-depth interviewing. In addition, groups of women and men managers were convened in various ministries and matched pairs of women and men, who had graduated together and entered the same field in the civil service, were contrasted in terms of their career progression. We should like to thank all those who gave their time and experience in talking to us, and, through their clarity, contributed to the picture we provide here.
5 For example, the International Labor Organization, USAID, the British Overseas Development Administration, the Canadian International Development Agency, the Swedish International Development Agency, and the European Community.
6 It has not been effective in improving the numbers of women in senior positions in the British Civil Service.

References

(1) Cornia, G. A., Jolly, R., and Stewart, F. (eds.) (1987) *Adjustment with a Human Face: Protecting the Vulnerable and Promoting Growth*. Oxford: Clarendon.
(2) Government of Tanzania (1985) *Economic Survey*.
(3) Government of Tanzania (1979–80) *Survey of Employment and Earnings*.
(4) Hansard Society for Parliamentary Reform (1990) *Women at the Top*. London: Hansard Society.
(5) Hollway, W., and Mukurasi, L. (1991) *The Position of Women Managers in the Tanzanian Civil Service*. Report to the Government of Tanzania and the British Overseas

Development Administration.

(6) *IBRD World Development Report* (1986) London: Oxford University Press.

(7) Institute of Development Management (1988) *A Report on the Workshop on Women Leaders in Tanzania*. Mzumbe.

(8) Institute of Development Management (1990) *A Study of Women in Management in Tanzania*. Mzumbe.

(9) Low, A. M. (1989) *Women in the Public Sector in Developing Countries*. Report to British Overseas Development Administration.

(10) Mukurasi, L. (1988) *Report for Workshop on Women Leaders in Tanzania*.

(11) Nyerere, J. K. (1967) *Socialism and Rural Development*. Dar es Salaam: Government Printer.

(12) Rweyemamu, J. (1973) *Underdevelopment and Industrialization in Tanzania*. London: Oxford University Press.

(13) United Nations (1986) *World Population Prospects*. New York: United Nations.

(14) United Republic of Tanzania (1971) *Government Standing Orders*. Section D.20.

(15) United Republic of Tanzania (1986) *Manpower Survey*.

21

ZIMBABWE

The Legacy and Opportunities for Women Managers in Zimbabwe

Helen J. Muller

The achievement of independence in 1980 transformed Zimbabwean society. The dissolution of white hegemony over political life enabled black Zimbabweans to ascend to positions of power in both the public and private sectors. Independence presented new opportunities in leadership and management, and their resultant dilemmas, to the women and men who the white Rhodesian settler regime had disenfranchised. Moreover, the new government, which was elected on a socialist political platform, intended to give women the chance to transcend the confines of traditional culture and colonial oppression. Despite a framework of legal equality, cultural, racial, and organizational issues have complicated women's ability to exploit the emerging opportunities.

Several historical legacies influence the political economy of gender and race relations in Zimbabwe. These legacies directly affect women's access to managerial and leadership positions in contemporary society. This chapter illustrates how the legacies of traditional culture, colonialism, and the liberation struggle have shaped the situation of women managers. It highlights how women's experiences and chances for advancement differ across organizational sectors. It assesses the constraints that women face in entering and retaining managerial positions within each sector. Examples of organizations and individual women managers are presented to illustrate their experiences.

Historical Context

Traditional background

The Shona and Ndebele are Zimbabwe's dominant ethnic groups. The Shona, who constitute about 80 percent of the population, trace their culture to A.D. 1200. The Ndebele, who constitute approximately 16 percent of the population, settled in Zimbabwe in the 1830s. Both cultures are patriarchal and patrilocal. The Shona economy was agriculturally based, the Ndebele economy was pastoral (61). Production in both was differentiated by gender (38;45;50), with individual women elevating their social status through hard work and by bearing children, especially sons (24).

Polygamy was widely practised, and bridewealth payment (*lobola*) was an important custom. *Lobola* compensated the bride's family for the loss of her labor and transferred the rights to a woman's labor to her husband's family (8). Although their origins are rooted in traditional economic transactions, these customs persist today among blacks. Describing precolonial society, Robert Mugabe, the current Executive President of Zimbabwe and the leader of the Zimbabwe African National Union (ZANU) political party said, "The general principle governing relationships between men and women has, in our traditional society, always been that of superiors and inferiors. Our society has consistently stood on the principle of masculine dominance – the principle that the man is the ruler and the woman his dependent and subject" (30:102).

Mugabe has actively supported equality among women and men. Although historical progress has affected social relationships, traditional roles for women and men remain significant in modern Zimbabwe. The amount of *lobola* is going up with increasing material consumption and legislation to limit the number of wives has been debated.

During the 1890s, white settlers and miners, under the direction of Cecil Rhodes, migrated north from South Africa to colonize the territory they subsequently named Southern Rhodesia. In opposition to the invasion, Mbuya Nehanda, a Shona spirit medium and still one of the two most powerful religious figures in Zimbabwe, organized the first protest and rebellion in 1896 (47;54). Sentenced to death and executed by the colonists in 1898, her role as a woman resistance leader was unique; she later inspired women in the liberation struggles.

Colonialism

In 1924 Southern Rhodesia became a self-governing British Crown Colony whose governance was restricted essentially to white males, even though they constituted only a tiny minority of the population (53). Racial segregation remained the norm in social and political life. Education was primarily directed at whites and some black men. In 1957, the franchise, heretofore restricted to men and British women, was extended to include black married women (but only the first wife in a polygamous marriage). Virtually no blacks, however, could vote because of restrictive income, property, and educational requirements (57). In 1965, under the leadership of prime minister Ian Smith, Southern Rhodesia declared her independence from Britain by invoking the Unilateral Declaration of Independence (UDI). Southern Rhodesia became an "illegal state" and continued the white supremacist regime despite international economic and arms sanctions.

To ensure the Rhodesians' high standard of living, black men were recruited from rural areas and forced into a migratory labor system to work in urban factories, in mines, and on white-owned farms. As a consequence, African women and children became the majority residents in the rural areas, where they assumed responsibility for subsistence agricultural production. Africans were forced to live in areas designated as tribal trust lands (now called communal areas), while the whites took the prime agricultural lands for themselves. Today 75 percent of the population is rural. For the most part, the movement of African women to urban areas is a recent phenomenon (13).

Liberation struggle

A protracted liberation struggle ensued during the late 1960s and 1970s. Thousands of young blacks fled to neighboring countries to train in guerilla warfare; tens of thousands fell victim to the widespread violence, especially in rural areas. Many Zimbabwean women played active roles either alongside their male comrades during the armed struggle (*Chimurenga*), by providing food and shelter, or by transporting and hiding supplies. Women, initially overlooked as potential soldiers, became active combatants for both the Zimbabwe African National Army (ZANLA, the ZANU armed forces) and the army of the Patriotic Front–Zimbabwean African People's Union (PF–ZAPU) (30;63).

By the end of the war, as many as one-quarter of the 30,000 guerrillas were women (51). As many as 250,000 women were actively involved in the struggle (3). The changing roles of women during the *Chimurenga* are captured by Naomi Nhiwatiwa: "We have women who train the cadres . . . we have women commanders who supervise . . . this is a change from when women weren't allowed to play a role in the community, into actually playing a major role in the revolution and being successful in being able to command men in the process" (56:248).

The common spirit and emergent roles of women and men liberation leaders, shaped by Marxism, resulted in the new state's eqalitarian policies and programs. A few of the most decorated women's liberation leaders became members of parliament and ministers in the Mugabe government. Then prime minister Mugabe and his wife, who were both *Chimurenga* activists, became vocal supporters of women's rights.

Women, Development, and Management

Only a tiny elite group of African women have been able to attain professional or managerial positions (16;31;46). The overwhelming majority of women remain subservient, economically dependent, illiterate, and in unskilled jobs in the secondary labor market and the agricultural sector (5;37).

Even today, development projects operate on the implicit assumption that women's status improves as a result of industrialization. Traditional modernization theory assumes that modernization is coterminous with industrialization and that the latter brings progress to both women and men. The increasing exploitation and continuing low standard of living of Third World women challenge the premises of this theory. There is growing awareness of the need to examine the political economy of gender in development strategies and the differential access that women and men have to power, including in economic and bureaucratic state structures (14;49). The material benefits of progress, for the most part, have gone to and are owned by men; and in Africa, until recently, this has meant European men.

British colonists brought Western management practices to Southern Rhodesia.

Professional management helped the Rhodesians to consolidate political power and develop a standard of living comparable to that of Europeans. The racist patriarchal capitalism of the colonists (10;18), grounded in Victorian values, justified the inferior status of blacks and ensured the subordinate status of white women to white men. At independence, the new government adopted a policy of national reconciliation that forbade nationalization of the private sector, thus recognizing the whites' vital contributions to the nation's economic development. As a result, whites remained in control of the industrialized private sector. The politics of black advancement in Zimbabwean organizations are largely influenced by this context of persisting white hegemony. The politics of women's advancement are also influenced by the inherent patriarchy of Western managerial practices.[1]

We must consider these historical factors when we analyze the situation of women managers in contemporary Zimbabwe. Although both black and white women have been subordinate to their male counterparts, they have fundamentally different role transitions with which to contend. White women must contend with the female-domestic-role–male-public-role transition, with its inherent managerial patriarchy. Black women must overcome the constraints of traditional African gender role distinctions, the legacy of colonialism and its inherent racism, as well as managerial patriarchy. Also, whereas black women's experience was in a rural agricultural society, white women's experience was predominantly urban and industrial.

Statistical Profile of Women

Zimbabwe has a population of about ten million, of whom 1.5 percent, or approximately 150,000, are white. A high percentage of people (47 percent) are below fifteen years of age (7), reflective of the high birthrate and declining mortality rates among blacks. The relative youth of the population, coupled with a high annual population growth rate of 3.3 percent (58), suggests that women have many children to care for and that pressure on the labor market for jobs will be relentless.

In 1986–1987, only 16 percent of all adult women were employed in the formal (modern) sector of the economy, compared to 43 percent of all adult men (7). Economically active women were found in agriculture (80 percent), industry (4 percent), and services (16 percent). The percentage distribution of economically active men was, respectively, 64 percent, 15 percent, and 21 percent. In this distribution, Zimbabwe is representative of Africa as a whole (15). Wages are relatively low; for example, in 1987 the average monthly wage in manufacturing was Z$527.90 (Z$2.25 = US$1 in 1990) (23).

Government labor force analyses, with data on professional and managerial women, differ substantially in their findings. The Zimbabwe Labor Force Sample Survey of 1986–1987 (23) reported more than double the number of employees reported by the Annual Occupational Survey of Employees of 1985 (2). The differences might be attributed to sampling error or poor data collection methods.

The Occupational Survey of Employees of 1985 found that women in the professional, technical, and related workers' category (including medical workers and teachers) constituted 26 percent of the 61,880 total workers in this category. The racial composition was African, 79 percent; European, 17 percent; and Asian/ Colored, 4 percent. Women in the administrative and managerial category (including legislative officials, government administrators, and managers) constituted 10 percent of the 6,025 total workers in this category. The racial composition was African, 29 percent; European, 60 percent; and Asian/Colored, 11 percent.

Whereas the proportion of Africans among professional women has increased in recent years, in management, European women continue to hold the majority of positions, despite their decline in the overall labor force. Moreover, the number of women in management may be overestimated. A survey of women in manufacturing found that women who identified themselves as top and middle managers were, in fact, mostly white secretaries and typists (26).

A tremendous surge in literacy and educational enrolment followed independence when the government enacted a nonracial policy and allotted about 20 percent of the budget to education (4;11). In the ten years between 1979 and 1989, primary school enrolment more than tripled and secondary school enrolment multiplied nine times (17). Yet disparities between women's and men's educational attainment persist. In 1990, the adult literacy rate (women as a percentage of men) was 81, and during 1986–1990, the enrolment ratio of women as a percentage of men in secondary school was 86 (58). Although the student body at the University of Zimbabwe grew from eight blacks and 68 whites in 1957 to 7,264 blacks and 300 whites in 1988 (9), the enrolment of women students as a proportion of men students remained static at undergraduate and postgraduate levels during the 1980s, with women making up only about one-quarter of the enrolled students (12).

A Framework for Women Managers

The status of women managers as well as their experiences and opportunities for advancement vary across organizational sectors. The private industrial sector, the public or governmental sector, and the nonprofit organizational sector are reviewed in this chapter with respect to their constraints and opportunities for women managers.[2] Some results from the author's recent exploratory study of senior level women managers in Zimbabwe are included.[3]

The following analysis of the issues that affect women's capacity to hold managerial positions unfolds at three levels:

1 Public policy and legal mandates that affect women's equality in political and economic life and their ability to actively participate as adults and self-sufficient persons;

2 Organizational attributes, both structural and behavioral, that shape women's ability to advance in the professions and into managerial ranks; and

3 Sociocultural traditions and expectations that mold women's roles in the family and that shape women's and men's expectations of themselves and what is acceptable behavior with the opposite sex at home and at work.

The New Policy Agenda

The new socialist government committed itself to redress the discriminatory practices that prevailed in colonial Zimbabwe. Legislation adopted in the early and mid-1980s provided a framework to support women's rights and their participation in modern economic and political life. The significant policy changes included the following:

Legal Age of Majority Act (LAMA) (1982) granted women, like men, majority status at the age of eighteen. Prior to LAMA, black women were minors for life – unless they were widows – and subordinate to the authority of their fathers or husbands. Formerly, white women attained majority status at age 21 and enjoyed full contractual rights. *Lobola* and "seduction damages" (a man engaging in sexual relations with a female minor without the father's consent could be legally sued) could now be claimed, in theory, by a woman who had reached majority status. Women could also sue for divorce and to establish credit.

Minimum Wages Act (1982) and Labor Relations Act (1984) established provisions for minimum wages, equal pay for equal work, and maternity leave. It became illegal for employers to discriminate on several grounds, including sex and race, in the areas of wages, recruitment, promotion, training, and retrenchment. Women who worked at least one year were entitled to maternity leave at three-quarters pay for three months, and were permitted time off during the day for breastfeeding, all at employer's expense.

Matrimonial Causes Act (1985) entitled women, upon divorce, to become beneficiaries of property that was acquired during marriage and to obtain custody of children. Previously women could not inherit property, had little opportunity for ownership of material property, and relinquished custody of their children to their husbands upon divorce.

Tax Law of 1987 permitted wives and husbands to be taxed according to their respective incomes. Previously wives and husbands were taxed at the highest rate that either one of them classified for – a measure that acted as a disincentive for women to work outside the home (35).

Today, only a few privileged women are able to take advantage of these legal rights. For the overwhelming majority of women, little change has been felt, and in some cases, there have been negative ramifications. For example, the private sector may resist hiring women because it has to pay for maternity leave. A senior governmental official explained that a small factory closed because the owners could not afford to pay for maternity leave. This example was evidence, she felt, that women were losing ground because of the new laws. However, a professional woman in government said that she was not afraid of losing her job as a result of her third pregnancy; and after maternity leave, she would be assured the same job at the same pay.

Heralded by some as landmark pieces of legislation (34;39;65), others have been more cautious and have pointed to the vast disparities between what the new laws permit and what African customary law and traditional culture allow (18;27;28).

Some claim that the state's policies toward women's reproduction and production are contradictory because the high birthrate and prohibition of abortion deter women from entering the public sphere and workforce (25).

Several women public policy experts explained that most women remain unable to make use of their legal rights because traditional cultural expectations are prevalent and the government's enforcement ability is weak. Also, most women lack the economic self-sufficiency necessary to survive were they to be socially ostracized for asserting their legal rights.

Public Sector Organizations

The government's policy toward employment of women manifests itself in the increasing inclusion of women in public sector jobs. A presidential directive enacted soon after independence called for greater representation by blacks in decision-making positions in the civil service. This policy was also a stimulus to affirm greater gender diversity in the civil service.

In early 1991, Dr. Eddison Zvobgo, the Minister of State for the Public Service, publicly reiterated the government's commitment to advancing women in public service and stipulated that women should hold 30 percent of civil service management positions. He said that the Public Service Commission would investigate the advancement of women and ensure that more women were promoted into management. As part of this effort, seminars on women in management, organized by the Zimbabwean Institute of Public Administration and Management, were held in 1991 (20;21).

The proportion of women at the level of assistant secretary or above in civil service positions increased from less than 1 percent in 1981 to 9 percent in 1984, with most positions in the health and education ministries (3). Statements from my sources in Zimbabwe suggest that women hold about 9 to 10 percent of current civil service management positions as well as publicly elected offices. After the 1990 election, women represented 5 percent of the members of parliament, a decline from 9 percent prior to the election (1).

There are three women, out of a total of 22 members, in the ZANU Politburo, the highest body of authority in the country (19). Angeline Makwavarara, Ambassador to Sweden, is the first Zimbabwean woman to receive an appointment as a government representative to a foreign nation.

Ministers are selected from the elected members of parliament. The three women ministers, who made up roughly 10 percent of the 29 cabinet members in 1990, all had important roles during the liberation struggle:

> Victoria Fikile Chitepo, the widow of ZANU's leader in exile during the resistance, Minister of Information, Posts, and Telecommunications
> Fay Chung, of Chinese origin with an MA from Leeds University, Minister of Education and Culture
> Joyce Teurai Ropa Mujuru, Minister of Community and Cooperative Development

Joyce Mujuru's background illustrates the unusual circumstances that some black Zimbabwean women endured in their rise to power. She was born in 1955 in one of the tribal trust lands. One of ten children, her education was aborted because of the *Chimurenga*. Comrade Mujuru encountered severe hardship when she lived in the guerilla camps in Zambia (41). There she contracted cerebral malaria, married, and gave birth to a child during the middle of a battle. Her husband was then the second in command of ZANLA and became commander in chief of the Zimbabwean army. She was a guerrilla officer, the director of politics at a refugee camp, and at the age of 22 became secretary of women's affairs and a member of the ZANU central committee. She became one of the world's youngest cabinet ministers and the first woman to hold a ministerial post in Zimbabwe (30).

Shortly after independence, in 1981, the Ministry of Community Development and Women's Affairs was established to oversee and spearhead the mobilization of women in economic and political affairs. Naomi Nhiwatiwa was appointed deputy minister and Joyce Mujuru became minister. The ministry has been the target of much controversy over the years (51;55). Recently, Women's Affairs was relegated to departmental status, with a deputy permanent secretary as head, and placed under the Ministry of Political Affairs. Several senior-level women with whom I spoke believed that Women's Affairs had not done enough in the way of advocacy, that its effectiveness had been compromised, and that its movement to Political Affairs is evidence that its role is to be diminished.

The regionally prominent University of Zimbabwe (UZ), with 10,589 students and 900 teachers is an important resource for women's professional development (17); several well-known women faculty conduct research on women. UZ's academic staff in the lower ranks was made up of 21 percent women lecturers. In the higher ranks of senior lecturer and above, constituting 29 percent of the academic staff, only 2 percent were women (12). The climate in the upper-level ranks is not hospitable to women, and although tacit discrimination exists throughout the university, particularly in higher-level positions, it is not openly acknowledged because discrimination is illegal.

The Faculty of Commerce (business and accounting) at UZ offers graduate and undergraduate business degrees. In 1990, out of 24 academic faculty members, most with master's degrees, there were three recently appointed women faculty, and only four out of 60 MBA students were women. A program administrator said that women MBA candidates find it difficult to complete their studies because they experience many familial and organizational obstacles. For example, when a problem in a student's family requires attention, it is the woman student who must attend to the problem. Because families place a higher value on men completing their education, their familial obligations in such situations are secondary to a woman's.

Private Sector Organizations

Zimbabwe has one of the largest and most diversified manufacturing sectors in sub-Saharan Africa, except for South Africa. In comparison to other African countries,

Zimbabwe's physical and business infrastructure is good, and its banking and financial sector is well developed (29).

About 50 percent of the industrial sector is foreign-owned (22), with transnational corporations and local nonindigenous capital controling over 80 percent of the productive sectors (43). Forty-four major foreign firms have subsidiaries in Zimbabwe, the majority being American- or British-owned (42). Forty-four American companies, of all sizes, have subsidiaries in Zimbabwe (60). Most American companies employ Zimbabwean managers to run their subsidiaries; a few employ women in management positions.

A survey of private sector firms for the Confederation of Zimbabwe Industries found whites (2 percent of the population) holding 62 percent of senior management, 35 percent of middle management, and 22 percent of junior management positions. The survey's author noted that white managers believe "blacks are incompetent and cannot do the job" (48:6). In many instances the appointment of blacks to higher management positions is more cosmetic than substantive, and whites still do not want blacks in charge of policy and overall company direction (10;43). Women occupy very few management positions at any level in the private sector (59), but white women have more opportunities for management positions than do black women (3).

The Coalition of Private Business Companies provides an example of some of the racial and gender issues with which organizations are struggling. The Coalition was organized to foster better working relationships between certain Zimbabwean subsidiaries of large multinational companies and Zimbabwean-owned businesses. For many years, the board of directors remained in the control of the Rhodesian men who managed the local subsidiaries of foreign-owned firms. They resisted bringing both women and black men into its membership. Within the last few years, the board has begun to diversify its membership as a result of the work of its executive director, a black woman who holds foreign citizenship. Paradoxically, while the board was resisting its own racial and gender integration, it was not averse to appropriating funds for organizing a group of local women business managers to help them improve their skills and develop a support network.

One of the major constraints to private sector growth in Zimbabwe is the lack of qualified senior and middle managers as well as technical personnel, in both the public and private sectors (29). Senior- and middle-management ranks in many large companies are dominated by white managers who have worked their way up the ladder with little formal business education. Few black Zimbabweans have had higher management experience. A number of interviewees in one study stated that black junior- and middle-level managers are often more educated than their white counterparts and than white senior managers (29).

With the encouragement of the government, several locally based and international organizations are involved in training women managers, assisting women entrepreneurs, and developing income-generating projects for women. The Zimbabwe Women Finance Trust, an affiliate of Women's World Banking, assists women entrepreneurs in rural and urban areas by providing credit, training, and technical assistance. In 1990, eight loans had been made, ranging from 2,000 to Z$10,000

(29). The Eastern and Southern African Management Institute has several women professionals, specializing in women-in-development and management, who conduct research and training.

The U.S. Agency for International Development (USAID) is involved in a major private sector initiative in Zimbabwe. USAID has tied part of its financial aid program to enhancing women's advancement in employment. One-third of its private sector training activities must address women's needs; for example, it specified that as a condition of its purchase of capital equipment for the Zimbabwean railroads, women have to be targeted for advancement to management.[4] The USAID contract with Labat-Anderson Inc. for private sector human resources training in Africa stipulates that one-third of the trainees have to be women.

Anecdotes in newspapers, a few consultant reports, and government officials' speeches reveal the behaviors and attitudes that thwart women's job retention and advancement in the formal labor market.[5] Women are held back due to the patriarchal concept of the importance of many children, which perpetuates multiple pregnancies; the objections of husbands who fear women's emancipation and liberation; the lack of education that women receive because parents place a low value on educating female children; the channeling of women into jobs that perpetuate sexual stereotypes; and pervasive sexual harassment on the job (10;26;33).

Nonprofit and Other Organizations

Nongovernmental organizations include a variety of nonprofit and quasi-governmental organizations. Many specifically focus on women's issues. Some examples are the Zimbabwe Women's Bureau, the Musasa Project (a domestic violence center), and the Women's Action Group (which publishes *Speak Out* and is involved in women's advocacy). *Parastatals* are quasi-governmental organizations; some, like the Zimbabwe Family Planning Council, focus on women. International organizations, such as the United Nations Fund for Women (UNIFEM) and the United Nations Family Planning Fund have offices in Harare and provide grants to nonprofit and *parastatal* organizations for services to women. The Canadian International Development Agency recently established a women's resource center in Harare.

The history of indigenous women's organizations can be traced to the introduction of Christianity in Zimbabwe when women organized groups around various church denominations (36). The groups were used as a vehicle to spread teachings of the church and eventually encompassed social service activities, including the YWCA and women's professional associations. Women's groups have actively, though informally, participated in spontaneous political activity such as strikes and public demonstrations in both urban and rural areas (62). Women have also been active in organized labor unions, with some holding administrative positions (32).

During the liberation struggle, the nationalist politicians organized women's leagues within their political parties. Since independence, many party committee structures have been organized in urban and rural areas to mobilize women for social action and employment-related activities. My contacts who spoke of the ZANU Women's League felt that more of its effort was directed at assisting male politicians than at getting women elected. The extent of women's influence in party political decisions has also been questioned (44).

The Ministry for Women's Affairs, several international organizations, and many nonprofit organizations are directly involved or contract work to mobilize and support women's groups throughout the country. My interviewees said that women manage most of these formal projects and organizations, and that the staff is often racially mixed. Perhaps due to their more recent history (many have developed since independence), these organizations have suffered less from the legacy of racism and sexism.

The Zimbabwe Women's Bureau, managed by a woman, actively promotes change in women's status and serves as a conduit for internationally funded aid projects to reach women at the grass roots. The Musasa Project for victims of violence is funded by several international organizations. In addition to counseling clients, it conducts training for the local courts and the police, most of whom are men. The founding director observed that wife beating is widespread in Zimbabwe and is not socially accepted as a reason for divorce, although it is legally accepted.

A Future Agenda

There is little published information on women managers in Zimbabwe. Bibliographies on African women do not contain references to managers (6;52). The findings reported here raise issues to be addressed in further research and change-oriented projects intended to develop women managers.

More than ten years have passed since independence. Although important legislation in the area of women's rights has been adopted, the implementation and extension of those rights remain problematic. Government social policies with regard to women appear contradictory. Conflict between civil law and African customary law persists. Men's attitudes and practices have not kept pace with women's own expectations and demands for more equal opportunity.

The duality of a public administration based on socialist ideology in partnership with private capitalism has contributed to the perpetuation of differential access by race and gender to management and leadership. The crucial role that women played during the liberation struggles seems to have been a high point for black women's advancement. Now the public sector provides them with the best opportunities to ascend to leadership positions. Although black men still lag behind their white counterparts as senior managers in the private sector, black women lag even farther behind in all management positions in private business. White women, on the other hand, occupy a disproportionately high percentage of management positions considering their small number in the general population.

Women managers in Zimbabwean private, public, and nonprofit organizations constitute a tiny elite portion of urban working women, who themselves constitute a small percentage of all working women. As the accomplishments of independence and the initial enthusiasm for women's equality recede with time, women's upward mobility beyond its current status may be inhibited. Traditional African gender-role distinctions, reinforced by managerial patriarchy, may preclude further advances in the public sector. In the private sector, even if African men make up the majority of managers, sexism may prohibit women from moving ahead.

The government's recent economic liberalization policy may produce adverse consequences for women's progress in the labor market (40). The contraction of jobs and price adjustments may negatively affect those most vulnerable; namely, women. The proposed fee at the primary school level would disproportionately affect women. Private sector enhancement is an agenda of the Mugabe government and of international aid organizations; yet its growth may not contribute to women's organizational advancement because of the historical contraints women have experienced in that sector. Massive training projects (directed at both women and men) will be needed to enable women to be equal competitors in the marketplace.

The climate for women in organizations is restrictive, for the most part, except in smaller organizations, many of which focus on projects aimed at women. Moreover, many of these depend on Western international aid donors rather than indigenous support. Larger organizations appear to have a "glass ceiling" at levels below management. Because nonindigenous firms dominate the private sector, it is conceivable that foreign governments and international aid organizations can pressure the recalcitrant management of some Zimbawean subsidiaries to hire and promote women. At present, this does not appear to be the case.

The position of women in the labor market, for the most part, appears to be consistent with the position of women within the family. Traditional gender-role distinctions still affirm women's subordinate role in the marital relationship and in the work environment, with few exceptions. Women professionals command *lobola* and while some favor its abolition, others feel it is women's only means of security in marriage.

What may result is that further class divisions among women will occur, with a growing percentage of women, although still a token in absolute numbers, advancing to management, while the vast majority remain in unskilled, low-paying jobs. Because Zimbabwe has a well-developed educational infrastructure, increasing numbers of educated women will search for employment. More of them, it is hoped, will advance organizationally and professionally. However, massive job market pressure from the burgeoning youthful population, coupled with the nation's inability to create needed jobs, may further heighten competition for scarce resources and further entrench those already in leadership positions. Opportunity for women's upward mobility could be stymied.

The preceding comments notwithstanding, Zimbabwe's comparatively well-developed educational system and business sector suggest that the nation's infrastructure provides comparatively good opportunities for aspiring women managers. These factors coupled with the national policy framework of equal rights and nondiscrimination suggest that Zimbabwe may be the prototype for other sub-Saharan nations (with the exception of South Africa) with regard to opportunities for women managers and leaders.

Notes

I gratefully acknowledge the Lobo Center Lecturership award from the Anderson Schools of Management at the University of New Mexico that provided partial financial support for this study. My friends and colleagues, Bongiwe and Jonathon Moyo in Harare, stimulated my inquiry into women's issues there. My daughter, Mala Nani Htun, became an invaluable guide and research assistant in Zimbabwe. My women colleagues in business studies at the University of Zimbabwe generously shared their expertise. Karen Fung, African specialist at the Hoover Institution Library, Stanford University, graciously directed me to the African literature and data. My heartfelt thanks to Nancy Adler and Dafna Izraeli, whose insightful comments significantly shaped the final outcome of the manuscript.

1 Managerial patriarchy has been described by Western feminist scholars as a male-centered ideology with values and behavioral standards that benefit primarily men. There is a developing literature in this area. A feminist interpretation of the interplay among Western managerial patriarchy, traditional Zimbabwean gender roles, and contemporary women managers in urban Zimbabwe is timely, but it is beyond the scope of this chapter.

2 Little statistical data were found to describe the extent to which women occupy middle- or senior-level positions in various industries or organizational sectors. Recent studies of the industrial sector (Chimanikire, 1987; Labat-Anderson Inc. and Probe Market Research, 1990; United Nations Industrial Development Organization, 1989) delineate some of the problems and issues that organizations and managers encounter in the modern economy, but the question of women managers is not addressed.

3 I held discussions, using a semistructured format, with approximately 25 senior-level managers and professional women and several professional men. I also participated in formal and informal group discussions on issues of women, politics, management, and gender roles. People with whom I spoke included high-ranking women in the Mugabe administration, male and female faculty members and senior-level women administrators at the University of Zimbabwe, and mid-level to senior-level women and men administrators in private industry and nonprofit organizations. A few of these people were non-Zimbabwean residents who worked in the Harare regional offices of prominent international organizations or who were on contract with local organizations. The discussions ranged from 30 minutes to two hours with the majority being on the longer side.

4 Kulsum Mohammed, USAID Harare, personal communication, May, 1991.

5 Two professors at the UZ (Wilson and Mbudze, 1989), who were interested in identifying attitudes toward achieving greater sexual equality, conducted a study targeting the reliable and valid assessment of attitudes toward women. The data obtained were unreliable and statistically insignificant, causing the authors to doubt the cross-cultural usefulness of attitudes scales.

References

(1) *Africa South of the Sahara (1991)*, 20th edn. (1990) London: Europa Publications.

(2) Batezat, E., and Mwalo, M. (1989) *Women in Zimbabwe*. Harare: Southern Africa Political Economy Series (SAPES) Trust.

(3) Batezat, E., Mwalo, M., and Truscott, K. (1988) "Women and Independence: The Heritage and the Struggle," in C. Stoneman (ed.), *Zimbabwe's Prospects: Issues of Race,*

Class, State and Capital in Southern Africa, pp. 153–173. Basingstoke, England: Macmillan.

(4) Bhola, H. S. (1990) "Adult Literacy for Development in Zimbabwe: The Third Phase of the Revolution Examined," in S. H. Arnold and A. Nitecki (eds.), *Culture and Development in Africa*, pp. 93–106. Trenton, N.J.: Africa World Press.

(5) Brydon, L., and Chant, S. (1989) *Women in the Third World: Gender Issues in Rural and Urban Areas*. New Brunswick, N.J.: Rutgers University Press.

(6) Bullwinkle, D. A. (1989) *Women of Eastern and Southern Africa: A Bibliography 1976– 1985*. New York: Greenwood Press.

(7) Central Statistical Office (1989) *Statistical Yearbook of Zimbabwe*. Harare: Central Statistical Office.

(8) Cheater, A. P. (1986) "The Role and Position of Women in Precolonial and Colonial Zimbabwe," *Zambezia* 13:65–79.

(9) Chideya, N. (1991) "Zimbabwe," in P. G. Altbach (ed.), *International Higher Education: An Encyclopedia*, Vol. 1, pp. 437–447. New York: Garland.

(10) Chimanikire, D. P. (1987) "Women in Industry: Legal and Social Attitudes," *Africa Development* 12(4):27–39.

(11) Chung, F. (1988) "Education: Revolution or Reform?" in C. Stoneman (ed.), *Zimbabwe's Prospects: Issues of Race, Class, State and Capital in Southern Africa*, pp. 118– 132. Basingstoke, England: Macmillan.

(12) Dorsey, B. J. (1989) "Factors Affecting Academic Careers for Women at the University of Zimbabwe," in *Highlights of the Research Programme at the University of Zimbabwe*, Issue 2, pp. 32–35. Harare: University of Zimbabwe.

(13) Drakakis-Smith, D. W. (1984) "The Changing Economic Role of Women in the Urbanization Process: A Preliminary Report from Zimbabwe," *International Migration Review* 18:1278–1292.

(14) Duley, M. I., and Edwards, M. I. (eds.) (1986) *The Cross Cultural Study of Women*. New York: The Feminist Press.

(15) Economic Commission for Africa (1990) *African Socio-economic Indicators 1987*. Addis Ababa, Ethiopia: Economic Commission for Africa.

(16) Erwee, R. (1988) "South African Women: Changing Career Patterns," in N. J. Adler and D. Izraeli (eds.), *Women in Management Worldwide*, pp. 213–225. Armonk, N.Y.: M. E. Sharpe.

(17) Europa Publications (1991) *The World of Learning 1991*, 41st edn. London: Europa Publications.

(18) Folbre, N. (1988) "Patriarchal Social Formations in Zimbabwe," in S. B. Stichter and J. L. Parpart (eds.), *Patriarchy and Class: African Women in the Home and the Workforce*, pp. 61–80. Boulder, Colo.: Westview Press.

(19) *Herald, The* (1990) April 18, p. 24.

(20) *Herald, The* (1991) "Zvobgo Speaks Out on Better Jobs for Women," February 28, p. 7.

(21) *Herald, The* (1991) "Third of Public Service Jobs to Go to Women," March 1, p. 7.

(22) Herbst, J. (1990) *State Politics in Zimbabwe*. Harare: University of Zimbabwe.

(23) International Labor Office (1990) *1989–90 Year Book of Labour Statistics*, 49th Issue. Geneva: International Labor Office.

(24) Jacobs, S. (1984) "Women and Land Resettlement in Zimbabwe," *Review of African Political Economy* 27:33–50.

(25) Jacobs, S. M., and Howard, T. (1987) "Women in Zimbabwe: Stated Policy and State Action," in H. Afshar (ed.), *Women, State, and Ideology: Studies from Africa and Asia*, pp.

28–47. Albany, N.Y.: State University of New York.

(26) Jassat, E. M., and Jirira, K. O. (1987) *Industrial Development in Zimbabwe: The Case of Women in Manufacturing Activities*, No. 7a. Harare: Zimbabwe Institute of Development Studies.

(27) Jirira, K. O. (1990) "The Condition of Women: Has It Improved?" *Southern Africa Political and Economic Monthly* 3(6):19–23.

(28) Kazembe, J. (1986) "The Women's Issue," in I. Mandaza (ed.), *Zimbabwe: The Political Economy of Transition 1980–1986*, pp. 377–404. Dakar, Senegal: Codesria.

(29) Labat-Anderson Inc. and Probe Market Research (LA-PMR) (1990) *Private Sector Training Needs Assessment USAID/Zimbabwe.* (Under Contract No. AFR-0463-C-00-8030-00).

(30) Lapchick, R. E., and Urdang, S. (1982) *Oppression and Resistance: The Struggle of Women in Southern Africa.* Westport, Conn.: Greenwood.

(31) Lungu, G. F. (1989) "Women and Representative Bureaucracy in Zambia: The Case of Gender-Balancing in the Civil Service and Parastatal Organizations," *Women's Studies International Forum* 12(2):175–182.

(32) Made, P., and Lagerstrom, B. (1985) *Zimbabwean Women in Industry.* Harare: Zimbabwe Publishing House.

(33) Made, P., and Lagerstrom, B. (1986) "Zimbabwean Women in Industry," *Isis International Women's Journal* 6:74–81.

(34) Made, P. A., and Whande, N. (1989) "Women in Southern Africa: A Note on the Zimbabwean 'Success Story,'" *Issue* 17(2):26–28.

(35) Mazura, D. (1987) "Tax Reforms Favour Women and Families," *African Business* 110:61.

(36) Ministry of Community Development and Women's Affairs (1985) *Women's Organizations in Zimbabwe.* Harare: Ministry of Community Development and Women's Affairs.

(37) Morrow, L. F. (1986) "Women in Sub-Saharan Africa," in M. I. Duley and M. I. Edwards (eds.), *The Cross Cultural Study of Women*, pp. 290–375. New York: The Feminist Press.

(38) Muchena, O. (1979) "The Changing Positions of African Women in Rural Zimbabwe-Rhodesia," *Zimbabwean Journal of Economics* 1(1):44–61.

(39) Mugabe, R. (1988) "Editorial: The President's Message to Zimbabwe Woman," *Zimbabwean Woman* 1(2):1.

(40) Mwanza, A. (1991) "Zimbabwe's Economic Liberalisation Programme: Justification and Expected Impact," *Southern Africa Political and Economic Monthly* 4(6):25–29.

(41) "My Story – A Woman Talking" (1988) *Speak Out* (October–December):27–28.

(42) National Register Publishing Company (1991) *International Directory of Corporate Affiliations 1991 Volume II.* Wilmette, Ill.: National Register Publishing Company.

(43) Ndoro, H. (1990) "Black Advancement in the Private Sector in Southern Africa," *Southern Africa Political and Economic Monthly* 3(8):3–5.

(44) Ong, B. N. (1986) "Women and the Transition to Socialism in Sub-Saharan Africa," in B. Munslow (ed.), *Africa: Problems in the Transition to Socialism*, pp. 72–94. London: Zed Books.

(45) Pankhurst, D. (1988) 'Women's Lives and Women's Struggles in Rural Zimbabwe," *Leeds Southern African Studies* 6(August):1–18.

(46) Perlez, J. (1991) "Elite Kenyan Women Avoid a Rite: Marriage," *The New York Times*, March 3, p. 8.

(47) Qunta, C. (ed.) (1987) *Women in Southern Africa.* London: Allison & Busby.

(48) Raftopoulos, B. (1990) "The Dilemma of Black Advancement in Zimbabwe," *Southern*

Africa Political and Economic Monthly 3(8):6–8.

(49) Robertson, C., and Berger, I. (eds.) (1986) *Women and Class in Africa*. New York: Africana.

(50) Schmidt, E. (1988) "Farmers, Hunters, and Gold-Washers: A Reevaluation of Women's Roles in Precolonial and Colonial Zimbabwe," *African Economic History* 17:45–80.

(51) Seidman, G. W. (1984) "Women in Zimbabwe: Postindependence Struggles," *Feminist Studies* 10(3):420–440.

(52) Sherwood, M. (1988) *Women under the Sun: African Women in Politics and Production – A Bibliography 1982–5*. London: Institute for African Alternatives.

(53) Sullivan, J. (1989) *Africa*, 3rd edn. Guilford, Conn.: Dushkin.

(54) Sweetman, D. (1984) *Women Leaders in African History*. London: Heinemann.

(55) Sylvester, C. (1991) "'Urban Women Cooperators,' 'Progress,' and 'African Feminism' in Zimbabwe," *Differences* 3(1):39–62.

(56) Thompson, C. B. (1982) "Women in the National Liberation Struggle in Zimbabwe," *Women's Studies International Forum* 5:247–252.

(57) United Nations (1989) *Statistics and Indicators on Women in Africa 1986*, Social Statistics and Indicators Series K No. 7. New York: Department of International Economic and Social Affairs Statistical Office.

(58) United Nations Children's Fund (1993) *The State of the World's Children 1993*. London: Oxford University Press.

(59) United Nations Industrial Development Organization (1989) *Skill Requirements for Industrial Development in Zimbabwe – The Prospective Role of Women*, V. 89-60868, November 3. Regional and Country Studies Branch Industrial Policy and Perspectives Division.

(60) Uniworld Business Publications (1987) *Directory of American Firms Operating in Foreign Countries*, 11th edn. Vol. 3. New York: Uniworld Business Publications.

(61) Weinrich, A. K. H. (1979) *Women and Racial Discrimination in Rhodesia*. Paris: United Nations Educational, Scientific and Cultural Organization.

(62) Weinrich, A. K. H. (1982) "Changes in the Political and Economic Roles of Women in Zimbabwe Since Independence," *Cultures* 8(4):43–62.

(63) Weiss, R. (1986) *The Women of Zimbabwe*. Harare: Nehanda Publishers.

(64) Wilson, D., and Mbudzi, M. (1989) "Correlates of Attitudes toward Women in Zimbabwe," *Journal of Social Psychology* 129(1):21–26.

(65) Zvobgo, E. (1983) "Removing Laws That Oppress Women," *Africa Report* 28(2):45–47.

PART V

NORTH AMERICA

22

CANADA

Women in Management: The Canadian Experience[1]

Caroline Andrew, Cécile Coderre, and Ann Denis

This chapter examines the relationship between the professional and private lives of middle- and senior-level women managers in Canada employed in the public and private sectors. The personal profiles of these managers underline their relatively privileged backgrounds – the occupational and educational levels of their parents and their own high educational levels. Canadian women managers' commitment to their professional work is very strong, but in most cases they are also highly committed to family and personal life. In addition, they demonstrate a high degree of female solidarity with other women rather than expressing concern solely with furthering their own careers.

Women still hold only a small minority of middle- and senior-level management positions in Canada, although their numbers have increased substantially since the 1970s. This chapter focuses on the changing lives of women managers and the patterns of these changes within the broader context of the trends in Canadian women's labor force participation.

Women's Labor Force Participation

Women's labor force participation rates in Canada climbed from 36 percent in 1970 (15) to 60 percent in 1991 (23). The increase was greater among married women, rising from 31 percent in 1970 to 63 percent in 1991 (23).

Educational attainment strongly influences women's labor force participation rates. Both in 1971 and 1981, educated women were more likely to join the labor market than were uneducated women. Over time, the increase in participation rates has been considerably greater among the most educated women (3;4).

Despite the increase in women's participation in the labor force, their occupational distribution has not changed significantly. Relative to men, women remain concentrated in a small number of occupations. For example, in 1984 one-third of all employed women worked in clerical jobs, whereas, no more than 12 percent of men worked in any single major occupational category (15;16). In general, therefore, the increase in women's participation rates took place without altering their prior distribution within the occupational structure.

Occupations in Management

Management as an occupational category has grown significantly since the early 1970s as a result of developing the tertiary sector, growth in the state sector, and increasing bureaucratization of the private sector. Between 1971 and 1991, management is the only occupational category in which the proportion of both the female and male labor force increased substantially. For women, this increase was from 3 percent to 10 percent, and for men, from 5 percent to 14 percent (15;20;22;24).

Within management, the proportion of women rose from 16 percent in 1971, to 25 percent in 1981, and to 33 percent in 1991. Although women remain underrepresented, their increase in this occupational category considerably exceeded their increase in the labor force as a whole.

A more detailed examination of the management occupation for 1971 and 1981, however, demonstrates a phenomenon that has been widely observed in the labor force, and not just in Canada: the more senior the position, the lower the percentage of women in it. In 1971, women accounted for 16 percent of all managers and 4 percent of senior management. By 1991, the figures were 38 percent of all managers, but only 21 percent of senior managers (20;24).[2]

In 1971, women managers did not differ significantly from the total labor force in terms of marital status, except for senior managers, who were less likely to be single. In 1981, women in all management categories were less likely to be single than women in the labor force as a whole (21). Managerial jobs seem, therefore, to be no more incompatible with marriage than labor force participation in general – indeed, to be more compatible today than in the 1970s.

Overall, therefore, the 1970s were a time of change for women in management. The sector as a whole expanded considerably, and the place of women within management grew even more rapidly. Women remain marginal at the senior management levels but, even there, growth has occurred during the past fifteen years. In order to understand these changes, it is important to understand how Canadian women managers experience their work world.

A Study of Canada's Women Managers

We interviewed 214 middle- and senior-level women managers in the public and private sectors in the provinces of Ontario and Quebec to learn about their professional lives and the relationship between their professional and personal lives.[3] In the public sector, the women managers worked in the federal, Ontario, and Quebec civil services in ministries that were relatively comparable in terms of function, including those with both economic and noneconomic missions. In the private sector, the women managers worked in large companies in finance, sales, and manufacturing, which are the major sectors employing women. Comparable companies with head offices in Montreal and Toronto were included.[4]

Cooperation was very high, with only three organizations refusing to participate, and only 2 percent of the women declining to be interviewed.[5] Of the 214 women interviewed, 114 worked in the public sector, and 100 in the private sector.[6] Each interview took, on average, an hour and a half to two hours and included both closed and open questions.[7] The interviews allowed us to establish a general profile of Canadian women managers in both the public and private sectors. This was important since differences in career patterns have been stressed between the two sectors (7;8;9;18;19).

We also focused on generational differences, because statistics indicate a growing presence of women in management. If this increase is accurate, to what extent does it change the kind of women found in management and the way in which women can and do operate in managerial positions? To answer questions such as these, we divided the women into three relatively equal age groups: those born in 1941 or before (71 women), those born between 1942 and 1947 (73 women), and those born in 1948 or later (70 women).

Empirically, age and the sector one works in are interrelated. Women managers in the private sector are younger than those in the public sector. Almost half of the private-sector managers were born after 1948, whereas this was true for fewer than one-quarter of the public sector managers. It is, therefore, important to be prudent in interpreting differences, since patterns that appear to be linked to differences between the public and private sectors may, in reality, reflect differences in generation.

A Profile of Canada's Women Managers

Half of the women managers were born after 1945, with birth dates ranging from 1921 to 1958. In terms of mother tongue, 38 percent spoke French, 53 percent spoke English, and 9 percent spoke another language.[8]

The women managers came from relatively advantaged backgrounds, as can be seen from the educational levels and occupations of their parents. Women who became middle and senior managers tended to come from family backgrounds that offered a model of high educational attainment, high-status occupations, and paid employment for women.

Looking first at parental levels of education, almost one-third of the fathers and one-quarter of the mothers had a university degree. Indeed, 15 percent of the fathers and 2 percent of the mothers had a postgraduate degree, which is a substantially higher proportion than that for the overall Quebec and Ontario population of the same age group (6). Women managers working in the public sector were more likely to have had parents with a university education. As Table 22.1 indicates, significant differences between public and private sector managers existed in relation to the levels of the mothers' education. Thirty-five percent of public sector managers had mothers with a university education, compared with 15 percent of those from the private sector. These differences are all the more striking in that the public sector managers are older than those from the private sector and therefore might be expected to have less well-educated mothers.

Parental occupations also indicate the relatively privileged background of these

Table 22.1 Parents' education of women managers by sector

Sector	Mother		Father	
	Less than secondary (%)	BA or more (%)	Less than secondary (%)	BA or more (%)
Public	42.5	35.4	35.4	37.2
Private	43.4	15.2	41.7	26.0
Total	42.9	25.9	38.3	32.1

Mothers: $\chi^2 = 14.7$; $P \leq 0.002$. Fathers $\chi^2 = 6.3$; $P \leq 0.10$

Source: Authors' translation from C. Andrew et al. (1988) "Entre les libertés et les contraintes," in F. Harel Giasson and J. Robichaud (eds.), *Tout savoir les femmes cadres d'ici*. Montreal: Les Presses H.E.C.

women managers. Forty percent of their fathers had most recently held a position in management or the professions, and a further 16 percent were in clerical or sales jobs. The most recent employment of 14 percent of the mothers was in professional positions, with another 26 percent in clerical and sales occupations. Sixty percent of the mothers worked outside the home.

Almost 70 percent of the women managers' mothers had been employed before marriage. By the time their respective daughters were fifteen years old, 40 percent of the mothers were in the labor force, a rate that is relatively high compared with that of the general Canadian female population (4;5). Many of the women managers therefore grew up in an environment in which there was a role model of women's employment outside the home.

The women managers' own educational levels also reflect their relatively privileged backgrounds. Fully 37 percent had studied at the postgraduate level, and only 10 percent had no more than secondary schooling. The high levels of education indicate relatively advantaged social origins. The high educational levels also indicate a considerable on-going investment in education as the majority of the women continued their studies after having begun to work. Almost half the women studied some aspect of administration, compared with one-quarter who studied the arts and social sciences, the next most frequently studied area. The public and private sectors differed in this regard. As Table 22.2 indicates, 51 percent of the public sector managers had at least begun studying at the postgraduate level, while this was true for fewer than one-quarter of the managers in the private sector.

If these women managers seem "exceptional" in terms of their socioeconomic backgrounds, they seem less so in terms of their life-styles. Many studies of women in management have emphasized the difficulties women face in combining family and professional responsibilities (8;9;12;13;14;18;19). Among the women we interviewed, however, the majority live within a family; in this, they neither differ from the Canadian women's labor force as a whole, nor from the entire population of women managers. Among the women managers, 14 percent were single, 50 percent were married[9], 14 percent were remarried, 19 percent were divorced or separated, and 2 percent were widowed. In this regard there is very little difference among age groups or between the public and private sectors.

Our data suggest that children rather than marriage pose career problems for

Table 22.2   Educational level of Canadian women managers by sector

Sector	BA or less (%)	Some postgraduate education (%)
Public	48.2	51.8
Private	79.0	21.0
Total	62.6	37.4

$\chi^2 = 21.5; P \leq 0.000$

Source: Authors' translation from C. Andrew et al. (1988) "Entre les libertés et les constraintes," in F. Harel Giasson and J. Robichaud (eds.), *Tout savoir les femmes cadres d'ici*. Montreal: Les Presses H.E.C.

women managers. Fifty percent of the women managers reported that they did not have responsibility for children (see Table 22.3). The figure was lowest for the middle-aged women and highest among the youngest women, in which 65 percent had not had responsibility for children; however, it must be recognized that these women were still of childbearing age. The women with children had had them at a later age than the overall Canadian population.[10] As shown in Table 22.4, women from the public sector had responsibility for more children than did their counterparts in the private sector.

Table 22.3   Number of children by year of birth of Canadian women managers

| Woman manager's year of birth | Number of children | | | |
	0 (%)	1 (%)	2 (%)	3 or more (%)
1941 or earlier	45.1	18.3	19.7	16.9
1942–1947	38.4	24.7	30.1	6.8
1948 or later	65.7	15.7	14.3	4.3
Total	49.5	19.6	21.5	9.3

$\chi^2 = 18.4; P \leq 0.005$

Source: Authors' translation from C. Andrew et al. (1988) "Entre les libertés et les constraintes," in F. Harel Giasson and J. Robichaud (eds.), *Tout savoir les femmes cadres d'ici*. Montreal: Les Presses H.E.C.

Table 22.4   Number of children by sector of Canadian women managers

| Sector | Number of children | | | |
	0 (%)	1 (%)	2 (%)	3 or more (%)
Public	40.4	17.5	28.1	14.0
Private	60.0	22.0	14.0	4.0
Total	49.5	19.6	21.5	9.3

$\chi^2 = 15.3; P \leq 0.002$

Source: Authors' translation from C. Andrew et al. (1988) "Entre les libertés et les constraintes," in F. Harel Giasson and J. Robichand (eds.), *Tout savoir les femmes cadres d'ici*. Montreal: Les Presses H.E.C.

Orientation toward Work

The women managers indicated a high level of satisfaction with the development of their careers. When asked, 52 percent replied that they were fully satisfied with their career development; 43 percent, that they were satisfied; and only 5 percent, that they were not very satisfied. Nevertheless, when asked at what level they thought they should be, taking into account their experience and aptitude, 40 percent thought they should be at a higher level (28 percent, one level higher; and 12 percent, two levels); 58 percent said that they should be at their present level; and only 2 percent thought they should be at a lower level.

The women described where they thought they would be five years hence. Their answers described four types of movement: vertical (moving up the hierarchy), developmental (content of job continuing to be challenging, with the focus on the content of the work, rather than upward mobility and level); stable (similar to present job); other (complete change of career, retirement, etc.). Almost 40 percent of the women defined their likely career development in terms of vertical mobility; and another 23 percent, in terms of development. Only 20 percent saw themselves as likely to stay at the same job level.

Not surprisingly, there were age differences. The youngest group was more inclined to see career development in terms of vertical movement (50 percent, compared with 30 percent of the oldest group) and less likely to see it as stable.

A similar picture of career commitment emerged from the women's descriptions of the characteristics they considered most and least important. The women selected from a list that included factors both related and unrelated to work. Among those related to work, there were both intrinsic job benefits (atmosphere, interest of work, etc.) and extrinsic benefits (possibility for training, job security, etc.). The women's descriptions indicated three strong trends: strong attachment to the work world, importance of the content of the work, and a desire to combine family and professional ties. Two-thirds of the women described interesting work as one of the two most important factors. The single most popular combination was interesting work and time with family (cited by 20 percent of the women), followed by interesting work and level of responsibility (cited by 12 percent of the women). The least important factors were job security, long-term career plans, possibility for training, salary, time with friends, and leisure time (each chosen by between one-fifth and one-third of the women as one of the least important factors). Concern for the content of work and for balancing private and public responsibilities clearly count for Canadian women managers.

Commitment to the work world was part of the women's world view from an early age. Two-thirds of the women indicated that as adolescents they had already planned to work as adults, and 13 percent said that their plans as adolescents had included marriage, children, and paid employment. These replies indicate that nearly 80 percent of the women grew up with the idea that as adults they would work outside the home. Sixteen percent said that they had seen their future in terms of marriage and children, and 5 percent said that they had not had a life plan during their adolescence. When the women were specific about the type of employment they had imagined, it was most often professional.

Women's Solidarity

The women demonstrated considerably less individualism and more concern for helping others than the literature and stereotypes would have us believe is true for successful women managers (10;11;17;25). One particularly interesting aspect of this is the degree of solidarity the interviewed women showed with other women managers. This solidarity was illustrated by the spontaneous comments the women made in explaining why they felt it important, despite very busy schedules, to participate in the study. This solidarity among women was also demonstrated in the answers the women gave to three questions: how important is it for women to support each other? have you served as a mentor for others? and have you ever given particular support to someone because she was a woman?

The first question assesses how important women managers thought it was for women to support each other. The number of positive replies was impressive: 60 percent of the women said that it was very important; and another 30 percent, that it was important. There were no differences between age groups or sectors on this question. All groups recognized the importance of women supporting each other. The "Queen Bee", who is geared to individual success, is certainly not the model for these managers, as is borne out by their practice, and indicated by their experience in acting as mentors.

The women managers' responses to the questions concerning whether they had served as mentors for other people and whether those people were primarily women, men, or both also illustrated, even more clearly, their sense of solidarity with other women. Eighty-five percent of the women said that they had been mentors, with slightly more than 40 percent primarily for women, 37 percent for both, and only 8 percent primarily for men. Considering the fact that most of these women have had mostly male colleagues, this is a particularly interesting finding. It may suggest that the women managers helped women who were in clerical jobs; however, it clearly seems to indicate that they have shown particular concern for helping their women peers. The women managers did not differ in their mentoring behavior in terms of employment sector or age.

Solidarity among women was also demonstrated by the women's answers to the question of whether the women managers had ever given particular support to someone because she was a woman. Twenty-eight percent said they had done so often, and 33 percent had sometimes done so, making a total of slightly over 60 percent who had given support to another woman primarily on grounds of women's solidarity. The other women were divided more or less equally between those who had not given such support and those who were opposed to doing so.

Women managers in the public and private sector differed on the question of mentoring (see Table 22.5). Women from the private sector were less likely to have supported other women because they were women, and more likely to oppose doing so. This difference may indicate an ideological difference between the two sectors,

Table 22.5   Support of other women by Canadian women managers, by sector

Sector	Often (%)	Sometimes (%)	Never (%)	Opposed to such support (%)
Public	31.6	43.0	15.8	8.8
Private	24.5	22.4	23.5	27.6
Total	28.3	33.5	19.3	17.5

$\chi^2 = 20.3$; $P \leq 0.000$

Source: Authors' translation from C. Andrew et al. (1988) "Entre les libertés et les constraintes," in F. Harel Giasson and J. Robichand (eds.), Tout savoir les femmes cadres d'ici. Montreal: Les Presses H.E.C.

with the private sector supporting individualism and equality of opportunity more. Equally likely, it may reflect differences in the functioning of the two sectors and in the positions occupied by women within each.

Perceptions of the Work World

The women managers described how they perceived the place of women in management and what they saw as the factors facilitating and blocking women's careers in management. The factor seen as most frequently blocking women was the small number of women managers. Some women suggested that this is because many men have not yet learned to work with, and, perhaps more importantly, to work for women. Men's attitudes cause problems for women and, as there are few women managers, these attitudes change slowly.

These attitudes realistically describe the present place of women in management, and yet permit women to envisage their careers with confidence. Far from "blaming the victims," the women clearly report that the problem lies in men's attitudes, but also that, with increasing numbers of women managers, these attitudes can change. Realistic but also optimistic, the solidarity of the women managers represents a collective strategy for change.

Summary and Conclusions

Our profile of women managers in Canada deals with both socioeconomic variables and elements relating to working conditions and work satisfaction. The socially advantaged background of the women managers was very clear. This finding supports the view that it is still exceptional in Canada for women to become middle- and senior-level managers and that those who succeed tend to come from family backgrounds with a tradition of salaried employment for women, high professional status, and high educational achievement.

There were important differences between women managers in the private and public sectors. These differences were, in part, socioeconomic – women managers in the public sector had, for example, mothers with higher levels of education – and, in part, generational, as women managers in the public sector tended to be older than those in the private sector. Managers in the public and private sectors also differed in their support for other women, with public sector managers showing more support for their sisters.

These sectoral differences should not, however, distract attention away from the areas of broad agreement among the women managers. The majority display beliefs and behaviors that reflect solidarity with other women. This strengthens our view of women as interested in career development, but in a somewhat different way from that portrayed in the stereotype of the overly career-oriented manager. These women managers are committed to their work, and show particular interest in its content and in its ability to offer them a constant challenge. A large percentage of the women combine a strong commitment to work with an equally strong commitment to family and personal life. In addition, these women appear more supportive of other people, particularly other women, rather than showing concern solely for furthering their own careers.

As more women move into management, can we say that they are changing the rules of the game in relation to the world of work? It is clearly too early to answer this question, but it is certainly worth asking.

Acknowledgments

We should like to thank the women we interviewed, and their employers, for their generous collaboration. We should like to acknowledge with thanks the financial support we have received for this research from the Women and Work Strategic Grants program of the Social Sciences and Humanities Research Council of Canada and from the University of Ottawa. We should also like to thank Nicole Lemire, Andrée Daviau, Béatrice Godard, Hyacinthe Irving, and Nicole Ollivier, who worked as research assistants on this project. Finally, we should like to thank Ginette Rozon, Louise Clément, and Phuong Chi Hoang, of the Faculty Research Secretariat, for the rapidity and quality of their typing assistance.

Notes

1 This chapter has been adapted from "Women in Management: The Canadian Experience," in Nancy J. Adler and Dafna N. Izraeli (eds.), *Women in Management Worldwide*. Armonk, N.Y.: M. E. Sharpe.

2 Determination of the position of women in management requires some manipulation of the census categories. The major category 11 in the Canadian census, administrative and related occupations, is homogeneous in that it includes only positions within large organizations, but it is heterogeneous in terms of the level of managerial responsibility, as it includes administrative support occupations through senior managers. One subcategory includes only senior managers, but excludes those in occupations unique to government. It is also possible to distinguish the subcategories that include all the middle and senior management positions. These distinctions are made in the censuses (Statistics Canada, 1975a, 1975b, 1983), but not in the quarterly labor-force surveys based on samples (Labour Canada, 1977, 1986).

3 Ontario and Quebec are the two most populous, and the two most industrial, of the ten Canadian provinces. The large majority of the Quebec population is French-speaking,

and of the Ontario population, English-speaking.

4 For budgetary reasons our interviews were limited to women working in Montreal, Quebec, Toronto, and Ottawa-Hull. In the case of the public sector, this included most eligible women – an indication of the high degree of geographic centralization of the public sector in Canada. In the private-sector companies, because of differences in recruitment and career-development practices between "head office" and "branch," we wished to include women in both. However, our financial constraints permitted inclusion of "branch" representatives only when these were located in one of the above four urban centers.

5 Our research strategy consisted of contacting the companies and ministries and asking for their collaboration. These initial contacts were directed to the vice-president, human resources (private sector), or to the deputy minister (public sector). We asked for lists of intermediate and senior women managers, explaining that we would contact these women directly. When lists were provided, we drew random samples. When organizational policies prevented names' being given out, the organizations distributed letters from us describing the project and asking for collaboration, and the women willing to be included contacted us directly.

6 Sixty-six of the public-sector respondents came from ministries with an economic mission, and 47 from those with a noneconomic mission. In the private sector, the distribution was as follows: 43 from the financial sector, 23 from sales, and 35 from manufacturing.

7 All the areas touched on in the questionnaire will not be discussed in this article. The questionnaire included questions about the current job of the respondent and past work experience. Career plans, both past and future, were explored, as was the respondent's experience with mentors, support networks, and organizational plans relating to women's careers within the organization. In terms of the personal dimension, questions were asked about education, family background, patterns of childcare, division of responsibilities, and allocation of time for various household activities.

8 Three-quarters of the women interviewed were born in Canada; 11 percent, in Great Britain; 1 percent, in France; and 12 percent, in other countries. By ethnic origin the distribution was as follows: 38 percent French, 40 percent English, and 23 percent other.

9 Includes those cohabiting, as does the married category in the Canadian census.

10 For a fuller discussion of this point, see C. Andrew et al. (1989).

References

(1) Andrew, C., Coderre, C., Daviau, A., and Denis, A. (1988) "Entre les libertés et les contraintes," in F. Harel Giasson and J. Robichaud (eds.), *Tout savoir les femmes cadres d'ici*. Montreal: Les Presses H.E.C.

(2) Andrew, C. et al. (1989) "La bureaucratie à l'épreuve du féminin," *Recherches féministes* 2(2):55–78.

(3) Armstrong, P., and Armstrong, H. (1978) *The Double Ghetto*. Toronto: McClelland and Stewart.

(4) Armstrong, P., and Armstrong, H. (1984) *The Double Ghetto*, 2nd edn. Toronto: McClelland and Stewart.

(5) Denis, A. (1983) "Women's Paid Employment and Subordination." Paper presented at annual meeting of the Canadian Sociology & Anthropology Association, Vancouver.

(6) Denis, A. et al. (1986) "Interrelations between the Public and Private Lives of Women in Management." Paper presented at the International Sociological Association Meet-

ing, New Delhi.

(7) Fogarty, M. P. et al. (1971) *Women in Top Jobs: Four Studies in Achievement*. London: Allen and Unwin.

(8) Fogarty, M. P., Rapoport, R., and Rapoport, R. N. (1971) *Sex, Career and Family*. London: Allen and Unwin.

(9) Fogarty, M. P., Allen, I., and Walters, P. (1981) *Women in Top Jobs 1968–1979*. London: Heinemann Educational Books.

(10) Giasson, F. H. (1981) "Perception et actualisation des facteurs de promotion chez les femmes cadres des grandes entreprises québécoises francophones du secteur privé." Doctoral thesis, Hautes Etudes Commerciales, Montreal.

(11) Gordon, F. E., and Strober, M. H. (eds.) (1975) *Bringing Women into Management*. New York: McGraw-Hill.

(12) Hennig, M., and Jardim, A. (1977) *The Managerial Woman*. Garden City, N.Y.: Anchor Press/Doubleday.

(13) Hupper-Laufer, J. (1982) *La Femininité neutralisée*. Paris: Flammarion.

(14) Jewell, D. O. (ed.) (1977) *Women and Management: An Expanding Role*. Atlanta: School of Business Administration, Georgia State University.

(15) Labour Canada (1977) *Women in the Labour Force. Facts and Figures* (1976 edn.), Part 1. Ottawa: Labour Canada, Women's Bureau.

(16) Labour Canada (1986) *Women in the Labour Force. Facts and Figures* (1985–86 edn.). Ottawa: Labour Canada, Women's Bureau.

(17) Rosen, B., and Jerdee, T. H. (1974) "Sex Stereotyping in the Executive Suite," *Harvard Business Review* 52:45–58.

(18) Sales, A., and Bélanger, N. (1985) *Décideurs et questionnaires*. Québec: Editeur Officiel du Québec.

(19) Simard, C. (1983) *L'Administration contre les femmes*. Montreal: Boréal Express.

(20) Statistics Canada (1975a) "Occupations by Sex Showing Birthplace, Period of Immigration and Ethnic Group, Canada and Provinces," *1971 Census of Canada* (Cat. 94–734, Vol. 3.3, Bul. 3.3–7). Ottawa: Statistics Canada.

(21) Statistics Canada (1975b) "Occupations of Females by Marital Status by Age for Canada," *1971 Census of Canada* (Cat. 94–733, Vol. 3.3, Bul. 3.3–6). Ottawa: Statistics Canada.

(22) Statistics Canada (1983) "Labor Force – Occupation by Demographic and Educational Characteristics," *1981 Census of Canada* (Cat. 92–917, Vol. 1, National Series). Ottawa: Statistics Canada.

(23) Statistics Canada (1993a) *Census 1991* (Cat. 93–324). Ottawa: Ministry of Industry, Science and Technology.

(24) Statistics Canada (1993b) *Census 1991* (Cat. 93–324). Ottawa: Ministry of Industry, Science and Technology.

(25) Stead, B. A. (1978) *Women in Management*. Englewood Cliffs, N.J.: Prentice-Hall.

UNITED STATES OF AMERICA

The Status of Women Managers in the United States

Ellen A. Fagenson and Janice J. Jackson

Current and Projected Status

Overview

By the year 2000, it has been predicted that the majority of new entrants into the United States labor force will be women (23). More working women are choosing management careers (61). Although they are finding that entry into the management profession is an achievable task, women are having great difficulty breaking through the "glass ceiling," the invisible barrier that separates women from positions of significant corporate power (58). This chapter discusses the current situation of women managers in the United States, ventures projections about their future, highlights differences between minority and nonminority women managers, looks at the barriers women managers face, and presents recommendations for how these barriers can be overcome.

Participation in the workforce and in management

In the last few decades, the number of women in paid employment and their rate of participation in the workforce have steadily increased (23). Only 34 percent of U.S. women were employed in 1950 (representing 30 percent of the labor force), 43 percent were employed in 1970 (38 percent of the labor force), and over half (52 percent) were working by 1980 (43 percent of the workforce) (23). In 1990, these numbers increased to 58 percent and 45 percent, respectively (59). The prediction is that by the year 2000, 61 percent of women will be in paid work, and they will constitute approximately 47 percent of the workforce (15).

Women are not equally represented in all segments of the labor force. They dominate in what are considered traditionally women's occupations (e.g., secretarial, clerical, nursing). In 1991, for example, women constituted 80 percent of administrative support workers, 99 percent of all secretaries, 95 percent of all registered nurses, and 67 percent of all retail and sales workers (60).

Women's participation rate in management, a traditionally male occupation (including the job titles of executive, manager, and administrator), is growing, albeit slowly.[1] In 1940, 4 percent of all women in the labor force were managers, com-

Table 23.1 Women executives, administrators, and managers (1900–1992)

Year	Number of women executives, administrators, and managers	Women as % of total executives, administrators, and managers
1900	74,374	4.4
1910	150,067	6.1
1920	190,627	6.8
1930	292,274	8.1
1940	414,472	11.0
1950	699,807	13.6
1960	1,099,000	15.6
1970	1,320,000	16.0
1980	2,849,859	26.1
1990	5,943,000	40.0
1992	6,128,000	41.5

Sources: D. L. Kaplan and M. C. Case (1958) *Occupational Trends in the United States, 1900–1950*. Washington, D.C.: Department of Commerce, Bureau of the Census; U.S. Department of Labor (1991b) *Employment and Earnings*, 1961, 1971, 1981, 1991, and 1993; *Unpublished tabulations from the Current Population Survey*. Washington, D.C.: U.S. Government Printing Office.

pared to 10 percent of men (49). In 1978, almost 40 years later, the proportions were 6 percent and 12 percent, respectively (53). In 1990, 11 percent of working women were managers, compared to 14 percent of employed men (55). The gap had narrowed significantly.

Of individuals who have become managers, a growing proportion are women. As shown in Table 23.1, in 1900 women represented only 4.4 percent of all managers.[2] Fifty years later, women represented 14 percent of the management profession. In 1980, they represented 26 percent, and by 1992 they were 42 percent of the managerial labor force. As indicated in Table 23.2, women managers are most heavily concentrated in the medical/health, personnel/labor relations, and education/administration areas.

Earnings

The number of women in management is increasing and approaching that of men. Women managers, however, have not achieved equity with their male counterparts in terms of their salaries (see Table 23.3). In 1992, women managers earned 66 percent of male managers' compensation. In the managerial category of "service organization managers," women's pay progressed to as much as 88 percent of male managers' earnings. Yet, in other managerial categories, such as "financial managers," women earned only 62 percent of the amount paid to men. Thus, whereas in some managerial categories the gap in salaries is narrowing, in others, it remains quite large.

Education

The increasing number of women in the management profession may be an outgrowth of the increasing rate of their graduation from U.S. colleges and universities.

Table 23.2 Numbers (in thousands) and percentages of full-time women and men executive, administrative, and managerial workers in specific management areas (1992)

Occupation	Totals[a]	Women	Men	Women as % of total employed[a]
Public legislators, chief executives, and general administrators	28	10	18	35.7
Public administrators and officials	541	237	304	43.8
Protective service administrators	49	10	39	20.4
Financial managers	517	239	278	46.2
Personnel and labor relations managers	104	61	43	58.7
Purchasing managers	113	37	75	32.7
Marketing, advertising, and public relations managers	516	174	373	33.7
Education and related fields managers	605	344	261	56.9
Medicine and health managers	364	238	125	65.7
Postmasters and mail superintendents	51	22	29	43.1
Food service and lodging establishment managers	1,142	471	671	41.2
Properties and real estate managers	436	198	238	45.4
Funeral directors	53	8	45	15.1
Service organization managers	473	231	243	48.8
Managers and administrators	5,822	1,783	4,039	30.6
Management-related occupations	3,960	2,064	1,897	52.1
Total executives, administrators, and managers	14,775	6,128	8,647	41.5

[a] Totals and percentages may not reflect calculation (addition or division) of line items because of the rounding of individual entries. Percentage calculations are by the authors.

Source: U.S. Department of Labor, Bureau of Labor Statistics (1993). *Unpublished tabulations from the Current Population Survey*. Washington, D.C.: U.S. Government Printing Office.

The U.S. Department of Education reports that the number of bachelor's degrees awarded to women has risen steadily since the 1970s; and in 1982, the number of women awarded bachelor's degrees began to exceed that of men, with this trend projected to continue through the year 2000 (51). Furthermore, since the 1970s, the percentage of bachelor's degrees awarded to women in the fields of business and management has grown significantly. As shown in Table 23.4, in the academic year 1969–1970, women earned 8.7 percent of all bachelor's degrees in business and management; this figure increased markedly to 47 percent in 1990–1991.

Women are increasingly securing more of the graduate degrees as well. The number of women awarded master's degrees began to exceed the number awarded to men in 1986; by the year 2000, the U.S. Department of Education predicts that women will be awarded the majority (54 percent) of all master's degrees (51). Women are also increasingly securing master's level degrees in business and management. As can be seen in Table 23.4, in 1969–1970, women received 3.5 percent of the master's degrees in these fields, while in 1990–1991, women received 34 percent of these degrees.

The number of women receiving doctorates has also increased steadily since

Table 23.3   Percentages and median annual earnings of full-time women and men executive, administrative, and managerial workers in specific management areas (1992)

Occupation	Totals[a] ($)	Women ($)	Men ($)	Women's earnings as % of men's
Public legislators, chief executives, and general administrators	45,960	37,894	49,342	76.8
Public administrators and officials	36,926	31,256	41,750	74.9
Protective service administrators	32,279	28,985	39,418	73.5
Financial managers	39,735	31,876	51,068	62.4
Personnel and labor relations managers	37,376	30,687	45,184	67.9
Purchasing managers	42,356	32,000	50,006	64.0
Marketing, advertising, and public relations managers	40,728	32,586	47,690	68.3
Education and related fields managers	40,133	35,182	45,395	77.5
Medicine and health managers	37,223	34,947	43,682	80.0
Postmasters and mail superintendents	36,728	34,405	39,626	86.8
Food service and lodging eestablishment managers	21,738	18,866	24,783	76.1
Property and real estate managers	26,507	24,792	28,506	87.0
Funeral directors	33,161	25,779	34,604	74.5
Service organization managers	29,381	27,223	30,850	88.2
Managers and administrators	29,417	26,417	46,209	57.2
Management-related occupations	30,866	26,364	36,809	71.6
Total executives, administrators, and managers	33,820	26,978	40,746	66.2

[a] The Bureau of Labor Statistics reports median weekly earnings. Calculations for median annual earnings and percentages are by the authors.

Source: U.S. Department of Labor, Bureau of Labor Statistics (1993). *Unpublished tabulations from the Current Population Survey*. Washington, D.C.: U.S. Government Printing Office.

1969–1970, and this trend is expected to continue through the year 2000. By the turn of the century, the total number of doctorates awarded to women is projected to equal the number awarded to men; by the year 2001, it is expected to exceed the number awarded to men (51). In the fields of business and management, the percentage of women doctorates (see Table 23.4) has increased significantly from a mere 1.7 percent in 1969–1970 to 24 percent in 1990–1991.

Middle- to upper-level management positions and corporate board positions

Although more women are obtaining college degrees and securing management jobs, they are having great difficulty securing middle- to upper-level management positions (58). The U.S. Department of Labor estimates that women fill only 1 to 2 percent of senior executive management positions (53).

In 1990, *Fortune* conducted a study to determine the number of women listed among the 4,000 highest paid officers and directors in approximately 80 percent of the 1,000 largest U.S. industrial and service companies and found that only 19 or 0.005 percent were women (13). In 1978, a similar study found that, 0.002 percent or ten out of 6,400 officers and directors were women (13).

Table 23.4 Percentage of degrees in business and management received by women

Degree	1969–1970 (%)	1976–1977 (%)	1980–1981 (%)	1987–1988 (%)	1990–1991 (%)
	8.7	23.4	36.9	46.7	46.7
Bachelor's	3.5	14.3	25.0	33.5	34.0
Master's	1.7	6.3	14.8	23.1	24.4
Doctorate					

Percentage calculations are by the authors.

Source: U.S. Department of Education, National Center for Education Statistics (1992). *Digest of Education 1992*. Washington, D.C.: U.S. Government Printing Office.

A 1990 survey by UCLA's Anderson Graduate School of Management and Korn/Ferry International investigated the representation of women and minorities in top executive positions in 1,000 of the largest corporations in the United States. The study revealed that women and minorities occupied less than 5 percent of these high-level managerial positions, a 2 percentage point increase from 1979 (58). Moreover, a very large telecommunications firm in the United States found that within its own ranks: "One out of every 21 white males has the opportunity to reach middle-level management and above; for men of color, the ratio was one out of 42; for white women, one out of 136; and for women of color, one out of 289" (33:3).

Women's presence on corporate boards also presents an interesting picture. In a 1992 study, Korn/Ferry International found that 60 percent of the *Fortune 1,000* companies had women on their board of directors. This figure was up from 36 percent in 1979 and 11 percent in 1973. An industry breakdown of the 1992 statistics reveals that banks and financial institutions had the highest percentage of women board members (74 percent), followed by insurance companies (67 percent) and billion-dollar industrial and service companies (63 percent). A decade ago, most women board members were drawn from academia. In 1992, senior executives accounted for the largest percentage of women board members (38 percent). While these numbers may sound encouraging for women, the great majority (41 percent) of these boards had only a single "token" woman as a member. A negligible proportion (2 percent) contained three or more women. Since the average size of corporate boards is thirteen, the presence and voting power of women on these boards are largely overshadowed by men (26).

Career and family

Women managers have not achieved equity with their male peers in terms of their ability to pursue a career and have a family. In 1988, only 60 percent of women managers were married, compared to 75 percent of men managers (53). Reflecting the growing tendency to delay childbearing, approximately 57 percent of women managers between the ages of 25 to 34 and 25 percent of women managers ages 35 to 44 are childless (38). Compared to their male colleagues, executive women are thirteen times more likely to be single, separated, divorced, or widowed (38). Moreover, executive women are significantly more likely to be childless (61 percent) than executive men (3 percent) (40). Thus, it appears that women who have made it into the executive suite have difficulty juggling both family life and a high-powered career.

Minority women

Minority women managers are not as well represented in the managerial ranks as are white women.[3] In 1992, 12 percent of white, 7.2 percent of black, and 7.7 percent of Hispanic women were managers (61). Black women represented only 7.1 percent and Hispanic women, 4.5 percent of all women managers (61). In 1986, only 3.3 percent of women corporate officers in the *Fortune* 1,000 companies were minority women (53).

In addition to their under-representation in the management ranks, Hispanic women managers earn salaries that trail behind white women managers' earnings. However, even when accounting for racial differences, the gap among these women's salaries in no way compares to the chasm between female and male managers' salaries. The annual median income of white women managers in 1992 was $26,944, representing 65 percent of the income of white men managers ($41,526) and 66 percent of all men managers' earnings ($40,746) (61). Black women managers earned $27,029, 103 percent of their white female counterparts' earnings, 96 percent of their black male counterparts' earnings ($28,264), but only 65 percent of white men managers' salaries and 66 percent of all men managers' salaries (61). Although black women managers' salaries have surpassed those of white women managers, the difference in salaries is too small to draw any meaningful conclusions at this juncture. Hispanic women managers fared even worse, earning only $24,951. This annual median income represented 93 percent of white women managers' earnings, 76 percent of their Hispanic male counterparts' earnings ($32,921), but a mere 60 percent of white men managers' earnings and 61 percent of all men managers' earnings (61).

Educationally, minority women are also lagging behind white women. Table 23.5 reports recent statistics regarding the percentage of business and management degrees awarded to minority and nonminority women. As revealed in this table, the overwhelming majority of women who received bachelor's, master's, and doctoral degrees in management and business were white.

Women who have broken through the glass ceiling

As we have seen, women are increasingly earning business and management degrees and are gaining entrance into the management profession. Women managers overall, however, are not being financially rewarded, promoted, or appointed to powerful positions at the same rate as men. Yet, a few women have been able to break through the glass ceiling and secure well-compensated, upper-level management jobs. Who are these women? How did they secure these positions? What are their personal and professional experiences? What follows is a profile of a typical corporate woman officer who achieved something very atypical – she made it to the upper echelon of her company.

Heidrick and Struggles conducted a study of corporate women officers in America's largest *Fortune* 1,000 industrial and service companies (18). Although

Table 23.5 Percentages of 1990–1991 business and management degrees conferred on women by race

Race	Bachelor's		Master's		Doctorate	
	% of all women's degrees	% of all degrees	% of all women's degrees	% of all degrees	% of all women's degrees	% of all degrees
White non-Hispanic	81.9	38.3	78.8	26.8	79.9	19.5
Black non-Hispanic	8.1	3.8	5.9	2.0	1.1	0.3
Hispanic	3.1	1.4	2.3	0.8	0.7	0.2
Asian/Pacific Islander	4.0	1.9	4.2	1.4	2.5	0.6
American Indian/Alaska Native	0.4	0.2	0.2	0.1	0.4	0.1
Nonresident Alien	2.5	1.2	8.6	2.9	15.4	3.8

Calculations are by the authors.

Source: U.S. Department of Education, National Center for Education Statistics (1992). *Digest of Education 1992*. Washington, D.C.: U.S. Government Printing Office.

none of the women in the study had reached the top rung of the corporate hierarchy, approximately 80 percent were at the vice presidential level or above. The typical corporate officer in this study was a 44-year-old white Protestant woman working at a $2 billion or more service organization headquartered in the eastern portion of the United States. Her annual compensation (base salary and bonus) was $116,810. Having worked for three employers in her career, she had been with her present firm for less than ten years. She devoted 55 hours a week to her work and spent less than 25 percent of her time on business travel. She was married, childless, and spent less than ten hours each week on homemaking tasks. She had been employed continuously throughout her career without interruption for family or homemaking responsibilities. She was likely to have had a background in finance or general management and was promoted to her present position from a job within the firm. She had one or more mentors (knowledgeable counselors) and sponsors (influential supporters) and reciprocated by serving in a similar capacity for others. She had a college degree and was likely to have earned an advanced degree.

The typical woman in the Heidrick and Struggles survey was greatly satisfied with her career progress and with her job (18). She felt that her work afforded her above-average pleasure. However, the women in this study acknowledged that personal sacrifices had to be made to accommodate their careers. Areas affected by their careers included the decision regarding whether to have children (30 percent), the success of their marriage (17 percent), the decision regarding whether to marry (15 percent), their parental effectiveness (13 percent), and their social/personal relationships (4 percent).

Thus, it appears that the women who have broken through the glass ceiling into upper-management levels have achieved professional success and fulfillment. However, this achievement has exacted a relatively high personal cost. Since the goal of many women managers is to achieve the level of success attained by these women, we present a discussion of five factors that may be impeding women's career progress and suggest how they can be overcome.

Barriers and Recommendations

Stereotypes and perceptions

A great deal of research in the management literature has demonstrated that women and men managers have similar values, traits, motivations, leadership styles, and skills and that women perform better than or equal to men (7;14;17;36;48). Yet, despite these overwhelming similarities, women and men managers are perceived to differ (7;14;19;40). Unfortunately, women managers are believed to be less likely than their male counterparts to possess the attributes characteristic of successful managers (1). Moreover, the attributes that are perceived to characterize successful managers are those that men and not women have been socialized to possess and display (1;19;43;44). Given these unflattering and prejudicial perceptions, it is not surprising that 81 percent of over 200 women CEO's identified stereotyping and preconceptions of women managers as a primary factor impeding women's ability to rise to the top of their corporations (18).

How can women overcome these biased perceptions? The images of women presented in books, advertisements, movies, and television programs overwhelmingly depict them as less competent than men (12). Societal representations of women as competent managers need to become the status quo. Moreover, research shows that stereotypes thrive in situations in which very little information beyond social group categorical data about individuals, such as race, sex, and so on, is known (24). Stereotyping is heightened when a minority group is isolated from or has very little opportunity to associate with members of the majority group (24). Increasing the number of women managers and their degree of interaction with male colleagues would help counter this process (35;40). Additionally, organizational programs in which individuals examine and discuss their preconceptions about women in general and women managers in particular would help sensitize the groups to one another and help change perceptions (40).

Mentorship and networking

In order for women to break through the glass ceiling, they need to associate with powerful individuals. Two methods that have been found to help in this regard are networking and securing a mentor.

Many studies have reported that women have been largely excluded from "old boy" networks, the traditionally male circles of power within the business world (9;20;24). In response to this exclusion, women have formed their own networks (32;35;62). Some women report that these networks have benefited their careers; others have found them to be lacking in value (18;35). Indeed, 53 percent of high-level women in one study stated that networking in professional women's organizations had not helped them advance in their professions (18). Thus, it appears that women need not only to form their own networks (35;62), but also to penetrate men's networks to a greater extent if they are to be promoted into positions of power in corporations.

Women perceive that they face great barriers to attaining mentors – that is, individuals who provide psychological and social support as well as career development to them as protégés (41). This is surprising since research consistently shows that women in organizations obtain mentors at the same rate as men and experience the same benefits as male protégés: they enjoy more promotions and power, greater job mobility, recognition, satisfaction, and easier access to powerful individuals in the organization than nonprotégés (8;10;11;41). Many women who have secured high-level corporate positions have acknowledged the help of their mentors (18;20).

In sum, to advance in their careers, women managers should engage in both networking activities and mentorship alliances. Engaging in one will facilitate the other. Networking can help women who are interested in breaking through the glass ceiling find a mentor. In turn, mentors can help women gain entrance into "old boy" networks (10).

Discrimination

The legal system has been both a help and a hindrance to women managers. Since the 1960s, sex discrimination in employment has been illegal. Federal protection from discrimination is covered by Title VII of the Civil Rights Act of 1964. It protects women from discrimination in hiring, job assignments, transfers, promotions, and discharges as well as other employment-related decisions (27). The Equal Pay Act of 1963 requires employers to pay women and men equally for the same work. Sex discrimination by recipients of federal contracts exceeding $10,000 is prohibited by Executive Order 11246, amended by Executive Orders 11357 and 12086, and requires employers to create and employ affirmative action policies (27).

While these laws are designed to protect the rights of women and minorities, they do not guarantee a discrimination-free work environment nor favorable court decisions. In fact, an analysis of the sex discrimination rulings issued in the federal courts between 1971 and 1980 revealed that women (managers and nonmanagers) won their discrimination cases based on the merits (as opposed to technicalities) only 34 percent of the time (27;30). In particular, women managers (or potential managers) who charged sex discrimination in hiring or promotion in the federal courts between 1983 and 1989 won (on the merits) only 29 percent of the time (27). As has been noted regarding the frequent failure of women managers to prove discrimination in the United States courts: "Given the difficult burden of proof that plaintiffs face, as well as judicial deference to the employer's evaluation of the plaintiff, this outcome is not surprising but it is discouraging for women contemplating filing sex discrimination charges" (27:250).

Legislative action has been and is being taken in the United States Congress to provide victims of sex discrimination with more protection and redress. With the passage of these laws, women managers should find it easier to fight against and receive compensation for the illegal actions taken by their employers. In fact, the

Civil Rights Act of 1991 supersedes several Supreme Court rulings that had severely limited the ability of job discrimination victims to prove their cases in court (27). The current law allows women who file a discrimination charge to have, for example, a jury trial and to sue for expanded compensatory and punitive damages, although the amount awardable is capped (27). Despite some progressive legal changes, the monetary, professional, and personal costs associated with pursuing legal remedies to rectify gender-based job discrimination still remain exceedingly high.

Family issues

As shown earlier, women managers are less often married and more likely to be childless than their male peers. However, some women try to "have it all", and become parents while pursuing careers in management, contrary to the advice of more than 70 percent of the high-level women surveyed at *Fortune 1,000* companies. They contend that in order to stay on the corporate fast track, women have to remain childless (18). Thus, it is not surprising that women who try to "have it all" experience a great deal of stress both at home and on the job (5;16;36).

How can women managers achieve what their male colleagues have achieved – remain on the fast track, marry, and have children? Research shows that women typically secure marital partners who earn more, and are higher in educational and occupational achievement than themselves (22;38;53). In seeking marital partners, heterosexual women managers may want to look in nontraditional places; that is, among younger, less accomplished men or among their professional colleagues and peers. The latter should be knowledgeable about the job demands placed on successful managerial women, value their competence, help them, and, it is hoped, not be threatened by them.

For women to be able to balance career and family responsibilities, women, men, and society at large will need to define the gender-role expectations of women and men more fluidly. Whether women work inside or outside the home, they are expected to, and in fact do perform the majority of household and childcare chores (21;38). As these chores are neither valued nor expected of men, men are reluctant to become involved. In order to reduce women's time on the "second shift" (21), more sharing of family responsibilities is needed. Alternatively, childcare assistance from relatives or the community should be sought. These options are particularly relevant for women who head their own households, a model that is becoming more common in the United States (3;56).

Organizations could also help women managers balance their career and family responsibilities by supporting flexible work schedules and childcare programs. Only 2 percent of all companies provide on-site daycare, despite the fact that several studies have shown that these programs result in lower employee absenteeism, lower job turnover, and greater job satisfaction and commitment (6;31;63). A growing, yet still small, number of companies are providing programs other than on-site childcare to support working parents. These include daycare referral services, flexible leaves, company-negotiated childcare discounts, subsidies, and tax savings (2). Programs such as these benefit both women managers and employers as childcare programs enhance recruitment, improve employee morale, and lower absenteeism and job turnover rates (2;6;28;39).

Recently a controversial suggestion called the "mommy track" was recommended as an intervention that organizations can use to help women balance their career and family lives (45;46). "Mommy track" programs identify women (and not men) who intend to have children early in their careers and place them on slower career tracks than women who choose not to have a family. This intervention has been widely criticized as being harmful and discriminatory against women (37). Gender-blind "parent tracks" have also been introduced in some organizations as have "daddy tracks." However, very few men take advantage of these programs (35).

Additionally, the United States government could support programs and legislation that would help women strike a balance between their dual roles. Until very recently, the United States and South Africa were the only two industrialized nations that had no national parental or maternity leave policy. However, on February 5, 1993 the Family and Medical Leave Act was signed into law in the United States leaving South Africa alone in this category. As a result of this law, individuals working in organizations with 50 or more employees will be allowed to take up to twelve weeks of unpaid leave for the birth or adoption of a child or a serious medical illness in their family. Still, more progress needs to be made in the area of government sponsored (or monitored) quality childcare, which is not readily available to all women managers who need it in the United States. However, some progress has been made in this area; in 1991 Congress passed a grant program to help states improve the availability and quality of childcare (34).

Becoming one's own boss

One way to overcome the difficulty of rising to the top of one's organization is not to attempt to climb the "corporate ladder" at all – that is, women managers need not wait for someone to promote them, they can promote themselves by becoming the chief executive officers of their own businesses. Women are increasingly choosing this option. As of 1987, the latest year for which statistics are available (based on U.S. census data collected and published every five years), American women owned 30 percent of all U.S. sole proprietorships and partnership businesses and collected 14 percent of the revenues.[4] As depicted in Table 23.6 the number of businesses owned by women in the United States increased by 58 percent between 1982 and 1987. This was four times the overall rate of new business creation in the United States. Table 23.6 also reveals that the major industries in which women owned the largest number of businesses in 1982 remained the same in 1987: services, retail trade, and finance, insurance, and real estate. Women owned over one-third of all firms in these industries and generated approximately 15 percent of the revenues (see Table 23.7).

What can account for this rapid increase of women entrepreneurs? Fifty-five percent of top women executive officers contend that it is the result of management's discomfort with women executives (18). This discomfort often manifests itself in the underestimation and under-utilization of the knowledge, skills, and abilities of women executives, who are viewed as either encroaching on traditionally male territory or who, at best, bring into the workplace qualities often associated with women (sensitivity and a preference for cooperation), qualities that have traditionally held a tenuous place in corporate America and have not been overwhelmingly appreciated (18). In utter frustration, many women executives have left corporations and begun their own businesses (4;42).

There are many advantages to be gained by women who head their own companies. By being their own bosses, women are able to set flexible work hours and flexible work policies; consequently, they become better able to sustain both a career and a family life. Indeed, research has shown that 71 percent of all women business owners are married, compared to 60 percent of all women managers and 52 percent of all high-level women executives who are not self-employed (38;40;54). Moreover, these women entrepreneurs should be particularly sensitive to their women employees' needs to balance work and family matters and, in turn, should adopt policies that are more flexible than those of traditional corporations (29). Of course, starting a business is a financially costly endeavor with no guarantee of success. Consequently, given these financial considerations, many women will not be able to pursue this option. However, for the woman who thrives on hard work, risk taking, and challenge, this option provides potential for success and personal satisfaction that entrepreneurs report is unparalleled (47).

Summary and Conclusions

Women have made a great deal of progress penetrating the management profession over the years. However, women have also experienced inequity in their level of

Table 23.6 Women-owned businesses by industry (in thousands) and percentage change between 1982 and 1987

	1982	1987	Percentage change 1982 to 1987
All industries	2,612.6	4,114.8	57.5
Agricultural service, forestry, and fishing	19.5	48.0	146.2
Mining	19.8	26.4	33.3
Construction	59.0	94.3	63.0
Manufacturing	44.9	94.0	109.4
Transportation, communications, and public utilities	38.9	79.8	105.1
Wholesale trade	32.1	82.5	157.0
Retail trade	631.3	798.7	26.5
Finance, insurance, and real estate	246.4	437.4	77.5
Services	1,284.8	2,269.0	76.6
Unclassified industries	235.8	184.8	−21.6

Calculations are by the authors.

Source: U.S. Department of Commerce, Bureau of the Census (1990). *1987 Economic Censuses: Women-Owned Business*. Washington, D.C.: Government Printing Office.

Table 23.7 Women-owned businesses as a percentage of all U.S. firms and receipts (1987)

	All U.S. firms		Women-owned firms		Women-owned firm receipts	
	Number	*Receipts*[a]	*Number*	*Percent*[b]	*Amount*[a]	*Percent*[b]
All industries	13,695,480	1,994,808	4,114,787	30.04	278,138,117	13.94
Agricultural services, forestry, and fishing	356,950	20,585	47,979	13.44	1,932,818	9.39
Mining	121,092	15,084	26,420	21.82	1,933,822	12.82
Construction	1,651,102	232,372	94,308	5.71	20,302,124	8.74
Manufacturing	432,971	226,824	93,960	21.70	30,914,089	13.63
Transportation, communication, and public utilities	592,751	76,355	79,768	13.46	10,936,278	14.32
Wholesale trade	439,200	298,264	82,513	18.79	42,804,558	14.35
Retail trade	2,241,494	544,768	798,692	35.63	85,417,525	15.68
Finance, insurance, and real estate	1,227,215	123,710	437,360	35.64	17,833,402	14.42
Services	5,937,671	417,105	2,269,028	38.21	61,123,430	14.65
Unclassified industries	695,034	39,741	184,759	26.58	4,940,071	12.43

[a] Receipts represent the dollar sales (in millions) received by all U.S. firms and the dollar sales amount (in thousands) received by women-owned firms.

[b] Some percentage calculations are by the authors.

Source: U.S. Department of Commerce, Bureau of the Census (1990). *1987 Economic Censuses: Women-Owned Business*. Washington, D.C.: U.S. Government Printing Office.

compensation, promotion, and appointment rates to powerful, middle- to high-level positions and with respect to sustaining both a career and a personal life. These roadblocks can be overcome, but women must challenge them on many fronts. Perceptions, stereotypes, and laws will need to be changed. Networks and mentors will need to be secured. Individuals, organizations, communities, and the government must provide support for family pursuits. Alternatively, women could potentially avoid these problems by becoming the chief executive officers of their own companies. Of course, women should not be forced to start their own companies because they cannot break through corporate glass ceilings. Instead, it is our hope that women and men managers will be treated equitably in corporations in the future and, as suggested by Elizabeth Dole, the former U.S. Secretary of Labor, "the glass ceiling [will] meet the same fate as the Berlin Wall" (57).

Notes

1 Before 1983, the managerial category, currently coded as "executives, managers, and administrators" was coded by the Bureau of Labor Statistics of the U.S. Department of Labor and the Census Bureau under several headings including but not limited to "managers, officials and proprietors, non-farm," "managers and administrators except farm," and so on.

2 In table 23.1 the coding for the managerial category has changed several times over the
   years.
3 With the exception of table 23.6, statistics and references to minorities make no distinction
   between blacks in general and blacks who are of Hispanic origin or whites in general and
   whites who are of Hispanic origin. Therefore, since Hispanics can be of either race, some
   of the statistics may inaccurately report racial/ethnic representation.
4 These figures are not based on large corporations.

References

(1) Brenner, O. C., Tomkiewicz, J., and Schein, V. E. (1989) "The Relationship between
     Sex Role Stereotypes and Requisite Management Characteristics Revisited," *Academy
     of Management Journal* 32:662–669.
(2) Burud, S. L., Aschbacher, P. R., and McCroskey, J. (1984) *Employer-Supported Child
     Care: Investing in Human Resources*. Boston: Auburn House Publishing Company.
(3) "Census Finds 26 percent of Families Fit 'Traditional' Description" (1991) *The Wash-
     ington Post*, February 2, p. A5.
(4) Cromie, S. (1987) "Motivations of Aspiring Male and Female Entrepreneurs," *Journal
     of Occupational Behaviour* 8:251–261.
(5) Davidson, M., and Cooper, C. (1986) "Executive Women under Pressure," *Interna-
     tional Review of Applied Psychology* 35:301–326.
(6) Dawson, A. G., et al. (1984) *An Experimental Study of the Effects of Employer-Sponsored
     Child Care Services on Selected Employee Behaviors*. Chicago: CRS, Inc.
(7) Donnell, S. M., and Hall, J. (1980) "Men and Women as Managers: A Significant Case
     of No Significant Differences," *Organizational Dynamics* (Spring):60–77.
(8) Dreher, G., and Ash, R. (1990) "A Comparative Study of Mentoring among Men and
     Women in Managerial Professional and Technical Positions," *Journal of Applied Psy-
     chology* 75:539–546.
(9) Fagenson, E. A. (1986) "Women's Work Orientation: Something Old, Something
     New," *Group and Organizational Studies* 11:75–100.
(10) Fagenson, E. A. (1988) "The Power of a Mentor: Protégés' and Non-Protégés' Percep-
     tions of Their Own Power in Organizations," *Group and Organization Studies* 2:182–
     194.
(11) Fagenson, E. A. (1989) "The Mentor Advantage: Perceived Job/Career Experiences of
     Protégés vs. Non-Protégés," *Journal of Organizational Behavior* 10:309–320.
(12) Faludi, S. (1991) *Backlash: The Undeclared War against American Women*. New York:
     Crown Publishers.
(13) Fierman, J. (1990) "Why Women Still Don't Hit the Top," *Fortune*, July 30, pp. 40–62.
(14) Freedman, S., and Phillips, J. (1988) "The Changing Nature of Research on Women
     at Work," *Journal of Management* 14:231–263.
(15) Fullerton, H. N., Jr. (1990) "New Labor Force Projections, Spanning 1988 to 2000,"
     in U.S. Department of Labor, Bureau of Labor Statistics, *Outlook 2000*, Bulletin No.
     2352, pp. 1–11. Washington, D.C.: U.S. Government Printing Office.
(16) Greenglass, E. R. (1987) "Anger in Type A Women: Implications for Coronary Heart
     Disease," *Personality and Individual Differences* 8:639–650.
(17) Greenhaus, J., Parasuraman, S., and Wormley, W. (1990) "Effects of Race on Organi-
     zational Experiences, Job Performance Evaluations and Career Outcomes," *Academy of
     Management Journal* 33:64–86.

(18) Heidrick and Struggles (1986) *The Corporate Woman Officer*. Chicago: Heidrick and Struggles.

(19) Heilman, M. E., et al. (1989) "Has Anything Changed? Current Characterizations of Men, Women and Managers," *Journal of Applied Psychology* 74:935–942.

(20) Hennig, M., and Jardim, A. (1977) *The Managerial Woman*. New York: Anchor/Doubleday.

(21) Hochschild, A. (1989) *The Second Shift: Inside the Two-Job Marriage*. New York: Penquin.

(22) Howard, A., and Bray, D. W. (1988) *Managerial Lives in Transition*. New York: Guilford Press.

(23) Johnston, W., and Packer, A. (1988) *Workforce 2000: Work and Workers for the 21st Century*. Indianapolis, Ind.: Hudson Institute.

(24) Kanter, R. M. (1977) *Men and Women of the Corporation*. New York: Basic Books.

(25) Kaplan, D. L., and Case, M. C. (1958) *Occupational Trends in the United States 1900–1950*. Washington, D.C.: Department of Commerce, Bureau of the Census.

(26) Korn/Ferry International (1993) *Board of Directors Annual Study*. New York: Korn/Ferry.

(27) Lee, B. (1993) "The Legal and Political Realities for Women Managers: The Barriers, the Opportunities and the Horizon Ahead," in E. A. Fagenson (ed.), *Women in Management: Trends, Issues and Challenges in Managerial Diversity*, pp. 246–273. Newbury Park, Calif.: Sage Publications.

(28) Magid, R. Y. (1983) *Child Care Initiatives for Working Parents: Why Employers Get Involved*. New York: American Management Association.

(29) Martin, P. (1993) "Feminism and Management," in E. A. Fagenson (ed.), *Women in Management: Trends, Issues and Challenges in Managerial Diversity*, pp. 274–296. Newbury Park, Calif.: Sage Publications.

(30) Maschke, K. J. (1989) *Litigation, Courts and Women Workers*. New York: Praeger.

(31) Milkovich, G. T., and Gomez, L. R. (1976) "Day Care and Selected Employee Work Behaviors," *Academy of Management Journal* 19:111–115.

(32) Morrison, A. M., and Von Glinow, M. A. (1990) "Women and Minorities in Management," *American Psychologist* 45:200–208.

(33) Munitz, B. (1991) "Women in Management: New Leadership for a Strong Economy: A Commentary," *Business Insights* 7:2–3.

(34) 1991 Legislative Column (1991) *Psychology of Women Newsletter* 18(1):12–13.

(35) Northcraft, G., and Gutek, B. (1993) "Discrimination against Women in Management: Going, Going, Gone – or Going But Never Gone?" in E. A. Fagenson (ed.), *Women in Management: Trends, Issues and Challenges in Managerial Diversity*, pp. 219–245. Newbury Park, Calif.: Sage Publications.

(36) Offermann, L., and Armitage, M. (1993) "The Stress and Health of the Woman Manager," in E. A. Fagenson (ed.), *Women in Management: Trends, Issues and Challenges in Managerial Diversity*, pp. 131–161. Newbury Park, Calif.: Sage Publications.

(37) Olofson, C. A. (1989) "Management Women: Debating the Facts of Life," *Harvard Business Review* 3:182–214.

(38) Parasuraman, S., and Greenhaus, J. (1993) "Personal Portrait: The Lifestyle of the Woman Manager," in E. A. Fagenson (ed.), *Women in Management: Trends, Issues and Challenges in Managerial Diversity*, pp. 186–211. Newbury Park, Calif.: Sage Publications.

(39) Perry, K. S. (1979) "Survey and Analysis of Employer-Sponsored Day Care in the United States." Doctoral dissertation, University of Wisconsin-Milwaukee, 1978.

(40) Powell, G. (1988) *Women and Men in Management.* Newbury Park, Calif.: Sage Publications.

(41) Ragins, B., and Cotton, J. (1991) "Easier Said Than Done: Barriers to Mentorship among Women and Men in Organizations," *Academy of Management Journal* 34:939–951.

(42) Rosin, H., and Korabik, K. (1990) "Marriage and Family Correlates of Women Managers' Attrition from Organizations," *Journal of Vocational Behavior* 37:104–120.

(43) Schein, V. (1973) "The Relationship between Sex Role Stereotypes and Requisite Management Characteristics," *Journal of Applied Psychology* 57:95–100.

(44) Schein, V. (1975) "The Relationship between Sex Role Stereotypes and Requisite Management Characteristics among Female Managers," *Journal of Applied Psychology* 60:340–344.

(45) Schwartz, F. (1989) "Management Women and the New Facts of Life," *Harvard Business Review* (January/February):65–76.

(46) Skrzycki, Cindy (1990) "Efforts Fail to Advance Women's Jobs: 'Glass Ceiling' Intact Despite New Benefits," *The Washington Post*, February 20, p. A1.

(47) Steinhoff, D., and Burgess, J. F. (1989) *Small Business Management.* New York: McGraw-Hill.

(48) Tsui, A., and Gutek, B. (1984) "A Role Set Analysis of Gender Differences in Performance, Affective Relationships and Career Success of Industrial Middle Managers," *Academy of Management Journal* 27:619–636.

(49) U.S. Department of Commerce, Bureau of the Census (1953) "Census of Population: 1950," in *The Report of the Seventeenth Decennial Census of the U.S.*, Vol. 2, pp. 1–267, Characteristics of the Population, Part I, U.S. Summary.

(50) U.S. Department of Commerce, Bureau of the Census (1990) *1987 Economic Censuses: Women-Owned Business.* Washington, D.C.: U.S. Government Printing Office.

(51) U.S. Department of Education, National Center for Education Statistics (1990) *Projections of Education Statistics to 2001*, NCES No. 91-683. Washington, D.C.: U.S. Government Printing Office.

(52) U.S. Department of Education, National Center for Education Statistics (1992) *Digest of Education 1992.* Washington, D.C.: U.S. Government Printing Office.

(53) U.S. Department of Labor (1989a) "Women in Management," *Facts on Working Women*, No. 89-4. Washington, D.C.: U.S. Government Printing Office.

(54) U.S. Department of Labor (1989b) "Women Business Owners," *Facts on Working Women*, No. 89-5. Washington, D.C.: U.S. Government Printing Office.

(55) U.S. Department of Labor (1990a) *Employment and Earnings.* Washington, D.C.: U.S. Government Printing Office.

(56) U.S. Department of Labor (1990b) "20 Facts on Women Workers," *Facts on Working Women*, No. 90-2. Washington, D.C.: U.S. Government Printing Office.

(57) U.S. Department of Labor (1990c) *Women & Work.* Washington, D.C.: U.S. Government Printing Office.

(58) U.S. Department of Labor (1991a) *A Report on the Glass Ceiling Initiative.* Washington, D.C.: U.S. Government Printing Office.

(59) U.S. Department of Labor (1991b) *Employment and Earnings.* Washington, D.C.: U.S. Government Printing Office.

(60) U.S. Department of Labor (1992) *Employment and Earnings.* Washington, D.C.: U.S. Government Printing Office.

(61) U.S. Department of Labor (1993) *Unpublished Tabulations from the Current Population Survey.* Washington, D.C.: U.S. Government Printing Office.

(62) Welch, M. S. (1981) *Networking: The Great New Way for Women to Get Ahead.* New York: Warner Books.

(63) Youngblood, S. A., and Chambers-Cook, K. (1984) "Child Care Assistance Can Improve Employee Attitudes and Behavior," *Personnel Administrator* 19:44–45.

INDEX